Sport Business Management in New Zealand and Australia
3rd Edition

Sarah Leberman, Chris Collins, Linda Trenberth

Sport Business Management in New Zealand and
Australia
3 Edition
Sarah Leberman, Chris Collins, Linda Trenberth
Daryl Adair, Lucy Atkinson, Chris Auld
Patricia Bradbury, Robyn Cockburn, Graham Cuskelly
Deborah Edwards, Margot Edwards, Lesley Ferkins
Ron Garland, Chris Gratton, Terry Kilmister
Richard Hollier, Trevor Meiklejohn, Ian O'Boyle
Farah Rangikoepa Palmer, Jenny Parry

Publishing editor: Ben Day
Production controller: EePin Pang

Any URLs contained in this publication were checked
for currency during the production process. Note,
however, that the publisher cannot vouch for the
ongoing currency of URLs.

For product information and technology assistance,
in Australia call 1300 790 853;
in New Zealand call 0800 449 725

For permission to use material from this text or product, please
email
aust.permissions@cengage.com

ISBN 978 0 17 021732 3
PP0626

Cengage Learning Australia
Level 7, 80 Dorcas Street
South Melbourne, Victoria Australia 3205

Cengage Learning New Zealand
Unit 4B Rosedale Office Park
331 Rosedale Road, Albany, North Shore 0632, NZ

For learning solutions, visit cengage.com.au

Printed in China by RR Donnelley Asia Printing Solutions
Limited.
1 2 3 4 5 6 7 16 15 14 13 12

Brief table of contents

Table of contents

List of figures

List of tables

Dedications and Acknowledgements

This text book is dedicated to Associate Professor Ron Garland who passed away suddenly in November 2011. He was a very active contributor to sport management and sport marketing education in New Zealand and Australia. Ron was an inspiration to his students, a generous colleague and good friend to many in the industry. His sense of humour, enthusiasm and energy will be missed.

We would like to thank all our contributors for their chapters, particularly given the tight turnaround time required. Our thanks also goes to Ben Day from Cengage who was very helpful in responding to questions readily and in a timely manner. A big thank you to Brigit Eames for her attention to detail, all the work in preparing the graphics and making sure all the files were consistent. Thank you for always being ready to assist in your friendly and highly professional way – we could not have met the deadline without your help.

Sarah has again enjoyed working with Chris and Linda. Despite being at different institutions in both hemispheres the process has been remarkably trouble free – just as well we have email! I would like to particularly thank Brett, for shouldering more than his fair share of being a Dad, looking after Phoebe, spending evenings alone and for always supporting me wholeheartedly in whatever I set out to do. I hope that in some small way this book will prepare future sport managers to the extent that Phoebe may benefit from their knowledge and expertise in years to come as she moves through the sporting world, and as such gains the enjoyment I have had from being involved in sport for as long as I can remember. I also wish to thank Julie Lyons, my PA for her unfaltering support and managing to free up my time, often at short notice, for me to complete the text.

Chris acknowledges the support and input of Naomi, his wife, who makes an important proof-reading and editing contribution to the text. Without her support, it would be difficult for me to remain involved given new role as a Chief Executive of a large public institution. Like Sarah, writing and editing texts is not overly compatible with family life. My delightful children, Abigail, Charlotte, Dominic and Jonathon, have had a highly distracted and weary father at various points, from late nights and very early morning starts; they've missed out on too many of their nightly wrestles. But I do trust that sport, and the way that it is managed in the future, will provide opportunity for mastery, excitement and joy for each of them, as it does for me. I wish to also acknowledge my senior colleagues at the Eastern Institution Technology, who have also put up with a slightly distracted CEO at times, and thank them for their forbearance and support. Finally, it was a very good decision to ask Sarah to take on the role of lead editor, given my own and Linda's changed circumstances; she has done an outstanding job.

Linda at Birkbeck, University of London, wishes to thank Sarah for taking on the lead with this new edition of managing the business of sport incorporating both New Zealand and Australia. So thank you Sarah and Chris for continuing the good work at home, to which I have been still able to make a contribution from abroad.

Introduction

Where there is genuine vision, people excel and learn, not because they are told to, but because they want to.

Peter M. Senge

Welcome to this new first edition of Sport Business Management in New Zealand and Australia. We hope that you are reading this book because you are passionate about sport and want to be a part of sport in New Zealand and Australia in the years to come. As inferred above, if you have a vision for how you would like to be involved in sport and make a difference to other peoples' experiences of sport, then you will excel and enjoy learning about the context and application of sport management in New Zealand and Australia, as detailed in this book.

This first edition of Sport Business Management in New Zealand and Australia builds on the previous texts which only focused on New Zealand, and reflects the significant changes that have taken place within the sport industry in New Zealand and Australia since 2006. Both New Zealand and Australia have seen changes in the way sport is managed and delivered over the past 5 years. For Australia the release of the Crawford Report in 2009, has heralded a number of significant changes to sport. The 2011 establishment of High Performance Sport New Zealand (HPSNZ) is bringing in a new era for high performance sport in New Zealand. At the same time there has been a continuing decrease in the amount of money available to sports organisations through the gaming trusts, meaning that future sport managers need to be well versed in securing funding to meet the demands of their stakeholders.

The importance of indigenous sport in New Zealand and Australian society is growing. With limited funds available for sport, strategic alliances are becoming more common in order to maximise sport opportunities. This is evidenced by the trend towards multi-sport clubs and an increasing number of partnerships between community and sporting organisations. The most recent one in New Zealand involves business and community leaders from within the Hawkes Bay coming together to become the Principal Partner of the Black Sticks through to the 2012 London Olympics.

The influence of globalisation on New Zealand society is all pervasive, and sport as an integral aspect of society, is increasingly being impacted by a number of global trends. At the same sport organisations are becoming more aware of the triple bottom line and the importance of corporate social responsibility (CSR) in the sporting context. Linked to this is the rise of sport-for-development, as a means of using sport as a vehicle to foster community development and peace in areas of conflict across the world. These developments are reflected in two new chapters one on CSR and the other on sport development.

The remaining chapters have been updated and rewritten to reflect the current sporting environment in New Zealand and Australia. The chapters in this book have been written in such a way that they can be read independently from each other, and as such the book does not need to be read in order. However, the book has been organised to follow a logical flow.

In the first four chapters we provide an understanding of the context within which sport management operates in New Zealand and Australia. Chapters 5 through 13 focus on key management themes as applied to sport. The third section of the book considers the business of managing sport and, as such, contains chapters with more practical applications.

The goal of this book is to provide students of sport management with a clear understanding of sport within the New Zealand and Australian context, a grounding in the key management concepts applicable to managing sport, followed with some practical knowledge to assist them once they leave their course of study. The chapters in this book are a starting point and you are encouraged to advance your understanding of particular areas by considering the sources listed at the end of each chapter. We hope you enjoy learning more about sport management in New Zealand and Australia, and through your passion and vision for sport will help to maintain and develop sport in these counties in the years to come.

Sarah Leberman, Chris Collins and Linda Trenberth
Editors

Chapter 1

The Sport Business Industry

By Sarah Leberman, Chris Collins and Linda Trenberth

OBJECTIVES

After completing this chapter, you should be able to:

- understand what is meant by 'sport as a social construction';
- define the terms sport, sport business management and sport industry;
- discuss how the environment impacts on the management of sport;
- describe the unique aspects of the sport product that make sport different from other products to manage.

Key terms

In this chapter, readers will become familiar with the following concepts and terms:
- sport
- management
- sport business management
- perishable commodity
- institutionalisation
- social construction
- sport industry

Introduction

For the last 100 years or so, sport has been a significant aspect of life in New Zealand and Australia. Sport has provided a source of enjoyment, challenge, escape, pride, and meaning for many individuals, and for others, alienation and conflict. Sport often features in our 'quests for identity', both as individuals and as a nation. Granted such quests have in the past usually been male-dominated and often based on 'invented or selected traditions', symbols, myths and nostalgia; nevertheless, sport has featured centre stage at various points in New Zealand's and Australia's history. The long significance of sport at the symbolic level, however, is arguably no longer now the primary driving force; sport is also increasingly becoming more significant at the economic level (Collins & Jackson, 2007).

Historian Jock Phillips (2000) notes the way in which the significance of sport has shifted in New Zealand since the 1960s. Prior to the 1960s he argues that sport primarily had symbolic meanings for

New Zealanders, and that its importance was mostly in character formation in a modern capitalist world. Sport had a moral imperative. It was seen as inculcating moral virtue, such as 'character' and 'patriotism'. Similar notions would also apply to the Australian experience of sport. These moral virtues embraced hard work, self-discipline, and team-work, which argues Phillips, were important in a new, disordered capitalist, urbanized world. A shift has now become increasingly powerful over the last 30 years, posits Phillips, where sport is now part of the mass media entertainment world in a post-industrialist society. "Its motivation is money. It is sport as economics, not sport as morality, which is the dominant force" (p. 324).This is particularly evident in the area of highly corporatised sport, where the challenge is to maintain the integrity of the sporting contest, whilst at the same time understand the commercial needs of businesses. This is a difficult balance to manage as can be seen with the challenge confronting organizers of the 2011 Rugby World Cup in New Zealand. Rugby World Cup 2011 Limited, the company set up to run the tournament, needed to manage and protect the rights of official advertisers and sponsors from the 'ambush marketing' strategies of other commercial operators, protect the coverage rights for accredited media from other media, generate substantial revenue primarily through ticket sales to meet the costs of hosting the tournament, whilst at the same time, ensure appropriate access to the 'stadium of 4 million people', a feature New Zealand organizers had promoted in their bid to host the tournament.

The monetary value of sport for the global media complex is clear when one considers the value of the television rights negotiated in recent times. Broadcasting and sponsors rights, for example, along with revenue generated during game days by ticket and match programme sales, together with merchandising, account for most professional sport revenue. While there has been recent pressure on the amounts of funding sport can negotiate, sport remains big business globally and is intensely competitive in a business sense. And it is not just the actual event of the sport contest that has become important, but the whole realm of spin-off associated activities, such as merchandising, magazines, newspapers and books. The global importance of merchandising in sport, is highlighted in chapter 4 where the case study on Nike indicates that despite the global recession in 2008/9, Nike's revenues grew to $19.2 billion in 2009 with net income at $1.9 billion, which was almost double what was achieved in 2004.There is no doubt, sport is increasingly aligned and enmeshed with a vast array of business activity, and hence, not surprisingly the practices and disciplines of the business world are now clearly evident in the organization and delivery of sport.

This growing significance of the business of sport has clearly been impacted on by the increasing globalization processes occurring in our societies. Westerbeek and Smith (2003) argued a number of trends were evident in the sport globalization processes, which further highlight the business aspects of sport. These trends, they suggested, include:

- the proliferation of sport in the media;
- the increasing value of sport global properties;
- the blurring between sport and entertainment;
- the vertical and horizontal integration of sport by media and entertainment companies;
- the way sport, leisure, and recreation are increasingly becoming part of the entertainment industry;
- the growth in the impacts and economic effects sport;
- the growth that is occurring in investment in transnational sport enterprises;
- the defragmentation of sport governance that is occurring;
- the way the less major sports and leagues are being marginalized even though they may be becoming more professionally managed;

- the convergence of economic power that is occurring in sport ownership;
- the greater use of technology to distribute sport globally;
- the increasing worldwide acceptance of sport as capitalism;
- the increasing 'Americanisation and westernization of sport'.

They argued that sport business trends also needed to be placed in the context of the nations in which sport is contested, arguing that in the US it is hyper developed; in countries such as Canada, Western Europe, Australia, and Japan it is developed; whereas it remains 'as developing' in many countries in South America and in Eastern Europe, and in countries such as China, India, and South Africa.In this sense it is probably fair to argue that in New Zealand sport is still in the developmental stage, with only a very small, though high profile segment of sport in this country, strongly developed at the commercial end of the spectrum. Nevertheless, the size of the broader sport and physical leisure sector in New Zealand is not insignificant when considered in the context of the economy, where it is now a large, diverse and vital component.

The first major study attempting to measure the size of the sector in New Zealand was in 1993, which clearly demonstrated the growing significance of the business of sport and physical activity (Jensen, Sullivan, Wilson, & Russell, 1993). Subsequent updates in 1996 (Hillary Commission, 1998) and in 1999 (Goodchild, Harris, Nana, & Russell, 2000) confirmed the sector has continued to grow. The most recent research by Dalziel (2011) estimates that the total value of sport and recreation to New Zealanders in 2008/9 was $12.2 billion. Sport and recreation including volunteer services contributed $5.2 billion to GDP, representing 2.8%. Without volunteer services, the amount is $4.5 billion or 2.4% of GDP. In the 2006 census 48,363people were employed in the sport and recreation sector making it the fifth highest industry in New Zealand by employment. The role of globalisation in sport is further discussed in chapter 4. Sport and recreation sector contributes about 2% of Australia's GDP. The value of volunteers to Australian sport and recreation is estimated at $3.9billion for 2006 (Frontier Economics, 2010). In Australia there were 75,155 people employed in the sport and physical recreation sector (2006 Census).

Sporting related events are now increasingly valued for their multiplier effect in the economy. In Western Australia, for example, the economic value of hosting the 2007 Australian Surf Life Saving Championships injected approximately $23million into the Western Australian economy (Government of Western Australia, 2009).This connection between sport and event tourism expenditure was clearly evidenced in an analysis on the value of rugby to the Taranaki region of New Zealand. For example, an All Blacks game vs. Manu Samoa in 2008 resulted in an impact of around $1.2million on regional GDP. The estimated value of hosting three of the rugby World Cup games in 2011, is valued at adding $5.2 million to the region's GDP (Venture Taranaki, 2009).A similar argument was mounted about the economic value of the 2011 Rugby World Cup hosted in New Zealand, in terms of the value of the tournament to the New Zealand economy even though the tournament itself was projected to make a loss. The broader economic gain was a key rationale for the Government becoming a financial backer of the tournament and even establishing a Government Ministerial portfolio of World Cup Minister to ensure some Governmental controls and influence. In spite of this, some lively debate occurred in the media leading up to the tournament about the accuracies of the cost-benefit analyses that had been put out into the public arena by Government and tournament organizers.

These highlights provide a glimpse at the scale and nature of economic activity connected to the sport and recreation sector, as well as demonstrate the importance of this sector to the New Zealand and Australian economy. This book is about the fundamentals of managing components of this sector, but before the fundamentals of management can be applied to sport business, the sport business industry and the environment in which it operates must be understood. This chapter will define the terms *sport* and *industry* in order to better develop an understanding of the sport industry. It will also define *sport business management* and describe, albeit briefly, certain environmental factors which can influence the growth, structure and processes of sport organisations. While sport today is considered a business and theoretically could be managed as any other business would be, there are unique features of sport that sport managers should be aware of and take into account in the management process. These unique features will be discussed as managers of sport must understand the nature of sport as a product.

What is sport?

Discussions about how we might define sport are bound to cause dissent. Frequently, attempts at definition are just as likely to reflect what people believe sport *should be*, rather than the shape they see it taking. This reflects some important inter-related aspects worth noting, the first of which is the changing nature of what society regards as sport.

A hundred years ago, the term 'sport' almost certainly differed from its present-day accepted meaning. This is not to suggest that our definitions are necessarily any more adequate than previous attempts, but more likely the forms and meanings of sport have changed; they are not in a static state. For example, we might not regard what was often referred to in the 1830s as 'football' as being 'real sport': the players didn't train; there was little in the way of any practised strategy; there were no established rules; there was no competitive league; and there was no over-arching administrative structure or organisation. To us it might have seemed much more like a school lunchtime game of 'scrag'. To those in the 1830s, however, what we often refer to as 'sport' they may well have perceived as being more like what they called 'work' (Collins, 2007c).

Sport as a social construction

Linked to this is the important point that there is nothing inherent within the phenomenon of sport that means that it should occur in a certain way or form. There is no 'pure essence' or 'pure nature' of sport. Rather, sport has come to mean different things within different settings. Its forms and meanings change (Collins, 2007c). For the sport manager, this has an important and rather obvious implication; namely, that as sport has no fixed or static state, the successful manager must be cognisant of ongoing change and be flexible enough to adapt structures and processes to suit. Dramatic change is relatively easy to detect, and is perhaps more likely to force shifts in management. Within the social setting, however, change is subtle and continual, and this will usually catch the unobservant organisation or manager unawares (Collins, 2007c).

The fundamental reason for this changing form and meaning is that sport is a socially constructed phenomenon. It is situated within a social context and is shaped by the social processes creating that context. Hence, the way that sport is defined and organised is not dependent on any supposed inherent feature or innate essence; rather, the way sport is defined and organised is dependent, in part, on the various social, political and economic resources that are mobilised by those with vested interests who attempt to shape sport to fit their interests and concerns. Furthermore, this fluid process involves ever-continuing processes of conflict, negotiation, compromise, coercion and subtle persuasion between various groups of people. The forms and meanings sport takes at any given time are determined by the intended and unintended consequences which flow from past and present interactions of interdependent people (Collins, 2007c).

This is why some scholars refer to sport as 'contested activities' (Coakley, Hallinan, Jackson, & Mewett, 2009). This isn't referring to the competitive nature of the activity, but rather, the fact that people differ in their ideas about what sport could and should be. These differences lead to struggles, which Coakley et al. suggest occur in three primary and interrelated areas, namely:

- what are the meaning, purpose and organisation of sport?
- who participates in sport and what are the conditions of that participation?
- why and how is sport sponsored?

Because of these struggles, Coakley et al. (2009, p. 6) argue that rather than limit analysis through attempting a precise definition of sport, many scholars are more interested in questions such as, 'what counts as sport?', and 'whose sport counts the most?'. These questions, they suggest, focus on the deeper social and cultural contexts which form ideas about physical activities.

Such questions are not the focus of this book (see Collins and Jackson, 2007, for such discussion of the New Zealand context); however there is value in retaining this insight when discussing any definition of sport. Definitions do add value, but they are only tools to aid our level of understanding and to help us to distinguish between one phenomenon and another. We need to be mindful, however, of a definition's in-built limitations, not only in terms of its precision, but also regarding the analysis that might result.

Defining sport

In most traditional definitions, sport is regarded as physical activity that is competitive, requires skill and exertion, and is governed by institutionalised rules. Coakley et al. (2009) provide a good example of such a definition and suggest that in many cultures today, sport can be defined as follows:

> ...institutionalised competitive activities that involve rigorous physical exertion or the use of relatively complex physical skills by individuals whose participation is motivated by a combination of personal enjoyment and external rewards.

(Coakley et al., 2009, p. 5)

INSTITUTIONALISATION IN SPORT GENERALLY INCLUDES THE FOLLOWING:
The rules of the activity are standardised. • *an official set of behavioural and procedural guidelines are established.*
Rule enforcement is taken over by official regulatory agencies. • *this could include a local rules committee to a highly centralised national or international rule-sanctioning body.*
The organisational and technical aspects of the activity become important. • *with competition and rule enforcement, the activity becomes increasingly rationalised (e.g., training, strategies) in order to improve chances of success.*
The learning of games skills becomes formalised. There are two major reasons this occurs: • *concern with success grows and guidance from experts is sought* • *the activity becomes more complex and so must be systematically learned*

Adapted from Coakley et al. (2009)

Apart from the features of competition, physical activity and relatively complex skills, an important aspect of this definition is the concept of 'institutionalisation'. By this, Coakley et al. are referring to the "processes through which behaviours and organisation become patterned or standardised over time from one situation to another" (2009, p. 5). In sport, they suggest that this typically includes the:

* standardisation of rules;
* establishment of official regulatory agencies that are responsible for rule enforcement;
* increasing importance of organisational and technical aspects of the activity;
* formalisation of the learning of game skills.

Concept Check

Institutionalisation

This refers to the processes through which behaviours and organisation become patterned or standardised over time from one situation to another.

Institutionalisation often involves bureaucratic organisation. Today the term 'bureaucracy' is often used colloquially in a negative and demeaning way, but its sociological sense is less value-laden and refers to certain features of organisation. It means a type of organisation that emphasises rational-legal authority, where authority is linked to positions rather than individuals, where there is the existence of specialised positions within clear-cut divisions of labour, where delegation of responsibilities occurs within the hierarchy and divisions of labour, and where there is a rational calculation and an efficient pursuit of organisational tasks and goals (Nixon & Frey, 1996).

Increasingly, as Nixon and Frey (1996) point out, sport also often has a corporate structure as well as a formal or bureaucratic one. By corporate, they refer to the way in which the commercial or business dimension takes on the greatest importance, so that corporate sport is organised to make money. In corporate sport, sport is essentially a commodity to be produced, packaged, marketed and sold.

Given this definition of sport, it is not difficult to see the link between sport and management, as institutionalisation implies some of the themes of management. Clearly, management practice is a central element of much sport as we know it today, as the more visible forms of sport are becoming increasingly highly institutionalised. While what occurs on the field or court may be spontaneous, relatively unplanned, and with uncertain results, the activity/event itself is also the result of the rational calculation and efficient pursuit of organisational tasks and goals.

Coakley et al's definition is a scholar's attempt to delineate a useful and accurate working definition of sport for the purposes of the study of sport. However, much broader definitions are likely to be utilised in more applied settings. For example, the financial data provided at the outset of this chapter with regard to the sport and recreation sector in New Zealand and Australia, are derived from much looser and broader definitions than that provided above. Likewise, the Sport and Recreation New Zealand Act 2002, which established the Crown entity Sport and Recreation New Zealand (SPARC) and dissolved the Hillary Commission, makes no attempt to define sport in the list of Interpretations in Clause 5 of Act. SPARC, on behalf of the Crown, is responsible for developing and promoting sport, physical recreation and physical activity, receives its mandate from the 2002 Act, and so not surprisingly also adopts a broad definition of sport. For the purposes of funding sport, SPARC excludes all activities that may be classified as part of 'the arts' such as dancing, music and theatre, as it is believed that these activities are able to gain funding from other sources. At a more informal level, however, when it comes to a question of funding sport, SPARC considers the nature of the activity (i.e., how physical is the activity) and the level of organisation behind the activity (i.e., what level of organisational structure does it have). Similarly, in the Australian Sports Commission Act 1989, there is no definition of sport, and its mandate is very clear to amongst other things Clause 6 1b "encourage increased participation and improved performance by Australians in sport". There is, however, no precise set of definitional criteria provided as to whether a certain activity might qualify as a sport. Perhaps not dissimilarly, the North American Society for Sport Management (NASSM) also uses the term 'sport' in a global sense as covering various forms of physical activities (Parkhouse, 2005). In terms of this book, the focus is also relatively broad, and is on what most people would commonly call 'organised sport'.

The terms 'sport' and 'sports' are often used interchangeably. Parkhouse (2005) suggests that 'sports' is singular in nature, whereas 'sport' is a more encompassing term. The NASSM uses the collective noun 'sport' (Parkhouse, 2005), and this book follows that lead.

Sport industry

The term 'sport industry' has been used by many scholars in its singular form. Considering that an industry is a group of organisations that produce the same or similar products that are substitutable for each other, the question arises, whether the sport industry is indeed a single industry. The contemporary sport industry is complex and is in fact a number of sport industries with unique legal, business and management practices and imperatives. It includes all organisations and groups involved in the private, public and voluntary provision of sport services, goods and programmes.

The industry embraces a considerable number of products and services, consumer market segments, service delivery system sectors and occupations. Its influence has widened considerably because of the interrelationships with several cognate industries, public and commercial health and fitness agencies, sport science and technology and medicine, sporting goods, entertainment, tourism and recreation – many of which have come into prominence only in recent years. Beech and Chadwick (2004) identified amongst others, players, clubs and their teams, leagues, governing bodies, player's associations, player's agents, stadia owners and operators, tournament and event organizers, sport equipment manufacturers and sponsors of players, clubs, leagues and events as participants in the sport industry. Parks, Quarterman, and Thibault (2010) suggest that the sports industry can be considered from three different perspectives. The first is by the types of sport that exist. The second is determined by the settings in which sport occurs. The third approach is based on industry models that highlight the interrelationships between elements in the sport industry. They provide three examples of this approach – the product type model, the economic impact model and the sport activity model.

Essentially, the sport industry revolves around sport clubs and associations, within the community, public and commercial sectors. The community-based or not-for-profit sector includes the organisation of local clubs, sport interest groups, private clubs, local and national associations. The commercial sector includes the provision of facilities, services, materials and equipment in the form of leisure centres, sports clubs, sponsorships, tourism in the form of sport packages and the formation of events such as triathlons. The public sector includes government servicing through formulating policy, developing strategic coordination of industry sectors and the provision of independent advice, guidance and responsibility for the allocation of funds. The sport industry, then, can be defined as the market in which the products offered to its buyers are sport, fitness, recreation or active leisure related and may be goods, services, people, places or ideas (Pitts & Stotlar, 2007).

Sport business management

'Management' can be defined as the process of getting things done in organisations through other people to achieve organisational objectives in an efficient manner (Inkson & Kolb, 2002). As management is often limited to subject matter that focuses on the functions of planning, organising, leading and controlling, the term 'sport management' can be misleading. Other business functions such as finance, marketing, sponsorship and public relations are all important and relevant to the sport manager. The term 'sport business management', then, seems a more accurate term to describe both the applied and academic aspects of the sport industry.

Hood (1997) noted in an address to New Zealand's sport leaders that the very juxtaposition of the terms 'sport' and 'business' still make many people uncomfortable with the connotations that 'business' brings, of entrepreneurial and 'for-profit' activities. A similar observation was made by Smith and Stewart (1999) when commenting on sport in Australia. Phillips (2000) highlights this lack of comfort in New Zealand, evidenced in the intensity of the hostile public reaction to the New Zealand yachtsman Russell Coutts leaving Team New Zealand to join the challenging Alinghi Team in the 2003 America's Cup, which was raced in New Zealand waters. For Coutts this was primarily a business decision as a professional yachtsman, whereas many New Zealanders regarded it as a lack of loyalty and betrayal, particularly given Alinghi's defeat of Team New Zealand and Coutts's leading role in Alinghi's victory. Similar debates occurred when NRL Rugby League player Sonny Bill Williams suddenly and without warning left his Sydney NRL Club the Canterbury Bulldogs in 2008, switched codes and joined a French based Rugby Union Club in Toulon. He had been regarded as one of the star players in the league, but his 'contract-breaking' departure was hotly debated, leading media news stories on both sides of the Tasman, with it being suggested by some that it was the most treacherous act in Australian sporting history (Ramus, 2011). Subsequently, in the lead up to the2011 Rugby World Cup, where Williams was an All Black squad member, mainstream news media coverage led with a new debate around Williams' unwillingness to commit to staying in New Zealand post-World Cup, demonstrating an ongoing public unease around an athlete's business imperatives connected with sport, verses a player's loyalty and commitment to New Zealand rugby and the All Black jersey.

Increasingly, however, New Zealanders and Australians are becoming more accustomed to athletes and teams making decisions on the basis of business considerations, in ways which would have been quite unimaginable even two decades ago. For people involved in the organisational and management levels of sport, there is a definite convergence of sport and business and there is a clear need for a business orientation with the appropriate managerial approach to their sport organisation.

'Sport business management' and the way it is used in this text, is a broad concept including all people, activities, businesses and organisations involved in producing, facilitating, promoting or organising sports, fitness and recreation products (Pitts & Stotlar, 2007). At the heart of sport business management is the application of management theory to the various sectors of the sport industry with all their distinctive characteristics that will be addressed below. However sport organisations do not operate in a vacuum. They operate within an environment which is shaped by various interdependent processes such as economic, social, political, legal and technological, which, although they may not have a direct impact on the operations of a sport organisation, can influence the industry in general ways that ultimately have an impact on the organisation (see chapter 5).

The environment

It is the ability of sport organisations to understand and respond to changes that are shaping the social and economic environment it has to work in which is an important contributor as to whether they will be successful or not. Sport managers cannot survive without acknowledging the changes taking place in the economy, in a deregulated environment, in demographics, in work patterns and in society generally. To this end, a number of different interdependent processes shaping the environment are briefly considered in relation to their impact on sport business management.

The economic environment

The increasing emphasis upon effective business management, the possible threats to the charitable status of sport organisations, less disposable income and decreasing local government subsidisation of resources and facilities as user-pays philosophies intrude into more and more areas of the lives of New Zealanders and Australians, all combine to have an economic impact on sport management.

Some of the factors that affect National Sports Organisations (NSOs) of sport include government funding, sport sponsorship, and disposable income. For example, SPARC's announced in 2011 the establishment of High Performance Sport New Zealand, a subsidiary of SPARC, responsible for developing and supporting the country's elite athletes, with the ultimate goal of winning more on the world stage. Other aspects of SPARC's funding are participation-focused and membership-oriented. Similarly, in Australia, the Australian Sports Commission (ASC) has responsibility for both high performance sport through the Australian Institute of Sport and sports participation at the community level.

Sport sponsorship has become increasingly important and competitive. However, over 80 percent of commercial sponsorship goes to high-performance or prestigious sports. The end result, therefore, is that there is an increasing dichotomy between elite media- and sponsorship-driven sports such as rugby, cricket, league and netball, and those which appeal more to mass participation at a lower competitive (or non-competitive) level, but which are not attractive to the media.

Economic decisions, such as the individual and household decision on how much time to devote to sport relative to work or other leisure activities, and how much limited income received from work effort will be allocated to sport rather than spent on consumer durables or food and clothing, are choices that are important for both economists and sport managers alike. However, the state of the economy significantly affects these choices; any downturn in the economy impacts on sport. Financial difficulties are a fact of life for most sport organisations and their managers. Increasing unemployment and decreasing incomes have created difficulties both in recruiting and retaining volunteers and in the recruitment of players. Sports, and local sport clubs in particular, that predominantly draw on participants from low- to middle-income earners, find they face considerable financial pressures. Many clubs at the local level already struggle to obtain players' subscriptions and there is evidence that unemployment is a factor in non-payment of fees (Collins, McLeod, Thomson, & Downey, 2007). Sport managers are having to be more innovative and enterprising in order to survive and must carefully consider the socio-economic profile of the area they draw from. The effects of economic downturns have been felt throughout sport, from a decrease in club bar-takings, subscriptions and gate-takings to the increasingly difficult pursuit of sponsorship, with sponsors being more discriminating and less generous in their support unless, of course, it is a major sporting event (Sawyer, Hypes, & Hypes, 2004; Parent & Seguin, 2008).

Obtaining media coverage, most particularly television, is becoming increasingly difficult for many sports. Minor sports, in particular, find themselves in a vicious circle of requiring television coverage to attract sponsorship, yet having to use sponsorship funds to pay the high cost of television coverage. Chapter 4 highlights the growing costs of coverage rights, noting that the SANZAR's Super Rugby rights for the 1996-2006 seasons were sold to News Corporation for US$555 million, 2006-2010 rights sold for US$323 million (a 16% increase per season), and 2011-2015 rights sold for US$437 million (a 35% increase per season).It is impossible for minor sports to compete with that. Major sports, and men's in particular, dominate media coverage (Bruce, Falcous, & Holly, 2007). Interestingly, despite the fact that netball has limited primetime coverage in comparison to rugby, figures for the year ending June 2010 in New Zealand, indicate that netball had the highest average television audiences (82,950) followed by rugby (74,010) (Dalziel, 2011).

Economic pressures and the commercialisation of sport are forcing change and even the large sport organisations find they need to look to protecting and, if possible, increasing their market share. Interestingly, Hood (1997) questions sport organisations that regard other sports as competitors, and challenges sport organisations to look for opportunities for cooperation and even alliances across codes. He argues that in the business world, firms are finding new ways to cooperate in order to save costs. An example of this occurring in sport is the use of the Melbourne Cricket Ground. Thirty years ago only one Australian football team had the Melbourne Cricket Ground as its home; now five teams use it and the intensive use of the facility has funded the further development of the stadium to its present high-quality level. This is just one example of how sport has responded to the impact of the economic environment. Hood (1997) argues that sports bodies should be looking for opportunities for cooperation whether from the large investment perspective which usually involves substantial facilities or the smaller opportunities which might involve shared office accommodation, administrative resources and information technology investments. Westerbeek and Smith (2003) also make the point that sport organisations need to expand, amalgamate and form alliances in order to acquire greater market leverage. They predict that the ownership and governance of large and influential sport organisations will increasingly fall under the control of fewer and fewer.

The general economic conditions in which a sport organisation exists (whether publicly or privately owned), the banking system in the country in which the organisation operates, fiscal policies and patterns of consumption are all components of the economic sector shaping the sport organisation's operating environment. The sport manager must be cognisant of these conditions.

Social

Changing social attitudes towards a range of issues such as competition in junior sport, women in sport, veterans' sport, violence in sport, equality and access in sport, and the disabled and ethnic minorities have all affected the way sport is organised and managed. Sport and business have to come to grips with changing community lifestyles as well. Fundamental lifestyle changes such as 7-day a week shopping, two-career families, more single-parent families, greater mobility, more competing sports and interests, computer games, and, not least, the advent of television eroding interest in watching second-best players when one can watch the best, all add up to enormous pressure being placed on sport organisations to maintain public interest and participation in their codes (Collins et al., 2007; Coakley et al., 2009).

Seven day a week shopping and the development of major shopping complexes have not only had an effect on children's sport traditionally played on weekends, but also on the input of significant numbers of parents and other volunteers. Nonetheless, despite all these various pressures which are undoubtedly eroding the volunteer base underpinning sport organisations, the value of the volunteer input in New Zealand and Australia remains significant, estimated as being equivalent to $3,867m in 2008/9 (Dalziel, 2011) in New Zealand and $3.9 billion in 2006 in Australia (Frontier Economics, 2010). The importance of volunteers in sport is discussed further in chapter 12.

There is a growing recognition of the need to understand the impacts of culture and ethnicity on sport consumption and to identify the consequent implications for sport management and marketing (Thomas & Dyall, 1999; Coakley et al., 2009). In New Zealand and Australia matters of culture and ethnicity have seen some focused attention, such as, the development of specific programmes targeted at increasing participation of Māori and indigenous people. In New Zealand Surfing New Zealand has been working with Te Puni Kokiri to invest particularly in administration, coaching and judging initiatives involving Māori. In Australia, the Shooting Goals Programme is delivered by the Swan District Football Club in the Pilbara region of Western Australia, using netball to increase school attendance and motivation amongst indigenous girls. Clearly there is a need for sport managers to manage and market sport in ways that are sensitive to cultural differences given the pluralistic communities we now all live in. This relies, however, on continuing to develop our understanding of how culture and ethnicity might contribute to the development of sport and sport management. Chapter 3 focuses on Māori and Indigenous sport and its management, which is pertinent to the New Zealand and Australian context.

Other socio-cultural factors that influence a sport organisation include the class structure of the social system, and the sporting traditions of the area in which the organisation is situated. Given the socially constructed nature of sport, as was discussed earlier, it is not surprising that often the administrative structures of many sport organisations reflect the inequalities of social life in terms of their class, race and gender (Coakley et al., 2009). Sport is created by people interacting with other people, and hence the socio-cultural processes shaping a particular social context, as already stated, will clearly also shape the forms and meanings of sport (see Collins and Jackson, 2007, for more full discussion on sport in New Zealand society).

Political

The prevailing political situation, the extent to which political power is concentrated and the ideology of the party in power are all factors which impact on sport organisations. Historically, government involvement in sport and recreation in New Zealand and Australia has been a proverbial football. In line with their respective political philosophies, successive governments have sought to establish and implement direct influence via programmes and agencies (Collins, 2007a, 2007b). Both countries invest heavily in sport and recreation from participation through to elite levels.

While the highly controversial days of the issues surrounding sporting contact with the former apartheid regime in South Africa are in the past, the intense public and political debate surrounding New Zealand Cricket's Black Caps' 2005 Tour of Zimbabwe and the Government's activities directed towards discouraging it, indicate the on-going interconnectedness of the political world with that of sport. This particular case presented major implications for managers of the sport, related to public opinion, sponsors, interactions with Government, the International Cricket Committee (ICC), and contractual obligations including anon-touring penalty fine from the ICC of $2.8m. New Zealand Cricket claimed the potential loss of non-touring were in the tens of millions of dollars. Intriguingly, the intense public debate of 30 years ago surrounding tours to South Africa were centred on the issue of should politics and sport be kept separate; in 2005, the defence from New Zealand Cricket made no such reference to moral and philosophical arguments, but were centred firmly on the business imperatives and contractual obligations, demonstrating how much sport had shifted towards a business orientation (Collins, 2007a, 2007b).

In general, however, the primary direction of government policy and philosophies in New Zealand and Australia is clearly in line with the trend towards increased commercialism. The role of the state as provider in sport and recreation has shifted from the more egalitarian goals of the 'welfare reformist' phase of the 1970s to a more business and performance orientation with policies which are more directed towards corporatist styles of sport management. Whereas facilitation and participation might have been the buzz words of the late 1970s and early 1980s, business values and processes such as strategic planning, profitability, accountability, efficiency and performance, have dominated sport since the 1990s (Collins, 2007b).

Legal

The growing commercialisation of sport has led to the increased involvement of the legal system, particularly on issues relating to the legal status of participants in contracts, as well as in contractual aspects relating to the organisation of sporting events, professional athletes' employment, sponsorships and grant-aid to sport organisations. A case in point is the Sports Disputes Tribunal of New Zealand. The Sports Disputes Tribunal was established in 2003 by the Board of SPARC as an independent body to determine certain types of disputes for the sports sector. Primarily the disputes surround anti-doping violations, appeals against decisions made by a national sport organisation, including selection decisions for New Zealand teams, and applications for assistance. At present the Tribunal consists of nine members, appointed for the expertise in law and/or sports (for more information see www.sportstribunal.org.nz). In South Australia, the State Sport Dispute Centre was established in 2008 to provide confidential and impartial mediation dispute resolution services to the sporting community. The strong relationship between sport and the law is also evident in areas such as the legal liability of participants in tort and criminal law; the self-regulation of sporting bodies through tribunals, penalties and appeals; and the legal doctrines of 'vicarious responsibility' and 'occupier's liability', which have in turn led to a range of legal solutions for administrators to remove or minimise risk. The latter tend to have been largely negated by the Accident Compensation Commission (ACC) in New Zealand, but changes to the eligibility of sport accidents may engender litigation (see chapter 16 for further discussion).

Technological

All sport organisations are affected by technological developments that may improve production and/or service (Parks et al., 2010). The wider business world is experiencing the massive impacts of communications and information technology, and in sport, technology is bringing global competition to our back door. Twitter, blogs and facebook are now used by most sports organisations as key ways of communicating with stakeholders.

Our sporting codes, even the most prominent ones such as rugby, will compete with global sports stars and clubs, such as, Tiger Woods, or Manchester United, for the public's dollar and attention. As Hood (1997) argues, the competition for brand value is global, just as it is for Coke®, McDonald's®, Nike® and IBM®. The NZRU, for example, clearly regard themselves as brand managers and are attempting to position the All Black brand on the global stage. Similarly, Netball Australia rebranded in 2009 to move from an organisation considered to be conservative and traditional, to one that is seen as exciting and relevant to the community. Part of this involved relocating their national headquarters to Melbourne and launching the Australian Netball Diamonds brand. This global level competition will call for more thoughtful and clever strategies in the years ahead for all sport managers and continued effort will go into building 'brands' (see chapter 14).Resources will need to be allocated to achieve success at elite levels, as winning captures the media and public interest. But there remains a challenge for sport codes to balance this with stimulating and growing local community involvement, and ICT advances are making communication and administrative tools more accessible to local as well as elite level sport (see following case study on Sportsground). Sports that build and support local leadership and more effective models for community involvement are likely to strengthen their competitive advantage.

There is a world-wide trend to sit at home and watch the world's most attractive athletes on television and to absorb the barrage of advertising that accompanies it. As in business, the protective barriers are gone and sport must invest in producing effective local leadership (see chapter 8) and cultivate their own icons much as they would cultivate a great brand.

Technology is also probably going to increase the wealth gap in sport. Funding already primarily flows to a few major sports such as yachting and golf, as well as team sports, such as rugby, rugby league and cricket. The sport-media complex is the main driver of this because, by way of example, television executives know that many more people will watch Manchester United, the Bull Dogs, Vixens or the Crusaders team than South Hampton, Wellington Rugby League, Western netball or Wanganui Rugby. Some sports overseas have recognised that the health of their code is dependent on achieving some significant redistribution or equalisation of funds, because maintaining evenness of competitiveness is seen as important to maintaining public interest. Hence, in US football the television rights are shared equally between teams and the result is that a small-town team such as Green Bay can win the Super Bowl. By contrast, baseball and English soccer operate on the basis of the survival of the fittest, and the teams with the largest inherited supporter base, or the largest population, are financially more secure. The emergence of significant television revenue will be largely siphoned off by the more powerful sports or clubs and will increase wealth disparity, and competition unevenness will result unless policies of redistribution are considered.

Improved technology may also, however, bring many opportunities for New Zealand and Australian sport. For example, Netball Australia has created 'Diamond Girl' a cartoonlike figure, to engage with young girls. Small-screen developments, such as digital television, and the twitter and facebook, for example, are areas that have major implications on the way sport and the public interact. Digital television will clearly make multi-channelling easier and cheaper and it is argued that sports programming opportunities abound for the establishment of niche services, such as dedicated sport channels, including pay-per-view options. For more minor sports, this may offer hope for some type of television coverage, although some industry commentators still express doubts about the economics of such coverage in a country the size of New Zealand. Nevertheless, sport managers will need to ensure they are abreast of such developments in order to gain the greatest advantages from such media and information communication technological developments.

CASE STUDY: CREATING A WEB-BASED SOLUTIONS COMPANY TARGETING SPORT ORGANISATIONS, 'SPORTSGROUND LTD – EASIEST, FASTEST, SMARTEST', WWW. SPORTSGROUND.CO.NZ

Mike Purchas is the CEO of Sportsground, a fast growing technology company servicing sport clubs and organisations with web-based services, such as self-edit websites. Sportsground supports hundreds of pages of content, documents, online registrations, group email, eNewsletters, and eCommerce. The service starts at zero cost under an advertising-supported model, or sport organisations can elect to pay a hosting fee if there is preference for a more customised website free of advertising.

Sportsground has grown to provide the websites to somewhere over 40% of all sports clubs and regional sports organisations in New Zealand. The company's capability statement (Feb, 2011) notes it is now the single largest provider of websites to Kiwi sport, with over 7,000 websites adopted by sports organisations, clubs, schools and teams, serving over one million page impressions per month.

CAPTURING THE SPORT SECTOR MARKET OPPORTUNITY

Mike's background was previously in financial markets. He was involved with a business in Australia that took global financial market information, aggregating and formatting the data into useable information in real-time, and providing subscription based services for financial traders and dealers, delivered via mobile devices and internet services.

With this prior knowledge and technical background Mike could see an opportunity and significant gap in provision of web-based services targeted at the sport sector. At the local or regional level in particular, there was lack of information and difficulty in finding out information about local sporting club activities. There was also difficulty for organisations at a local or regional level to get up-to-date information out to members and the wider public, or to cope with the information and data gathering that is required in a club or a regional sports organisation.

At the same time social media, such as Facebook, were gaining significant momentum and were demonstrating a different type of business model around such technology use. Mike could see an opportunity to target the information and administration needs of the sport not-for-profit sector, which was largely ignored by commercial providers of web-based services.

Building and maintaining conventional web-based solutions, services and web pages was costly; commercial builds were usually customised, taking it out of the financial range of the typical community

(Continued)

sports club. If a club had a site, it was usually built by a volunteer who had specific expertise, which left the club reliant on that volunteer. Most such sites and services quickly became dated, and provided little in terms of real-time information and services. It was usually too labour intensive for a volunteer to build and maintain real time services. Yet even in a country as small as New Zealand, the number of clubs and organisations numbered in the thousands. Mike could see the potential for web-based services and support, which, if well designed, could open up an entirely new level of service and functionality for clubs and organisations, particularly if they were easy to use, relevant functionally and low cost.

UNDERTAKING THE RESEARCH AND DEVELOPMENT

By 2007, now based in Hawke's Bay, New Zealand, Mike and a small team engaged in extensive research and development to build an IT CMS (content management system) for web-based internet services, which specifically targeted the needs of sports clubs and organisations. The key challenges to building successful web-based solutions were to:
- meet the typical needs of a sports club or organisation
- be low cost – i.e., cost of use was not a barrier to participation by clubs with scarce resources
- be easily scalable for the development company – i.e., same solution across a high numbers of users
- be easily transportable across different codes – i.e., not code specific
- be very easy to use – i.e., the CMS had to be highly intuitive, regardless of the technical knowledge or ability of members of clubs and regional sport organisations. These people were likely to be volunteers who had probably worked mostly with paper based processes and systems in the club, and possibly had limited or no technical knowledge.

Mike wanted a system where a club official could work, update, and edit information on club web pages, and see what it would look like as they worked. He wanted web-based solutions where people could manage for themselves the club information, data needs or club services. As the CMS development progressed, the testing of developing solutions even occurred with his own children (6 and 8 years of age), to "watch what the kids did when they used it", to "see where they went with the mouse", all aimed at ensuring intuitive solutions were being designed.

Parallel to this IT development work, extensive research and database gathering occurred to build a database of potential users and contacts across the thousands of clubs and sport organisations in New Zealand. With club contact details changing all the time, building a data base presented a significant, but nonetheless critical task to getting the business off the ground.

Early investors, who could see the potential and value of such a service, provided important early capital for the emerging company. Securing a major mainstream sponsor in Toyota was also critical. Early piloting occurred with the Millennium Institute for Sport and Health and the Cougar Athletics Club on the North Shore in Auckland, and with Eastern Region Netball in the North Island, all aimed at ensuring the system met the needs of the targeted sports market.

SPORTSGROUND COMPANY IS LAUNCHED

With the CMS developed and the database ready, Sportsground was launched in October 2008. A direct marketing campaign was undertaken with a mail out to more than 7000 contacts, which was followed up with email and outbound calling, at over 10,000 outbound calls a month. The goal was to achieve 15% participation from the target market in the first year – Sportsground achieved that in the first 4 months. By the end of the first year 25% growth had been achieved. Growth was measured by two factors:
- the percentage of penetration of the number of organisations that joined;
- and the percentage of the size of the audience, as determined by on-going 'page views'.

(Continued)

Growth continues at about 5 % each month, which means Sportsground is potentially doubling its size every 12-16 months. New services rolled out in 2010 included on-line registrations, membership databases, professionally formatted group email Newsletters, photo printing and new layouts for websites for clubs requiring a more customised look.

Large numbers of local sports clubs, Regional Sports Organisations, Regional Sports Trusts and National Sport Organisations across New Zealand have now become active uses. The goal of 'ease of use' and 'relevance of the services' appears to have been achieved, if high uptake of Sportsground services is anything to go by. The 'no-cost' ability for a club to utilise the services was clearly also attractive for organisations with scarce resources.

How does the Company generate revenue? Revenue is primarily generated via advertising on the web-sites, and for clubs and organisations requiring 'advertising-clean' web based solutions to enable use of their own sponsor branding, subscription based services are available.

Other added value web-based solutions and services continue to be developed and brought online for subscription based usage, creating additional revenue streams. During 2011 services launched or under development include: Club Online payments alongside Online Registrations; the ability to create national databases and smart communications for NSOs and associations; team information management tools; Club E-Commerce options to allow members and the wider community to buy and sell online; fundraising products and solutions; further integration with online accounting such as Xero and MYOB software; development of website portals that showcase community sport and share knowledge between clubs and organisations; optional photo products for club galleries; and options for greater customization of website design.

To see a snapshot of some of the activity across the Sportsground channel, see www.sporty.co.nz. To see some examples of organisations using Sportsground websites, see www.mahedrysdale.com, www.waterpolo.org.nz, www.sportauckland.co.nz, www.sporthb.co.nz, www.csa.org.nz, www. harbourhockey.co.nz, www.1boat2girls.co.nz, www.netballwellingtonregion.org.nz, www.hvsa.org. nz, www.primarysportwellington.org.nz, www.wellingtonunited.org.nz and www.wvcc.org.nz, www. pgarena.co.nz, www.magpies.co.nz, www.hbunited.co.nz.

Source: Developed from C. Collins interview with Mike Purchas, 2011.

QUESTIONS TO PONDER:

- How does the sport club you are involved with manage its information communication needs with members and wider public?
- Can you think of different and emerging forms of developing information communication technologies that sport organisations could make use of?
- What are the risks of becoming more heavily reliant on ICT in the operation of a club, and how might a sport manager mitigate some of those risks?

The unique aspects of sport business management

While much of sport operates in the business environment, there are arguably, some unique aspects of the sport product that render the management of sport different from the management of other business enterprises. While there are strong parallels, there are some differences in the way sport organisations have to market their product/service, as well as structure and finance their organisations as a result of the unique aspects of sport.

Mullins, Hardy, and Sutton (2007) for example, note that the sport product is invariably intangible and subjective. What each sport consumer sees in a sport is quite personal and this makes it difficult to ensure a high probability of consumer satisfaction. No other product evokes such strong personal identification and such emotional attachment as sport, which can have both positive and negative effects.

Unique aspects of managing sport

- The sport product is intangible and subjective making it difficult to ensure consumer satisfaction.
- The sport product is inconsistent and unpredictable. Consumer-product marketers market consistency whereas sport products market the excitement of unpredictability.
- The sport product is a perishable commodity, developed in anticipation of demand and produced and consumed simultaneously.
- Aspects of financing and budgeting for sport organisations differ from those of a typical business and direct income from competition is usually seasonal.
- For the manager there is a highly complex network of stakeholders ranging from government agencies to sponsors, volunteers and members.
- Sport enterprises earn significant income from sources extraneous to the sale of the service (e.g., sponsorship and television rights).
- Managers of sport leagues must heighten competition to be successful, not eliminate it.
- Competition cannot take place without coordination and collaboration with competitors.

Second, the sport product is inconsistent and unpredictable. Those providing the sport experience cannot predict the outcome because of the spontaneous nature of the activity, the inconsistency of various events and the uncertainty surrounding the results. Consumer-product marketers sell consistency whereas sport products market the excitement of unpredictability. There are, in marketing terms, product extensions such as a facility's amenities, clean restrooms, concessions, food, and entertainment, to ensure some consistency and provide a baseline of satisfaction. Given that the result cannot be guaranteed in sport, as much emphasis must be placed on the product extensions, as on the core product.

Sport is a perishable commodity, developed in anticipation of demand and produced and consumed simultaneously, notwithstanding delayed broadcasts and videotaping. The majority of sport products are perishable commodities requiring pre-selling. No other product evokes such strong personal identification and such emotional attachment as sport, and this can have positive and negative effects. A backlash can occur when the fans' favourite players are moved or when product modifications are made, for example. Marketers of sport face special challenges dictated by the nature of the enterprise (see chapter 10). Similar points have been made by Stewart and Smith (1999). They argue that sport managers must be aware of "the features that distinguish sport from other forms of business" (p. 87), in order to maximise the performance of sports organisations.

The financing and budgeting for sport organisations also differs from that of a typical business in a number of ways. Although their income might be more definite in that subscription levels are set and their membership levels and grants may be known in advance, their cash flow is likely to be more erratic. Their objectives will also be more varied and difficult to quantify, with the likelihood

Figure 1-1: (cartoon)

Source: New Zealand Herald, 14–15 November 1998 (used with kind permission of Malcolm Evans)

of greater problems of accountability due to the spreading of responsibility among members. While this situation is slowly changing with increasing professionalism and concomitant restructuring (see chapters 5 and 9), this structural issue is still pertinent, with the sporting landscape littered with examples of sporting codes which respond too slowly, if at all, to the changing environments within which they operate because of their cumbersome organisational structures.

With regard to revenue, sport enterprises earn significant income, not from the sale of service (e.g., a game or a 10 km run), but from sources extraneous to the sale of the service (e.g., sponsorship and television rights). Sport managers compete for the discretionary dollar of consumers through the sale of items that may or may not be related to what might be thought of as the primary focus of the enterprise. As a result of such a unique financial base, sport managers require a different practice within their setting from that which occurs in business, although obviously similar basic accounting and budgeting principles apply (see chapter 11).

It could also be argued that the economics of sport are unique. Undoubtedly the goal for those in the business of baked beans production is not only to be the best baked beans producer, but to also be the only producer. The goal is to eliminate competition. Sport, however, requires competition for its economic survival. Managers of sport leagues find themselves striving for a state of affairs where participants are able to remain competitive in relation to other participants. Owners/managers of teams need to be the best, but only just the best, not to be so much better than the others that there is a loss of spectacle. The Americans are masters at manipulating the variables to ensure even competition and therefore spectator appeal and economic success. Rule changes and draft systems are obvious examples that are increasingly being used. For example, in 2006 the SANZAR Super Rugby competition expanded from 12 to 15 teams, with five from each country, with each country forming their own conference and using a bonus point system, a significant change from the Super

12 competition which ran between 1996-2005. The new competition meant that teams played more games in their home country, and the extension of the finals to include more teams and games at the knock out phase, were designed to heighten final phase of the competition. SANZAR have since invited Argentina to join the competition from 2012, to create a four nations tournament to develop a southern hemisphere championship. The success of this evolving development is yet to be determined, but will be dependent on establishing an evenness of competition across the countries by spreading top players, and securing broadcasting rights and revenue associated with the new market opportunities.

The interdependence between public sector activity (especially local government), the commercial sector and club provision of facilities; the role of sponsorship; the voluntary nature of much organisational activity; the nature of competition between clubs in both organised games and for members; the blurring distinction between amateur and professional sport; and the requirement of being a team player are all distinctive features of the business of sport.

Bottom line – implications for management/policy

- Precise definitions of what constitutes a sport are difficult to articulate, and definitions still require levels of arbitrary judgment, thus they possess inbuilt limitations. Nonetheless for those managing sport and developing policy, definitions can provide a guide.
- Sport is socially constructed by people, usually in an attempt to fit their interests. This means the forms and meanings of sport are dynamic and changing. Policy development and management must be cognisant of these changing dynamics if they are to be effective.
- Dramatic change is always relatively easy to detect, and is perhaps more likely to force shifts in management or policy. However, on-going subtle change is a continual aspect of social processes, and this is what will usually catch the unobservant manager or policy developer unawares.
- Sport is interconnected with wider social processes, such as the economy, technological and political environments. The shapes, forms and meanings of sport are also the outcome of unintended actions arising from widely interdependent people involved in these wider processes. As a result, policy makers and management have a limited ability to completely control outcomes given the socially constructed dynamic nature of sport. While managers and policy makers cannot anticipate all the unintended outcomes, it is important to monitor policies so that unanticipated outcomes can be identified quickly and, if necessary, corrective action taken.
- Often there is a powerful connection between sport, ideology and wider power relations in society. Policy developers should attempt to understand these power relations when formulating policy. In particular, policy is required for those individuals or groups in society who might be disadvantaged in terms of prevailing attitudes and ideas, and/or through lack of resources, in order to ensure access, participation for all, and opportunity for pursuit and achievement of excellence for the talented.

(From Collins, 2007c)

Summary

Clearly New Zealand's and Australia's sport managers are involved in a multi-million dollar industry representing a significant component of the New Zealand economy and making unique demands on its personnel. As managers they face increasing legal technicalities, complexities of technology, financial responsibilities, sponsor requirements, media demands, public and private sector negotiations and an increasingly discerning and demanding membership. To meet the complex demands a new breed of specialist is emerging – the sport business management specialist. The intention in this book is to highlight the key management processes that are required to make sport happen.

CASE STUDY: THE CHALLENGES OF MANAGING SPORT

Charlotte is a new Chief Executive Officer who has responsibility for a regional netball franchise. The franchise has a team in the national elite-level semi-professional netball league and has been struggling for a while. Charlotte is typical of the new breed of sport manager: she holds postgraduate-level qualifications relevant to sport and leisure management, and she has strong event management experience in the sport and leisure sector and some commercial experience. While she has been an active and successful sportswoman across a wide range of sports herself and is still active at a social level in some sporting activities, she is not that well connected with the sport of netball, having not played the sport for some years, and having only played at a more social level.

She has had her first meeting with the board, and this poses some concerns for her. First, she is aware that there is a high level of expectation related to her appointment. Second, she is not sure that the board is going to give her enough management autonomy, as several members seem to have strong ideas on how the Chief Executive Officer should undertake certain tasks. She is also a little apprehensive as to how much actual help the board will be to her in terms of their levels of expertise. Clearly they have strong knowledge and networks in netball, which will be important, but are more limited in thinking through the key strategic issues facing the franchise. She was hoping for a greater level of business experience to support her.

The first and major task confronting Charlotte is the need to dramatically increase the funding base of the franchise; it must generate a greater level of income to remain viable and competitive. This will require the development and successful implementation of a major sponsorship and income generation strategy. While everyone recognises the importance of maintaining a place in the league, Charlotte knows that attracting the necessary sponsorship dollars and finding ways of generating more income is going to be very difficult. The track record of her league team has not been good; other men's sports have a higher profile in her region; some players have unrealistic expectations regarding what they might receive by way of support or payment; the internal politics surrounding the appointment of the coaching staff has been divisive; and several of the feeding associations/unions are struggling financially.

Apart from the financial issues, she also has to manage other areas such as the establishment of a successful talent development and identification programme, which will require developing a coordinated network of support with the various unions that feed into the franchise. Also important to success will be the development of a higher profile for the franchise, and Charlotte knows that the development of a comprehensive marketing and public relations strategy requires some urgent attention.

Charlotte is aware that she faces long hours and significant hurdles in order to be successful. She knows, too, that she faces the dilemma of many sport managers, namely that her success is going to be tied to the success of her team on the court, and she has limited control over that. But whoever said that managing sport was going to be easy?

Review questions

- How would you define 'sport' for the purpose of managing sport?
- What is sport business management?
- What is the sport industry? Give some examples.
- How does sport contribute to the economy? Describe its size.
- What do you think will be the major technological impacts on sport in the next decade?
- Identify the unique features of the sport product that make it important for sport managers to understand the nature of sport when managing a sport business.
- Discuss how the environment impacts on the way sport is managed.

References

Beech, J. (2004). Introduction. In J. Beech & S. Chadwick (Eds.), *The business of sport management* (pp. 3–24). Harlow, UK: Prentice Hall.

Bruce, T., Falcous, M., & Holly, T. (2007). The mass media and sport. In C. Collins & S. Jackson (Eds.), *Sport in Aotearoa/New Zealand society* (pp. 147–169). Melbourne: Thomson-Dunmore.

Coakley, J. J., Hallinan, C., Jackson, S., & Mewett, P. (2009). *Sports in society: Issues and controversies in Australia and New Zealand.* Sydney: McGraw-Hill.

Collins, C. (2007a). Politics and sport connections. In C. Collins & S. Jackson (Eds.), *Sport in Aotearoa/New Zealand society* (pp. 190–207). Melbourne: Thomson Dunmore.

Collins, C. (2007b). Politics, government and sport in Aotearoa/New Zealand. In C. Collins & S. Jackson (Eds.), *Sport in Aotearoa/New Zealand society* (pp. 208–229). Melbourne: Thomson Dunmore.

Collins, C. (2007c). Studying sport in society. In C. Collins & S. Jackson (Eds.), *Sport in Aotearoa/New Zealand society* (pp. 1–22). Melbourne: Thomson Dunmore.

Collins, C., & Jackson, S. (Eds.) (2007). *Sport in Aotearoa/New Zealand society.* Melbourne: Thomson Dunmore.

Collins, C., McLeod, T., Thomson, R., & Downey, J. (2007). Challenges ahead: The future and sport in Aotearoa/New Zealand. In C. Collins & S. Jackson (Eds.), *Sport in Aotearoa/New Zealand society* (pp. 443–466). Melbourne: Thomson Dunmore.

Dalziel, P. (2011). *Valuing sport and recreation in New Zealand.* AERU Research Unit, Lincoln University. Retrieved from http://www.nzae.org.nz/conferences/2011/Papers/Session2/25_Dalziel.pdf

Frontier Economics. (2010). *The economic contribution of sport to Australia.* Retrieved from http://www.frontier-economics.com/_library/publications/Frontier%20publication%20-%20The%20economic%20contribution%20of%20sport.pdf

Football stars cash in on fame game. (2005, June 12). The Guardian, reprinted by *Sunday Star Times*, A17.

Goodchild, M., Harris, F., Nana, G., & Russell, S. (2000). *The growing business of sport and leisure: The impact of the physical leisure industry in New Zealand, An update to the 1998 report.* Wellington, New Zealand: Business and Economic Research Limited.

Government of Western Australia, (2009). *More than winning: The value of sport and recreation in Western Australia.* Department of Sport and Recreation.

Gratton, C., & Taylor, P. (2000). *Economics of sport and recreation.* London: Spon.

Harrison, M. (2005, June 28). Glazer's Man Utd bid unfair says academic. *The Independent.* Retrieved from http://www.independent.co.uk/news/business/news/glazers-man-utd-bid-unfair-says-academic-496854.html

Hillary Commission. (1998). *The business of sport and leisure: The economic impact of sport and leisure in New Zealand.* Wellington, New Zealand: Hillary Commission.

Hood, J. (1997). Sport management through business eyes. Paper presented to *Running Sport Conference*, 16–17 May, 1997.

Horne, J. (1996). Kicking racism out of soccer in England and Scotland. *Journal of Sport and Social Issues, 20*, 45–68.

Inkson, K., & Kolb, D. (2002). *Management perspectives for New Zealand* (3rd ed.). Auckland, New Zealand: Pearson Education.

Jensen, B., Sullivan, C., Wilson, N., & Russell, D. (1993). *The business of sport and leisure: The economic impact of sport and leisure in New Zealand.* Wellington, New Zealand: Hillary Commission.

Market Economics Ltd. (2003). *Comparison of America's Cup economic impacts, 2000–2003.* Ministry of Tourism, New Zealand.

Mullins, B., Hardy, S., & Sutton, W. (2007). *Sport marketing.* Champaign, IL: Human Kinetics.

New Zealand Institute of Economic Research. (1997). *The economics of high performance sport, the role of government: Report for the New Zealand Sport Foundation*.NZIER: Wellington.

Nixon, H., & Frey, J. (1996). *A sociology of sport*.San Francisco, CA: Wadsworth Publishing.

Parent, M. M., & Séguin, B. (2008). Toward a model of brand creation for international large-scale sporting events: The impact of leadership, context, and the nature of the event. *Journal of Sport Management*, 22(5), 526–549.

Parkhouse, B. L. (Ed.). (2005). *The management of sport: Its foundation and application* (4th ed.). New York: McGraw Hill.

Parks, J., & Quarterman, J. (Eds.). (2003). *Contemporary sport management*. Champaign, IL: Human Kinetics.

Parks, J. B., Quarterman, J., & Thibault, L. (2010). Managing sport in the 21st century. In P. M. Pedersen, J. B. Parks, J. Quarterman, & L. Thibault (Eds.), *Contemporary sport management* (4th ed.) (pp. 4–27). Champaign, IL: Human Kinetics.

Phillips, J. (2000). Epilogue: Sport and future Australasian culture. In J. Mangan & J. Nauright (Eds.), *Sport in Australasian society: Past and present* (pp. 323–332). London: Frank Cass.

Not half as barmy as they seem (2005, June 2). *The Dominion Post*, p. A5.

Pitts, B., & Stotlar, D. (2007). *Fundamentals of sport marketing* (3rd ed.). Morgantown, WV: Fitness Information Technology.

Ramus, D. (2011, May 4). *League's most hated player?* Retrieved from http://www.bigpondsport.com/leagues-most-hated-player/tabid/91/newsid/70796/default.aspx

Sawyer, T. H., Hypes, M., & Hypes, J. A. (2004). *Financing the sport enterprise*. Champaign, IL: Sagamore Publications.

Smith, A., & Stewart, B. (1999). *Sports management: A guide to professional practice*.Sydney: Allen & Unwin.

Sport and Recreation New Zealand Act 2002. Public Act; 2002 No 38, 17 October 2002.

Stewart, B., & Smith, A. (1999). The special features of sport. *Annals of Leisure Research*, 2, 87–99.

Thomas, D., & Dyall, L. (1999). Culture, ethnicity and sport management: A New Zealand perspective. *Sport Management Review*, 2, 115–132.

Venture Taranaki. (2009). *The value of rugby to Taranaki*. Venture Taranaki and Taranaki Rugby Union in association with BERL.

Westerbeek, H., & Smith, A. (2003). *Sport business in the global marketplace*. New York: Palgrave Macmillan.

Chapter 2

Structure of Sport and its Management in New Zealand and Australia

Sue Walker and Sarah Leberman

OBJECTIVES

After completing this chapter, you should be able to:

- understand sports participation in New Zealand and Australia;
- understand the strategic and planning context;
- understand the organisational structures for sport in the two countries;
- identify the key 'players' in the public, private and voluntary sectors and their main roles;
- understand how sport is funded, managed and delivered from the grassroots (community sport) to the world stage (high performance).

Key terms

In this chapter, readers will become familiar with the following concepts and terms:
- patterns and trends in sports participation
- the sport and recreation pathway
- strategic, whole-of-sport plans
- community and high performance sport
- public, private/commercial, voluntary and informal sectors
- national, state/territory, regional and local levels of sport
- national sports organisations (NSOs)
- regional sports trusts (RSTs)
- funding for sport
- sportsvilles

Introduction

This chapter describes the strategic and planning context for community and high performance sport in New Zealand and Australia. It then examines the organisational structures for sport in the two countries and describes the main sources of funding. The chapter will describe the different types of organisations at a national, regional, and local level and how they work together to deliver sport to participants along the sport pathway from the foundation to the high performance phase. By the completion of the chapter, the complexity of the structures will be apparent, as will the main similarities and differences between the two countries.

To understand the environment within which sport is managed and delivered, the section for each country begins by briefly describing participation in sport and recreation and recent trends. As well as participating in sport and recreation organised by the sectors described below, many New Zealanders and Australians also participate on an informal or casual basis. This can range from family or friends getting together for a game of cricket on the beach to more structured events run by community groups, iwi and hapu.

For both New Zealand and Australia, the private sector includes a wide range of organisations that provide services and products for profit. Examples include: retailers of sports goods and equipment (such as Rebel Sport); manufacturers (and retailers) of clothing and equipment (such as Canterbury - CCC - and Elite Fitness); facility managers and owners; event organisers; service providers like sports psychologists and instructors and guides (such as ski instructors and mountain guides). The fitness industry is also a large part of the private sector. FitnessNZ reports that there are 300 to 400 fitness centres in New Zealand (Dalziel, 2011). Around 1.73 million Australians are estimated to use fitness centre services, contributing about $872.9 million to the Australian economy in 2007-8 (Access Economics, 2009).

The private sector also supports sport by sponsoring sportspeople, sports teams, and events. High profile sponsorships include adidas' sponsorship of the All Blacks and Emirates' sponsorship of Team New Zealand. Holden is the sponsor of the Australian Netball Diamonds. Sponsors also support junior sport such as Persil's recent sponsorship of the Small Whites and Milo's longstanding support for cricket's junior development programme. At the other end of the spectrum, the private sector also caters for people who do not want to join a sports club or commit to playing for a season by offering opportunities for pay-for-play. There is anecdotal evidence that this type of participation is growing but little data to support this assertion.

Sport in New Zealand and Australia is organised and delivered by national, state/territory, regional and local organisations in the public, private and not-for-profit sectors, although the demarcation between these sectors is blurring (Hayes, 2006). International organisations also have a role to play. Sport can be informal or casual, such as friends getting together for a game of football or to shoot some hoops, or a family game of frisbee at the park. Table 2-1 provides examples of sports organisations by sector and level of provision.

Table 2-1: Examples of sports organisations by sector and level of provision				
LEVEL	PUBLIC SECTOR	PRIVATE SECTOR	NOT-FOR-PROFIT	INFORMAL
International	World Health Organization	adidas Les Mills IMG	International Olympic Committee World Anti-doping Agency (WADA)	Friendly competitions arranged as part of a family/clan reunion
National	SPARC High Performance Sport NZ Australian Sports Commission (ASC) Department of Health & Aging (DHA)	Rebel Sport Canterbury – CCC	National sports organisations (NSOs) New Zealand Olympic Committee (NZOC) Australian Olympic Committee (AOC)	National participation campaigns

(Continued)

Table 2-1: Examples of sports organisations by sector and level of provision (Continued)				
State/Territory	State Departments of Sport & Recreation (SDSR)	Kelly Sports	NSW Hockey	State indigenous sports festivals Be active campaigns
Regional	Regional councils	Bowling Venues Fitness Centres	Regional sports organisations Parafed Otago	Tramping, climbing, sailing Māori Sports Festival - Christchurch
Local	Local councils	Indoor Sports Centres	Swan Districts Football Club	Family play in the back yard or skateboarding in the park

Source: Adapted from Hayes (2006, p. 47)

Sport and recreation in New Zealand

Participation in sport and recreation

Sport and recreation are an important part of New Zealanders' lives. People engage in a wide range of activities as participants, volunteers, spectators and supporters. Sport and recreation are not easily defined. Depending on the context and the participant's view, many activities can be classed as sport and recreation. For example, cricket is usually thought of as sport, but when played by a family in the backyard it is often seen as recreation. This chapter is about sport and recreation, but for convenience uses *sport* to refer to both types of activity.

Participation in sport by young people and adults

Information available shows that a high proportion of both young people and adults play sport, but participation rates and patterns vary with gender and age. There is limited recent information on young people's participation in sport. This will be remedied shortly as SPARC began a nationwide survey of five to 18-year-olds in August 2011, with results due in the first quarter of 2012. Surveys of young people (SPARC, 2003; Carnachan, 2010) show that:

- almost all (9 out of 10) young people play at least one sport and, on average, play for around half-an-hour a day;
- most young people play sport at school or with family and friends;
- club sport is played by around one-third of young people; and
- participation rates vary with gender and age: boys spend more time playing sport than girls and are more likely to play club sport and get coaching; and participation rates decline as young people enter their teenage years.

Traditional preferences for activities are evident, with rugby the number one sport for boys and netball for girls, although soccer was the number two activity for both genders. These were the preferences a decade ago and some evidence, from the NZSSSC's census for example, suggests teenagers' sporting choices are changing. Individual sports (like cycling and orienteering), event-based activities, and those allowing participants the ability to train, compete and move onto something else are becoming more popular than traditional, season-based, team sports (Carnachan, 2010).

The best source of data for adult participation in sport is SPARC's 2007/08 Active New Zealand survey (SPARC, 2008). This shows that:

- like young people, almost all adults (9 out of 10) take part in some sport; this provides a measure of total participation and participation rates decrease to around eight out of 10 if the two most popular recreation activities (walking and gardening) are excluded;
- adults spend, on average, around two and a half hours a week playing sport (this figure doubles if walking and gardening are included);
- club sport is played by around one-sixth of adults;
- almost four out of ten adults receive some coaching and a similar proportion take part in organised competitions or events;
- as for young people, adults' participation varies with gender and age: participation rates are only slightly higher for men than women, but men spend, on average, an hour more a week playing sport than women; and younger adults are more likely to play sport than older adults - figures range from over nine out of 10 for 18 to 24-year-olds to around six out of 10 for those 65 years and over; and
- gender differences are also evident in the ways in which people participate, with men more likely to play club sport and more likely to play competitively than women.

Trends in participation

The surveys of young people in 1997/98 and 2000/01 (SPARC, 2003) pointed to a decline in overall participation. The decline in participation rates (from 93% in 1997/98 to 88.5% in 2000/02) was statistically significant, but it is not possible to know whether the trend continued over the next decade. The decline was apparent for boys and girls and across a number of settings, including at school. However, the level of participation in club activities did not change, either for all young people or by gender or age.

For adults, comparing results from Active NZ with those from earlier surveys shows that overall participation in sport has remained at a similar level over the ten years from 1997/98 to 2007/08. Participation over this period for men remained at the same level, while for women the figures suggest that participation increased.

Elite participation

Some New Zealanders are able to earn high incomes as international sports stars, for example, Michael Campbell as a professional golfer (winner of the US Open Championship in 2005) and Ryan Nelsen, ONZM, as a professional footballer playing for Blackburn Rovers in the English Premier League since 2005. New Zealanders are also employed as professional rugby players and coaches around the world. Professional teams compete in Australasian competitions including the ANZ Netball Championship, the Hyundai A League (football), the National Basketball League, the National Rugby League (NRL) and Super 15 Rugby.

A small group of elite sport participants receive funding as part of government investment in high performance sport. A national network of high performance operations supports elite athletes and their support personnel to compete on the world stage. In 2010, 700 athletes and support people from 29 sports were recognised and funded as elite sportspeople. This includes *carded athletes* who are eligible for an allocation of performance services as determined by their national sport organisation. As at 11 February 2011, there were 522 carded individuals from 16 sports (Table 2-2).

Table 2-2: Carded athletes as at 11 February 2011			
SPORT	NUMBER	SPORT	NUMBER
Athletics	39	Paralympics	31
Bike	68	Rowing	79
Canoeing	24	Swimming	36
Curling	2	Taekwondo	13
Equestrian	17	Triathlon	26
Football	28	Winter Sports - Snow Sports	12
Hockey	47	Winter Sports - Ice Sports	3
Netball	45	Yachting	52

Source: SPARC (2011c).

Participation in sport - the pathway

The previous section highlighted the importance of sport to New Zealanders, whether they play sport informally or compete on the world stage. To understand more about how people participate and to structure support programmes and investments, SPARC uses a pathway that describes the key stages of a participant's engagement (Figure 2-1). There are three key stages in the pathway:

- **Foundation phase (explore and learn)**, the entry level to sport (and recreation activities), where development is fostered through providing playful, fun and supportive environments for children to *explore* and *learn* skills.
- **Community sport and recreation phase (participate)**, where there is a need to provide for dual aspirations of social and competitive participation and diverse ranges of activities.
- **High-performance phase (perform and excel)**, where the performance potential of people is realised and participants are identified and supported to transition to *perform* and excel.

The pathway is a participant-focussed model that recognises the dual outcomes of lifelong participation and high performance. It also recognises that people participate socially and competitively and that changes in the way people participate over their lifetime are common, with people taking up new activities. Movement through the pathway occurs when an individual is ready, rather than at a pre-determined stage.

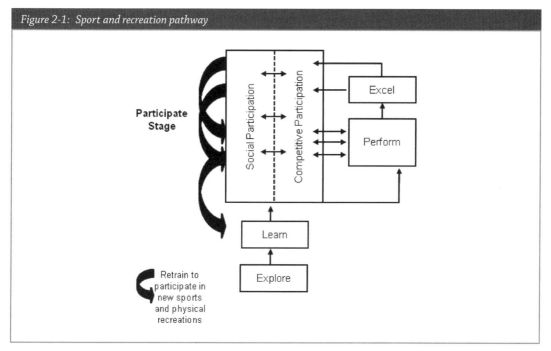

Figure 2-1: *Sport and recreation pathway*

Source: SPARC (2011d)

Strategy and roles

The pathway forms part of SPARC's strategic approach to sport. SPARC's strategic plan for 2009 to 2015 (SPARC, 2009a), along with the strategies and plans of the national and regional sport and recreation organisations and local councils, provides the strategic and planning context for sport in New Zealand. Results against strategic and annual targets are reported in organisations' annual reports, which also include reporting on financial performance. As a Government agency, SPARC's 3-year priorities and annual performance targets are also set out in its yearly Statement of Intent, which is prepared in consultation with the Minister for Sport and Recreation. Results showing how SPARC has achieved its performance targets are reported in the Annual Report to Parliament (recent reports are available at: www.sparc.org.nz/en-nz/resources-and-publications/Publications-2/Sparc-Corporate/).

SPARC

SPARC's five-year strategic plan provides the national context for sport and recreation and reflects the Government's priorities for the sector. High performance sport is further guided by a high performance strategy for 2006 to 2012 (revised in 2010, see SPARC, 2010a).

SPARC's strategy focuses on meeting the sport and recreation needs of New Zealanders. The plan sets out three high-level goals:

- more kids in sport and recreation;
- more New Zealanders in sport and recreation; and
- more winners on the world stage.

The plan contains measurable increases for each of these goals, which are being assessed by a programme of work set out in SPARC's performance measurement framework (SPARC, 2011a).

Guided by the high-level goals, SPARC's priority areas for 2009-2015 are:

- young New Zealanders – with an initial focus on increasing participation in organised sport and recreation;
- grassroots sport – with a focus on getting more resources to clubs, teams and young people's sport;
- recreation – the focus here is on outdoor recreation as described in the Outdoor Recreation Strategy (SPARC, 2009b);
- high performance – to enhance high performance sport and see more New Zealanders winning or on podiums in pinnacle events and global competitions; and
- partner capability – improving the capability of sport and recreation organisations (for example, RST, NSOs) to deliver sport and recreation opportunities to New Zealanders.

The plan describes SPARC's tactics for delivering its strategy - the *Game Plan*, as well as highlighting some of the challenges that must be addressed to achieve the five-year goals. SPARC's describes its role - as leading, investing and enabling –a move away from developing and implementing programmes such as Green Prescriptions (note: this programme is being continued by the Ministry of Health - www.moh.govt.nz/greenprescription).

Central government supports sport across a range of portfolios, including a sport and recreation portfolio. Other portfolios that contribute to the management and/or delivery of sporting opportunities include education, conservation, economic development (including New Zealand Major Events), racing, transport, and agriculture and forestry. The Accident Compensation Corporation (ACC) also invests in injury prevention programmes to reduce the social costs of sport and recreation injuries.

SPARC and HPSNZ are the largest central government organisations responsible for sport. SPARC is a Crown entity and HPSNZ is a Crown entity subsidiary of SPARC. Each organisation is governed by a Board, with the Minister of Sport and Recreation appointing the SPARC Board. SPARC was formally established on 1 January 2003 under the Sport and Recreation New Zealand Act 2002 (www.legislation.govt.nz/act/public/2002/0038/latest/DLM157117.html). Under the Act, SPARC has 14 functions that can be summarised as policy, research and public education, targeting population groups, funding and infrastructure delivery, and dispute resolution.

SPARC's performance is overseen by the Ministry of Culture and Heritage, which also administers Vote Sport and Recreation (i.e., the funding allocated by Government to sport and recreation). As well as direct Vote funding, SPARC receives money from the Lottery Grants Board. SPARC (2009, p. 14) describes its role as:

- **leading**, providing clear and strong leadership for the sport and recreation sector;
- **investing**, on behalf of Government, in organisations that are able to help SPARC achieve its outcomes; and
- **enabling**, which means building the capacity of partner organisations by providing expert advice, resources, research and good practice to improve; for example, governance and management, the use of information technology, the management of human resources, the use of research, and monitoring.

High Performance Sport New Zealand (HPSNZ)

HPSNZ, established in August 2011 as a subsidiary of SPARC, is following the existing high performance strategy, which will be reviewed after the Olympics in London in 2012. The strategy recognises that New Zealand has a smaller talent pool and less funding than most other sporting nations and so argues that the high performance system needs to be wiser, savvier, more innovative and more strategic.

The strategy describes nine tactics to achieve the mission of *More New Zealanders winning on the world stage*. These include: leadership; targeted investment (up to 75% of high performance investment is targeted at results-capable sports and athletes); athlete development (the perform and excel stages of the pathway in Figure 2-1); world-class coaching; knowledge capture and transfer; cutting-edge services to athletes (previously delivered by the two New Zealand Academies of Sport, but now part of HPSNZ); world-class facilities; major events (including effective event-hosting strategies in New Zealand and attendance strategies outside New Zealand); and using technology and innovation to generate competitive advantage.

HPSNZ began operation on 8 August 2011 and is responsible for developing and supporting New Zealand's elite athletes. HPSNZ was formed through a merger of SPARC's high performance unit and the two New Zealand Academies of Sport. As well as developing high performance athletes, HPSNZ will develop a network of world-class training facilities in partnership with the private sector.

The new structure allows HPSNZ to operate independently by having its own Board, its own Chief Executive reporting directly to the Board and its own brand. At the same time HPSNZ is integrated with SPARC in that the Boards will have the same Chair, four members of the SPARC Board (including the Chair will be on HPSNZ's Board, the Chief Executive of SPARC will be an ex officio member (non-voting) of HPSNZ's Board, HPSNZ's Chief Executive will be an ex officio member of SPARC's senior leadership team, and SPARC will provide corporate services to the new entity through a Shared Services Agreement. SPARC retains responsibility for all reporting and accounting to Government. SPARC's team of Relationship Mangers continues to be the main point of contact for the national sport and recreation organisations. While HPSNZ is operating already, details of its management structure will not be finalised until the Chief Executive Alex Baumann, takes up his position in early 2012. Information about the structure and operation of the new organisation will be available on its website: www.hpsnz.org.nz.

SPARC's and HPSNZ's strategic goals are mirrored and developed in the plans of strategic partners, principally NSOs and RSTs.

National Sports Organisations

NSOs are responsible for developing and implementing strategic high performance plans and each NSO has a high performance director/manager responsible for leading the development of the plan. These plans identify all the critical areas that have the ability to impact on athlete performance and set out strategies and tactics to address these.

NSOs are also being encouraged to produce community sport plans; with seven NSOs having developed or are in the process of developing these plans to increase their focus on community participation (see SPARC's 2009/10 Annual Report for details (SPARC, 2010b)). Some sports are taking an integrated approach and producing whole-of-sport plans, linking community and high-performance sport.

New Zealand Football's Whole of Football Plan is one example and explains the purpose as follows:

> With international success, a higher profile and greater financial stability, we now have the chance to implement a national development structure to benefit participants at all levels. It involves everyone in the game working together, which is why it's called the Whole of Football Plan (WOFP). This master plan aligns all our development programmes to provide a unified pathway into the game and deliver a consistent experience to all participants. It's not just about players– it also involves the ongoing development of coaches, referees and administrators.
>
> *(New Zealand Football, n.d., p. 2)*

Hockey New Zealand (2010a) also recognises that "the profile and market attractiveness of hockey has not moved with the times" and to counter this describes Six Priority Projects in its Whole of Hockey Business Plan, which the Chief Executive describes in a letter to Hockey New Zealand's Boards of Associations, Boards of NHL Regions and Councils as "not…Hockey New Zealand's plan, it is our plan, the Hockey Community's plan" (Hockey New Zealand, 2010b).

Sustaining and growing their sports is also a key objective for many sports organisations. To achieve this goal, organisations recognise that they need to be strategic, and understand the environment they work in and the changing needs of their participants. In its 2009-2012 Strategic Plan, Netball New Zealand (n.d., p. 4) aspires to be "New Zealand's leading sport by 2020" and "the biggest participation sport" but acknowledges that it is competing with other sports and forms of entertainment and needs to "be flexible enough to meet the changing needs of participants in terms of delivery, scheduling and forms of the game" (p. 7).

As another example, Athletics New Zealand's vision is to see "all New Zealanders engaged in Athletics" (Athletics NZ, 2011 p. 2) and to achieve this they aim to provide "new opportunities for participation through events and services" (p. 3) and a transformation project has been launched to achieve these changes (for details see: www.athletics.org.nz/Article.aspx?ID=5836).

To sustain and grow participation, NSOs are also focussing on more and better facilities and, among others, Athletics New Zealand, Bike New Zealand, Hockey New Zealand and New Zealand Football, have developed national and/or regional facilities strategies.

Incorporated societies are governed by a board or a committee (whose members may be elected or appointed) and managed by paid staff and/or volunteers and include most of the national and regional sport and recreation organisations (NSO, NROs and RSOs) and community sport and recreation clubs. NSOs are responsible for the overall administration and development of their sports. Netball New Zealand, for example, describes its work as "high performance, game development, marketing, finance and administration", while the New Zealand Rugby Union (NZRU) says its role is "fostering, developing, administering, promoting and representing the game of rugby in New Zealand" (for more details see: www.mynetball.co.nz and www.nzru.co.nz). Both organisations work with regional organisations. Netball New Zealand works with 12 Regional Entities (managed by regional managers) to administer, promote and develop the game nationwide and the NZRU works in partnership with 26 Provincial Unions. Both Netball New Zealand and the NZRFU also work with professional and semi-professional franchises to compete in the ANZ Championship (netball) and the Rebel Sport Super 15 (rugby).

Regional organisations, in turn, work with clubs and other local groups. Netball, for example, has over 1,000 clubs in 92 centres catering for over 135,000 registered members and a further 80,000 people playing in social competitions; the centres provide facilities and support for teams to play nationwide and are linked to Netball New Zealand's Regional Entities. The NZRU's Provincial Unions support more than 500 clubs throughout New Zealand, which have over 140,000 members.

These are examples of two of the larger NSOs, but visiting the web sites of a number of the smaller sports organisations shows that their purpose and aims are similar, even if their regional and local structures differ.

Regional Sport Trusts

RSTs strategic plans share many of the goals and priorities of SPARC's strategic plan. For example, Sport Bay of Plenty (2010) describes its priorities for 2010 to 2013 as: young people, grassroots sport and improving capability. It also adds Active Lifestyles (ensuring all of the Bay of Plenty has the opportunity to be active so that More People, are More Active, More Often) as a priority, reflecting the fact that RSTs have other stakeholders whose focus is on health and physical activity. As another example, Sport Wellington (2010) describes it strategic outcomes as: more kids with a life-long love of sport and recreation; great delivery of and access to sport and recreation; and strong partners who consistently deliver.

Trusts are not-for-profit organisations governed by a Board of Trustees. Examples include the 17 RSTs, which are independent not-for-profit organisations whose Boards of Trustees are drawn from the local community. Other examples are the John Walker Find Your Field of Dreams Foundation (a charitable trust aiming to encourage young people in Manukau in South Auckland to pursue a more active lifestyle through sport and physical recreation) and the Wellington Regional Stadium Trust (which manages the Westpac Stadium).

The RSTs act as network hubs and have strong working relationships with sports organisations, local councils, health agencies, education institutions, local businesses and the media. As 'umbrella' organisations, RSTs work across the broad sport and physical recreation spectrum, assisting regional sports organisations, schools and club, as well as supporting individuals and community groups participating in less structured physical activity. They provide a regional voice for their sport and recreation communities. RSTs are accountable to a variety of stakeholders and often have contractual relationships with local councils, health agencies, community trusts and commercial sponsors, as well as SPARC. RSTs are linked by a national network – Sport*net* NZ.

Other sport organisations

National Recreation Organisations (NROs) are key players in creating and sustaining recreational opportunities that encourage more New Zealanders to be more active more often. Examples include the YMCA, Girl Guides Association of New Zealand, NZ Alpine Club, as well as umbrella organisations like the New Zealand Recreation Association (NZRA).

Regional Sport Organisations are organisations established to develop and support sport regionally. Most RSOs are responsible for the strategic direction of the sport in their region, organising local competitions, representative teams, and coaches' and officials' education.

Clubs are central to the delivery of community sport and recreation. There are an estimated 15,000 clubs in New Zealand varying in size and catering for single or multiple sports. There is not a comprehensive list of clubs but NZ Sport (www.nzsport.co.nz) and Sportsground (www.sportsground .co.nz) are two organisations building directories. Clubs are increasingly being encouraged to establish links with schools to help young people transition from school to community sport and so continue participating or volunteering in sport throughout their lives.

Clubs and other organisations in the not-for-profit sector could not operate without volunteers. There are an estimated three-quarters of a million sports volunteers of all types in New Zealand who donate over 50 million hours of their time over the course of a year (Dalziel, 2011). The main roles include: coaches/instructors who contributed 16.6m million hours, referees and other officials (6.6 million hours), administrators and committee members (10.6 million hours), and parent helpers (14.9 million hours).

Local government

Long Term Plans (LTPs, also known as Long Term Council Community Plans - LTCCPs) are the vehicle used by local councils to describe their activities to achieve community outcomes, which are identified after consulting with their communities. Long Term plans, which have a ten-year perspective, are produced after a review every three years (Annual Plans are produced in each of the other two years).

As one example, one of Wellington City Council's community outcomes is "Wellingtonians will enjoy recreation and be amongst the most active in New Zealand" (Wellington City Council, 2009, p. 122). The Council translates this into its own outcome as "More actively engaged: Wellington residents will be actively engaged in their communities, and in recreation and leisure activities". To achieve this outcome the plan sets out Recreation Activities and Components that include swimming pools, sports fields, synthetic turf sports fields, recreation centres, playgrounds, and marinas, as well as recreation partnerships and programmes and grants. The Council says that it knows that it will have achieved its outcome "When the number of recreation programmes, and participation rates in our programmes, continue to achieve performance targets and when resident participation in physical activities continues to increase".

Local government (11 regional councils, 67 territorial authorities, 13 city councils and 54 district councils) plays a key role in providing facilities, programmes and services for sport. As Dalziel (2011, p. 57) explains:

> Councils are responsible for caring for and maintaining lakes, rivers, beaches, parks, camping grounds, sports fields, stadiums, swimming pools, recreation centres, gymnasiums, cycle-ways, walkways, playgrounds, picnic areas and botanic gardens. The new Auckland Council, for example, reports that the region has more than 4,219 parks covering 83,164 hectares (16.6 per cent of the Auckland land area).

Auckland Council's website (http://www.aucklandcity.govt.nz/whatson/sports/) also says that they have:

- nine recreation centres
- 12 swimming pools
- three public golf courses

- more than 100 public tennis courts
- 550 sports fields
- 13 skate parks.

The policy and strategic direction of councils are set by elected representatives (councillors) and implemented by staff and managers. As described above, councils set out their priorities and work programmes for a 10-year period in their LTPs.

Local councils are increasingly considering facility partnerships with schools and community organisations as an efficient and cost-effective way to meet the sporting needs of communities as well as students. A recent guide (Visitor Solutions, 2011) sets out the benefits, challenges and opportunities of these partnerships to assist organisations considering partnerships.

SPARC encourages the sport and recreation sector to get involved in the consultation and reviews processes for Long Term Plans to make councils aware of the issues facing the sector and underline the importance of councils' role as a provider and funder of sport and recreation facilities and services.

Figure 2-2 shows the links between, and roles of, organisations in the public and not-for-profit sector.

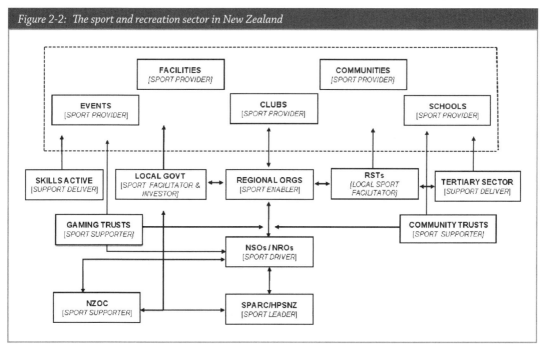

Figure 2-2: *The sport and recreation sector in New Zealand*

Source: SPARC (2011)

Funding for sport

Funding for sport comes from central government, local government, philanthropic trusts, gaming and community trusts. Support also comes from the private sector in the form of sponsorship, which may be in cash or kind. Using The Estimates of Appropriations 2010/11, Dalziel (2011, section 5.2) estimated that, for the year ending June 2010, central government spent $483.1 million on sport; this includes spending on sport-related education, recreation, outdoor recreation and racing, as well components of tourism spending and spending on activities like search and rescue.

Investment in community sport and recreation and high performance sport has grown significantly over the last six years as a result of increasing government financial support for the sector, which is administered by SPARC and now HPSNZ. Information about SPARC's funding and expenditure each year is in its Annual Reports to Parliament. In 2009/10 SPARC invested $35 million in community sport and recreation programmes. Investment in community and school sport has increased as a result of KiwiSport, launched in August 2009 and providing $82 million over four years. KiwiSport funding has two components. The Direct Fund is allocated by the Ministry of Education, providing new funding to primary schools and replacing Sportfit funding to secondary schools. The KiwiSport Regional Partnership Fund is allocated to RSTs by SPARC and administered by RSTs for use in their communities. RSTs are using the fund to encourage new partnerships involving schools, clubs, local and community groups to get more young people involved in sport and recreation. Examples of the way KiwiSport funding is being used are on SPARC's website.

Investment in high performance sport in 2009/10 was $38 million. This sum will increase substantially over the next 3 years and by 2012/13 will be over $60 million annually. This increase is to fund high performance facilities, increase resourcing to athletes and build a stronger focus on high performance sport.

SPARC targets its investment into organisations and programmes that will help it to achieve its goals. Funding is targeted to create a sport and recreation environment where more New Zealanders participate, support, and win. SPARC's approach means partnerships are established with organisations at the national and regional level, and in local sport and recreation communities. Key partnerships are with NSOs, NROs, RSTs and local councils.

Funding to NSOs includes funding targeted at those organisations that are able to achieve high performance and community outcomes and contestable funding. Regional sports trusts are contracted to help SPARC achieve its outcomes and to meet the sport and recreational needs of their communities. Local councils are given priority for SPARC's Active Communities funding, which supports innovative project-based initiatives that demonstrate a collaborative approach to reducing barriers to participation in sport and recreation at a community level. The initiative supports pilot projects targeting new/modified methods of delivery to increase participation in sport and recreation and lessons learned are shared with the sector (for more details see: www.sparc.org.nz/en-nz/communities-and-clubs/Active-Communities/Sharing-Good-Practice/).

Other funding sources for high performance sportspeople include:
- Prime Minister's Athlete Scholarships, which are managed by SPARC on behalf of the Government. The Government established this programme in late 2000 to enable emerging and talented New Zealanders to concurrently pursue tertiary study and elite-level sport development (further details and examples of recent recipients are available at: www.sparc.org .nz/en-nz/high-performance/PM-Scholarships/Prime-Ministers-Athlete-Scholarships/). Prime Minister's Athlete Gold Level Scholarships also allow athletes to study after they retire or are de-carded.

- The Prime Minister's Officials, Coaches and Support Teams Scholarships, also managed by SPARC, are to develop the skills of elite-level officials, coaches and support teams (team managers, high performance managers, support services coordinators, sports scientists, sports medicine providers, and other sports specialists whose work underpins elite athletes' achievements).
- Performance Enhancement Grants (PEGs) which provide world-class athletes with financial support to enable them to dedicate time to training and competing, in order to maximise their sport potential. PEGs nominations must be endorsed and submitted by the athlete's NSO (for more details see: www.sparc.org.nz/en-nz/high-performance/Athletes/Performance-Enhancement-Grants-PEGs/).

Local government invests hundreds of millions of dollars annually in sport and recreation partnerships, facilities, programmes, and major events. Chapter 18 provides more detailed information on the amount spent on facilities.

Gaming trusts invested $81 million into sport, recreation and physical activity in 2010, with just over $73 million going to sport (SPARC, 2011b). The largest amount of sport-related funding ($32 million) went to local clubs, followed by regional organisations ($21 million). Comparing investment in 2010 and 2007 showed a decrease of 17.7% (from $98.5 million to $81 million). This decrease was due partly to a decrease in funds from class four gaming machines (pokies), which was down by 10.6 percent over this period, and partly to the merger of two of the trusts part-way through 2010 (the Lion and Perry Foundations). The purpose for which grants are made has varied considerably, other than for the major item of salary support, which has held steady at around $18 million, although this has increased as a percentage of total funding from 18.5% in 2007 to 22.1% in 2010. Some of the major sports are particularly reliant on this type of funding, leaving their staffing reliant on discretionary funding that may not be sustained if the priorities of the trusts change.

Community Trusts, such as The ASB Community Trust and the Community Trust of Southland, also invest significant sums in sport and recreation.

Despite a range of funding streams, like other not-for-profit organisations, funding and financial management are critical issues for sports organisations and clubs. A study by Cordery and Baskerville (2008, p. 1) of six sporting codes (rugby, netball, cricket, hockey, squash and golf) found that "more than 40% of sports clubs have noncurrent (i.e., long-term) debt and, generally, smaller clubs have higher ratios of total liabilities: total assets. These debts pose a risk to the clubs' financial sustainability". This work is currently being extended by looking at the financial statements for football and golf for RSOs and NSOs, as well as clubs, to see what the key sources of funding show about financial vulnerability and to see what non-financial resources can strengthen sports clubs' finances and contribute to organisational effectiveness.

Sport and recreation clubs have traditionally operated independently and often as single-purpose clubs. However, as financial and other challenges grow, initiatives are underway to bring clubs together in what are referred to as sportvilles or sportsvilles.

Burley reviewed eight such initiatives and concluded:

> Those that are successful are generally very successful. They display healthy financial positions, and are able to demonstrate growth in sport participation by the constituent

clubs that formed them. They are able to show much more than this. Many of the successful clubs provide a range of programmes that they support as a result of the increased human capital and infrastructure they created out of forming collectives.

(2008, p. 3)

A more recent example is described in the Hutt City sportsville case.

CASE STUDY: HUTT CITY SPORTSVILLE

Hutt City sportsville is establishing sports club partnerships in the Hutt Valley. The project aims to increase club capability, provide sustainable, long-term governance structures for sport, and give sponsors and funders more surety of return on investments in sports facilities and programmes.

A sportsville is owned by member clubs but operated independently of the clubs with its own board of directors. It is not an amalgamation of clubs and doesn't take decision-making away from clubs.

Sportsvilles aim to engage and attract young people, develop partnerships with schools, lead to new participation initiatives, and create quality, affordable experiences for club members, as well as increasing pay-for-play options for local residents.

In Hutt City, Fraser Park and Petone sportsvilles are already up and running and Wainuiomata is next in line.

Fraser Park, for example, was established by eight founding clubs and associations and plans are being discussed for a central clubroom catering for rugby, football, cricket, hockey, softball and squash – replacing four existing bars/clubroom – and for more and better sports fields and turfs for all of these sports.

Source: Hutt City Council - www.huttcity.govt.nz/sportsville

Sport and recreation in Australia

Participation in sport and recreation

The Australian Bureau of Statistics reports that in 2009-10, 10.5 million Australian participated in sport and physical recreation. Of these 80% took part in non-organised sport, and just over 40% participated in organised sport (Australian Bureau of Statistics, 2011).

Participation in sport by young people and adults

Of the 2.7 million children aged 5 to 14 years in Australia between April 2008 and April 2009, 63% had played sport outside of school hours, organised by school, a club or an association (Australian Bureau of Statistics, 2009). The participation rates basically the remained same between 2003 and 2009. Interestingly, the rate of participation in bike riding over the same period declined for both boys and girls. Participation overall in organised sport was highest amongst 9-11 year olds, and higher for boys across all age groups. The greatest difference was in the 12-14 year age group where 74% of boys participated in organised sport compared with only 55% of girls. The most popular sport for boys was soccer and for girls was swimming representing 20% of the participants respectively (Australian Bureau of Statistics, 2011).

In 2009, the number of Australians over 15 years of age who participated in regular physical activity (at least three times a week) remained the same as in 2008 at 8.2 million, but decreased as a percentage of the population from 49.3% to 47.7%. Similarly, the percentage of people over 15 years of age who only exercised once a week also decreased from 71.5% in 2008 to 69.5% in 2009 (Standing Committee on Recreation and Sport, 2009, 2010). In 2010 the total participation rate in any physical activity, was an estimated 14.4 million persons aged 15 years and over, or 82.3% of the population participated at least once annually in physical activity for exercise, recreation or sport. An estimated 12.2 million persons aged 15 years and over, or 69.4% of the population, participated at least once per week, on average, in physical activity. The regular participation rate of at least three times per week was an estimated 8.3 million persons, or 47.7% of the population (Standing Committee on Recreation and Sport, 2011).

Strategy and roles

The responsibility for sport in Australia at a Federal level has changed over the years largely reflecting the Government of the time. The latest move in 2008 was to the Department of Health and Aging (DHA), where sport is regarded as a division housing the Australian Sports Commission (ASC) and the Australian Sports Anti-Doping Authority (ASADA). Sport and recreation policy advice is delivered through the Sport Performance and Participation program, which aims to both increase participation and achieve on the world stage. Whilst the ASC and ASADA operate under the DHA, they are independent agencies, but inextricably linked with the DHA.

The DHA also supports the Sport and Recreation Ministers' Council (SRMC), which provides a forum for co-ordination and co-operation between the Commonwealth, State and Territory governments on matters relating to the development of sport and recreation in Australia, and the ministers responsible for sport and recreation in New Zealand and Papua New Guinea (ASC, 2011a). For example, in June 2011 the SRMC signed off a national policy on match-fixing in sport in order to protect the integrity of sport using a national approach. They also agreed that the state and territory institutes and academies of sport would work together with the AIS and NSOs to support athletes through agreed high performance plans. All apart from NSW agreed to this. The Ministers also endorsed the National Sport and Active Recreation Policy frame work aimed at increasing participation, success on the international stage and a strong nation al competition (ASC, 2011b). Similarly, the Standing Committee on Recreation and Sport (SCORS) comes under the DHA and is responsible for the annual exercise, recreation and sport survey, as well as for example, the development on policies for women in sport.

Federal government

The Australian Sport Commission (ASC) "is the Australian Government body that supports, develops and invests in sport at all levels in Australia. It works with NSOs, state and local governments, schools and community organisations to support the development of the Australian sport system from the grassroots community level to high performance sport" (ASC, 2010, p. 6). The ASC was established by the Australian Sports Commission Act 1989, including the Australian Institute of

Sport (AIS) which had been operating independently since 1981. The key outcomes are seen in Table 2-3.

Table 2-3: Key outcomes of the ASC
Outcome 1: Improve participation in structured physical activity, particularly organised sport, at the community level, including through leadership and targeted community-based sports activity.
Program 1.1: National sport system development Key strategic directions: - Growth in sport participation - Best practice management and governance of sport - Maintaining the integrity of Australian sport - Enhanced leadership in the international sports community
Outcome 2: Excellence in sports performance and continued international sporting success by talented athletes and coaches, including through leadership in high performance athlete development, and targeted science and research.
Program 2.1: National elite athlete development Key strategic directions: - Sustained achievements in high performance sport - The Australian Institute of Sport – a world centre of excellence

Source: ASC (2010, p. 7)

The release of the independent review of sport in Australia in November 2009, *The Future of Sport in Australia*, called the Crawford Report after the chair David Crawford, highlighted the lack of a national sports policy in Australia and also questioned the overemphasis on the elite spectrum of sport at the expense of participation. Please consider the following extract from the Crawford Report and consider the advantages and disadvantages of adopting the recommendations.

CASE STUDY: THE CRAWFORD REPORT – REFORMING THE ASC TO LEAD THE SPORT SYSTEM

The current Australian sports system is very complex, inefficient and cumbersome. Delivery of sport involves all three tiers of government and its various arms including sport and recreation, health, education, and other portfolios. Most of the NSOs also have 'federal' structures consisting of several layers of governance and control. As well, the sports system involves the participation of many other players, including the Australian Olympic Committee, private providers, universities and the school system.

The result is that every aspect of sport has to be managed across multiple organisational boundaries by voluntary collaborative effort involving many stakeholders. This takes time and effort and does not always happen. There is frequently poor co-operation between stakeholders, leading to inconsistent and ineffective delivery. The Panel was frequently told that the level of co-operation across the sports system has been deteriorating and is less effective than it was before Australia hosted the 2000 Olympic Games. The ASC is seen by most to be the logical 'broker' across the system, building collaboration and bringing various parties to the table to secure agreement. The ASC itself understands how important this is and in its submission declared that it is ready to "lead the strengthening of relationships among stakeholders and across all jurisdictions…".

This is welcomed by the Panel. But to fulfil this promise, the ASC will not only have to change its style but also be restructured to remove activities that give it a 'conflict of interest' with those organisations it must support and bring to the table.

(Continued)

There are at least two important areas where the ASC is 'conflicted'. The ASC 'owns' the Australian Institute of Sport (AIS) which has been increasingly viewed by the state and territory institutes and academies of sport (SIS/SAS) and private providers as a competitor. It comes into further conflict when the ASC negotiates the provision of government funding for the NSOs who are deciding whether or not to use the AIS.

Furthermore, the ASC's role in the Active After-school Communities (AASC) program is that of service deliverer and, as such, the ASC is competing with NSOs, other government agencies, non-government organisations or private providers who might also deliver the program.

The Panel believes those activities that create, or have the potential to create a conflict for the ASC, be removed from its operations. Specifically, the AIS should be separated from the ASC and the AASC program should be contracted out by the ASC to appropriate providers at agreed performance standards.

The Panel was told by many respondents in the sports sector that the ASC has not contributed enough to resolving problems and proposing initiatives in key areas of sport. This view is shared by the Panel.

There are many areas where the absence of data or analysis has been telling. We have already noted the dearth of data on total government spending on sport—and make the obvious point that no sensible sports strategy is possible without data on where the money is currently being spent.

While there is talk of rapidly changing demographic and lifestyle shifts in Australian society with significant impact on participation, little research or analysis appears to have been conducted on what this means for sports planning. There seems to have been little attempt to measure outcomes in sport beyond medal counts and certainly there is a paucity of data on the state of community sport. We have been repeatedly told of the need for systems to support volunteers; for locating alternative sources of funding for NSOs and their increasing competition for the 'entertainment' dollar; for creating an inventory of facilities, and for providing whole sector funding packages. The only information that exists on past AIS scholarship holders is through a voluntary alumni association, and little is known about whether they are still engaged in their sports. These are just some of the examples cited through the course of the review.

The Panel believes that the ASC has focused overwhelmingly on elite Olympic sport to the detriment of other sports as well as participation and community sports. It is time this changed. Even, in its own submission, the ASC suggested "community sport was on the brink of collapse" and called for a national plan to rectify the problem.

The areas of elite and community sport are strongly related and the link needs to be reflected at the policy and strategic level. There is an obvious link between the size of the participation base and the flow of talented athletes to the elite end. Elite sports are now recognising that building and 'owning' their grassroots participation structures is an avenue to securing new revenue streams and elite success. The Panel believes it is important that policy and funding decisions are made in ways that recognise the links between elite and participation sport. The ASC's role is defined as covering both elite and participation sport and this linkage needs to be strengthened.

The Panel believes—along with the ASC—that the sport system needs change but that change is also needed at the ASC. Removal of those activities that give it a conflict and strengthening its commitment to building collaboration and problem solving are needed. And to ensure that these changes are driven from the top, the board and executive leadership needs to be reconstituted to ensure that the right skills are in place to meet its objectives.

The Panel's view is that a spill of the current ASC board should take place and the Minister for Sport should take advice on nominations for the new board to ensure the proper skills-set is achieved. The board should have no more than eight non-executive directors plus the chief executive officer (CEO) as a board member. Board members should be chosen on a skills basis but with relevant and diverse experience and a truly national perspective. A chairman and CEO who can best bring the skills and

(Continued)

vision appropriate to meet this new challenge should be appointed. The 'new' ASC should be a much smaller organisation but one that provides strong and empathetic leadership to the entire sports system.

RECOMMENDATIONS:

2.1 Recognising the complex nature of the Australian sports system, a single point of focus is required to provide leadership. That point of focus should be the Australian Sports Commission.

2.2 Consistent with the Australian Sports Commission's leadership role, it should not be involved in service delivery. Those activities that give the Australian Sports Commission a 'conflict' with the other organisations it is supposed to deal with and support should be taken away from it. Specifically, the Australian Institute of Sport should be separated from the Australian Sports Commission and the Active After-school Communities program should be contracted out to appropriate providers at agreed performance standards.

2.3 The Australian Sports Commission should be responsible for developing the overarching strategy framework in light of Australian Government policy, proposing and measuring national outcomes, contributing to policy proposals, solving problems, allocating Australian Government money to elite and community organisations and strengthening and evaluating the national sporting organisations. And very importantly, it should be building collaboration across the sports system.

2.4 The Australian Sports Commission board and executive leadership should be reconstituted to ensure that the right skills are in place to meet the Australian Sports Commission's new objectives. The Australian Sports Commission board should be reconstituted with no more than eight non-executive directors plus the chief executive officer as a board member. Board members should be chosen on a skills basis but with relevant and diverse experience and a truly national perspective. A chairman and chief executive officer who can best bring the skills and vision appropriate to the new challenge should be appointed (Commonwealth of Australia, 2009, p.12–15).

The report included a number of recommendations to the Australian government which were each addressed in the 2010 report, *Australian Sport: The Pathway to Success* (Commonwealth of Australia, 2010). According to the ASC 2009 Annual Report, they are leading reforms to the high performance system in collaboration with national sporting organisations (NSOs); peak bodies such as the Australian Olympic Committee, Australian Paralympic Committee and Australian Commonwealth Games Association; and state and territory institutes and academies of sport (SIS/SAS). The key planks of reform are:

- a new Collaborative Partnership Agreement with SIS/SAS and peak bodies;
- a new national elite athlete support scheme;
- an enhanced high performance program planning model;
- an enhanced National Talent Identification and Development (NTID) program;
- an improved Australian Institute of Sport (AIS) service delivery model; and
- an improved National Athlete Career and Education program (ASC, 2010).

The ASC is also seeking to build stronger relationships with all the sport system partners, but particularly the state departments of sport and recreation (SDSRs).

The Annual Report suggests that:

> Generally the Australian sports system has solid and mature 'horizontal' relationships and somewhat tenuous 'vertical' relationships. Strengthening the ASC/SDSR relationships will provide the ASC with improved connectivity to state and territory sporting organisations

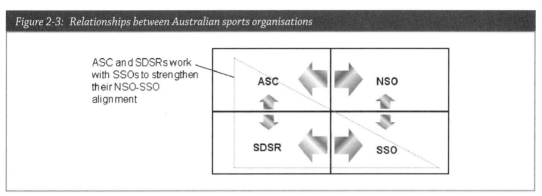

Figure 2-3: Relationships between Australian sports organisations

Source: ASC (2010, p. 9)

and help drive stronger alignment with their respective NSOs. Strengthening the SDSR relationships will also provide the ASC with a vital link to what is happening on the ground. SDSRs are more closely connected to local government and community clubs and thereby are integral players in the government sector's responses to many of the challenges facing sport.

(ASC, 2010, p. 9)

Australian institute of sport

The AIS was established as a result of poor medal performances in the Montreal Olympic Games, with the AIS opened in 1981 leading to a strong medal performance at the Los Angeles Olympic Games in 1984. The concept of the AIS was to have one location for elite athletes to live and train surrounded by the best sport support staff, including coaching, sport scientists, sports medics and athlete career advisors. The delivery of this service has spread across the country including high performance bases in Adelaide, Brisbane, the Gold Coast, Melbourne, Perth and Sydney. The AIS offers 36 sport programs in 26 sports with a range of scholarships available to Australia's best athletes. (For more information please see http://www.ausport.gov.au/ais). In 2009.10 $158.7 million was allocated to high performance sport of which 4143.8 million came from government funding. It also provides around 700 scholarships a year to athletes from across Australia.

All states have their own institutes of sport with varying objectives. Prior to the Crawford Report there was much competition between state institute of sports and the links between them and the AIS. Three key recommendations arose from the Crawford Report resulting in the government adopting a new national approach to deliver a more aligned, co-ordinated and effective sport system at the elite level. The following principles are highlighted in *Australian Sport: The Pathway to Success* (Commonwealth of Australia, 2010, p. 14):

- whole-of-pathway focus
- federal, state/territory government partnership, shared investment, influence and accountability
- national outcomes in the context of the National Sport an d Active Recreation Policy Framework
- local flexibility and integrated decentralised delivery options catering for individual athlete and local needs

- NSO high performance plans developed collaboratively, with the involvement of all key stakeholders and delivery partners
- Institutes an d academies as partners not just service providers
- Economic efficiency gains at all levels.

State and local government

One of the key challenges in Australian sport is managing the interface between the three levels of government involved in the provision of sport – federal, state/territory and local. One of the outcomes of The Crawford Report has been the recommendation to have all levels of government working more closely together at all levels of the sport spectrum from participation through to elite, focusing on a 'whole of sport approach'. All of Australia's states and territories have a government department responsible for sport and recreation. The location of sport within these government agencies may change, reflecting the political changes in government. All of the agencies focus on increasing participation in sport and physical activity and promote the concomitant health benefits associated with regular physical activity.

Each State/territory has a slightly different approach depending on the government in power. For example, in Tasmania, Sport and Recreation Tasmania is located in the Department of Economic Development, Tourism and the Arts, Sport and Recreation Victoria is in the Department of Planning and Community Development and in Western Australia they have their own department the Department of Sport and Recreation. Regardless of their location, each unit has a focus on increasing participation in sport and physical activity and providing opportunities at all levels of the sport spectrum. Similar to New Zealand local government is responsible for providing the infrastructure and services associated with sport delivery.

In South Australia for example the majority of sport and recreation facilities are provided and maintained by State (40%) and local government (50%). At the community level the following infrastructure needs were identified:

- Pool facilities – there are three indoor pools in the metropolitan area and an inequitable distribution of 50-metre indoor pools in the state. Within metropolitan Adelaide, some areas lack 25-metre indoor pools while other areas experience some duplication.
- Indoor courts – there is an inequitable distribution of indoor courts for community use (e.g., suitable for basketball, netball and badminton). Some areas lack such facilities; others have an oversupply, which makes maintaining quality a challenge. New courts developed for schools are often three-quarter size, making them unsuitable for use by the broader community.
- Recreational trails – continued sustainable development of the state recreational trails network is required to meet the growing demand for unstructured recreation, particularly walking and cycling, and to support tourism initiatives.
- Soccer pitches – an increase in the popularity of soccer, particularly among girls, has resulted in a deficiency of pitches in the metropolitan area (http://210.247.132.180/alt-host/assets/pdf_file/0010/5203/rec_sport.indd.pdf).

As another example is the relatively new (established in 2009) Department of Communities New South Wales (CNSW) focuses on improving the quality of life for people in NSW, including sport and recreation, as well as arts and culture and community development. One of its four key goals is to "increase the number of people participating in sporting activities and physical activity by 10% by 2016" (2010, p. 7) Most of CNSW's funding comes from the NSW Government, with the remainder generated from entry fees, charges for programmes and services, concessions and leases across their many venues (Communities NSW, 2010).

National sports organisations

Much like in New Zealand, NSOs are responsible for the development of sport in their respective codes. There are over 90 NSOs in Australia and the Crawford Report argued that NSOs had often focussed on the elite end of their sport to the detriment of participation. Other areas highlighted by the report included the need to strengthen the governance capability of NSOs, stronger links with the ASC and the needs for NSOs to review their structures which in many cases consists of representatives from each state/territory, which then in turn each have their own CEO meaning decision making is often cumbersome and not to the overall best advantage for the sport. The six key recommendations made in The Crawford Report have been supported by the Government meaning that:

- NSOs will have primary responsibility for developing their own high performance programs with assistance from the ASC
- The ASC should make the adoption of appropriate and national skills-based governance structures that reflect diversity of membership a funding condition for NSOs
- NSOs need to place engagement of recreational participation as a key priority backed by government policy at all levels.
- NSOs will be judged on five-year national plans where they are highly dependent on public funding based on set targets and measures
- To address duplication of functions, the ASC will encourage ventures that provide shared functions to sporting clubs an d bodies an d make sharing a condition of financial support to identified NSOs
- Olympic NSOs should explore events to raise their profile outside of the Olympics

The NSOs also have links to the Australian Olympic Committee (AOC) and the Confederation of Australian Sport (CAS). For the NSOs associated with professional sport such as rugby league, basketball, cricket, rugby, netball and tennis, the impact of their business arm created a need to clarify their different roles. As an example Hockey Australia's vision is "we will be respected as an Australian and international sporting leader, demonstrating innovation and excellence in everything we do" (Hockey Australia, 2010, p. 4). They are responsible for game development at the participation level through to high performance and have national training centres in eight states.

State/territory sports associations

Given the federal system most NSOs have an equivalent body in the states/territories in Australia and beneath these sit the regional associations and clubs. So for example if you look at the 2010 annual report for Hockey Australia you will see that the report includes a summary from all the state/territory associations. Then look at the Hockey Queensland website (http://www .hockeyqld.com.au/) and their Annual Report to see that their mission is "to promote, preserve, foster and encourage the growth and enjoyment of the sport of hockey, for players, officiators and spectators".

Funding for sport

Similar to New Zealand, funding for sport comes from federal government, state/territory government, local government, philanthropic trusts, gaming and community trusts. Support also comes from the private sector in the form of sponsorship, which may be in cash or kind. Interestingly the Crawford Report indicated that the

> panel was unable to ascertain the total level of funds spent by Australian Government Departments or agencies on sport or sport related matters. There is no central registry of amounts spent on sport and no requirement to inform any central agency. Sports related payments identified included subsidies, infrastructure, tourism, trade, education, welfare, Indigenous affairs and so on.

> *(Commonwealth of Australia, 2009, p. 46)*

The Australian Government has committed $325 million to Australian sport from 2010-2014, the largest single increase, based on its new 2010 strategy *Australian Sport: The Pathway to Success*. The Australian Sport Commission allocated a total of $4.5million to more than 500 elite athletes through the Australian Government Sport Training Grant Scheme. The 2010-11 Budget by the ASC for national sport system development was $82,810 million and $190,392 million for national elite athlete development (ASC, n.d.).

Similar to the New Zealand situation much sport and recreation funding comes from grants and other funding sources such as gaming trusts. For example, the Western Australian State Government through the Department of Sport and Recreation and Lotterywest provides significant financial assistance to sport in Western Australia through the Sports Lotteries account, amounting to $10 million each year (Government of Western Australia, 2011).

The services and funding to the sporting community in NSW for 2009-2010 are detailed below in Table 2-4:

Tasmania will be used as an example to highlight the value of investing in sport and recreation (Muller, Wadsley, Adams, Arthur, & Felmingham, 2010). Sport and recreation contributes $819.3 million directly to the Tasmanian economy employing over 13000 people. For every $1 invested, Tasmania receives over $4 in benefits, with the combined value of these benefits estimated at $5.6 billion. Tasmanian volunteers contribute over three million hours of work each year, equating to nearly 1800 full-time jobs. The value of sport and physical recreation to Tasmania is summarised in Figure 2-4, signifying the wide range of benefits to society as a whole well beyond health and fitness.

Table 2-4: Services and funding to the sporting community in NSW, 2009-10			
	NSW GOVERNMENT FUNDING 2009-10		
DIVISION	RECURRENT $'000	CAPITAL $'000	NUMBER OF SERVICES TO THE COMMUNITY
Sport, Recreation and Parklands cluster			
Sport and Recreation	68 472	10 535	• 194 000 people attended Sport and Recreation Centre programs, including 76 000 children in outdoor education programs • 22 500 indigenous people attended regional sport and recreation programs • $21.1 million in grants for over 870 sport and recreation projects.

Centennial Park and Moore Park Trust	1 637	2 900	• over 10 million visitors, including:
			  – 6 million visitors to the parklands open space
			  – 4 million visitors to the Moore Park sporting and entertainment precinct
			  – 206 000 attendees at major events in the parklands
			  – 513 000 participants in organised sporting competitions
			• 330 000 visits to the website.

Hunter Region Sporting Venues Authority	0*	0	• over 826 000 people attended 236 events.

Illawarra Venues Authority	0*	1 800	• over 270 000 people attended 87 events, including:
			  – 128 200 attendees at 35 events at WIN Stadium
			  – 143 800 attendees at 52 events at WIN Entertainment Centre.

Parramatta Park Trust	4 465	0	• 1.7 million visitors, including:
			  – 23 300 children in school groups
			  – 25 000 visitors in sporting groups
			  – 148 000 people at major public events
			  – 13 000 people at private or commercial events.

Parramatta stadium Trust	0*	0	• 152 000 people attended events including:
			  – 139 000 at sporting events
			  – 11 000 at the Hindu Deepavali Fair, an Indian cultural festival
			  – 1 700 attended the under-18 dance festival, Springbreak
			  – 11 000 attended Super Cross Motor racing.

Sydney Olympic Park Authority	34 196	11 145	• 9.5 million visitors, including:
			  – 2.2 million visitors to the parklands
			  – 1.1 million attendees at concerts
			  – 1.6 million attendees at major sports events
			  – 1.1 minion participants in sporting activities
			  – 900 000 attendees at business or commercial events
			  – 900 000 attendees at the Royal Easter Show.

Western Sydney Parklands Trust	9 588	0	• over 1.6 million visitors.

* This agency is self-funding through revenue raised by its management of the assets and services it administers on behalf of the government.

Source: Communities NSW (2010, p. 18)

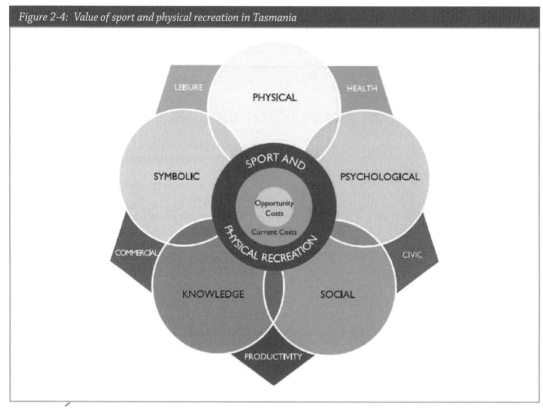

Figure 2-4: *Value of sport and physical recreation in Tasmania*

Source: Muller et al. (2010, p. 2)

Specialist sector organisations in New Zealand and Australia

In both countries several organisations meet the needs of people with physical and intellectual disabilities:

- Special Olympics New Zealand and Special Olympics Australia, offer year-round programmes of sports training and competition for children and adults with intellectual disabilities. (more details are available at: www.specialolympics.org.nz/ and at http://www.specialolympics.com.au/ for Australia).

- Paralympics New Zealand and the Australian Paralympic Committee support and encourage sporting opportunities for people with disabilities to participate in all levels, from club level, regional and national competition through to international competition. (more details are available at: www.paralympicsnz.org.nz/page/about_pnz.html and http://www.paralympic.org .au/ for Australia).

The Deaf Sports Federation of New Zealand and Deaf Sports Australia and Blind Sport New Zealand and Blind Sports Australia cater for the needs of deaf and blind and visually impaired athletes.

Sport support organisations in New Zealand and Australia

A number of organisations support the work of the sport and recreation sector. Some of these currently include:

- Drug Free Sport NZ (DFSNZ), which is the government organisation responsible for providing a doping-free environment for New Zealand athletes. Its responsibilities include: athlete testing, which is conducted all over the world wherever New Zealand athletes compete and/or train; investigations to apprehend those involved in doping; education to ensure all athletes and support staff understand their rights and responsibilities; and research to measure the trends in sport and the effectiveness of programmes. DFSNZ is bound into the World Anti-Doping Programme (WADA) both through the Sports Anti-Doping Act and its status as a Signatory to the World Anti-Doping Code. DFSNZ contributes to the Regional Anti-Doping Organisation (RADO) in Oceania and an inter-governmental agreement on collaboration (IADA) (more details are available at: www.drugfreesport.org.nz).

- The Sports Tribunal of New Zealand, which is an independent statutory body that determines certain types of disputes for the sports sector. The Sports Tribunal was established in 2003 by the Board of SPARC under the name of the Sports Disputes Tribunal of New Zealand. The Tribunal has been continued under the name of the Sports Tribunal of New Zealand because of s 29 of the Sports Anti-Doping Act 2006 (the Act). This part of the Act came into force on 1 July 2007. The Act sets out the sorts of disputes the Tribunal can hear and allows the Tribunal to determine its own practices and procedures for performing the Tribunal's functions under the Act. The aim of the Tribunal is to ensure that national sport organisations and other parties to a sports dispute, such as athletes, have access to an affordable, just and speedy means of resolving a sports dispute (more details are available at: http://www.sportstribunal.org.nz).

- The New Zealand Olympic Committee (NZOC), which is an independent organisation responsible for providing New Zealand athletes the resources they need to achieve their goals at Olympic, Commonwealth and Youth Games. In addition, the NZOC actively promotes the history and values of the Olympic Movement through a wide variety of cultural and educational programmes, and operates according to the Olympic Charter and Commonwealth Games Federation Constitution. The NZOC is funded principally through corporate sponsorship, trusts, SPARC and the International Olympic Committee (more details are available at: www.olympic.org.nz).

- Australian Sports Anti-Doping Authority (ASADA) replaced the Australian Sports Drug Agency in 2006, to protect Australia's sporting integrity through the elimination of doping (ASADA, 2010a). As of July 2010 Australia implemented a new anti-doping framework with the inclusion of an anti-doping rule violation panel to maintain a register of findings and make recommendations to Australian sport on appropriate sanctions for athletes and support personal.

- Australian Olympic Committee (AOC) is an independent organisation responsible for providing Australian athletes the resources they need to achieve their goals at Olympic, Commonwealth and Youth Games. In addition, the AOC actively promotes the history and values of the Olympic Movement through a wide variety of cultural and educational programmes, and operates according to the Olympic Charter and Commonwealth Games Federation Constitution. The AOC is funded principally through corporate sponsorship, licensing and an annual distribution from

Figure 2-5: Australia's new anti-doping framework

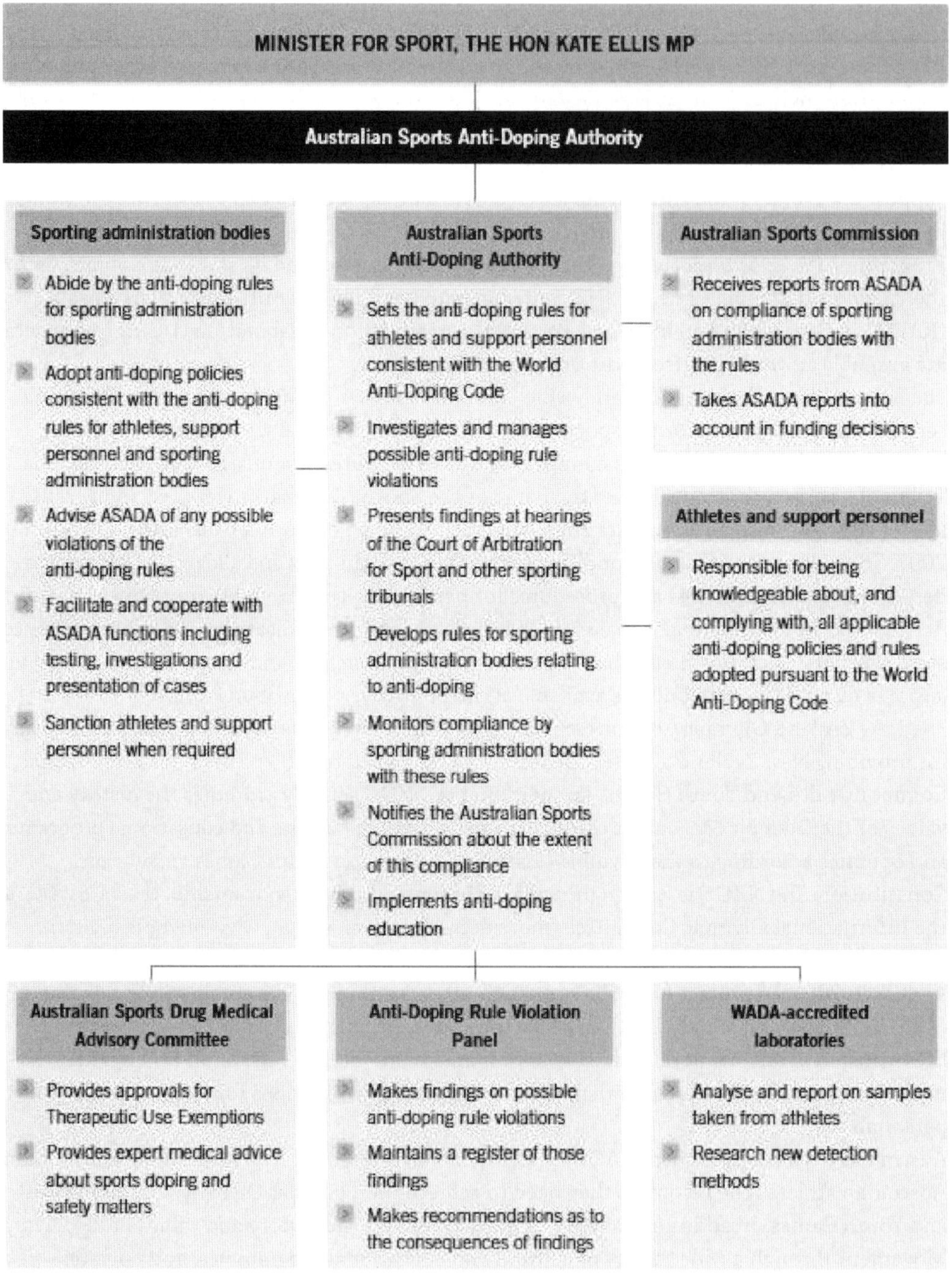

MINISTER FOR SPORT, THE HON KATE ELLIS MP

Australian Sports Anti-Doping Authority

Sporting administration bodies

- Abide by the anti-doping rules for sporting administration bodies
- Adopt anti-doping policies consistent with the anti-doping rules for athletes, support personnel and sporting administration bodies
- Advise ASADA of any possible violations of the anti-doping rules
- Facilitate and cooperate with ASADA functions including testing, investigations and presentation of cases
- Sanction athletes and support personnel when required

Australian Sports Anti-Doping Authority

- Sets the anti-doping rules for athletes and support personnel consistent with the World Anti-Doping Code
- Investigates and manages possible anti-doping rule violations
- Presents findings at hearings of the Court of Arbitration for Sport and other sporting tribunals
- Develops rules for sporting administration bodies relating to anti-doping
- Monitors compliance by sporting administration bodies with these rules
- Notifies the Australian Sports Commission about the extent of this compliance
- Implements anti-doping education

Australian Sports Commission

- Receives reports from ASADA on compliance of sporting administration bodies with the rules
- Takes ASADA reports into account in funding decisions

Athletes and support personnel

- Responsible for being knowledgeable about, and complying with, all applicable anti-doping policies and rules adopted pursuant to the World Anti-Doping Code

Australian Sports Drug Medical Advisory Committee

- Provides approvals for Therapeutic Use Exemptions
- Provides expert medical advice about sports doping and safety matters

Anti-Doping Rule Violation Panel

- Makes findings on possible anti-doping rule violations
- Maintains a register of those findings
- Makes recommendations as to the consequences of findings

WADA-accredited laboratories

- Analyse and report on samples taken from athletes
- Research new detection methods

Source: ASADA (2010b)

the Australian Olympic Foundation. Each state/territory also has an Olympic Council responsible for raising additional funds (for more information see http://corporate.olympics.com.au/).

Review questions

- The sport and recreation pathway requires an integrated sports system that achieves the dual outcomes of lifelong participation and high performance sport. To what extent does the current organisation, delivery and funding of sport in New Zealand and Australia achieve this and what, if anything, needs to change to achieve better integration?
- It is always interesting to look at Annual Reports and see what is reported first – participation or high performance. Take a look at some of these for sports you are interested in and gauge how this reflects the mission of the sport.
- Consider one NSO and evaluate how they organise and fund both participation and high performance programs.
- Compare the New Zealand and Australian sport system and discuss the merits of each one.
- Identify the key challenges for government agencies responsible for sport over the next 10 years and how you would go about addressing these.

References

Access Economics. (2009). *Let's get physical: The economic contribution of fitness centres in Australia*. Retrieved from http://www.fitness.org.au/the_economic_contribution_of_fitness_centres_in_australia_report___july_09_2.pdf

Athletics New Zealand. (2011). *Strategic Plan*. Wellington: Athletics New Zealand. Retrieved from: http://www.athletics.org.nz/Resource.aspx?ID=12329

Australian Bureau of Statistics. (2009). *Children's participation in cultural and leisure activities*. Retrieved from: http://www.abs.gov.au/ausstats/abs@.nsf/mf/4901.0

Australian Bureau of Statistics. (2011). *Sports and physical recreation: A statistical overview*. Retrieved from http://www.abs.gov.au/ausstats/abs@.nsf/Latestproducts/4156.0Main%20Features12011?opendocument&tabname=Summary&prodno=4156.0&issue=2011&num=&view

Australian Sports Anti-Doping Authority. (2010a). *About ASADA*. Retrieved from http://www.asada.gov.au/about/index.html

Australian Sports Anti-Doping Authority. (2010b). *2009:2010 annual report*. Retrieved from http://www.asada.gov.au/publications/annual_reports/asada_annual_report_2009_10/overview/snapshot.html

Australian Sports Commission. (n.d.). *Agency resources and planned performance*. Retrieved from http://www.ausport.gov.au/__data/assets/pdf_file/0006/368601/ASC_2010-2011.pdf

Australian Sports Commission. (2010). *Annual report 2009-2010*. Retrieved from: http://www.ausport.gov.au/__data/assets/pdf_file/0004/398695/Annual_Report_2009-2010.pdf

Australian Sports Commission. (2011a). *Sport and Recreation Ministers Council*. Retrieved from http://www.ausport.gov.au/information/scors/about_us/council

Australian Sports Commission. (2011b). *Sport and Recreation Ministers' Council Communique*. Retrieved from http://www.ausport.gov.au/__data/assets/pdf_file/0011/436754/SRMC_Communique.pdf

Burley, P. (2008). *SPARC Sport Partnership Project: A review of eight high profile sport club partnerships*. Retrieved from http://www.sparc.org.nz/Documents/Communities%20and%20Clubs/Active%20Communities/SPARC_Sport_Partnership_Project.pdf

Carnachan, G. (2010). *School sport, trends, barriers, opportunities*. Presented at the PENZ National Conference, 2010. Retrieved from http://www.penz.org.nz/b_Publications.asp

Commonwealth of Australia. (2009). *The future of sport in Australia*. Retrieved from http://

www.sportpanel.org.au/internet/sportpanel/ publishing.nsf/Content/540DAC9B7F50B132CA2 5766B0014E8A6/$File/front_cover.pdf

Commonwealth of Australia. (2010). *Australian sport: The pathway to success.* Retrieved from http://www.ausport.gov.au/__data/assets/ pdf_file/0011/368597/Australian_Sport_the_ pathway_to_success.pdf

Communities NSW. (2010) *Vibrant sustainable inclusive communities: Annual Report 2009-10.* Retrieved from http://www.communities.nsw .gov.au/assets/pubs/corporate/CNSW_AR_2009- 10_CNSW.pdf

Cordery, C. J., & Baskerville, R. F. (2008). *Financing sports organisations in New Zealand: The impact of governors' choices.* Report prepared for Sports and Recreation New Zealand. Wellington: Victoria University of Wellington.

Dalziel, P. (2011). *Valuing sport and recreation in New Zealand.* AERU Research Unit, Lincoln University. Retrieved from http://www.nzae.org.nz/ conferences/2011/Papers/Session2/25_Dalziel .pdf.

Government of Western Australia. (2011). *Sports lotteries account.* Retrieved from http://www.dsr .wa.gov.au/sportslotteriesaccount

Hayes, L. (2006). The structure of sport and its management in New Zealand. In S. Leberman, C. W. Collins, & L. Trenberth (Eds). *Sport business management in Aotearoa/New Zealand* (2nd ed.) (pp. 42–61). Melbourne: Dunmore Press.

Hockey Australia. (2010). *2009/2010 Annual Report.* Retrieved from http://www.e-brochures.com.au/ hockey_australia/annual_report_2010/

Hockey New Zealand. (2010a). *Whole of Hockey's business plan to drive the growth and sustainability of hockey throughout New Zealand.* Auckland: New Zealand Hockey. Retrieved from http://www .hockeynz.co.nz/resources/administration/

Hockey New Zealand. (2010b). *CEO update from Hilary Poole, 19th October 2010 final.* Retrieved from http://www.hockeynz.co.nz/documents/CEO%20 UPDATE/

Muller, P., Wadsley, A., Adams, D., Arthur, D., & Felmingham, B. (2010). *The value of sport and physical recreation to Tasmania.* Australian Innovation Research Centre, University of Tasmania, Australia. Retrieved from http://www .sportandrecreation.tas.gov.au/__data/assets/ pdf_file/0016/47122/Summary_-_12_July.PDF

Netball New Zealand. (n.d.). *Strategic plan for Netball New Zealand Inc 2009-2012.* Auckland: Netball New Zealand. Retrieved from http://www .mynetball.co.nz/netball-nz/organisation-profile .html

New Zealand Football. (n.d.). *Whole of Football plan.* Auckland: New Zealand Football. Retrieved from http://www.nzfootball.co.nz/index.php?id=917

SPARC. (2003). *SPARC facts: Results of the New Zealand Sport and Physical Activity Surveys (1997-2001).* Wellington: SPARC.

SPARC. (2008). *Sport, recreation and physical activity participation among New Zealand adults: Key results of the 2007/08 Active New Zealand survey.* Wellington: SPARC. See also: http://www .activenzsurvey.org.nz

SPARC. (2009a). *Sport and recreation. Everyone. Every day. Sport and Recreation New Zealand's strategic plan 2009-2015.* Wellington: SPARC.

SPARC. (2009b). *Outdoor recreation strategy 2009- 2015.* Wellington: SPARC

SPARC. (2010a). *High performance strategy 2006 – 2012.* Wellington: SPARC. Retrieved from http:// www.sparc.org.nz/en-nz/high-performance/ High-Performance-Strategy/

SPARC. (2010b). *Annual report for the year ended 30 June 2010.* Wellington: SPARC.

SPARC. (2011a). *Statement of intent 2011-14.* Wellington: SPARC. Retrieved from http://www .sparc.org.nz/Documents/Publications/SOI/ FINAL-SOI-2011-WEB.pdf.

SPARC. (2011b). *Gaming funding into the sport and recreation sector: An update for 2010 and comparison with 2007.* Wellington: SPARC.

SPAC. (2011c). *Carding.* Retrieved from www.sparc.govt .nz/en-nz/high-performance/Athletes/Carding/

SPARC. (2011d). *The sport and recreation pathway.* Retrieved from www.sparc.org.nz/en-nz/About- SPARC/Who-we-are/The-Sport-and-Recreation- Pathway/

Sport Bay of Plenty. (2010). *Strategic plan 2010-2013.* Gisborne: Sport Bay of Plenty. Retrieved from http://www.sportbop.co.nz/sport-bop-strategic- plan-2010-2013

Sport Wellington. (2010). *Strategic plan 2010-2013: Summary.* Retrieved from http:// www.sportwellington.org.nz/assets/About-us-/ SPW3750Strategic-Plan-2010PRESS-2.pdf

Standing Committee on Recreation and Sport. (2009). *Participation in exercise, recreation and sports survey 2008, annual report.* Retrieved from http:// www.ausport.gov.au/information/scors/ERASS/ exercise,_recreation_and_sport_survey_past_ reports/erass_2009

Standing Committee on Recreation and Sport. (2010). *Participation in exercise, recreation and sports survey 2009, annual report.* Retrieved from http:// www.ausport.gov.au/information/scors/ERASS/ exercise,_recreation_and_sport_survey_past_ reports/erass_2010

Standing Committee on Recreation and Sport. (2011). *Participation in exercise, recreation and sport survey, 2010 annual report.* Retrieved from http://www.ausport.gov.au/__data/assets/pdf_file/0018/436122/ERASS_Report_2010.pdf

Visitor Solutions. (2011). *Territorial authority / school partnerships: A guide. A report to SPARC.* Retrieved from: http://www.sparc.org.nz/en-nz/our-partners/Territorial-Authorities/Research-Policy-and-Strategy/

Wellington City Council. (2009). *Long term plan 2009-19.* Wellington: The Council. Retrieved from http://www.wellington.govt.nz/plans/annualplan/ltccp/vol1.html

Chapter 3

Indigeneity, Race Relations and Sport Management

Farah Palmer and Daryl Adair

Objectives

After completing this chapter, you should be able to:

• consider how terms and concepts like race, ethnicity, Indigeneity and diversity influence sport management policies, practices and programmes;

• apply race relations theories to sport management experiences and concepts;

• critically understand how the socio-cultural circumstances of Indigenous people relate to the structure and institution of sport;

• critically analyse what impact stereotypes, assimilation, segregation, and self-determination may have on sport management initiatives as they relate to Indigenous and ethnic minority groups and individuals;

• engage in discussion with others involved in sport management and governance about the influence of symbolic racism on sport organisations and initiatives;

• critically discuss race relations theories such as social distance theory, segregation theory, and symbolic racism as they apply to sport management;

• realise the differences and similarities between Indigenous experiences in sport in Australia and Aotearoa New Zealand.

Introduction

In 2008, a conference titled 'Sport, Race and Ethnicity: Building a Global Understanding' was staged by the University of Technology, Sydney. The conference provided a chance to discuss opportunities and obstacles to sport being a site of inclusion and exclusion, and of diversity and difference, as well as how 'race', ethnicity and indigeneity influence, and are influenced by, the global phenomena known as sport. As a direct result of this conference, six special issues of journals and an edited book were produced: "Unlevel playing fields: 'Race' and sport in Australia", *Australian Aboriginal Studies* (2009); "Narratives of 'race' and racism", *Sporting Traditions* (2009); "'Race', ethnicity and indigeneity – challenges and opportunities for embracing diversity in sport", *Cosmopolitan Civil Societies* (2010); "Managing ethnocultural and 'racial' diversity in sport: Obstacles and opportunities" *Sport Management Review* (2010); "Interrogating boundaries of 'race', ethnicity and identity", *International Review for the Sociology of Sport* (2010); "Sport, 'race', ethnicity and identity: Building global understanding", *Sport in Society* (2011); and *Sport, race and ethnicity: Narratives of difference and diversity*, FIT publishing (2011). Among those who attended the conference and contributed to these publications were academics, sport practitioners and policy makers with a particular focus on Indigenous issues relating to sport in contemporary Aotearoa New Zealand (ANZ) and Australia (Bruce & Wensing, 2009; Edwards, 2009; Klugman & Osmond, 2009; Nelson, 2009; Norman, 2009; Tatz, 2009; Cottle & Keys, 2010; Gorman, 2010; Hippolite & Bruce, 2010; Palmer & Masters, 2010; Stronach & Adair, 2010; Thomson, Darcy, & Pearce, 2010). This chapter is an attempt to challenge the reader to consider how sport management concepts and race relations theories may be applied to Indigenous people and communities, and how Indigenous people influence sport policies and practices in Australia and ANZ.

As nations with Indigenous populations located in a similar region, Australia and ANZ have much in common historically and culturally, yet there are also important differences. First, the urban societies of both countries were created by the British over the last three centuries; they were built as an outcome of the annexation of Indigenous land and the imposition of colonialism on Indigenous populations. Second, both countries have evolved to become more demographically and culturally diverse, which has created avenues for migrants and ethnic communities to flourish. However, the turn to multiculturalism has too often failed to meet the needs of Indigenous people and their claims of redress in respect of human rights violations. Third, although the Indigenous peoples of Australia and ANZ both underwent similar processes of colonisation, there were important differences of experience and structure. Māori tribes signed a Treaty (in Māori and English) with representatives of the British Crown, while Aboriginal and Torres Strait Islanders (ATSI) were unable to negotiate such terms; the Australian land mass was deemed *terra nullius* (unoccupied and thus available for settlement) (Miller, Ruru, Behrendt, & Lindberg, 2010). Fourth, the demographic proportions of Indigenous communities across the Tasman Sea are starkly different: ATSI's comprise around 2.5% of the total population of Australia, while Māori are around 14.5% of ANZ's total population. This has profound implications in terms of the collective voice and political power of these two Indigenous groupings. Another key contrast is that Māori and English are recognised languages in ANZ, but in Australia there is no formal recognition of Aboriginal languages (of which there are many). A fourth commonality is that both nations pride themselves on having strong sporting cultures, and Indigenous people play a very significant part in this – particularly in the major football codes. This chapter will analyse how indigeneity impacts sport management and vice versa by applying race relations theories commonly used in a North American context to ANZ and Australian sport environments. Before this can occur, however, an overview of key terms and concepts is needed.

Glossary of terms

- **Race:** Despite substantial scientific literature discounting the biological validity of the term 'race', it has not prevented its common usage as a way to explain the social world, and it cannot be denied that 'race' continues to impact on the lives of some racialised individuals and groups.
- **Racism:** The ideological belief that people can be classified into 'races' is manifested as racism when people treat each other as either superior or inferior on the basis of skin colour and associated assumptions of status thereof.

- **Ethnicity:** The most common meaning refers to the categories or labels used by people to identify themselves or others. These labels may be based on family, language, religion and nationality. Unlike 'race', however, ethnicity is a fluid term because individuals born into ethnic communities can reject this connection and recast themselves with a different sense of self.
- **Culture:** Refers to the meaning systems and lifestyles of a particular group of people. The term culture makes no reference to biological characteristics, such as skin colour or 'race' and refers to learned patterns of behaviour. It is often, however, used interchangeably to refer to traditions and lifestyles of particular racialised or ethnic groups and the culture of the dominant social group is often invisible.
- **Mana:** In Māori philosophy all power and authority came from higher spiritual forces or *mana atua* (Durie, 1998). The term *mana tangata*, in contrast, was a reflection of human expertise, possibly assisted by the gods but essentially an acknowledgement of the skills and knowledge that allowed certain people to direct day-to-day activities within their communities. As *iwi* began to work closely together in pursuit of common goals generally and collective Māori political awareness increased, the concept of *mana Māori* became applicable. Nowadays the term *mana* is simplistically and widely used by Māori and non-Māori to refer to status, influence, and power (Mead, 2003) or charisma in contexts such as sport, business and leadership roles.
- **Rangatiratanga:** When applied at an individual level, rangatiratanga is about qualities of leadership and chieftainship over a social group, hapū or iwi in Māori culture. The term can also be associated with political issues such as sovereignty, chieftainship, leadership, self-determination and self-management and rangatiratanga is discussed extensively in relation to the Treaty of Waitangi, Article 2 (Mead, 2003).
- **Indigeneity:** The term 'Indigenous' is applied to people who inhabited 'nations' before colonisation by imperial powers. These include the Māori (*tangata whenua*) in ANZ as well as Aborigines and Torres Strait Islanders (ATSI) in Australia. Indigeneity refers to the Indigenous identity of these people. Indigenous identity, however, can be complex and diverse rather than homogenous when the distinctive languages, customs and histories of ancestral tribes are considered.
- **Diversity:** This term involves coming to terms with alterity (otherness) and negotiating inclusion (togetherness). Achieving diversity can be a challenge but also an opportunity in a range of environments, such as business, education and sport. (Adair, Taylor, & Darcy, 2010).

Conceptualising Indigeneity: Colonialism, 'race' and hybridity

In basic terms, Indigenous people can be understood as those groups and individuals "who have maintained a relationship through descent, self-identification, and community acceptance with the precolonial populations" in their ancestral homeland (Paradies, 2005, p. 1). This physical environment, a source of Indigenous knowledge and productive engagement, has also been important to Aboriginal communities as a site for traditional cultural practices and spiritual expressions (Armstrong, 2010). The term 'pre-colonial' infers that Indigenous peoples have gone onto endure colonialism and been subject, through this process, to treatment as a *colonised* 'other' (Ahmed, 2000). This has had important implications for the status and power of Indigenous groups subsequently. As Paradies has put it, in historical terms, "non-Indigenous approaches to defining and understanding Indigeneity have focused on the need to survey and control the socialisation, mobility and biological reproduction of those with…descent from pre-colonial peoples" (Paradies, 2006, p. 335). In the case of colonial New Zealand and Australia, Māori and ATSI peoples were in protracted and sometimes violent struggles with European regimes, seeking to either maintain or regain their connection with the land and (re)establish their cultures, languages and right to self determination (Belich, 1986; Reynolds, 2007).

Ideas of 'race' were central to the imperial mindset in the Antipodes. Paterson, in a critique of settler attitudes towards Māori in the 19th century, argues that "more than just skin colour or cultural difference separate[d] the colonizer and colonized"; fundamentally, the two were "deemed to be different according to nature" (Paterson, 2010, p. 135). They were considered racial opposites. There was and is, however, no scientific basis to racial categories: they are social inventions inspired by the fallacy of biological determinism (Graves, 2001, pp. 1-7). Nonetheless for centuries, ideas about skin colour and racial hierarchy – with whites at the top and blacks at the bottom – have been used by dominant powers to justify stereotypical assumptions about identity and status. The racial subjugation of Māori and ATSI was part of the British imperial mission; in Australia it even involved attempts at genocide (Tatz, 2010).

The post-colonial identity of Aboriginal peoples has long been complex and remains so. Many ATSI and Māori people have links to an ancestral tribe with its own distinctive dialects and customs. They are, therefore, ethnically divergent despite being classified in popular thought as homogeneous (Kukutai, 2004; Paradies, 2006). Moreover, skin colour is hardly the sole barometer of Indigeneity; some individuals, while fair-skinned in appearance, claim for themselves a coloured identity that connotes blackness, or at least non-whiteness, such as with a small, but significant minority of Indigenous Australians (Cowlishaw, 1987; Tomkinson, 2001). There are also difficult debates about what is thought to constitute an 'authentic' Māori, Aborigine, or Torres Strait Islander. Some of this revisits racially conservative discourses about 'half-caste' Indigenous people (Anderson, 2009; Paterson, 2010). Yet there are also progressive views in which parents with white, black or brown combine to produce offspring of varying colour, and who choose to identify with a Māori or ATSI heritage (Kukutai, 2007). Today there is a greater acceptance of hybridity within Indigenous communities and, as a consequence, more spaces in which to engage positively with intercultural diversity (Callister, 2008; Kukutai & Callister, 2009).

Hokowhitu (2010) contends that any transcultural Indigenous collective needs to be based on difference and contradiction in order to create a place of relativity, multiplicity of truth and ambiguity as opposed to a location that promotes singularity of truth. Debates regarding the rights of Indigenous people in relation to ideologies such as neo-liberalism, diversity and globalisation will continue to occur, as they should. In addition, Indigenous studies must continue to develop as an embryonic and ambiguous discipline by:

- encouraging epistemic challenge (self-critique) to confront how the world has been constructed within universalising discourses and under the colonial gaze;
- engaging in 'transcultural Indigenous dialogue' where locally indigenised truths are analysed in a realm that recognises the multiplicity of Indigenous subjectivities. Studies of Indigeneity, therefore, must investigate contradictions as well as comparisons across Indigenous cultures (Hokowhitu, 2010).

With these points in mind this chapter presents issues of Indigeneity, 'race' and ethnicity in ANZ and Australian sport in a way that acknowledges both commonalities and difference.

Sport, Indigeneity and race relations: New Zealand

According to the 2006 Census, 14.6% of ANZ's population identify as Māori, 67.6% as European (the largest group in this category being New Zealand (NZ) European or Pākehā), 9.2% as Asian, and 6.9% as Pacific Island (Statistics New Zealand, 2007). Lines separating all of these ethnic groups are often blurred, and mixed ethnicity is common (James & Saville-Smith, 1989; Walker, 1990). Of those who identify as Māori, for instance, 52.8% identify as Māori only, 42.2% as Māori and European, 7% as Māori and Pacific Island, 1.5% as Māori and Asian, and 2.3% as Māori and 'New Zealander'. The increasingly diverse composition of ANZ society, a growing sense of independence from the colonial past, and the quest for competitive advantage in a globalised market, have created a level of uncertainty with regards to Indigenous rights and how this relates to wider policies promoting ethnic diversity and multiculturalism.

Māori people, considered the tangata whenua of ANZ (which implies Indigenous status), have made significant progress in terms of reducing relative economic and social disparities, yet they continue to be one of the most marginalised groups in the country (Te Puni Kōkiri, 2009). One of the few areas where Māori tend to feature positively in the public realm is in sport. The popularly held and often internalised belief reinforced in the media and historically through education, is that Māori are innately 'gifted' in physical pursuits related to work and leisure (Hokowhitu, 2003b), and are over-represented in some aspects of ANZ sport (Hyde, 1993; Te Puni Kōkiri, 1993, 1995a, 1995b, 2005, 2006). Māori play a prominent role in many team sports that receive media attention in ANZ and Australia, such as rugby union, rugby league, basketball, netball and hockey. There are also a small number of high profile Māori athletes in individual sports. Prominent Māori sportspeople in recent times include Michael Campbell (golf), Temepara George (netball), Benji Marshall (rugby league), Kayla Sharland (hockey), Storm Uru (rowing), Joelle King (squash), Quade Cooper and Piri Weepu (rugby union).

Indigenous sport participation: New Zealand

According to the latest 2007/2008 Active NZ Survey (SPARC, 2008), participation in organised sport and recreation competitions/events is higher among Māori (44.2%) than the total population (36.9%). A higher percentage of Māori are also members of clubs/centres (37.7%) and receive instruction for sport/recreation (45.1%) compared to the overall population (34.9% and 39.9%). The survey also revealed that 97.2% of Māori took part in at least one sport or recreation activity in a year, and touch football and rugby union were the most popular sporting activities. Māori have played a significant role in the history of ANZ sport and in particular rugby union (Hokowhitu, 2005, 2009; Mullholland, 2009; Ryan, 1993), which is widely considered ANZ's national sport (Te Puni Kōkiri, 2005). In 2011, for instance, 22% of professional players at the Super rugby level, 21% at the professional provincial level, and 18% at the All Black (national team) level identified as Māori. Players of Pacific Island ethnicity also featured disproportionately in the professional ranks of rugby, with 31% at Super Rugby level, 27% at professional provincial level, and 15% at the All Black level in 2011 (from New Zealand Rugby Union [NZRU] 2011 player database).

If indeed the sporting world was a level playing field as purported "… then the workplace of the SportsWorld would be comprised of trained professionals from different race and ethnicities, cultures, genders, religion, sexualities, national origin, age, and ability status mixing together equally …" (Smith & Hattery, 2011, p. 107). In the United States (US), Smith and Hattery (2011) suggest racial diversity has lagged at every level of sport management, including coaching, leadership/administration, marketing and ownership. A cursory glance at research currently being completed on ethnic diversity in ANZ sport leadership by Ryan Holland (Holland, Leberman, Palmer, & Walker, 2010) suggests that sport management in ANZ, like that in the US, continues to be racialised in the interests of white dominance (Fink & Pastore, 1999).

The high visibility of Māori athletes on the national and global stage, in combination with the dominant perception of sport as a key agent of identity formation and inter-racial assimilation in ANZ's history (Watson, 2007), suggests that sport is an ideal context within which to study the nation's Indigenous, racial and ethnic issues. Such topics, however, have not been extensively developed in ANZ sport studies (Palmer, 2006; Thompson, Rewi, & Wrathall, 2000), historically (Watson, 2007) or in sport management specifically (Palmer, 2006; Thomas & Dyall, 1999). Watson (2007), in a review of research on sport and ethnicity in ANZ, noted that much of the scholarly work has focused on case studies, biographies and chronologies of particular sporting codes (e.g., Crawford, 1999; Bergin, 2002; Fougere, 1989; Hapeta & Palmer, 2009; Hippolite, 2008; Masters, 2006; McCausland-Durie, 2007; Melnick, 1996; Melnick & Thomson, 1996; Mullholland, 2009; Murchie, 1984; Palmer, 2000, 2007a; Ryan, 1993; Te Rito, 2006, 2007; Thompson, et al., 2000). Much less attention is given to sport experiences of other ethnic minority groups in ANZ (e.g., Grainger, 2006; Leckie, 1989; Ryan, 2007; Watson, 2005).

Critical scholarly work specific to Māori and physicality has been conducted in particular by Brendan Hokowhitu (Hokowhitu, 2003a, 2003b, 2004, 2005, 2007, 2009; Hokowhitu & Scherer, 2008; Jackson & Hokowhitu, 2002). In his critical scholarly work, Hokowhitu argues that although the number of Māori and Polynesian players achieving in sport is sometimes cited as evidence of the inherent equality of ANZ society, success in sport has not seen these ethnicities accorded equality in citizenship. There are also emerging scholars: a recent article by Hippolite and Bruce (2010), based on Hippolite's thesis work, is especially illuminating of the 'unspoken' racism in ANZ sport as it relates to Māori, which is alluded to in the following case study.

CASE STUDY: NEW ZEALAND RUGBY – IS THEIR EVIDENCE OF RACISM IN RUGBY?

In an article by sports journalist Richard Boock in 2008, titled "She'll be white bro", the issue of racism was described as ANZ rugby's 'dirty little secret'. Boock wrote that "Racist British and European football fans tend to yell and chant their warped abuse at the ground on game day; Aussies favour hurling obscenities and/or missiles. Over here it's whispered among friends and behind backs, and rationalised into a language that attempts to deodorise the stench of the core message: that it's OK to judge folk on the basis of race" (Boock, 2008). In another article in response to Boock's provocative claim, Ex-All Black Va'aiga Tuigamala agreed the sport could do more to tackle what is a societal rather than just a sporting problem. He cited examples overseas of racism in sport and stated: "we're nowhere near as bad as over there but it's a real shame we can't even talk about our situation. We are fast becoming a country that doesn't want to talk about real issues" (Sunday Star Times, 18 October 2008). New Zealand Rugby Union chief executive Steve Tew responded by saying that "racism is not tolerated in rugby and there is no place for it, fullstop". He added that the theory that Pacific Islanders were unsuited to certain positions on the field, which are said to require more brain power, had been debunked; rugby therefore didn't need to implement a campaign to educate those who subscribed to such misplaced views. Tew concluded: "We have given people of all walks of life an opportunity to demonstrate they are capable of becoming leaders and I can't think of any better examples of that than Piri Weepu captaining Wellington, Tana Umaga the All Blacks and Pat Lam coaching the Blues. We are working really hard to grow everyone in our game and Māori and Pacific Island players are taking those opportunities better than anyone. That's a better response than any direct action". (Sunday Star Times, 18 October, 2008)

Thompson (2004) contends that critical analyses of race and ethnic relations in ANZ sport may be limited because in the conservative framework of the national sporting culture there are many who would consider statements made by sociologists, who critically investigate sport, as tantamount to treason. In addition, 'race' and ethnic relations in ANZ sport may have avoided critical analysis because the claim that Māori are privileged in sport has, until recently, been taken for granted, celebrated and internalised by Māori and New Zealanders in general (James & Saville-Smith, 1989). In his review of sport and ethnicity research in New Zealand, Watson (2007) concluded that Australian scholars have been ahead of their New Zealand counterparts in casting a critical eye on the relationship between sport and ethnicity, especially as it relates to Indigeneity (e.g., Adair & Stronach, 2011; Coram, 2007; Elder, Pratt, & Ellis, 2006; Gardiner, 2003; Hogan, 2003; McNeill, 2008; Tatz, 1995; Tatz, 2009; Taylor, 2001, 2004; Taylor & Toohey, 1999).

Sport, Indigeneity and race relations: Australia

In the 21st century, Aborigines and Torres Strait Islanders (ATSI), once the sole custodians of the Australian continent, constitute less than three per cent of the national population. The pernicious legacy of colonialism remains with Indigenous disadvantage evident across virtually every socio-economic indicator. ATSI people have, as examples, significantly lower life expectancy than other Australians, much higher levels of unemployment, considerably lower levels of education and income, and are vastly over-represented in the nation's prisons (Adair & Stronach, 2011). Compared to all of the above, some key areas of professional sport appear to be a "good news" story for Aboriginal people (Adair, 2006, p. 69). In recent years they have been statistically over-represented in the two major football codes – Australian Rules (AFL) and rugby league (NRL) – with ratios of around 10 per cent (AFL, 2007; Masters, 2009). Several Indigenous sportspeople have also become celebrities in other sports, such as champion boxers Anthony Mundine and Daniel Geale and track and field star Cathy Freeman.

However, this widespread engagement in elite sport and public adulation thereof are both relatively recent. During the 19th century and for most of the 20th century, Australian society and sport was riven by laws, rules and customs that excluded, marginalised and compromised Aboriginal and Torres Strait Islander involvement in 'mainstream' sporting activities organised by whites (Nielsen, 2009; Sampson, 2009; Stephen, 2009; Tatz, 1995, 2009). Moreover, when ATSI athletes eventually 'made it' into the big time of sport, they were not necessarily made welcome. As Indigenous footballers became more commonly involved in the AFL and the NRL from the mid 1980s, it was customary for racist language to be directed at them, and no penalties for doing so. This did not change until Indigenous footballers in the AFL took a stand, effectively forcing their organisation to respond with a set of rules outlawing racial vilification (Gardiner, 1997). Today there is a much greater acceptance that racist epithets – whether directed by players or spectators – are unacceptable in both sport and society.

Indigenous sport participation: Australia

ATSI people are, as we have seen, now high profile performers in a small number of professional sports. Does this mean that there is a propensity for sport participation and physical activity among Indigenous communities more generally? The Australian Human Rights Commission (AHRC) has pointed out that "while many sporting organisations have dedicated Indigenous sporting programmes, some have yet to develop specific initiatives to promote Indigenous participation in sport" (Oliver, 2006, p. 20). The AHRC has also emphasised that "Aboriginal and Torres Strait Islander people are ... not represented proportionally in sporting organisations, and very few have represented at the elite and national level" across the wide spectrum of sports played in Australia (Oliver, 2006, p. 19). In making these observations the AHRC bemoaned that "while there is a plethora of information available on the general number and characteristics of Australian people who participate in sport and recreational activities (including age, gender, frequency and type of participation), very little data focuses on the ethnic or cultural background of participants" (Oliver, 2006, p. 19). There is, however, limited data on levels of physical activity according to these criteria. The Australian Bureau of Statistics (ABS) has contended that 'after adjusting for differences in the age structure between populations, Indigenous Australians were more likely than non-Indigenous Australians to be sedentary or to exercise at low levels' (ABS, 2008). This has serious health implications: the ABS has argued that 'physical inactivity was the third leading cause of the burden of illness and disease for Indigenous Australians in 2003, accounting for 8% of the total burden and 12% of all deaths' (ABS, 2008). A challenge for sport and physical activity stakeholders, therefore, is how to improve opportunities for ATSI Australians to improve health and wellbeing outcomes from routine engagement in sport and exercise.

CASE STUDY: AUSTRALIAN RULES FOOTBALL AND 'OLD FASHIONED' RACISM

Debates about racism in sport were renewed dramatically when a former Australian Rules Football star mockingly referred to Indigenous players of the 1960s and 1970s as "little cannibals", complaining that he had trouble seeing them in the poor light of night games owing to their dark skin. Mal Brown's flippant remarks to a Melbourne football lunch were dismissed by him as comical, and he later reminded critics that he was a champion of Indigenous player recruitment into West Australian football.

AFL chief executive Andrew Demetriou said he was disgusted by remarks that reflected a bygone era and did not represent the sport's present culture. The AFL has been working to clamp down on racism since former Essendon player Michael Long stood his ground in 1995, leading to the introduction of a racial vilification code. The AFL is strongly supported in many Aboriginal communities and has produced a growing number of indigenous stars: in the sixteen AFL teams in 2010 there were 83 registered players who identified as Indigenous (Ansley, 2010).

The next section explores the decline and revival of Indigenous games and pastimes in New Zealand and Australia. A brief description of this process may allow those in sport management to understand why and how these games and activities can assist in the revival of Indigenous culture and the enhancement of well being for all individuals involved.

The revival of Indigenous games: New Zealand

Prior to contact with Europeans, Māori as members of specific whānau, hapū and iwi groups had their own games and active contests referred to as "ngā mahi a te rehia"(Best, 1925, Makereti, 1986, cited in Thomas & Dyall, 1999, p. 120). The manual dexterity, agility, calculation skills, mental alertness and ability to memorise displayed in these activities were used as elementary training for battle or adult tasks, such as gardening, and emphasised important skills and knowledge forms for Māori to pass from one generation to the next. Early observations and accounts of Māori as a collective ethnic group were as an energetic, healthy, and virile population that had developed a society where physical pursuits and games of skill were participated in enthusiastically by men and women.

Aspects of colonisation and capitalism, such as structural domination, state legislation, the Anglo-Māori wars, introduced diseases, deprivation of land, and assimilation of the Māori body and mind, had a detrimental impact on Indigenous wellbeing. Soon after the signing of the Treaty of Waitangi (in Māori and English), Māori were assimilated through institutions such as school and sport to reflect the attributes, skills, and practices of the dominant culture. Māori students in native and public schools were discouraged from continuing with ngā mahi a te rehia because these were considered to be antagonistic to Christian and Western educational ideals (Tuhiwai Smith, 1992). Instead, sporting and recreational activities of the British settlers were encouraged, and as inter-ethnic group interaction increased due to urbanisation, some members of the Māori population adopted and often excelled in these European forms of sport and recreation (Crawford, 1981).

The resurgence of Māori language and culture since the 1980s has also revived interest in 'nga taonga takaro', the treasured games of Māori ancestors (Brown, 2010a, 2010b). Nga Taonga Takaro have become a transformative agent in the areas of health, sport and education as a result of being ingratiated into the ANZ school system (Brown, 2010a, 2010b) as well as community health initiatives targeting Māori (Palmer, Graham, & Mako, 2009). What is more intriguing is the growth of Māori games overseas. In the US, for example, the ball game ki-o-rahi was introduced into 31,000 elementary schools by their curriculum directors in 2004, while the board game mu torere has been used since World War 2 in many American university mathematics programmes, even to doctorate level (Brown, 2010a, 2010b). In a review of ki-o-rahi initiatives in the Manawatu (Palmer et al., 2009) it was found that this traditional ball game and its variations:

- were a user-friendly learning activity enjoyed by Māori and non-Māori alike;
- enhanced the education of Māori students;
- empowered Māori by being able to speak Māori while playing;
- provided leadership opportunities;
- fostered cohesion and co-operation (whanaungatanga); and
- elevated the sense of self-worth of Māori engaged in the game and its holistic kaupapa.

The revival of Indigenous games: Australia

Aboriginal societies are typically spatially aware and physically dexterous; they needed these attributes when fishing and hunting for food. It was here that play, games and sports provided input. Within Australian Indigenous communities there were strategy and play activities requiring athleticism and poise. Footraces promoted speed, ball games fostered agility, while spear and boomerang throwing contests demanded eye-to-hand coordination important for hunting (Howell & Howell, 1992). However, with the onset of European annexation, traditional Aboriginal sports and games began to lose their functional relevance, with the meaning and significance of such activities not passed onto later generations. Recently, there have been efforts to trace, record and revive traditional Indigenous games. Using the medium of oral history, non-Indigenous researcher Ken Edwards has spent many years talking with Aboriginal and Torres Strait Islander elders. Through this dialogue, as well as by reading early anthropological accounts, he has established a formidable record of customary Aboriginal recreation (Smith, 2000; Edwards, 1999). That knowledge now has applied significance because Edwards, with the assistance of the Australian Sports Commission, has produced a user friendly booklet for schools and community groups that explains the purpose of particular Indigenous games and how they may be played today (Edwards, 2008). This is a significant development: through sport and recreation all Australians can be made aware about aspects of a culture centuries old. Too often Indigenous history and customs are neglected as 'irrelevant' in discourses of modernity in Australia.

Race relations theory and sport management

The world of sport is often touted as a domain in which merit is the sole criterion for engagement and success: the idea of sport being open to all, an exemplar of cultural diversity and, unlike many other areas of society, a level playing field in terms of recognition and reward. Smith and Hattery (2011) reject this view, arguing that if the world of sport was indeed so representative and meritocratic then we would see a wide diversity of social groups engaged across all of the areas of sport participation and management. Since the late 20th century, several major global and national sporting bodies have introduced equity-based reforms to encourage participation among minority groups and people of colour. However, the policy rhetoric of social inclusion and cultural diversity has too often not translated into sport management and institutional practice (Cunningham, 2006; Singer, 2005; Spracklen, Hylton, & Long 2006). Smith and Hattery (2011) note that although professional sport now includes people from various ethnic and 'racial' backgrounds, the same cannot be said for other areas of the sport industry, such as coaching, marketing and sponsorship, public relations and media. These domains, where considerable economic and organisational power lies, continue to be overwhelmingly dominated by white males.

How might such inequities be explained for people of colour? Smith and Hattery (2011) provide a succinct overview of race relations theories that might be drawn upon by sport management researchers engaged in critical inquiry. Three approaches are dealt with here. First, social distance theory postulates that sport provides an elusive sense of interracial harmony. While white fans typically cheer athletes of any colour, they may be reluctant to embrace them in other social contexts. Distance allows for ersatz relations; proximity, which provides a basis for intimacy, is a better measure of social acceptance. Smith and Hattery (2011) argue that whites who claim to be non-prejudicial are sometimes confronted by lived experience. In the world of sport, these are the type of people who applaud non-white athletes but would prefer not to socialise with non-whites on the golf course and similar settings. Second, the social distance perspective is underpinned by segregation theory; the greater the level of proximity and intimacy between people and sport, the more likely there is to be conservative resistance to racial equity. This means renewed efforts by those in power to set role and power boundaries between whites and people of colour, even though in the 21st century – an era in which anti-racism shapes sport policy – this is not officially sanctioned. Instead, segregational impulses are realised by strategic appointments within the sport industry, such as whites rather than blacks to managerial positions. Third, the most recent addition to theory is the concept of symbolic racism. This approach is concerned with the implications of a widespread assumption in American society that "overt [race] discrimination has largely ended and ... the playing field is more or less level" (Smith & Hattery, 2011, p. 113). That type of view, while idealistic, is more important in another sense; it infers that little more is needed to achieve racial harmony. Some commentators even tout the realisation of a 'colour blind' society. In terms of sport, the symbolic racism perspective reminds us how difficult it is likely to be to transform the management of sport from an industry dominated by whites to one that proactively engages people of colour.

Applying race relations theory to sport management issues, policies and practices regarding race relations and indigeneity could provide researchers and sport practitioners with a way of addressing the following:

- Identifying instances of social distance, segregation and symbolic racism within sport.
- How sport provides a rich context within which to investigate race and ethnic relations in Australia and ANZ.
- How sport management policies, practices and initiatives can be adapted or created to cater to Indigenous rights and needs.

Race relations theory and Australian sport

How might race relations theory help sport managers to make sense of complex scenarios? The Sydney 2000 Olympics are an intriguing example for exploration. The Games were staged amidst a racially charged backdrop of political disquiet; critics had condemned the Australian Government's refusal to officially apologise for state policies that underpinned what has been dubbed the Stolen Generations (Neilson, 2002). This refers to the forced removal of Indigenous children from parents and their relocation as wards of the state with non-Indigenous families – a process that took place, more or less surreptitiously, from the 1870s to the 1970s (Wilson, 1997). There were suggestions by Aboriginal political activists that the Olympic Games were a legitimate site for Indigenous protest about the Stolen Generations and a number of other major grievances. By and large, though, this did not happen: a key reason was that Olympic organisers had liaised with Aboriginal leaders to assure them that the Games would be a platform within which ATSI people would be given symbolic prominence (Morgan, 2003). Nowhere was this more obvious than at the opening ceremony, with an emphasis on Indigenous cultures and a strong message of reconciliation, including musicians who made a statement by wearing t-shirts with a 'sorry' slogan (St John, 2001). Renowned Indigenous athlete Cathy Freeman was given the role of lighting the Olympic cauldron – an iconic ceremonial moment. Her famous victory, subsequently, in the 400 metres track final allowed Freeman to celebrate her dual identity – Aboriginal and Australian (Elder et al., 2006).

From a social distance perspective, the reformist narrative in the Olympic ceremony allowed liberal-minded Australians to vocalise their desire for reconciliation but not have to deal with the day-to-day realities of Indigenous disadvantage. In cheering Cathy Freeman across the finish line, these armchair supporters were de facto applauding *themselves* as champions of reconciliation. The Sydney Games can also be interpreted from a segregation perspective. Although Indigenous culture was instrumental to the Festival of Dreaming and the Olympics themselves, "neither the Australian Olympic Committee (AOC) nor the Sydney Organising Committee for the Olympic Games (SOCOG) included an Indigenous representative" (North, 2002, p. 1). Finally, the event can be read from a symbolic racism perspective. While the selection of Cathy Freeman in the role of torch bearer was widely applauded in the media and among liberal-minded commentators, some observers were scathing in their criticism. Opponents regarded the appointment as an example of political correctness (i.e., that Freeman was 'rewarded' for being Indigenous); she was not, claimed some complainants, representative of the wider Australian community, but only a small section of it. Some critics felt that the selection of Freeman actually did harm to race relations cause: they reasoned that everyone had an equal chance in 21st century Australia, so privileging someone on the basis of their 'race' was tantamount to discrimination against others (Bruce & Wensing, 2009).

Race relations theory and Aoteaoroa New Zealand sport

In Australia, the 2000 Olympics provided an opportunity for Indigenous issues relating to sport and national identity to be discussed. Likewise, the Rugby World Cup (RWC) 2011 provides the same opportunity for New Zealand. Indigenous culture featured heavily in the opening ceremonies and events and race-related issues featured in media stories associated with the tournament. First, Springbok coach Peter de Villiers claimed that there was an over-exposure to the haka at the RWC 2011, and this meant he was losing respect for it (Watson, 2011). This was a curious statement: was de Villiers also losing respect for the national anthems being played before each match? Second, a member of the Samoan rugby team claimed they had been unfairly treated by the International Rugby Board (IRB) with regards to game scheduling (Kelly, 2011): his side had only a few days rest before lining up against one of the stronger teams. The scheduling, to him, was both inequitable and disrespectful. Third, a South African rugby journalist claimed that he was the victim of racism by Police in Taupo (Russell, 2011). The reaction from organisations and institutions such as the New Zealand Police, the International Rugby Board, and event organisers has largely been to downplay such claims. However, racism has long been a part of ANZ sport, especially in the form of stereotyping and symbolic racism alluded to in the article by Smith and Hattery (2011).

Stereotypes associated with Māori and Pacific Island athletes tend to be lumped together as representative of all 'brown' athletes, consistent with the rhetoric surrounding the Polynesianisation of New Zealand sport since the 1990s (Hyde, 1993). This occurs despite 'brown' athletes being influenced by diverse Pacific Island cultures (e.g., Samoa, Tonga, Niue, Cook Islands, Fiji), tribal groups (e.g., Ngati Porou, Tuwharetoa, Kai Tahu, Tainui, etc), and levels of assimilation and cultural knowledge (Hirini & Flett, 1999).

In an article in the early 1990s entitled 'White men can't jump', Lois Muir, a well- known national netball selector and coach, recalled how "people had always looked at Polynesian players as 'one offs'. They had no stickability, so people weren't prepared to put their shirts on them" (cited in Hyde, 1993, p. 67). In the same article, other statements made about Polynesian athletes included: "naturally superior to us in talent...but they didn't have the discipline", "Polynesian flair", as well as "unpredictable and innovative" (Hyde, 1993, p. 68). In 2003, Martin Crowe, a Pākehā sports commentator and former captain of the New Zealand cricket team stated that "traditionally not many Māori make good cricketers ... They don't have the patience or the temperament to play through a whole day, let alone over a Test match" (see Gamble, 2003).

These stereotypes are based on the belief that the success of Māori and Polynesian athletes is attributed to innate and instinctive attributes rather than due to the influence of training, discipline, work ethic, and intellect. As a result, opportunities for Māori and Polynesian athletes in other aspects of the SportsWorld such as coaching, governance, and management are limited which suggests a social distance perspective could be applied – where Māori and Polynesians are embraced on the field but not welcomed with open arms in the boardroom. In research conducted by PhD candidate Ryan Holland (see Holland et al., 2010), National Sporting Organisations (NSOs) registered with Sport and Recreation New Zealand (SPARC) were asked to complete a survey in 2010. Of the 613 people serving on the 84 NSOs who responded to the survey (93% response rate), 4 were identified as Pacific and 33 as Māori (5.3%). Four NSOs had an ethnic requirement for Māori or Pacific representation on their board, six NSOs had policies specific to Māori and/or Pacific stakeholders, and nine NSOs had sub-committees relating specifically to Pacific and Māori matters. Only 16.6% of national team/athlete leaders (i.e., coaches, managers, medical staff, etc) were identified as Māori.

The predominantly Pākehā leaders and administrators of ANZ sport suggests a void with regards to cultural understanding between Māori athletes and non-Māori leaders in sport may exist. A study by Wrathall (1996) based on interviews with 13 female Māori elite athletes found that for many of these athletes cultural insensitivity, intolerance, manipulation, isolation and exploitation were experienced. More specifically, whānau decision-making was of major importance to these athletes when considering their athletic careers, and yet they felt there was little understanding of Māori lifestyles and attitudes from their predominantly Pākehā administrators and coaches. Wrathall (1996) concluded that for these women at least, they had little input into the design and delivery of sport policies and programmes that directly affected them suggesting segregation along racial lines still occurred in some aspects of ANZ sport and society. Hippolite and Bruce (2010) also reported similar experiences from their participants who mentioned cultural differences lead to misunderstandings with major repercussions for Māori players and teams, including non-selection, increased surveillance by officials, Māori feeling they did not have the mana to be heard, or even deciding to withdraw from particular sports and competitions because of racism.

Palmer and Masters (2010) conducted research from a relational perspective to determine what impact the intersection of gendered and Indigenous identities had on the experiences of four Māori women involved in sport leadership. Despite accessing leadership opportunities themselves, the participants mentioned barriers and constraints in sport management, which included: institutional racism in the form of tokenism; always having to justify the inclusion of Māori perspectives; not having genuine decision-making power; and losing mana in Pākehā-dominated contexts and in the presence of older Māori males. Structural issues that impacted negatively on the wellbeing and effectiveness of the Māori women as leaders and managers included the continual fight to access more resources and the related feeling of being over-worked and under-valued. Other negative impacts on their effectiveness included: lack of visionary guidance and support from members of the governing body; lacking the mana or mandate to lead in a Māori context; and working in a Pākehā organisation that did not incorporate Māori values or practices. Similar experiences from Māori were mentioned by Hippolite and Bruce (2010) where many of the participants' interactions with Pākehā-dominated sport systems made them feel inferior, frustrated, hurt, disillusioned and angry.

Despite evidence that racist stereotypes and attitudes exist at the individual level, any frank or in-depth discussion about racism at the socio-cultural or structural level is perceived as negative (Wetherell & Potter, 1992), and immediately denied or responded to with "considerable hostility and resistance" by Pākehā (Consedine & Consedine, 2005, p. 158) suggesting symbolic racism is alive and well in ANZ sport and society. For example, claims by famous Pākehā former All Black Andy Haden that a successful rugby franchise had long operated a racially-based quota system of three Polynesian players were immediately dismissed and attention re-directed away from a possible example of institutional racism towards a critique of his use of the term "darkies" and calls for him to quit his role as a Rugby World Cup 2011 ambassador (Watkins, 2010). Interestingly he maintained his role as a rugby ambassador until he made public comments about women and rape (Gay, 2010). Hippolite and Bruce (2010, p. 31) also refer to this scenario in an attempt to highlight how conversations regarding racism in New Zealand tend to be shutdown.

CASE STUDY: RUGBY, 'RACE' RELATIONS AND POWER IN AOTEAROA NEW ZEALAND

According to the received version of ANZ history, rugby was a key agent in the integration of Māori and Pākehā, and Māori ability in rugby was one of the few occasions where Māori were admitted to full citizenship (Hokowhitu, 2005). This status, however, was conditionally awarded and did not prevent Māori being barred from All Black teams which toured South Africa in 1928, 1949 and 1960. A compromise was reached in 1970, when four players of Māori and Polynesian heritage were permitted to tour South Africa as 'honorary whites'. The international and domestic pressure regarding ongoing contact between the Springboks and the All Blacks during the Apartheid era came to a head during the 1981 Springbok Tour protests.

Even thirty years after these protests about race relations in South Africa and ANZ, rugby continues to be a site where Māori both gain and lose mana (Hokowhitu, 2005). The New Zealand Māori Rugby Board (NZMRB) for instance, is an advisory board to the NZRU who have limited power with regards to decision-making and allocation of resources regarding the NZ Māori team. Playing for the Māori rugby team can also provide players with an opportunity to reaffirm and strengthen their cultural identity (Hirini & Flett, 1999), yet the team's existence remains conditional on the goodwill of the NZRU. The fluctuating status of the NZ Māori Rugby team and the NZMRB are examples of how power struggles play out along racial lines. The increasingly business-like approach taken by the NZRU reflects the broader social shift from imperialism through biculturalism to multiculturalism and the status of the Māori team as something 'for Māori' is threatened and emblematic of broader issues of reverse racism and political correctness rhetoric (Hokowhitu & Scherer, 2008).

After scrapping the NZ Māori programme in favour of the Junior All Blacks in 2009, the NZRU were under pressure from Māori stakeholders to re-instate the team for 2010, a year that also happened to mark the centenary year of the NZRU sanctioned Māori team. After confirming test games would take place the NZMRB and NZRU proceeded to invite past players and their whānau to luncheons and games hosted in Whangarei, Rotorua and Napier. Perhaps as a result of heightened media attention, the significance of the year to Māori, and the coinciding publication of a book on the history of Māori rugby by politically savvy Malcolm Mullholland (2009) the call for an 'apology' to Māori players excluded from tours to South Africa started to rouse (Bidwell, 2010). Initially, the NZRU did not respond immediately or favourably to such a request which only intensified demands. Eventually the NZ and South African rugby unions caved in to public and international pressure and apologised to Māori players who were excluded from All Black teams touring South Africa in 1928, 1949 and 1960. As a post-script to the apology however, the NZRU explained it hadn't apologised earlier because of advice from the NZ Māori Rugby Board that it would be inappropriate to be critical of Apartheid-era decisions made in particular by Māori administrators.

What does this scenario illustrate with regards to sport management and governance? It suggests that the status of Māori teams and 'advisory' groups fluctuate depending on what resources are being allocated and whose privilege and power is being threatened. When the NZ Māori team was dropped in 2009, the NZMRB were not consulted, but when the apology was requested, they were. This example also illustrates how threats to privileged status can influence the decision-making processes of Māori as well as Pākehā involved in sport governance.

Sport management and Indigeneity: Australia

Tatz (2009) contends that sport is more important to ATSI people than any other group of Australians. In an era when Indigenous health, poverty, education, incarceration and suicide are each problematic, sport provides a sense of purpose. As an Aboriginal observer remarked recently: "for the Tiwi people [Australian Rules] football means hope, it means pride and most of all it means life" (Moodie, 2008, p. 105). As noted previously, though, Indigenous participation rates in regular physical activity appear to have declined in the early 21st century. This is something of a conundrum because ATSI athletes feature more strongly than ever in elite-level sport. Programs to improve Aboriginal health, which include exercise and diet, have been introduced in every state and territory, such as Victoria's Physical Activity and Aboriginal Health initiative, which involves the provision of resources and training to schools and localities serviced by the state's twenty-four Aboriginal Community Controlled Health Organisations (Go for your Life, 2011). Some sport programmes have arisen as an outcome of corporate social responsibility ventures on the part of major companies, such as the mining giant Rio Tinto, which has funded the Kickstart Indigenous Football Program, targeted particularly at children in remote regions (Walker & Oxenham, 2001). Other programs have been conceived as philanthropic gestures, such as the Red Dust Role Models initiative, which is presented as a case study in chapter 15 on Sport Development.

In recent times, professional sporting bodies have more consistently contributed resources to Indigenous engagement in sport at the grassroots level. While this has been prompted by a sense of goodwill, including a commitment to improving the life experiences of ATSI people, there is also a strategic imperative. Talent scouts now roam the nation in search of Indigenous athletic talent, particularly for the AFL and the NRL. Many of the young men identified come from rural or remote regions, and are expected to relocate to a major city in order to become professional footballers. Until recently, many sport organisations failed to understand the support needs of Indigenous athletes during the complex process of acclimatisation. Programs are now emerging that are dedicated to inducting ATSI players into professional football, with Indigenous mentors and culturally appropriate support mechanisms (Campbell & Sonn, 2009).

According to Adair and Stronach (2011), however, Aboriginal success at elite-level has an unintended down side in that it is widely assumed that Indigenous people are 'naturally' talented at sport, but not similarly 'gifted' in academic or intellectual pursuits. This presumption of physical acumen at the expense of mental dexterity is held widely: in terms of sport it is a means of limiting Aboriginal advancement in off-field positions of responsibility, such as after retirement from a playing career. A key problem, however, is that researchers have found that many Aboriginal athletes have low levels of self-efficacy beyond playing sport; too often they have assumed that the stereotype of high physical capital and low mental capital applies to them (Godwell, 1997, 2000). It is all the more important, then, for Indigenous professionals in sport to develop skill sets to prepare them for life beyond the playing field. Indeed, recent research has indicated that many ATSI athletes who have retired from sport have had serious problems adjusting to a new life and a different career (Stronach & Adair, 2010). A major challenge for sport managers, therefore, is to liaise with Indigenous people to meet their needs – not only when coming into sport but also transitioning productively thereafter.

Sport management and Indigeneity: New Zealand

Research by Tina Masters (see Palmer & Masters, 2010) and Raima H. Hippolite (see Hippolite & Bruce, 2010) suggest Māori have implemented strategies to negotiate barriers and racism they experience in ANZ sport. These strategies include adopting an approach to leadership/decision-making that reflects a partnership implied by the Treaty of Waitangi; using networks in the Māori and sporting worlds; speaking out to bring about change from within their sport; being solution-focused and outcome-oriented; being willing to learn; developing supportive relationships with governing bodies, kaumatua and staff; initiating their own training and development; and incorporating Māori values and practices into organisational culture and management styles to improve their well-being, the well-being of their staff, and the effectiveness of their organisation. In some cases the strategy used was to re-evaluate their commitment to sport and/or opt out of sport altogether.

The Declaration on the Rights of Indigenous Peoples (non-binding) adopted by the UN General Assembly in September, 2007 included reference to the right of Indigenous peoples to maintain and strengthen their own institutions, cultures and traditions and to pursue their development in keeping with their own needs and aspirations. Interestingly the four states that voted against adopting the Declaration were Australia, Canada, USA and New Zealand all of whom have significant Indigenous populations. What this highlights is that the rights of Indigenous people tend to run counter to the neo-liberal, 'equal opportunities for all' ideology that is manifest in discourse regarding diversity and globalisation. The Declaration nonetheless acknowledges the unique place Indigenous peoples have within a multicultural society. Academics and practitioners advocating for diversity to be valued and understood in organisational and management studies must also consider the different histories and contemporary circumstances between Indigenous groups and 'other' ethnic minority groups. This resonates with what Māori leaders are seeking in New Zealand. Sir Mason Durie, for instance, developed broad aims of self-determination or tino rangatiratanga based on advancement of Māori people through "economic self-sufficiency, social equity, cultural affirmation and political power" (Durie, 1998, p. 239). These objectives, he argues, stand equally with a firm cultural identity as Māori. How can sport assist Māori in their aspirations to achieve rangatiratanga or self-determination in the broadest sense? The following New Zealand case studies are examples of Indigenous initiatives from within Te Ao Māori, from within the SportsWorld, and as a partnership arrangement.

CASE STUDY ONE: IRONMĀORI EVENT

Te Timatanga Ararau Trust was established in December 2007 to support Māori to make lifestyle changes through increased exercise and improved diet and nutrition. In December 2009 after running several small hikoi/fun run events, the Trust hosted its first Māori-based half ironman event under the IronMāori brand. To achieve its vision the Trust developed a range of initiatives to support participants developing physical, emotional and social wellbeing as they prepared for the event. This included weekly swimming and cycling clinics, monthly information evenings, an information website and an interactive Facebook page. The Trust also promoted the benefits of being smoke, drug and alcohol free at all its events. The event is not exclusively for Māori but in 2009 Māori made up more than 90% of

(Continued)

the competitors. This initiative could be considered to have originated within a Pākehā-centric sporting organisation by a Māori organisation which is visually represented in Figure 3-1.

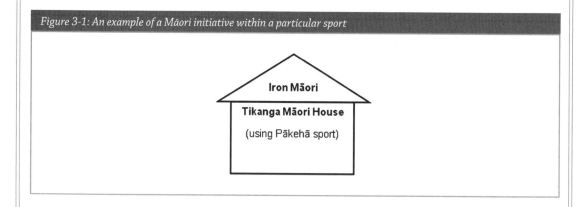

Figure 3-1: An example of a Māori initiative within a particular sport

Iron Māori

Tikanga Māori House

(using Pākehā sport)

CASE STUDY TWO: MĀORI TOUCH NZ AND TOUCH NZ PARTNERSHIP

Māori Touch New Zealand was formed in 1998 with the aim of improving Māori, iwi, hapū and whānau outcomes through a game with a high number of Māori participants. Guiding principles for Māori Touch NZ as an organisation, and in partnership with iwi, hapā and takiwā (regions) include mana (authority, prestige), rangatiratanga (self-determination), oritenga (creating provision for learning), kaitiakitanga (guardianship and protection), and whakapapa (ancestral relationships). See Ngawati, Paenga and Ngawati (2008) for more detail regarding these principles. Criteria developed for positive outcomes included autonomy over development and outcomes, and access to Te Ao Māori (the Māori world), including traditional knowledge, te reo (Māori language) and practices. Touch was envisaged as a positive vehicle for traditional knowledge and well-being, relevant to Māori specifically through the implementation of the Māori Touch NZ National Tournament and the World Indigenous Tournament. With both events, partnership relationships between Māori Touch NZ and the National Sporting Organisation (NSO), Touch NZ (TNZ) needed to exist. The most significant step toward partnership between Touch NZ (TNZ) and Māori Touch NZ occurred in 2004 when a partnership agreement was established in 2004. The agreement contained the following aspects:

- The importance of the well-being of the game of Touch in Aotearoa/NZ.
- Access by Māori Touch NZ to TNZ technical resources (including expertise).
- The individual player (if selected) has the right to state his/her eligibility for either organisation.
- TNZ reserves the first right of selection of players.
- Māori Touch NZ selections are only made at Māori Touch tournaments.
- TNZ recognises and supports the Māori Touch NZ Tournament date.
- TNZ supports Māori Touch NZ membership to Federation of International Touch (FIT) and participation in World Cup events and international competition.

According to Ngawati et al. (2008) this partnership agreement was not always successful in bridging the divide because despite being a binding document, it relied on goodwill from both parties in order to be implemented. A partnership agreement based on the Treaty of Waitangi, however, promotes the creation of distinct spaces in which the cultures can naturally evolve in their own way. The model also outlines the principles, guidelines and conditions in which these two discrete "houses" can interact with

(Continued)

one another under the auspices of the "Treaty of Waitangi House" (Royal, 1998). According to this model, Māori Touch NZ and TNZ could continue to operate as organisations in their own right with shared resources and support from the Treaty of Waitangi House (i.e., SPARC) in the spirit of partnership for the well-being of the game. This is visually represented in Figure 3-2.

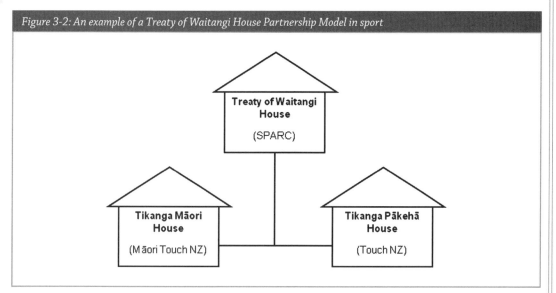

Figure 3-2: An example of a Treaty of Waitangi House Partnership Model in sport

Source: Adapted from Royal (1998) and Ngawati et al., (2008)

CASE STUDY THREE: HE ORANGA POUTAMA

The Sport and Recreation Act (2002) affirms that one of the functions of SPARC is to "promote and support the development and implementation of physical recreation and sport in a way that is culturally appropriate to Māori". SPARC delivers this function through its He Oranga Poutama (HOP) programme; and invests funds into appropriate organisations with the strategic goal to "increase participation and leadership as Māori in sport and traditional physical recreation at community level". The HOP strategic goals sit on a foundation based on the principles of the Treaty of Waitangi – Partnership, Participation and Protection (see Table 3-1 for more detail). The focus on participation 'as Māori' is a key distinction of this programme which has 3 key outcomes:

- Kaiwhakahāere participating as leaders in their community.
- Increased opportunities for whānau to explore, learn and participate in sport and traditional physical recreation.
- Development/revitalisation of sport and traditional physical games.

In 2011, there were 12 providers contracted by SPARC to deliver initiatives under the HOP programme: five Regional Sports Trusts (RSTs) and seven iwi/Māori organisations. SPARC's work with providers has identified five key elements that contribute to defining what it means to participate as Māori in the context of HOP.

In conclusion self-determination or rangatiratanga is about creating the greatest extent possible for independence and autonomy of Māori communities, not necessarily in isolation from wider society

(Continued)

but certainly apart from controls and regulations imposed from outside the would-be self-determining community. The Treaty of Waitangi articles and principles have been theoretically applied to sport in the past (see McConnell, 2000; Palmer, 2007b) and practically applied as evidenced in these case studies. Table 3-1 provides a basic guideline for how the principles of the Treaty of Waitangi could be applied to sport management.

Table 3-1: Possible ways the Treaty Principles could be applied to Sport Management policies, practices and programmes		
ARTICLE	PRINCIPLE	POSSIBLE APPLICATION TO SPORT MANAGEMENT
Article One Governance	Partnership Kotahitanga	• What is the governance relationship between Māori and mainstream organisations? • Does this relationship portray a genuine partnership that includes sharing decision-making responsibilities and resources or is it tokenistic? • Are Māori stakeholders considered in allocation of resources and development of policies and practices?
Article Two Ownership Guardianship	Protection Kaitiakitanga	• Are Māori taonga relating to sport protected? This could include: use of Māori symbols, rites and rituals (e.g., haka, art forms); traditional games and pastimes; and well-being (holistic) • Are there some sport tournaments, games, teams and events that are better protected under the guardianship of Māori for Māori?
Article Three Inclusiveness	Participation Urunga-Tu	• Are steps being taken to provide opportunities for Māori to participate and excel in all aspects of sport (as athletes, coaches, volunteers, staff and leaders)? • What right/need do Māori have to participate as Māori on the international stage? • Are there opportunities to participate in sport as Māori within Māori cultural frameworks and contexts?

Summary

In focusing on sport management and society, this chapter has highlighted commonalities and differences between two Indigenous communities – Aboriginal and Torres Strait Islanders (ATSI) of Australia and Māori of Aotearoa New Zealand (ANZ). The terms indigeneity, race and ethnicity are complex and when combined with hybridity, assimilation and globalisation these concepts are even more difficult to understand with regards to sport management, especially when the rhetoric around sport is that it is a level playing field irrespective of race, colour or creed. The examples illustrated in this chapter, however, challenge that rhetoric. Despite claims that Māori and ATSI are well represented in sport, a closer and critical analysis reveals that Indigenous people are basically absent in some sports. Moreover, even in sport where ATSI and Māori athletes are well represented, this has not translated into similar involvement in the management of sport, including marketing and sponsorship, public relations and media, coaching and sport science. Just as importantly, the high profile presence of so many Māori in rugby union and ATSI in Australian Rules and rugby league, does not insulate Indigenous athletes from racist attitudes and behaviours. According to the theories of social distance and segregation, it also does not guarantee Indigenous athletes full citizenship in other aspects of Australian or ANZ society. Symbolic racism occurs in both countries: in the realm of sport, as stressed by Hippolite and Bruce (2010), race relations can only be improved if those in power to confronting and challenging issues of discrimination and inequity. To date, those in power tend not to demonstrate any interest in confronting or challenging the issue of racism in ANZ sport, especially at the cultural and institutional levels. Australian sport has been more proactive in this area, but it is still a work in progress.

Recommendations for sport managers

- Ethnoculturally diverse pools of applicants for sport management positions should be encouraged as part of any major recruiting of volunteer and paid roles in sport. This must involve women and men; gender representation is a crucial part of human resource equity.
- Recruiting for sport management positions should be conducted in ethnoculturally diverse environments, including schools, coaching clinics, and Indigenous contexts. This is intended to encounter 'closed' appointments under an 'old boys' network'.
- Systematic reviews of sport management practices and policies should be conducted every 3-5 years by an independent body, such as a Human Rights Commission, to monitor the degree which sporting bodies are ethnoculturally inclusive.
- Sport management personnel must be trained in decoding the language of symbolic racism so that they can deflect or combat problems that arise.
- Liaise with ATSI and Māori community groups to ascertain how Indigenous values, beliefs, models and practices might be incorporated into the organisational culture of a sport.
- Actively target and train Indigenous people for sport management roles, especially those with leadership and decision-making capacity.

Review questions

- What are some of the key differences between Indigenous peoples and other ethnic minority communities and how does this relate to the management of sport?
- How do stereotypes of people based on beliefs regarding race and ethnicity influence opportunities and experiences in sport?
- How can sport management organisations and personnel influence perceptions and attitudes toward Indigenous communities and individuals in a way that benefits the organisation and the individuals involved?
- What are the benefits and costs of having sports teams and events for particular ethnic groups?
- How can cultural diversity and multiculturalism be implemented while considering the rights and needs of Indigenous groups in sport?
- Consider a sport governing board that you are aware of. What is the ethnic composition of this board and how does this influence decision making and allocation of resources, if at all?
- How can incorporating values, practices and protocols from an Indigenous or ethnic minority culture improve the performance of a sport organisation? Can you think of some examples of this occurring in your experiences of sport management?

- How can genuine ethnocultural integration take place within all levels of sport? What are your thoughts on affirmative action, quotas, and legislation in order to achieve equity in sport?
- Consider examples of symbolic racism that you have experienced or been aware of. How can this symbolic racism be addressed?
- What sport programmes, policies and practices could be changed to be more inclusive of Indigenous communities?
- Consider the principles of the Treaty of Waitangi and how they could be applied to sport management policies, practices and programmes you are aware of. Could these be applied to other cultural contexts outside of New Zealand?
- How can more ethnic minority individuals be encouraged to pursue leadership opportunities in coaching, sport management and governance?
- How have aspects of Indigenous culture been used to promote national identity or to market a sport brand? From an ethical standpoint, what are the benefits and costs of using Indigenous culture in this way for Indigenous people and for the organisations/brands involved?
- How can cross-cultural communication and understanding be promoted within a sport organisation, team, and between individuals from diverse ethnicities?

Māori Glossary

Haka Dance used during a wero (challenge), powhiri (welcome) and on many ceremonial/celebratory occasions

Hapū Refers to sub-tribes and translates as pregnant

He Oranga Poutama A programme funded by SPARC with the strategic goal of increasing participation and leadership as Māori in sport and traditional physical recreation at community level.

Hikoi Walk or march (often associated with organised walks for a significant purpose)

Hoe waka Traditional canoe races

Hui Gathering/meeting

Iwi Refers to the larger tribal communities (e.g., Ngati Porou, Kai Tahu, Tuwharetoa, Ngati Kahungunu, Te Arawa) and also translates as 'bones' (i.e., where are your bones from?)

Kaitiakitanga guardianship, ownership and protection

Kaiwhakahāere Individuals responsible for co-ordinating the He Oranga Poutama programme

Kaumatua elderly person who because of their status, knowledge and experience in a Māori context are respected and honoured and may fulfil formal duties for the people they represent

Kaupapa Purpose, objectives

Ki-o-rahi Ball game that is considered an ancestral game for Māori and incorporates tikanga and te reo Māori elements

Kotahitanga Governance, unity

Mana Status, having influence or power; authority or prestige

Mana atua Status of the gods

Mana tangata Status of the people

Mana Māori Status of Māori as a people

Marae Ceremonial courtyard. Meeting place where Māori protocol and customs are carried out (e.g., Waipatu and Ngāruawāhia Marae)

Mu torero Traditional board game

Ngā mahi a te rehia Term used to refer to traditional games and pastimes

Ngā taonga takaro Term used to refer to treasured games of Māori ancestors now being taught in schools and health programmes

Oritenga Creating provision for learning

Pākehā New Zealander of British ancestry whose cultural values and behaviour have been primarily formed from the experiences of being a member of the dominant group in New Zealand society

Rangatiratanga Depending on the context can mean leadership, chieftainship (at individual level) and self-determination at the collective level

Tainui One of the ancestral waka (canoe) that Māori came to Aotearoa on

Takiwā Regions

Tangata Whenua People of the land (implies Indigeneity)

Taonga Property; anything highly prized

Te Ao Māori The Māori world (or worldview)

Te Papa Takaro o Te Arawa Iwi organisation in the Te Arawa area which focuses on holistic well-being through the vehicle of sport and physical recreation

Te Puni Kōkiri Ministry of Māori Development

Te Reo The language (often used to refer to the Māori language)

Te Timatanga Ararau Trust A Māori organisation in the Ngati Kahungunu iwi

Te Whetu Rēhua A model used by SPARC and Māori to guide decision-making with regards to appropriate activities for He Oranga Poutama programme

Tikanga Culture motives. Tikanga Māori refers to protocols, customs and beliefs associated with Māori culture

Tino rangatiratanga Self-determination

Treaty Often refers to the Treaty of Waitangi (English version) which was a covenant signed by some Māori chiefs and representatives of the Crown in 1840. In this chapter, it is a term used to refer to both the English and Māori version known as Tiriti o Waitangi

Urunga-Tu Inclusiveness

Whakapapa ancestral relationships and geneology

Whānau Family unit in Māori context; art of giving birth

Whānaungatanga Relationships

Whare House/home (symbolic and actual)

References

Adair, D. (2006). Shooting the messenger: Australian history's warmongers. *Sporting Traditions, 22*(2), 49–69.

Adair, D., & Stronach, M. (2011). Natural born athletes? Australian Indigenous people and the double-edged lure of professional sport. In K. Spracklen & J. Long (Eds.), *Sport and Challenges to Racism* (pp. 117-134). London: Palgrave MacMillan.

Adair, D., Taylor, T., & Darcy, S. (2010). Managing ethnocultural and 'racial' diversity in sport: Obstacles and opportunities. *Sport Management Review, 13* (4), 307–312.

Ahmed, S. (2000). *Strange encounters: Embodied others in post-coloniality.* London: Routledge.

Anderson, W. (2009). Ambiguities of race: Science on the reproductive frontier of Australia and the Pacific between the wars. *Australian Historical Studies, 40*(2), 143–160.

Ansley, G. (2010, 18 June). Racism storm sweeps through sporting codes. *New Zealand Herald.* Retrieved from http://www.nzherald .co.nz/

Armstrong, J. C. (2010). Indigeneity: The heart of development with culture and identity. In V. Tauli-Corpuz, L. Enkiwe-Abayao, & R. de Chavez (Eds.), *Towards an alternative development paradigm: Indigenous peoples' self-determined development* (pp. 79–88). Philippines: Tebtebba Foundation.

Australian Bureau of Statistics (ABS). (2008). *4704.0 The Health and Welfare of Australia's Aboriginal and Torres Strait Islander Peoples, 2008.* Retrieved from http://www.abs.gov.au/Ausstats/abs@.nsf/0/D059DE84AB99BE60CA2574390014BE51?opendocument.

Australian Football League (AFL). (2007, May 22). *AFL indigenous round: Round nine.* Retrieved from http://www.afl.com.au/Season2007/News/NewsArticle/tabid/208/Default.aspx?newsId=43746

Belich, J. (1986). *The New Zealand wars and the Victorian interpretation of racial conflict.* Auckland: Auckland University Press.

Bergin, P. (2002). Māori sport and cultural identity in Australia. *The Australian Journal of Anthropology, 13*(3), 257–269.

Bidwell, H. (2010, 5 May). NZ rugby 'owes Māori apology'. *The Press.* Retrieved from http://www.stuff.co.nz/

Boock, R. (2008, Nov 11). 'She'll be white, bro'. *The Sunday Star Times.* Retrieved from http://www.stuff.co.nz/

Brown, H. (2010a). Nga taonga takaro: The growth of cultural sport in our society. *New Zealand Physical Educator*, pp. 28–30.

Brown, H. (2010b). Nga taonga takaro – 'the treasured games of our ancestors' *Australasian Parks and Leisure, 13*(1), 11–14.

Bruce, T., & Wensing, E. (2009). "She's not one of us": Cathy Freeman and the place of Aboriginal people in Australian national culture. *Australian Aboriginal Studies, 2,* 90–100.

Callister, P. (2008). Skin colour: Does it matter in New Zealand? *Policy Quarterly, 4*(1), 18–25.

Campbell, E., & Sonn, C. C. (2009). Transitioning into the AFL: Indigenous Football Players' Perspectives, *Athletic Insight, 11*(3). Retrieved from http://athleticinsight.com

Consedine, R., & Consedine, J. (2005). *Healing our history: The challenge of the Treaty of Waitangi* (2nd ed.). Auckland: Penguin Books.

Coram, S. (2007). Race formations (evolutionary hegemony) and the 'aping' of the Australian indigenous athlete. *International Review for the Sociology of Sport, 42,* 391–409.

Cottle, D., & Keys, A. (2010). The blindside flick: Race and rugby league. *Cosmopolitan Civil Societies: An Interdisciplinary Journal, 2*(2), 1–11.

Cowlishaw, G. (1987). 'Colour, culture and the Aboriginalists'. *Man* (new series), *22*(2), 221–37.

Crawford, S. (1981). Māori legacy: The Māori in New Zealand sport and physical education. *Action: British Journal of Physical Education, 12*(1), 14.

Crawford, S. (1999). Rugby and the forging of a national identity. In J. Nauright (Ed.), *Sport, power and society in New Zealand: Historical and contemporary perspectives, ASSH studies in sports history No. 11* (pp. 1–19) Sydney: Australian Society for Sports History.

Cunningham, G. B., & Fink, J. S. (2006). Diversity issues in sport and leisure. *Journal of Sport Management, 20*(4), 455–65.

Durie, M. (1998). *Whaiora. Māori health development* (2nd ed). Victoria, Australia: Oxford University Press.

Edwards, K. (1999). *Choopadoo: Games from a dreamtime.* Brisbane: Queensland University of Technology Press.

Edwards, K. (with Meston, T.) (2008). *Yulunga: Traditional Aboriginal games.* Canberra: Australian Sports Commission.

Edwards, K. (2009). Traditional games of a timeless land: Play cultures in Aboriginal and Torres Strait Islander communities. *Australian Aboriginal Studies,* (2), 32–43.

Elder, C., Pratt, A., & Ellis, C. (2006). Running race: Reconciliation, nationalism and the Sydney 2000 Olympic Games. *International Review for the Sociology of Sport, 41*(2), 181–200.

Fink, J. S., & Pastore, D. L. (1999). Diversity in sport? Utilizing the business literature to devise a comprehensive framework of diversity initiatives. *Quest, 51*(4), 310–327.

Fougere, G. (1989). Sport, culture and identity: The case of rugby football. In D. Novitz & B. Willmott (Eds.), *Culture and identity in New Zealand* (pp. 110–122). Wellington: GP.

Gamble, W. (2003, 25 January). Outspoken Crowe pleads for a fair go. *New Zealand Herald.* Retrieved from http://www.nzherald.co.nz

Gardiner, G. (1997). Racial abuse and football: The Australian Football League's racial vilification rule in review. *Sporting Traditions, 14*(1), 3–25.

Gardiner, G. (2003) Running for country. *Journal of Sport and Social Issues, 27*(3), 233–260.

Gay, E. (2010, 9 July). Haden's future in doubt. *New Zealand Herald.* Retrieved from http://www.nzherald.co.nz

Go for your Life (2011, June). Physical activity and Aboriginal Health. *Active Inform.*

Godwell, D. (1997). *Aboriginality and rugby league in Australia: An exploratory study of identity construction and professional sport.* (Unpublished Masters thesis). Dept of Kinesiology, University of Windsor.

Godwell, D. (2000). Playing the game: Is sport as good for race relations as we'd like to think? *Australian Aboriginal Studies*, (1), 12–19.

Gorman, S. (2010). Sporting chance: Indigenous participation in Australian sport history. *Cosmopolitan Civil Societies: An Interdisciplinary Journal*, 2(2), 12–22.

Grainger, A. (2006). From immigrant to overstayer: Samoan identity, rugby and cultural politics of race and nation in Aotearoa/New Zealand. *Journal of Sport & Social Issues*, 30, 45–61.

Graves, J. L. Jr. (2001). *The emperor's new clothes: Biological theories of race at the millennium.* Piscataway NJ: Rutgers University Press.

Hapeta, J., & Palmer, F. (2009). TŪ TOA – 'Māori youth standing with pride as champions' in sport and education. *Journal of Australian Indigenous Studies*, 12(1–4), 229–247.

Hippolite, H. R. (2008). Towards an equal playing field: Racism and Māori women in sport. *Mai Review*, 1, 1–12.

Hippolite, H. R., & Bruce, T. (2010). Speaking the unspoken: Racism, sport and Māori. *Cosmopolitan Civil Societies Journal*, 2(2), 23–45.

Hirini, P., & Flett, R. (1999). Aspects of the Māori All Black experience: The value of cultural capital in the new professional era. *He Pukenga Kōrero*, 5(1), 18–24.

Hogan, J. (2003). Staging the nation: Gendered and ethnicized discourses of national identity and Olympic opening ceremonies. *Journal of Sport and Social Issues*, 27(2), 100–123.

Hokowhitu, B. (2003a). Māori masculintiy, post-structuralism, and the emerging self. *New Zealand Sociology*, 18, 179–201.

Hokowhitu, B. (2003b). 'Physical beings': Stereotypes, sport and the 'physical education' of New Zealand Māori. *Culture, sport, society*, 6(2/3), 192–218.

Hokowhitu, B. (2004). Tackling Māori masculinity: A colonial geneology of savagery and sport. *The Contemporary Pacific*, 16(2), 259–284.

Hokowhitu, B. (2005). Rugby and tino rangatiratanga: Early Māori rugby and the formation of traditional Māori masculinity. *Sporting Traditions*, 21(2), 75–95.

Hokowhitu, B. (2007). Māori sport: Pre-colonisation to today. In C. Collins & S. J. Jackson (Eds.), *Sport in Aotearoa/New Zealand Society* (2nd ed.) (pp. 78–95). Melbourne: Thomson Dunmore Press.

Hokowhitu, B. (2009). Māori rugby and subversion: Creativity, domestication, oppression and decolonization. *International Journal of the History of Sport*, 26(16), 2314–2334.

Hokowhitu, B. (2010). Introduction: indigenous studies, research, identity and resistance. In B. Hokowhitu, N. Kermoal, C. Andersen, M. Reilly, A. Petersen, I. Altamirano-Jemenez, & P. Rewi (Eds.), *Indigenous identity and resistance: Researching the diversity of knowledge* (pp. 9–20). Dunedin: Otago University Press.

Hokowhitu, B., & Scherer, J. (2008). The Māori All Blacks and the decentering of the white subject: Hyperrace, sport, and the cultural logic of late capitalism. *Sociology of Sport Journal*, 25(2), 243–262.

Holland, R., Leberman, S., Palmer, F., & Walker, R. (2010). Diversity in sport governance/leadership roles in national sport organisations. In J. Davies (Ed.), *16th Sport Management Association of Australia & New Zealand Conference* (pp. 21). Wellington, New Zealand: Sport Management Association of Australia & New Zealand.

Howell, R. A., & Howell, M. L. (1992). *The genesis of sport in Queensland*. St Lucia: University of Queensland Press.

Hyde, T. (1993, September). White men can't jump: The Polynesianisation of sport. *Metro*, 62–69.

Jackson, S. J., & Hokowhitu, B. (2002). Sport, tribes and technology: The New Zealand All Blacks haka and the politics of identity. *Journal of Sport and Social Issues*, 26(2) 125–139.

James, B., & Saville-Smith, K. (1989). *Gender, culture and power. Challenging New Zealand's gendered culture. Critical issues in New Zealand society.* Auckland: Oxford University Press.

Kelly, A. (2011, 20 September). *Samoan faces sanction over IRB blast.* Retrieved from http://au.sports.yahoo.com/news/article/-/10297428/samoans-twitter-blast-for-irb/

Klugman, M., & Osmond, G. (2009). That picture – Nicky Winmar and the history of an image. *Australian Aboriginal Studies*, 2, 80–91.

Kukutai, T. (2004). The problem of defining an ethnic group for public policy: Who is Māori and why does it matter. *Social Policy Journal of New Zealand*, 23, 86–108.

Kukutai, T. (2007). White mothers, brown children: Ethnic identification of Māori European children in New Zealand. *Journal of Marriage and Family*, 69(5), 1150–1161.

Kukutai, T., & Callister, P. (2009). A "main" ethnic group? Ethnic self-prioritisation among New Zealand youth. *Social Policy Journal of New Zealand*, (36), 16–31.

Leckie, J. (1989). From race aliens to an ethnic group - Indians in New Zealand. In M.C. Howard (Ed.), *Ethnicity and nation-building in the Pacific* (pp. 169–197). Tokyo: United Nations University.

Masters, R. (2009, April 24). League's Polynesian powerplay muscles in on indigenous numbers. *Sydney Morning Herald*, p.??.

Masters, T. (2006). *Ngā kaiwhakahaere wāhine Māori: Māori women sport managers*. (Unpublished masters thesis). Massey University, Palmerston North, New Zealand.

McCausland-Durie, Y. (2007). *Retention issues for Māori girls in netball*. (Unpublished masters thesis). Massey University, Palmerston North, New Zealand.

McConnell, R. (2000). Māori, the Treaty of Waitangi and sport: A critical analysis. In C. Collins (Ed.), *Sport in New Zealand society* (pp. 227–239). Palmerston North: Dunmore Press.

McNeill, D. (2008). 'Black magic', nationalism and race in Australian football. *Race & Class, 49*(4), 22–37.

Mead, H. M. (2003). *Tikanga Māori: Living by Māori values*. Wellington, New Zealand: Huia.

Melnick, M. J. (1996). Māori women and positional segregation in New Zealand netball: Another test of the Anglocentric hypothesis. *Sociology of Sport Journal, 13*(3), 259–273.

Melnick, M. J., & Thomson, R. W. (1996). The Māori people and positional segregation in New Zealand rugby football: A test of the Anglocentric Hypothesis. *International Review for Sociology of Sport, 31*(2), 139–154.

Miller, R. J., Ruru, J., Behrendt, L., & Lindberg, T. (2010). The Doctrine of Discovery in Australia. In R. J. Miller et al. (Eds.), *Discovering indigenous lands: The doctrine of discovery in the English colonies* (Vol. 1)(pp. 171–187). Oxford: Oxford University Press.

Moodie, D. (Ed.). (2008). *Tiwi footy Yiloga*. Singapore: F11 Productions.

Morgan, G. (2003). Aboriginal protest and the Sydney Olympic Games. *Olympika, 12*, 23–38.

Mullholland, M. (2009). *Beneath the Māori moon: An illustrated history of Māori rugby*. Wellington, NZ: Huia Publishers.

Murchie, E. (1984). *Rapuora: Health and Māori women*. Wellington: Māori Women's Welfare League.

Neilson, B. (2002). Bodies of protest: Performing citizenship at the 2000 Olympic Games. *Continuum, 16*(1), 13–26.

Nelson, A. (2009). Sport, physical activity and urban Indigenous young people. *Australian Aboriginal Studies, 2*, 101–111.

Ngawati, R., Paenga, M., & Ngawati, C. (2008). Indigenous partnership strategies in sport: Māori touch as a vehicle for traditional knowledge and well-being and Whanau/hapu/iwi development. In J. S. Te Rito & S. M. Healy (Eds.), *Proceedings of the Traditional Knowledge Conference, 2008* (pp. 219–225). Auckland, New Zealand, Nga Pae o te Maramatanga (New Zealand's Centre of Research Excellence).

Nielsen, E. (2009). Profound indifference: Amateur athletics and Indigenous Australians in the early twentieth century. *Sporting Traditions, 26*(2), 31–46.

Norman, H. (2009). An unwanted corroboree: The politics of the New South Wales Aboriginal Rugby League Knockout. *Australian Aboriginal Studies, 2*, 112–122.

North, I. (2002). Staraboriginality. *Hawke Institute Working Paper Series, 20*, University of South Australia, 1–21.

Oliver, P. (2006). *What's the score?: A survey of cultural diversity and racism in sport*. Human Rights and Equal Opportunity Commission, Sydney.

Palmer, F. (2000). *Māori girls, power, physical education, sport and play: 'Being hungus, hori, and hoha'*. (Unpublished doctoral thesis). University of Otago, New Zealand.

Palmer, F. (2006). Māori sport and its management. In S. Leberman, C. Collins, & L. Trenberth (Eds.), *Sport business management in Aotearoa/New Zealand* (pp. 62–88). Melbourne, Vic: Thomson Dunmore Press.

Palmer, F. (2007a). Body image, hauora and identity: Experiences of Māori girls in sport. *Childrenz Issues, 11*(2), 12–19.

Palmer, F. (2007b). Treaty principles and Māori sport: Contemporary issues. In C. Collins & S. Jackson (Eds.). *Sport in Aotearoa/New Zealand society* (2nd ed.) (pp 307–334). Melbourne: Thomson Dunmore Press.

Palmer, F., Graham, M., & Mako, N. (2009). *Ki O Rahi Evaluation and Scoping Project*. Te Au Rangahau, Māori Business Research Centre, Massey University and Best Care (Whakapai Hauora) Charitable Trust.

Palmer, F. R., & Masters, T. M. (2010). Māori feminism and sport leadership: Exploring Māori women's experiences. *Sport Management Review, 13*(4), 331–344.

Paradies, Y. (2005). Anti-racism and indigenous Australians. *Analyses of Social Issues and Public Policy, 5*(1), 1–28.

Paradies, Y. (2006). Beyond black and white: Essentialism, hybridity and indigeneity. *Journal of Sociology, 42*(4), 355–367.

Paterson, L. (2010). Hawhekaihe: Māori voices on the position of 'half-castes' within Māori society. *Journal of New Zealand Studies, (9)*, 135–155.

Reynolds, H. (2007). *The other side of the frontier: Aboriginal resistance to the European invasion of Australia*. Sydney: UNSW Press.

Royal, T. A. C. (1998). *Mātauranga Māori paradigms and politics*. Paper presented to the Ministry for Research, Science and Technology. Retrieved from http://www.charles-royal.com/assets/mm-paradigmspolitics.pdf

Russell, A. (2011, 27 September). South African RWC journalists cry 'racism'. Retrieved from http://www.newstalkzb.co.nz/newsdetail1.asp?storyID=205568

Ryan, G. (1993). *Forerunners of the All Blacks. The 1888–89 New Zealand Native football team in Britain, Australia and New Zealand.* Christchurch, NZ: Canterbury University Press.

Ryan, G. (2007). Few and far between: Māori and Pacific contributions to New Zealand cricket. *Sport in Society, 10*(1), 84–100.

Sampson, D. (2009). Culture, 'race' and discrimination in the 1868 Aboriginal cricket tour of England. *Australian Aboriginal Studies, 2*, 44–60.

Singer, J. N. (2005). Addressing epistemological racism in sport management research. *Journal of Sport Management, 19*(4), 464–79.

Smith, A. (Ed.), (2000, November 10). *Games from the dreamtime.* [ABC Radio National Interview with Ken Edwards]. Online transcript retrieved 4 April 2008 from http://fulltext. ausport. gov.au/fulltext/2000/sportsf/s210119.htm.

Smith, E., & Hattery, A. (2011). Race relations theories: Implications for sport management. *Journal of Sport Management, 25*(2), 107–117.

SPARC. (2008). *Sport, Recreation and Physical Activity Participation Among New Zealand Adults: Key Results of the 2007/08 Active NZ Survey.* Wellington: SPARC

Spracklen, K., Hylton, K., & Long, J. (2006). Managing and monitoring equality and diversity in UK sport: An evaluation of the sporting equals racial equality standard and its impact on organisational change. *Journal of Sport & Social Issues, 30*(3), 289–305.

St John, G. (2001). Australian (alter)natives: Cultural drama and indigeneity. *Social Analysis, 45*(1), 122–140.

Statistics New Zealand. (2007). *QuickStats about Māori.* Retrieved from http://www.stats.govt.nz/NR/rdonlyres/095030F8-BD62-4745-836D0EF185619C37/0/2006censusquickstatsaboutmaorirevised.pdf

Stephen, M. (2009). Football, 'race' and resistance: The Darwin Football League, 1926–29. *Australian Aboriginal Studies, 2*, 61–77.

Stronach, M., & Adair, D. (2010). Lords of the square ring: Future capital and career transition issues for elite Indigenous Australian boxers. *Cosmopolitan Civil Societies Journal, 2*(2), 46–70.

Sunday Star Times (2008, 18 October). Inga: we must tackle racism in rugby. *Sunday Star Times.* Retrieved from http://www.stuff.co.nz

Tatz, C. (1995). *Obstacle Race: Aborigines in sport.* Kensington, NSW: University of NSW Press.

Tatz, C. (2009). Coming to terms: 'Race', ethnicity, identity and Aboriginality in sport'. *Australian Aboriginal Studies, 2*, 15–31.

Tatz, C. (2010). The destruction of Aboriginal society in Australia. In S. Totten & R. Hitchcock (Eds.), *Genocide of indigenous people: A critical biographical review* (Vol. 8)(pp. 87–116). New Brunswick, NJ: Transaction Publishers.

Taylor, T. (2001). Cultural diversity and leisure: Experiences of women in Australia. *Society and Leisure, 24*(2), 535–555.

Taylor, T. (2004). The rhetoric of exclusion: Perspectives of cultural diversity in Australian netball. *Journal of Sport and Social Issues, 28*(4), 453–476.

Taylor, T., & Toohey, K. (1999). Sport, gender and cultural diversity: Exploring the nexus. *Journal of Sport Management, 13*, 1–17.

Te Puni Kōkiri. (1993). *The Healthy Lifestyle Programme: An evaluation.* Wellington: Ministry of Māori Development.

Te Puni Kōkiri. (1995a). *Health through the marae. Nga tikanga hauora o nga marae.* Wellington: Te Puni Kokiri.

Te Puni Kōkiri. (1995b). *Omangia te oma roa: Māori participation in physical leisure.* Wellington: Te Puni Kokiri.

Te Puni Kōkiri. (2005). *Te Māori i te whutupōro: Māori in rugby* (Fact Sheet 23). Wellington: Te Puni Kōkiri.

Te Puni Kōkiri. (2006). *Ngā Māori i ngā mahi tākaro. Māori in sport and active leisure* (Fact Sheet 25). Wellington: Te Puni Kōkiri.

Te Puni Kōkiri (2009). *Māori earnings. Te Puni Kōkiri Fact Sheet.* Retrieved from http://www.tpk.govt.nz/en/in-print/our-publications/fact-sheets/maori-earnings.

Te Rito, P. (2006). *Leadership in Māori, European cultures and in the world of sport* (Internal Research Report). Auckland: Ngā Pae o te Maramatanga.

Te Rito, P. R. (2007). *Māori leadership: What role can rugby play?* (Unpublished masters thesis). Auckland University of Technology, New Zealand.

Thomas, D. R., & Dyall, L. (1999). Culture, ethnicity and sport management: A New Zealand perspective. *Sport Management Review, 1*, 115–132.

Thompson, S. (2004). Sociology of sport in service mode: How does it fit as a sport science provider? *Journal of Physical Education New Zealand, 37*, 17–28.

Thompson, S., Rewi, P., & Wrathall, D. (2000). Māori experiences in sport and physical authority: Research and initiatives. In C. Collins (Ed.), *Sport in New Zealand Society* (pp. 241–255). Palmerston North: Dunmore Press.

Thomson, A., Darcy, S., & Pearce, S. (2010). Ganma theory and third-sector sport-development programmes for Aboriginal and Torres Strait Islander youth: Implications for sports management. *Sport Management Review, 13*(4), 313–330.

Tomkinson, M. E. (2001). 'Is it in the blood? Australian Aboriginal identity'. In J. Linnekin & L. Pyer (Eds.), *Cultural identity and ethnicity in the Pacific* (pp. 191–218). Honolulu: University of Hawaii Press.

Tuhiwai Smith, L. (1992). Māori women: Discourse, projects and mana wahine. In S. Middleton & A. Jones (Eds.), *Women and Education in Aotearoa 2* (pp. 33–51). Wellington: Bridget Williams.

Walker, R. (1990). *Ka whawhai tonu matou: Struggle without end.* Auckland: Penguin.

Walker, R., & Oxenham, D. (2001). *A sporting chance: An evaluation of the Rio Tinto AFL Kickstart Program in the Kimberley region.* Perth: Curtin Indigenous Research Centre, Curtin University of Technology.

Warren, I., & Tsaousis, S. (1997). Racism and the law in Australian Rules football: A critical analysis. *Sporting Traditions,14*(1), 27–53.

Watkins, T. (2010, May 31). Haden saved by Holmes' cheeky darkie. Retrieved from http://www.stuff.co.nz/national/3759664/Haden-saved-by-Holmes-cheeky-darkie

Watson, G. (2005). Affirming Indian identities? An analysis of imperial rhetoric and orientalism in the tours of Indian hockey teams to New Zealand in 1926, 1935 and 1938. *Sporting Traditions, 21*(2), 119–140.

Watson, G. (2007). Sport and ethnicity in New Zealand. *History Compass, 5*(3), 780–801.

Watson, M. (2011, September 19). Haka losing respect – Springboks coach. *The Dominion Post.* Retrieved from http://www.stuff.co.nz/

Wetherell, M., & Potter, J. (1992). *Mapping the language of racism: Discourse and the legitimation of exploitation.* New York: Columbia University Press.

Wilson, R. (1997). Bringing them home: A guide to the findings and recommendations of the National Inquiry into the Separation of Aboriginal and Torres Strait Islander children from their families. Sydney: Human Rights and Equal Opportunity Commission. Retrieved from http://www.austlii.edu.au/au/ special /rsjproject/rsjlibrary/hreoc/

Wrathall, D. A. (1996). *Sports policy and the Māori woman athlete from a Māori perspective.* (Unpublished masters thesis) Victoria University, New Zealand.

Chapter 4

Sport in the Global Marketplace

Chris Gratton and Sam Richardson

OBJECTIVES

After completing this chapter, you should be able to:

- define the sport market and its component parts;
- recognise and comprehend the changing business environment in which the sport industry operates;
- review and critically evaluate the theories, concepts and principles underlying increasing globalisation in the sport market.

Key terms

In this chapter, readers will become familiar with the following concepts and terms:
- globalisation
- outsourcing
- sport market
- sport goods sector
- sport services sector
- consumer expenditure
- sports market
- sporting mega-event
- broadcasting rights
- global sports company
- global marketing strategy
- global brand
- corporate responsibility

Introduction

This chapter analyses the increasing economic importance of sport and the emergence of what is now recognised as a sport industry. It begins by defining the sport market and analysing consumer spending on sport in New Zealand and Australia. It then goes on to look at changes in the sport market since the 1970s. The changes in New Zealand and Australia reflect what has been happening to sport in most Western developed countries over this period. There are significant transnational forces operating in the sport market that have led to increasing globalisation of this market. The remainder of the chapter concentrates on analysing these forces in an Australasian context and supplementing these observations with a case study of the global sports company, Nike.

Concept Check

Globalisation

A range of developments that has led to the same products being made available throughout the world through the globalised marketing of brands as described in the Nike case study. National markets become less important as companies look to market their products on a global basis.

Definition of the sport market

Sport is now recognised as an important sector of economic activity. Sport accounts for close to 2% of Gross Domestic Product, employment and spending in Australia and New Zealand. 1.8% of consumer expenditure in Australia in 2003/04 was spent on sports and physical recreation, while 2.2% of consumer expenditure was spent on physical recreation in New Zealand in 2000. Although most recent attention has focused on the amount of money involved in sport at the elite level including sponsorship, payments for broadcasting rights and players' salaries, consumer expenditure on sport is not dominated by payments related to major professional sports. Consumer expenditure in the sport market consists in the main of expenditure related to the consumer's own participation in sport rather than to the viewing of sport.

Figure 1 gives a diagrammatic breakdown of consumer expenditures in broad terms on physical recreation and sport in Australia and New Zealand. These sectors are discussed in the following sections.

The sport goods sector

The sport market consists of the sport goods sector and the sport services sector. The sport goods sector includes all products which are bought for use in sport, such as, sport clothing, sport footwear, and sporting equipment, which includes sport and recreational vehicles and boats. The sport goods sector could be expanded to include sport-related publications, including newspapers, books and magazines. This is not included in the calculation of the sport goods sector, which means the importance of the sector is understated when compared to measures that include this sub-sector. The potential size of this sub-sector is evident when one notes that in the United Kingdom, for example, in 2008 sport-related publications were estimated to be worth 2.7% of the value of the sport market.

The sport services sector

The sport services sector is measured slightly differently between Australia and New Zealand. The broad groupings of sub-sectors are reasonably consistent, however. The largest sub-sector within the sports services sector is clubs, venues and facilities operation. In Australia this sub-sector

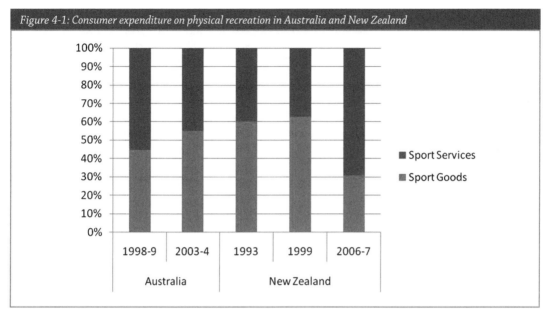

Figure 4-1: Consumer expenditure on physical recreation in Australia and New Zealand

Source: Australian Bureau of Statistics, BERL (2000); Dalziel (2011)

includes club subscriptions, admission fees and facility hire charges. The next sub-sector is lessons/ instruction and related services. The final sub-sector is health/fitness centres and gyms. This could be categorised as part of facilities operation, but it is recognised as an important sub-sector in its own right. The relative size of each sub-sector is detailed in the following sections. The calculation of the sport services sector in Australasia excludes potentially important sub-sectors that are included in other countries measures of the sport market. By way of example, these include sport-related gambling (estimated to be approximately 14% of the size of the UK sport market in 2008) and the production of sport-related television and DVD (estimated to be worth almost 13% of the value of the UK sports market in 2008). The omission of these from the calculations is important to note, and suggests that the measure of the services sector in Australia and New Zealand may well be significantly understated.

The size of the sport market

Total consumer expenditure on sport and physical recreation in Australia was AU$6.2 billion in 2003/4. In New Zealand in the 1999 study, it suggested that consumer expenditure on physical leisure was NZ$961 million. In Australia, annual consumer expenditure on sport and physical recreation increased by 29% between 1998/9 and 2003/4, while in New Zealand total household expenditure on physical leisure increased by 39% from 1993 to 1999. It is quite clear that the sport market is a growing market, and it is likely to have increased even further in both countries since these figures were calculated.

Table 4-1: Expenditure on selected sports and physical recreation products, by Australian households, 2003-2004.			
	AVERAGE HOUSEHOLD EXPENDITURE $/WEEK	TOTAL HOUSEHOLD EXPENDITURE $M/YEAR	NUMBER OF HOUSEHOLDS REPORTING EXPENDITURE(A) '000
Sports and recreation vehicles			
Bicycles	*0.13	*52.4	(b)61.1
Boats, their parts and accessories	0.98	395.3	(c)51.8
Total	1.11	447.7	112.9
Sports, physical recreation and camping equipment			
Camping equipment	0.33	133.1	72.6
Fishing equipment	0.46	185.5	178.3
Golf equipment	0.20	80.7	82.2
Sports or physical recreation footwear	1.14	459.8	228.0
Swimming pools	3.41	1 375.4	(b)86.7
Other sports and physical recreation equipment	2.03	818.8	441.1
Total	7.57	3 053.3	978.4
Sports and physical recreation services			
Hire of sports equipment	*0.06	*24.2	33.8
Health and fitness studio charges	1.44	580.8	332.2
Sporting club subscriptions	1.04	419.5	236.1
Spectator admission fees to sport	0.73	294.4	278.6
Sports facility hire charges	2.30	927.7	1 225.1
Sports lessons	1.05	423.5	294.3
Physical recreation charges n.e.c. (d)	0.40	161.3	444.9
Total	7.02	2 831.5	2 169.2
Total expenditure on selected sports and physical recreation products	**15.70**	**6 332.5**	**2 717.7**
Total expenditure on all products	886.63	357 617.4	7 735.8

(Continued)

*estimate has a relative standard error of 25% to 50% and should be used with caution

(a) Households reporting expenditure in the two week enumeration period unless otherwise noted.
(b) Households reporting expenditure in the twelve months prior to interview.
(c) Households reporting expenditure in the twelve months or two weeks prior to interview for different commodities within this category.
(d) This is a new expenditure category for 2003-04 and includes charges for horse riding, ice-skating, snooker and related games, swimming pool admission, parasailing and skydiving. For 1998-1999 these were all included in an expenditure category which was predominantly out of scope of sports and physical recreation.

Source: ABS data available on request, Household Expenditure Survey, 2003-04

Source: Australian Bureau of Statistics

The size of the sport goods market

The sport goods market in Australia in 2003/4 accounted for 55.3% of all sport-related consumer expenditure (see Table 4-1), with the most important item being expenditure on swimming pools, accounting for more than a third of annual household expenditure on sport goods. Expenditure on other sports and physical recreation equipment is 26% of the total expenditure on sport goods, and is likely to include sport clothing, while expenditure on footwear is the next largest amount at 15%. In New Zealand (see Table 4-2) in 2006/7, the value of the sports good market is estimated to be around 31% of the overall sports market. Major contributors to the sport goods sector were boat building and repairs (29%), sports and camping equipment – wholesale and retail (32%), and amusement and other activities (21%).

The size of the sport services market

Expenditure on sport services in Australia in 2003/4 accounted for 44.7% of total consumers' expenditure on sport. The corresponding value in New Zealand in 1999 was 37.3% of total sport-related spending, while updated figures for 2006/7 indicated that it comprised almost 69%. As mentioned earlier, the difference in proportions between Australia and New Zealand is likely due to different methodologies used in calculating the sectors. The largest sub-sector of the sport services market in Australia was sport facility hire charges, accounting for 14.6% of total consumer expenditure on sport. Health and fitness studio charges accounts for a further 9.2% of the total. This market has expanded rapidly since the early 1990s. The admission fees for the spectator sport sub-sector is comparatively small, contributing just 4.6% of total consumer expenditure on sport. In New Zealand, expenditure on grounds and facilities in 2006/7contributed over 21% of total expenditure on sport. While it is not clear exactly what is included in this sub-sector, it is likely to include the major components of the Australian sport service sector. Health and fitness centres and gyms accounted for almost 15% of the value of the sports services market, while clubs and sports professionals contributed the same percentage (21%) of total expenditure on sport as grounds and facilities operation.

Future trends in the sport market

There are often considerable time lags involved in the calculations of the sports market from country to country. The data discussed in the chapter to date, while appearing somewhat dated, is the most recent available data. It is useful at this juncture to consider what the 2011/12 statistics for the sport market might look like for both New Zealand and Australia. If recent (2008) estimates from the UK are anything to go by, there are likely to be substantial changes to the nature of the sport market in New Zealand and Australia in the not-too distant future. Recent statistics for the UK indicate that the sport services market is approximately 61% of the sport

Table 4-2: Contribution to GDP of sport and recreation industries, 2006/07.	
INDUSTRY	CONTRIBUTION TO GDP ($ MILLIONS)
Toy and Sporting Goods Wholesaling	144.8
Sport and Camping Equipment Retailing	185.0
Boatbuilding and Repair Services	297.8
Amusement and Other Recreation Activities (not elsewhere classified)	220.0
Turf Growing	2.2
Horse Farming	35.6
Toy, Sporting and Recreational Product Manufacturing	46.6
Sports and Physical Recreation Instruction	103.3
Physiotherapy Services	129.9
Nature Reserves and Conservation Parks Operation	320.7
Health and Fitness Centres and Gymnasia Operation	343.1
Sport and Physical Recreation Clubs and Sports Professionals	485.2
Sports and Physical Recreation Venues, Grounds and Facilities Operations	491.8
Sport and Physical Recreation Administrative Service	190.6
Horse and Dog Racing Administration and Track Operation	79.0
Other Horse and Dog Racing Activities	156.5
Amusement Parks and Centres Operation	105.0
TOTAL (measured in 2006/07 values)	3,337
TOTAL (measured in 2008/09 values)	3,844
Contribution to GDP (percent)	2.1%

Source: Statistics New Zealand, National Accounts Data and Census 2006 data

Source: Dalziel (2011)

market, with the sport goods market contributing the remaining 39%. This reflects a greater use of services in the UK, with a major contributor being the increased popularity of gym and fitness clubs in recent years. Indeed, the 2006/7 New Zealand figures do not appear too far away from the UK estimates, although the Australian figures are markedly different. As mentioned in the earlier sections, potential inclusion of omitted sub-sectors in up-to-date estimates is likely to also influence the size of each sector of the sport market. Increased exposure to and involvement in international competitions in recent years, combined with the hosting of major sporting events in the two countries, suggest that there is every reason to expect the size of the sport services market to increase in importance over time.

Recent changes in the sport market

If we were to go back forty years, the sport market would look radically different to the market we observe today. For one thing, the public and voluntary sectors were the major providers of sporting opportunities through voluntary sector sport clubs and public sector indoor and outdoor sport facilities. There was tremendous growth in public sector sport provision in Australia and New Zealand in the 1960s and 1970s, mainly through the establishment of national sports bodies, and massive investment in indoor sport facilities, as well as swimming pools. The Ministry of Recreation and Sport and the Council for Recreation and Sport were established in the early 1970s in New Zealand, which assisted in the planning and support of national the sport and recreational strategies. Around the same time the Federal Ministry of Tourism and Recreation was set up in Australia with the aim of assisting in the provision of sports facilities and providing support for national sporting bodies. The UK and many European countries experienced a similar expansion in public sector investment in sport during this period. The Australian Institute of Sport (AIS) was established in 1981 in Canberra, and is thought by many to be the catalyst for the increase in success of Australian athletes in recent times. The AIS offers programs in Adelaide, Brisbane, Gold Coast, Melbourne, Perth and Sydney. The Hillary Commission was established in 1987 in New Zealand, a body that was predominantly publicly funded. Sport and Recreation New Zealand (SPARC) was set up in 2002 to replace the Hillary Commission with a view to enhancing participation in sport and recreation as well as enhancing the development of national strategies.

Sport participation

Alongside the rapid expansion in sport facilities in the 1970s and 1980s there was strong growth in sport participation particularly in indoor sport and amongst women. Women's sport had experienced growth from the 1950s and 1960s in Australia and New Zealand with the profile of performances by Olympic gold medallists Dawn Fraser (swimming – Australia) and Yvette Williams (athletics – New Zealand) and the growth in netball during this period being especially influential.

Sport participation overall in Australia and New Zealand has been static in recent years (see Figure 4-2). Approximately two-thirds of Australian adults (aged 15 years and older) participated in at least one sport or physical recreation activity in the past year in 2010. In New Zealand, the corresponding figure for 2007/8 was almost 96%. Men and women's participation rates were similar for both countries, and the age group with the highest participation rate was the youngest group in

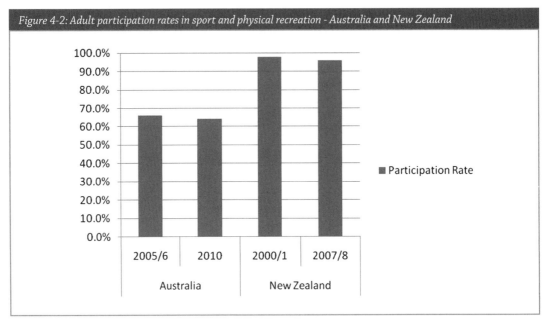

Figure 4-2: Adult participation rates in sport and physical recreation - Australia and New Zealand

Source: Australian Bureau of Statistics (2011); SPARC (2008)

each country (from 15 to 17 years in Australia (79%) and from 16-24 in New Zealand (97.2)). This is a promising sign for future growth of the sports market in these countries. Survey results in the UK, in stark contrast, show a decline in the participation of younger people.

Within this overall picture of static sport participation in recent years, there has been growth in some activities (matched by decline in others). In Australia, the most popular activity in 2010 was walking for exercise (23%), aerobics, fitness and gym activities (14%) followed by swimming and/ or diving (7%). In New Zealand, the most popular activity in 2007/8 was walking (64%), followed by gardening (43%) and swimming (35%). Equipment-based exercise was enjoyed by almost 27% of New Zealanders, suggesting that, like Australians, New Zealanders enjoy hitting the gym for fitness. In Australia, the age groups that found gym fitness activities most popular were the 18-24 and 25-34 years groups. In New Zealand the corresponding age groups in terms of popularity of gym fitness activities were also the youngest – 16-24 (34%) and 25-34 years (32%). Indeed, one of the most significant developments within this area has been the growth in the number of commercial health and fitness clubs in the past twenty years, catering to this increasing interest in a healthy lifestyle in which regular exercise plays such an important part.

Many of the sub-sectors of the overall sport market are dependent on the level of sport participation: sport clothing and footwear, sport equipment, boats, admission/ membership fees, accommodation, among others. The more people taking part in sport, then the greater the expenditure in all these categories will be. This has important implications for the sport market, and particularly for the producers of equipment. As we shall see with the Nike case study later in this chapter, demand for sport clothing, equipment and footwear will be supplied by transnational companies such as Nike with their production dominated by China and other low-wage Asian countries.

Sport participants now spend a lot more on sport clothing, equipment and footwear than they did 10 or 15 years ago. Similarly, overall entrance and membership fees have risen on average with the increasing importance of the relatively high-priced commercial health and fitness clubs. There has been some switching from relatively cheap sporting activities to relatively more expensive ones which has allowed the value of sport markets to rise in real terms. Whatever the activity, however, people taking part spend more money on clothing, shoes and equipment than previously. Over the longer term, however, the single most important variable that determines the economic health of the sport market is the level of sport participation.

Sport spectating

If a large part of the sport market is dependent on how many people take part in sport, the rest is largely dependent on how many people watch sport, either because they are interested in the sport or because they have a bet on the outcome. Many spectators are also participants, so there is a large overlap between the two parts of the market.

While there are no readily available figures of sports spectating for New Zealand, these statistics have been recorded in Australia. In 2009/10, 43 percent of Australians aged 15 and over attended a sporting event (the corresponding figure in 2005/6 was 44%). Interestingly, the only age group to experience a statistically significant change in attendance rates between 2005/6 and 2009/10 was the 18-24 years age group, falling from 57% to 51%. The top ten sports activities in terms of attendance rates are as shown in Figure 4-3.

The most popular event attended was Australian Rules football, with over 16 percent of people attending games in 2009/10. Of the six events that displayed a statistically significant change in

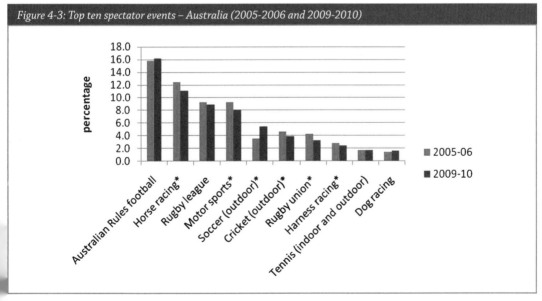

Figure 4-3: Top ten spectator events – Australia (2005-2006 and 2009-2010)

Note: * denotes statistically significant change.

Source: Australian Bureau of Statistics

attendance rates between 2005/6 and 2009/10, five of them (horse racing, motor sports, cricket, rugby union and harness racing) experienced significant falls. The only one to break the trend was outdoor soccer, with attendance rates rising from 3.5 to 5.4 percent.

Spectator interest in sport is likely to be influenced by broadcasting, particularly events that are broadcast either live or delayed by radio or television. Indeed, much of the research in this area suggests that broadcasting of events reduces the attendance at the event itself. With more and more people seemingly choosing to watch top-level sport in the comfort of their living rooms, the role of the broadcast has changed the sport market landscape considerably in recent years. There is perhaps no better illustration of this than the dramatic escalation of the cost of television rights to major sporting events around the world. This is discussed in more detail in the next section. People now pay substantial amounts of money for something they used to get at zero marginal cost. There is a lesson here for the sport market in general. Consumers of sport, whether spectator or participant, are now spending more on their sport consumption than ever before even though the numbers consuming has not risen substantially. This phenomenon alone suggests an optimistic future for the sport market. If the industry could also expand the number of its consumers, then the industry would be looking at a very healthy future.

The rise of the sporting 'mega-event' in Australasia

Since the economic success of the 1984 Olympic Games in Los Angeles, there has been an increased interest in the hosting of sporting events as a vehicle for economic development, with benefits including the creation of jobs and the generation of income. Events such as the Olympic Games had been held successfully before 1984 (Melbourne hosted the Games in 1956, the first city in the Southern Hemisphere to do so), but what made the Los Angeles experience different was that the event was profitable. A major contributing factor towards this outcome was the use of facilities that were largely already in place, and the level of public funding was relatively small. Since 1984, the benefits of sporting mega-events such as the Olympic Games, Football World Cup, Commonwealth Games, Winter Olympics, and Rugby World Cup, among others have been widely publicised, which has led to considerable interest from cities in this part of the world in the hosting of these events. Australia and New Zealand have been able to attract several of these events, most recently with the Olympic Games (Sydney 2000), Rugby World Cup (NZ/Australia 1987, Australia 2003 and New Zealand 2011), Commonwealth Games (Melbourne 2006) and the America's Cup regattas (Fremantle 1987, and Auckland 2000, 2003), among others. The profile associated with these events have significantly raised local interest and awareness in the respective sports, and alongside broadcasting, discussed in detail below, has unquestionably played a significant role in the growth in the sports market in Australasia, and will likely continue to do so.

Sport in the global marketplace

Increasingly it is becoming more and more appropriate to talk about the global sport market. A small, but increasing, part of every country's sport market is international or global. There already exist sporting competitions that are of truly global dimensions. Over two thirds of the world's population (over 3.5 billion people) watch some part of the global television coverage of the summer Olympic Games, while the cumulative global television audience for soccer's World Cup is over 40 billion. A particularly revealing insight into the changing nature of the demand for television viewing of global sport can be seen with the recent estimates of the reach of television for the Rugby World Cup. The inaugural Rugby World Cup hosted by New Zealand and Australia in 1987 was watched by an estimated 300 million viewers. The 2007 Rugby World Cup in France was viewed by an international audience of 4 billion viewers from 238 countries. Large sports-related companies such as Nike and Adidas target such major sporting events for their marketing campaigns. Not only will they have advertising slots around the world when these events are being broadcast but such campaigns will themselves involve the top players or athletes taking part in these competitions and on contract to one of these major global companies. Changes in the relationship between sport and broadcasting have been important in accelerating the globalisation of the sport market. This is demonstrated by the role of Kerry Packer's Nine Network and Rupert Murdoch's News Corporation in re-defining three of the major sporting codes in Australasia.

Packer, Murdoch and their roles in re-defining major Australian sport

Australian media magnate Kerry Packer was a prominent player in sports broadcasting in Australia as the owner of the Nine Network, a free-to-air channel. Taking over Nine in the mid 1970s, Packer embarked on a strategy to boost Nine's ratings through increased sports programming. Packer's influence of Australian sport began in the late 1970s with the creation of World Series Cricket, a rebel competition that involved many of the world's leading players at the time being signed up to play. This competition led to major changes in cricket, not the least of which was the introduction of day-night one-day matches. Other changes included the marketing of cricket and the introduction of coloured team strips, which led to the sale of merchandise. The Nine Network also held the broadcast rights of the Australian Football League (AFL) and the then New South Wales Rugby League (NSWRL) competition, later named the Australian Rugby League (ARL) competition after expansion of the league from its traditional Sydney base to Auckland, North Queensland, South Queensland and Perth in 1995.

News Limited, owned by Australian media giant Rupert Murdoch, sought to acquire the broadcast rights of rugby league to boost the popularity of pay-per-view television in Australia. This was part of a global strategy, including chasing the rights for Premier League football in the UK and for the NFL in the US. The resulting 'war' between News Limited and the Packer-backed Optus Vision resulted in two rugby league competitions between 1996 and 1997 – the News Limited-aligned Super League and the Optus-aligned Australian Rugby League. The dramatic increase in player salaries as a result of the competition for players between the two competitions was unprecedented in the sport's history. In 1998 a single competition under the National Rugby League (NRL) banner was formed as a compromise between News Limited and the Australian Rugby League. News Limited's Fox Sports pay television channel broadcast every match live, with Packer's Nine Network broadcasting delayed coverage of feature matches each weekend. In 2005, the broadcasting rights for the NRL were sold to Fox Sports and Nine for a combined A$500 million over six years.

In 1995, at the same time the Super League war broke out in rugby league, rugby union was facing a war of its own. The formation of the World Rugby Corporation saw the New Zealand and Australian Rugby Unions work alongside the South African Rugby Union with News Limited to create the SANZAR (South Africa New Zealand Australia Rugby) group, with the result being two fully professional annual competitions – the franchise-based Super rugby and the international Tri-Nations competition between the three countries. The Super competition has expanded throughout its history, from 12 teams in 1996 to 15 teams in 2011. The broadcast rights for 1996-2006 were sold to News Corporation for US$555 million. The 2006-2010 rights were sold for US$323 million (an increase of 16% per season on the previous deal), and the rights for the 2011-2015 SANZAR competitions were sold for US$437 million (an increase of 35% increase per season from the previous deal).

Sport and broadcasting

The escalation in the price of broadcasting rights for sport is the single largest factor affecting the global sports business. In addition to the figures detailed in the previous section, there are many global examples. The rights to the largest event in the sporting world, the Olympic Games, from 1996 to 2008 were sold to US broadcaster NBC for US$4 billion. The next most important global sports competition, the World Cup in soccer, saw the broadcasting rights for the 2002 and 2006 competition sold to Kirch of Germany for US$2.36 billion. The three competitions 1990, 1994, and 1998 had previously been sold to a consortium of mainly public broadcasters for a total of US$314 million. In early 1998, American broadcasters agreed to pay US$18 billion for the rights for the National Football League for eight years. The previous deal for 1995-1998 was for $1.58 billion. This previous deal involved Fox for the first time, which is owned by Rupert Murdoch's News Corporation, also owners of UK pay television company BSkyB. This deal projected Fox to be one of the big four broadcasters in the USA together with NBC, CBC, and ABC.

The top eight television programmes in the United States are sports events. Around 130 million watch the Super Bowl on television. Advertising rates are at a premium during the televising of such events, and the large sports companies such as Nike, adidas, and Reebok want to attach their advertising slots to this and other major televised sports competitions.

Coverage of the NFL by Fox in the United States and the English Premier League by BSkyB in England has been crucial to the economic success of these broadcasting companies. They have also been a major force in the globalisation of the sports market. NFL games and Premier League matches are now broadcast live across many countries. Global demand for major sporting competitions has not only raised the broadcasting rights fees but has also led to escalation in the price of sponsorship deals for both the events themselves and the athletes that take part in them. These sponsors are sometimes the major global sports companies, Nike, adidas, or Reebok, but more often they are non-sport companies (e.g., Coca-Cola, McDonalds) operating in the global marketplace and wanting to be associated with such globally significant events. The following case study profiles Nike, one of the world's largest sports clothing and footwear manufacturers.

CASE STUDY: NIKE

Nike is a classic case-study of how the sport market has been affected by globalisation. Nike dominates the world sports shoe industry, an industry that has shown phenomenal growth over the last twenty years. Nike accounts for nearly a third of the total sales of sports shoes worldwide.

Nike started out as a company called Blue Ribbon Sports, based in Oregon, USA, and distributing running shoes produced by a Japanese company, Onitsuka Sports. By the early 1970s the company had severed ties with Onitsuka and was designing, marketing, and distributing its own running shoes. In 1978 Blue Ribbon Sports changed its name to Nike. This company very quickly established itself in the lead in one of the fastest growing leisure markets in the world. Although Nike produces other sportswear, sports shoes are its main area of activity and 75% of the company's turnover comes from shoes.

(Continued)

There is some literature relating to the global production, distribution, and marketing approach of Nike (Clifford, 1992; Willigan, 1992). What is perhaps surprising is that Nike is not a manufacturing company at all. All manufacturing is done by contractors, 99% of them in Asia. Clifford (1992) described how Nike kept the cost of production down by constantly seeking out lowest cost producers in the late 1980s and early 1990s:

> The company is forever on the lookout for cheap production sites. If costs in a particular country or factory move too far out of line, productivity will have to rise to compensate, or Nike will take its business elsewhere. The firm uses about 40 factories; 20 have closed in the past five years or so and another 35 have opened.
>
> (Clifford, 1992, p. 59).

This tremendous dynamism and flexibility in the organisation of production is illustrated by Nike's response to soaring labour costs in South Korea in the late 1980s. In 1988, 68 per cent of Nike's shoes were produced in South Korea. By 1992, this percentage had fallen to 42 per cent (Clifford, 1992). Over this period Nike switched an increasing proportion of production to contractors in the cheaper labour cost countries of China, Indonesia, and Thailand. In 1988, these countries accounted for less than 10 per cent of Nike's production. By 1992, this had increased to 44 per cent.

Not only was Nike able to move production rapidly in search of lower and lower costs. It was also able to alter its global distribution network in response to world events. Clifford (1992) reports that Nike was faced by a potentially dangerous commercial threat in September/October 1992. Having moved much of the production of sports shoes to China, the US government became involved in a dispute with China over demands to open up the Chinese markets to American goods. The USA threatened to impose punitive tariffs on Chinese goods unless agreement was reached by October 10th. In response to this threat Nike planned to switch most of the output from Chinese factories to Europe. It also made an agreement with its Chinese suppliers that any loss resulting from any remaining shoes entering the US market would be split equally between Nike and the Chinese suppliers. In the end the dispute was resolved and no action was needed.

Willigan (1992) emphasised how Nike developed its global marketing strategy in the late 1980s and early 1990s. One of Nike's major characteristics in marketing was the association of the product with the athlete: Michael Jordan with Air Jordan the basketball shoe, John McEnroe, Andre Agassi, and Pete Sampras with tennis shoes and clothing. This association was an ideal way of marketing to a global market. The global media coverage of major sports events allowed Nike to establish a global marketplace for its products as this quote from Ian Hamilton, Nike's tennis marketing director, illustrates:

> When I started at Nike tennis, John McEnroe was the most visible player in the world, and he was already part of the Nike Family. He epitomised the type of player Nike wanted in its shoes - talented, dedicated, and loud. He broke racquets, drew fines, and, most of all, won matches. His success and behaviour drew attention on and off the court and put a lot of people in Nikes.
>
> (Willigan, 1992, p. 95).

Similarly a further quote from Phil Knight stresses the importance of the association of the product with the athlete:

> The trick is to get athletes who not only can win but can stir up emotion. We want someone the public is going to love or hate, not just the leading scorer...To create a lasting emotional tie with consumers, we use the athletes repeatedly throughout their careers and present them as whole people.
>
> (Willigan, 1992, p. 98)

(Continued)

Thus as John McEnroe got older and Andre Agassi replaced him as the fiery newcomer, Agassi became the promoter of Challenge Court, the exciting and colourful tennis range, while John McEnroe launched a new more subdued range, Supreme Court.

This policy of breaking down each individual sport into smaller and smaller sub-markets is another major characteristic of Nike's marketing approach. Thirty years ago there was only one type of basketball shoe on the market and very few specialist running shoes. A trainer was an all purpose sports shoe catering to a wide variety of sporting activities. Now there are different shoes and equipment for every sport. The Air Jordan basketball was a concerted effort by Nike to create a completely new market for basketball shoes. It succeeded and later Nike further segmented the market with two other basketball shoe ranges, Flight and Force.

In the mid-1980s, Nike was losing out to Reebok, which was then the dominant force in the sport-shoe market. In 1987, Reebok had a 30 per cent market share of the US sports footwear market compared to Nike's 18 per cent. Nike's aggressive global marketing, alongside its massive expenditure on athletes' endorsement contracts, projected Nike way ahead of Reebok. By 1996, Nike had a 43 per cent share of the US footwear market while Reebok's share had dropped to 16 per cent. In the 1997 financial year alone, Nike increased its global revenue by 42 per cent to $9.2 billion (see Figure 4-4). Only three years earlier in 1994, Nike's global revenues stood at only $3.8 billion.

At this point in time Nike was spending over $1 billion annually on marketing and athlete endorsement contracts compared with a spend of around $400 million by Reebok. In January 1998, Reebok announced that it would no longer attempt to compete head-on with Nike anymore largely because it could not match this massive investment in marketing its brand. Although Nike won the 'trainer wars' battle with Reebok, while it was going on, adidas expanded in 1997 to become the second largest sports company in the world with global sales of over $5 billion spread across sports shoes,

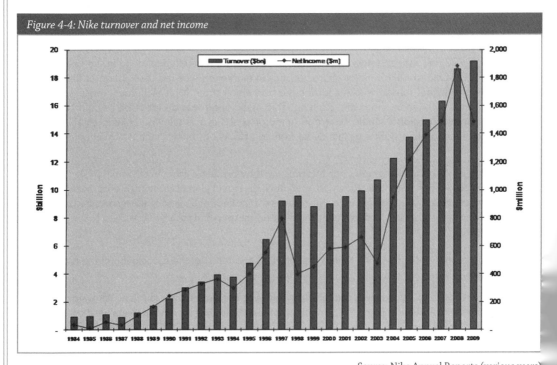

Figure 4-4: Nike turnover and net income

Source: Nike Annual Reports (various years)

(Continued

clothing, and equipment. Adidas had followed Nike in moving most of its manufacturing to Asia and aggressively marketing its brand with global advertising and athlete endorsement contracts.

However, things started to go wrong for Nike after its record breaking 1996/7 financial results. As Naomi Klein, author of the book, *No Logo*, reports:

> Nike CEO Phil Knight has long been a hero of the business schools. Prestigious academic publications such as The Harvard Business Review have lauded his pioneering marketing techniques, his understanding of branding and his early use of outsourcing. Countless MBA candidates and other students of marketing and communications have studied the Nike formula of "brands not products". So when Phil Knight was invited to be a guest speaker at the Stanford University Business School - Knight's own alma mater - in May 1997, the visit was expected to be one in a long line of Nike love-ins. Instead, Knight was greeted by a crowd of picketing students, and when he approached the microphone he was taunted with chants of, "Hey Phil, off the stage. Pay your workers a living wage". The Nike honeymoon had come to a grinding halt. No story illustrates the growing distrust of the culture of corporate branding more than the international anti-Nike movement - the most publicized and tenacious of the brand-based campaigns. Nike's sweatshop scandals have been the subject of over 1,500 news articles and opinion columns. Its Asian factories have been probed by cameras from nearly every major media organization, from CBS to Disney's sports station, ESPN.
>
> *(Klein, 2002, pp. 365-6).*

Nike's problem was also the source of its financial success as Table 4-3 illustrates. The 1990s Nike Air Carnivore retailing in the United States for $140 actually cost $4.40 in total labour cost. Chinese and Indonesian workers producing Nike's products were reported to earn $0.4 per hour. There were further allegations of use of child labour in Pakistan for sewing Nike footballs, and of sexual exploitation in factories producing Nike products.

Table 4-3: *The Nike Air Carnivore*		
THE NIKE AIR CARNIVORE		
Retail Price	$140.00	
Price at arrival in US	$38.10	
Shipping		$1.40
Transport and warehousing in SE Asia		$7.20
Ex factory	$29.50	
Raw materials		$17.70
Labour cost		$4.40
Other costs		$7.40

Source: Brookes & Madden (1995).

(Continued)

Nike's initial response that it did not own these factories satisfied nobody. As Figure 4-4 shows, the long rise in Nike's turnover and profitability was reversed and Nike could not afford to ignore the protests. As Holmes (2004) indicates: "When Nike was getting pummelled on the subject in the 1990s, it typically had only two responses: anger and panic. Executives would issue denials, lash at out critics, and then rush someone to the offending supplier to put out the fire. But since 2002, Nike has built an elaborate program to deal with the charges of labour exploitation". A new Vice-President for Corporate Responsibility was appointed and the first corporate responsibility report contained the admission that Nike knew far too little about what was happening in the factories and that it's monitoring system was mot working well enough.

By the end of the fiscal year ending May 2004, Nike was back on its growth trajectory. Its turnover shot up 15% on the year before (see Figure 4-4), jumping from $10.7 billion to $12.3 billion. Its net income doubled from $474 million to $946 million. As Figure 4-4 indicates, this growth trajectory in turnover and net income then continued right through to the start of the global recession in 2008/9, with revenues peaking at $19.2 billion in 2009 and net income at $1.9 billion, both at almost double their 2004 values.

As Holmes (2004) indicates, this turnaround in financial performance was also associated with a turnaround in business approach: "The New Nike ...No longer the brat of sports marketing, it has a higher level of discipline and performance". Nike even became official US Olympic sponsor for Beijing 2008 and "toned down its anti-Establishment attitude" (Holmes, 2004). The financial turnaround was not only brought about by greater emphasis on corporate responsibility, but also by greater concentration on global business performance.

Not everything has changed. Nike still invests up to 13% of turnover in marketing. It still has 31% of the global sports footwear market and this generates over half of its revenues. However, overseas sales are now larger and growing faster than US sales. Sales in China, for instance, increased by more than 50% in 2009 alone, the year of the global recession.

Concept Check

Outsourcing

This is part of the process of globalisation where products are designed in rich economies, such as, the United States but produced in low wage economies, mainly in Asia.

CASE STUDY: OBO, A GLOBAL COMPANY

Adapted from a case study by Jan Charbonneau, Department of Marketing, Massey University: Charbonneau, J. (2005). Designed by goalkeepers for goalkeepers: www.obo.co.nz. In P. Ramburuth, & C. Welch (Eds.), *Casebook in international business: Australian and Asia-Pacific perspectives* (pp. 165-170). Sydney: Pearson Education. Also available from Rachel D'Cruz at Presence, Auckland.

Established in 1992 in Palmerston North, New Zealand by part time university marketing lecturer, part time entrepreneur, Simon Barnett, OBO specialises in the manufacture of field hockey goalie equipment. From the outset OBO was a global company, treating New Zealand like any other market,

(Continued)

with one sole agent. OBO set out to be a global player in the niche market of protective gear. This market is growing globally with safety becoming increasingly important in all sports, particularly the head and face. The brand name OBO was chosen as it was short, with no existing meaning that could be used in a multitude of languages, and was easy to say – perfect for an international brand. Attention to detail is a hallmark of OBO. The logo was created with joined letters so that it could easily be cut out and bonded to the foam based goalkeeping equipment.

OBO's product range includes everything a goalie needs from helmets, through chest protectors, protective pants and leg guards, with lines designed for specific age groups and skill levels. Each product line combines the design features required for 'performance enhancing sports protection equipment' with a not insignificant amount of colour, style and name appeal. For example, the Robo line drew its design inspiration from the futuristic world of the movie Robocop.

OBO's products were launched at the 1994 Field Hockey World Cup in Sydney Australia and agents from the US, Japan, South Africa, Argentina quickly lined up for exclusive rights to sole distributorships in their areas, impressed by both the functionality and design. At this time a small European distribution centre was also established. When you are attempting to develop a global market with a highly specialised product, Simon Barnett says distributors are among your most important customers. For OBO, selecting distributors and ensuring they are driven by the OBO vision has been a critical consideration. A key factor has been selecting agents for whom OBO represents a significant amount of their business, ensuring the brand gets a high degree of commitment.

Originally subcontracting the manufacturing, OBO now does the majority of its own manufacturing. From a 10,000 square foot facility 14 full time staff work 24 hours a day, five days a week producing an annual turnover of between NZ$ 3 and 4 million. Put in the context of worldwide market share, OBO has captured and retains a 60% share against four main competitors in Taiwan, the UK and Czechoslovakia. Players say the name OBO is shorthand for excellence - evidenced by the fact that at the Athens Olympics 77% of Hockey Goalies wore OBO. Even more tellingly, none of the players were paid to wear OBO equipment as is the norm with gear in other sports.

Through an ever-expanding network of agents and retailers, OBO products are now sold in 48 countries, from Argentina to Barbados to Canada. Barnett attributes the success of OBO to focusing on a niche market, long term thinking, patience, investment and talented and dedicated people. OBO operates a sharp end style of business which aims to meet the latent needs of consumers, by being in control of design, manufacture, branding and distribution.

Barnett's emphasis has been on generating competitive advantage in his selected niche market through a continual focus on product development and refinement with as much input as possible from goalkeepers and a constant search for new needs to fulfill. By specialising, OBO is able to focus on doing a few things very well and controlling much of their operating environment, keeping overheads low. As the largest customer of their New Zealand foam supplier for example, they have been able to not only negotiate lower prices but also create the bright jazzy colours that have now become a hallmark of their equipment, despite initial supplier reluctance.

In 1997, OBO joined the world Internet craze, registering on every available search engine, becoming the first field hockey brand with its own website www.obo.co.nz. Unlike many companies, however, OBO went online only after careful analysis and planning, taking into consideration the purchase process undertaken by their customers and the potential for channel conflict while minimising capital outlay, consistent with maintaining low overheads. Purchasing goalkeeping equipment is high risk. The wrong equipment can seriously hamper performance, increase the chance of injury and set the customer back $200-600 NZ per item. To reduce these risks, goalkeepers seek out information- a classic risk reduction strategy. OBO has always been aware

(Continued)

of the need to provide agents and retailers with as much technical and performance information as possible but have, in the past, relied on agents passing this on to customers and then customers passing it amongst themselves.

A key priority for the OBO website has been to be as information rich as possible. The site not only provides the standard 'product brochure' type information but 3D models of key equipment. A section called 'community' is billed as the 'online meeting place for goalkeepers' where goalkeepers can find product tips, player opinions, competitions and gain email access not only to the experts at OBO but also the international battery of OBO sponsored players. Customers are, in Barnett's words, 'nurtured'. All player communication is taken very seriously, and all OBO staff are clear that the goalkeeper is the final focus of their efforts. While OBO relies mostly on its products to drive consumer preference, a small number of sponsorships are offered online, and via national agents. Sponsored players get free products, business cards and are integrated into the promotional activities of the agents. They also get an opportunity to share their expertise online.

Good relations with agents have been another major source of OBO's competitive advantage. Mindful of the potential for channel conflict and irritated agents, OBO will only sell on-line in a geographic area where an agent or retailer is not established. Good communication and honest interactions calmed initial channel concerns when OBO went on-line. Only if there was no agent in the area will OBO sell direct (with the added benefit of 24 hour turnaround and free shipping), otherwise all orders are routed through the agents. Even though most of OBO's target market is young and likely to be high users of the Internet, most sales are still made through specialist retailers. The website allows OBO access to new markets but perhaps more importantly has been a source of potential agents, especially in smaller developing markets.

Barnett sums up what the Internet does for OBO in one word – it 'connects'. It connects OBO with customers, agents and suppliers, connects agents with customers, and connects players with players. The Internet has not changed what OBO does but how it does it. Consider OBO's operations 'before and after' it went online. Notice how the Internet has facilitated two-way communication amongst different stakeholders (see Figure 4-5).

Prior to the Internet, OBO had virtually no direct contact with its worldwide player base, relying heavily on agents and retailers to pass information back to OBO. Product research was by necessity based mainly on input from local goalkeepers. Post Internet, OBO is truly connected to its customer base, increasing the credibility of their slogan 'designed by goalkeepers for goalkeepers'.

The three areas of enhancement OBO focuses on are better playing performance, better durability and ensuring goalies look great. This is being achieved by knowing more about the dynamics behind the art of goal-keeping than goalies themselves. This means that Barnett and his chief designer have observed goalies in action and carefully listened to their feedback to the point where they have become biodynamic experts in an area in which there are no other experts – and transfer what they have learned directly to their designs. A key principal for OBO has been to design their products first and consider the manufacturing ramifications second. This means that design thinking is never limited by potential manufacturing limitations.

The degree of investment and commitment to such a small niche is challenging for larger multinational competitors for whom hockey goalie protective equipment is a decimal place rounding in their overall output. While it is viable for Simon Barnett to invest a significant amount of OBO's $4 million annual turnover in R&D, it is more difficult for a large corporate to justify such an investment, given the relatively small size of the market.

By keeping close to goalies and being part of their community OBO significantly reduces its need for traditional marketing communications. Through their dedication to goalies, OBO has built a loyalty and credibility among its customers that is hard for competitors to combat in any way other than price.

(Continued)

Figure 4-5: Effect of internet on OBO's operations

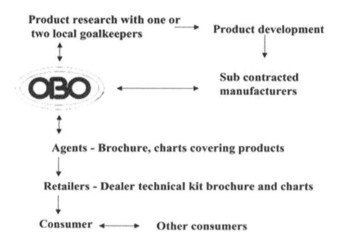

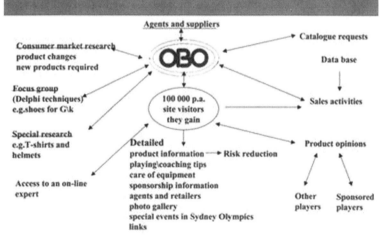

Simon Barnett 2001. Used with permission.

Summary

Up until the 1960s sport was predominantly a local activity. People played sport locally and supported their local teams, both professional and amateur. People who played professionally received modest incomes and the only way to watch professional sport was to pay to attend the matches. The voluntary sector (i.e., sports clubs) was the leading sector and the size of the sports economy was insignificant. Both New Zealand and Australia played host to major sports events after World War Two – Auckland hosted the 1950 Commonwealth Games while Melbourne became the first Southern Hemisphere city to host the Olympic Games in 1956. These events and subsequent exposure to international competition created significant momentum in the sport markets in Australasia. In the 1970s, the increasing importance of international sporting competitions created the need for national policies and strategies for elite sport. At the same time there was a desire to get people more involved in sport and recreation through emphasising the health and social benefits of sport and recreation. During this period many countries created national agencies for sport and the role of government in sport became increasingly important. Since the start of the 1980s, we have seen increasing globalisation of media coverage of major sports events, global recognition of top athletes taking part in such events, and association of these athletes with global sports brands. The main characteristics of this increasingly globalised sports market are: the escalation in the price of broadcasting rights for major sports events; global marketing of major sports products using images that are recognisable worldwide, with global sports celebrities as the most important part of these images; and the escalation in the prices of sponsorship deals for both events and athletes by both sport and non-sport sponsors. Alongside these changes on the supply-side of the sports market we have seen rapid acceleration in the growth of consumer expenditure on sport with expenditure on sectors such as health and fitness and sport related broadcasting expenditure rising from virtually nothing in the early 1990s to become significant components of the sport market today. The sports economy is no longer an insignificant part of a modern developed economy.

Review questions

- Choose any sport and analyse how the globalising forces discussed in this chapter have changed the sport over the last twenty years?
- How do you think increasing globalisation of the sports market has changed the traditional role of the voluntary sector in sport?
- What have been the main economic changes that have happened in Australian and New Zealand professional sport over the last twenty years to create a global market for the sport and what factors have caused these changes?

Advancing your understanding

Allison. L. (Ed.). (2005). *The global politics of sport*. London: Routledge.

Andreff, W. (2008). Globalization of the sports economy. *Rivista Di Diritto Ed Economia Dello Sport*, 4(3), 13-32.

Andreff, W., & Szymanski, S. (2006). *Handbook on the economics of sport*. Boston, MA: Edward Elgar.

Giulanotti, R., & Robertson, R. (Eds.). (2007). *Globalization and sport.* London: Blackwell Publishing.

Giulanotti. R., & Robertson, R. (2009). *Globalisation and football.* London: Sage.

Gratton, C., Liu, D., Ramchandani, G., & Wilson, D. (2011). *Economics of sport in the global market.* London: Routledge.

Gratton, C., & Taylor, P. (2000). *The economics of sport and recreation.* London: E. and F. N. Spon Ltd.

Szymanski, S. (2009). *Playbooks and checkbooks: An introduction to the economics of modern sports.* Princeton, NJ: Princeton University Press.

References

Australian Bureau of Statistics. (2011). *4156.0 Sports and physical recreation: A statistical overview.* Retrieved from http://www.abs.gov.au/ausstats/abs@.nsf/mf/4156.0

Brookes, B., & Madden, P. (1995). *The globe-trotting sports shoe.* London: Christian Aid.

Business and Economic Research Limited (BERL). (2000). *The growing business of sport and leisure: The impact of the physical leisure industry in New Zealand. An update to the 1998 report.* Wellington, New Zealand.

Clifford, M. (1992). Nike roars. *Far Eastern Economic Review, 155*(44): 58–59.

Dalziel, P. (2011). *Valuing sport and recreation in New Zealand.* Lincoln, New Zealand: AERU Research Unit, Lincoln University.

Holmes, S. (2004, September 20). The new Nike. *Business Week,* 78–86.

Klein, N. (2000). *No logo.* London: Flamingo.

Sport and Recreation New Zealand. (2008). *Sport, recreation and physical activity participation among New Zealand adults: Key results of the 2007/08 Active NZ survey.* Wellington, New Zealand: SPARC.

Willigan, G. (1992). High performance marketing: Nike. *Harvard Business Review, 70*(4), 90–101.

Chapter 5

Organisational Theory and Sport Management

Christopher Auld and Graham Cuskelly

OBJECTIVES

After completing this chapter, you should be able to:

- understand the relationship between organisational theory and the structure and management of sporting organisations;
- appreciate the significance of the development of organisational theory and its influence on contemporary sport management behaviour;
- articulate a range of organisational structure and design possibilities available to sport managers;
- describe how internal and external factors influence organisational structure;
- understand the concepts of culture, power and decision-making and their role in the organisational context;
- appreciate the evolving nature of organisational theory.

Key terms

In this chapter, readers will become familiar with the following concepts and terms:
- authority
- bounded rationality
- centralisation
- complexity
- culture
- decision-making
- differentiation
- environment
- formalisation
- mechanistic and organic structures
- organisational structure
- power and politics
- rationality
- satisfice

CASE STUDY: "WHO HAS THE POWER? WHO SHOULD HAVE THE POWER? WHO WILL HAVE THE POWER?"

At the AGM of a high profile provincial sporting body, the incumbent President had been nominated for re-election to a further term. However, her previous term had not been without controversy. Issues had included unsuccessful attempts to work with and bring together some previously disenfranchised stakeholder groups – groups that were unhappy due to longstanding and bitter personal conflicts that had plagued the organisation for over a decade. Furthermore, a number of members were concerned about the composition of the current board and the process of board appointments.

As a consequence of these old and long running disputes, organisational governance and overall performance (especially financial management) had suffered to the extent that the national body intervened 5 years ago and assumed control over the running of the organisation. Subsequently, as part of a plan to allow the provincial body to again operate independently, the national body appointed a President as well as a new board comprised almost entirely of 'external/independent' members not connected to existing clubs. This was an attempt by the national body to elevate governance to a broader state wide perspective and beyond the narrow interests and petty squabbles that had previously characterised the organisation. Importantly, the board was given the power to self appoint its members although these 'nominations' were to be subsequently ratified at the AGM – for many in the organisation this was a major concern as they felt that the traditional democratic and representative approach to board composition (and thus control of the organisation) had been usurped.

The President and board were well aware of these concerns and had been working gradually towards reform of the constitution that would facilitate a blended board structure – a mix of independent board members together with club representatives albeit with the independents holding the majority (4 independents and 3 club representatives). However, some members felt the pace of change was too slow, did not want any independent board members and furthermore, also resented the inclusive nature of the process adopted by the board as it forced together the warring factions of the past and opened up old wounds that they were unwilling to let go. On a more positive note, the organisation had progressed very strongly under the new leadership approach with participation growing strongly and was also in a strong financial position for the first time in many years.

However, at the AGM the President's nomination for a further term was rejected. This result was pushes through by an individual with strong informal power who had sought and gained a large number of proxy votes that eventually resulted in a significant majority. The outcome was unexpected (at least to the board, who had not seen it coming and had not been alerted either formally or informally as to what was being planned). However, the voting block that overturned the President's nomination did not have an alternative for President or indeed a plan for change –the action was largely done as a protest against the current situation without any considered thought about the consequences. Subsequently the organisation was left with a rudderless board that included a number of new members and thus who were unwilling to step forward to act as President.

This outcome set in turn a chain of events with some board members resigning and a concerted effort over the next 12 months by the informal voting group to initiate constitutional reform to alter the board composition. Their desired structure was a 6 + 3 model the majority of members being club representatives. While for many this was a positive step forward, there were also concerns that the old and lingering personal animosities that had resulted in the previously ineffective board, were again the key catalyst of these changes and the organisation now could slide back into the bad old days of bickering and conflict and thus ineffective governance.

(Continued)

DISCUSSION
- What are the potential implications for the organisation if the informal voting block succeeds? What may have prevented these events occurring?
- As the Executive Director of this organisation, how would you respond? What are the pros and cons to both you and the organisation resulting from your proposed actions?

Introduction

Despite working in what many believe is a very practical and applied area, sport managers have a great deal to learn from organisational theory. Amis and O'Brien (2001) suggested that organisational theory provides a framework to understand why organisations are structured and function in different ways. Robbins and Barnwell (2002) further argued that it may be beneficial to integrate intuitive judgements with the results from systematic research about organisations and to learn about organisational design in order to be able to structure an organisation to best achieve its goals. On a more general level, as organisations are responsible for achieving many of society's goals, it is important to understand how they function and how they might be improved. This is even more the case in the contemporary management context as the "problems and opportunities facing organisations today are complex and changing. All of society's institutions feel the pressure of a new and very challenging environment" (Schermerhorn et al., 2011, p. 87).

Sport is delivered to its clients and members by a variety of different organisations including for example, large highly centralised bureaucratic organisations (e.g., Australian Sports Commission), smaller less structured, bureaucratic organisations (e.g., NRL clubs) and a significant number of third-sector organisations with varying levels of professionalism, structure and bureaucracy (e.g., national, provincial and local sport organisations). But what do these terms (e.g., bureaucracy, centralisation) actually mean and what are the implications of varying degrees or types of structure for the people who work within, volunteer for, or receive services from sport organisations? This chapter will first present an overview of organisational theory and then explore a number of critical topics within the organisational theory literature and how they relate to the management of sport organisations.

Changes in the sport delivery system

The sport system and its operating environment have changed substantially in the past twenty-thirty years and consequently, so too have the roles and structures of sport organisations. For example, many sport organisations now have a significant number of paid staff, participate in a wide range of revenue-generating activities and must be more accountable to more demanding government agencies, sponsors, media interests and other stakeholders. Consideration of the manner in which New Zealand and Australian provincial Rugby Union was structured and managed in 1995 compared to 2011, demonstrates the significant changes undergone by many sport organisations. The development of more professional rugby placed new demands on organisational structures, processes and governance models.

An appreciation of the nature of these changes, why they occurred and what their consequences are for stakeholders is important for sport managers. Organisational theory can help develop this understanding. For example, it is widely acknowledged that the employment of paid staff heralded a new period of development for sport. Resultant changes included increased complexity, formalisation and centralisation (more about these terms later), and yet it would appear that little if any consideration has been given to the implications and consequences of such structural changes for sport organisations (e.g., in terms of goal achievement, decision-making processes, authority relationships and governance) and for the people that are affected by such changes (e.g., employees, volunteers, participants, members, sponsors and spectators). Sakires, Doherty, and Misener (2009) noted that uncertainty in organisations could intensify with the addition of paid staff. In many cases, it appears that paid staff have been simply 'tacked on' to existing structures with little thought about the best means to integrate them with traditional volunteer based governance systems and to build new structures that function more effectively.

Therefore, to achieve a more strategic rather than ad hoc approach to organisational design, it is imperative that sport managers are aware of the implications of structural changes for their organisations and its stakeholders. Smith, Evans and Westerbeek (2005) suggested an understanding of theory assists sport managers in making informed decisions about the most appropriate organisational adaptations to an increasingly turbulent and dynamic environment. Furthermore, internal structures influence employees and thus understanding this relationship can assist managers in predicting employee behaviour (Robbins, Judge, Millett, & Boyle, 2011).

Organisational theory – definition and overview

For the purposes of this chapter, organisational theory is defined as "... the discipline that studies the structure and design of organisations" (Robbins & Barnwell, 2002, p. 8). This definition, and subsequently this chapter, reflects a somewhat conservative paradigm. However, it is critical that the basic tenets of organisational theory are understood before considering the nature of more recent adaptations of this body of knowledge. As suggested by Schermerhorn et al. (2011) the legacies of the history of management must be understood in order to be effective in the new conditions and challenges of 21st century management. "Knowledge gained through past experiences can and should be used as a foundation for future success" (p. 87).

Concept Check

Organisational theory

Organisational theory is concerned with the structure and design of organisations. It depends upon how an organisation aligns its structural elements as to how effectively it will achieve its goals. Organisational theory looks not only at the organisation's characteristics, but also at the characteristics of the environment and the departments and groups that make up the organisation.

Organisational theory has undergone a number of different transformations during its relatively short history. Robbins and Barnwell (2006) argued that the field could be broken down into five broad approaches or periods of development since 1900 (see Table 5-1), some of which have been minor incremental adjustments to previous theoretical approaches, while others have adopted a radically different perspective.

Table 5-1: Summary of the development of organisational theory	
DEVELOPMENT PERIOD	MAIN POINTS
1) Classical Organisation Theory (1900-1930s)	Using scientific rigour to analyse management with the aim of raising productivity. Consequently jobs became more specialised and power was centralised at the management level. Theorists promoted the idea that there was one best way to rationally structure and manage the organisation.
2) Organisational Behaviourists (1930s-1960s)	This period was characterised by an appreciation of the behavioural implications of management behaviour. Theorists concentrated on why people work, what motivates work behaviour, and how to democratise work and make it more interesting.
3) The Unmanageable Organisation & Decision Making (1950s-1970s)	Researchers and theorists grappled with complexity of information processing and decision making in large, impersonal and bureaucratic organisations. Organisations were viewed as systems with extensive environmental interactions.
4) Contingency (1960s-1980s)	Organisations were viewed as rational but the best structure was dependent on the situation. Theorists recognised that contingency factors such as the environment, technology and strategy influenced an organisation's behaviour.
5) Paradigm Proliferation (1980s-present)	This period reflects an increasing diversity of approaches and research. Organisations are viewed as social movements thus promoting the study of culture and organisational meaning. Studies also focus on the complexity of the competitive environment, organisational networks, gender in organisations and often adopt postmodern and critical theory perspectives. Conflict, power and influence are seen as inevitable elements of organisational life.

Source: Adapted from Robbins & Barnwell (2006)

The early classical theorist viewed organisations as having machine like properties, that there was one best way to structure the organisation to optimise production and that the best approach could be determined by analysis and scientific measurement. Furthermore, this approach assumed that people and organisations act in accordance with rational economic principles with Weber's concept of bureaucracy perhaps the best known example. Although they have subsequently been criticised for their simplicity, the approaches utilised in this period left a lasting legacy which still influences both practitioners and theorists (Slack, 1993; Frisby, 1995; Papadimitriou, 2002).

Subsequently, the 'behavioural' approach began to focus more on the human element in organisations and recognised that organisations shape behaviour and influence perceptions of such things as work, interactions, communication and leadership. The focus was on accommodating human needs in work practices and although still adopting a closed systems perspective, concentrated on the social rather than the production aspects of the system. The challenge for managers was how to incorporate a more humanistic attitude in structures and processes without compromising efficiency.

The next period shifted the concern of theorists to improving the manageability and decision making processes in organisations. This approach was influenced by the advances in knowledge about organisations that became available in the post-war period and addressed design issues such as specialisation, span of control, formalisation, centralisation, differentiation and complexity. The concentration on decision making introduced ideas such as: limits to rationality; organisations consist of individuals, not positions; the formation of coalitions; and that organisations may not be maximising rational goal-seeking entities, but instead are more likely to 'satisfice'. By recognising the irrational nature of decision making, this approach highlighted the role that power and politics play in organisational life.

Concept Check

'Satisfice'

'Satisfice' is a combination of the words 'sufficient' and 'satisfactory'. A satisficing solution is one that may not necessarily be the best choice or the one that will maximise the outcome, but one that will be good enough in the circumstances – therefore to satisfice is to make do.

These ideas were further developed in the next period which focussed on an open systems perspective, contingencies and determining the most appropriate structural form. This approach was influenced by systems theorists and therefore emphasised the interconnections and interdependencies of organisations and relationships with the external environment. As a consequence of interacting with the environment, organisations were viewed as dynamic – in a constant state of change and adaptation. However, organisations did not have an infinite number of forms and structures were somewhat predictable depending on the contingency factors – although size was viewed as a critical determinant of structure. The organisational forms that survive are those that the environment 'selects' based on such criteria as economies of production and degree of specialisation.

The current phase (from the 1980s onwards) has been characterised by the emergence of a number of new frameworks many of which have been facilitated by a multidisciplinary approach to organisational research. Amis and Silk (2005) noted the inherently multidisciplinary nature of sport management research. One of the consistent themes during this period has been the recognition of the political nature of organisations. Organisational power and politics is suggested as being responsible for the areas unexplained by contingency factors. Organisations are not necessarily single rational entities that pursue shared or common goals. Rather, they are instruments for the furthering of stakeholder interests and goals and the means by which this is determined is via the allocation of scarce organisational resources. Such an approach suggests competition amongst stakeholders for resources and fluid balances of power among flexible coalitions (Shafritz & Ott, 1996).

Other themes include organisational culture and symbolic management that assume that most organisational decisions and behaviours (and therefore structures) are 'pre-determined' by the basic assumptions, beliefs and values held by organisational members. These approaches argue that cultural norms, assumptions and beliefs, rather than formal rules and procedures control people's behaviour. This is typically referred to as 'the way we do things around here'. More recent developments include organisational economics (people will act in opportunistic and selfish ways), institutional theory (organisational responses tend to be repetitive and follow past actions) and the study of gender in organisations (focussing on the marginalisation of women and the positive contribution of the feminisation of management).

Issues in sport management

A continuing debate in the sport management literature has revolved around the domination of research and practice by what is usually referred to as 'traditional' or 'classical' organisational theory (e.g., Frisby, 1995, 2005; Slack, 1993). Frisby (1995) suggested that sport management may have much to learn from the incorporation of alternative theoretical paradigms into research about the practice of sport management. She suggested, for example, that critical, feminist and post-modern organisation theory would assist in furthering knowledge and methodology in the area. Frisby (2005, p. 2) later argued that to better understand and reflect on organizational practices "and how we teach, research and theorize about sport management" research should adopt multiple paradigms including a critical social science perspective that went beyond the typical search for more efficient organisational designs. Importantly Amis and Silk (2005, p.360) argued that sport researchers should be aware that sport industry practices can "reproduce gender, race, sexual orientation and social class stereotypes and even contribute to consumer practices that are harmful to personal health and the environment". Amis and Silk (2005) also advocated the adoption of a wider array of approaches and reinforced the need for sport management research to understand the sport management context and its impact on people. This trend has continued with regular calls for, as well as examples of, the adoption of new and innovative approaches to sport management research. These have included:

- ethnography and postmodernism (e.g., Skinner & Edwards, 2005);
- cognitive optimality theory (e.g., Smith, 2009);
- integrating frameworks of power impacting on culture of diversity (e.g., Doherty, Fink, Inglis, & Pastore, 2010);
- institutional theory (e.g., Washington & Patterson, 2010);
- institutional field and isomorphism (e.g., Skille, 2010).

The views of many of the authors discussed above echoed those of Slack who advocated the incorporation of alternative images (based on the work of Morgan, 2006) into sport management research and practice. Morgan developed an 'alternative' approach to understanding organisational theory (see Table 5-2) and argued for the adoption of a different paradigm rather than those based originally on the classical structural school. He advocated a typology founded on the premise that our perceptions of organisations are "based on implicit images and metaphors that lead us to see, understand and manage organisations in distinctive yet partial ways" (Morgan, 2006, p. 4).

Table 5-2: *The Morgan Metaphors*	
METAPHOR	MAIN POINTS
Organisations as Machines	The perception of organisations are made up of interlocking parts each of which play defined role
Organisations as Organisms	Organisations belong to different species and interact with and adapt to the environment
Organisations as Brains	Focuses on the concepts on information processing, learning and intelligence
Organisations as Cultures	Organisational life is guided by values, beliefs and other patterns of shared meaning
Organisations as Political Systems	Organisational activities are shaped by interests, conflicts and power plays
Organisations as Psychic Prisons	People are trapped by their own thoughts beliefs, ideas and subconscious preoccupations
Organisation as Flux and Transformation	Focuses on the nature of organisational change which is shaped by social forces
Organisations as Instruments of Domination	Organisations use employees, host communities and the world economy to achieve their own ends

Source: Adapted from Morgan (2006)

Metaphors imply a way of thinking and a way of seeing. Morgan argued that successful managers have the capacity to read a situation from a variety of perspectives and this 'wide' reading strategy facilitates a broader range of 'action possibilities'. However, Morgan also suggested that each perspective only offers a partial insight and because no theory provides an 'all-purpose' view, managers need to be flexible and adaptive.

The structure of sport organisations

Structure is one of the enduring themes of organisational theory as it is a critical determinant not only of organisational effectiveness, but also of the ways in which humans interact within the organisation and to the sport industry external to the organisation (e.g., clients, spectators and the media). Indeed, the influence of structure on human behaviour may be a significant factor in organisational functioning. For example, Amis, Slack, and Berrett (1996) found that structural features (especially differentiation and interdependency) precipitated conflict between organisational sub-units and more recently, Parent (2010) identified structural dimensions as one of four key drivers of decision making in sport event organising committees.

Components of structure

The basic structure of any organisation can be broken down into three essential components. These are:

- formalisation – the degree to which jobs are standardised and the number of rules and procedures to control work;
- centralisation – the degree to which decision-making power is dispersed throughout the organisation; and
- complexity – the relationship between horizontal, vertical and spatial attributes of the organisation.

Spatial differentiation refers to the geographical dispersion of an organisation. For example an organisation such as the Auckland Warriors NRL club with one central location is less spatially differentiated, and in this respect more easily managed, than Netball New Zealand which has a number of regional associations.

Horizontal differentiation refers to the number of different areas of work specialisation in an organisation. In a sport organisation these may include areas such as coaching, administration, marketing, media relations, junior development, membership and fundraising. As the variety of specialisations increases so too does the level of horizontal differentiation. Subsequently, to cope with the increased complexity caused by more horizontal differentiation, organisations usually increase the number of vertical levels by adding additional layers to reduce the number of different specialist positions reporting to one person. Therefore, as organisations grow in size, they tend to increase both horizontal and vertical differentiation.

The number of different people reporting to one person is known as the 'span of control' and the way in which this is manipulated is a critical determinant of the number of vertical layers. Usually if an organisation chooses to have a 'wide' span of control (that is, with more people reporting to a single supervisor), that organisation is likely to have fewer administrative levels (and therefore less vertical differentiation) for the same number of employees (see Table 5-3). A wider span of control therefore results in what are termed 'flatter' organisations, while a narrow span of control tends to mean a taller, more hierarchical organisation design. Table 5-3 reveals that by changing the span of control from four to eight, an organisation can fit the same number of operational staff into five hierarchical levels rather than seven. Furthermore, this also reduces the number of supervisors from 1365 to 585.

Table 5-3: Relationship between span of control, horizontal and vertical differentiation (organisational members at each level)		
LEVEL	SPAN OF CONTROL = 4	SPAN OF CONTROL = 8
1	1	1
2	4 (1)*	8 (1)
3	16 (4)	64 (8)
4	64 (16)	512 (64)
5	256 (64)	4096 (512)

*number in brackets refers to the number of supervisors

Source: Adapted from Robbins et al. (2011)

Similarly, the more differentiation that exists, the greater the level of complexity and the more difficult it is to effectively manage the organisation. This is quite an intuitive relationship. The interaction of these factors with formalisation and centralisation can create a variety of different structures and these variables can be further manipulated to create new structures. This may include, for example, increasing rules and procedures (increasing formalisation), facilitating more involvement by employees, members and volunteers in decision-making (becoming more decentralised), and increasing complexity (by increasing horizontal, vertical and spatial differentiation). For example, most sport organisations tend to increase both horizontal and vertical differentiation as a 'natural' consequence of the addition of specialist staff (e.g., development officers, marketing, media and sponsorship specialists, event managers) (see Figure 5-1).

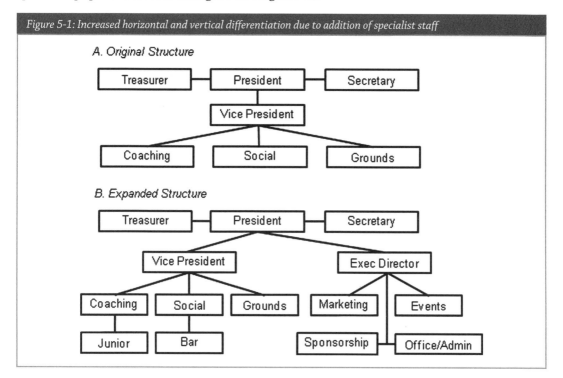

Figure 5-1: Increased horizontal and vertical differentiation due to addition of specialist staff

Concept Check

Organisational structure

Organisational structure defines the way in which the tasks of the sport organisation are broken down and allocated. The structure subsequently influences the context, nature and flow of interactions. Organisational structure is determined by formalisation, centralisation and complexity.

What determines structure?

There are a number of factors that influence structure. Although managers have a high level of control over the final design of their organisations, it is not necessarily absolute control. Organisations do not operate in a vacuum and are therefore shaped by a variety of internal and external forces. Thus managers may sometimes be forced to adopt structures to suit particular circumstances even if it is not their preferred option. The degree of influence attributed to any of these forces reflects to a large extent on the approach to organisational theory to which the manager subscribes.

The environment

Most of the literature has identified the environment as a critical determinant of structure. However, Amis and O'Brien (2001) argued there is little use in managers attempting to deal with every factor external to the organisation. Managers should focus on two aspects of the environment: those factors which are more distal and over which they have little likelihood of control (e.g., changing community values and attitudes, demographics or the economy); and those proximal factors which are of more immediate concern to the organisation (e.g., clients, members, volunteers, sponsors, competitors, suppliers, media, politicians and government officials). While not suggesting that the general environmental factors are not important, most efforts should be directed at the proximal issues over which the organisation may be more able to exert influence.

The external environment shapes structure because organisations seek to reduce uncertainty. In stable and predictable environments, organisations can take advantage of the efficiencies offered by increased centralisation and formalisation. However, in uncertain, dynamic and discontinuous environments organisations must divert more effort into interacting with the environment in order to obtain more information. Subsequently, managers usually decrease formalisation and centralisation in order to maximise flexibility and increase the capability of the organisation to process information coming in from the outside. For example, more staff may be involved in what are called 'boundary spanning' activities; that is, interacting with and interpreting information from the environment and then communicating this internally within the organisation. Development officers, marketing and media staff as well as talent scouts fulfil such roles in sport organisations.

Strategy

Another factor which can influence structure is organisational strategy. As organisations face new challenges and environmental changes, they often adapt new means or strategies of dealing with them. Schermerhorn (2002, p. 288) argued that organisational structure should match strategy if the 'desired results are to be achieved'.

> Strategy is essentially like a coach's game plan. It is designed to help a sport organisation achieve its objectives by addressing such issues as what products and/or market segments to compete in; how to best allocate resources; and whether to diversify, expand or even shut down certain aspects of the organisation.
>
> *(Amis & O'Brien, 2001, p. 78).*

For example, Schermerhorn (2002, p. 288) argued that growth strategies require a structure that "allows for internal flexibility and freedom to create new ways of doing things". Expansion of the AFL and Super Rugby competitions are examples of growth strategies. However, a stability strategy is more suited to bureaucratic/mechanistic designs. There are a range of possible strategy types available to organisations. These are summarised in Table 5-4.

Table 5-4: *Organisational strategy overview*	
STRATEGY	SUMMARY
Growth	Diversifying by moving into new markets or products; horizontal integration by buying out a competitor; vertical integration by purchasing suppliers and distributors.
Defensive	Turnaround decreasing revenues and/or rising costs through cost cutting; divesting part of the business; liquidate assets to gain capital.
Stability	Maintain current position with no plans to grow; maintain market share and same level of service.
Combination	Combination of the three strategies summarised above.

Source: Adapted from Amis & O'Brien (2001)

Power and politics

In sport there are many issues related to power and politics. They may include for example: inter-organisational relationships (e.g., power relations between clubs and league competition organisers or between government and sporting bodies – see Dickson, Arnold & Chalip, 2005); national sporting bodies versus state and provincial associations; and, conflicts between different stakeholders (e.g., sponsors versus media organisations). However, what is of most interest from the perspective of organisational theory is how internal politics influence structure.

The power and politics perspective argues that a key factor which shapes organisational design is the self-interest-seeking behaviour of stakeholders. Individuals who gain power will attempt to structure the organisation in order to help maintain their grip on the reins. Slack (1997) reported that size, environment and other contingency variables may still leave almost 40 per cent of variance in structure unexplained. This suggests that although factors such as the environment and strategy play significant roles in shaping organisational structures, they act as 'constraining' forces rather than the sole determining factors (Robbins & Barnwell, 2002). Consistent with this view, Papadimitriou (2002, p. 217) found in a study of sport clubs that their structures were inconsistent with the influence of size and age as suggested by organisational theory. It was argued that this may have been partly due to the "values and beliefs of the voluntary boards which constitute the most powerful constituency" in such clubs. Amis, Slack, and Hinings (2004, p. 158) later found that national sport organisations that were able to effect strategic change did so because volunteers were willing to share power with paid staff. However, those organisations unable to transform themselves were characterised among other things, by a structure where power was "retained centrally by volunteer board members."

Managers therefore have some degree of autonomy over structural choice. However, implicit in this view is that the resulting structure may not be designed to optimise organisational goal achievement, but rather personal or coalition interests. For example, Auld (1997a) indicated that coalitions formed between the presidents and executive directors of national and state sport organisations in Australia, may act to inhibit involvement of other board members in decision-making. However, in a later study Schulz and Auld (2006) found that lower levels of role ambiguity among board chairs and executive directors were associated with more organic organisational structures. Parent (2008) utilised stakeholder theory to examine issue management in a sport event organising committee and found that issues became less strategic as one moved down the hierarchy and further, that interests (e.g., political, symbolic) varied between different stakeholders. Some authors (e.g., Macintosh, Bedecki, & Franks, 1986; Macintosh & Whitson, 1990) suggested that the use of power by an 'external' stakeholder (in this case government) has influenced the shape of organisational structures. It has also been argued by these authors that executive directors, because they were largely dependent on government funding for their positions, became 'internal' agents for government policy and aided in this structural change process. Government, which has been instrumental in providing financial support to assist in improving the effectiveness of sporting organisations, was also interested in developing structures that were more rationalised and bureaucratised in order to protect its 'investment' and to facilitate accountability and increasing compliance requirements. The critical importance of stakeholders was noted by Hoye and Cuskelly (2007) who suggested that poor performance by sport organisations may result in the withdrawal of government funding.

The issue of power and influence is therefore one that has great significance for sport organisations. There is some evidence of shifting power bases in sport (e.g., from volunteer members to paid staff), but this process is evolving, and what is an appropriate power balance in one organisational structure may not be the same as that required in an organisation which is structured differently. The extent to which power and influence is shared may also change over time for a particular organisation.

Culture

Organisational culture is another factor that plays a major but often subtle role in establishing organisational structure. Structures and behaviours are to a certain extent determined by the underlying assumptions, beliefs and values held by organisational members and are often described as the 'way we do things around here'. As suggested by Robbins et al. (2011) an organisation, like an individual, has a personality. These authors argue that organisational culture is a system of shared meanings and values within an organisation that largely determines how employees and managers see and respond to the world, and therefore behave. They further suggest that the definition implies culture is a perception that exists in the organisation, not in the individual, and that organisational culture is a descriptive rather than an evaluative term.

Schermerhorn (2002) argued that culture can be classified as either observable or core. Observable culture is comprised of those things that are more easily identified by organisational stakeholders and may include how employees deal with clients, how people dress, the language used, and how employees interact with each other. Core culture on the other hand, is the reason we observe some of these features. It is the underlying values and beliefs (e.g., about such things as ethics, work quality and work behaviour) that determine the observable culture. Based on this level of analysis, cultures can also be described as strong or weak (or thick or thin as suggested by Slack, 1997) and subcultures may also exist in different elements within the larger organisations. It is generally agreed that strong cultures are characterised by organisations in which core values are firmly held and widely shared. Furthermore, strong cultures are very difficult to change, can impact on managerial behaviour (e.g., limiting decision options) and also influence structural variables. For example, strong cultures influence employee behaviour and can result in fewer rules and policies (i.e., lower levels of formalisation) therefore allowing more worker discretion (and thus more decentralised decision-making).

As identified by Slack (1997) and Colyer (2000) there has been limited research on the culture of sport organisations. However, Thibault, Slack, and Hinings (1991) argued that the introduction of professionals challenged the culture of amateur sport organisations. Further, Smith and Stewart (1995) found that the success of an Australian Rules Football Club could be attributed in part to its culture, which was characterised as masculine, achievement-oriented, disciplined and featured collective identity. Other authors who have examined this issue in a sport context include McConnell (1996) who undertook an exhaustive study of culture in the All Blacks, and Weese (1995, 1996) who examined the link between leadership and culture. Weese (1996) reported a significant relationship between culture strength and organisational effectiveness, but Lewis (2001) argued that there is no direct link between culture and performance. Colyer (2000) found evidence of tension between volunteers and paid staff and suggested this indicated the existence of two subcultures in state sporting organisations in Western Australia. More recently Smith (2009) utilised cognitive optimality theory to explore the mechanisms underpinning the cultural transmission of concepts and meaning in sport organisations especially related to the degree of counterintuitive content embedded in the stories - thus making them more memorable and assisting with the construction of sport organisation culture.

Size

Organisational size is a significant influence on organisational design. Slack (1997) suggested that in most cases size refers to the number of employees. Most organisations begin as more organic and flexible in nature and gradually become more mechanistic/bureaucratic as they grow. In general, increasing size is associated with increasing levels of both horizontal and vertical differentiation (see Table 5-3 and Figure 5-1). As the level of complexity is also increased as a result of these changes, most organisations institute more policies, rules and procedures to attempt to manage this complexity. Consequently, an organisation adopts more formalised and bureaucratic features. Amis and Slack (1996) argued that size is related to organisational structure, although this is mediated to some extent by different possible combinations of volunteers and professional management. However, Slack (1985) had earlier found that voluntary sport organisations gradually evolve to become more bureaucratic and that the employment of paid staff may serve to accelerate the process.

Two organisational designs

The process of assembling the different components of organisational structure outlined in the preceding sections is termed 'organisational design'. The literature (e.g., Robbins et al., 2011) generally suggests that there are two main alternatives at opposite ends of the design continuum. These alternatives are termed 'mechanistic organisations' (sometimes called bureaucratic) and 'organic organisations' (sometimes called adaptive) (see Table 5-5). This perspective reflects a contingency approach to organisation design which argues that there is no one best way to design a structure that will suit all situations. In broad terms, when the environment is uncertain and changing rapidly, an organic structure which is flexible and adaptable is advocated. This is because the organisation needs to be able to interact readily with its environment and respond appropriately. However, when the environment is perceived to be more stable and predictable, then the organisation can take advantage of the efficiencies offered by a more mechanistic structure. Although it is generally accepted that organisations become more mechanistic as they age (this is often related to increasing size), Theodoraki and Henry (1994) found no differences in organisational design types existed between older traditional collectivist sports and new individualised sports.

Table 5-5: Continuum of organisational design alternatives		
BUREAUCRATIC ORGANISATIONS MECHANISTIC DESIGNS		ADAPTIVE ORGANISATIONS ORGANIC DESIGNS
Centralised	Authority	Decentralised
Many	Rules and Procedures	Few
Narrow	Spans of Control	Wide
Specialised	Tasks	Shared
Few	Teams	Many
Formal/Impersonal	Coordination	Informal/Personal

Source: Adapted from Schermerhorn et al. (2011)

Schermerhorn et al. (2011) argued that more contemporary organisational design trends include: flatter organisations with less vertical differentiation; more teams and flexibility in supervisory arrangements; wider spans of control; more delegation and empowerment to employees to make decisions; and, using technology to retain control in more decentralised structures. These trends reflect the findings of Papadimitriou (2002) who reported that sports clubs were moving towards more loosely structured and less bureaucratic operations.

Authority and power in sport organisations

Centralisation is concerned with the distribution of formal authority in organisations. Robbins and Barnwell (2002, p. 487) defined authority as the 'formal rights inherent in a managerial position to give orders and expect to be obeyed'. This construct had its origins in the classical theory era which assumed that people were rational and would therefore obey an order purely on the basis that it had come from a person with more authority who was higher up the hierarchical ladder. The degree to which authority (e.g., in making decisions) is dispersed throughout the organisation determines the extent of centralisation (authority restricted to one location – usually at the top) or decentralisation (authority more diffused throughout the organisation). Although the impacts of centralisation on organisational success may be situational, Morrow and Chelladurai (1992) found that structure consistent with theoretical specifications was consistent with organisational success, but some stakeholders (e.g., coaches) viewed increasing centralisation as detracting from organisational effectiveness.

One of the key issues for sport managers is the degree of delegation that occurs within the organisation. Delegation requires a decision about what work will be done by the manager and what will be entrusted to others. Delegation is critical as it is related to issues of power distribution and the degree of centralisation or decentralisation that exists in an organisation. It is also important in relation to employee motivation. As discussed by Schermerhorn et al. (2011), delegation involves the assignation of responsibility to another person and then granting that person the authority to act. They should not feel they have to report back to their supervisor to ask permission to carry out tasks related to the responsibility they have been assigned. However, authority carries with it the accountability for results.

Sources of power

The concept of formal authority is closely associated with that of power which is frequently defined as the ability to influence people. Individuals in organisations derive their power from two basic sources: positional and personal. Position power is that level of legitimate authority that 'belongs' to the position regardless of the person who is occupying it at the time. Classical theorists did not take into account personal sources of power as this suggested a non-rational approach to power in organisations; that is, people who do not have a high level of formal authority may nonetheless exert considerable influence due to their personal characteristics such as expert knowledge and/or charisma. It should also be noted that some individuals may also exercise power due to holding a structural position that has little formal authority but which has control over scarce resources (e.g., finances, information, contacts, getting time with the club president or executive director). More contemporary approaches to organisational theory have embraced the importance and critical role of informal power.

The main source of formal authority in most third-sector sport organisations is vested within the elected board of directors or management committee. Within these groups there are also a few individuals who are elected to more senior positions (e.g., president, treasurer) and therefore occupy positions with a higher level of formal authority than do 'ordinary' committee members. Despite the impact of change on sport organisations over the past two to three decades, the board has tended to retain its position of formal and legal authority contained within the constitution of most sporting organisations (see Papadimitriou, 2002; Amis et al., 2004; Hoye & Cuskelly, 2007). However, there may be many examples where some individuals who do not hold a high (or any) position in the hierarchy still exert influence. These may include the paid administration or coaching staff, or even an ex-star player, or long-serving volunteer with significant levels of credibility and respect.

Sport managers should therefore be aware that power is not always located only in the 'formal structure' of the organisation (see Figure 5-1). In particular, much power may reside in what is called the informal structure that sits alongside the formal structure and, as some authors have suggested, actually makes the formal structure work. The informal structure is comprised of the personal networks and contacts that arise in any organisation and people quickly learn who they should go to if they want something done. That person may not always be the individual with the designated formal authority in that specific area. Schermerhorn et al. (2011) argued that informal structures assist with getting needed work done and are necessary for organisational success as informal employee interactions help overcome the inefficiencies of the formal operating system (e.g., problems solved in the lunch room rather than sending a memo which may have to go through two to three sets of hands before reaching that person – not forgetting that it then has to come back). However, the impacts of informal processes are not always positive. In a study of the professionalization of the English Rugby Union, O'Brien and Slack (2003) found that when key actors were not included in decision making, they engaged in coalition building and used political and coercive pressures that resulted in organisational uncertainty and conflict. Auld (1997a) found that informal alliances between presidents and CEOs in sport organisations tended to result in more centralised decision making and the 'exclusion' of board members.

Decision-making in sport organisations

Power and authority are strongly related to organisational decision-making. Those individuals that have legitimate formal authority are more likely to make decisions and as previously discussed, the main purpose of boards is to make decisions on the organisation's behalf. Research has reinforced this view. Doherty and Carron (2003) in a study of sport committee members found that while volunteers become involved to make a contribution to the work of the committee as well as to develop social relationships, task cohesion (rather than social cohesion) was a significant predictor of volunteer effort and intent to remain with the committee.

Despite appearing to be a straightforward process, organisational decision-making has attracted a great deal of research interest. Research findings suggest that decision-making is a complex process that requires significant attention by sport managers. The classical theory approach to decision-making was based on the assumption that people were rational; that is, they would rigorously search for the best (or optimal) solution to any problem. Implicit in this approach is that the decision-making process would generate a large number of possible solutions and that the very act of making a decision meant choosing from among these alternatives. Consequently, most decision-making models tend to have a series of linear steps culminating in the selection of the 'best' alternative (see Figure 5-2).

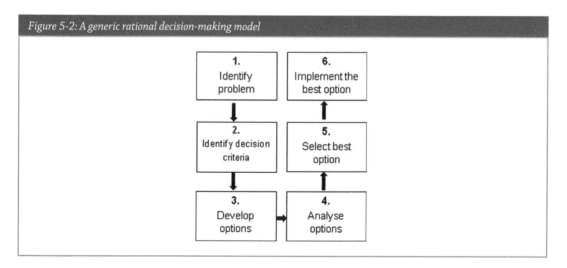

Figure 5-2: A generic rational decision-making model

However, the assumption of rationality fails to consider the human element (such as self-interest, rapidly increasing access, facilitated by technology, to large amounts of information but somewhat conversely constrained by the limited ability of people to process information) and other possible constraints such as a lack of time to generate and assess an exhaustive list of alternatives, organisational culture and/or policies that may prohibit certain solutions, lack of information and, ambiguity about the nature of the real problem. Simon (1960) argued that there were such limits to rationality and coined the phrase 'bounded rationality' to describe the actual process of decision-making rather than the prescribed or theoretical approach. He observed that although people will attempt to be rational in their decision-making process in order to optimise the outcome, they do so within certain parameters. The result was not a maximising outcome but one that he termed 'satisficing'.

Board and staff relationships in sport

As the previous sections have described, power, politics and decision-making are important issues for sporting organisations. This is especially the case in the area of board and staff relationships. A significant issue with which sport is still grappling is the impact that increasing numbers of paid staff have had on the organisations and people that employ them.

Paid staff are often employed by volunteer boards and work in a number of different administrative and decision-making roles with those boards. Depending on how the relationship between the board and paid staff evolves, there may be various levels of involvement in the actual process of decision-making by different individuals and therefore a different amount of organisational power accrues to those people. While it seems that all of the power previously held by the volunteer committee is now shared with paid staff, the full impact of increasing numbers of paid staff on sport organisations is unclear. For example, research in Canada has indicated that increasing bureaucratisation and professionalisation has not occurred uniformly in amateur sporting organisations (Kikulis, Slack, Hinings, & Zimmermann, 1989; Thibault et al., 1991), has resulted in varying levels of volunteer involvement in decision-making, and a potentially problematic relationship between paid staff and the volunteer board. Although some of the Canadian research found evidence to support the gradual takeover by professional staff, Kikulis, Slack, and Hinings (1995) reported that an overall shift in control from volunteers to professionals had not occurred. However, research by Auld (1997a, 1997b), Auld and Godbey (1998) and Inglis (1997a, 1997b) on both Canadian and Australian sporting organisations indicated that board members were perceived to have less influence in decision-making than did paid staff, and also wanted less influence in the future than the professionals. Auld argued that these findings indicated that professionalisation was impacting on board and staff relations by gradually pushing volunteers from the core to the periphery of decision-making. However, in many organisations there is a vast amount of 'corporate memory' vested in board members, and this resource should be utilised to its fullest potential. Therefore, sport managers must ensure that the growth and subsequent restructuring of their organisations facilitates rather than inhibits active involvement by board members (see chapter 7 for discussion on sport governance).

A further issue in the sport management context is the varying level of influence between paid staff and volunteers in different decision areas. This is often summarised and separated into strategic (policy making) and operational (policy implementation). The normative view argues that there should be a clear split between these functions: the board formulates policy and staff then implement those decisions. However, research has found that the clear delineation of policy development and implementation was not evident in national sport organisations (Auld, 1997a, 1997b; Auld & Godbey, 1998; Kikulis, 2000; Papadimitriou, 2002). Ferkins, Shilbury, and McDonald (2009) later found that greater involvement in strategy development by board members enhanced the ability of the board to perform its strategic function and emphasised the importance of shared leadership between the board and the CEO. Reinforcing this, other research found that task, relationship and process conflict within sport organisation boards may be negatively related to decision quality (Hamm-Kerwin & Doherty, 2011).

CASE STUDY: GOVERNANCE AND MANAGEMENT

During the lunch break at a sport management conference, a newly appointed CEO is complaining to her counterpart from another NSO. 'I don't know how much longer I can stay in this job. The Board won't let me make any decisions, even hiring and firing casual administrative support staff. They want to be involved in the recruitment and selection process and question me about day-to-day operational decisions like correspondence to potential sponsors and government departments. Even about the costs of a new computer for the Coaching Director! They have implemented a lot of rules and reporting procedures and I seem to spend all my time doing these compliance tasks for them rather than the job they hired me for.'

'And to make things worse, they call me at all hours – even 11 p.m. at home – to tell me what should be done on certain issues and then half of them want it done one way and the other half another way – I can't win! They don't seem to trust me. You've been in this game for a long time – what can I do? If I can't resolve some of these things I'll have to resign. I can see now why they've had four people in this position in the last six years!'

'I know just how you feel' replied her more experienced colleague. 'I've been putting up with this type of stuff for years. All I can say is that sometimes it gets better depending on who gets voted onto the board each year. I tried developing some strategies to help decide what areas were the boards responsibility and what were mine – things like job descriptions for board members based around specific policy portfolio areas - it worked for awhile but then new people came in and wanted to make an impact on the organisation and it all fell over again.'

DISCUSSION

Use the concepts discussed in this chapter to offer solutions to this problem. Some of the concepts you may wish to consider are:

- centralisation/decentralisation,
- structure,
- formalisation,
- board–staff relations,
- power and politics, and
- delegation.

Summary

There is little doubt that sport organisations in New Zealand and Australia are facing turbulent and challenging times. A dynamic environment has implications for sport managers as they search for the most appropriate way to deal with sometimes rapidly changing circumstances. That a structure or process worked in the past is no guarantee that it will continue to function effectively in the future. Even more disquieting is that in an era of discontinuity, history and past trends may provide little guidance in determining what may occur in the future. Some of these changes may involve commercial impacts, an increasingly crowded sports market, increasing professionalisation, changing interests and values of members, participants and spectators, more demanding external stakeholders and, in general, a world that is increasingly influenced by technology in ways that will continue to affect the manner in which sport organisations deliver their services. As suggested by a number of authors (Amis & Silk, 2005; Frisby, 1995, 2005) a common theme throughout these changes will be the need for sport managers to adopt a critical stance about their activities and become more aware the role of theory in guiding their responses to the challenges ahead.

Review questions

- Why is it important that managers understand organisational theory?
- Discuss your view of sport organisations in the context of the different approaches to organisational theory. Which one best seems to fit your view of the world? Why?
- Differentiate between mechanistic and organic organisation structures. Under what circumstances would it be best to make a sport organisation more organic?
- How would you facilitate more decentralisation in a National Sport Organisation? What are the likely benefits (and to whom)?
- What is the relationship between power and delegation? How would you go about delegating to an employee?
- How would you describe the culture of a sport organisation with which you have been involved (e.g., as a participant, member or employee)? What have been the positive and negative outcomes?

Advancing your understanding

- International Journal of Organization Theory and Behavior
  - (http://pracademics.com/ijotb.html): The International Journal of Organization Theory and Behavior brings together researchers and practitioners who are in the areas of organization theory, management, development, and behaviour. This journal covers all private, public and not-for-profit organizations' theories and behaviour
- Journal of Sport Management
  - (http://journals.humankinetics.com/jsm): JSM is the official journal of the North American Society for Sport Management. JSM publishes thought-provoking editorials, research articles, and reviews that frequently examine how management theory applies to sport.
- Sport Management Review
  - (http://www.elsevier.com/wps/find/journaldescription.cws_home/716936/description); SMR is the official journal of the Sport Management Association of Australia and New Zealand and is published as a service to sport industries worldwide. It is a multi-disciplinary journal concerned with the management, marketing, and governance of sport at all levels and in all its manifestations.

References

Amis, J., & O'Brien, D. (2001). Organisational theory and the study of sport. In B. L. Parkhouse (Ed.), *The Management of Sport: Its Foundation and Application* (3rd ed.) (pp. 72–92). New York: McGraw Hill.

Amis, J., & Silk, M. (2005). Rupture: Promoting critical and innovative approaches to the study of sport management. *Journal of Sport Management, 19,* 355–366.

Amis, J., & Slack, T. (1996). The size–structure relationship in voluntary sport organisations. *Journal of Sport Management, 10,* 76–86.

Amis, J., Slack, T., & Berrett, T. (1996). The structural antecedents of conflict in voluntary sport organisations. *Leisure Studies, 14,* 1–16.

Amis, J., Slack, T., & Hinings, C. R. (2004). Strategic change and the role of interests, power and organizational capacity. *Journal of Sport Management, 18,* 158–198.

Auld, C. J. (1997a). Centralisation and decision-making: The influence of executive directors, presidents and board members. Paper presented to the 1997 Sport Management Association of Australia and New Zealand Conference, Massey University, Albany, New Zealand.

Auld, C. J. (1997b). Professionalisation of Australian sport administration: The effects on organisational decision-making. *European Journal for Sport Management, 4,* 17–39.

Auld, C. J., & Godbey, G. (1998). Influence in Canadian national sport organisations: Perceptions of professionals and volunteers. *Journal of Sport Management, 12,* 20–38.

Colyer, S. (2000). Organizational culture in selected Western Australian sport organizations. *Journal of Sport Management, 14,* 321–341.

Dickson, G., Arnold, T., & Chalip, L. (2005). League expansion and interorganisational power. *Sport Management Review, 8,* 145–165.

Doherty, A. J., & Carron, A. V. (2003). Cohesion in volunteer sport executive committees. *Journal of Sport Management, 17,* 116–141.

Doherty, A., Fink, J., Inglis, S., & Pastore, D. (2010). Understanding a culture of diversity through frameworks of power and change. *Sport Management Review, 13,* 369–381.

Ferkins, L., Shilbury, D., & McDonald, G. (2009). Board involvement in strategy: Advancing the governance of sport organizations. *Journal of Sport Management, 23,* 245–277.

Frisby, W. (1995). Broadening perspectives on leisure service management and research: What does organisation theory offer? *Journal of Park and Recreation Administration, 13,* 58–72.

Frisby, W. (2005). The good, the bad, and the ugly: Critical sport management research. *Journal of Sport Management, 19,* 1–12.

Hamm-Kerwin, S., & Doherty, A. (2011). Intragroup conflict in nonprofit sport boards. *Journal of Sport Management, 24,* 245–271.

Hoye, R., & Cuskelly, G. (2007). *Sport governance.* Oxford: Elsevier.

Inglis, S. (1997a). Shared leadership in the governance of amateur sport: Perceptions of executive directors and board members. *Avante, 3,* 14–33.

Inglis, S. (1997b). Roles of the board in amateur sport organizations. *Journal of Sport Management, 11,* 160–176.

Kikulis, L. (2000). Continuity and change on governance and decision making in national sport organizations: Institutional explanations. *Journal of Sport Management, 14,* 293–320.

Kikulis, L., Slack, T., & Hinings, C. R. (1995). Does decision-making make a difference? Patterns of change within Canadian national sport organisations. *Journal of Sport Management, 9,* 273–299.

Kikulis, L. M., Slack, T., Hinings, B., & Zimmermann, A. (1989). A structural taxonomy of amateur sport organisations. *Journal of Sport Management, 3,* 129–150.

Lewis, D. (2001). Organisational culture – theory, fad or managerial control? In R. Wiesner & B. Millett (Eds), *Management and organisational behaviour* (pp. 121–134). Brisbane: Wiley.

Macintosh, D., Bedecki, T., & Franks, C. E. S. (1986). *Sport and politics in Canada: Federal government involvement since 1961.* Montreal: McGill-Queen's University Press.

Macintosh, D., & Whitson, D. (1990). *The game planners: Transforming Canada's sport system.* Montreal: McGill-Queen's University Press.

McConnell, R. (1996). Inside the All Blacks: Lessons for leadership and management. A presentation to the 1996 Conference of the Sport Management Association of Australia and New Zealand, Lismore, NSW.

Morgan, G. (2006). *Images of organisation* (updated ed.). Thousand Oaks: Sage Publications.

Morrow, W. W., & Chelladurai, P. (1992). The structure and processes of Synchro Canada. *Journal of Sport Management, 6,* 133–152.

O'Brien, D., & Slack, T. (2003). An analysis of change in an organizational field: The professionalization of English Rugby Union. *Journal of Sport Management, 17,* 417–448.

Papadimitriou, D. (2002). Amateur structures and their effect on performance: The case of Greek voluntary sports clubs. *Managing Leisure, 7,* 205–219.

Parent, M. (2008). Evolution and issue patterns for major sport organizing committees and their stakeholders. *Journal of Sport Management*, 22, 135–164.

Parent, M. (2010). Decision making in major sport events over time: Parameters, drivers and strategies. *Journal of Sport Management*, 24, 291–318.

Robbins, S. P., & Barnwell, N. (2002). *Organisation theory: Concepts and cases* (4th ed.). Frenchs Forest: Pearson Education.

Robbins, S. P., & Barnwell, N. (2006). *Organisation theory: Concepts and cases* (5th ed.). Frenchs Forest: Pearson Education.

Robbins, S. P., Judge, T. A., Millett, B., & Boyle, M. (2011). *Organisational behaviour* (6th ed.). Frenchs Forest: Pearson Education.

Sakires, J., Doherty, A., & Misener, K. (2009). Role ambiguity in voluntary sport organizations. *Journal of Sport Management*, 23, 615–643.

Shafritz, J. M., & Ott, J. S. (1996). *Classics of organisation theory* (4th ed.). Belmont: Wadsworth.

Schermerhorn, J. (2002). *Management* (7th ed.). New York: Wiley.

Schermerhorn, J., Davidson, P., Poole, D., Simon, A., Woods, P., & Chau, S. L. (2011). *Management foundations and applications* (1st Asia Pacific ed.). Milton: John Wiley & Sons.

Schulz, J., & Auld, C. J. (2006). Perceptions of role ambiguity by chairpersons and executive directors in Queensland sporting organisations. *Sport Management Review*, 9, 183–201.

Simon, H. (1960). *Administrative behaviour* (2nd ed.). New York: Macmillan Co.

Skille, E. A. (2010). Change and isomorphism: A case study of translation processes in a Norwegian sport club. *Sport Management Review*, 14, 79–88.

Skinner, J., & Edwards, A. (2005). Inventive pathways: Fresh visions for sport management research. *Journal of Sport Management*, 19, 404–421.

Slack, T. (1985). The bureaucratization of a voluntary sport organisation. *International Review for the Sociology of Sport*, 20, 145–166.

Slack, T. (1993). Morgan and the metaphors: Implications for sport management research. *Journal of Sport Management*, 7, 189–193.

Slack, T. (1997). *Understanding sport organisations: The application of organisation theory*. Champaign, IL: Human Kinetics.

Smith, A. (2009). An exploration of counter-intuitive conceptual structures in organizational stories. *Journal of Sport Management*, 23, 197–206.

Smith, A. C., Evans, D. M., & Westerbeek, H. M. (2005). The examination of change management using qualitative methods: A case industry approach. *The Qualitative Report*, 10, 96–121.

Smith, A. C., & Stewart, B. (1995). Sporting club cultures: An exploratory case study. *Australian Leisure*, December, pp. 31–37.

Theodoraki, E., & Henry, I. P. (1994). Organisational structures and contexts in British national governing bodies of sport. *International Review for the Sociology of Sport*, 29, 243–268.

Thibault, L., Slack, T., & Hinings, B. (1991). Professionalism, structures and systems: The impact of professional staff on voluntary organisations. *International Review for the Sociology of Sport*, 26, 83–97.

Washington, M., & Patterson, K. (2010). Hostile takeover or joint venture: Connections between institutional theory and sport management research. *Sport Management Review*, 14, 1–12.

Weese, W. J. (1995). Leadership and organisational culture: An investigation of Big Ten and Mid-American Conference campus recreation administrations. *Journal of Sport Management*, 9, 119–134.

Weese, W. J. (1996). Do leadership and organisational culture really matter? *Journal of Sport Management*, 10, 197–206.

Chapter 6

Strategic Management

Trish Bradbury

OBJECTIVES

After completing this chapter, you should be able to:

- define strategic management and strategic planning;
- understand and explain why strategic planning is a necessity for sport organisations;
- recognise how strategic planning is hierarchically related to shorter-term, narrower-focus tactical and operational planning;
- understand the nature of strategic planning as the first stage of a strategic management process;
- identify the steps in the strategic management process;
- discuss the realities of strategic management and planning;
- apply the principles learned to the case studies provided and to other sport organisations.

Key terms

In this chapter, readers will become familiar with the following concepts and terms:
- planning
- SMART
- strategy
- hierarchy of plans
- strategic planning
- tactical plans
- strategic management (process)
- operational plans
- SWOT analysis
- emergent
- strategic control
- content
- mission and/or vision statement
- process
- goals and/or objectives
- KPIs

Introduction

This chapter introduces how sport organisations can base their management on a *planned* approach. This involves using strategic management to determine the long-term direction of the organisation and making strategy the basis of all actions. The terms *strategic management* and *strategic planning* are often used interchangeably. Strategic planning is at times considered to refer only to strategy formulation, the creation of the plan (Gamble & Thompson, 2011; Nolan, Goodstein, & Goodstein, 2008), while strategic management is a broader term including strategy formulation, implementation, and evaluation (David, 2011; Pearce & Robinson, 2011; Schermerhorn et al., 2011).

A strategic plan is a detailed road map of an organisation's objectives and the resultant actions it will pursue during the time period for which it has been developed, and it is integral to the entire process of management. The main function of a strategic plan is to set direction and clarify an organisation's purpose, intended outcomes, capabilities, and operational details. It should therefore not be thought of as an extra or as something separate from the management of the sport organisation. As sport is considered a business in today's world, sport organisations must think strategically like businesses. Strategic planning offers them the opportunity to do so.

Strategic management can help a sport organisation realise and achieve its goals. Both Sport and Recreation New Zealand (SPARC) and the Australian Sports Commission (ASC) provide written documentation and mentor national sport organisations (NSOs) to help in strategic planning efforts and to realise the resulting benefits at the high performance and participatory levels of sport. In addition, NSOs in both New Zealand and Australia must develop strategic plans in order to be eligible for government funding. SPARC and the ASC believe strategic management is fundamental to the success of NSOs. Therefore, it is imperative that students, the potential future managers of New Zealand and Australian sport organisations, learn about and engage in the strategic management process.

Sport has taken strategic management on board. The language of strategic management is parallel with that of sport, with use of such terms as *game plan*, *competitive advantage*, *goals*, and *performance outcomes*. This chapter shows how sport organisations can plan for the future through careful advanced planning known as strategic planning. Examples of strategic planning, and in fact the entire strategic management process, are demonstrated in case studies of the North Harbour Softball Association's (NHSA's) journey to pitch the perfect game and Gymnastics Australia's (GA's) advanced planning.

CASE STUDY: PITCHING THE PERFECT GAME – PLANNING THE FUTURE OF SOFTBALL IN THE NORTH HARBOUR REGION

BACKGROUND

The North Harbour Softball Association (NHSA), a member of Softball New Zealand (SNZ), is a regional sporting organisation representing seven softball clubs in the North Harbour area. Its vision, as stated in the 2009-2014 Strategic Plan, is for softball "To be a leading sport in the North Harbour Region", and their mission is "To contribute to the success of softball at all levels of participation through the provision of competition that provides enjoyment for all sectors of the community" (North Harbour Softball Association, 2010, p. 2).

The NHSA's 2009-2014 strategic plan is the second plan developed by the organisation. The 2004-2008 plan was largely ignored due to lack of resources and commitment; therefore, most of the plan's

(Continued)

objectives were not achieved. The Board of Directors is tasked with managing the strategic plan and is adamant that the current plan will achieve the intended outcomes. The Board acknowledges that it has been dysfunctional and thus blames itself for the failure of the 2004-2008 plan. It has rectified this by seeking guidance from Harbour Sport, an organisation with the mandate to "lead and support the development of the sport and recreation community within North Harbour" (www.harboursport.org.nz), and by individual Board members' taking ownership of various aspects of the plan.

FORMULATION

In preparation for creation of the 2009-2014 plan, the 2004-2008 plan was reviewed. The review showed the majority of targets had not been reached and were out of date. The NHSA Board saw value in revising the plan, as parts of it were still relevant, so the Board conducted a thorough process that would provide the strategy required to attain the targets. In addition, the NHSA were required to have a plan to enter a team in the National Fastpitch Championships, and they wanted to align their plan with SNZ's. Figure 6-1 is a flow chart noting the strategic questions asked in order to aid the plan's revision.

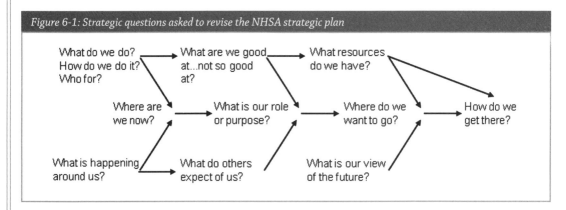

Figure 6-1: Strategic questions asked to revise the NHSA strategic plan

    The Board put together a draft plan and then gained input from Harbour Sport, who facilitated the design of a questionnaire in early 2010 from which valuable feedback was received. The feedback contributed to the revision of the 2004-2008 SWOT (strengths, weaknesses, opportunities, and threats) analysis and was used for development of the 2009-2014 strategic plan. Examples of the Association's strengths and weaknesses are below in Table 6-1.

Table 6-1: Examples of NHSA's strengths and weaknesses

STRENGTHS	WEAKNESSES
Facilities – sufficient number of diamonds (including two of international standard) and clubrooms	Limited volunteer base with many over-worked
Good representative programmes	Lack of professional staff
All games played at Rosedale Park so facilities are not duplicated at club level	Funding sources not sufficiently diverse to ensure long-term sustainability
Well-established softball clubs meeting player needs across the region	Reluctance of members to pay realistic fees for services provided
Competition available at all levels of play	Substandard image and media presence

(Continued)

Finally, a meeting was held with all stakeholders to present the plan and gain more comments. The plan was finalised in late 2010 and is a "living document" and considered a "work in progress" (North Harbour Softball Association, 2010, p. 6), meaning that revisions can, and will, be made as changes take place internally in the organisation and externally in the environment. Key outcomes of the 2009-2014 strategic plan are:

- provide access to quality softball competition,
- maintain and manage facilities for the development of the game, and
- drive an effective and structured organisation to oversee and govern softball.

CHALLENGES

The Board did not want to make the same mistake again of ignoring their strategic plan but they faced challenges early on.

The 2009-2014 plan was only finalised in late 2010. No tactical or operational plans, or key performance indicators (KPIs, defined in the Gymnastics Australia case at the end of the chapter), have been identified yet to assist in the realisation of the outcomes. Another continuing challenge is the lack of resources to implement the strategies and outcomes identified. The lack of resources - human, financial, time, and skill - is causing the Association to be rudderless and consequently be reactive rather than proactive.

Plans are always subject to challenges, and strategic planning is not the answer to all problems. It must go hand in hand with the capability and resources to act on it, as well as the willingness to follow it through. The NHSA has the willingness, but the resources, mainly human ones, have let them down in the past. This is a challenge they plan to hit out of the ballpark this strategic planning period.

A copy of the strategic plan and further information on the North Harbour Softball Association can be found at www.northharboursoftball.co.nz.

The hierarchy: Levels of planning

Planning has been defined as the process of documenting objectives and determining how best to accomplish them. More simply put, planning is deciding in advance what to do, how to do it, when to do it, and who is to do it. Planning takes place at all levels of an organisation and can be viewed from three interrelated perspectives: strategic, tactical and operational.

Sport organisations engage in diverse activities which must be encompassed in a single plan – the strategic plan. The strategic plan is the organisation's grand plan, its statement of how, over an extended time period, it will respond to its internal and external challenges. It determines what an organisation's long-term goals are, how an organisation will ensure it has competitive advantage, and the steps for allocating resources at each level to achieve the goals. A hierarchy of plans exists at different levels. At the top of the hierarchy, a strategic plan sets the game blueprint for tactical and operational planning.

Concept Check

Planning hierarchy

Planning moves from the general to the specific, the abstract to the concrete, the long-term to the immediate and from the organisation to the division to the individual.

The process of creating a strategic plan has been defined by many researchers (Bertocci, 2009), but all descriptions include the concepts of setting a mission and/or vision and goals and objectives, as well as the five steps of completing a thorough analysis of internal strengths and weaknesses and external opportunities and threats (SWOT), considering alternatives, choosing the best direction, implementing the plan, and finally monitoring and evaluating it.

Strategic plans cover the whole organisation and generally last a period of three to five years, but can be longer. Most sport organisations work on a four-year plan coinciding with major competitions such as the Olympic Games or a World Championship. Of the two cases in this chapter, the NHSA operates on a five-year plan and GA on a four-year plan.

Concept Check

Strategic plan

An organisation's long-term statement of its identity, its direction, and how it intends to respond to its environment typically states:
- what business the organisation is in;
- what vision it has for the future;
- what objectives it seeks to achieve;
- what actions it intends to take to achieve these objectives;
- what method it intends to implement to monitor the plan's progress.

Tactical plans are proposed ways to execute strategic plans. In tactical planning, the strategic plans are broken down to more specific plans, so that each division's plans are complementary to and contribute to the overall strategic plan. These plans have a shorter time frame, perhaps a year or two, than strategic plans.

Operational plans identify the explicit activities necessary to realise strategic outcomes. In operational planning, day-to-day activities of the organisation such as specific tasks and measurable targets are specified and actioned, so each person in each division has a plan and responsibility for his or her work. Staff daily diaries, and project action lists or to-do lists are examples of operational planning. Operational plans comprise an even shorter time frame than tactical plans.

The strategic, tactical, and operational plans form a planning hierarchy in the organisation. They should be linked in sequence and be congruent with each other. The top-down planning – including the vision and mission – needs to be decided at the top level before the lower-level tactical and operational plans can be slotted in. The process is two-way. Many organisations make provision for bottom-up planning, as did Gymnastics Australia, in which ideas flowed upwards as well as downwards.

The strategic management process

Planning can be divided into the concepts of *content* and *process*. The content of planning is the actual plans that emerge. The process is all the activities – gathering information, thinking, analysing, discussing, negotiating and objective setting – that people in the organisation go through in order implement the plan.

The term *strategic management* implies conducting all management on a strategic basis so that decision-making, leadership, control and the management of change are all driven by strategic planning. It is based on a view that strategic management is future-oriented, deliberate, long-term, informed and rational. Strategic management includes strategic planning; once the strategic plan is formulated then strategic management takes over. It must be noted that many authors such as David (2011), Pearce and Robinson (2011), and Schermerhorn et al. (2011) include formulation as part of the strategic management process, whereas others like Gamble and Thompson (2011) and Nolan et al. (2008) consider the whole process as strategic planning.

The strategic management process has basic characteristics and typically follows a series of consecutive steps as shown in Figure 6-2 below. Some textbooks may provide fewer/more steps but all processes are intended to arrive at the same place. Many break the process down into three stages: strategy formulation (Steps 1-4), strategy implementation (Step 5), and strategy evaluation (Step 6).

Figure 6-2: The strategic management process

> **1.** Analyse and determine the organisation's mission and vision, and associated goals and objectives.
>
> **2.** Explore the organisational (internal) and environmental (external) factors.
>
> | Organisational | S | Strengths |
> |---|---|---|
> | | W | Weaknesses |
> | Environmental | O | Opportunities |
> | | T | Threats |
>
> **3.** General possible strategic alternatives.
>
> **4.** Choose strategic direction.
>
> **5.** Plan implementation.
>
> **6.** Monitor and control the plan.

Source: David (2011); Inkson & Kolb (2002).

1. Mission and vision, and associated goals and objectives

Organisations should have central statements of mission and vision. Some authors incorporate the vision statement as part of the mission statement, while others recognise the importance of keeping them separate (Bertocci, 2009). The mission statement provides answers to the questions, *What is our core purpose?* and *What business are we in?*, while the vision answers the question, *Where are we going?* (Bertocci, 2009; Gamble & Thompson, 2011). The main difference between a mission and a vision statement is that a mission statement describes an organisation's present business and purpose, while a vision statement identifies the organisation's future business (Gamble & Thompson, 2011). Good mission and vision statements, constantly reinforced, provide clarity, guidance, and a strong reminder to members of the strategic questions *Why we are here?*, *Where we are going?*, and *How do we get there?* A careful re-reading of the NHSA's vision and mission statements will reveal whether they meet the above criteria.

These statements are normally formulated at the top of the organisation (possibly following a consultation process), but provide guidance for the entire organisation and its stakeholders. They should be communicated so they can provide direction and be relatively enduring. However, a problem with such statements is that they can be non-specific and of little direct help in defining what is special about the organisation.

Goals and objectives are also a necessary part of a strategic plan. They convert the mission and vision statements into specific aims which the organisation strives to reach. A goal is an enduring and timeless aim or target; in other words, it is a desired future state, representing intentions rather than predictions and responding to the vision statement in answering the question, *where are we going?*

Objectives involve short-term action steps to achieve the goals, providing clear direction for actions. The objectives lead to the development of strategies that form the heart of the plan. They encourage a different way of thinking about work by focusing on the *outputs* rather than the *inputs*, and on the *specific results* rather than the *general goals*. The assessment of how well the divisions and individuals are working toward those goals and implementing the strategies involves KPIs, as seen in the Gymnastics Australia case.

Through goal- and objective-setting, the hierarchical principle of planning can be used to tie together the plans of different organisational levels. The principle of hierarchy enables the goals and objectives to cascade down through the organisation.

Effective objectives have certain characteristics that sport managers should strive for. These are represented by the acronym SMART.

- *Specific:* clearly stated and relevant to goal achievement.
- *Measurable:* a target must be set to know if the goal has been achieved.
- *Achievable:* setting goals that challenge and motivate – goals that can be too easily achieved do not stretch the organisation to higher levels of performance.
- *Realistic:* within the potential – it is de-motivating to be expected to strive for objectives which cannot be attained.
- *Time-Bound:* time limits must be set in which to achieve the objectives and subsequently to evaluate the performance of the achievement.

2. Analysing organisational (internal) and environmental (external) factors

Strategy must be based on accurate, up-to-date information. In determining goals and objectives, organisations must take into account the importance of internal organisational factors such as employee morale, skill expertise, and the services offered. As well, organisations must take into account external environmental factors, such as socio-cultural/demographic changes, technological developments, economic cycles, and competitive forces. Sport organisations, for example, have to deal with factors such as:

- the fluctuating disposable income of members and potential members;
- competition from and trends in other sports (including fads and fashions);
- legislative changes in matters such as risk management and volunteer involvement; and
- the mixture of paid and unpaid (volunteer) staff.

An analysis of strengths, weaknesses, opportunities, and threats, commonly called by the acronym SWOT, is completed to capitalise on the strengths, minimise the weaknesses, take advantage of the opportunities, and defend against the threats.

Strengths and weaknesses comprise positive and negative features of the *internal* environment; that is, of the organisation itself. These are features that the organisation has control over. This internal organisational analysis asks the question, *What is going on in here?* The NHSA has strengths, for example, in the number of superior coaches and the number and quality of diamonds, but has weaknesses in its volunteer base, professional staff, and financial position. Analysing these strengths and weaknesses objectively is difficult but necessary.

Opportunities and threats are aspects of the *external* environment, which the organisation has no control over and which can either create a positive strategic situation or a potentially negative one. This analysis answers the question, *What is going on out there?* The NHSA, for example, might see an opportunity in the fact that the local school's softball coach is a club member and encourages talented youth to join the club. A threat might come from the sudden growth, or competition, of other sports in the catchment area.

3. Generating possible strategic alternatives

Once the organisation knows where it wants to go - that is, it has identified goals and objectives - it must decide *how* to get there. Alternative options are brainstormed aiming at capitalising on the organisation's strengths and opportunities, neutralising or overcoming its weaknesses, and taking advantage of opportunities while protecting itself against, or combating, threats. A number of possible ways forward may be discerned, providing strategic choices.

4. Choosing strategic direction

At this point, the organisation makes choices from among the alternatives and commits itself to a particular way forward. The intent is to choose a direction that will give the organisation an advantage over competing organisations, secure its mission and vision, lead to its goals and objectives, and sustain its advantage over a longer period of time. Once the choices have been made, the plan's detail can be set.

5. Plan implementation

In this stage the plan is finally translated into action (Nolan et al., 2008). Here resources are allocated, tactical and operational plans created, and strategies put into action. Steps 5-6 are the most demanding and time-consuming of the strategic management process (Gamble & Thompson, 2011). In order to implement the plan:

- the mission and vision, and goals and objectives, must be *shared* so members of the organisation can visualise the goal posts;
- mechanisms for detailed planning must be made to translate the plan into tactical and operational planning, so that divisions and individuals can see their *own* roles in the strategy;
- resources of finances, time, skills and competencies must be *sourced* and made *available*;
- stakeholders need to *support* the strategy, which is easier if they have been involved in its development and are *committed* to its execution;
- implementation of the plan must be *communicated* so people will understand the goals, be motivated to implement it, and work to achieve desired outcomes.

"Successful strategy formulation does not guarantee successful strategy implementation" (David, 2011, p. 213), as can be seen in the NHSA case. It was easy for the Association to plan what they wanted to achieve, but actually doing it was a challenge. Some other challenges that an organisation might face when implementing a strategic plan include:

- the organisation and its structure do not fit or match the plan;
- staff do not have the skills, competencies, and knowledge to implement the plan;
- staff and leaders lack commitment to the plan;
- responsibility and accountability for carrying out the plan are not clearly assigned (Nolan et al., 2008). Some authors refer to these challenges as failures of *substance* and failures of *process*.

6. Monitor and control the plan

Finally, all aspects of the plan must be measured and evaluated, as in any management process. Three key activities that must be completed within this step include an examination of the strategy, comparison of expected results with actual results, and taking of corrective action, if needed (David, 2011).

Strategies must be monitored and controlled, as these systems assess where the organisation is or appears to be heading in relation to the mission and vision statements and set goals and objectives. Monitoring takes place throughout the entire strategic management process. If the plan is going off track, then revisions must be made before it goes too wayward. It is quite common for plans to be revised, as internal organisational and external environments constantly change.

Planning as a philosophy of management

The North Harbour Softball Association's and Gymnastics Australia's strategic plans, and the strategic management processes by which they were created, embody a philosophy of planning. This philosophy states that an organisation seeks to be in charge of its own destiny. Such an organisation does not entrust its future to the forces of fate; rather it creates its own future by specifying that future in advance. It plans and provides clear direction through goal and objective setting, against which all actions can be measured, stating where it is going to go and how it is going to get there.

Features of the NHSA and GA cases illustrate some widely-practiced principles of strategic management (Thompson & Strickland, 2003).

- The planning process takes account of organisational and environmental circumstances through a SWOT analysis. It enables the organisation to survive and prosper in a specific environment.
- The plan provides clear direction for the organisation. It defines specific goals, objectives and targets, many of them precisely. These objectives provide a guide to decision-making and a basis for evaluating performance.
- As well as specifying goals and objectives, the plan specifies the means to reach objectives; in other words, not just what the organisation wants to achieve but what it intends to do, and how it intends to do it, in order to achieve the objectives.
- Plans are not dictated from the top but emerge following a consultative process. This enhances the commitment of stakeholders towards making the plan work.
- The strategic plan is a unifying force to be communicated, creating a common view among organisation stakeholders, especially employees, about what is to be achieved.

- The strategic plan enables a hierarchy of subsidiary plans to be created. The objectives for the whole organisation can be broken down into shorter-term tactical and even shorter operational plans providing targets for specific divisions and for specific individuals respectively.
- The strategic plan is a living document designed for constant use and guidance. Because it is, in a sense, dynamic and alive, the plan can be revised on an ongoing basis as circumstances change.

Realities of strategic management and planning

The processes of strategic management and planning may seem clearer, more rational, and more organised than they usually are in reality. In practice, the stages of strategic management may be difficult to differentiate. Planning may take place untidily and unevenly, with feedback loops between steps. In some sport organisations, the strategic plan will be written down and widely distributed; in others the process may result in nothing tangible, just a shared commitment to pursue broad objectives. In some cases strategic management will be neatly timetabled; in others the organisation will lurch through the process unevenly. Evidence suggests that organisations that take an organised, planned approach usually perform better than those that let strategy evolve.

Nolan et al. (2008) believe that if plans are not organised in every detail then the planning process will fail. They say that "Strategic planning provides a road map to the desired future state, and the planning process is worthless if this road map is not used to guide the organization on its path" (p. 130). But even if the content of the plan is not wholly achieved, the process may be worthwhile in terms of the focused thinking that everyone does about the organisation and its future. Imagining the future often generates feelings of self-confidence among organisation members. The value of the exercise comes as much from the learning done by the participants as from the final plan itself.

Some managers believe that as environmental change takes place with increasing speed and conditions become less predictable, strategic management becomes more difficult. In these circumstances, strategy is not so much planned as *emergent* or created by events. Anecdotally one manager said, "The environment changes so quickly these days that our plan gets out of date, so we are constantly revising it. It is almost better to see what is happening, and then decide what our strategy will be". In this view, managers must be able to alter direction quickly in response to rapid change, take advantage of opportunities that suddenly appear, and manage less rationally and more intuitively. However, some managers who say they do this may simply be making an excuse for poor planning!

Table 6-2: Should a sport organisation have a strategic plan?	
ARGUMENTS FOR	ARGUMENTS AGAINST
• sets direction to clarify purpose, direction, and future intentions	• the external environment changes too quickly; thus plans go out of date too quickly
• sets the stage for tactical and operational planning	• lack of knowledge and know how
• aids competitive advantage	• lack of time, money, people….
• assists in decision-making	• lack of flexibility
• minimises mistakes and surprises	• lack of commitment
• exposes opportunities and threats	• inaccurate forecasts
• provides targets to measure expected results with actual results	• fear of failure

CASE STUDY: PLANNING FOUR YEARS IN ADVANCE – GYMNASTICS AUSTRALIA

Case Authors: Lisa Gowthorp and Popi Sotiriadou, Griffith University, Gold Coast, QLD

This case reflects on the process of strategic planning and strategy implementation (i.e., strategic management) for Gymnastics Australia (GA). More specifically, it explores how the process of setting strategic priorities is organised and facilitated.

Every four years sport organisations are called upon by the Australian Sports Commission (ASC), the statutory authority responsible for providing leadership, resources and service to sports in Australia, to do two things: (a) to report on their previous success in reaching their key performance indicators (KPIs), and (b) to set their strategic priorities for the next four years. A KPI is a measureable goal that allows performance to be measured against the world's best within each sport. The KPI is set against a major international sporting event, such as a World Championships or the Olympic Games. For example, GA identified the 2011 World Artistic Gymnastics Championships as a key event in which to measure performance of potential Olympic competitors. Australia hoped to achieve the following KPIs in these Championships:

- Team to finish Top 8
- All-around competition – 1 athlete in Top 12
- Apparatus competitions – 1 athlete in the Final
- Australia to win 1 medal

Gymnastics Australia is the national governing body of gymnastics, and its purpose is to represent the interests of gymnastics in Australia. Its mission is "To promote, develop and increase participation in gymnastics from grassroots to elite through the provision of best quality programmes, products and services". Gymnastics Australia is comprised of various gymsports which include three Olympic disciplines (Artistic, Rhythmic and Trampoline) and various non-Olympic disciplines (Acrobatics, Cheerleading, Sport Aerobics, and Gymnastics for All).

Between January and March 2007, head coaches and programme managers were invited by GA to participate in a workshop to discuss and prepare their 2009–2012 strategic plan. The result of that workshop was the identification of goals, strategic priorities, key performance areas (KPAs), key focus areas (KFAs) and KPIs for each gymsport. This planning process ensures that while each gymsport is working towards its own unique outcomes and targets, all are also contributing to the overall achievement of GA's vision, mission and goals. The goals represent an agreed picture of success for gymnastics in Australia by 2012.

Each goal is broken down into goal-related objectives. For instance, in order for GA to achieve the goal of raising its profile, it needs to:

- deliver Olympic medals and sports stars to provide positive, public role models;
- be widely accessed through the media which reinforces its contemporary, national profile;
- be exposed to a large, active, virtual community;
- improve the spectator appeal of gymnastics events.

Strategic priorities for GA are clear sets of priorities within the overall goals that are essential for the sport, given the finite resource base. Each strategic priority is evaluated against four KPAs: Governance, Management, Sport Development, and High Performance

Each KPA, in turn, is comprised of various KFAs. For example, Sport Development is comprised of several focus areas including: membership services, club services, participation, gymsports, volunteers, coaching and officiating, education and training, disability, pathways and programmes, and events and competitions.

Once the KPAs and their KFAs were identified, coaches and managers set their strategic priorities, identifying outcomes, strategic actions, tasks, and KPIs. Each gymsport applied those KPAs and KFAs in shaping its own strategic plan within the framework of the seven strategic priorities. For example, Women's Artistic Gymnastics, an Olympic sport, shaped their strategic plan based on the same KPAs

(Continued)

and KFAs as every other gymsport; however, the High Performance KFA would have a distinct Olympic strategic focus and measurable KPIs, such as "to win one medal at the 2012 Olympic Games".

The case of GA illustrates that their strategic plan is prepared through a well-coordinated effort that included an extensive review, evaluation and consultation process. This process began well before the start of the new Olympic cycle (i.e., 2007 for the 2009-2012 plan). The draft document was then presented to GA's Board of Directors. Before the end of 2008, GA was ready to give the ASC a full report on previous results and submit their new 2009-2012 strategic plan.

This strategic management process represents a bottom-up approach, as GA called for the contribution and consultation of staff in preparing the strategic plan. This approach is effective, because employing the staff to develop and enact the strategic plan means they are empowered to follow through in its implementation.

Any plan is only as good as its implementation. The strategic priorities, when successfully implemented, can contribute to the future goals of the sport. Sport organisations, typically run by volunteers unfamiliar with planning or strategy processes, quite often do not understand a plan and cannot operationalise it. Such plans are set by administrators or Board members who are unfamiliar with the day-to- day operations of the sport. It seems pointless to invest effort and resources into a plan that sits in a drawer because its goals are unrealistic and the day-to-day tasks unattainable. Making sure staff who work in the operational aspects of the sport are included in the planning process can help ensure the strategic plan is achievable and realistic.

In their 2009 annual report, GA noted that 2009 would be remembered with great pride as the year Australia won three medals at the World Artistic Championships. With such impressive milestones achieved within the first year of their strategic plan, GA was well on its way to realising it.

A copy of the strategic plan and further information on Gymnastics Australia can be found at *www.gymnastics.org.au.*

Summary

Strategy is the overall pattern of an organisation's response to its internal and external environment. Strategic management is used by organisations to determine their long-term futures and uses strategic plans as a basis for all management action. It is viewed as a best practice effort to create a successful and sustainable organisation in an ever-changing environment.

The strategic management process involves a number of steps. Mission or vision statements define the basic purpose of the organisation. Goals and objectives are set to guide the organisation to goal achievement. Next, relevant environmental and organisational factors are identified and analysed often by a SWOT analysis. Strategic alternatives are determined and chosen from; and finally, the strategy is implemented and monitored throughout the process, and evaluated at the end of its planning cycle.

Planning is hierarchical. Strategic planning (top-level, long-term) sets the stage for tactical planning (middle-level, medium-term) and operational planning (lower-level, short-term). In practice, planning is not purely rational but involves informal elements and often goes less smoothly than this chapter and the framework in Figure 6-2 suggest.

Strategic management and planning require good implementation, and in particular, good leadership (see Chapter 8). However, even when plans aren't achieved, the planning process may bring other benefits. Management guru Peter Drucker summarises strategic management well by saying it is not a box of tricks or a bundle of techniques. It is analytical thinking and commitment of resources to action" (as cited in Bertocci, 2009, p.11).

Remember, there are three types of organisations: those who make things happen, those that watch things happen, and those who wonder what happened. Strategic management makes things happen, minimising the watching and wondering, if the implementation goes right.

Review questions

- Is strategic management essential in the ever-changing sport world? Why? Why not?
- Briefly describe the six steps required to develop a strategic plan.
- What should the North Harbour Softball Association and Gymnastics Australia consider in their next strategic management cycles?
- Sport organisations frequently spend a lot of time and energy producing detailed plans, but then file them away and forget about them. Why do you think this is?
- Write a mission and vision statement for a sport organisation you are familiar with.
- How would you use the principles of strategic management to develop a plan for your life over the next three to five years?

Advancing your understanding

Mintzberg, H., Ahlstrand, B., & Lampel, J. (2005). *Strategy bites back: It is a lot more, and less, than you ever imagined....* Harlow, UK: Pearson Education Limited.

Slack, T., & Parent, M. (2006). *Understanding sport organizations: The application of organization theory.* Champaign, Ill.: Human Kinetics.

References

Bertocci, D. I. (2009). *Strategic planning and management: A roadmap to success.* Lanham, Maryland: University Press of America, Inc.

David, F. (2011). *Strategic management: Concepts and cases* (13th ed.). Upper Saddle River, NJ: Prentice Hall.

Gamble, J. E., & Thompson, A. A. (2011). *Essentials of strategic management: The quest for competitive advantage* (2nd ed.). New York: McGraw-Hill Irwin.

Harbour Sport. (2011). *What we do.* Retrieved from http://www.harboursport.org.nz

Inkson, K., & Kolb, D. (2002). *Management: Perspectives for New Zealand.* Auckland, New Zealand: Pearson Education.

Nolan, T. M., Goodstein, L. D., & Goodstein, J. (2008). *Applied strategic planning: An introduction* (2nd ed.). San Francisco, CA: Pfeiffer.

North Harbour Softball Association. (2010). *Downloads & forms: NHSA 2009-20f14 Strategic Plan Ver 1.5.* Retrieved from http://www.northharboursoftball.co.nz

Pearce, J. A., & Robinson, R. B. (2011). *Strategic management: Formulation, implementation, and control.* New York: McGraw-Hill/Irwin.

Schermerhorn, J. R., Davidson, P., Poole, D., Simon, A., Woods, P., & Chau, S. L. (2011). *Management* (4th Asia-Pacific Edition). Milton, Queensland: John Wiley and Sons Australia.

Thompson, A. A., & Strickland, A. J. (2003). *Strategic management: Concepts and cases* (13th ed.). Boston, Mass.: McGraw-Hill/Irwin.

Chapter 7

Sport Governance

Lesley Ferkins and Terry Kilmister

OBJECTIVES

After completing this chapter, you should be able to:

- define sport governance and the role of the board in sport organisations;
- describe selected theories and apply them to sport governance challenges;
- explain the board's responsibility to its 'owners' and stakeholders;
- analyse the board-chief executive relationship and discuss the notion of shared leadership;
- discuss the board's strategic role and involvement in organisation strategy;
- discuss the board's monitoring and evaluation role.

Key terms

In this chapter, readers will become familiar with the following concepts and terms:

- sport governance
- stakeholders
- monitoring
- board roles
- shared leadership
- evaluation
- sport governance challenges
- strategic direction
- performance assessment
- owners
- strategic thinking
- independent board members
- foresight
- oversight
- insight
- directorship
- managerial hegemony theory
- stewardship theory
- institutional theory
- Chief Executive performance evaluation
- Board performance assessment

Introduction

This chapter addresses the concept of sport governance which includes both the work of the board within a sport organisation and the role governing bodies can play across a sport system. We explore the concept of sport governance, discuss various theories used to understand governance, and apply them to sport governance challenges and issues. The board's responsibility to its 'owners' and stakeholders is explained and the critical relationship between the board and CEO is addressed. Finally, two key elements of governance, that is, the board's strategic or forward looking role, and the board's monitoring and evaluation role are also considered. Two case studies are offered which provide a representation of the work of the board in sport organisations and highlight the concepts discussed.

CASE STUDY: YEARS OF WISDOM HELP TRIATHLON NEW ZEALAND

Over the past 30 years Patrick (not his real name) has forged a very successful career out of helping boards of sport organisations govern. His work across not only sport but other not-for-profit organisations, government agencies and companies in New Zealand and Australia means he can also draw on and share insights from those contexts. Triathlon New Zealand was, therefore, fortunate to have the guidance of Patrick to assist with changes to its governing model. These changes were necessary as part of the organisation's ongoing transition from a small, amateur sport to a multi-million dollar organisation with governing responsibility for a rapidly growing sport, following Olympic Games success and booming participation at all levels.

Before we detail the changes in Triathlon New Zealand's governance model, we offer some of Patrick's accumulated wisdom which highlights how, in Patrick's experience, the *insight* role of the board (explained within this chapter) has been underplayed.

REFLECTIONS OF A SPORT GOVERNANCE SPECIALIST: AN UNDERPLAY OF THE INSIGHT ROLE

Of the three aspects of a board's overarching role (foresight, oversight, insight – see body of chapter), it's the insight aspect that is the most difficult to discuss and is the most neglected by sport boards.

In my mind, it is the real value-adding stuff that directors can offer; it's about thinking, reflecting and understanding. I consider that the board is a pool of wisdom available to the sport organisation and this wisdom really only gets released when directors engage in thoughtful discourse and philosophic reflection. Without this, sport boards can become rather too mechanical. My experience is that few boards offer intellectual challenge to their chief executive or, indeed, to their own thinking. It's just too hard and many just want to tick boxes and go home.

The best boards exercise the brains of their members and management and are prepared to go beyond the easy to address, superficial layers. Not-for-profit sport organisations have the opportunity to consider societal-level issues and to address such questions as: What does sport offer to community cohesion? What contribution does sport make to moral development? Why is winning so important, if indeed it is, and how does sport address the issues faced by losers, as indeed there must be if there are winners? These issues are at the heart of strategic thinking for sport organisations. An example of this is rugby league in South Auckland. After the church, the local league club appears to be the next most important community building organisation in the area.

These questions do not need to be constantly addressed, but it is my experience that they are not addressed at all. On a more practical note, sport boards should have the opportunity to reflect on the effectiveness of strategies, and try to understand why some work while others don't. They should dig into

(Continued)

the assumptions that underpin the chief executive's thinking and challenge their veracity, as appropriate. After 30-odd years of working with sport boards in New Zealand and Australia, I'm of the opinion that far too little thinking takes place in boardrooms.

Notice how this wisdom is used to guide a change to board composition for Triathlon New Zealand. We begin with a rationale for seeking 'outside' appointments to the Triathlon New Zealand board. Like many sport organisations in New Zealand and Australia, boards of national sports have traditionally been comprised of elected members from the regions or states. It is only recently that constitutional changes have been made to allow for the appointment of board members from 'outside' the sport's structure. Triathlon New Zealand was seeking to appoint two independent board members to complement its four elected board members. The directorships are unpaid but the return for their involvement is the opportunity to 'make a difference' and to contribute to a hugely successful and exciting sport with a growing world-wide reputation for producing top-class athletes. The board meets ten times per year.

WHAT WERE THE REASONS FOR SEEKING OUTSIDE APPOINTMENTS TO THE TRIATHLON NEW ZEALAND BOARD?

- The organisation has shifted from a small amateur organisation with a turnover of just $200,000 per annum, to a professional entity with a multi-million dollar turnover.
- As a consequence, it needed directors who could assist in the professionalisation process of the sport's governing body in New Zealand.
- Some of the existing directors were professional people but were so passionate about the sport that board meetings easily dropped into discussing the next or last event. The organisation needed help to 'lift the board's view'.
- The board was aware of the need for it to govern at a strategic level rather than working with the chief executive in running the organisation and the sport.

WHAT PROCESS WAS UNDERTAKEN?

- A Board Appointment Panel was formed which included an experienced board member, a SPARC representative and Patrick, as a governance specialist. The chief executive assisted in the process.
- Advertisements were placed in internal networks and newsletters, national newspapers and on the Institute of Director's website.
- The advertisement called for two directors with the ability to think strategically, that is, able to see the 'big picture' and to drive the organisation towards the achievement of a challenging vision.
- Applications were screened against criteria that included start-up/commercial experience, financial and general business skills, marketing, communication fluency, governance experience, strategic thinking, enthusiasm, special issue experience (e.g., gender, geography), and, finally, a personal subjective feel for the applicant.
- 20 applications were received. In Patrick's view, all were of a very high quality.
- The field was narrowed to seven for a telephone interview, whereupon four were selected for a final face-to-face interview.
- Patrick considered there was an extraordinarily high quality of applicants.

WHAT WAS THE IMPACT OF THE INDEPENDENT BOARD POSITIONS ON BOARD FUNCTION?

Oversight

In continuing to work with the Triathlon New Zealand board and chief executive, Patrick considered that the two independent board members brought highly-developed financial skills and attention to risk. They

(Continued)

asked questions that other board members would not have known to ask. As a consequence, they also formed a two-person Finance and Risk Committee.

Foresight

Patrick also sought ongoing feedback from the board and chief executive who noted that the contribution to strategic thinking and the foresight of the independent board members was significant. They kept board discussion at a strategic level (rather than operational details), and made a very strong contribution to the annual planning day. They were also very supportive of the 'passion' element of triathlon but tested the board's thinking at all times.

Insight

Patrick also observed that as a result of their 'weekend warrior' experience (i.e., their own participation in the sport), both members were able to shift into 'triathlon thinking' mode. While they found it challenging at times because of their business experience, both took time to come to terms with the not-for-profit, volunteer ethos, which contrasts sharply with a well-resourced business ethos in which a drive for profit-making can dominate. Both were good philosophical thinkers and helped the board to explore deeper issues free from the distraction of the next event. Given Patrick's reflections, this ability was perhaps the most significant contribution of the independent appointments to the Triathlon New Zealand board.

The concept of sport governance

What do we mean by the term 'sport governance' and how might it differ from other forms of governance?

Governance is a contested term, in other words, it means different things to different people (Bradshaw, 2009). As a consequence, you will find a range of definitions in the literature pertaining to governance. Part of the confusion is to do with the range of contexts within which the notion of governance is applied. Those who study governance often divide the various contexts into public (government departments and agencies drawing primarily on tax take), not-for-profit (member-based organisations where profits are invested back into the organisation), and commercial (where profits are paid to shareholders) (Ferkins et al., 2005). Sport, of course, falls across all three settings. So, while there is no universally agreed definition of governance, a search of the literature does reveal common elements. These elements generally focus on the forward-looking role of the board, sometimes called 'performance' but let's call it *'foresight'*; and the monitoring or accountability role of the board, sometimes called 'conformance'. Let's call it *'oversight'*.

Relative to other industries, sport is a young sector and is still in transition from amateur and voluntarily run organisations to business-like professional organisations. The governance of sport organisations, which includes the work of the board as we currently know it, is therefore a relatively new phenomenon and has come to be known as 'sport governance'. Ferkins and Shilbury (2010, p. 235) offered the following definition. In essence, sport governance "is the responsibility for the functioning and overall direction of the organization and is a necessary and institutionalized component of all sport codes from club level to national bodies government agencies, sport service organizations and professional teams around the world"

This definition captures the idea that sport governance incorporates both the work of the board within an organisation and the governing role played by entities across a sporting code. For example, the International Tennis Federation (ITF) plays a governing role globally that reaches across nation states, and Tennis Australia plays a national governing role for the sport code within Australia.

In their definition, Hoye and Cuskelly (2007) nicely capture and expand on the two elements noted above, foresight and oversight, in describing sport governance as, "establishing a direction or overall strategy to guide the organization and ensuring that organizational members have some say in how that strategy is developed and articulated" (p. 10). So the idea of a foresight role for the sport organisation is expanded into the responsibility for establishing the strategic priorities on behalf of others. Hoye and Cuskelly (2007) also described sport governance as "controlling the activities of the organization, its members and staff so that individuals are acting in the best interests of the organization and working towards an agreed strategic direction" (p. 10). Here, the idea of oversight is described as the responsibility for controlling, that is, monitoring and evaluating the CEO and organisational activities. Hoye and Cuskelly (2007) also noted that regulating behaviour is a third element of governance, which entails "setting guidelines or policies for individual members or member organizations to follow" (p. 10). This final aspect of their definition captures the governing role some sport organisations play across a sport system, rather than just within organisational boundaries. The case study at the end of this chapter highlights some of the tensions and challenges faced by those who govern beyond organisational boundaries.

Concept Check
Sport governance

Sport governance "is the responsibility for the functioning and overall direction of the organization and is a necessary and institutionalized component of all sport codes from club level to national bodies, government agencies, sport service organizations and professional teams around the world" (Ferkins & Shilbury, 2010, p. 235).

Why the board exists: General principles of governance

Despite the characteristics of sport organisations (which fall across public, not-for-profit and commercial settings and have to deal with governance beyond organisational boundaries), there are many aspects of sport governance that are universal to the notion of governance per se. At the heart of governance is the work of the board. Indeed, a board's overarching role is that of governance. To fulfil this role it must successfully tackle and carry out many tasks and functions. Above the role and the functions, it is generally agreed that there are four high-level reasons for the existence of the board (Garratt, 2005; Kilmister, 2006):

To protect the legal entity

The legal entity under which the organisation operates exists in its own right separate from the members. The board's first duty is to ensure that the legal entity meets all requirements in law so that it might continue to exist for those people whose interests it serves. For example, the legal entity of Squash Australia is a separate legal entity from its state associations (e.g., Squash Victoria). This notion of protection aligns with the concept of *oversight* noted above.

To secure a prosperous and successful future for the sport organisation on behalf of its owners/members

The board adopts a long-term view with a concern for the 'big picture'. Members want their organisation to exist over time and entrust to the board the responsibility for ensuring this. The notion of a prosperous future aligns with the concept of *foresight* noted above. Many not-for-profit sport organisations in New Zealand and Australia have been in existence for well over 100 years. While the governing role and concept has evolved over that time, it has always been the responsibility for those who have governed to ensure a viable future for their sport organisation whether at the club, regional/state or national level.

To provide a vehicle for owner/member input into the affairs of their sport organisation

The board is not bound to simply reflect owner opinions and views in its thinking and planning; its job is to think beyond both owner/member and staff input to protect the best interests of the entity, present and future. Nevertheless, the board does provide a vehicle for owners/members to participate in the processes which go beyond the day-to-day, month-to-month management carried out by staff. Here, again, we see the idea of *foresight* extended to establishing the strategic priorities on behalf of others. For example, the board of Squash New Zealand works with its eleven districts (regional associations) for input into the strategic direction of the sport. In so doing it is not beholden to one or other of the districts, rather it is charged with considering the best interests of the sport, nationally. This is not an easy thing to achieve. In order to balance the need of the whole with individual (district) needs (which may be conflicting), let's introduce the notion of *insight*. The governing role is also one of *insight*, that is, the ability to 'read' and understand a complex situation as part of the decision-making process. The *insight* role is highlighted in the first case study (Triathlon NZ) by the reflections of our governance specialist, Patrick.

To provide a point of accountability for the chief executive

Without a board as employer, the senior manager has no point of accountability. The board as employer and the executive as employee are the starting points for most organisations as they define the separate but inter-dependent roles of governance and management. The accountability role highlights the idea of *oversight*. For example, the CEO of the Australian government agency for sport the Australian Sports Commission (ASC), is accountable to the board of the ASC.

Concept Check

Generic governance: Foresight, oversight and insight

The exercise of establishing and monitoring the necessary controls and strategic direction-setting so that an organisation is equipped to respond to the changing circumstances and situations in the external and internal environments in order to meet the expectations and demands of owners and other key stakeholders. In other words, governance is about *foresight*, *oversight*, and *insight*, irrespective of context.

The board's role

What is a board and how does it carry out its governance role?

Having established the general notions of governance and sport governance, we now become more specific in considering the role of the board and the tasks and functions carried out by those who sit around a boardroom table. Once again, there are varying perspectives regarding what the board of a sport organisation actually does. There have been a small number of studies that have sought to clarify the board's role. Inglis (1997) investigated roles of the board in amateur sport organisations in Canada. She identified four board roles: setting the organisation's mission, strategic planning, monitoring the chief executive, and engaging in community relations. In a study of state sporting organisations in Australia, Shilbury (2001) identified roles of the board as: setting financial policy, advocacy and community relations, hiring of the chief executive, long-range planning, representing constituents, setting governance policy, and budget allocation. Despite these two pieces of research taking place in two different countries, several common elements exist. In fact, Kilmister (2006) established a list of common themes that emerged from the governance literature regarding the role of the board. They include:

- overseeing the organisation's systems, processes and actions to ensure that there is compliance with externally-imposed requirements and that the internal policies and rules are honoured;
- managing the relationship with the chief executive – hiring, firing and setting performance criteria;
- setting the organisation's mission, vision and strategic direction, i.e., the upper level components of the organisation's strategy;
- setting and monitoring policies, including risk management policies;
- monitoring progress towards long-term strategic objectives and monitoring short-term results;
- expressing accountability to members and other key stakeholders;
- accepting ultimate accountability for all organisational actions.

In moving away from a list of roles, Carver (2002) considered that the board's job is to create the future, not mind the shop. This statement accentuates the *foresight* role and the need for the board to contribute at the strategic level, and cautions against being captured by the day-to-day demands of the organisation. It also brings us back to the interplay between the concept of governance and the work of the board. In essence, governance is what the board is charged with doing.

Garratt (2005) also emphasised the board's *foresight* role and considered that many boards find it difficult to balance the *oversight* or conformance role with the need to consider the organisation's future. In an earlier thought-provoking text, he described the role of the board in the following way:

> As I see it, the key to organisational health is a committed and thoughtful board of directors, not managers, at the heart of the enterprise. It is the board's job to keep striking balances between the external and internal pressures on the organisation to ensure survival. The board must give a clear direction to the business and create an emotional climate in which people can align and attune to that direction...Directing (the board's role, thus directors) is essentially an intellectual activity. It is about showing the way ahead, giving leadership.
>
> *(Garratt, 1996, p. 3-4)*

This statement introduces the notion of *directorship* and, in fact, many board members of sport organisation are now called directors. This label is consistent with the title used to describe board members within commercial or corporate organisations and, once again, signals the transition of sport organisations from an amateur to a more business-like ethos in the discharge of their duties. In fact, the term 'governance' comes from the Latin verb 'gubernare' meaning 'to steer' (Shilbury, 2001), a similar idea to that of directing.

Concept Check
Board of directors
The governing body of a legal entity with legal powers as defined, usually, by the sport organisation's constitution. Terms used in sport such as board of control, management committee or council have been superseded by the title, 'board of directors', which captures the *foresight, oversight,* and *insight* roles of the board.

Theories and challenges of sport governance

While a good theory can help guide practice, one of the main roles of theory is to explain why things occur in the way they do. Employed in this manner, theories can help make sense of governance tensions, dilemmas, and challenges. At present, no universal theory of governance has been agreed upon within the literature (Huse, 2009; Hoye & Doherty, 2011). However, we are starting to gather together several theories, borrowed from other spheres of organisation studies, and apply them to the sport governing role. Some of the most frequent theories used in sport governance and beyond include managerial hegemony theory, agency theory, stewardship theory, and institutional theory. At the risk of introducing too many theories, the use of multiple theories can help us to understand each theory by highlighting their contrasting approaches. Each theory or 'way of looking' at governance, also offers something different in our search to make sense of the tensions and dilemmas of the governing role (Cornforth, 2003).

Managerial hegemony theory: A theory of CEO dominance

Managerial hegemony theory asserts that while the board has power by legal right, the real responsibility for the organisation is assumed by management or the chief executive (Stiles, 2001). This view of governance points out that, in many cases, the board has unrealised or latent power. For example, in a research study undertaken by Ferkins et al. (2009), they found a situation where the board of New Zealand Football collectively brought a high level of capability and experience but were not involved enough in designing the strategic direction for the sport. As one board member stated, "We need a board that is not marching to the CEO's or any other person's agenda". In other words, a board that is "operating as being in charge…where the tail is not wagging the dog" (Ferkins et al., 2009, p. 258). Using managerial hegemony theory to offer insight into this situation, the researchers worked with the board of New Zealand Football to create greater board involvement in strategy and, in particular, designed an agenda which facilitated greater strategic discussion by the board and less CEO reporting.

Agency theory: An over-emphasis on the oversight role

Agency theory encourages us to think about the purpose of governance as being focussed on the need to control and monitor the actions of the CEO and/or senior management, that is, the *oversight* role. It is a theory that has emerged because of the separation of ownership (largely within the commercial sector) between those who govern and those who manage (Fama & Jensen, 1983). Agency theory assumes that owners of an organisation will have interests that are different from those who manage it. In sport, agency theory, at least in part, helps to explain how management and board members often unwittingly draw the board's attention away from its real job of looking ahead and out into the wider environment, instead causing them to look inwards and backwards, checking management and staff actions over the preceding period. While monitoring the financial and non-financial performance of the organisation is an important and necessary component in the board's role, it is not the exclusive component. While the board will undoubtedly spend some of its valuable time looking into the past and the near future, its real value is in its ability to use its collective wisdom and creativity to look to the medium- and long-term future and to ensure alignment between its vision for the organisation and the changing external environment (Garratt, 2005).

Stewardship theory: A theory of CEO-board partnership and collaboration

In contrast to agency theory, stewardship theory views the role of the board as one where board members and the CEO have similar aspirations for the organisation. It is a more collaborative or partnership-oriented approach to thinking about the governance of sport (Davis & Schoorman, 1997; Hoye & Cuskelly, 2007). It is a theory that also encourages an emphasis on the board's strategic role because, with interests aligned, the opportunity for the board and CEO to work collaboratively on organisation strategy is afforded (Cornforth, 2003). However, while this sounds good, such an approach takes a great deal of insight on behalf of the board because of the competing and conflicting roles between the board and CEO. SPARC, the government agency for sport in New Zealand, demonstrated in its governance guidelines how the board-chief executive relationship is full of contradictions.

> The chief executive is usually a full-time professional employed by part-timers who are mostly amateurs in the operation of the business being governed. That brings special challenges. The chief executive controls operations, including the information necessary for the board to make its governance decisions, yet the board carries ultimate

accountability for these decisions. The chief executive is expected to provide leadership to the organisation and, at times, to the board. Yet the board is the ultimate leadership body. In short, it depends on the chief executive to make things happen, but the chief executive's only authority is granted by the board. These contradictions can only be resolved when the board and chief executive work as a team – partners and colleagues working together. Some directors and chief executives find this difficult to accept.

(Sport and Recreation New Zealand, 2006, p. 80)

Institutional theory: It's the way we do things around here

Institutional theory provides insight into why the practice of governance is repeated across so many different sporting codes and in a similar way. According to institutional theory, it is because governance frameworks adopted by sport organisations are "the result of external pressures to conform to accepted business practice, including legal requirements for incorporation" (Hoye & Cuskelly, 2007, p. 13). Such pressures can come from funding agencies such as SPARC and the ASC who also provide governance guidelines for sport. In essence, institutional theory is about organisational practices that become embedded because of the need to conform to expectations and appear legitimate ('it's the way we do things around here'). In fact, the concept check earlier, setting out a definition of sport governance, includes this notion of institutionalised practice. Playing into this is the issue that many sport boards (particularly at the state or regional level) do not have a role description or terms of reference, and there is typically little or no attention paid to the induction of new members into the board's affairs. Training often takes the form of 'on-the-job, watch and learn, just do what we do'. This often results in wasted potential while the new member 'waits and watches', a lack of constructive criticism about current practices, and a lack of incentive to explore new or improved ways of carrying out the board's business. Often this situation leads to the CEO playing a dominating role as the trained, paid professional. Both managerial hegemony theory and institutional theory provide some insight into this challenging scenario.

Table 7-1: Summary box - theories and challenges of sport governance	
THEORIES USED TO UNDERSTAND SPORT GOVERNANCE	SPORT GOVERNANCE CHALLENGES
Managerial hegemony theory	CEO dominance – the board has the legal authority but the real responsibility for the organisation is assumed by the CEO. Summed up by the following statement: the 'tail is wagging the dog'.
Agency theory	The board is too focussed on monitoring and control of the CEO and organisation (oversight) and not engaged in the forward looking or strategic (foresight) role.
Stewardship theory	The board's and CEO's interests are aligned and, therefore, the board and CEO work in partnership. However, there are still many conflicting and competing roles between the two.
Institutional theory	Governance structures and decision-making are taken for granted, institutionalised, and thus resistant to change. This explains why there may be a lack of constructive criticism about current practices, and a lack of incentives to explore new or improved ways of carrying out the board's business.

Concept Check

Sport governance challenges

Many not-for-profit boards, including boards of sport organisations, demonstrate problems that are typically associated with a lack of role clarity and understanding of governance.

Stakeholders: Owners, members and others

Every sport organisation has stakeholders who stand to benefit or gain from its existence. At the top of the list of stakeholders is a group we will refer to as the organisation's 'owners'. Strictly speaking there are no 'owners' of not-for-profit organisations in the legal sense. The concept of 'ownership', however, can be helpful when thinking about the board's responsibility to certain stakeholders or groups of stakeholders. Almost without exception, the 'owners' of not-for-profit sport organisations are the paying members. For example, the 'owners'/members of Netball New Zealand are its 12 regional entities, such as Canterbury Netball or Netball Wellington. In turn, the 'owners'/members of Netball Wellington are its five centres (e.g., Kapiti/Paraparaumu Netball). Individual players, coaches, and umpires can become members of the clubs and centres which are, in turn, members of the regional entity.

In each case, it is the 'owners'/members for whom the organisation was originally established. As the professionalisation process has occurred in sport, the notion of 'ownership' and control has become contested (Ferkins & Shilbury, 2010 - refer case study on Tennis New Zealand). If there is doubt about who the members/owners of a sport organisation are, the answer to the questions, 'Who has the power to alter the constitution?', 'Who has voting rights for the election of board members?' and 'Who has the authority to close the legal entity and distribute the assets?' will, in most instances, quickly identify the legal members/owners. In a general sense, it is to the owners that the board owes its primary accountability. There are a small number of sport organisations in New Zealand that have private ownership. Examples include the New Zealand Breakers (basketball), the New Zealand Warriors (rugby league), and the Wellington Phoenix (soccer/football). More private ownership of sport exists in Australia (e.g., in basketball, soccer/football and rugby league). As a point of clarification, the notion of 'membership' referred to above is used differently from the idea of 'membership' of a professional sports team, such as, a member of the North Melbourne Australian Rules football club, which could also refer to a season-ticket holder.

There may also be other people close to the organisation, for example, major funders, sponsors, and broadcast partners, staff, and fans who also stand to benefit from its existence. They, too, are stakeholders. However, their stake is not as 'owner'. A major funder, for example SPARC, may provide a significant portion of the organisation's operating costs, perhaps to the point where it could not exist without those funds. This alone does not make the funder an owner. Unless the organisation's constitution accords to the funder, membership, or some other special status, it has no power to affect the basic rules of the organisation or to elect or appoint the members of its governing body. Certainly, it may be a significant stakeholder, so significant that the board is obliged to give careful consideration to any instruction or suggestion offered, but the board has the choice to ignore them and make its own decisions. In terms of its composition, many boards of contemporary not-for-profit sport organisations in New Zealand and Australia are considered to be hybrid boards. In other words, the board group is made up of a mix of both elected members and independent appointments. The Triathlon New Zealand case study highlights the importance of independent appointments and the skills that may be added to the board mix.

Concept Check

Stakeholders

There are different categories of stakeholders in a sport organisation. A board must have a clear appreciation of which ones it is accountable to, and how it should respond to others.

Board–Chief Executive relationships

At the heart of any effective board is an effective chief executive and a good board-executive relationship (Hoye & Doherty, 2011). Historically referred to as an executive director, executive officer, or general manager, the relationship between a chief executive and the board begins at the time of appointment. Ideally, the board is clear about what outcomes it wants this key employee to achieve, and matches them against the skills, experience and attitudes brought to the position. The chief executive is employed to benefit the sport organisation by achieving results, rather than the organisation being there to benefit the chief executive by providing employment. This distinction is highlighted by the contrasting positions of agency and stewardship theory. Hoye and Doherty (2011) in their review of literature on sport board performance concluded that not only was the relationship between the board and chief executive a key to board performance, but there also exists a critical role between the board chairperson and chief executive. Drawing on an earlier study by Hoye and Cuskelly (2003), Hoye and Doherty (2011, p. 278) asserted that, "board performance was related to positive relationships between the board and paid staff". In fact, this relationship is "built on the basis of mutual trust, the centrality of the executive in the provision of information, and the positive sharing of leadership between a dominant coalition of board members, the board chair, and the executive".

Knowing about operations, but staying out of them

Indeed, boards of sport organisations face many and varied challenges in managing the relationship with the chief executive. Most corporate boards comprise professional directors with vast experience of their governance role and no wish to become involved in any way in operational activities. Many sport organisation board members, by contrast, seek membership of the board on the misconception that they can become involved in their organisation's operational affairs. Sometimes there is a desire to address certain operational matters that the individual believes need 'putting right'. Quite simply, they want to help run their association, bringing their hands-on operational skills to the board. When a new board member whose motivation is so directed joins a well-functioning governing board, frustration is a likely outcome. Such a board member is likely to quickly discover that he or she has misunderstood the board's role. Delegated authorities, clearly defined in writing and setting out the boundaries between executive and board authority, can assist the two parties to set about carrying out their respective roles so that they complement rather than compete or overlap (Carver, 2010). As noted above, trust and respect are essential elements in the formation of this relationship. Inglis (1997), in a study of Canadian sport organisations, described this relationship as shared leadership. The use of this concept helps us view the board-chief executive relationship as a partnership, much like the perspective offered by stewardship theory.

Focussing on the right information

In order for the board to have control over, but be free from, the complexity of staff-managed operations, there needs to be clearly-stated and agreed processes for reporting to the board. While many board members will want to know about the details of day-to-day actions and events, in themselves they are often of little use to the board in carrying out its governance responsibilities. A board needs to move beyond merely rubber stamping management actions to a level of meaningful engagement but without interference (Bradshaw, 2009). Instead of merely reporting on the operational actions, the chief executive should interpret them in terms of the board's duties, interests and concerns. In this way, there is an ongoing dialogue between the chief executive and the board. There may, however, be times when the chief executive is called upon to describe or explain operational strategies and actions in order to facilitate board understanding of a high-level issue. It is generally accepted that if the dialogue around operational issues is designed to provide 'context', such dialogue is an acceptable part of the governing role (see Carver, 2010). When operational reporting becomes the norm at board meetings or, worse, when board members take the opportunity to impose their authority on operational decision-making, this practice is likely to damage the integrity of the board-chief executive relationship (Kilmister, 2006).

Concept Check

Shared leadership

A successful board-chief executive relationship is in the nature of a partnership in which both parties have clearly-defined expectations of each other.

Strategic role and involvement in organisation strategy

Like many of the terms and concepts associated with the governing role, defining the board's strategic role is also a source of much debate within the literature and an unclear concept in practice. A number of scholars have concluded there exists a 'fuzziness' associated with the notion of the board's strategic role (Edwards & Cornforth, 2003; Ferkins et al., 2009; Pugliese & Wenstøp, 2007). Edwards and Cornforth (2003, p. 78) considered that a primary issue in seeking clarity regarding the board's strategic role is the "fuzziness of the boundary between operational detail and strategic focus". In picking up on this point, Ferkins et al. (2009, p. 249) explained that "operational detail may be an important aspect of strategic decision-making and, therefore, needs to be presented in a manner that enhances strategic function". Pugliese and Wenstøp (2007) also asserted that, "Board strategic involvement, albeit challenged by many scholars, is widely recognised as one of the major tasks of the board.... However, we still lack consensus about the boundary of board strategic involvement" (p. 385).

In their study on small firms, Pugliese and Wenstøp (2007, p. 386) adopted a definition that "board strategic involvement, in general, refers to shaping mission, vision and values, identifying important strategic activities and scanning the environment for trends and opportunities". While this is a useful definition in considering the board's strategic role in a generic sense, Ferkins and Shilbury (2012, in press) in a study of sport organisations in New Zealand, established four elements that serve as reference points in 'mapping out' meanings associated with board strategic capability specifically for national sport organisations. These are:

- the need to have capable people who are able to 'think strategically';
- the need to have a frame of reference (i.e., an articulated strategic plan);
- facilitative board processes, (e.g., an agenda that allows for strategic discussion, a board charter and protocols that encourage a strategic focus etc.); and
- facilitative regional relationships (e.g., relationships with member organisations such as regional entities, where input into the sport's strategic direction is sought so that the strategic delivery mechanism can function).

Figure 7-1 sets out this mapping of elements. The second case study expands on the fourth element, facilitative regional relationships, in setting out the Tennis New Zealand story.

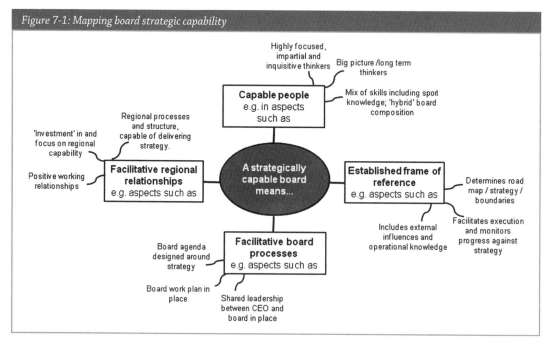

Figure 7-1: Mapping board strategic capability

Source: Ferkins & Shilbury (2012, in press)

The research findings explained above emphasise that a board's leadership role and the fact that it is ultimately accountable for organisation outcomes, demands that it take full responsibility for determining organisational direction. However, this is not done so in a vacuum. There is much consensus in the literature that a board should involve not only its chief executive and senior staff, but key members (e.g., regional entities, centres, clubs, and individual members) and external stakeholders (funders, sponsors, community, fans) in the discussion of organisation direction, as appropriate (Ferkins & Shilbury, 2010; Kilmister, 2006). The expected results have to be achievable and also acceptable to a wide range of interested parties. If these discussions are effective and real, they build commitment and ownership throughout the organisation and lead to better decision-making. Chapter six sets out the process of strategy development and strategic planning, noting the importance of involvement by those who will be affected by the setting of strategic priorities.

Ongoing strategic thinking

Just because the board has articulated its strategic direction does not mean that it has completed its strategic work – far from it. The work that the board puts into developing the upper-level statements not only forms the basis for operational level planning (for which the CEO is responsible), but also forms the platform for the board's essential ongoing strategic thinking role.

Strategic thinking is the process used by the board to continually measure the progress made towards its stated outcomes or goals, and to better understand the environment within which the organisation operates (Garratt, 2005). Strategic thinking assists board members to stay abreast of a wide range of strategic issues relevant to the organisation and its success. For example, such thinking could include consideration of:

- changes in member/consumer expectations or demands, e.g., professionalism in a sport raises the demand, breadth and level of delivery of player services;
- changes in economic circumstances, e.g., an anticipated grant does not eventuate requiring reconsideration of the programmes or services offered to members, or rapidly growing membership and thus an increase in revenue from subscriptions provides the opportunity to hire staff for the first time;
- legislative change, e.g., awareness of the impact of employment law, environmental law etc.;
- changes in the playing environment of the sport itself.

Using a well-framed agenda and strategic thinking tools such as a SWOT analysis, stakeholder analysis, brainstorming, and scenario analysis, the board can create at every meeting the time and opportunity to use the experience and skills of its members. In this way, the board adds value to the work done by the chief executive and staff by focusing on the implications of operational actions and placing them in the context of the big picture. The process of strategic review and ongoing strategic thinking is at the heart of the board's governance role.

Ferkins et al. (2009), in their study of national sport organisations, found that boards can develop their strategic capability by becoming more involved in strategy design. They developed a continuum that builds on the idea that the board should be involved in shaping strategy, but that there exist varying degrees to which this involvement occurs. They advanced the work of McNulty and Pettigrew (1999), who challenged the prevailing view that the chief executive designs strategy and the board approves it. Ferkins et al. (2009) promote the benefits of increased involvement by the board in strategy design. Figure 7-2 sets out the four stages of increased board involvement in strategy design.

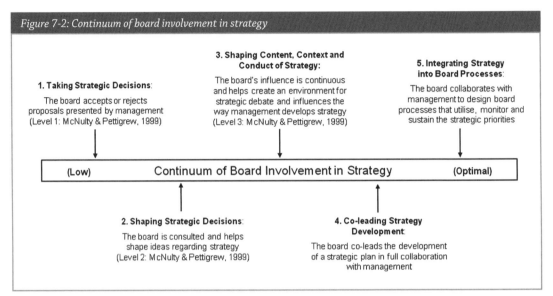

Figure 7-2: Continuum of board involvement in strategy

3. Shaping Content, Context and Conduct of Strategy:

The board's influence is continuous and helps create an environment for strategic debate and influences the way management develops strategy (Level 3: McNulty & Pettigrew, 1999)

5. Integrating Strategy into Board Processes:

The board collaborates with management to design board processes that utilise, monitor and sustain the strategic priorities

1. Taking Strategic Decisions:

The board accepts or rejects proposals presented by management (Level 1: McNulty & Pettigrew, 1999)

(Low) Continuum of Board Involvement in Strategy **(Optimal)**

2. Shaping Strategic Decisions:

The board is consulted and helps shape ideas regarding strategy (Level 2: McNulty & Pettigrew, 1999)

4. Co-leading Strategy Development:

The board co-leads the development of a strategic plan in full collaboration with management

Source: Ferkins et al. (2009, p. 271)

Concept Check

Setting strategic direction

The board's role is to establish the strategic direction for the sport organisation. The chief executive is responsible for the design of the operational plan/s. The board makes an ongoing contribution to the achievement of organisational outcomes through involvement in high-level strategy design and strategic thinking.

Monitoring and evaluation

An essential component of the board's role is its duty to ensure that the organisation is performing to desired standards and delivering the outcomes required (Kilmister, 2006). In order to do this, the board needs information. Although boards receive information from a variety of sources, its main source is the chief executive. Boards need information for two core purposes. Their duty of care requires that they are sure that the 'right things' are being done, or have been done. Information to facilitate this is monitoring information. Boards monitor the organisation's finances and other system components to be sure that internally- and externally-imposed requirements are being met, and organisation risk is assessed and appropriately managed. The monitoring process is, almost without exception, based on an objective assessment of facts. The monitoring process is aimed at determining whether or not 'things' are 'right' or 'wrong' or 'have' or 'have not' been done as required. Monitoring is, typically focussed on past events. Ideally, this type of information is set against pre-determined criteria. In this way, monitoring is easily and quickly carried out, saving the board time that can be more usefully spent discussing future rather than past matters (Carver, 2002).

The evaluation process, by contrast, is typically more subjective in nature, requiring the board to make judgments about its satisfaction with the results or outcomes achieved, as described in the strategic plan. While evaluation information might contain factual data, it will be aggregated to create a picture of something that is greater than the sum of the various facts. Board members will be asked to sift through a range of information and to analyse and interpret it in order to build a picture of a result that they can be satisfied with. In this, the board engages in both the *oversight* and *insight* role. While a board will undoubtedly form an opinion about the competence of its chief executive, based on whether or not things are being done 'right', that is, the exercise of monitoring, the ultimate test faced by most chief executives is whether the board's evaluation of the achievement of big picture outcomes results in a positive score card.

Concept Check

Monitoring and evaluation

Boards monitor the organisation's finances and other system components to be sure that internally- and externally-imposed requirements are being met, and that risk is assessed and appropriately managed. The evaluation process is, typically, more subjective, requiring the board to make judgments about its satisfaction with the results or outcomes achieved, as described in the strategic plan.

Evaluating the Chief Executive's performance

One of the tasks in their annual calendar that boards of sport organisations find most difficult, is the evaluation of their chief executive's performance in the role. To compound this situation, many sport organisations still exhibit an amateur ethos (Shilbury & Ferkins, 2011) which can mean that few boards or board chairpersons are trained in performance evaluation. To set the framework for the appraisal, it is helpful to go back to basics and examine the board and the chief executive roles, respectively. The board is charged by the organisation's owners (typically club or organisation members) with achieving certain outcomes. In turn, the chief executive is employed to achieve those outcomes.

Ultimately, the chief executive is accountable to the board for his/her performance in the role. For this reason, it is important the board makes clear exactly what this most senior officer is accountable for. If the chief executive does not succeed in his or her job, the organisation will not succeed. Chief executive success is, thus, synonymous with organisational success. The accountability of the chief executive is thereby derived (Charan, 2005). Maintaining a focus on performance at the macro-organisational level will help the board to keep the process as objective as possible. Additionally, board appraisal of the chief executive's performance should be ongoing and continuous rather than an annual event (Charan, 2005). This approach is an expression of the "...board's leadership and is a way of forcing the board to probe and reach consensus about how the chief executive could improve" (Charan, 2005, p. 87).

If the chief executive uses each board meeting to report progress towards the achievement of strategic goals, and if the board is vigilant in its monitoring and compliance with policies, then every board meeting becomes a vital piece in the overall board evaluation of the chief executive's performance. When the chief executive engages with the board in dialogue about strategic matters of significance to the organisation, board members will inevitably make personal judgments about the value that is added as the result of such input. If, in addition to the regular evaluations there is an annual, formal performance appraisal, it becomes a 'wrap-up' – the chance to evaluate the whole year's performance, to set personal development goals and to reflect on the chief executive–board interrelationship and, if appropriate, to discuss salary expectations and any changes to the job or performance contract.

Concept Check

Chief executive performance evaluation

Board appraisal of the chief executive's performance needs to be ongoing and continuous rather than a yearly event.

Evaluating the board's performance

While most boards (led by the chairperson) annually review their executive officer's performance, few apply a disciplined process to evaluate their own performance. Several obstacles have stood in the way (Kilmister, 2006). The seniority of directors and of the board itself has resulted in many directors viewing themselves as 'above performance assessment'. Secondly, because so much of what boards discuss is viewed as confidential, there is resistance to allowing an outsider evaluate. There has also been reluctance for directors to subject themselves to judgment by their peers or by outsiders, sensing that their performance is less than they might wish and that they are 'just volunteers'. Another attitude often encountered is that board evaluation has never been done before, so why do it now? This issue can, in part, be explained by applying the ideas of institutional theory. Either the board chair might lead this process or an independent governance specialist might undertake an evaluation which typically involves anonymous self- and peer-assessment of each other and the board as a whole (Charan, 2005).

Based on agreed criteria

Like any performance assessment, it is imperative that the board assesses itself against pre-agreed criteria, preferably criteria that have formed the basis for the board's own operating procedures. Typical questions address the following matters which also serve as a summary of board performance.

- *Role and structure* – understanding of the governing roles and duties, appreciation of the separate but inter-dependent roles of the board and chief executive, board composition, board competencies.
- *Strategic leadership* – the extent of strategic thinking and direction-setting and the effectiveness of strategy formulation.

- *Board systems* – the effectiveness of policy formulation and monitoring, organisation performance monitoring, risk management, financial monitoring, compliance monitoring, delegation to the chief executive, director and office holder succession planning, induction of new directors, professional development for directors and the board, and remuneration.
- *Board meetings* – agenda design, meeting management including the role of the chairman, information management and record-keeping.
- *Board-chief executive relationship* – performance management, reporting expectations and information supply, nature and quality of the relationship.

Concept Check

Board performance assessment

Just as boards expect to evaluate the effectiveness of their chief executive and for the person in that role to ensure that there is performance evaluation of all other staff, so, too, should the board assess its own performance and the performance of individual board members.

CASE STUDY: CHANGING THE GOVERNING STRUCTURE OF TENNIS IN NEW ZEALAND

"Tennis New Zealand is hamstrung by associations and associations are the same. There is little convergence or alignment of goals" (Tennis New Zealand, 2004b, p. 4). This statement was made by the chief executive of Tennis New Zealand (TNZ) in a presentation to members of the tennis community in 2004. In referring to the then governing structure of 25 associations, the chief executive, supported by the board, stated that the sport in its current form is ungovernable.

In the years following this 2004 speech the board and chief executive of TNZ embarked on a most challenging process of change involving the governing structure of the sport. This proved an extremely difficult process as many association members were uneasy at the thought of such major change to a sport which was over 125 years old. Such views, entrenched in historical practice, reflect the ideas of institutional theory.

> The historical evolution of tennis structures in New Zealand means that clubs and associations are obliged by separate constitutions to comply with narrow and sometimes 'self-interested' objectives. As a result, Tennis NZ has neither the human nor financial resources to offer genuine leadership to the sport, and clubs and associations operate in isolation with varying degrees of success.
>
> (Tennis New Zealand, 2004b, p. 7).

One initial proposal for change put forward to the regional associations (i.e., members) for comment by a working party commissioned by the TNZ board, was a 'unitary' model of governance (Tennis New Zealand, 2004c). This model would see the 25 regional associations disbanded to become part of TNZ. In other words, the associations would give up their independent legal status and, instead, become

(Continued)

regional offices of the national body. Again, there was opposition to this proposal. Arguments against such radical change to the governing structure included:

- risk of disenfranchising long-serving volunteer stakeholders;
- perceived loss of democracy – TNZ controls the game without the usual checks and balances operating at regional level;
- potential loss of revenue from local trusts and sponsors as the focus of activity is perceived to be national;
- significant 'opportunity costs' of any structural re-engineering.

The rationale put forward by the working party for fundamental change included:

- centralises the leadership and resources of the sport (TNZ absorbs 25 associations and 6 affiliates);
- allows professional management of valuable tennis resources and creates efficiencies by avoiding duplication of effort and expenditure;
- enables effective national planning and implementation of key strategies;
- opens up the prospect of new revenue streams for national initiatives;
- relieves the current debt burden of some associations by consolidation of assets and liabilities into a single balance sheet;
- financial and information management will be driven centrally, creating improved service to member clubs.

(Tennis New Zealand, 2004c).

Irrespective of the arguments for and against fundamental change toward a unitary governing model, there was widespread agreement that tennis in New Zealand was suffering some major issues. These included, low media profile of tennis, aging facilities, shrinking membership, confused and complex governance, eroding financial base, duplication of effort, and risk of hi-jack by commercial interests (Tennis New Zealand, 2004a).

On the eve of what was to be a three-year process to achieve structural change, the chairperson of the board made the following statement: "Whatever the outcome of the restructure, it will be better than what we currently have, but will it be the best? Or will parochialism, politics, fiefdoms and fear of change get in the way? That's the challenge" (Tennis New Zealand, 2004c, p. 5). Much of this forecast was to become reality as the national body and regional entities appeared to have contrasting views of their respective governing roles.

In an article on the Tennis New Zealand situation, Ferkins and Shilbury (2010, p. 245-246) commented that issues of ownership and control appeared to be at the heart of the debate regarding change to the governing structure. The two frameworks of agency and stewardship theory noted earlier in this chapter can be applied here. Stewardship theory of governance advocates behaviour and decision-making that is collectivistic where those who govern consider they do so as stewards of the organisation (Davis & Schoorman, 1997). In contrast, agency theory focuses on the concept of ownership of the sport and, therefore, invokes the need for control. If the board of TNZ considered that their role is to act as 'stewards' on behalf of the organisation, the collective principles of stewardship theory could apply. "However, if the concept of governing was considered from an ownership perspective (i.e., the TNZ board was there to govern on behalf of the owners) then why would the owners (i.e., regional centres) risk being disadvantaged by collective decisions that may not address their regional concerns?" (Ferkins & Shilbury, 2010, p. 245-246). To summarise, there appeared to be two distinct points of view relating to issues of ownership and control, which were brought to the fore by the re-structuring process. According to Ferkins and Shilbury (2010, p. 246), they were:

- TNZ view: the regional entity exists to deliver national priorities and programmes and keep the sport 'alive' at the regional level.
- Regional view: the national body exists to co-ordinate our wishes as owners of the sport. We tell them what to do and what the strategic priorities are.

In the end, at a special general meeting of TNZ on 12 August, 2006, the motion to replace the existing TNZ constitution with a new constitution mandating six geographical areas, known as regional

(Continued)

centres, was approved unanimously by the members (i.e., 25 regional associations) of TNZ. Despite much controversy relating to regional autonomy and TNZ governing authority, "this was arguably the most significant change to the national body since it was established and, as such, a major achievement for all concerned" (Ferkins & Shilbury, 2010, p. 246). While not a unitary model, such a change set the sport up to engage in a power-sharing approach to the governance of the sport. Figure 7-3 sets out a representation of the structural change from a traditional hierarchical model of TNZ's governing relationships, to a 'networked' model. These two contrasting models also align with the contrasting theories of agency (Model A) and stewardship (Model B). In particular, the language used to explain each model represents a different philosophy in relation to governance. This model was prepared in 2007 and published by Ferkins and Shilbury in 2010. While the structural aspects of the model are accurate, the governing philosophy, suggested by the language used, is not necessarily a reflection of what has happened since.

Figure 7-3: *Hierarchical vs. networked governing models. (A) Traditional hierarchical model of TNZ's governing relationship with regional entities. (B) Networked model of TNZ's governing relationship with regional entities*

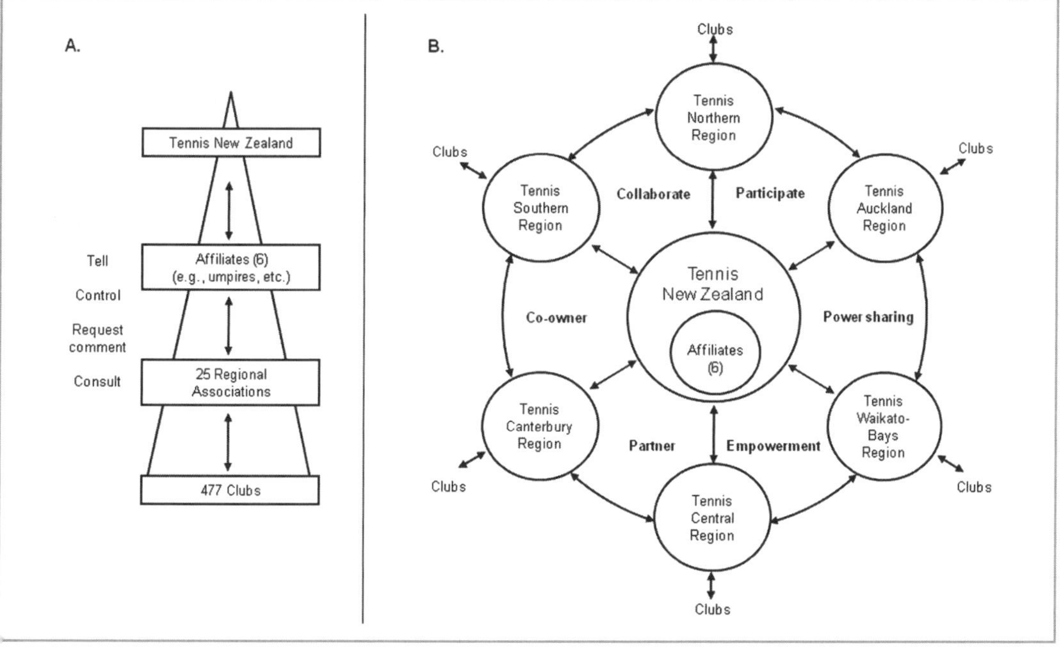

Source: Ferkins & Shilbury (2010, p. 251)

CASE STUDY: REVIEW QUESTIONS

- Using institutional theory, explain why you think there was opposition to the proposed unitary model of governance.
- List the reasons given for why a change to the governing structure was needed. Why else do you think change might have been needed?
- In considering Figure 7-3, discuss the strengths and weaknesses of (A) Traditional Hierarchical Model, versus (B) Networked Model.
- Find out more about the change to TNZ's governing structure by visiting its website. How has TNZ implemented this major change and what have been the issues it has faced since?

Summary

Good governance is not easy to achieve, nor is it easy to develop and maintain the kind of chief executive–board relationship advocated by most writers on governance. By their very nature, good chief executives are focussed, goal-driven and often practical. They are achievers; that is why they are chief executives and not everyday staff. Good governors are thinkers. They take the high view and engage in dialogue about outcomes, values, vision and high-level strategic direction rather than operational strategies and goals. They establish a sound, working partnership with their chief executive and make clear their expectations of that role. Effectively operating boards add value to the organisation governed that is over and above the value added by the chief executive and staff. Good boards 'make a difference', and that difference makes a real contribution to the life of the sport organisation that is demonstrated in the delivery of superior outcomes to those people on whose behalf the board exists.

Review questions

- What special rights do owners of a sport organisation have that are not available to other stakeholders?
- Give three reasons why sport organisations should have a board.
- Briefly describe how chief executives, when reporting to the board, can ensure that the board stays at the governance level in its discussions and deliberations?
- Describe a theory used to explain governance issues and apply it to some of the problems associated with governance of sport organisations.
- What are some of the essential components of an effective board-chief executive relationship?
- Discuss the concept of 'shared leadership' in the context of the board's strategic role.

References

Bradshaw, P. (2009). A contingency approach to nonprofit governance. *Nonprofit and Voluntary Sector Quarterly, 20*(1), 61–81.

Carver, J. (Ed.). (2002). *John Carver on board leadership: Selected writings from the creator of the world's most provocative and systematic governance model*. San Francisco: Jossey-Bass.

Carver, J. (2010). A case for global governance theory: Practitioners avoid it, academics narrow it, the world needs it. *Corporate Governance: An International Review, 18*(2), 149–157.

Charan, R. (2005). *Boards that deliver*. San Francisco: Jossey-Bass.

Cornforth, C. (Ed.). (2003). *The governance of public and non-profit organisations: What do boards do?* London: Routledge.

Davis, J. H., & Schoorman, D. F. (1997). Toward a stewardship theory of management. *Academy of Management Review, 22*(1), 20–48.

Edwards, C., & Cornforth, C. (2003). What influences the strategic contribution of boards? In C. Cornforth (Ed.), *The governance of public and non-profit organisations: What do boards do?* (pp. 77–96). London: Routledge.

Fama, E. F., & Jensen, M. C. (1983). Separation of ownership and control. *Journal of Law and Economics, 26*, 307–325.

Ferkins, L., & Shilbury, D. (2010). Developing board strategic capability in sport organisations: The national-regional governing relationship. *Sport Management Review, 13*, 235–254.

Ferkins, L., & Shilbury, D. (2012, in press). Good boards are strategic: What does that mean for sport governance? *Journal of Sport Management*.

Ferkins, L., Shilbury, D., & McDonald, G. (2005). The role of the board in building strategic capability: Towards an integrated model of sport governance research. *Sport Management Review, 8*, 195–225.

Ferkins, L., Shilbury, D., & McDonald, G. (2009). Board involvement in strategy: Advancing the governance of sport organizations. *Journal of Sport Management, 23*, 245–277.

Garratt, B. (1996). *The fish rots from the head*. London: Harper Collins Business.

Garratt, B. (2005). The real role of corporate directors: Balancing prudence with progress. *Journal of Business Strategy, 26*(6), 30–36.

Hoye, R., & Cuskelly, G. (2003). Board-executive relationships within voluntary sport organisations. *Sport Management Review, 6*, 53–73.

Hoye, R., & Cuskelly, G. (2007). *Sport governance.* Sydney, Australia: Elsevier.

Hoye, R., & Doherty, A. (2011). Nonprofit sport board performance: A review and directions for future research. *Journal of Sport Management, 25*, 272–285.

Huse, M. (2009). The value-creating board and behavioural perspectives. In M. Huse (Ed.), *The value creating board: Corporate governance and organizational behavior* (pp. 3–9). New York: Routledge.

Inglis, S. (1997). Shared leadership in the governance of amateur sport. *AVANTE Journal, 3*(1), 14–33.

Kilmister, T. (2006) Governance. In L. Trenberth and C. Collins (Eds.), *Sport Business Management in Aotearoa New Zealand* (pp. 184–201). Palmerston North, New Zealand: Dunmore Press.

McNulty, T., & Pettigrew, A. (1999). Strategists on the board. *Organization Studies, 20*(1), 47–74.

Pugliese, A., & Wenstøp, P. (2007). Board members' contribution to strategic decision-making in small firms. *Journal of Management & Governance, 11*, 383–404.

Shilbury, D. (2001). Examining board member roles, functions and influence: A study of Victorian sporting organisations. *International Journal of Sport Management, 2*, 253–281.

Shilbury, D., & Ferkins, L. (2011). Professionalisation, sport governance and strategic capability. *Managing Leisure, 16*, 108–127.

Sport and Recreation New Zealand. (2006). *Nine steps to effective governance: Building high performance organisations* (2nd ed.). Wellington, New Zealand: Sport and Recreation New Zealand.

Stiles, P. (2001). The impact of the board on strategy: An empirical examination. *Journal of Management Studies, 38*, 627–651.

Tennis New Zealand. (2004a). *The regional association health check survey*. Auckland, New Zealand: Tennis New Zealand.

Tennis New Zealand. (2004b, September). Current issues and challenges ahead: Address by Chairman and CEO, Tennis New Zealand. Paper presented to the International Club, Auckland.

Tennis New Zealand. (2004c). *For the good of the game: Report of the T21 working party*. Auckland, New Zealand: Tennis New Zealand.

Chapter 8

Leadership

Sarah Leberman

OBJECTIVES

After completing this chapter, you should be able to:

- have an understanding of the different types of leadership theories;
- understand how these have been applied to the sport management area;
- understand difference between quantitative and qualitative approaches to studying leadership;
- have a better understanding about what leadership is in sport management;
- importance of socially constructed notion of leadership, context and stakeholder views.

Some of the theoretical sections of this chapter have been reprinted with permission from: Kihl L., Leberman, S. I., & Schull, V. (2010). Stakeholder constructions of leadership in intercollegiate athletics. *European Sport Management Quarterly*, *10*(2), 241–275.

Key terms

In this chapter, readers will become familiar with the following concepts and terms:
- mainstream leadership approaches
- critical leadership approaches
- social construction
- context
- stakeholder theory

Introduction

Headlines such as 'Wanted: Great NZ leaders' (Birchfield, 2010), 'The heart of leadership: Gut feel and inspiration' (Gautier, 2011) and 'Leadership's looming crisis: Managers drowning in complexity' (Birchfield 2011) highlight that leadership is at the forefront of organisational challenges. This latest article focuses on the findings of the 2011 Global Leadership Forecast, which is based on interviews with 12,423 leaders and 2000 human resource professionals in 74 countries. The findings suggest that organisations with the highest quality leaders outperform their competition in key metrics including employee engagement customer satisfaction, quality of products and services, as well as financial performance. The most critical leadership skills needed in the future were identified in order of importance as – driving and managing change, identifying and developing future talent, fostering creativity and innovation, coaching and developing others, executing organisational strategy, building customer satisfaction and loyalty and improving employee engagement (Winter, 2011). So do any of these findings apply to sport organisations? Let's have a look at some examples. Before we do this have a look at the activity

Activity

Describe the attributes that you think are important in a leader and name three leaders who are important to you.

If we look at how sport recognises leadership in sport organisations, New Zealand's SPARC, instituted a 'leadership excellence in sport' award in 2009, with the inaugural winner being Kerry Clark Chief Executive Bowls New Zealand. The accompanying press release stated:

> Bowls New Zealand (Bowls NZ) is the national not-for-profit governing body for the sport of lawn bowls. Kerry's achievements were possible through a combination of the following competencies and attributes:
>
> * a passion for the sport of bowls, and an outstanding knowledge of all aspects of the game;
> * knowledge-seeking for personal development and for the benefit of the sport;
> * excellent financial management and fundraising ability;
> * a clear understanding of operational and governance issues;
> * a very good working relationship with his Board;
> * ability to interact effectively with all stakeholders within, and beyond, the sport;
> * a preparedness to make tough decisions;
> * a resilience to the 'knockers' and personal attacks;
> * bigger-picture vision;
> * commitment to 'walking the talk'; and,
> * innovative thinking and influencing skills
>
> *(Eden, 2009)*

The 2010 winner was Dave Beech, CEO Triathlon New Zealand, and in 2011 it was Jim Doyle, CEO, New Zealand Rugby League. The following reasons were cited.

> Doyle was appointed as NZRL Chief Executive in 2009 after a turbulent time for the sport. Many of the organisation's financial backers and sponsorship partners had deserted the sport, national and international affiliations had disassociated themselves from the organisation, and staff morale was at an all-time low. SPARC Chief Executive Peter Miskimmin said the focus of the award is leadership shown throughout the 2010 year, and during that time, Doyle turned around a troubled sport. "Jim Doyle is a clever guy who used his considerable commercial nous to reinvent New Zealand Rugby League," Miskimmin said. "He galvanised the entire league community through passion, a strong communication process and admirable leadership that deserves recognition. He got them winning on and off the field. He inspired new sponsors to the game, built up the game's grassroots backbone, and is recognised by the players, staff, and the International League Federation as being a very good CEO"
>
> *(Wallace, 2011)*

Considering leadership

Leadership covers a vast area of research which is well beyond the scope of this chapter. So my objective is to point you in the direction of further resources which will give you the background on the main leadership theories that have informed thinking in the area, and use the space I have to expose you to some of the more recent developments. I should note upfront, that I concur with Grint (2005) who argues that it is virtually impossible to learn leadership from a book, it is a process that is learned, over time, through experience and reflection. In addition, whilst traditionally leadership has been attributed to individuals, it is I believe inherently relational. Overall, I would argue that leadership is about being a person of influence in whatever context you are operating in, family, team, club, not-for profit or profit making sport organisation.

Looking at leadership through different lenses can also assist us in understanding the complexity of this topic (Grint, 2005). Depending on the lens we adopt, we will attribute leadership to different factors. Broadly there are four different ways of 'seeing' leadership. Grint (2005, p. 1) summarises these four ways by asking the following questions:

- *Person:* is it WHO 'leaders' are that makes them leaders?
- *Result:* is it WHAT 'leaders' achieve that makes them leaders?
- *Position:* is it WHERE 'leaders' operate that makes them leaders?
- *Process:* is it HOW 'leaders' get things done that makes them leaders?

By looking at leadership through the person lens we tend to attribute leadership to things like personality, traits, personal style, charisma and heroes or villains. In contrast, a position lens attributes leadership to job title, holding power, hierarchy and holding power. In sport is the results lens is often used, where leadership is attributed to winning or losing, performance, outcomes and measurables. The process lens attributes leadership to things like interactions, language, systems, ideologies and power.

Mainstream approaches to leadership

This chapter will require you to think about your own experiences with leadership and grapple with what the term means to you in theory and practice. This chapter will not detail all the different perspectives, as there are many text books which cover these – for a good summary of the key approaches with an Asia-Pacific focus please look at for example, Daft and Piola-Merlo (2009). They discuss the main approaches to understanding leadership, including the trait approach, behaviour approach and contingency approaches. Another very useful book is Jackson and Parry's (2008) 'A very short, fairly interesting and reasonably cheap book about leadership'.

Following is a brief overview of the key themes highlighted in mainstream leadership research over the last 50 years. Traditional leadership studies (e.g., Bryman, 1992; Bennis & Nanus, 1985) influenced by the "great man" theory have focused on individual leaders and the traits and characteristics they possess (Stogdill, 1974), as well as behaviours or styles that contribute to their effectiveness (Bass, 1985). Burns (1978) first introduced transforming leadership, which focused on the leader's ability to motivate and empower followers, developing into what Bryman (1992) called the "new leadership" perspective. The various approaches that make up the "new leadership" perspective include charismatic (Bryman, 1992), transformational and transactional (Bass, 1985) and visionary (Bennis & Nanus, 1985), and share the common theme of influencing followers in achieving organisational goals. The constant evolution of leadership teamed with widespread criticism that leadership research lacks substance, usefulness, and understanding has challenged researchers (Yukl, 2006).

Traditional methodologies of leadership research have also been criticised for their positivistic approach and neglecting to explore leadership as a social influence process (Alvesson & Deetz, 2000). In response to this critique and as a result of the development of the new leadership approaches, some movement towards a variety of qualitative methodologies to address this perceived weakness and to move the field forward (Ospina & Schall, 2001) has occurred. Many theories on leadership have been introduced, embraced and in some cases abandoned in favour of the new buzzwords in leadership research, such as "authentic leadership" (Garger, 2008) or "ethical leadership" (Brown & Trevino, 2006). Despite these developments, most of the leadership research literature has been developed from the experiences of white males in the corporate, political and military sector, and often lacks explicit links between leadership, context and culture (Elliott & Stead, 2008). In essence, most leadership inquiry assumes a leader-centric approach, which limits the exploration of leadership as a phenomenon experienced by people within a group setting.

Leadership research in sport management

Over the last 20 years there has been wide ranging research associated with leadership in sport management (Amis, Slack, & Hinings, 2004; Branch, 1990; Doherty, 1997; Doherty & Danylchuk, 1996; Ferkins, Shilbury, & McDonald, 2005; Hoye & Cuskelly, 2003; Kellett, 1999; Kent & Chelladurai, 2001; Quarterman, 1998; Scott, 1999; Sherry & Shilbury, 2009; Smart & Wolfe, 2003; Soucie, 1994; Steen-Johnsen & Hanstad, 2008; Weese, 1995). Most of the research undertaken in the North American context adopted a quantitative approach (Branch, 1990; Doherty, 1997; Doherty & Danylchuk, 1996; Kent & Chelladurai, 2001; Quarterman, 1998; Scott, 1999; Smart & Wolfe, 2003; Soucie, 1994; Weese, 1995), with many employing leadership questionnaires including the Leadership Orientation

Survey, the Multi-factor Leadership Questionnaire, the Leadership Behaviour Questionnaire and the Leader Member Exchange Questionnaire. In addition, the study of leadership and/or management in intercollegiate athletics (ICA) and sport has been influenced by traditional 'great man' approaches (Soucie, 1994). Many of these studies examined leader characteristics to assess athletic director and organisational effectiveness (Branch, 1990; Scott, 1999; Soucie, 1994), job satisfaction of employees (Snyder, 1990), influences of leadership style and program goals on occupational stress (Ryska, 2002), and leaders' self-perceptions of skills needed to manage effectively (Quarterman, 1998).

The research specific to ICA has been limited and most research in this area focused on understanding coaches and or subordinates perceptions of leader behaviours and/or the impact on them (Branch, 1990; Doherty, 1997; Snyder, 1990). Branch (1990) found that leaders in effective organisations are more prone to goal and task characteristics than developing relationships with subordinates. Gender and age differences in transformational/transactional behaviour were reported by Doherty (1997), where female and younger athletic administrators displayed more transformational leader behaviours, than their male and older counterparts. While Snyder (1990) reported that leader behaviour in terms of degree of consideration significantly impacted perceptions of job satisfaction and supervision.

New leadership approaches within sport management have examined transformational leadership behaviours related to perceived leadership effectiveness and departmental commitment (Doherty & Danylchuk, 1996), the influence of transformational leadership on organisational culture (Weese, 1995), the impact of leader-member exchange theory on perceptions of transformational leadership (Kent & Chelladurai, 2001), leadership within sport organisation boards (Hoye, 2004, 2007), and the effect of leadership characteristics on transformational/transaction leader behaviour (Doherty, 1997). Some studies have used a follower-leader perspective however, these focused on leaders and the importance placed on their behaviours, characteristics, and/or characteristics, rather than taking a stakeholder perspective (e.g., Branch, 1990; Doherty, 1997; Kent & Chelladurai, 2001; Snyder, 1990). Stakeholder research has been the focus of Parent's work on sport events (2007, 2008) and was applied in the ICA context by Wolfe and Putler (2002), but the linking of stakeholder perceptions with leadership appear to be absent in the sporting context. The qualitative research in leadership and organisational change tended to be either European or Australasian (Ferkins et al., 2005; Hoye, 2004, 2007; Inglis, 1997; Hoye & Cuskelly, 2003; Kellett, 1999; Sherry & Shilbury, 2009; Steen-Johnsen & Hanstad, 2008), with the exception of Amis et al. (2004), which was based on Canadian NSOs. In addition, many of these studies have focused on issues around board performance, rather than considering leadership within the management side of the organisation (e.g., Hoye, 2004, 2006; Inglis, 1997).

Leadership/management debate

Before we consider some of the more recent thinking on leadership, it is important to think about the different aspects of leadership within an organisation – all of which are interrelated. Most sport organisations have a board, a CEO or General Manager and other management staff. So what is the difference between them? How are leaders and managers different or similar? For example, it is often said that 'managers do things right, while leaders do the right thing' (Bennis & Nanus, 1985). Another way of looking at these different processes is to consider the functions and types of questions they focus on. The board for example, has ultimate accountability for the organisation, as well as legitimising what it does. Their role is to consider how the organisation is viewed and manage any risks the organisation is exposed to. The functions of the CEO are about identity, purpose and direction – who are we? Why are we here? And where are we going? Obviously there is a certain amount of overlap in many sports organisations, as many boards are still operating in a management, rather than governance role, particularly at the regional and club level. Similarly many CEOs have management functions including control, co-ordination, organisation and monitoring, which in business situations are often undertaken by line managers. Their focus is on the - who, what, where and when questions.

A different perspective of the leadership management debate is that there are "two forms of authority rooted in the distinction between certainty and uncertainty" (Grint, 2005, p. 1463). What Grint argues is that managers deal with certainty and how to solve a problem, whereas leaders primarily deal with uncertainty. Both ways of framing the debate are useful when thinking about the differences and similarities between management and leadership. Similar to the elusive definition of leadership – there is a lack of consensus in this area too.

Whether we are leader or manager, a critical skill set of either, is the ability to be reflective of one's practice. To date there has been little research in the area of reflective practice within sport management with an article on the topic by Edwards (1999) being one of the few. He highlights the importance of being able to reflect critically on what is happening in sports organisations in order to not only improve personal professional practice, but also that of the organisation.

Activity

What do you think? Which framework to you favour and why? Can we make this distinction in sport organisations?

CASE EXERCISE

Consider the following events which have arisen in sport over the past few years which have hit the media headlines. Given what you have been reading what kind of interpretations can you offer for these occurrences and who is to be held responsible for these situations? If you were in a leadership position within these organisations what would your plan for the future be?

MELBOURNE STORM

In 2010, the Melbourne Storm had their 2007 and 2009 titles taken away, were fined A$500,000 and were forced to return A$1.1 million in prize money after committing breaches of at least A$1.7 million. They were also stripped of all their 2010 competition points, as an investigation by the Australian National Rugby League identified that the club had breached the salary cap regulations over a period of 5 years.

NEW ZEALAND ROWING

Following an independent review of the 2010 World Rowing Championships in New Zealand, Rowing New Zealand was left with a debt of NZ$2.2 million, despite a successful event for New Zealand in the medal tally. Financial mismanagement by Karapiro 2010 the company set up to run the event was identified as the key factor.

Critical perspectives on leadership

In sport as in other contexts, individuals are rewarded for leadership, such as in the SPARC awards; however, recent research is calling for a new approach. In a sense, individual leaders cannot be 'successful' on their own – they need the support of followers and the systems that underpin their organisation. If we think of a successful sports team – it is about group success, rather than only attributable to just the captain or coach – without the team there would be no success. We will now focus on some of the current more critical thinking around leadership and in particular on the work of Amanda Sinclair (2007, 2010) and Donna Ladkin (2010). In her book 'Leadership for the disillusioned' (2007) Amanda Sinclair challenges the existing theories of leadership by arguing that we need to think "about leadership as a way of being that is reflective and thoughtful about self; that values relationships and the present; that is connected to others and embodied; that is not narrowly striving or ego-driven; and that is liberating in its effects' (p. XV).She encourages readers to reflect upon their own experiences of leadership and how these experiences inform the way they are both leaders and followers. Similarly, she highlights how the leaders we should aspire to are often business leaders and questions how the voices and knowledge of certain groups of society are marginalised or privileged.

Activity

What are your earliest experiences of leadership? How has your heritage and upbringing shaped the way you think about leadership?

Sinclair provides a very useful framework for considering the different ways of affecting change by being a person of influence, focused on two dimensions – strength of articulating concern (voice) and location (see Figure 8-1). In many ways this is similar to the sentiments expressed by Meyerson (2008) in her book "Rocking the boat". Figure 8-1 illustrates different ways of affecting change depending on your personality and circumstances. Some people influence change quietly from the inside – quadrant 1. Others are more vocal and often choose to be in high-profile positions to make a difference – quadrant 2. For more broader societal change it is often necessary to move outside your organisation and this is represented by quadrants 3 and 4.

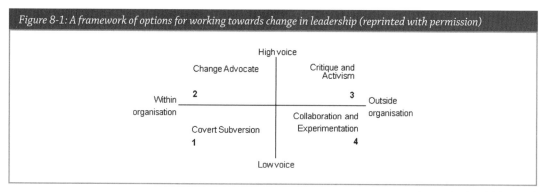

Figure 8-1: A framework of options for working towards change in leadership (reprinted with permission)

Source: Sinclair (2007, p. 87)

Activity

Think about how you might place yourself in these quadrants? What examples from sport can you think of that would fit into each quadrant?

In her most recent work Sinclair (2010) focuses on the importance of knowing your sense of place when learning and reflecting on leadership. Her key argument is that identities and places have been largely absent from the leadership literature and yet form such an important part of thinking about both leadership and what it means to be a leader. She argues that we have multiple identities and often these are contradictory, requiring constant negotiation depending on the situation we are in. Drawing on Brewis (2004) she challenges us to think about 'how we might all resist, delay, and interrupt the need to be, and the need to be seen as a leader, in order to do the leadership work better?" (p. 454).

Sinclair argues for the importance of placing ourselves by thinking about the places we have come from and are in and the multiple identities that we have, when we are thinking, studying and writing about leadership. Where do I come from? How do I situate myself within this? In a sense what is my story and experience of leadership in response to the established theories and are there new or more appropriate ways of studying and explaining leadership? These are important questions as they frame the way we interpret and view leadership theories - do they resonate with us? Do they help explain our experiences? Can we engage with them? Much leadership is about knowing yourself and Sinclair focuses this strongly on identity work with her students - where they come from in family and history as this provides the lens through which we see everything we do. Similar to Grint (2005), Sinclair strongly advocates an experiential and reflective approach to studying leadership.

This is particularly important for us in New Zealand and Australia, when much of what we read is informed by North American or European experiences, which may be quite different to our own. An often neglected aspect of leadership research is that from gender and indigenous perspectives. As Elliott and Stead (2008) contend most of the leadership research literature has been developed from the experiences of white, males in the corporate, political and military sector, and often lack explicit links between leadership, context and culture. With women increasingly assuming leadership roles it is important to identify women's experiences of leadership and develop models of leadership representative of their experiences. In their study, six British women from a range of contexts, including politics, community work, sport and medicine were interviewed regarding their experiences of leadership. The findings suggest that for these women their upbringing shaped their leadership behaviour and influenced the environments they worked in. Their multiple experiences provided a leadership focus centred on the community and they adopted a relational approach to leadership. A community–orientated social capital conception of leadership is suggested as an alternate model of representing leadership.

Palmer and Master's (2010) provide a greater understanding of the socio-cultural and structural issues that arise from the intersection between indigeneity and gender. Their research highlights how Māori women are one of the most marginalised groups in New Zealand society, and explores the experiences of Māori women within organised sport – "one of the most privileged, Eurocentric and masculine institutions in New Zealand" (p. 332). The research is based on in-depth interviews with four Māori women working within sport organisations, using a *kaupapa* Māori approach. This approach is coupled with a Māori feminist approach and intersectionality theory. The findings highlight how these women came to be in sport leadership positions, as well as the barriers they experienced, the strategies they used to negotiate these and the impact of identities on their sport leadership experiences. The rich data presented in the article not only provides insight into these women's experience, but also illustrates the realities of indigenous issues in sport and emphasises the importance of 'hearing' indigenous voices when attempting to manage diversity in sport management.

Similar to Sinclair, Ladkin (2010) also questions the traditional approaches used for studying leadership. She takes a phenomenological approach to exploring the notions of leadership and leaders. The focus of her book is on leadership, seen as "a collective process" (p. 11) including both leaders and followers within "particular social and historical contexts" (p.11). Most existing leadership theories have been based on the positivist paradigm, where leadership is predominantly focused on one person the 'leader' and individual variables are separated out and evaluated. What these theories omit is any reference to time and context. Phenomenology focuses on the lived experiences of people and the meaning they attribute to these qualitatively, rather than quantitatively.

Ladkin uses the analogy of a cube to explain how phenomenology can assist in rethinking the way we conceptualise leadership. In Figure 8-2 below you will see a cube which has six 'sides', but at any one time it is impossible to see all of them. Similarly, depending on which way you move the cube will vary the 'aspect' with which you see the cube. Now transfer these notions to leadership – a side could be 'leader', 'follower', 'the organisation', 'the community' or 'historical situation'. In terms of aspect – imagine how a parent will view what is happing in a sports organisation differently to the CEO, the coaches or the children – perspective is therefore crucial when considering questions of leadership. For example, Messner and Bozada-Deas (2009) investigated leadership roles in youth soccer from the perspective of coaches. They draw on a combination of statistical background figures for US Youth

Figure 8-2: The leadership cube

Soccer and Little League Baseball/Softball in Southern California, field observation, participant observation and 50 interviews with women and men coaches. The findings suggest that whilst the notion of choice was raised by many participants, this choice is constrained by the social environment within which operates. This means that the terms 'coach' and 'team mom' are inherently gendered and reflect the gender divisions inherent in the family and work lives of most of the participants. Similarly, as in family and work situations, men are in the visible leadership roles, whilst women are in the invisible support roles. The term, 'soft essentialism', is used by the authors to describe this notion that men in a sense have a destiny to be leaders and therefore coaches, whereas women exercise a choice to do so. This research has implications for sport managers on many fronts. If we are to change the culture of youth sport where women are just as likely as men to be seen in leadership roles as coaches, sport managers need to consider the way in which opportunities to take on these roles are presented and supported. It is moving beyond the formal, to consider the 'way things are done' and raise awareness about the informal ways in which gender segregation in youth sport is perpetuated.

Equally important to the side and angle is the notion of 'identity'. Whilst our cube is an inanimate object, it will have different properties depending on whether it is a child's building block made of wood, or a die. Whilst phenomenology suggests that it is never possible to completely articulate ones identity or indeed identities, acknowledging and expressing this is vital to understanding leadership, as also advocated for by Sinclair (2007, 2010).

In addition to 'sides', 'aspects' and 'identity', the notions of 'wholes', 'pieces' and 'moments' are important when trying to understand a phenomenon from a phenomenological perspective. "Wholes are clearly distinguishable, independent and separate things...and are comprised of 'pieces'" (Ladkin, 2010, p. 25). Things like weight, colour and size can never be independent, "phenomenologists call such things 'moments'" (Ladkin, 2010, p. 25). Following this line of thought, Ladkin argues that leadership is a 'moment' of social relation, as it cannot exist independently – it requires people, a context, a purpose and a point in time, and therefore moves beyond the focus on one aspect namely that of the leader. The way we interpret this leadership moment is very much dependent on our own perspective, experience and how we are positioned in relation to that moment. Are we the parent, coach, umpire or CEO? Leadership is inherently about people and great leaders get the best team together to achieve set objectives.

Reinforcing this perspective, recent work by Raelin (2011) shifts the focus from leadership as an individual act – to leadership as the process of people working together to accomplish a particular outcome. The emphasis is therefore on understanding "where, how and why leadership work is organised and accomplished" (p. 196), rather than on who the individual is. The implication for research is that studies taking a leadership-as-practice approach will focus on observing actual practice, including for example the artefacts, language, emotions and technologies involved in 'doing leadership'. Process and context are therefore vitally important, instead of the outcome per se. Raelin argues that leaderful practice, as distinct from leadership-as-practice, requires collectiveness, concurrency, collaboration and compassion. Leaderful practice focuses on the democratic approach involving all stakeholders in working towards outcomes. What this means for sport management researchers is that it may be time to move away from the more individualistic approaches to leadership which have provided the majority of leadership research in sport management, towards research that takes more account of context and the multiple realities of leadership. In addition leadership development therefore needs to take place in the context for which it applies. Focusing on lists of competencies may therefore not be readily transferable to the multiple settings that students may find themselves in after University. Finally, given that leadership is viewed as a process and a practice, reflection is crucial to enable learning to occur, as already mentioned earlier in this chapter.

As an example take a look at the job advertisement for the CEO of Hockey New Zealand and the resulting whole of sport plan since the appointment of Hilary Poole to the position. Hockey has seen a dramatic turnaround in its world rankings since her appointment. The question for you to consider is what factors might she have contributed to enable this to happen. What role does the board play and does leadership off the field result in high performance on the field?

CASE: HOCKEY NEW ZEALAND CEO RECRUITMENT ADVERTISEMENT (2009)

Hockey in New Zealand has a proud sporting tradition and a large player base across the country. Its athletes have always demonstrated strong sporting values and been admired for their contribution to the country's sporting history. This Olympic sport faces many challenges, both in funding high performance programmes on the national and international stage and in enhancing player participation through local associations.

Hockey New Zealand seeks a CEO who has a proven drive and ability to grow the revenue base that supports the national body and the sport as a whole. The successful applicant will demonstrate an ability to lead and enhance the future participation and performance of the sport and its administration across the country. The CEO will be the public face of Hockey and be responsible for managing relationships with stakeholders such as sponsors, funding agencies, local associations, media and the wider Hockey community. He/she will be highly focussed on ensuring that funding and sponsorship is in place to continue to develop the sport to world class standards at all levels.

Outstanding leadership and management skills, together with strong commercial and fundraising abilities are pivotal in the position. Relationship management and communication skills are also key to ensuring the future success of Hockey New Zealand.

Strong financial management, staff performance and development skills must also be demonstrated.

While hockey experience is not essential an affinity to sport would be required.

Following this advertisement and the appointment of Hilary Poole to the position, Hockey New Zealand began work on a 'Whole of Sport' Strategy for Hockey in 2009. This includes nationwide strategies for our sport from grass roots through to high performance. In the 2010 Annual Report the following strategic framework for hockey was presented.

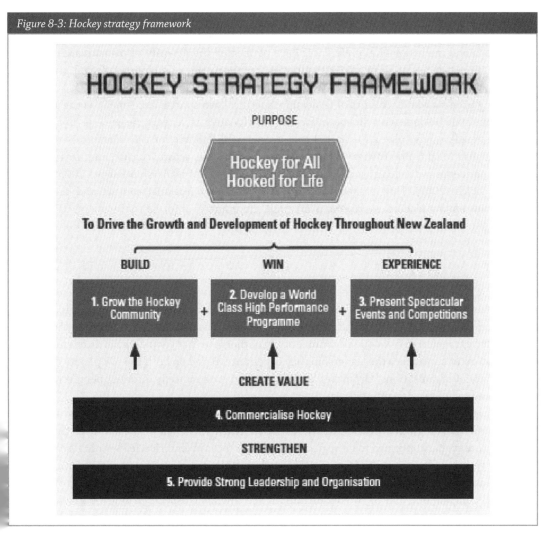

Figure 8-3: Hockey strategy framework

The importance of context, social construction, and stakeholder theory

As already highlighted above in particular by Sinclair (2007, 2010) and Ladkin (2010), the leadership literature to date, has primarily taken a post-positivist and leader-centric approach, used quantitative methodologies, while neglecting stakeholders' perspectives of leadership (Bligh & Schyns, 2007; Meindl, 1995) and the importance of context in their constructions of leadership (Alvesson & Deetz, 2000; Ford &

Lawler, 2007). As a result, considerable discontent exists about our understanding of leadership (Alvesson & Deetz, 2000; Alvesson & Sveningsson, 2003). More importantly, taken for granted assumptions of what leadership is and methodological preferences have permeated the majority of mainstream leadership research "at the expense of losing understanding of how the intrinsic and interconnected processes of leadership take place in complex organizational settings" (Gilstrap, 2007, p. 96).

Missing from standard accounts of leadership, specifically in sport management, is the subjective voice, from stakeholders who are both formally designated as leaders, as well as not formally designated leaders, who play an essential role in leadership interactions. Leadership is embedded in the organisational context where the environment, structure, actors, culture, and organisational processes influence individuals' socially constructed meanings of leadership (Grint, 2005; Osborn, Hunt, & Jauch, 2002). How stakeholders interpret the organisational context and the various relationships among leaders, superiors, peers, and subordinates informs their construction of the nature of leadership and its effectiveness within specific institutional settings (Pye, 2005).

Context

Fielder (1967) first hinted at the importance of context in the study of leadership with his contingency model, which emphasised that different situations called for different leadership approaches. By recognising the importance of context, attention is drawn to the fact that leadership theories cannot necessarily be transferred from one environment to another, and that people within different settings, to a certain extent, influence the leadership they experience. Based on both the complexity of context and diversity of organisations, Osborn et al. (2002) called for a radically different perspective in the study of leadership as a dynamic process.

Similarly, in a review of the leadership literature, Porter and McLaughlin (2006) found that there has been greater recognition of the importance of context in leadership research over the past 15 years, yet context has continued to be neglected as a major focus in empirical leadership research. They offered suggestions to improve the future of leadership study including: 1) an increased emphasis on the organisational context as a "primary object of interest" (p. 573); 2) to study interactions of multiple contextual components; and 3) to concentrate on the "dynamic aspects of organizational context relationships" (p. 574). Iszatt-White (2011) argues that more leadership research needs to take account of how context shapes our understanding of leadership practices and that we cannot necessarily simply transfer learning about leadership from one context to another. She therefore advocates adopting an ethnomethodologically-informed ethnography, which implies that the context and phenomena within it will drive what data is and how best to collect it. Iszatt-White argues that previous research (situational and contingent leadership models) has focused on leader effectiveness within certain contexts, rather than the context being the determinant of leadership. Her main argument is that "the practice of leadership is a necessarily situated occurrence" (p. 122). Understanding leadership means that researchers need to observe, listen to, and be part of the situated environment within which leadership occurs. Her study was conducted within the road transport and construction sector and focussed on safety management, and she acknowledges that one of the limitations of adopting an ethnomethodologically-informed approach is the lack of transferability to other settings prevalent in more positivistic research. This, however, is her key point that in order to understand leadership we need to have the many contexts within which sport management takes place tell their own story. We cannot assume that what we learn in one context will apply in another and that leadership is socially constructed by the people in those settings.

The importance of history and context has been emphasised by Osborn et al. (2002) who "argue that leadership is embedded in the context. It is socially constructed in and from a context where patterns over time must be considered and where history matters" (p. 798). Steen-Johnsen and Hanstad (2008) suggested that one of the key reasons for organisational change not taking place in the Norwegian Olympic and Paralympic Committee and Confederation of Sports was the historically fragmented organisational culture. The authors conclude that in order to affect change, leadership within voluntary organisations must include political skills, as well as visionary and integrative skills, because organisational change operates within the context of the historical and institutional set-up of the organisation.

Social construction

The social constructionist perspective is focused on the idea that leadership emerges from the constructions and interactions of people in organisations. Stakeholders within organisations are involved in a social process in which shared meanings are developed to understand the roles of leaders and followers (Ospina & Schall, 2001). This perspective "emphasizes followers and their contexts for defining leadership itself and for understanding its significance" (Meindl, 1995, p. 330). The follower-centric approach highlights the assumption that many individuals are involved in the construction of leadership. It allows a focus on the experience and the informal patterns of leadership that occur within organisations, rather than simply examining what a leader does (Bresnen, 1995; Yukl, 2006). Similar to Ladkin's (2010) work, emphasising stakeholder perceptions highlights that leadership has multiple frames of reference and meanings and that there are different paths to understanding leadership and how it evolves within diverse organisations (Schneider, 2002).

Concept Check
Social construction
Social construction arises from the interactions of people within different settings, and takes account of the context within which they are situated.

Leadership and its effectiveness are generally dependent upon the context (Alvesson & Sveningsson, 2003; Grint, 2005; Osborn et al., 2002). Changing the context changes leadership and the type of leadership patterns considered effective (Osborn et al., 2002). Socially constructed leadership distinguishes itself from contingency theories of leadership, because contingent leadership assumes that good leadership is based upon the correct analysis of a situation (Grint, 2005). It is context dependent and highlights how individual organisational stakeholders' perspectives of the context will influence understandings of the phenomenon. Grint (2005) argues that "leadership involves the social construction of the context that both legitimates a particular form of action and constitutes the world in the process" (p. 1471). How leadership is situated within a specific context acknowledges the interlinking nature of leadership with a situation, rather than leadership being independent of the environment. Social constructivism therefore assumes that language is the vehicle to construct reality and is a dynamic and collective phenomenon. Hence organisations and their stakeholders are co-creators and owners of what counts as leadership, an aspect often ignored in previous research.

Stakeholder theory

The use of stakeholder theory in organisational studies is not new (Laplume, Sonpar, & Litz, 2008); however, its impact on the leadership literature has been limited. Bass and Steidelmeier (1999) suggested that leadership studies could benefit from being placed in the context of contemporary stakeholder theory, due to the complexity and diversity of organisations.

Concept Check

Stakeholder theory

Stakeholder theory suggests that an organisation should recognise the interests of a wide range of constituents who have a stake in the organisation.

Stakeholder theory posits that an organisation is composed of various internal and external constituencies each possessing a stake in the organisation, while maintaining their own values, beliefs, interests, and resources (Buchholz & Rosenthal, 2005). This is particularly true in sport organisations considering the complexity and diversity of stakeholders such as administrators, staff members, coaches, athletes and sponsors (Parent, 2008).Furthermore, similar to Ladkin (2010) research focused on the various stakeholders' perceptions of leader or manager effectiveness have found that different stakeholder groups will have different perceptions based largely on their perspective and the organisational context (Fraser & Zarkada-Fraser, 2003).However, as Wolfe and Putler (2002) indicated stakeholder groups themselves are not necessarily homogeneous in their perception of issues, as was highlighted in the case of an ICA. In addition, Laplume et al. (2008) indicated that understanding stakeholder perspectives is important in building long-term organisational sustainability, because of the link provided to the community, which is particularly important for local clubs and regional sports organisations, where much funding comes from the local community. The example provided earlier of Hockey New Zealand emphasises the importance of involving as many stakeholders as possible in order to provide this long term organisational sustainability.

Summary

As I finalise this chapter the Rugby World Cup 2011 is only a few weeks away. There is no doubt that the team has a highly respected leader on the field in Richie McCaw and time will tell whether leadership in the board room and by the CEO will translate into success on the field for New Zealand. Similarly, the London Olympic Games are less than a year away and both Australian and New Zealand athletes will seek to bring home as many medals as possible – so how can sports organisations provide the leadership for their athletes have the best chance of doing so? Well respected Harvard professor Rosabeth Kanter (2004), in her book 'Confidence' argues that in order to be successful on the field or court, an organisation needs to cultivate a culture of confidence, which includes accountability, collaboration and initiative

Having studied winning and losing sports teams across the world she concluded that "the ability to stay calm, learn, adapt and keep on going – separates the winners from losers" (Kanter, 2011, p. 34).

Activity

Having now read this chapter, reconsider the first activity. Describe the attributes that you think are important in a leader and name three leaders who are important to you. Have you changed your mind? If so why and if not why not?

Review questions

- What does it mean to be a leader?
- Who do you consider to be a leader in sport? On the field, in the board room, as the CEO?
- Do different situations require different types of leadership?
- What are the different ways in which leadership has been researched?
- What is the difference between individual and organisational leadership?

References

Alvesson, M., & Deetz, S. (2000). *Doing critical management research*. Thousand Oaks, CA: Sage Publications.

Alvesson, M., & Sveningsson, S. (2003). The great disappearing act: Difficulties in doing "leadership". *The Leadership Quarterly, 14*, 359–381.

Amis, J., Slack, T., & Hinings, C. R. (2004). The role of interests, power and capacity in strategic change. *Journal of Sport Management, 18*, 158–198.

Bass, B. M. (1985). *Leadership and performance beyond expectations*. New York, NY: Free Press.

Bass, B. M., & Steidlmeier, P. (1999). Ethics, character, and authentic transformational leadership behaviour. *The Leadership Quarterly, 10*, 181–217.

Bennis, W. G., & Nanus, B. (1985). *Leaders: The strategies of taking charge*. New York: Harper & Row.

Birchfield, R. (2010, August). Wanted: Great NZ leaders. *New Zealand Management: The Leaders' Magazine*, 30–33.

Birchfield, R. (2011, July). Leadership's looming crisis. *New Zealand Management: The Leaders' Magazine*, 16–21.

Bligh, M. C., & Schyns, B. (2007). Leading question: The romance lives on: Contemporary issues surrounding the romance of leadership. *Leadership, 3*, 343–360.

Branch, D. (1990). Athletic director leader behavior as a predictor of intercollegiate athletic organizational effectiveness. *Journal of Sport Management, 2*, 161–173.

Bresnen, M. J. (1995). All things to all people? Perceptions, attributions, and constructions of leadership. *The Leadership Quarterly, 6*, 495–513.

Brewis, J. (2004). Refusing to be 'me'. In R. Thomas, A. Mills, & J. Helms-Mills (Eds.). *Identity politics at work: Resisting gender, gendering resistance* (pp. 23–39). Abingdon, UK: Routledge.

Brown, M. E., & Trevino, L.K. (2006). Ethical leadership: A review and future directions. *The Leadership Quarterly, 17*, 595–616.

Bryman, A. (1992). *Charisma and leadership in organizations*. London: Sage Publications.

Buchholz, R. A., & Rosenthal, S. B. (2005). Toward a contemporary conceptual framework for stakeholder theory. *Journal of Business Ethics, 58*, 137–148.

Burns, J. M. (1978). *Leadership*. New York: Harper Row.

Daft, R.L., & Pirola-Merlo, A. (2009). *The leadership experience*. Asia Pacific Edition. Melbourne, Australia: Cengage Learning.

Doherty, A. J. (1997). The effect of leader characteristics on the perceived transformational/transactional leadership and impact of interuniversity athletic administrators. *Journal of Sport Management, 11*, 275–285.

Doherty, A. J., & Danylchuk, K. E. (1996). Transformational and transactional leadership in interuniversity athletics management. *Journal of Sport Management, 10*, 292–309.

Eden, S. (2009). Kerry Clark Chief Executive Bowls New Zealand - Winner leadership excellence award. Retrieved 15 July 2011, from http://www.sparc.org.nz/en-nz/About-SPARC/Media/Media-Releases/Kerry-Clark-Chief-Executive-Bowls-New-Zealand—Winner-Leadership-Excellence-Award-/

Edwards, A. (1999). Reflective practice in sport management. *Sport Management Review, 2*, 67–81.

Elliott, C., & Stead, V. (2008). Learning from leading women's experience: Towards a sociological understanding. *Leadership, 4*(2), 159–180.

Ferkins, L., Shilbury, D., & McDonald, G. (2005). The role of the board in building strategic capability: Towards an integrated model of sport governance. *Sport Management Review, 8*, 195–226.

Fielder, F. (1967). *A theory of leadership effectiveness.* New York, NY: McGraw Hill.

Ford, J., & Lawler, J. (2007). Blending existentialist and constructivist approaches in leadership studies: An exploratory account. *Leadership & Organization Development Journal, 28*, 409–425.

Fraser, C., & Zarkada-Fraser, A. (2003). Investigating the effectiveness of managers through an analysis of stakeholder perceptions. *Journal of Management Development, 22*, 762–783.

Garger, J. (2008). Developing authentic leadership in organizations: Some insights and observations. *Development and Learning in Organizations, 22*, 14–16.

Gautier, A. (2011, July). The heart of leadership: Gut feel and inspiration. *New Zealand Management: The Leaders' Magazine*, 22–27.

Gilstrap, D. L. (2007). Phenomenological reduction and emergent design: Complementary methods for leadership narrative interpretation and metanarrative development. *International Journal of Qualitative Methods, 6*(1), 95–113.

Grint, K. (2005). *Leadership: Limits and possibilities.* New York: Palgrave Macmillan.

Hockey New Zealand. (2010). *Annual report 2010.* Retrieved from (http://www.hockeynz.co.nz/documents/Annual%20Report/HNZ%20 2010%20AR_low%20res%20FINAL%20 %281%29.pdf).

Hoye, R. (2004). Leader-member exchanges and board performance of voluntary sport organizations. *Nonprofit Management and Leadership, 15*, 55–70.

Hoye, R. (2007). Leadership within Australian voluntary sport organization boards. *Nonprofit Management & Leadership, 16*, 297–313.

Hoye, R., & Cuskelly, G. (2003). Board power and performance in voluntary sport organisations. *European Sport Management Quarterly, 3*, 103–119.

Inglis, S. (1997). Shared leadership in the governance of amateur sport: Perceptions of executive directors and board members. *Avante, 3*, 14–33.

Iszatt-White, M. (2011). Methodological crises and contextual solutions: An ethnomethodologically informed approach to understanding leadership. *Leadership, 7*(2), 119–135.

Jackson, B., & Parry, K. (2008). *A very short, fairly interesting and reasonably cheap book about studying leadership.* London: SAGE.

Kanter, R. (2004). *Confidence: How winning streaks and losing streaks begin and end.* New York: Crown Business.

Kanter, R. (2011). Cultivate a culture of confidence. *Harvard Business Review, 89*(4), 34.

Kellett, P. (1999). Organisational leadership: Lessons from professional coaches. *Sport Management Review, 2*, 150–171.

Kent, A., & Chelladurai, P. (2001). Perceived transformational leadership, organizational commitment, and citizenship behavior: A case study in intercollegiate athletics. *Journal of Sport Management, 15*, 135–159.

Ladkin, D. (2010). *Rethinking leadership: A new look at old leadership questions.* Cheltenham, UK: Edward Elgar.

Laplume, A.O., Sonpar, K., & Litz, R. A. (2008). Stakeholder theory: Reviewing a theory that moves us. *Journal of Management, 34*(6), 1152–1189.

Meindl, J. R. (1995). The romance of leadership as a follower-centric theory: A social constructionist approach. *The Leadership Quarterly, 6*, 329–341.

Messner, M. A., & Bozada-Deas, S. (2009). Separating the men from the moms: The making of adult gender segregation in youth sports. *Gender & Society, 23*(1), 49–71.

Meyerson, D. E. (2008). *Rocking the boat: How to effect change without making trouble.* Boston, MA: Harvard Business Press.

Osborn, R. N., Hunt, J. G., & Jauch, L. R. (2002). Toward a contextual theory of leadership. *The Leadership Quarterly, 13*, 797–837.

Ospina, S., & Schall, E. (2001). Leadership (re) constructed: How lens matters. Paper presented at the Association for Public Policy Analysis and Management Research Conference, Washington, DC.

Palmer, F. R., & Masters, T. M. (2010). Māori feminism and sport leadership: Exploring Māori women's experiences. *Sport Management Review, 13*, 331–344.

Parent, M. M. (2008). Evolution and issue patterns for major-sport-event organizing committees and stakeholders. *Journal of Sport Management, 22*(2), 135–164.

Parent, M. M., & Seguin, B. (2007). Factors that led to the drowning of a world championship organizing committee: A stakeholder approach. *European Sport Management Quarterly, 7*(2), 187–212.

Porter, L. W., & McLaughlin, G. B. (2006). Leadership and the organizational context: Like the weather? *The Leadership Quarterly, 17*, 559–576.

Pye, A. (2005). Leadership and organizing: Sensemaking in action. *Leadership, 1*(1), 31–49.

Quarterman, J. (1998). An assessment of the perception of management and leadership skills by intercollegiate athletics conference commissioners. *Journal of Sport Management, 12*, 146–164.

Raelin, J. (2011). From leadership-as-practice to leaderful practice. *Leadership, 7*(2), 195–211.

Ryska T. A. (2002). Leadership styles and occupational stress among college athletic directors: The moderating effect of program goals. *The Journal of Psychology, 136*(2), 195–213.

Schneider, M. (2002). A stakeholder model of organizational leadership. *Organizational Science, 13*, 209–220.

Scott, D. K. (1999). A multiframe perspective of leadership and organizational climate in intercollegiate athletics. *Journal of Sport Management, 13*, 298–316.

Sherry, E., & Shilbury, D. (2009). Board directors and conflict of interest: A study of a sport league. *European Sport Management Quarterly, 9*, 47–62.

Sinclair, A. (2007). *Leadership for the disillusioned: Moving beyond myths and heroes to leading that liberates.* Crows Nest, NSW: Allen & Unwin.

Sinclair, A. (2010). Placing self: How might we place ourselves in leadership studies differently? *Leadership, 6*(4), 447–460.

Smart, D. L., & Wolfe, R. (2003). The contribution of leadership and human resources to organizational success: An empirical assessment of performance in major league baseball. *European Sport Management Quarterly, 3*, 165–188.

Snyder, C. (1990). The effects of leader behavior and organization climate on intercollegiate coaches' job satisfaction. *Journal of Sport Management, 4*, 59–70.

Soucie, D. (1994). Effective managerial leadership in sport organizations. *Journal of Sport Management, 8*, 1–13.

Steen-Johnson, K., & Hanstad, D. V. (2008). Change and power in complex democratic organizations: The case of Norwegian elite sports. *European Sport Management Quarterly, 8*, 123–143.

Stogdill, R.M. (1974). *Handbook of leadership: A survey of theory and research.* New York, NY: Free Press.

Wallace, J. (2011). *Winners announced at 2011 New Zealand Sport and Recreation Awards.* Retrieved 15 July, 2011, from http://www.sparc.org.nz/About-SPARC/Media/2011-Media-Releases/Winners-announced-at-2011-New-Zealand-Sport-and-Recreation-Awards/

Weese, W. J. (1995). Leadership and organization culture: An investigation of Big Ten and MidAmerican Conference campus recreation administrators. *Journal of Sport Management, 9*, 119–134.

Winter, C. (2011). Best in the boardroom. *Leadership, 4*, 34–35.

Wolfe, R. A., & Putler, D. S. (2002). How tight are the ties that bind stakeholder groups? *Organization Science, 13*(1), 64–80.

Yukl, G. (2006). *Leadership in Organizations* (6th ed.). Upper Saddle River, NJ: Pearson Prentice Hall.

Chapter 9

Change Management
Margot Edwards

OBJECTIVES

After completing this chapter, you should be able to:

- understand the interaction of the force of external environmental change with internal organisational change to create organisational change;
- have an appreciation of the human factors in organisational change, forces underlying resistance to change and methods of overcoming this resistance;
- appreciate some of the different types of change which can take place in organisations, and the difference between reactive and proactive change;
- understand key principles of organisation development;
- apply the principles learned to understanding the case studies outlined in the chapter and to other sport organisations with which they are familiar.

Key terms

In this chapter, readers will become familiar with the following concepts and terms:
- organisational change
- alignment
- organisational restructuring
- strategic change
- external forces for change
- internal forces for change
- proactive action
- change agent
- culture change
- reactive action
- resistance to change
- coercion
- participation
- manipulation
- co-optation
- technological change

- negotiation
- facilitation
- education
- organisational development

Introduction

This chapter considers why and how organisations change. It deals particularly with management-induced change aimed at improving the organisation and at external and internal forces which promote change in organisations. It considers the 'people' issues in organisational change and ways of gaining support for change. It details types and methods of organisational change, and shows how managers can proactively avoid problems by ensuring organisational change. It outlines the practice of 'organisational development', which provides a set of principles and methods for undertaking organisational change.

CASE STUDY: CHANGING THE VOLUNTEER CULTURE

Sport management researchers (see, for example, Cuskelly, 2004) have reported a significant drop in the number of sport volunteers since the mid-1990s. This drop is potentially disastrous for sport and, as a matter of some urgency, sport governors have devised a range of change strategies to reinvigorate the volunteer culture. One strategic development 'Game Plan 2012', published by the New South Wales Department of Sport and Recreation (NSW DSR), aims to create a 'culture of inclusion' and make sport volunteers feel valued (NSW DSR, n.d., p. 10). The strategic plan also aims to provide better incentives for volunteers in recognition of their contribution to the community.

Brendan Lynch, Principal of exSport, an organisation that specialises in strategic planning, organisational development, change management and workforce planning, highlights one structural aspect related to the NSW DSR strategy that is very applicable to small sports clubs. He suggests that each volunteer role is split into small bite sized pieces, each with a very specific job description. For example, a parent might be assigned to one small, specific task each week, such as writing the club newsletter or running a BBQ. The key consideration is that everyone knows what they are signing up for. They know exactly where to be and for how long they are required. This enables them to plan ahead and trust that the job will not escalate beyond their capabilities or time resources.

GROUP DISCUSSION

Read the volunteer strategy in 'Game Plan 2012' (NSW DSR, n.d., p. 7). The list of strategies and action steps provided by the NSW DSR provide an excellent array of ideas. Importantly, they set a specific target, an increase of one-percent in volunteer numbers, against which they can measure their success. In a group, discuss the following questions:

- How can indigenous peoples' needs and perspectives be incorporated into such change strategies?
- What cultural factors might impact on decisions to volunteer in sport?
- Using experiential knowledge of your own sports, how important are financial reward systems compared to other systems, such as certificates and medals?

Organisational change

Change in organisations is functional. Organisations which do not change cannot adapt to the changes around them and die. It is a principle of natural selection similar to that governing the survival of species (Hannon & Freeman, 1977). The necessity of change may seem self-evident, but it is easy for managers to ignore it, concentrating on the administration of current activities. As change takes place at an ever-increasing rate, "as the world becomes more connected and interdependent, information and communication is made to be instantaneous and omnipresent", organisations need to become more adaptable, and to anticipate change (Lee, 2011, p. 72). Consider the changes in recent years in the wider context affecting sport organisations, which include:

- the professionalisation of sport;
- the reconceptualisation of élite sport as an entertainment whose primary beneficiary is the spectator, rather than a form of physical exercise where the primary beneficiary is the athlete;
- the commercialisation of sport, including the developing ability of television to show sport instantaneously, anywhere in the world;
- the development of sport sponsorship at all levels;
- the growing competition from other sports that each sporting code faces for both participants and audience;
- new sports (e.g., touch rugby, rough skiing and new forms of motor sport) and alternative leisure activities including television, shopping malls, casinos and overseas travel;
- changing public knowledge and attitudes concerning the health-related benefits of fitness;
- technological developments in computing and information transmission and rapid mass transportation.

Much of this may seem more relevant to commercial sport organisations than not-for-profit organisations or small local neighbourhood sports clubs and teams which have functioned well enough for a long time by techniques of maintaining and developing their facilities and looking after their members. All organisations, large and small, must adapt to external changes. A tennis club that fails to upgrade its courts or offer a bar and lounge to members risks losing those members to better resourced or more proactive clubs, or even to other sports or recreational opportunities. Change in organisations does not occur in isolation. Organisations consist of integrated parts. Changing one part of an organisation (such as structure) tends to cause 'ripple' effects in which other aspects also change (such as culture).

External and internal forces of change

The pressures on organisations to change come both from the environment and from within the organisation, including members pushing for change. In the NSW DSR case, change was necessary in order to halt the decline of volunteers. In this case, the state organisation may have responded to the concerns of grass roots organisations because they lacked the necessary resources or competencies to drive their own changes (Francis, Bessant, & Hobday, 2003).

External pressures for change are often beyond the organisation's control. For example, consider the external forces affecting local cricket club:

- the establishment of an alternative local cricket club;
- economic cycles affecting how much money people have to spend on club membership;

- the fortunes and profile of the current national cricket teams;
- legislative changes affecting the club's liquor license and gaming machines;
- new costs such as rates and electricity charges;
- policy changes by the sport's governing body;
- the emphasis given to cricket in neighbouring schools;
- demographic changes in the neighbourhood population.

The list could go on indefinitely. These variables can create opportunities for the club to prosper, or threats to its existence. The club needs to monitor such trends and consider how it can adapt. Ignoring external changes is unwise, since they commonly attract attention in due course through some crisis threatening the organisation's wellbeing. In a sport organisation the crisis might be the departure of some of the best players, relegation to an inferior league, shrinking attendances, declining membership, or a refusal by the bank to extend the overdraft.

Dealing with change depends on the internal resources of the organisation to make an appropriate response. Again, there are many such forces:

- the goals of the club and of those within it and their congruence with the external changes.
- the energy or inertia of club members – how set are they in their ways? Do they want change?
- the organisation's structures – do its constitution and formal organisation encourage rapid change or tend to slow things down and maintain the 'status quo'?
- the physical resources available – how many members are there? How willing are they to work for change? What are their skills?
- the 'habits' of change. Is the club used to change? Is the culture innovative?
- the availability of 'change agents' – people with special skills in facilitating change. Are the club's leaders natural change agents? If not, can change agents be acquired, possibly temporarily, from elsewhere?

Change tends to be effective only when both sets of pre-conditions – both external and internal – are met. An organisation may change its internal dynamics – its goals, structure, resources and culture – so that it will respond productively to change pressures.

Paying attention to change

Good organisations always pay attention to both the external environment and their own internal dynamics. They strive to remain relevant to their stakeholders and respond to 'new realities', described by Beerel (2009, p. 1) as "forces that herald change". In doing so, they gather information about key external changes taking place or likely to take place in future: "What's going on out there? How are we set up in here?" should be constant questions.

One problem is that many people in sport organisations are very focused on the sport itself. They are less interested in the wider context of social-cultural, market, legislative and other changes. They are, as it were, production-oriented – interested in sport and sports performance as products – rather than market-oriented – interested in the market for the sport and the way that market is changing. Every organisation needs to involve itself in environmental scanning – reviewing community changes, threats and opportunities on an ongoing basis, paying attention to the media, watching out for dangerous competition, etc.

But effective change also depends on internal review of what is going on inside: for example, club membership levels, revenue, costs, attendance, participation in competitions, members' compliments and complaints. In most cases a few key parameters between them provide a good guide to the organisation's sporting, financial and psychological health, and consequently the possible need for change.

One phenomenon, which applies particularly well to sport organisations, is the so-called 'boiled frog' syndrome. If you put a frog in a beaker of boiling water it will immediately save its own life by leaping out. However, if you put the frog in a beaker of cold water and then gradually heat it to boiling, the frog will stay where it is until it dies: it does not have the sensitivity to notice gradual changes. It is similar in organisations: an ongoing, gradual decline in membership, a rise in complaints, a reduction in bar-takings, or a drop-off in performance by teams is often unnoticed until there is a crisis.

Concept Check

Alignment

The act of alignment refers to the way the organisation attempts to match the internal and external challenges and opportunities. The process of alignment occurs when the activities associated with change are aligned so that they can be carried out simultaneously. As Lee (2011, p. 72) explains, "the culture, strategy and social arrangements in an organisation require continuous alignment with forces of change and variation". This concept is similar to the oft quoted saying having your 'ducks in a row'.

Change is about people

In any organisation, sport or non-sport, change is about people (Kotter & Cohen, 2002). It is *people* who decide that change is needed, lead change, and implement change, and ensure that plans to change are actually carried out. It is people who are affected, positively or negatively, by change. People may support change, and work to make it successful. Alternatively, they may oppose change by withholding cooperation from change programmes, by resisting change, and sometimes by leaving the organisation.

In recent years, many people have experienced substantial, life-affecting changes in the organisations in which they work. Deregulation has led to many companies restructuring, rationalising and downsizing. This can mean drastic changes in the job people do, and in some cases they are made redundant. Such changes can cause distress, alienation, trauma, and plummeting organisational morale. But overall, in time, most New Zealanders have adapted well to change. For example, many have quickly learned new jobs, new occupations, and new skills (Arthur, Inkson, & Pringle, 1999).

This does not mean that the change methods which have been applied to New Zealand's commercial companies and public services will work in a sport organisation; there is a vital difference. Companies have employees whose commitment is based on an 'effort-for-money' contract and who represent a major cost to the organisation. The same applies to a few 'commercial' sport organisations, such as the Paramatta Eels, but most sport organisations have members rather than employees and their commitment is voluntary. Members who don't want change may go elsewhere.

While it is advantageous in most organisations to consult with members and perhaps even involve them in determining change, in voluntary organisations such as sports clubs it is essential.

Change agents

Organisational change nearly always involves 'change agents'. A change agent is not necessarily someone who changes things directly but rather someone who assists and facilitates change. Frequently the top manager of the organisation – for example, the CEO of a business or the chair of a sport organisation committee – can use his or her position and respect or 'mana' to promote change. Board members are also important change agents as they influence strategic decision making. In addition, most organisations probably have 'hidden' change agents, people who have good ideas about the direction and process of change, who have not previously been asked to contribute.

Another type of change agent is the external one. Internal people may be 'too close to the action', and not able easily to visualise the organisation in any mode other than the one it is in. An external change agent can bring in specialist knowledge of change processes, or act as 'honest broker' or 'facilitator' to taskforces and meetings. External organisations such as Regional Sports Trusts offer services as change agents to assist sport organisations through processes of change.

CASE STUDY: CHANGE-MAKER BRENDAN LYNCH

Brendan, a keen rugby player and rower, studied physical education at Sydney University but as he didn't wanted to teach, and because of the lack of sport management courses available at that time, he decided to work in the building industry. At this stage, his main involvement in sports was as a volunteer. In the early 1990s, he left the building industry and accepted a position at the Australian Catholic University (ACU) located in Canberra, the city that hosted the 1996 Australian University Games. As ACU were co-hosts of this event, Brendan accepted responsibility for the volunteer programme. A key aspect of his role was to develop a model that encouraged students to take on volunteer roles that were very closely related to their field of study and course work, whether it was media, sport management or medical studies. This model was highly successful and as a result Brendan was eventually appointed to the Sydney Olympic Games Organising Committee (SOCOG) for the Sydney Olympics in 2000, where he accepted the challenge of attracting more than 50,000 volunteers. He estimated that about half of the volunteers would need specialist skills and developed a programme to recruit from 22 Australian universities, as well as other specialist organisations.

Brendan recalled the difficulties associated with setting up the volunteer programme:

> In terms of Sydney, we didn't get a lot of great information from the previous games so we had to plan, re-plan and keep doing it until we got it right. Since 2000, the International Olympic Committee (IOC) has recognised the importance of prior knowledge and has formed the Olympic Games Knowledge Service to make it easier for organisations who are bidding for, or running, Olympic Games and this makes it so much easier in terms of planning because they are not actually starting from zero each time.

Brendan has an in-depth knowledge of sport, key sporting issues and how sport actually works, built up over any years as a participant and volunteer. However, he considers that the skills he picked up

(Continued)

in the building industry, especially the ability to plan, have been crucial for his role as change maker. Brendan also highlights the importance of communication and people skills:

> When you go into an organisation you have to do a lot of listening. I like to work very closely with the chief executive officer, to get a really strong relationship with that person, to make sure that we are both on the same wavelength, that we are developing a plan together. And while we are obviously working with the board and the directors in setting the strategy, the CEO is the one who is going to be responsible for driving a plan and implementing change in the organisation. So getting to know that person really well is very important.

Brendan believes it is very important to work closely with organisations through the entire change process. This is especially necessary in smaller sports organisations because they are often run by one or two key people who simply get overloaded with day-to-day operational matters and find it difficult to engage with strategic issues. Brendan argues that the implementation phase is a key responsibility of the change maker's role.

> In most of our sports organisations, the CEO is a very lonely job. They often don't have a second in command to help with the operational stuff. If big changes need to be made, I work with them to help them implement the change plan.

Brendan highlights the connection between change management and sport business development. His focus, for example, in terms of strategic planning, is on 'having good governance models, sound financial management and solid communications strategies in place'. As a change agent, Brendan emphasises the catch phrase 'structure follows strategy'.

> We get the strategic plan right before we look at the organisational structure, which may need to be redesigned to support the strategy. Following that, we look at the people. And if there are existing people, we see how they might fit into the existing structure, if they don't quite fit we ask how we can we up-skill them, develop them or help them change. However, in some cases we need to consider the adage 'If you can't change the people then change the people'.

Brendan also notes the importance of open and honest consultation prior to changes being decided. The staff and key stakeholders must be involved in every stage of the development of the strategic plan. If you involve the staff in the planning and development of changes, they will have a greater understanding of the need for the changes and it will make the implementation process easier.

Managing change then, in sporting organisations or any organisation, is about planning, communication and relationships. It's about having a vision and enacting that vision with the support and participation of all involved with the organisation.

Resistance to change

A common phenomenon where change is proposed is individual 'resistance to change'. People resist change for at least three reasons (Kotter & Schlesinger, 1979):

- *Uncertainty*: Change substitutes the unknown for the known. There may be new routines, new methods, new skills. Familiar patterns disappear, yet we cannot be sure what they will be replaced by. Extra effort may be required. The familiar may not be perfect, but we know what it is.
- *Loss*: We invest in organisations as they are. We build security, status, skills, relationships and achievement based on current systems. If the system changes, we may lose our investments. On the whole, the longer we have been in the organisation, the greater the potential loss.

- *Concern for the Organisation*: We may genuinely believe that change is not in the best interests of the organisation.

Similarly, Francis et al. (2003) describe 'pre-action barriers' that can foster resistance. They describe these as avoidance, indecision, poverty, insularity and inability. In effect it is important to clearly articulate and make sense of perceptions of change within the organisation.

Resistance to change tends to subvert change, slow it down, and reduce commitment to change. Those supporting change can use various techniques to overcome resistance (Kotter & Schlesinger, 1979). These techniques involve varying degrees of involvement of people in determining and implementing the change process. Often the techniques are used in combination. They are as follows:

- *Coercion*: This means using threats to impose one's will. For example, 'anyone who opposes this plan will be considered as a disruptive influence in the club and may have their membership terminated'. Coercion is quick and simple, but often arouses anger and even greater resistance. In a voluntary organisation which depends on members' goodwill for its survival, coercion is usually inappropriate.
- *Manipulation and Co-optation*: Manipulation involves covert influence; for example, altering the facts to make change seem attractive or making promises which can't be kept. Co-optation is 'buying off', or securing the compliance of the leaders of the forces of resistance. For example, 'if you keep your opposition to yourself, we guarantee you a seat on the committee after the change is made'. Again, these tactics can lead to short-term success, but like coercion they may be morally unacceptable and may cause long-term problems when people become aware that they have been manipulated.
- *Negotiation and Agreement*: This involves offering benefits to resistors in return for their compliance. For example, 'if you agree to the new membership drive, then we will ensure special privileges for those who have been members for more than ten years'. Major resistance can often be avoided in this way, but at the cost of compromising the changes that need to be made. It also encourages others to seek additional benefits.
- *Facilitation and Support*: Here resistance is reduced by offering support in the form of training, assistance or counselling. For example, 'to help you adjust to the change, members of the committee will be happy to meet people on a one-to-one basis to explain the background and help them to adjust'. This approach often helps people to adjust to change, but is very time-consuming and can backfire if undertaken poorly.
- *Participation and Involvement*: In this method, people are involved in the decision to change and its implementation. For example, 'any change will occur after a series of discussions open to all members, and will be voted on'. Involvement increases the resources available by enabling members to add their knowledge and skills to the process. It also tends to increase commitment to the decision. On the other hand, people may not have appropriate expertise and may arrive at a poor decision. Involvement tends to complicate matters and is time-consuming. The change desired by the initiators may be rejected by the participants.
- *Education and Communication*: This means maximising communication about the change so that people can better understand it. For example, 'every member is being sent a comprehensive plan explaining what is intended, why the change is needed and how it will benefit the organisation'. Proposals for change often suffer because of misunderstanding and rumour. Information gives people a more secure basis for committing to change. However, this method depends on the credibility of the communicators and may not work if there is distrust. Again, it can be time-consuming and expensive.

Reactive v. proactive action

An organisation can be 'reactive' or 'proactive' about change. A reactive organisation 'reacts' to external events by changing in response to them. Often reactive changes take place hurriedly in an atmosphere of crisis. A 'proactive' organisation anticipates external change, plans for it and implements changes ahead of time. Often it has additional prior consultation with those likely to be affected. Proactive change is often better thought through, smoother and more acceptable to those involved, although there is always the danger that by acting ahead of time, the organisation will anticipate events wrongly.

While no organisation can anticipate every eventuality, and while all organisations should be able to respond appropriately to short-term events, the ability to be proactive to anticipate change is also very important and is lacking in many sport organisations.

Types of change

Organisations consist of sets of interdependent overlapping components intended to support each other in the pursuit of the organisation's objectives. Major overlapping systems are:
- the financial component – the cash assets, investments, financial records, plans and expertise of the organisation;
- the technological component – physical assets, buildings, land, facilities, equipment, and information technology of the organisation;
- the structural component – the constitution, organisation structure, rules and regulations determining the formal functioning of the organisation;
- the cultural component – the traditions, attitudes, values, norms, rituals and ways of thinking of the people currently in the organisation;
- the human component – the people in the organisation – managers or committee members and rank-and-file members, and the pattern of relationships between them.

Any component can be changed. For example, financial assets can be built up through cost-cutting or revenue-generation, or different or controlled investments. Under 'structure', new organisation forms can be developed, such as larger or smaller committees, different job descriptions, changed rules and regulations. Determining desirable changes in these areas often needs technical expertise to ensure the decisions are the correct ones.

Because of the centrality of people, much attention needs to be devoted to the 'people' and 'culture' components. A common view is that 'changing the culture' is the key to changing the whole organisation. Once people have new values and expectations, it is argued, they will more quickly make the necessary changes. Unfortunately, as Brendan Lynch's experience suggests, this is not always the case because cultures develop over long periods, become deeply ingrained in organisations, and are not necessarily easy to change. Considerable effort may have to go into determining the current values of members and encouraging re-examination and change.

Although the human element will always be very important to sport organisations, more recently, technological advances such as email and web-based resources have made it possible for sport managers to re-think methods. Many organisations have made financial commitments to adopt software packages aimed at simplifying time consuming tasks, such as, athlete registrations, subscription payments and resource provision. The following case illustrates how one sport club has adopted social media as a way of improving communication.

CASE STUDY: NEW SOLUTIONS FOR AGE-OLD PROBLEMS

Laurie Hartley has been involved in sport management and coaching since graduating from the School of Physical Education at the University of Otago in 1961. He has had extensive involvement in school, club and provincial rugby. His greatest headaches when managing First XV teams at secondary schools were generally around communication issues, for example, organising billets, dealing with last minute cancellations, tracking uniforms and dealing with the local rugby union.

Recently, as president of his local rugby club, he focuses on making communication changes in order to attract more school leaver players and also to increase the number of spectators at club games.

This year, at the suggestion of a sport management practicum intern, Laurie has approved the creation of a club Facebook page in order to enhance the club's relationship with members.

Since the creation of the Facebook page, attendances at the under 85kg games have trebled, largely because Facebook has allowed the club to connect with the local school's old boys population. An unexpected bonus has been an increase in the numbers of young men trialling for club teams. The changes planned for next season are on-line season tickets, promoting key events through Twitter and improving on-line subscription payment options. Future possibilities include sponsoring an online 'e-sport' rugby competition and hosting the prize giving at the club, a strategy designed to 'get new boys in the door. (For a discussion on change and e-sport see Jonasson & Thiborg, 2010).

High-tech innovations, for example, the Internet, e-mail, computers and advanced management information systems, have increased the rate of change in sports organisations (Lussier & Kimball, 2009). Such changes often impact on strategy and structure and must be considered fully before implementation, but reported success stories, for example, the University of Utah Football team (Steinbach, 2010) and the Cincinnati Flying Pig Marathon (Schoenstedt & Reau, 2010), suggest many technological ideas are worth serious consideration. A comprehensive list of free websites, utilities and social media apps, relevant to sport team management, community-building, event planning and promotion and fundraising is provided by Hannan (2011).

Table 9-1: Advantages and implications of technological change	
IMMEDIATE ADVANTAGES	WIDER IMPLICATIONS
Provides effective and fast communication.	Implementations costs can be large, for example, new computers may be necessary.
The organisation keeps abreast of recent technological advances.	Staff may be resistant to new procedures and advanced training and on-going support may be necessary.
Staff are up-skilled.	Electronic communication has disadvantages e.g., it is difficult to conduct complex discussions on-line.
Saves costs in printing and advertising.	Stakeholders need to be trained/educated.
Professionally designed web sites are attractive to sponsors.	Highly trained staff may demand more pay or seek new employment opportunities.

Organisational development

'Organisational development' is a phrase used to represent a range of theories and techniques for inducing organisational change. Organisational development focuses on the 'people' and 'culture' components of the organisation. Organisational development methods have been pioneered among large commercial organisations, but the principles may be adapted to smaller organisations such as sports clubs.

French, Bell, and Zawacki (2005, p. 2) define organisational development (OD) as a prescription for a process of planned change in an organisation in which the key prescriptive elements relate to:

- the nature of the effort or programme (it is a long-range, planned, system-wide process);
- the nature of the change activities (they utilise behavioural science interventions of an educational, reflexive, self-examining, learn-to-do-it-yourself nature);
- the targets of the change activities (they are directed toward the human and social processes of organisations, specifically individuals' beliefs, attitudes, and values, the culture and processes of work groups – viewed as basic building blocks of the organisation – and the processes and culture of the total organisation);
- the desired outcomes of the change activities (the goals are *needed changed* in the targets of the interventions that source the organisation to be better able to adapt, cope, solve its problems, and renew itself).

In this definition can be seen a number of desirable principles for the practice of change, including some already referred to in this chapter, such as alignment. The emphasis is on the long term. It is not so much about dealing directly with immediate issues as it is about changing the organisation so that it becomes better able to solve both the immediate problems and the longer-term ones. Thus the emphasis is on both 'problem-solving' (immediate, tangible) and on 'renewal' (to increase the organisation's problem-solving capacity).

In addition, it is clear that the prime focus of OD is on changing the culture of values, attitudes and expectations of organisation members. It is an implicit value of OD that 'participative', 'collaborative' and 'educational' methods of change will be more effective than methods such as coercion, manipulation, and negotiation (see section on 'Resistance to Change'). The implicit suggestion here is that because things get done in organisations through people working together, the team may be a better unit of analysis than the individual. Thus, OD efforts may involve 'taskforces' to accomplish specific objectives and 'team-building' to improve cohesion and synergy in existing teams. The nature of sport means that sport organisations often have a special appreciation of the nature and value of teamwork, making this an especially appropriate emphasis.

The definition also emphasises the importance of collaborative solutions. A criticism of much research, for example, research on organisation change, is that it separates itself from the more mundane business of organisational action, such as attempting to make organisational changes. 'Action research' makes investigation of a problem a key part of finding the solution. For example, members might be surveyed by a questionnaire on their attitudes to a new strategic direction and then take part in an educational or collaborative workshop at which their questionnaire results are fed back and used to increase learning and explore new ideas (see, for example, Frisby, Reid, Millar, & Hoeber, 2005).

CASE STUDY: TWO REFEREES FOR RUGBY?

Controversy during the 2011 Super Rugby competition, has led to a call by senior players for two referees. The controversy arose in the match between the Crusaders and the Reds on May 29th in Brisbane. According to media coverage after the game, the referee missed crucial infringements in the later stages of the game, finally decided in favour of the Reds by 17 to 16. (Watch the video on http://tvnz.co.nz/rugby-news/call-two-referees-in-1-38-video-4201229/video). Following the game, experienced players voiced their support for a change to appoint two referees to each match because they think the increased pace of the game makes it more likely that mistakes will occur. For example, All Black Jimmy Cowan argues that having two referees would be beneficial for both teams 'one to keep an eye on the ruck and one to keep an eye on the defence structure' (TVNZ, 2011, May 31).

DISCUSSION QUESTIONS:
- What effect will this change have on the game?
- How should such a change be implemented?
- What strategies could be used to win over the traditionalists, who are against such a change?
- Can you think of any unintended consequences if the proposal to use two referees was adopted?

Summary

This chapter considers why and how organisations change. It deals particularly with management-induced change aimed at improving the organisation.

Organisational change is caused by external forces such as market pressures and internal forces such as the attitudes of organisation members. Both sets of forces need to exist in order for productive change to take place. Managers must constantly monitor the environment and the internal workings of the organisation to understand the direction of change and the best ways of bringing it about.

Change impacts on people in organisations and requires their support. Often people are resistant to change because of uncertainty, the likelihood of personal loss following change and the possibility of damage to the organisation. Techniques for overcoming resistance to change include a range from coercion and manipulation to communication and involvement. In applying these, short-term efficiency must often be traded against long-term effectiveness.

Change requires internal or external change agents with special responsibility for, and interest in, bringing about change.

The organisation has many components which can be changed. Usually a change in one will cause change in others, so change must be dealt with in an integrated way. The most fundamental forms of organisational change are: cultural change, which relates to people's personal values and attitudes; and strategic change, which relates to the organisation's long-term goals.

The theory and practice of organisational development provide a set of principles and methods for undertaking organisational change.

Review questions

- Consider a sport organisation that you know. Write a list of external factors and internal factors promoting change for the organisation at present and a list of any internal factors that may limit change.
- What are the similarities and differences between commercial companies and voluntary clubs in the ways they and their members handle change?
- Imagine you are on the committee of a sport club. Your committee decides it would be a good idea to amalgamate with a neighbouring club to share resources. The amalgamation will necessitate changing the club's name and selling the present premises. But there are many members who are proud of the history of the club, its name, its facilities and its independence. How would you implement the change?
- Read the article by Hannan (2011) and decide which types of technological advances would work in a sport organisation known to you. What changes would need to be considered before the advantages were realised?
- Is the practice of 'organisational development' relevant to sport clubs? Justify your answer.

Advancing your understanding

Anderson, D., & Ackerman Anderson, L. (2010). *Beyond change management: How to achieve breakthrough results through conscious change leadership* (2nd ed.). San Francisco: Pfeiffer.

Covell, D., Walker, S., Siciliano, J., & Hess, P. (Eds.). (2007). *Managing sport organisations: Responsibility for performance* (2nd ed.). Boston: Elsevier Butterworth-Heinemann.

Cunningham, G. B. (2009). Understanding the diversity-related change process: A field of study. *Journal of Sport Management, 23*, 407–428.

Girginov, V., & Sandanski, I. (2008). Understanding the changing nature of sports organisations in transforming societies. *Sport Management Review, 11*, 21–50.

Goff, B. (2005). *From the ballfield to the boardroom: Management lessons from sports.* Westport, CT: Praeger.

Kikulis, L. M. (2000). Continuity and change in governance and decision making in national sporting organisations: Institutional explanations. *Journal of Sport Management, 14*, 293–320.

Ladkin, D., Wood, M., & Pillay, J. (2010). How do leaders lead change? In D. Ladkin (Ed.), *Rethinking leadership: A new look at old leadership questions* (pp. 127–152). Cheltenham, UK: Edward Elgar.

Maguire, J., & Nakayama, M. (Eds.). (2006). *Japan, sport and society: Tradition and change in a globalised world.* New York: Routledge.

Parent, M., & Slack, T. (Eds.). (2007). *International perspectives on the management of sport.* Boston: Elsevier Butterworth-Heinemann.

Robinson, L. (2004). *Managing public sport and leisure services.* London: Routledge Taylor Francis Group.

Smith, A. C. (2004). Complexity theory and change management in sport organisations. *Emergence: Complexity and Organisaton*, Special Double Issue, 6(1–2), 70–79.

References

Arthur, M. B., Inkson, K., & Pringle, J. K. (1999). *The new careers: Individual action and economic change*. Thousand Oaks, CA: Sage Publications.

Beerel, A. (2009). *Leadership and change management*. London: Sage.

Cuskelly, G. (2004). Volunteer retention in community sport organisations. *European Sport Management Quarterly, 4*, 59–76.

Francis, D., Bessant, J., & Hobday, M. (2003). Managing radical organisational transformation. *Management Decision, 41*(1), 18–31.

French, W. L., Bell, C. H., & Zawacki, R. A. (2005). *Organisation development and transformation: Managing effective change* (6th ed.). New York: McGraw-Hill Irwin.

Frisby, W., Reid, C. J., Millar, S., & Hoeber, L. (2005). Putting 'participatory' into participatory forms of action research. *Journal of Sport Management, 19*(4), 367–386.

Hannon, M. (2011, February). Facebook, friends, freemiums, and fundraising: Killer apps for park agencies and volunteer groups. *Parks and Recreation*, 73–74.

Hannon, M. T., & Freeman, J. (1977). The population ecology of organisations. *American Journal of Sociology, 82*, 929–964.

Jonasson, K., & Thiborg, J. (2010). Electronic sport and its impact on future sport. *Sport in Society, 13*(2), 287–299.

Kotter, J. P., & Cohen, D. S. (2002). *The heart of change: Real life stories of how people change their organisations*. Boston, MA: Harvard Business School Press.

Kotter, J. P., & Schlesinger, L. A. (1979). Choosing strategies for change. *Harvard Business Review*, March–April, 106–114.

Lee, J. (2011). Aligning organisations for positive change: The role of leadership in matching strategy, culture, and social networks to vital organisational challenges. *Advances in Global Leadership, 6*, 71–94.

Lussier, R. N., & Kimball, D. (2009). *Applied sport management skills* (Rev. ed.). Champaign, IL: Human Kinetics.

New South Wales Department of Sport and Recreation. (n.d.). *Game plan 2012: NSW Sport and Recreation Industry Five Year Plan: Shaping our community for a sustainable future*. Retrieved from http://www.sportnsw.com.au

Schoenstedt, L., & Reau, J. (2010). Running a social-media newsroom: A case study of the Cincinnati Flying Pig marathon. *International Journal of Sport Communication, 3*, 377–386.

Steinbach, P. (2010, August). Facebook value: Social media offers ideal ways for ticket departments to build relationships and boost revenue. *Athletic Business*, 58–60.

Television New Zealand. (2011, May 31). One News [Video file]. Retrieved from http://tvnz.co.nz/rugby-news/call-two-referees-in-1-38-video-4201229/video

Chapter 10

Sport Marketing

Ron Garland and Lesley Ferkins

OBJECTIVES

After completing this chapter, you should be able to:

- appreciate that sport marketing follows basic marketing principles but with a change of emphasis to suit particular sporting contexts;
- recount how marketing's role can be applied to sport and sport organisations with special emphasis on service marketing's '7 Ps';
- evaluate the application of marketing strategies and tactics to chosen sport codes;
- identify the management information needs of sport marketers;
- describe the purpose of sport market research and identify different groups of sport fans;
- understand the role marketing planning and marketing management play in staging a sport event.

Key terms

In this chapter, readers will become familiar with the following concepts and terms:
- market research
- marketing plan
- marketing information system
- barriers to conversion
- the '7 Ps' – product, price, promotion, place, physical evidence, people, process
- relationship marketing
- sponsorship
- marketing mix
- public relations
- conversion chain
- intangibility
- performance measures
- brand

Chapter outline

Sport marketing addresses the satisfaction of sport consumer needs with sport products and services. In this chapter, we examine the role of marketing in sport and its specificities

A sport marketing plan contains a variety of marketing mix elements. The chapter's primary goal is to address sport marketers' information needs for the design, and execution, of their marketing strategies. As a result, the chapter analyses the services marketing mix (the 7 Ps: Shilbury, Westerbeek, Quick, & Funk, 2009) with a special focus on marketing planning for sport organisations. The reader is urged to read this chapter in conjunction with Chapter 14 Sponsorship which highlights the special focus on the role of sponsorship in the promotion of sport products and services.

The marketing of sport activities in Australasia has only achieved business status since the 1970s. As other chapters in this book show, marketing has had a marked effect on the manner in which sport is organised and even the way in which it is played and presented. After discussing the essential elements of marketing at a generic level, this chapter will use examples from New Zealand Football, International Beach Volleyball, New Zealand Rugby's domestic rugby championship and New Zealand Cricket to demonstrate customer segmentation and how elements of the marketing mix have been implemented.

CASE STUDY: A 'WHOLE' LOTTA FOOTBALL: NEW ZEALAND FOOTBALL GETS STRATEGIC

Prepared by Jan Charbonneau, Massey University

New Zealand Football (www.nzfootball.co.nz) is the body responsible for leading, governing and regulating football. It is responsible for coordinating the grass roots efforts of seven independent member federations across the country, running national league competitions, and overseeing New Zealand's teams at international competitions such as the FIFA World Cup and the Olympic Games. New Zealand Football (NZF) has three clear priorities:

- increase the number of participants in the game and the quality of their experience;
- achieve success at the elite level that creates a sense of identity and pride and inspires participation; and
- ensure the game has a clear strategic direction and is well-governed at every level.

Clear objectives, but these have not always been easy to achieve. At the start of 2000, NZF coordinated 30 grass roots Federations so getting agreement as to how football should be administered was challenging. High levels of duplication and costs at the grass roots level and NZF's need to also focus on international high performance meant financial resources were severely depleted. What followed was a period of consolidation including reducing the regions down to a manageable seven and efforts to achieve financial sustainability. The same forward thinking strategies, experience and skills the players, coaches, referees and managers applied to playing football were applied to revamping New Zealand Football into a 'lean, mean, high performing sporting machine'. Extensive consultation with the restructured Federations, and jointly developed shared vision and strategy for the development of the game in New Zealand, ensured that all players had a common purpose.

What were the results? 2010 was an exceptionally good sporting year for New Zealand Football. The All Whites' unbeaten record at the World Cup in South Africa captured the hearts and minds of all New Zealand sports fans. Even the football-proud British press referred to New Zealand as the 'feel good hit of the summer'. The All Whites went on to win the Team of the Year, Coach of the Year (Ricki Herbert), and Supreme Award at the Halberg Awards, New Zealand's premier sporting awards.

(Continued)

This was the first time football had claimed a Halberg Award since 1949 when Bert Sutcliffe won the inaugural 'Sportsman of the Year' title. The New Zealand public even voted Winston Reid's last minute goal against Slovakia as their SPARC 2010 Favourite Sporting Moment. The All Whites had definitely engaged with New Zealand's sports fans and New Zealand Football had a great opportunity to build on these high levels of fan engagement.

2010 was also a particularly good financial year with the organisation reporting a $7.7 million surplus - much of that thanks to prize money from the All Whites' performance in South Africa. 2011 got off to a good start when New Zealand won the rights to host the 2015 FIFA Under-20 World Cup, an event that has seen marquee players like Diego Maradona compete and that promises a massive international television audience.

Football is arguably the world's most popular sport and the biggest revenue earner with its World Cup marquee event. The failure to capitalise on New Zealand's dramatic qualification at its first appearance on the world stage at the 1982 World Cup in Spain was a stark reminder that success at the international level was no guarantee of future success and NZF was determined not to miss this golden opportunity of increased media attention and general public interest. The big question facing NZF was what specifically to do.

NZF knew continuing solid performance on the world's sports stage would be needed to keep the level of fan engagement with football at the levels achieved after the 2010 World Cup. All White captain Ryan Nelsen was considered a 'home grown' player and New Zealand Football knew they needed a strong programme with elite level coaching to fill the ranks of future All Whites. The same was true for the Football Ferns, New Zealand's elite female football team. NZF was determined 'to not take its eye off the ball' when it comes to high performance teams like the All Whites, Football Ferns and national teams and put programmes in place to ensure that New Zealand sports fans continued to enjoy world class success.

NZF also knew that football was the country's most popular participation sport for children aged 12 and under - both boys and girls - but players often changed over to a range of different sports as they got older. For example, males tended to move to rugby while females tended to favour netball. Netball was still considered the primary female sport in New Zealand with female players aspiring to fill the ranks of the Silver Ferns and ANZ Championship teams. While kids were attracted to football and loved playing the game, what was offered at the various age levels and across the member federations was often inconsistent.

New Zealand Football spent three years accumulating world's best practice, culminating in the development and rollout in late 2010 of its *Whole of Football Plan* - a solid strategic plan including both market and product development. As the name implies, this strategic plan is designed to generate engagement at *all* levels - administrators, coaches, referees and male and female players of all ages, motivations and locations.

The *Whole of Football Plan* aligns all of New Zealand Football's development programmes to provide a unified pathway into the game and deliver a consistent sporting product and experience to all participants regardless of gender, age, motivation or role within the game. The plan, rolled out in three stages of Junior, Youth and Senior, has the backing of the member federations as well as key long-term partners ASB and SPARC. The reason for the staged roll-out is to ensure Federations and clubs have in place the necessary structures to deliver consistency - lessons hard learned in the past.

The first stage specifically targets children under 12, including age appropriate instruction and programming - First Kicks played three-a-side for 4 - 5 year olds, Fun Football played four-a-side for 6 - 8 year olds and Mini Football for 9 - 12 year olds. These programmes are designed specifically to give players more time with the ball and more time to develop their physical and mental skills.

Girls are also specifically targeted with programming such as girls-only summer leagues so as not to compete with netball and its winter programming and specific recruitment drives focusing on moms and daughters. While the media focus has been primarily on the success of male elite footballers, female athletes such as Ali Riley, who played for New Zealand in the 2008 Olympics and has won a raft of

(*Continued*)

sporting awards, show clearly that females can also have a pathway to elite football performance and perhaps a spot on the Football Ferns at the next World Cup, the largest single-sport event for women.

The Plan focuses on consistency at all levels of the sport's administration (coaches, managers, referees and administrators) to ensure that appropriate training is provided to all players, whether they are high performance talent or a weekend 'kicker'. The Plan also looks at more channels for participation as football has tended to be viewed as a club and winter sport. Fun Football Centres, Football Festivals and user-pay after-school and holiday programs played in school sporting fields are all designed to make the sport more accessible year round.

By improving the level of coaching, providing age-specific instruction, and creating a consistent, positive experience at the grass roots level, the aim is to keep more of the promising male and female players as well as recreational players who currently drift away to other sports as they age, kicking 'the round ball'. New Zealand Football is not just about creating football players but football 'families' of participants, game leaders and spectators.

Source: Adapted from Solomon, M., & Charbonneau, J. (2012), *Marketing: Real people, real choices* (2nd ed.). Pearson Education New Zealand (publication pending).

QUESTIONS

Access the *Whole of Football Plan* at www.nzfootball.co.nz.
* How does the plan reflect New Zealand Football's three priorities?
* Explain how the plan is designed to generate engagement at all levels, ages, motivations and locations.
* Select one local sport. What lessons could this sport learn from New Zealand Football?
* Select one national sport. What lessons could this sport learn from New Zealand Football?

Introduction

Increasingly, marketing has assumed a prominent role in Australasian sport organisations. Despite sport marketing being in its infancy as an academic field of study, marketing principles have been applied to sport organisations worldwide for several decades. Earlier definitions of sport marketing such as 'the process of designing and implementing activities for the production, pricing, promotion and distribution of a sport product' (Pitts & Stotlar, 1996, p. 80) have now been supplemented by recognition of service relationships and by societal goals (in addition to managerial goals) leading to:

> Sport marketing is a social and managerial process by which the sport manager seeks to obtain what sporting organisations need and want through creating and exchanging products and value with others.

> *(Shilbury et al., 2009, p. 15)*

It is well to remind the reader that a financial perspective should always be present: meeting an organisation's financial objectives (for example, 'breaking even and staying in business') is obvious but sometimes overlooked.

Sport marketing, and its operational underpinning of marketing management, were probably first enunciated in 1978 in the United States in *Advertising Age* (Shilbury et al., 2009; Fullerton, 2010). Over the next three decades the term 'sport marketing' has become synonymous with two different, although converging marketing genres, being marketing 'of' sport, and marketing 'through' sport.

Shilbury et al. (2009) and Fullerton (2010) agree that marketing 'of' sport covers the deliberate, planned efforts by sport organisations to influence consumer demand (from participants and spectators) for a variety of sport products and services.

> Ultimately, the goal is to ensure the ongoing survival of the sport in rapidly changing environmental circumstances. This aspect of marketing has only recently developed in sporting organisations. Survival depends largely on the principal purpose of the sporting organisation. National sporting organisations predominantly associated with elite-level professional sporting competitions will be striving to develop their marketing mix [the 7 Ps of services marketing: see below] to ensure that the sport product is attractive as a form of live entertainment and live broadcast through television, the internet and other mobile outlets. Sports-governing bodies will also be responsible for ensuring that participation in their sport remains healthy. Participants are the lifeblood of sport, as they become the next generation of champions and spectators.
>
> *(Shilbury et al., 2009, p. 15)*

Notice that the sport marketer's emphasis is upon influencing spectatorship and participation. While marketing a sport is a business function (and is usually overseen by someone with 'marketing' in their business title), the marketing of any product or service, sport included, should be a total corporate or organisational effort. Every employee or volunteer has the responsibility to cater for customer needs. In effect, then, every employee is a 'part-time marketer' (Gronroos, 2007).

Yet there is another layer to sport marketing: that of the sporting goods and services domain, with sports equipment, apparel, footwear and the processes (services) that are put in place (for example, ticketing, e-commerce, media processes) to assist the distribution and selling of these goods and services. This is where the other genre of sport marketing emerges – marketing 'through' sport (almost always involving some form of sponsorship) – which is the way organisations (usually large corporations)

> use sport as a vehicle to promote and advertise their products, usually to specifically identifiable demographic markets known to follow a particular sport. Sports with significant television time are very attractive to firms seeking to promote their products through an association with sport. Developing licensing programs [paying for the right to use a sport logo to place on products to stimulate sales] is another example of marketing through sport.
>
> *(Shilbury et al., 2009, p. 15)*

Despite our best attempts at defining sport marketing, there is still debate and contention about definitions. Yet sport marketing need not be made difficult; marketing practice has a unity irrespective of the product or service being sold. The challenge comes in the choice of those concepts, tools and tactics that are appropriate in each context. In sport contexts, marketing is not just the 'contest on the field'. Of equal importance are issues of pricing, promotion and distribution of that contest to different groups of customers in either real time or recorded time.

The role of marketing

With today's intense competition for consumer discretionary dollars, successful sport organisations have adopted marketing processes into their business function for a host of reasons as outlined in the 'Bottom line - implications for management' box.

Bottom line – implications for management

- Segment the markets of a sport organisation and select the target markets for today and the months after.
- Guide this organisation in its design and selection of the 'sport product' (which includes more than the 'contest on the field') and its *target* customers.
- Identify and monitor the activities of business competitors.
- Develop and implement suitable pricing strategies in regard to the position of the organisation in the competition context (do the prices have to be lower, higher or equal to those of competitors?).
- Develop and implement suitable promotional strategies (what is the most relevant commercial endorsement for a brand? What are the values and messages that the sport organisation should use to promote its products?).
- Develop and implement distribution strategies (that is, getting the sport product to the customers or vice versa) and distribution processes.
- Develop and implement (preferably in conjunction with the Human Resources manager) human resource strategies to deliver sport products and processes.
- Coordinate the research and information needed to carry out the marketing functions (above), audit their performance, and help ensure their repeated success.

Therefore, marketing is a process that needs to be managed like any other process. It is much wider than merely promoting an event or activity and its lifeblood is information. Herein lies the necessity for the sport marketer to have a sound grasp of market research, if not the nuances of data analysis, then at least a sound working knowledge of market research process. That becomes important for briefing and working alongside market research consultants. While gaining and gathering information is part of the marketing function, storage and retrieval of that information is also required. Often this is managed using a *marketing information system* (MIS) (Shilbury et al., 2009, p. 56) which can be anything from a few index cards in a shoe-box to an advanced computer system.

Sport marketers require knowledge of the external environment (the so-called PEST analysis – political, economic, social and technological domains) of their customers and of their business competitors, both current and potential, for informed decision-making about their sport's direction. Identifying particular types of consumers for a sporting code is in essence a method of selecting the *target* market. Stanton, Miller, and Layton (1995) suggested that market segmentation is the process of dividing the total heterogeneous market for a product or service into several segments, each of which tends to be homogeneous in all similar aspects. According to Harris and Elliott (2007, p. 128; see also, Mullin, Hardy, & Sutton, 2007, p. 129), this can be done according to demographic characteristics (e.g., gender, age, presence or absence of children, etc.), psychographic characteristics (personality, lifestyle, psychological), behavioural characteristics or geographical characteristics but also location, attitudes to and involvement in the sport, prior participation, level of spectator patronage, etc. Irrespective of how they are selected, target markets become the basis of marketing strategy because they identify who the sport product is aimed at. Marketing mix decisions involving pricing, promotion, distribution, and facility and event planning are subsequently made with these prospective customers in mind. Herein lies another challenge for a sport marketer – an appreciation of their customers', and potential customers' behaviour. At the very least, an appreciation of sport fan segmentation – focussing on the different behaviours, and requisite different marketing mixes – for *aficionados* (or hard-core fans), *fair-weather fans* and *theatre-goers* is required. The 'Typical Rugby Crowd' case study illustrates how target customers can be selected.

CASE STUDY: TYPICAL RUGBY CROWD

Garland, Macpherson, and Haughey (2004) studied rugby fan attendance at four New Zealand rugby national championship games, two in Wellington and two in Palmerston North. Fans were assigned to one of three groups using a simple behavioural segmentation (based on level of attendance at home games, season ticket holder status, and level of involvement in rugby as either a spectator, a player cum spectator, spectator plus administrator/referee or all three categories). The three groups or customer segments that emerged were aficionados (hard-core fans) accounting for 29% of the crowd, fair-weather fans (27% of the crowd) and theatre-goers (44% of the crowd), with the latter group being the majority of the 'walk-up' crowd. As Quick (2000) suggested, not all fans are motivated by the same factors. Typically theatre-goers, and to some extent fair-weather fans, display temporal or situational, that is 'time and place' based involvement with their chosen sport/team. By contrast, aficionados display enduring involvement, that is, they are committed for a very long time. Aficionados were not deterred by adverse weather conditions but were somewhat distressed by the (poor) behaviour of other fans and also rather critical of the stadium's facilities. In contrast, fair-weather fans made their attendance decisions more upon the quality of the opposition, the home team's performance to date in the season, and the time in the season of the matches in question (e.g., ordinary pool game or semi-final). Not surprisingly, the theatre-goer attends the game almost exclusively for its entertainment value, the general atmosphere generated in the stadium; in short, a 'packaged' outing. These three quite distinct fan segments require different though complementary strategic responses from sport marketers. Aficionados deserve reinforcement of their behaviour to at least hold their levels of commitment and if possible increase their level of game attendance, their level of purchase of team merchandise and their contribution to club/team fund-raising. Rewarding these loyal fans through economic incentives and preferential treatment (sometimes connected to a loyalty scheme) are typical tactics. Seeking ways of increasing the psychological commitment of fair-weather and theatre-going fans to the home team and its home games is less easy. More access to the players, aligning attendance with a relevant social cause (cause-related marketing) and presenting home games as 'entertainment packages' are often fruitful tactics.

Implementing the overall marketing strategy for a sport will involve service marketing's 7 Ps. These are the mechanisms used by sport marketers to try and influence potential customers to patronise their sport, that is, to buy their 'product'. The knowledge for informed decision-making about the 7 Ps comes from marketing research and the central role of the organisation's marketer(s) is to combine the first four (product, pricing, promotion and place – distribution) of the 7 Ps in such a way as to meet the sport organisation's objectives (Shilbury et al., 2009).

Concept Check

Marketing

Marketing is a business process that includes researching consumer needs and wants in order to select the best way to meet those needs and wants to achieve the organisation's perform-ance objectives. *Sport marketing* addresses sport consumer needs and wants either directly by the sport organisation, team, etc or indirectly by intermediaries (such as sport equipment, apparel and footwear manufacturers, event promoters, sponsors, consultants, etc).

The services marketing mix: The 7Ps

Product

Sport as a 'product' differs somewhat from other competitive leisure and recreational activities. The unpredictability of the product (the event), inconsistency of product quality, strong emotional attachment and identification (with a team, nation or individual), and the subjectivity of judgement of the consumers with respect to the product typifies sport. Now also, the quality of venues, the 'entertainment' experience that surrounds any major event, the types of promotion used to garner interest, the accessibility of the venue, etc all impinge on the customer experience. The 'main event' in a sport product is intangible and, as Veeck and Linn (1965, p. 20) stated, 'the customer comes out of the park with nothing except a memory'. Thus, sport marketers need to have their minds firmly focused on their participants, spectators and supporters. Sport managers are often lovers of the game they are marketing – there is nothing wrong with this provided that management is not blind to such fundamentals as insufficient demand for their 'product' or living the sport through their own eyes rather than through those of their potential customers. This phenomenon is sometimes referred to as 'marketing myopia' (Mullin et al., 2007). A number of failures in the marketing of sport have come from assuming that consumers will want the sport 'product' merely because it is 'available'. If it was this simple, there would be no need for marketing or marketers.

Seeking to satisfy consumer wants (i.e., demand) by offering sport products and services, which may be tangible or intangible, is at the centre of the sport business. The way these products and services are priced, promoted and 'placed' (i.e., offered to the market) becomes crucial in their sale. The 'contest on the field' is, of course, the core service product yet that is only the 'tip of the iceberg'. The stadium, arena or ground in which the contest is held, the team web site, the variety of merchandise (apparel, banners, gifts, etc.) available, the entertainment provided before, during and after the game, the role of sponsors and the amount of community involvement are examples of the 'peripherals' or wider view of a sport service product (Shilbury et al., 2009). Many of these 'peripherals' are services. Any sporting event is simultaneously staged and viewed or participated in. It cannot be stored (or at least the live action cannot be stored) meaning unsold seats become lost sales (although the size of media right contracts and sponsorships in some modern professional sporting leagues makes empty stadiums - lost sales – less problematic than in the past). Service intangibility (not being able to sample the experience before engaging in the experience) forces the sport consumer into a reliance on the reputation of the event, the event manager and the 'peripherals' (service product extensions) such as venue, facilities, entertainment, atmosphere created, etc. Sport marketers use a variety of ways to 'tangibilise the intangible' as discussed below under 'physical evidence'.

Branding a sport product or service is about differentiation from competitors, that is, making a service product sufficiently different and distinct from rival offerings. The core service product, the 'contest on the field' can be difficult to differentiate. Thus the branding of sport and sport organisations tends to focus on the peripheral elements. Not every team in a competition can win all the time or have the best players. As a result, sport marketers help sport organisations to find their points of difference and then help them to emphasise these as elements of their brand in order to stand apart from their rivals. Despite inherent difficulties in differentiating core product, some sports have been successful in doing just that. For example, different forms of rugby (7 a-side, 15 a-side) and cricket (indoor cricket, twenty-20; one-day limited over cricket, 3-day or 4-day domestic cricket, 5-day international 'test' cricket) show that product differentiation by time duration, player numbers, rule changes, etc., is possible. Obviously these points of difference or brand elements need to be important to the consumer. In the world of international rugby, the power and relevance of the All Black brand with its connotations of strength, history, tradition, winning and striving for perfection is plain to see. Nonetheless, the financial value of the All Blacks' brand was not fully appreciated until the professional rugby era from 1995 onwards. As an example, the New Zealand Rugby Union receives substantial revenue from brand licensing arrangements with corporate partners such as adidas and Lion Corporation (Australasia's leading brewer) for its All Black brand.

Concept Check

Branding

Branding in sport involves sport organisations using their images (names, logos, symbols) in such a way as to differentiate their product and services from those of their competitors. Often corporate partners can be involved in licensing arrangements to promote the sport organisation brand to the mutual benefit of both parties.

Price

What price should be charged for a sport event? Buying any sport product will be affected by its perceived value, comparisons with competitive products, feedback from friends, relatives and significant others, whether it is unique or a copy. Like any business, a sport 'product' has its own costs of production which are usually reflected in the entry price (for participants) or seat price (for spectators). As all spectators know, different viewing positions (in a stadium) can be charged out at different prices. Increasingly sport organisations are charging different consumers different prices for the same product at different times or different 'locations'. Amid growing concerns that premium pricing (price skimming – charging high prices over the short-term without special regard to long-term, repeat purchase customers) can be damaging, especially to family-based sport attendance, some sport organisations are exploring more 'repeat-attendance' strategies, based on the philosophies of relationship marketing. Winning the ongoing support of a proportion of the fan base is the objective (see the 'Typical Rugby Crowd' case study) bearing in mind that entry fees to the contest on the field are only one of several sport 'products being offered for sale. Pricing strategies involving price discrimination will often apply unless a sport event is so popular that demand for entry always exceeds supply (such as the Australian Tennis Open final, Wimbledon finals, Summer Olympics Opening and Closing ceremonies, etc).

Promotion

Sport marketers have to be careful to not confuse promotion - the 'exciting part of the marketing mix' - with marketing *per se*. The sheer visibility of promotion, particularly advertising, create misconceptions. Sport marketers, like any marketer, can use a myriad of methods (known as the promotional mix) to promote their product as shown in the summary box on the promotional mix.

The promotional mix

- Advertising (print, television, radio, internet, mobile telephony).
- Sponsorship (naming rights, media rights, cause-related sponsorship), direct mail, special deals, special packages involving other goods and services.
- Pre-match entertainment, corporate 'boxes', merchandising paraphernalia (caps, key rings, collectibles, posters, etc.) and clothing (tee shirts, casual wear, dress clothing, replica team wear, etc.).
- Signs and signage, games programmes, 'Old Timers' days, 'Meet the Players' days, exhibition games to promote the sporting code, coaching clinics for young fans, autograph sessions and autographed photos and sporting equipment, free-to-enter competitions, internet gaming and gambling, etc.
- Public relations and social media.

Any or all of these are promotion. The sport organisation's promotional aims are to inform its targeted customers about the sport product and to encourage purchase of that 'product'. Marketers have to decide if their promotional mix methods can be used separately or together. Advertising refers to a classical way of promoting products and services. Except for its timing, (usually immediately before a sporting event), advertising does not often present important specificities in the promotion of sport products or services. These are attended to in pre-match entertainment, signs, games programmes, etc. which are part of what marketers call 'experiential marketing' - a 'global' method allowing the fan to not only be a spectator of the show but a part of it too. 'Experiential marketing' is used to enhance the link between the fan and the team, the event or the players. It is a relevant way to promote the brand and to develop emotion, passion and enthusiasm. Allied to experiential marketing is sponsorship, the promotional mix method so fundamentally important to sport. Certainly other domains – culture, media, etc. – are dependent upon sponsorship yet Slack and Amis (2004, p. 270) estimated 'two-thirds of all global investment in sponsorship is devoted to sport. Sponsorship is mainly used in 'marketing through sport' strategies to promote products or services. Sport sponsorship strategies can be designed depending on firstly, the objective that marketers want to reach (awareness, image, turn over, teambuilding) and secondly, the choice of the commercial endorsement to support a player, a team, an event or an organisation. (See Chapter 14 Sponsorship for more details on the role of sponsorship in the marketing of sport organisations.)

Concept Check

Marketing mix

The *marketing mix* is the strategic combination of the 7 Ps. By adding the service elements of physical evidence, people and process to the traditional marketing mix of product, price, promotion and place, sport marketers engage in *relationship marketing* with its emphasis upon the development and maintenance of enduring relationships (rather than one-off transactions) with their stakeholders.

Place

'Place' is *where* and *how* customers can buy the sport product. Any sort of active participation or spectatorship by customers means travelling to a sport venue, whereas consumption of the sport product through mediated elements – television, internet, mobile telephony – is more passive participation or spectatorship. The sport service product's simultaneity of production and consumption (and hence its perishability) means nothing is 'manufactured' until the contest begins. As a spectator, if the live action is missed, the first opportunity and its inherent excitement and tension is missed.

Distribution (place) also covers ticketing. From where and how do potential patrons buy tickets for sports events? Sport marketers can choose to mount their own ticketing operations or subcontract them to intermediaries (wholesalers, agents, etc.). Yet it is the liaison with the sport event's venue and facilities in respect of staging events that offers considerable challenge for a sport marketer. Couple that with the array of communication possibilities (discussed above) one might have with fans and stakeholders (Shilbury et al., 2009) and one can appreciate the complexity of 'distribution' issues.

Fans and participants expect up-to-date information about draws, results, players, coaches, teams, tactics, the club, etc., from sport organisation web sites along with opportunities to buy tickets, special offers, merchandise, sponsors' products and services, etc. Archived match coverage can be made available for 'history buff fans', chat rooms with the players for younger fans, online gaming and online gambling for older fans and virtual stores for online shoppers. Depending upon contractual arrangements with television networks, there can be possibilities for net casting some home games.

The marketing mix with its emphasis upon integrating each of the 7P's is an integral part of the marketing process. Yet, carried out in isolation from one another (such as an emphasis on promotion alone or in an absence of a focus on relationship building) usually courts disaster as the sport service product is bought repeatedly by the same customers. Therefore, sport marketing needs to incorporate a relationship focus into its processes, emphasising the building of long-term relationships with stakeholders. Nowhere is this more obvious than in event planning when not only are product, price and promotion brought together at a venue (or venues), but also the operations (people and processes) to make the event happen. Services marketers call these aspects 'physical evidence', 'process' and 'people' (Shilbury et al., 2009).

Concept Check

Unique aspects of the sport product

Sport is inconsistent and unpredictable, invariably intangible and subjective, and a perishable commodity which evokes strong personal identification. The marketing emphasis often has to be placed on the product extensions rather than on the core product to achieve some consistency, and sport organisations simultaneously compete and cooperate.

Physical evidence

We have seen already that much of the sport service product – 'the contest on the field' – is intangible. It is advantageous for the sport marketer to try and 'tangibilise' the sport service product for customers.

to assist participation and spectatorship (demand). Sport marketers try to enhance the sport service product with physical evidence – thus the emphasis is upon product extensions rather than the core service product. The venue – often a stadium – is an obvious example and many stadia in their own right have become attractive to spectators, even to the extent of the stadium becoming the draw card as much as the event for some spectators (for example: the Melbourne Cricket Ground in Melbourne, Australia; Old Trafford in Manchester, England; the Allianz Arena in Munich, Germany; and various 'domes' in USA like the new Yankee Stadium, New York). One not only expects all the facilities associated with a modern stadium, but additional features such as the most up-to-date technology for in-depth viewing, museums, exhibitions, etc., to encourage demand and help produce a memorable experience for spectator and participant alike. The types of promotion used to promote an upcoming event help too, along with event organisers' reputations (based on past events), the types and range of sponsors, the reputation of the athlete endorsers used to endorse the event, etc., all help to provide 'physical evidence' to consolidate an event's reputation.

Process

For any event, the venue is the point of convergence for the marketing and operational functions. Gronroos (2007) highlighted the roles played by marketers, and others, in service delivery. Delivering service to customers is not exclusive to those people with 'marketing' or 'customer service' in their job title; everyone in a sport organisation is a 'part-time marketer' with responsibilities for delivering an enjoyable worthy customer experience. The 'process' part of the marketing mix is the 'how' of service delivery: how the sport service product in its entirety is planned, produced and delivered to sports fans and participants. Consider for a moment the service provider encounters that spectators of a major sporting event might have from the time they decide to attend that event to the time they return home after attendance; a considerable amount of 'process' is involved.

People

All those sport service providers encountered in the consumption of the major sporting event alluded to above are the 'people' component of the marketing mix.

> The selection and training of human resources for service delivery in sport are tasks in which the sport marketer should have strong involvement. The level of training, skills and abilities of potential employees of the sporting organisation become 'people variables' that will make the difference between mediocre and excellent service provision.
>
> (Shilbury et al., 2009, p. 135).

Marketing strategy

Sport managers must try and identify those issues beyond their control, such as environmental factors, social conditions, economic conditions, legal changes, technology challenges and, of course, business competition. Like any other business management process, the sport marketing process should be strategically and systematically planned. Well managed marketing is essential in the development of a successful sport. Yet even with the best intentions, well managed marketing will never offset an organisation's fundamental problems (for example, environmental and financial problems). Sport marketing strategies and tactics can be applied to a whole sport (a large task) as well as to the somewhat smaller tasks at club or regional levels. Irrespective of the level, the decisions that face a sport marketer are illustrated in the case study about beach volleyball's entry to the Summer Olympics.

CASE STUDY: KEEPING THE PARTY GOING – LESSONS LEARNED BY BEACH VOLLEYBALL AT SUCCESSIVE SUMMER OLYMPIAD

By Jan Charbonneau, Massey University, New Zealand

You've already got sun, sand, bronzed athletes, and a crowd in party mode. How do you improve Beach Volleyball… and why would you want to? If you're the competition manager for Beach Volleyball for London 2012 the answer is simple… it's your job. And Beach Volleyball's survival as an Olympic sport depends on it!

To understand the challenge facing the competition manager, you have to appreciate that competition at the Olympics is not limited to the track, pool or court. The Olympics are, by any measure, the largest and most successful sporting event in the world. Millions of spectators watch athletes compete live, with many more watching the Games from the comfort of their homes. Consider that for Beijing 2008, 6.5 million tickets were sold for live events, 4.3 billion viewers in 220 countries watched over 61,700 hours of television coverage, the Games' internet channel on YouTube generated over 21 million video views, and Beijing2008.cn, the Games' official website, had over 100 million hits in August 2008 alone (IOC 2002, 2004, 2008a).

The Olympics is also big business, with broadcasting, corporate sponsorships, tickets and licensing generating $US 3 billion for Sydney 2000. For Athens 2004, broadcasting rights alone generated almost US$ 1.5 billion (IOC, 2004); for Beijing 2008 this rose to over US$ 1.7 billion. Global corporate sponsors - including Coke, McDonald's and Visa - paid US$ 866 million to sponsor Turin 2006 (winter Olympics) and Beijing 2008 (IOC, 2008). And for this kind of money, broadcasters, sponsors, ticket holders and licensees expect value!

The International Olympic Committee (IOC) finds itself in the enviable position that 'more sports want to participate in the Olympic Games, more athletes want to compete in the Olympic Games, more people want to attend the Olympic Games, and more media want to cover the Olympic Games' (IOC, 2002). Adding new sports adds audience, allowing this tradition-steeped organisation to maintain a modern image. For example, introducing Table Tennis increased television audiences in Asia, Handball increased Scandinavian television revenues, and Snowboarding and Beach Volleyball have drawn in a younger demographic.

However, each new sport or discipline not only adds audience but increases the size, time, complexity and resources required to stage the Games. Each new sport brings athletes, coaches and officials that need to be housed, fed and transported, and competitions that need venues and other infrastructure requirements. The IOC realises that future growth must be limited to ensure that the Olympics' unique features of atmosphere, athlete experience, universality and brand value are not lost. Resisting the temptation to extend competition over multiple host cities, the IOC has officially limited the duration of competition to sixteen days, capped the number of sports at 28 and competitors at 10,500, and committed to a single host city (IOC, 2000; IOC, 2003; IOC, 2008b).

To keep within these parameters, the IOC carefully evaluates new sports seeking Olympic status (IOC 2002). For Beijing 2008, the IOC received 18 applications for inclusion of new sports. For Rio 2016,

(Continued

seven applications were received, with Rugby Sevens and golf making the cut, assuring themselves a place at both the 2016 and 2020 games. The continued inclusion of existing Olympic sports is also evaluated on a per Games basis (IOC, 2002).

Six main criteria are used in these evaluations:
- history and tradition (e.g., competitive history)
- universality (e.g., number of affiliated federations & continental participation)
- popularity of sport (e.g., spectator attendance & media interest)
- image and environment (e.g., gender equity & anti-doping policies)
- development of the international federation (e.g., financial viability)
- costs (e.g., competition costs & complexity of television production)

Olympic sports now find themselves in the unenviable position of having to compete to stay within the Olympic family.

BEACH VOLLEYBALL AS AN OLYMPIC SPORT

As a sport, Beach Volleyball has a long history, staging its first competitive tournament in California in 1930 and now played in more than 150 countries on five continents. Beach Volleyball was officially recognised as an Olympic sport in 1994, debuting at Atlanta 1996. The FIVB (Fédération Internationale de Volleyball), Beach's International Federation, had modest objectives for Atlanta – make a good first showing. By Sydney 2000, according to Blair Harrison, Competition Manager, Beach Volleyball, SOCOG (Sydney Olympic Organising Committee), the objective was 'to ensure its long term future as an Olympic sport'.

In regular competition, Beach Volleyball has a tradition of combining sport and entertainment, creating a beach party atmosphere with entertainment enhancers such as music, announcers and dancers. Athletes train specifically for the 'party atmosphere' so music and dancers do not present a distraction for players. The FIVB incorporates this sports/entertainment theme into their slogan, billing itself in corporate communications as 'The Leader in World Sports Entertainment'. At all times, the overriding objective of the FIVB is not to disappoint their fans, whether at local competitions, World Championships or at the Olympics. At Sydney 2000, extensive use was made of music and scripted match entertainment including lifesaver themed characters and mock beach rescues to 'push the entertainment envelope'. The end result was a vibrant party atmosphere that generated positive spectator and media reactions.

For Athens 2004, according to Nikos Sofianos, Competition Manager, Beach Volleyball, ATHOC (Athens Olympic Organising Committee), the FIVB had three objectives:
- Add value to spectator and television viewer experiences.
- Maintain or increase attendance and media coverage.
- ensure Beach Volleyball's position in the top five overall sports.

The IOC criteria 'Popularity of Sport' offered the most potential for Beach Volleyball to differentiate itself from other Olympic sports. According to Andrew Hercus, FIVB Control Committee, Beach Volleyball sought to carve out a niche for itself in the Olympic family, combining the sport's athleticism and robust competition with its existing regular competition 'entertainment culture'.

ATHENS 2004 – ADDING SPECTATOR VALUE

A typical spectator spends five hours at a Beach Volleyball session. The FIVB did not want its Olympic spectators to be passive viewers but to take an active role in creating the party atmosphere. Downtime was minimised within and between matches by expediting side switches and limiting time outs. During these times, music was provided and announcers actively encouraged spectators to cheer and sing to

(Continued)

songs like Men at Work's 'Land Down Under' and the Village People's 'YMCA'. The FIVB employed DJs instead of the usual audio operators, providing them with scripts to hype up the crowd. As one announcer said 'You'll never hear us say 'quiet please' at Beach Volleyball' (Charles, 2004). The players also got into the act, encouraging spectators to cheer, sing and dance. And dance they did – especially when the bikini-clad dance troupe, Personal Plus, took to the sand. This troop of female dancers entertained with choreographed routines in timeouts and between matches, keeping crowd energy high. The aim, according to Chronis Chichlakis, Beach Volleyball Venue Coordinator for Sports Presentation, ATHOC, was to 'provide enough entertainment to keep audiences occupied, without compromising athlete performance'.

Two mock Olympic match courts were constructed, providing both spectators and volunteers with their own Olympic competition venue. Olympic competitors were contracted by the FIVB to play spectators on these courts. SWATCH, the FIVB's World Tour Sponsor, provided speed servicing guns, allowing spectators to compare their speed of service with the athletes.

To reinforce their commitment to maximizing the entertainment value for spectators and television viewers, one member of the FIVB's Control Committee was assigned the task of monitoring all entertainment features, feeding back to both the FIVB and ATHOC on a daily basis.

ATHENS 2004 – ADDING TELEVISION VALUE

For many sports, the duration of an individual match is not easily defined, presenting particular challenges for television broadcasters. Recognising this, the FIVB changed its scoring system to ensure that each match would last under an hour (80% certainty) – ideal for both television and Olympic scheduling. Under the new scoring system, a point was scored on each serve, adding excitement as the score quickly advanced, providing lots of opportunities for crowd cheers.

To accommodate the demands of television broadcasting, the FIVB made several rule changes for Athens 2004. Defining the time between rallies as 12 seconds reduced delays (no playing action), while being sufficient for television broadcasters to insert a replay and on-site announcers to play a short music clip or engage the crowd.

Referees were connected directly by earpiece to TV producers, allowing producers to advise referees on a continuing basis of their requirements. TV producers utilised three calls: Hold, indicating the need for a replay; Go, indicating play could recommence; and Stop, indicating a significant stoppage such as equipment failure. A new hand signal was developed to indicate a call of 'Hold'. If the arm was held vertically outwards from the referee, players knew that TV producers had requested a delay in commencement of play. Approximately 6 – 8 of these occurred per match, with announcers and dancers entertaining spectators during these 'television breaks'.

Twenty-two cameras, including super slow motion, net cam and aerial shots, were employed at Athens 2004, up from nine at Sydney 2000. Ball and line colours were changed to maximize contrast and microphones embedded in nets and under sand to provide referee/player audio. Media and stadium announcers were provided with extensive guides including biographies and match histories of all competitors for adding flavour to commentaries. The FIVB consulted official host broadcasters concerning match scheduling to ensure that home country matches would air in their home country prime viewing times.

ATHENS 2004 – MAINTAINING ATTENDANCE AND MEDIA COVERAGE

The Beach Volleyball venue at Athens 2004 held approximately 10,000 spectators. 2200 seats were reserved for Olympic sponsors, media, guests and other dignitaries, leaving 7800 for the FIVB and ATHOC to fill. Selling out finals and evening games (especially when Greece played) at the top ticket price was not a problem. However, filling seats for morning and afternoon games in the Athens heat

(Continued

presented the FIVB with a real challenge. To fill the venue, ATHOC agreed to price tickets for these sessions in the lowest price category.

According to Nikos Sofianos, Competition Manager, Beach Volleyball, ATHOC, 'sponsor seats were heavily utilised', with attendance for publicly available seats averaging between 3 – 6000 for morning sessions and 4 – 6000 for afternoon sessions. While down from the 98% capacity reached at Sydney 2000, Beach Volleyball outperformed most other Olympic sports at Athens 2004. On a daily basis, Beach Volleyball was in the top 5 sports in terms of percentage fill of capacity. Even the Olympic mascots, Athená and Phévos, whose attendance was dictated by spectator attendance and appreciation, were regular spectators.

HOW DID BEACH VOLLEYBALL SCORE AT ATHENS 2004?

The Washington Post referred to Beach Volleyball, Athens 2004 as a 'sell-out, foot-stomping success', calling it 'one of the most popular spectator sports at the Olympics' since its debut in Atlanta (Charles, 2004). Beach Volleyball's appeal extends from spectators at live competitions to television viewers. At Sydney 2000, Beach Volleyball attracted the fifth largest television audience of the 28 sports (Charles, 2004). For Athens 2004, Beach Volleyball was judged the most popular sport in terms of TV viewer hours (IOC, 2005).

Did the FIVB achieve its objectives for Athens 2004? Attendance and television viewership figures, especially when compared to some sports, would suggest that spectator, television viewers and broadcasters expectations were satisfied. Not only was Beach Volleyball going to Beijing 2008, its place was confirmed for London 2012 and Rio de Janeiro 2016!

BEIJING 2008 – DID THE FIVB TOP ATHENS 2004?

The bar was set high for Beijing. The objective, according to FIVB president Dr Acosta, was simple - ensure Beach Volleyball was the most successful sport in the Games (Jingyu, 2008).

While 6.5 million tickets were sold, organisers grappled with low actual attendance, eventually employing yellow t-shirted state trained 'cheer squads' to fill empty seats. Beach Volleyball tickets sold out within three days and fared better than many sports in terms of actual attendance, filling most of its 12,000 seats. The 'girls of Athens' were back on the sand, again often sharing their dances with official mascots, the Fuwa. This time, however, the proviso was that half of the dancers had to be Chinese and routines had to include traditional Chinese dances featuring red fans and nunchuks. Not that this mattered to the crowds or media. Also back were the professional DJs, many of whom were Chinese, spinning out well-known tunes and cranking up the crowds to shout 'jia you!' to encourage the athletes. Even then US President George W Bush attended and joined in the beach party. According to MSNBC. com 'Beach Volleyball + 10,000 fans + beach girls = formula for fun', referring to Beach Volleyball as 'one of the best produced events of the Olympics' (Wu, 2008). Beach Volleyball was able to 'keep the party going' for Beijing 2008, meeting attendance and media coverage targets.

But the lessons learned from Beach Volleyball at Athens 2004 were not lost on other sports or BOCOG (Beijing Organizing Committee for the Olympic Games). 'Entertainment enhancers' were not just employed by other sports but BOCOG itself, eroding Beach's competitive advantage. A pep squad of 200,000 volunteers trained in simple dance routines and 28 elite squads of 400 cheerleaders trained by the New England Patriot's football team's professional cheerleaders were employed by BOCOG to 'stir up spirit for any national team that needs it' (Huang, 2008). At Beijing 2008, the 'party' was not just on the beach but spread to all venues.

All of this begs the question - what will Beach do for London 2012 and beyond? Will its competitive advantage of using a party atmosphere to add value to spectators and media be further eroded? Will the 'party atmosphere' become the Olympic standard? Or will Beach remain Beach, '... the perfect

(Continued)

combination of sport, music and sex'. Tom Blauemauer, Stadium Announcer, Beach Volleyball, Athens 2004 (USA Today).

SOURCES: ALL ACCESSED ONLINE

IOC (2000), *Coordination Commission for the Sydney 2000 Olympic Games Final Report*; IOC (2002), *Olympic Games Study Commission*; IOC (2003), *Olympic Games Study Commission*; IOC (2004), *Athens 2004 Marketing Report*; IOC (2005), *Global Sport Report*; IOC (2008a), *Marketing Report Beijing 2008*; IOC (2008b), *Olympic Marketing Fact File*; Charles, D. (2004), 'Capacity Crowds at Beach Volleyball Rock the Joint', *Washington Post.com*, August 17; Duncan, C. (2004), 'Dance Team Stirs Up Beach Volleyball Venue', *Washington Post.com*, August 17; Anon (2004) 'Fans Party at Beach Volleyball', *USA Today*, September 15; Shipley, A. & Fan, M. (2008), 'Beijing all dressed up, but no one is going', *Washington Post.com*, August 13; Jingyu, W. (2008), 'FIVB President expects volleyball to peak in Olympics', *News.Xinhuanet.com*, August 16; Wu, S. (2008) 'Nightlife: Eye candy at beach volleyball leads to fun times', *MSNBC.com*, August 18; Huang, C. (2008), 'China trains 200,000 cheerleaders - for other Olympic teams', *CSMonitor.com*, July 8.

Interviews: Blair Harrison, Competition Manager, Beach Volleyball, SOCOG; Nikos Sofianos, Competition Manager, Beach Volleyball, ATHOC; Chronis Chichlakis, Venue Coordinator for Sports Presentation, ATHOC; Andrew Hercus, Control Committee, Beach Volleyball, FIVB, Atlanta, Sydney, Athens & Asian Games.

QUESTIONS

* As the Competition Manager for Beach Volleyball at the next Summer Olympics, what opportunities do you see for improving Beach Volleyball's position as an Olympic sport? What challenges do you see? What would you recommend to the FIVB for the next Olympiad?
* Select one of the less popular Olympic sports. What lessons could this sport learn from Beach Volleyball?
* Select a professional, regional or local sports team/code. What lessons could this sport learn from Beach Volleyball's Olympic package?
* Some within the athletic community and media question how far the entertainment 'envelope' can be pushed before the primary focus becomes the entertainment, at the expense of sport's athleticism. Discuss.

Based on: Charbonneau, J., & Hercus, A. (2007). 'The perfect combination of sport, music and sex': Beach volleyball's efforts to attract Olympic spectators and media'. In Quester, McGuiggan, Perreault & McCarthy (Eds.), *Marketing* (5th ed.). Australia: McGraw Hill.

Sport marketing in Australasia

Successful sport organisations are now obliged to become market-driven, and to recognise the need to adapt sport and associated products to both participant and spectator requirements (Shilbury et al., 2009). A particular example is cricket (see case study below) where the relatively new Twenty-20 version of the game, with its fast-action, entertainment-rich format delivers cricket to a 'time-poor' target market. In rugby, rugby league and netball, certain variations and changes to the rules have improved the flow and speed of the game. Each of these three sports has introduced marketing techniques to meet customer requirements and challenge competing activities. There has also been more competition for and rivalry between sports for consumer attention and this can be seen in the rise of the newer entrepreneurial sports emanating from the United States – basketball, baseball and gridiron. With these and similar sports comes the concept of *franchising* of a sports team or club, where a commercial organisation or entrepreneur 'owns' a club, team or sporting activity. In New Zealand, clubs that have a franchise in an Australian League such as rugby league's New Zealand Warriors, basketball's Breakers and soccer's Phoenix are current examples, while rugby union and netball also both have franchises (owned by the respective sport's governing body). They all buy and contract players, sometimes with help from sponsors and the proceeds of the club's marketing activities. Additionally, clubs are becoming 'international', with several Australasian franchises in rugby, rugby league and soccer holding financial interests in British clubs.

Sports now compete with each other for a share of the public's leisure expenditure and uncommitted time. Witness the plethora of Xtreme Sport events now seen in Australasia which have almost all arisen since year 2000. Available 'purchase opportunities' have increased substantially. Increased media communications, increasing wealth, major improvements in mobility and transportation have led to vast competition not only from other sports but also from a wide variety of travel, leisure and recreational opportunities. Sport has become almost a promotional medium in its own right with its ability to target, segment (categorise), promote and produce sport products. Sport marketing can use the emotional attachment of fans to their sporting heroes, their teams and their codes, to allow corporate sponsors to position their own products and services in a 'better light'. The thorny debate of tobacco industry sponsorship in sport and the rising societal unease with alcohol sponsorship are illustrations of the way sport is used as a medium for promotion. Increasingly, major corporations are becoming the conduit for fans to gain access to particular 'events', especially where these corporations offer tickets, or discounts on ticket prices, in exchange for proof of purchase of various products (often the sponsors' own products). Further testimony to sport as a marketing medium in its own right is that sport fans can now engage in sport betting on their favourite code, with the legalising of sport gambling in Australia late last century and the formalising of sport betting in New Zealand through the state-owned Totalisator Agency Board (TAB) in 1996.

CASE STUDY: DOES SHOWCASING TWENTY-20 CRICKET BENEFIT THE GAME?

Just as with beach volleyball morphing out of 'traditional' volleyball, Twenty-20 cricket represents the same conscious effort that sport organisations use for product diversification. Earlier criticism from cricket *aficionados* about Twenty-20 being frivolous has all but disappeared. Twenty-20 is now legitimate; to date two Twenty-20 World Cups have been staged and the Indian Premier League (IPL) has been integrated into the already cluttered international fixtures' calendar. Shilbury et al. (2009) placed Twenty-20 into its context: 'cricket, a popular but not global sport, has consistently sought to expand its market by working to develop new markets and by varying its product to better suit the needs of television' (p. 4). First it was the 'one day format' developed in the 1970s. Now it's Twenty-20 cricket with a guaranteed result packaged in a compressed, action-packed and entertainment-based format. Twenty-20 has become the leading weapon for many cricket nations' national authorities to showcase cricket to a wider target audience (especially youthful and female audiences), broadening the target away from the 'traditional middle-class, male and over 50 years of age' (Hopwood & Edwards, 2007, p. 262). Australia and New Zealand, like all leading cricket nations, have their own domestic Twenty-20 competitions and currently each nation is enjoying increased crowd attendances, enhanced television rights' contracts and enhanced sponsorship deals on the back of Twenty-20's success. Showcasing cricket to a wider audience has been achieved. Cricket Australia's CEO James Sutherland stated, 'the analogy I like to use is previously fathers were taking their sons or their kids [to the cricket], but what we saw last year with the Big Bash [Australia's domestic Twenty-20 competition] all of a sudden it was the kids dragging their parents along' (Ahmed, 2010, p. B6). Now the challenge is to convert some of these new spectators 'up the loyalty ladder' to other forms of the game.

The marketing plan

A well conceived marketing programme that identifies and seeks to satisfy consumer wants is a crucial aim of a marketing plan. The first step is to gather information on who the consumer might be. This is achieved by building a picture of consumer demographic characteristics and barriers, as well as participation in order to define the target market and the manner in which it is to be satisfied. A marketing plan or strategy needs to be highly focused and directed at specific categories of consumers or consumer groups. Sport marketers should also focus on individual brands or products within the sport which best satisfy requirements and direct marketing efforts accordingly. They may choose to segment the market and to classify potential consumers on the basis of their needs and the ability of the sport to satisfy these needs. A marketer must not only define the target market but also the manner in which it is to be satisfied. Taking New Zealand Cricket as an example, the most lucrative target market has become the *theatre-goers* (and some *fair-weather fans* - see Typical Rugby Crowd case study for definitions of these segments) with members of each segment attending mainly for the entertainment and not necessarily for the intricacies of the game of cricket itself. Hence the beauty of Twenty-20 cricket for showcasing the game to *theatre-goers*. As a result of the marketing research it obtained, over time, New Zealand Cricket improved its venue facilities, restructured its pricing policy, changed its presentation of the core 'cricket' product, upgraded entertainment activities involved with each event and targeted its promotional activities (e.g., Twenty-20 to youth, female and 'time-poor' segments). Effective marketing usually means implementing simultaneously many of the strategies and tactics described above.

Bottom line – implications for management
Marketing cricket

Improving facilities involved:
- more toilets and improvements to existing toilet facilities;
- more food and beverage outlets; and
- bigger and better replay screens.

The review of pricing resulted in:
- uniform pricing across all venues;
- the introduction of family group pricing; and
- free entry to some international matches for children belonging to a cricket club.

Improvements in the way cricket (the product) was *presented* included:
- better coloured uniforms for the players;
- playing the national anthem;
- better crowd control, allowing a better experience for all;
- better programme material;
- distribution of player profiles, match information, etc., to the media;
- increased branding in the promotional activity, including at the venues;
- increased attention to merchandising at the venues;
- increased attention to sponsor relationships.

The upgrading of entertainment accompanying each event saw:
- 'pop' bands playing in the intervals (for example, between innings, lunch times);
- special displays in the intervals;
- use of the replay screen and playing music over the speaker system;
- engaging professionals to run entertainment, competitions, etc., at the venue.

For high-profile sport in New Zealand, promotion is dominated by television. However, restricted access to television coverage (for all but the 'richest' sports) places pressure on the marketing planning for those sports not in the 'high-profile league'. Other promotional methods such as direct marketing and sales promotions come to the fore, along with advertising in the less expensive print and radio media. New Zealand Cricket has devised various sales promotions for promoting fixtures to encourage attendance. These include competitions, discounted entry for volume tickets (e.g., families, 'bring a friend for free'), all manner of package deals (tickets, travel accommodation), merchandise at the venue, pre- and post-match entertainment, etc. The objective is to involve the supporting public and encourage their further participation. Hopefully this compensates for the discounting of the current event by cementing loyalty in the form of future patronage.

Price is another important element of the marketing plan. However market research indicates that pricing does not always have a major influence upon the decision of the consumer to attend an event or participate in a sporting activity. It is important though for pricing to be competitive with the pricing of other similar events or activities. Prices can be determined by a number of factors, such as, the recovery of costs, market conditions, value, competition, scarcity, and special features that include social acceptability and status. For example, the prices for the Henley Rowing Regatta, Wimbledon Tennis and Lords Cricket Test bear little relation to value offered as a sports event, but do have added value in terms of social status and scarcity. Prices can also be directed to assist with the image the sport wishes to project. For instance, the creation of a favourably priced family pass at the different formats, especially Twenty-20 cricket, has led to a considerable increase in the number of families and young people attending. The key to successful pricing strategies is to react to market demands and the elasticity of that demand. The effect of minor price fluctuations has historically appeared not to affect demand. In most cases it appears price alone does not affect demand – promotional strategies and the quality of the product may alter perceived values and accordingly affect reaction to price.

Consumers can equate price with value, and discounted or free products can be equated with little or no value. Veeck and Linn (1965) declared that they would never give tickets away; no matter how poorly their teams were performing, as tickets are their one product to sell, to give them away would be to cheapen the product. No doubt this stance will continue to be hotly debated.

Marketing the benefits of sport

The sport product is a mixture of both product and service. Products and services are offered for sale, and both satisfy the needs of customers. However, it is the benefits derived from the products or services (rather than the products themselves) that actually persuade customers to buy a product or service.

The services aspect of sport is easy to understand. The 'Ps' of physical evidence, process and people discussed above reinforce this notion. Like any service, a sporting event or competition is staged (created) and consumed simultaneously and cannot be stored (that is, the *live* action cannot be stored). Hence the service part of sport is a perishable commodity. Empty seats or unsold tickets are opportunity losses, sales lost forever. The intangible nature of services (that is, not being able to see or test the experience before participating) means the consumer has to rely on the reputation of the contest, the stager of the event and the product extensions (venue, facilities, etc). As mentioned already, the sport product by itself is unlikely to fully satisfy consumer needs. In a modern competitive situation the product extension such as venue, facilities, entertainment and atmosphere become crucial to the total product.

Sport events and activities in themselves are intangible and subjective; a good experience judged by one person may be considered indifferent by another. In preparing to market an event or sport activity, the sport marketer should undertake market research to modify the product in an effort to satisfy consumer ends and adapt to market requirements. Cricket as a product in the 1970s was in decline until the advent of the amended One-Day Limited-Over game which provided a dramatic surge in crowd attendance. Interest in cricket again began to dwindle through the 1990s and into the early years of the 21st century when, with the inception of the Twenty-20 format, cricket again enjoyed a new 'high' (see Twenty-20 case study).

Note that many of the above factors are beyond the control of the sport marketer, and they reflect the need for a continued business relationship between the sport marketer, the venue marketer, the participants, the media, the sponsors and the consumer. When assessing the value of the product, account must be taken of all these elements, while the promotion of the event will also highlight aspects of the product extension which will serve to influence or reinforce a consumer decision to attend an event.

Summary

Marketing sport today is akin to the marketing of many services. Most sport codes and sport organisations recognise that marketing and promotion of their sport or activity is essential for its survival. The advance of professional and demanding sponsors, sophisticated media outlets, professional playing teams and increased communications has meant sport organisations are recognising and reacting to the need for marketing. Sport marketing will continue to develop to satisfy consumer needs and in the process has an exciting future with increased opportunities and entertainment. The major factors influencing sport marketing will include items highlighted in the Summary Box.

Summary box

Factors influencing sport marketing

- increasing competition from all forms of leisure activity
- increasing cultural awareness
- continued growth of sport in general, and Xtreme Sports in particular
- expansion and improvement of electronic media and communications, with emphasis on Internet communication
- increasing use of electronic aids

- high standards of performance
- increasing reliance on revenue from sponsorship, media rights
- increasing importance of role models
- substantial improvement to venues and facilities
- innovative product extensions and promotional gimmicks
- increasing leisure time
- increasing wealth

Sport organisations need to project their plans out to a longer-term horizon - three-to-five-years and beyond. While visualising the market, social conditions and sport's place in society several years ahead is difficult, that exercise should involve the sport marketing manager in conjunction with the sport organisation's governing body (Board, Executive Committee, etc). The Beach Volleyball case study exemplified the use of planning and implementation of marketing strategies. Considerable market research and analysis was backed by an integrated process of marketing: production, pricing, promotion and 'placing' (distribution) of the sport service product as entertainment for targeted customers.

Review questions

- Review the role of market research in any of the cases attached to this chapter and then try and adapt their lessons to a sport organisation of your choice.
- Show how sport's selling points (or consumer benefits) are affected by economic, social and cultural factors.
- Demonstrate how sport marketing can help match the varying needs from sport with those that both players and spectators have.
- Review the role of sport sponsorship in a marketing communication plan (for promotion of both products and services) then outline the key factors to make your sponsorship strategy successful.
- A sport event is both a product and a service. List the product and service features of such an event and review the differences between products and services.
- Outline your argument for convincing a friend to attend your favourite sport event rather than visiting a fast-food restaurant to spend her or his leisure dollar.
- You have been hired as a marketing consultant to market your favourite sporting code at national level from next year. Using any of the examples in this chapter, what marketing actions would you recommend to help your code's success in the next five years?

References

Ahmed, N. (2010, December 12). Cricket: more cash in bashes than Ashes. *(NZ) Sunday Star Times*, p. B6.

Fullerton, S. (2010). *Sports marketing* (2nd ed.). New York: McGraw-Hill Irwin.

Garland, R., Macpherson, T., & Haughey, K. (2004). Rugby fan attraction factors. *Marketing Bulletin*,

15, Article 3, 12 pages. Retrieved from http://marketing-bulletin.massey.ac.nz

Gronroos, C. (2007). *Service management and marketing: customer management in service competition approach*. Chichester, England: Wiley.

Harris, K., & Elliott, D. (2007) Segmentation, targeting and positioning in sport. In J. Beech & Chadwick, S. (Eds.), *The marketing of sport* (pp. 123–142). Harlow, England: Prentice Hall.

Hopwood, M., & Edwards, A. (2007). "The game we love. Evolved.": Cricket in the 21st century. In S. Chadwick & D. Arthur (Eds.), *International cases in the business of sport* (pp. 257–269). Sydney: Butterworth-Heinemann.

Mullin, B., Hardy, S., & Sutton, W. (2007). *Sport marketing* (3rd ed.). Champaign, Illinois: Human Kinetics.

Pitts, B., & Stotlar, D. (1996). *Fundamentals of sport marketing.* Morgantown, WV: Fitness Information Technology.

Quick, S. (2000). Contemporary sport consumers: Some implications of linking fan typology with key spectator variables. *Sport Marketing Quarterly, 9*(3), 149–156.

Shilbury, D., Westerbeek, H., Quick, S., & Funk, D. (2009). *Strategic sport marketing* (3rd ed). Sydney: Allen & Unwin.

Slack, T., & Amis, J. (2004). 'Money for nothing and your cheques for free?'. In T. Slack (Ed.), *The commercialisation of sport.* New York: Routledge.

Stanton, W.J., Miller, K.E., & Layton, R. (1995). *Fundamentals of marketing* (3rd ed.). Sydney: McGraw-Hill.

Veeck, W., & Linn, E. (1965). *The hustler handbook.* New York: Pitman.

Acknowledgement

The authors wish to acknowledge and thank Jan Charbonneau of Massey University for her contribution to this chapter.

Chapter 11

Financial Management

Jenny Parry

OBJECTIVES

After completing this chapter, you should be able to:

- understand the objectives of financial management and its role within an organisation;
- understand the purpose of a budget;
- describe the budget planning process and understand how to develop one;
- identify the components of a Balance Sheet and an Income Statement and understand the differences between them;
- understand the importance of the Cash Flow Statement in relation to the Balance Sheet and Income Statement.

Key terms

In this chapter, readers will become familiar with the following concepts and terms:

- financial management
- balance Sheet
- financial planning
- income statement
- profits and losses
- cash flow statement
- budgets
- variances

Introduction

This chapter will emphasise the importance of financial management and budgeting to the successful operation of a sporting organisation or club. All sporting bodies require funds in order to function. Unfortunately, in many instances, income, in the form of subscriptions, merchandise sales, sponsorship, is insufficient to cover the organisation's expenses. In the past, financial expertise or planning ability was not considered important. Today, however, the situation is significantly different and successful organisations have experienced administrators who forecast their future financial requirements and prepare budgets for submission to their boards.

This chapter will highlight the role that financial management plays to ensure that the financial decisions made by the Board are for the optimal benefit of the organisation and its members. Financial management techniques, including budgeting, play a crucial part in ensuring that the organisation has sufficient funds readily available to meet all its goals as set down by the Board.

CASE STUDY: 'WHEN YOU'RE DOWN IT'S HARD, OR VIRTUALLY IMPOSSIBLE, TO GET UP AGAIN!'

All professional and amateur sports organisations should use financial management techniques to ensure that sufficient funds are on hand when the need for them arises. In order to do this successfully, it is important to undertake financial planning activities not only for the coming year, but for the next 3-5 year period. Consideration must be given to how projects will be funded and how transfer fees (in the case of soccer players) are covered. Investment decisions must be made carefully so that liquidity is preserved, contractual debt obligations are managed, and the value of the organisation is maintained. Once an organisation finds itself in financial difficulties it is often very difficult to break the trend of bad financial decisions – a situation Leeds United Football Club in the UK faced for many years.

Leeds United was runner-up in Division 2 in the 1955-1956 season and, after a 10 year spell in this league, the team was promoted to Division 1. However, due to a fire that destroyed the underinsured West Stand the club became desperately short of money and was forced to sell its best player. As a result, the Club was less successful on the field and was relegated to Division 2 at the end of the 1959-1960 season. In 1961 the nucleus of a good team was once again present, but the Club found itself still short of money. Three board members lent the Club funds so that they could acquire additional top class players. Consequently, the Club was promoted back to Division 1 in 1964.

Financial and hiring mismanagement practices arose once more in 1974 when the manager, Brian Clough, arrived only to be expensively removed after 44 days! Bad practices occurred yet again in 1981-1982 when Peter Barnes was bought for £930,000 and failed to live up to his earlier ability. By the end of the season the Club's poor performance saw them relegated to Division 2. In the following season the manager was sacked and the club saddled with large debts and insufficient funds to pay the wages of the top players. Funding constraints continued until the 1988-1989 season when the manager made several cheap, or free, transfers. This eventually culminated with Leeds United becoming League champions in 1992.

At the start of this century Leeds United borrowed against the value of their playing squad in the expectation of gaining admission to the UEFA Champions League. However, although the Club had implemented the cost structure required for the competition, they failed to qualify and hence received no income from participation. In addition, income from a contract for television rights to football league matches with ITV Digital did not eventuate and that company went into liquidation when it could not raise the required number of subscribers. United's debt commitments could not be paid and once again they were forced to sell their best players at considerably reduced prices thereby further undermining the strength of the team.

In 2003 the new Chairman, Professor John McKenzie, admitted that the £78 900 000 debt was a major concern, but believed that operating costs could be reduced and revenues increased without the sale of more players. However, in November 2004 a sale-lease back agreement was arranged on the Club's Elland Road ground to reduce debt and in January 2005 an agreement to sell 50 percent of the Club to the Geneva-based Forward Sport Fund was made. The Fund's representative, Ken Bates, said that the first task was to develop short-, medium- and long-term plans to secure the club's financial future. (http://www.leedsunited.com; Trenberth, 2003). The Club continued to struggle financially, even seeking liquidation in 2007. In doing so they incurred a 10 point penalty that saw them relegated to the Third

(Continued)

Division. The liquidators put the Club up for sale and as a result this incurred a 15 point sanction from the Football League. Since then the team has had consistent periods of winning and losing. In 2010 after beating Bristol Rovers 2-1 they were at last promoted to Division 2. http://www.leedsunited.com/pottedhistory/20061120/club-history_2247643_930776).

The problems that have befallen Leeds United have also occurred in other English soccer clubs. Two clubs, Manchester United and Arsenal, however, are generally considered the best managed and most financially affluent in the English Football League. However, they too rely on sponsorship funds from wealthy business men or corporations.

Organisational decision-making

The Board should establish short-term (i.e., within a year) and long-term (i.e., periods greater than a year) goals for their club and identify any constraints that may impede their implementation. Short-term goals should only be considered if they enhance the club's long-term goals and profitability. Short-term decision-making involves internal variables, such as cash flow, and the contractual obligations of debt.

Long-term decisions, however, are future oriented and can be more creative due to the uncertainty surrounding future prospects. However, successful plans require accurate information so that members of the Board can interpret the information correctly. For example, while the decision to hire an exceptionally talented coach is a long-term decision, due to the expectation that they will be associated with the organisation for a number of years, the funds that have been expended will have an impact in the short-term because they will not be available for other purposes. While the benefits from this investment may not be immediately apparent (because the advantages of the new programme the coach intends to implement may take some time to come to fruition) ticket sales, marketing and the recruitment of new players would still need to be undertaken in order to ensure the success of the organisation.

The Executive Director (ED), who is a member of the Board, develops the guidelines for achieving the goals set by the Board. These are then communicated to the heads of the various sections of the organisation who, in turn, develop budgets to meet these goals. That is, they will compile a bid for resources that will allow them to achieve the objectives set down by the ED. The underlying assumption is that the resources awarded to a particular area will be maximised to the section head's best efforts and to the benefit of all members of the organisation.

The role of financial management

Financial management's ultimate goal is to maximise the financial wealth of the organisation. It does not matter if the organisation is a sole proprietor, a large multinational corporation or a sporting club. For the rest of this chapter, the term 'organisation' will be used to cover the organisation(s) or club(s) concerned. Financial management consists of the decisions and activities performed in order to meet the financing and investment objectives of the body concerned. If the activity is done well, then the Organisation's predetermined goals and objectives will be achieved and the operations of the Organisation will not be compromised through financial constraints. It is important to realise that nowadays many major sporting organisations operate along similar lines to the businesses that sponsor them. Hence, the financial management practices of a large multinational corporate sponsor, such as Nike, operate precisely in the same way as a professional sporting organisation, albeit at rather different scales of activity.

Many sporting organisations, such as the New Zealand Rugby Union, are 'not-for-profit' organisations whose main objective is to break even each year. These organisations have a treasurer who is responsible for the organisation's financial affairs. In larger organisations a more formal structure exists and paid administrators and accountants are employed. Those sporting organisations that have become companies and which are listed on their national stock exchange have rigorous financial requirements that must be followed in order to meet the regulations set down in the relevant Companies Acts and Stock Exchange Listing Rules.

Financial management provides a platform for appropriate planning by listing all expected income and expenditure for the coming year from all sections of the organisation. Done properly, these practices inform the Board, or Committee, of the organisation's financial position and highlight potential problems early so that steps can be taken to avoid them. However, the final decisions regarding these inputs will depend on the availability of funds. Financial management can be broken down into three areas:

- *Financial planning*: this is an ongoing process whereby the future goals and objectives of the organisation are converted into financial terms. Based on these forecasts investment and financing requirements will be identified and the resultant cash flows monitored through the development of a budget. The aim is to set financial goals that will satisfy the organisation's objectives by managing available funds in the best way possible.
- *Finance*: this involves obtaining the funds necessary to achieve the objectives or goals identified by the organisation. Funds may be raised internally (from subscriptions, catering, or the sale of memorabilia) or externally from funding bodies such as the community trusts, SPARC or corporate sponsors). Professional sporting organisations may also use a mix of debt (i.e., loans), or equity (i.e., shares), in order to fund particular projects.
- *Investment*: this involves deciding how to use the funds that have been raised in order to maximise the benefits to the organisation (Parry, Black, & Bennett, 2009).

Concept Check

Financial management

Encompasses the activities and decisions performed to meet an organisation's financing and investment objectives.

The role of budgeting

Budgeting is a financial planning tool used to forecast an organisation's financial transactions for th coming year and is primarily used to estimate the organisation's future financial requirements. I other words, budgeting is part of the overall planning process for an organisation and is the key t ensuring that the established goals are met by making sure there are sufficient funds on hand, whe required, to achieve them. Budgeting has two main purposes: firstly, it is used to estimate the resourc requirements for the coming period and, secondly, it provides a system of monitoring, controlling and evaluating an organisation's financial affairs.

Budget

A budget is a financial planning tool and is based on current and past practices together with forecasts for the coming year, expressed in financial terms. This allocates resources to defined objectives and, when completed, is approved by management. A budget forecasts the expected income and expenditure that will aid the planning and control of an organisation in achieving its goals and as such is an excellent decision-making aid. One of its most important functions is making sure that there are sufficient funds on hand to achieve the goals set by the organisation. It can also be used to communicate to the organisation's members the reasons why decisions have been made to, say, raise subscriptions or reduce spending in a particular area.

Because the annual budget assists the Board in establishing goals and objectives for the organisation, it becomes a financial plan for the future and as such can be incorporated into the organisation's business plan. The business plan should be very comprehensive, contain an economic and industry overview, details of the business, its location and marketing strategies, the management team and number of staff employed, as well as full proforma or forecast financial statements.

Each Section Head receives the goals and requirements pertinent to their area and from this information develops a budget that will ensure the targets are met. When all Section Heads have provided their input, a combined budget is prepared and submitted to the Board for approval. If during the course of the year unplanned events occur, the budget can be amended to incorporate these changes. A similar process should occur at the smaller club level, although it usually takes place in a less formal way.

Requirements of a budget

A budget should be:

- Carefully planned and developed
- Realistic and have achievable goals
- Flexible so that any unexpected income or expenditure that may arise can be incorporated
- Readily understood by all who are affected by it
- Reviewed monthly so that any variances from expected figures can be investigated.

Planning

Board members undertake the short- and long-term planning for an organisation. While long-term plans are developed, and arrangements for their incorporation into the organisation are noted, they are only included in the current budget of the year in which they will eventuate. Short-term goals are communicated to each section of the organisation so that they can provide a budget for their area.

Realistic goals

The resulting budget must be realistic with goals that are measurable, achievable within the time frame and stated in specific terms. If the stated objectives cannot be achieved with the resources that are on hand then these will have to change in order to fit within the resource constraint. This activity will also highlight the level of additional funding that may be required to meet the organisation's goals.

Budgets are not set in stone and should be developed so that if subscriptions, say, are less than forecast, then revenue reduction will be offset by a compensating fall in expenses. When these situations arise the budget should be reworked to show the impact of any amendments. Budget compilation is iterative and the revision process will continue until all goals can be met or an acceptable compromise achieved.

Flexible

In order to cope with changing financing requirements a budget must be flexible so that any unexpected income or expense can be included. Hence a budget is, in effect, a living document and one that changes to cope with the requirements of each organisation.

Readily understood

A budget must be readily understood by those who are responsible for it. Therefore, a successful budget is one that contains information that can be understood by non-financial people. For example, the information emanating from the Board must be clear and concise so that each section head is fully cognisant of what is required of them. The information provided to the Executive Director must also be in a form that is readily integrated into the budget for the whole organisation. Budgets are revised in order to meet required goals and hence, it may be that due to funding constraints some projects may be omitted or postponed. Alternatively, it may be possible to increase revenues and/or decrease expenses so that all goals can be achieved.

Variances

Budgets are usually compiled on a monthly basis so that the actual results which have occurred can be compared against the planned performance. Variances that are greater than a set level should be examined carefully and adjustments made if necessary. Section Heads will be advised of any significant deviations that have occurred within their area as these may herald a change in policy and necessitate proactive management action.

A budget is the key to financial planning as it forecasts the future performance of the organisation from its past and current situation. It should be adapted to take into account changes in the economic environment that may affect the organisation and its market. It is an important aid to the organisation's goal development and business objectives and, because it is future-oriented, it can be said that a budget is the future plan for the organisation set out in financial terms.

In order to be effective, however, the budget must be realistic - its goals must be measurable and achievable. These goals must be understood, stated in specific terms and be able to be achieved within the timeframe that has been established. If the stated objectives cannot be achieved with the resources on hand then the former will have to be altered to fit within the resource constraint. This activity will also highlight the level of additional funding that may be required to meet the organisation's goals.

Concept Check

Budget

A budget is a financial planning tool, based on current and past experiences together with forecasts for the coming year - that is, it is a plan for the coming year's operations. It is expressed in financial terms and allocates resources to defined objectives and, when completed, is approved by management.

Types of budget

There are three main forms of a budget. These are:
- *Capital budgets*: that record the organisation's future capital expenditure projects
- *Cash budgets*: that record the inflows and outflows of cash
- *Operating budgets*: that project the income and expenses each month for the coming year or predetermined period.

The operating budget is the most common form of budget and it aggregates each month's items to form an annual budget. When the budget is broken down into monthly segments any funding shortfalls can be highlighted and steps taken to either raise the funds required, reduce expenses or amend the goals so that a deficit for the year does not occur.

Accountability for the budget's performance

Accountability is a very important part of budgeting. The Board, via the ED, has communicated the goals of the organisation to the section heads in the expectation that they will be met. The ED is accountable to the Board and the section heads are accountable to the ED. Each section head will develop a budget based on the targets established for their area of operations. Depending on the requirements established for the area and the level of funding available, the budget will be either approved or modified. When approval is granted each section will be responsible for ensuring their expenditure does not rise higher than the funds allocated to them.

Figure 11-1: Levels of accountability

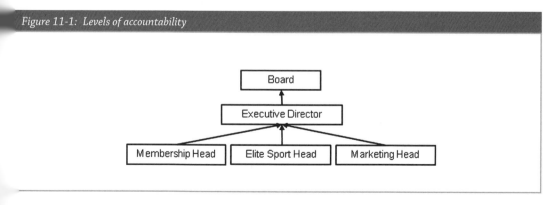

The budget process

Budget preparation for the coming year takes place once the goals have been determined by the Board. The budget should adhere to the organisation's objectives and amendments will be made, where necessary, so that the process achieves internal consistency within the organisation, i.e., that the organisation's goals can be achieved using the resources available. Once this has been achieved the budget is ready to be approved by the Board. Approval should be granted at least a month prior to the start of the financial year and be recorded in the Minutes prior to the financial period to which they relate. It is important to note that approval brings with it accountability, because the performance of all staff associated with their section of the budget will be judged positively or negatively depending on whether the goals set for their area have been met.

It is important to know how much income is expected to be received, the timing of the funds, and when expenses will be incurred. For example, the income from a golf club would be received at the beginning of the season when annual subscriptions are paid, with additional income being generated throughout the year from green fees, the professional's shop, competitions as well as summer and twilight memberships. That is, income will come in blocks throughout the year so that a very high income stream will occur in some months, whereas in other months very little income will be generated. In order to ensure that resources are available when required the expected activity levels should be established on a weekly or monthly basis. This exercise will show when expenses may exceed income and will highlight periods when additional funds will be required. If there is a shortfall in funding, additional funds can be obtained either in the form of a bank loan, by rescheduling some of the capital expenditure planned for projects, or by delaying payments to creditors.

The preparation of a budget requires that it adheres to the organisation's objectives and that its goals can be achieved using the resources available. In most instances, the demand for funds will exceed the supply so that in order to optimise the benefits to the organisation and its members, an iterative process, as shown in Figure 11-2, is performed to maximise the allocation of funds to cover the desired outcomes. The figure shows the lines of communication that flow between the various groups. If the funds available equal or exceed the budget requests from each section of the organisation, it can be presented to the Board by the ED. However, if the request for funds exceeds the level of funding available then each section will be required to rework their budgets until the goals can

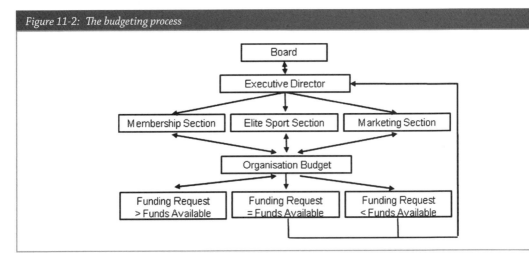

Figure 11-2: The budgeting process

be fully funded. In some instances, if the level of funds available is too low the ED may have to ask the Board to revise their programme or accept a more conservative one.

Although Figure 11-3 shows that the budget cycle can be performed step-by-step, many of the procedures that are undertaken, such as planning, coordinating and interpreting, are interrelated. Budgets are usually based on the previous year's data with adjustments incorporated to reflect changes in the income and expenditure patterns expected to occur during the coming year. As a result the process provides additional information that will be required for the budget in the year following.

Figure 11-3:   The annual budgeting cycle

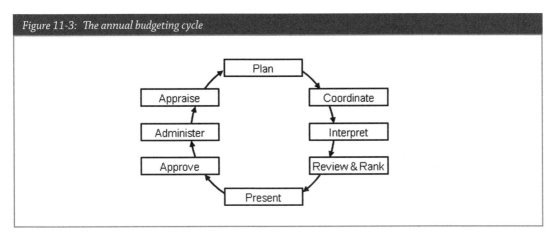

Budget development process

Plan
The business plan provides information regarding the direction and requirements of the organisation. If a current budget is available then consideration of how the items in it may change in the coming year should be considered with regard to forecasts of the direction of the economy and requirements of the target market. Information from the organisation's Board regarding its requirements for the coming year will also provide information concerning existing projects or contracts they want terminated as well as new ventures they want the organisation to follow.

Coordinate
Information will come to each section head from their staff. This information will be combined to form the budget for that section. Budgets from the various section heads will be integrated to form a single budget for the organisation. However, if one section's budget requires alteration it is important to consider budgets from all sections in order to make sure that the changes made to one section do not impact detrimentally on other sections. At this stage the ED will become aware of any funding shortfalls that will arise if the objectives set by the Board are to be fulfilled.

Interpret
It is important that the budget is fully understood by those who are affected by it and who are required to develop the budget for their section. If the budget's requirements have not been

communicated properly then it will be very difficult for it to be interpreted correctly by others and, prepared successfully. If the budget has been incorrectly interpreted by the section heads then wrong information will have been included and ED will require that the budget be amended.

Review and rank

Inevitably there will be insufficient income available to achieve all the goals set by the Board. As a result it will be necessary to review each project and assess its importance to the organisation. Once this has been done the projects can be ranked in order of priority with those considered to have the most benefit to the organisation selected.

Example

Assume that the Board of the Rotorua Rebels Rugby Club has $1.8 million available for projects for the coming year. These are listed below:

Training room refurbishment	$ 175,000
Corporate sponsorship promotion programme	$ 225,000
Minibus replacement	$ 45,000
Ground surface replacement	$ 560,000
Board room refurbishment	$ 225,000
Brand development programme	$ 125,000
Junior league promotion	$ 75,000
Player purchases	$ 750,000
Total funds required	$2,180,000

After considerable deliberation the Board decided that projects benefitting current and potential players were the most important, and the ranking of projects for the coming year would be as follows:

1. Player purchases	$750,000
2. Ground surface replacement	$560,000
3. Junior league promotion	$ 75,000
4. Corporate sponsorship promotion programme	$225,000
5. Minibus replacement	$ 45,000
6. Training room refurbishment	$175,000

7. Brand development programme	$125,000
8. Board room refurbishment	$225,000

The board decided to proceed with projects 1-6 even though the total funds to be committed were $30 000 greater than the sum available. The shortfall in funding could be obtained by reducing the amounts allocated for the purchase of new players and seeking to increase corporate sponsorship.

Present

If the coordination and interpretation of the instructions from the Board have been done well, then the presentation by the ED to the Board will be clear and concise. In general, this will result in approval being granted. Graphics and power-point presentations should be used to clarify difficult areas.

Approve

Budget approval is a management decision. If the groundwork has been done well then the budget will reflect the input from both management and others. A few Board members may want to see some of the individual budgets, as well as the coordinated one in order to assess the total impact of the future funding requirements on the organisation and its component units.

Administer

Accounting procedures are used to ensure that the budget is implemented properly and that funds are allocated to the various sections and their programmes. The purchase department verifies all purchase requisitions so that the programme providers are only required to review the budget reports and ensure the charges made against their accounts are correct. However, in those instances when the programme is income-producing the procedure becomes more complicated and the programme providers become more accountable for the transactions undertaken in running the programme. In these cases the programme providers are accountable for the receipt of funds and their allocation to those expenses relating to the programme.

Appraise

Appraisal is an ongoing process throughout the year. Each month the actual performance is compared against the expected performance and any variances from the expenditure reported back to the managers concerned. Significant variances, if they occur, are investigated and the reasons for the variance found so that the budget can be amended if necessary (Langley & Hawkins, 2004).

The annual budgeting cycle provides additional information required for setting next year's budget. If income is guaranteed then the organisation can pursue long-term goals and contracts with players as well as embark on capital improvements to the organisation and its facilities. However, if the income fails to materialise, these contractual undertakings and other commitments must still be paid requiring additional funds to be raised. In some cases, liquidation may be the only avenue open to the organisation. Some organisations may raise debt in order to pursue their goals in the expectation that when the goals are met additional revenue will follow. Although some organisations have a big demand for team memorabilia, problems satisfying this demand will arise if they do not have the cash to pay the suppliers.

Example

The example below provides figures for the month of May as forecast at the start of the financial year when the Club's budget was compiled. The actual amount that was received or spent is compared with this figure so that any variances greater than 3 percent can be investigated further.

	BUDGET AMOUNT	ACTUAL AMOUNT	VARIANCE	>< 3%	NOTES
Table 11-1: Rotorua Rebels Rugby Club budget showing variances					
INCOME					
Subscriptions	154 000	-4 500	-4 500	F*	
Merchandise expenses	58 000	61 500	3 500	F	1
Catering expenses	196 000	188 000	-8 000	U*	2
Total	408 000	399 000	-9 000	F	3
EXPENSES					
Team expenses	30 900	31 910	1 010	U	2
Merchandise expenses	33 720	34 150	430	F	1
Catering expenses	115 300	121 500	6 200	U	2
Electricity and Gas	10 200	10 300	100	F	1
Salaries and Wages	45 000	45 000	0	F	1
Printing and Stationery	3 200	3 250	50	F	1
Repairs and Maintenance	38 000	38 400	400	F	1
Total	*276 320*	*284 510*	*8 190*	*F*	*3*
Profit/Loss	*131 680*	*114 490*	*17 190*	*U*	*3*

*F = Favourable
*U = Unfavourable

Notes:
1. All items in this category were within the 3 percent deviation from the budgeted figure as required by the Board.
2. All items in this category exceeded the amount of variance required by the Board and will be investigated individually in order to determine the reasons for the discrepancies.
3. The totals for both Income and Expenses fell within the 3 percent variance requirement. However, the resulting loss exceeded this threshold which is unsatisfactory. The reasons for the discrepancy should come to light once the analysis of each item denoted as 'U' is investigated.

Example: Budget preparation

The Rotorua Rebels Rugby Club was formed 30 years ago in Rotorua. The Rebels home ground is situated on the exposed hilly side of Springfield Road. Due to a) the changing weather patterns that have prevailed over the past few years and b) a number of complaints from opposing teams and some Club members, the Board has developed a 5-year plan to upgrade the facilities at the ground. The planned schedule is as follows:

Year 1	Upgrade changing facilities and toilet blocks	$ 750 000
Year 2	Modernise catering facilities, shop and entrance turnstiles	$ 600 000
Year 3	Enlarge the stadium and modernise it to meet new safety regulations. Phase 1	$1 200 000
Year 4	Stadium development. Phase 2	$2 300 000
Year 5	Replace boundary fences and landscape park and grounds	$ 350 000

The Club has received a number of bequests over the years and has $3 800 000 in short- and medium-term investments. In order to raise the additional funds required to complete the projects the Board has recommended that investments of $300 000 be redeemed when they mature in the current year. In addition, $3 500 000 of investments will be retained until year 3 when a further $1 200 000 will be redeemed. The ED has been requested to reduce costs by 10% and increase revenues by 15% in the coming year. Due to the current strong economic climate and high employment levels, the ED considers that entrance fees and membership subscriptions could be increased for the first time for a number of years. In addition, additional corporate sponsors will be sought. The following cost reductions were achieved:

- A 9% reduction in catering costs
- A 17.5% saving on the cost of playing strips by changing to a cheaper manufacturer
- A 12% reduction for grounds and maintenance expenses as a result of implementing a tender programme
- a rate concession was granted by the City Council for the Club's grounds and facilities.

The budget shown below incorporates these cost savings, as well as the increase in entrance fees and subscriptions. The budget shows that the Club's income and expenditure does not occur evenly throughout the year. For example, subscriptions are paid at the start of the rugby season, game-related income and player expenses occur during the playing season, and the Club's terminal tax is paid in February and provisional tax payments are made in March, July and November. As a result a deficit occurs from October to December. However, due to the surpluses that have occurred in previous months, sufficient funds are available to cover these deficits and upgrade the Club's changing facilities and toilet blocks. Due to the Club generating sufficient income in year 1, the ED would recommend that the Board does not redeem the investment of $300 000.

ROTORUA REBELS RUGBY CLUB LTD
Budget for the year ending 31 December 2011

Income	January	February	March	April	May	June	July	August	September	October	November	December	Total
Subscriptions			295 000	426 000	154 000								875 000
Ticketing			94 000	126 000	112 000	128 000	124 000	124 000	132 000				840 000
Merchandise			38 000	74 000	58 000	47 000	35 000	31 000	53 000				336 000
Catering			164 500	220 500	196 000	224 000	217 000	217 000	231 000				1 470 000
Advertising	175 000	228 000	207 000	94 000	49 000	49 000	57 000	56 000	61 000				976 000
Interest	14 583	14 811	14 781	15 549	17 124	17 887	18 089	17 959	18 248	18 531	17 909	17 230	202 701
Total Income	**189 583**	**242 811**	**813 281**	**956 049**	**586 124**	**465 887**	**451 089**	**445 959**	**495 248**	**18 531**	**17 909**	**17 230**	**4 699 701**
Expenses													
Purchases: Catering			96 765	129 706	115 294	131 765	127 647	127 647	135 882				864 706
Merchandise			22 093	43 023	33 721	27 326	20 349	18 023	30 814				195 349
Team: Uniform			10 000										10 000
Transport & Accom.			20 900	25 850	25 850	25 850	25 850	25 850	25 850				176 000
Laundry			700	1 550	1 550	1 550	1 550	1 550	1 550				10 000
ACC and Physio	300	300	1 268	2 895	3 450	3 550	3 200	3 460	3 960	2 584	300	300	25 567
Umpires			3 200	5 200	5 200	5 200	5 200	5 200	6 400				35 600
Security	5 000	5 000	9 000	12 000	12 000	12 000	12 000	12 000	12 000	5 000	5 000	5 000	106 000
Promotion and Adv.	62 000	75 000	90 000	52 000	32 000	28 000	28 000	25 000	30 000	5 000	5 000	8 000	440 000
Repairs and Maint.	6 000	7 500	52 000	45 000	38 000	38 000	38 000	34 000	31 000	8 500	5 600	4 200	307 800
Telecommunications	4 500	4 500	9 600	9 600	9 600	9 800	9 800	9 700	9 900	5 000	4 500	4 500	91 000
Rates and Insurance			25 000	75 000		25 000			25 000	63 000	12 000	25 000	250 000
Printing and Stat'y	1 500	1 500	4 500	3 200	3 200	3 200	3 400	3 300	3 400	1 500	1 500	1 600	31 800
Salaries and Wages	20 000	20 000	54 000	45 000	45 000	45 000	45 000	45 000	48 000	45 000	20 000	20 000	452 000
Electricity and Gas	2 500	2 500	7 500	10 200	10 200	11 000	11 000	11 000	10 600	2 500	2 500	2 500	84 000
Depreciation	23 000	23 000	23 000	23 000	23 000	23 000	23 000	23 000	23 000	23 000	23 000	23 000	276 000
Bad Debts					1 500	1 800	1 800	1 800	1 800	1 500	1 000		11 200
Interest and Bank Ch.	4 000	4 000	6 000	6 500	6 500	7 000	7 500	7 500	6 000	4 000	4 000	4 000	67 000
Accounting and Legal	10 000	20 000	45 000	25 000	3 500	3 500	3 500	3 500	3 500	15 500	3 500	3 500	140 000
IRD Payments		71 197	95 420				95 420				95 420		357 457
GST Payments/(Refund)	10 631	14 273	51 236	63 924	35 194	15 622	18 337	18 882	18 802	-13 875	-5 098	-6 977	220 951
Total Expenses	**149 431**	**248 770**	**627 182**	**578 648**	**404 759**	**418 162**	**480 553**	**376 412**	**427 458**	**168 209**	**178 222**	**94 623**	**4 152 430**
Income – Expenses	**40 152**	**-5 959**	**186 099**	**377 401**	**181 365**	**47 725**	**-29 464**	**69 547**	**67 813**	**-149 678**	**-160 313**	**-77 393**	**547 295**
Cumulative Total	**40 152**	**34 193**	**220 292**	**597 693**	**779 058**	**826 783**	**797 319**	**866 866**	**934 679**	**785 001**	**624 688**	**547 295**	

Financial statements

The budget as described above is a working document that is used within the Club during the course of the year. There are three financial statements used by organisations which are published annually that reflect the financial performance of the organisation, its financial position and any changes in the organisation's cash position during the year. These are:

- Income Statement
- Balance Sheet
- Cash Flow Statement

Income Statement

The Income Statement measures the financial performance of the organisation by recording its income and expenditure over a specified period of time, usually a year, in order to calculate the profit or loss that has been generated. The process is shown in equation form as:

Profit (Loss) = Income – Expenditure

The Income Statement records transactions on an accrual basis, whereby income and expenditure are recorded when they occur and not when the funds are received or paid for the transaction. For example, merchandise sales may be on credit with payment to be made in the next reporting period. The transaction is recorded in the current period, but the following period's cash balance will increase when payment is made.

The Income Statement also includes non-cash items such as depreciation, as well as accruals and the purchase or sale of Fixed Assets. As a result the profits that are made do not reflect cash that is available to spend. Hence the situation could arise where an organisation was profitable but may not be liquid, i.e., does not have sufficient cash available to use. In order to overcome this problem a Cash Flow Statement is compiled to show the inflow of cash generated from operations or raised from additional financing activities.

Concept Check

Income statement

An Income Statement measures the financial performance of the organisation over a period of time. It shows the organisation's profits or losses that result from its income and expenditure over the period.

Balance Sheet

The Balance Sheet measures the organisation's financial position as at a certain date (the organisation's balance date). There are two sides to it – one that shows what the organisation owns and the other side shows how much the organisation owes. This can be represented by the following equations:

Assets = Liabilities + Owners' Equity

or

Owners' Equity = Assets – Liabilities

Assets are items that are owned by the Club and can be separated into two categories – Current and Fixed (or Non-Current). Current Assets can be converted into cash within a year, for example, cash, debtors, inventory, whereas Fixed Assets are owned for periods greater than a year, such as equipment, buildings, long-term investments.

Liabilities can also be separated into Current and Long-Term items that are owed to others by the organisation. Current Liabilities are short-term debts that have been incurred by the organisation and must be paid for within a year. These include, for example, creditors, bank overdraft. Long-term Liabilities are debts that the organisation owes that will mature within the next two or more years.

Owners' Equity (or Shareholders' Funds if a listed company) represents funds provided by the owners. Any profits or losses made during the course of the year belong to the owners and are added to (or subtracted from) this figure. In other words the financial performance of the organisation as shown by the Income Statement represents the changes in the organisation's financial position since the previous Balance Sheet was prepared.

Concept Check

Balance Sheet

The Balance Sheet reflects the organisation's financial position at a given date. It is a statement of the organisation's assets and liabilities as at a certain date.

Cash Flow Statement

The Cash Flow Statement records the changes in cash available to an organisation over a period of time. Cash receipts or payments are recorded when they are actually received or spent. The Cash Flow Statement also records the outflow of cash to purchase assets required by the organisation over a set period of time. The Cash Flow Statement is divided into three parts:

- Operational activities: cash flows associated with the income and expenditure from operations.
- Financing activities: cash flows acquired from raising and servicing debt and equity.
- Investment activities: cash inflows or outflows arising from the sale or purchase of assets.

Both the Income Statement and the Cash Flow Statement affect the Balance Sheet in the following way:

- Income Statement profits (losses) increase (decrease) Owners' Equity in the Balance Sheet.
- Cash Flow Statement reflects changes in the Owners' Equity, Assets and Liabilities sections in the Balance Sheet.

Concept Check

Cash Flow Statement

The Cash Flow Statement highlights changes in the organisation's cash inflows and outflows over a set period of time.

Therefore, the Owners' Equity in the Balance Sheet will increase or decrease depending on whether a profit or loss has been made during the year. The Cash Flow Statement builds on this by highlighting the changes in assets (i.e., sale or purchase of Fixed Assets) and liability (i.e., increases or decreases in debt or equity) values between balance dates.

Critical Argument Summary Box

Financial management in sport

Financially sound clubs can:
- purchase top players
- acquire the best coaches and support staff
- retain these coaches as the team's performance is high

Clubs with poor financial management:
- cannot afford to buy top players and good players leave when offered a more lucrative contract from another club
- are unable to attract elite coaches or support staff
- change coaches regularly because the team is not performing well. This process is unsettling to players and not conducive to good player performance.

Summary

Financial management and its role in any organisation was the first area covered in this chapter. The technique includes the decisions and activities required to meet the organisation's goals and objectives and, in the process, ensures that sufficient funds are on hand to do so.

The financial planning activity of budgeting is used to forecast the financial transactions of an organisation annually and includes the development of a budget. The budget is used to ensure that a) sufficient funds are available to meet the organisation's requirements and b) a system of monitoring, controlling and evaluating these activities are in place.

The chapter included a discussion of the five requirements of a budget, i) the levels of accountability, ii) its annual cycle of planning, coordinating, interpreting and reviewing, iii) its presentation to the Board, iv) the Board's approval and v) the administering and appraising during the year. The process of developing a budget was illustrated using a fictitious rugby club and showed that, even though a cash deficit may occur in some months, the surpluses of other months can assist the club meet its established goals.

The chapter concluded by describing the three financial statements that are used to show the organisation's financial performance (the Income Statement), its financial position (the Balance Sheet) and changes in cash (the Cash Flow Statement).

CASE STUDIES
1. ESSENDON FOOTBALL CLUB, AFL

This Club, at one time, did not have good financial management practices in place but did have a very strong subscription base that assisted it in avoiding financial problems. By having sufficient funds available to them meant that they could buy top players from other clubs in the competition whenever they were required. Other Australian Football Clubs, however, were not as fortunate and, as a result, did have financial management difficulties (Parkin & Bourke, 2004).

2. ALL BLACKS

The Rugby Union in New Zealand requires funds to support the development of potential All Blacks and to cover the salaries of top players. This is generated primarily from broadcasting income, All Blacks match revenues and sponsorships. Although the Union has shown a deficit for the last few years they have cash reserves. Naturally, their objective is to breakeven if at all possible so projects are carefully ranked and monitored to ensure that cost over-runs are minimised.

The players also receive money management advice and are offered the assistance of independent financial advisers to assist them manage their income (Paul Dalton, Commercial Manager, NZRU (2011) personal communication).

3. SYDNEY SWANS, AFL

All new players who are inducted into the Swans draw up a budget to record their income and expenditure. From day 1 emphasis is placed on commencing a saving plan so that by the end of year 2 sufficient funds have been accumulated to start an investment programme. As a result, by year 4 a number of players are able to pay the deposit for a house, the average value of which is more than $A600 000. This would not have been possible if financial management practises had not been encouraged on the personal level (Parkin & Bourke, 2004).

Review Questions

- Define financial management and describe its three functions.
- What is the objective of financial planning? Why is it necessary?
- Describe the budgeting process.
- Discuss the purpose of a budget and list its advantages.
- Describe the budget planning cycle.
- Compare and contrast the Balance Sheet and Income Statement.
- Discuss the purpose of the Cash Flow Statement and how it affects the Balance Sheet.

Advancing your understanding

Blayley, R. E., & McLean, D. D. (2008). *Financial resource management: Sport, tourism and leisure services*. Champaign, IL: Sagamore.

Bodie, Z., Kane, A., & Marcus, A. J. (2009). *Investments* (8th ed.). Boston, MA: McGraw-Hill Irwin.

Brealey, R. A., Myers, S. C., & Allen, F. (2011). (2003). *Principles of corporate finance* (10th ed.). New York: McGraw-Hill Irwin.

Brown, M. T., Rascher, D. A., Nagel, M. S., & McEvoy, C. D. (2010). *Financial management in the sport industry*. Scottsdale, Ar.: Holcomb Hathaway.

Fried, G., Shapiro, S. J., & DeSchriver, T. D. (2008). *Sport finance* (2nd ed.). Windsor, Ontario: Human Kinetics.

Gilson, C., Pratt, M., Roberts, K., & Weymes, E. (2001). *Peak performance: Business lessons from the world's top sports organizations*. London: HarperCollins.

Gitman, L. J., Juchau, R., & Flanagan, J. (2010). *Principles of managerial finance* (6th ed.). Frenchs Forest, NSW: Pearson.

Hiller, D., Grinblatt, M., & Titman, S. (2008). *Financial markets and corporate strategy* (European ed.). Boston: McGraw-Hill Higher Education.

Ross, S. A., Westerfield, R. W., & Jordan, B. D. (2010). *Fundamentals of corporate finance* (9th ed.). Boston: McGraw-Hill Irwin.

Sawyer, T. H., Hypes, M., & Hypes, J. A. (2004). *Financing the sport enterprise*. Champaign, IL: Sagamore.

Shibli, S. (2003). Budgeting and Financial Control. In L. Trenberth (Ed.), *Managing the business of sport* (pp. 185-208). Palmerston North, New Zealand: Dunmore Press.

Stewart, B. (2007). *Sport funding and finance*. Oxford: Elsevier Sport Management Series.

Viney, C. (2003). *McGraths financial institutions, instruments and markets*. Sydney: McGraw-Hill.

References

Langley, T. D., & Hawkins, J. D. (2004). *Administration for exercise-related professions* (2nd ed.). Belmont, CA: Thomson/Wadsworth.

Parkin, D., & Bourke, P. (2004). *What makes teams work*. Sydney: Pan Macmillan.

Parry, J., Black, C., & Bennett, A. (2009). *Fundamentals of finance* (3rd ed.). Auckland, New Zealand: Pearson Education.

Trenberth, L. (Ed.). (2003). *Managing the business of sport*. Palmerston North, New Zealand: Dunmore Press.

Websites

- Leeds United football club, http://www.leedsunited.com

Chapter 12

Human Resource Management

Graham Cuskelly and Christopher Auld

OBJECTIVES

After completing this chapter, you should be able to:

- understand the importance of the nexus between volunteer and paid staff in human resource management in sport organisations;
- define human resource management from the traditional perspective and its key functions of acquiring, developing, and retaining volunteers and paid staff;
- articulate the process of human resource planning;
- understand the recruitment, selection, orientation, training, and performance management functions of human resource management;
- describe the concept of organisational commitment and its importance in the retention of paid staff and volunteers;
- appreciate the complexity of and factors that affect human resource management in sport organisations.

Key terms

In this chapter, readers will become familiar with the following concepts and terms:
- human resource management (HRM)
- organisational commitment
- orientation
- performance appraisal
- performance management
- position description
- position specification
- recruitment
- remuneration
- replacement
- retention
- selection
- training and development
- turnover
- volunteer manager

CASE STUDY: THE NATIONAL DIRECTOR OF COACHING IS NEVER IN HER OFFICE

The President of a prominent National Sport Organisation sits down for a coffee with one of his board members and bemoans the fact that he can never get in contact with Director of Coaching (DoC). The DoC was appointed six months ago, shortly before the President was voted into his position after four years of loyal service as a National Board member and many years previously in a voluntary role as National Coach. About two years ago, the President retired from a large accounting firm, where he was a senior partner, with supervisory responsibility for 20 staff. Prior to her appointment, the new DoC signed a three-year performance-based employment contract that was approved by the National Board and the current President. A high priority on the position description (PD) was for the DoC to develop and strengthen networks of coaches across all levels of the sport. Although directly answerable to the National Executive Director (NED), the PD called for the DoC to work within broad policy guidelines and to report her activities to the National Board monthly meeting. A criticism that was frequently levelled at the previous DoC was that he lacked initiative. For all but relatively minor day-to-day tasks, the previous DoC constantly phoned the President and former National Coach to seek advice before he made a decision. The previous President was the prime mover in completely redesigning the PD for the role of DoC.

In an annoyed tone, the President looks over his coffee and says to the board member, "I never seem to be able to get in contact with the DoC. When I drop into the office, either she's not in or her assistant tells me she's in a meeting and can't be interrupted. When I phone, she is either out of the office or is on another call. Last week, the office assistant said it might be best if I make an appointment if I have something to discuss with the DoC." Raising his voice, the President goes on to say, "I've had enough. If things don't improve, I'm going to recommend to the Board that we call for her resignation."

Abruptly the board member says, "That sounds a bit harsh. After all, she has made significant improvements to the development of coaching across all levels in the sport and unlike her predecessor, complaints about a lack of communication and consultation by the DoC have been few and far between. Doesn't her employment contract require her to meet coach development targets and that she can approach the job how she sees fit? I think she's doing a great job."

"No, I don't think that I can put up with this situation any longer," grumbled the President, "being told that I should make an appointment to see *my* Director of Coaching is the last straw. Just two weeks ago, when I called, she was away with the national team, probably living it up in some five-star hotel. When I called her mobile, all I got was her voice mail." Board member: "Did she get back to you?" President: "Well, yes, she did, but that's not the point. She should tell me when she's going to be out of town. No, I don't care what sort of job she's doing; she's just got to go."

Two weeks later, the agenda paper lands on the NED's desk. Item #1 of the President's report is 'Review of the DoC employment contract'. As the NED, how will you prepare for the meeting? What specific issues or points would you bring to the Board's attention? Would you take sides on this matter? Why or why not?

Introduction

It is with and through human resources that sport is delivered to communities. The management of sport and the delivery of sport programmes and services are reliant upon the involvement and commitment of a large number of volunteers and a smaller but increasing number of paid staff. Volunteers are often described as the 'backbone' of sport systems, and 25.3 % or one in four New Zealand adults volunteered for a sport or recreation activity (SPARC, 2008). In Australia the rate is lower with 11% or 1.7 million adults volunteering in sport and recreation (ABS, 2011). Such a large discrepancy in volunteer participation rates may be accounted by differences between definitions and data collection methods. The delivery of sport in many communities would be curtailed or may not occur without the time and effort contributed by volunteers and paid staff. The management of sport however, is in a constant state of change and the increasing professionalisation of its workforce has led to increased numbers of paid employees in sport. In New Zealand in 2009 the sport industry accounted for 1.1% of the labour market, or more than 24,160 jobs (Department of Labour, 2010). In the 2006 census in Australia, 75, 155 (0.8%) people listed their main occupation in sport and recreation (ABS, 2011).

The management of sport organisations has become increasingly complex due to a range of influences, including the demands of members, government policy initiatives, contractual obligations to sponsors and incursions from the legal system. More than a decade ago Kikulis, Slack, and Hinings (1995) recognised that the management of sport has progressed from the kitchen table to executive office and boardroom operations. Volunteers can sometimes find it difficult to cope with the demands of successfully managing contemporary sport organisations, particularly those who are under increasing pressure to be more professional in their approach to service delivery and more accountable to a widening circle of stakeholders. Sport organisations are becoming more reliant on paid staff to realise strategically important goals and to manage their day-to-day operations.

As the trend of employing paid staff continues to rise, the nexus between volunteers and paid employees has emerged as a critical component in the success of sport organisations. This nexus is critical to the quality and timeliness of service delivery through management systems that are less impoverished than under the traditional 'kitchen table' approach. However, it has long been argued that volunteers do not integrate into organisational systems as completely as do employees (Simon, 1957). The relationship between volunteers and employees can break down as the two parties have different expectations of one another and of their own relationships with the sport organisation. Employees in sport sometimes complain about the unrealistic demands placed upon them by members of voluntary boards. They also feel that volunteers cannot be relied upon to complete tasks or meet deadlines. Volunteers, on the other hand, are sometimes resentful when paid staff place demands on them to complete tasks, especially when a task is perceived as a functional responsibility of an employee. A further layer of complexity in the relationship between volunteers, paid staff and sport organisations is evident because many of those employed in third-sector sport organisations are directly responsible to voluntary board or committee members. Pearce (1993, p. 177) contends that "tension can exist between volunteer and employee co-workers' which tends to undermine the legitimacy of the others" efforts because of differing relationships to the organisation.

This chapter provides an overview of a model of human resource management (HRM) which is based on traditional personnel management. The focus of this chapter is on the management of human resources, both paid and volunteer. Important differences between paid staff and volunteers in relation to HRM are highlighted. It is recognised that there is a range of HRM paradigms and that a HRM model based on traditional personnel management has weaknesses as well as strengths. All HRM models make the assumption that

> management's interests are the most legitimate...HRM must ultimately fit the competitive environment. . .that organisations be less ad hoc in their management decision making and more strategic. . .[and]. . .that HRM innovations will be in the long-term social interest of employees, employers, and the nation.
>
> *(Pinnington & Lafferty, 2003, p. 25).*

The role of Human Resource Management (HRM)

Human resource management (HRM) is a process whereby the needs and expectations of individuals are matched with organisational requirements within the context of broader social norms. The coordination and delivery of sport is labour-intensive and involves seasonal, casual, part-time, full-time, permanent and contracted staff, some of whom are paid and many others who are volunteers and unpaid. Often volunteers have direct managerial responsibility for other volunteers within sport organisations. Under different circumstances but within the same organisation, volunteers manage paid staff, paid staff manage volunteers, and paid staff have line management responsibility for other paid staff. Whether staff are unpaid or paid, the management of human resources is of fundamental importance to the success of sport organisations.

Concept Check

Human Resource Management (HRM)

HRM is that part of management dealing directly with people. It involves the productive utilisation of people in achieving the organisation's goals and the satisfaction of individual paid staff and volunteer needs.

Volunteers and paid staff often work at both strategic and operational levels within sport organisations (see Table 12-1). Individuals who hold multiple roles (e.g., as a coach and as a board member) are often required to divide their time between strategic and operational matters. Depending upon the size and financial resources available to a sport organisation, a job, such as a referee, might be a paid position at a particular organisational level but voluntary at a lower level within the same organisation. The interrelationships between volunteers and paid staff are complex. Volunteers are either appointed or elected to a designated position within a sport organisation and are not directly remunerated for the work that they do. Paid staff members are recruited and appointed, part-time or full-time, to a designated position on a permanent or contract basis for which there are particular working conditions and financial remuneration. For the purposes of this chapter, the terms 'volunteer' and 'unpaid staff' are used interchangeably. The functions of HRM in relation to players, members, parents of junior players, supporters, spectators and other non-managerial roles is beyond the scope of this chapter.

Table 12-1: Examples of paid and volunteer positions with operational and strategic foci within sport organisations

ORGANISATIONAL LEVEL	VOLUNTEER (UNPAID)	PAID
Operational	Official, umpire, referee Coach Team manager Bus driver	Referee Education Director Coaching Development Officer Front-office staff / secretary Event Operations Coordinator
Strategic	Board or committee member President / chairperson Vice-President Volunteer coordinator	Executive Director Chief Executive Officer Secretary-Manager Sport Development Officer

Sport organisations are often well versed in communicating their mission and goals, putting into place plans, structures and strategies and acquiring the necessary resources to attain their goals. It is the human resources that enable sport organisations to acquire the financial and physical resources needed to achieve strategically important goals. HRM is an essential function of sport management and is conceptualised as a sequential and cyclical process (see Figure 12-1). HRM plans and organises for the recruitment, selection, orientation, training, development, and performance management of paid and unpaid staff in sport organisations. The functions of HRM can be categorised as acquiring, developing and retaining human resources. The performance of individual staff is underpinned by their ability to do the job, the commitment and effort they are prepared to put into the job and the support provided by the organisation. The role of HRM is to bring appropriate staff and volunteers into the organisation, develop a sense of commitment to the organisation and to their role, provide training and development opportunities, offer appropriate support, retain those who contribute positively to the organisation's goals, and recognise and reward their performance.

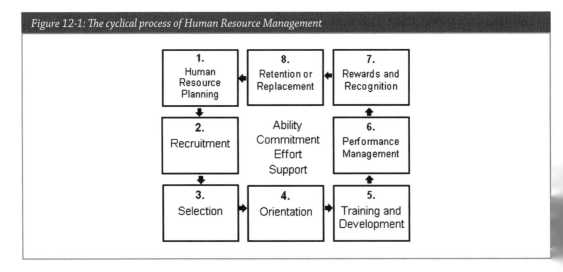

Figure 12-1: The cyclical process of Human Resource Management

Factors affecting the HRM function

The HRM function is impacted by a range of internal and external factors. Internal organisational factors such as culture, size, finance and structure, strategic plans, geographic dispersion, and the relationships between paid staff and volunteers are critical to the implementation of HRM activities. For example, the position of coaching development officer at a local hockey club would be unpaid in most cases, whereas a larger more financially secure regional association may be in a position to appoint a paid person on a part or full-time basis. The external environment also has an important role to play in the management of human resources. Government funding policies and legislative requirements – including anti-discrimination and equal opportunity, unions, and legislation which impacts on the HRM practices within sport organisations, particularly those which employ paid staff. In New Zealand this legislation includes the Health and Safety in Employment Act (1992), Employment Relations Act (2000), Human Rights Act (1993) and Minimum Wage Act (1983).

Australia has equivalent legislation such as the Model Work Health and Safety Act (2010), Fair Work Act (2009) and the National Employment Standards (2010).

Human resource planning

A strategic approach to HRM requires a long-term view and the process of human resource planning begins with a review of the sport organisation's strategies and objectives. Salaries and wages for paid staff account for a substantial proportion of the operating budgets of many sport organisations. Human resource planning, sometimes referred to as staffing, analyses current and future organisational needs for volunteers and paid staff in relation to existing and planned programmes, services and events. The purposes of human resource planning (staffing) are fitting the skills of individuals with the requirements of the job and ensuring that individuals fit with the culture, values and goals of the organisation (Chelladurai, 2006) As a starting point, the officer responsible for HRM develops an inventory of the qualifications, education and experience of individual volunteers and staff and the positions that they hold. The inventory is updated regularly as people move from one position to another or leave the organisation. The objective of this process is to indicate where the organisation has an actual or projected shortage or surplus of volunteers or paid staff.

Where a need for a new staff member or volunteer is identified, a job analysis is used to construct a position or job description and a position or job specification. Through consultation and observation, a description of the job requirements is prepared in which the organisation identifies the tasks it needs done in order to achieve its strategic objectives. A position *description*, sometimes known as a job description, specifies the title, duties, supervision (who the person supervises and by whom the employee is supervised), relationships and key contacts, working conditions and possible risks. A position *specification* provides details about the education, qualifications, skills, abilities and experience required to perform the job. It provides a firm foundation for recruitment and criteria for selecting the most appropriate staff member with the best 'fit' for the organisation. Consideration is given to the potential supply of human resources from inside and outside the organisation and whether the pool of potential applicants is likely to be large or small. Different qualifications may have to be written into a position specification depending upon whether the position is voluntary or paid and the estimated size of the pool of potential applicants.

Concept Check

Human Resource Management planning

HRM planning identifies what must be done to ensure that a desired number of persons with the correct skills are available at a specified time in the future. HRM planning must be an integrated part of an organisation's strategic planning processes.

A limitation of traditional human resource planning when applied to sport organisations is that it is modelled on work organisations in which labour demands are estimated and human resources are recruited. Paid staff are appointed to their positions because of their qualifications, skills, experience, and fit with an organisation's culture and strategic direction. They are financially compensated to fulfil a specified role within a sport organisation. Volunteers, in contrast, are often elected to a position and may not have the necessary qualifications, skills and experience to fulfil the role for which they are elected. In other circumstances, a volunteer might be recruited rather than elected because the organisation needs an extra 'pair of hands' and not because they have particular skills or abilities. Such situations are difficult to manage and are often exacerbated by an under-supply of volunteer labour relative to organisational needs. Human resource planning endeavours to align staffing requirements with strategic plans and priorities.

The process of human resource planning raises the issue of who should be responsible for HRM in sport organisations. SPARC (2000) recommends the appointment of a volunteer manager. The Australian Sports Commission in its module Volunteer Management: A Guide to Good Practice (Auld & Cuskelly, 2000) also recommends that a volunteer manager is key to HRM in sport organisations. The design and implementation of a human resource plan specifically for volunteers is more likely to occur in sport organisations that have taken the time to select a motivated and suitably qualified volunteer manager. Among the volunteer manager's responsibilities is determining where volunteers are needed, preparing position descriptions and planning a recruitment campaign. They may also be required to analyse training needs and to keep a human resource inventory up-to-date. At a club level such a manager is likely to be a volunteer. Sport organisations or sport events with sufficient financial resources might consider the appointment of a paid person to this position because of the strategic importance of recruiting and matching volunteers to appropriate positions. Volunteer managers usually hold a board or committee-level position because they need to be fully aware of their organisation's strategic plans and priorities. Where a sport organisation employs paid staff, the volunteer manager might also have a role in determining the position descriptions of paid employees, particularly in relation to lines of responsibility between paid staff and volunteers.

Recruiting volunteers and paid staff

The major purpose of the recruitment process is to attract a pool of qualified applicants. It is likely that paid positions will attract a number of suitably qualified applicants. For volunteer positions, the recruitment process is often much less formal and being able to attract a sufficient number of qualified applicants is a more difficult task. For some volunteer positions, sport organisations do not have the power to recruit individuals. Organisations are often bound constitutionally to elect board members or to appoint particular members on an ex-officio basis. For other positions, sport organisations might also consider whether an appointment needs to be made at all. Specific one-off limited-term jobs, such as running a special event or securing sponsorships may be contracted out to avoid some of the costs of recruiting, training and retaining a paid employee as well as establishing and maintaining office space and a suitable work environment.

When a decision is made to proceed with the recruitment process, consideration needs to be given to the type and level of appointment. The approach taken to recruitment will vary in relation to whether the job specification calls for a volunteer or paid employee and whether the position is operational or strategic. The appointment of a CEO is of much greater strategic importance to a sport organisation than the appointment of a development officer. Decisions also have to be made about whether to search for qualified applicants internally, advertise externally, or both. Searching for applicants internally provides individuals with incentives to work towards a more senior position but limits the size of the pool of potential applicants. An alternative to conducting the recruitment and selection process in-house is to contract a recruitment agency or consultant to act on behalf of the organisation. This approach is increasingly being used to fill senior appointments in major sport organisations.

The recruitment of paid staff and volunteers should provide potential applicants with a realistic preview of what a job entails. Benefits and conditions need to be clearly specified so that applicants are in a position to make an informed decision about whether a job might suit their skills, experience, expectations and availability. When recruiting volunteers it is important to emphasise the benefits for volunteers rather than the needs of the organisation. Many volunteers give up their free time to assist sport organisations. They may not be attracted by work-like recruitment campaigns. Volunteers and paid staff need to feel valued by sport organisations and not feel as though they are being recruited to fill a position that no one else wanted.

The selection process

The selection process involves choosing the individual who best meets the position specification from the pool of applicants. Depending upon the level of the position and its importance to the organisation's mission, the selection process can involve a number of steps which include resumé screening, formal interviews, testing, reference checks and a physical examination. The outcome of the selection process is a decision on whether to make a job offer to one of the applicants. All applicants should be kept informed about the progress of their application. Resumés are screened to compare the qualifications, skills and experience of applicants with the criteria for the position. Applicants who do not meet the essential criteria do not usually progress beyond the first step in the selection process. Before the position is offered to an applicant a formal interview and reference check should be completed.

The selection of volunteers can be quite a different process. An important consideration is whether a position is one that is usually appointed or elected. Committee or board members are often elected to their positions and the selection process is largely redundant. In contrast, the appointment of individuals to operational level unpaid positions, such as the coach of a junior club netball team, may involve a formal recruitment and selection process. Child protection legislation mandates background checks in many jurisdictions when appointing someone to a position that involves close contact with children.

Orientation

MINI-CASE: "SO YOU'RE THE NEW VOLUNTEER".

A notice is posted in a local school newsletter seeking a volunteer to coordinate the equipment store for the local cricket club. Your daughter plays cricket with the club. Feeling as though you would like to help, you telephone the President. The President asks you to come down to the clubhouse on Saturday morning at 8:30 a.m. "Someone will be there to meet you and tell you what the job entails". After arriving on time, you hang about for about half an hour until one of the coaches over at the nets notices you. He introduces you to the President, who promptly apologises for forgetting that he was organising the meeting. After a brief chat about his recent outing in the corporate box at the Third Test, he says, "Well, here are the keys to the equipment shed. It's great to have someone willing to help out. None of the members seem to have the time. Lock the doors at 11:00 a.m. and I'll see you next Saturday." He heads off as you peer into a disorganised, dark and dusty equipment store.

The transition period from being an outsider to taking up a new position is a critical time for both the individual and the organisation. A new appointee cannot be expected to understand the requirements of their position or how the organisation functions on a daily basis from their first day on the job. For example, a recently appointed under-10s netball coach needs to know where the equipment is stored, how to access it, what times the courts are available, what to do in case of an emergency and so on. A well designed orientation process reduces stress on new employees and volunteers, makes them feel welcome and may reduce the likelihood of early turnover.

Orientation is the process of assimilating new staff and volunteers into an organisation. The purpose of orientation is to ease transition into the organisation by ensuring that people feel comfortable about their new position and learning about the organisation and the people with whom they will work (Taylor, Doherty, & McGraw, 2008). Some organisations run formal orientation programmes as a forerunner to more detailed training and development programmes. In many sport organisations, the orientation process is somewhat less formal, but no less important if a paid staff member or volunteer is going to successfully perform their new role.

Training and development

An important factor in the extent to which the strategic goals of sport organisations are achieved is the level of competency of its paid and volunteer staff. After becoming part of a sport organisation, volunteers and paid staff should be provided with appropriate and timely opportunities for training and personal development. Chelladurai (2006, p. 176) refers to training as "the process of cultivating job-related skills, interpersonal skills, and organisational values . . . and learn[ing] the culture of the organisation." There are a number of steps in the process of preparing for and implementing a training and development programme. It is important to establish needs, set objectives, select and implement appropriate methods, and evaluate the effectiveness of training and development.

The process of training and development should be cognisant of individual needs and organisational goals. Needs are established through an assessment of the organisation's strategic goals, its human resource plan and in consultation with existing paid staff and volunteers. Where gaps exist, objectives are set to provide for improved levels of staff competencies. There is a wide choice of training and development methods and programmes available in sport management. The selection of a method is constrained by costs, timing, specificity and relevance, flexibility, mode of delivery and prerequisite knowledge. However, there is an increasing range of delivery modes and formats to suit the wide-ranging needs of individuals and organisations. For example, training and development can be generalised or specific, formal or informal, and undertaken on or off the job. The world-wide web is becoming an increasingly important resource for flexible delivery, particularly for people with busy schedules and those living in isolated regions. Decisions have to be made about whether training is optional or compulsory and who pays for the direct (e.g., course fees) and indirect (e.g., travel and subsistence allowances) costs associated with attendance at training and development programmes. In both Australia and New Zealand a range of training programmes have been specifically developed to meet the needs of paid and volunteer staff in sport. Examples of these programmes in New Zealand include: Coaching New Zealand's Getting Started and Levels 1-3, the Prime Minister's High Performance Coach Scholarships and SPARC's Running Sport 1 (club level administration) and Running Sport 2 (regional and national organisations). In Australia, the National Coaching Accreditation Scheme has similar coaching schemes to those in New Zealand, with level 1 through to high performance programmes. In addition the Australian Sport Commission (ASC) has a large range of modules, including Volunteer Management: A Guide to Good Practice, to assist those working and volunteering in sport.

Performance management

Individual job performance is influenced by personal (e.g., level of ability, motivation) and organisational factors (e.g., working conditions, management practices), which in turn impact on the achievement of organisational goals. Performance management is a process used by organisations "to try to achieve strategic goals consistently through better formal and informal motivation, monitoring, evaluating and rewarding performance" (Pinnington & Lafferty, 2003, p. 158). Performance management is widely practiced in the private and public sectors but tends to be much less utilised in sport organisations with small numbers of employees. According to Pinnington and Lafferty (2003) performance management has four major components. These are determining performance expectations, supporting performance, reviewing and appraising performance, and managing performance standards.

Performance appraisal is an important but sometimes controversial component of performance management because it is prone to bias and inaccuracies. Performance appraisal is the process of evaluating the performance of paid and unpaid staff and providing them with feedback. It is often a basis for rewarding or disciplining individuals in relation to their job performance. Performance appraisals sometimes act as a catalyst for dismissing an employee. However, there are legal considerations in terminating paid staff who are accorded the protection of employment contract and industrial relations legislation. With volunteers, because there is no employment contract, the situation is not as clear. For example, a volunteer whose performance is inadequate may not be able to be dismissed because of a lack of constitutional provision for dealing with such matters. If a paid or unpaid staff member is to be dismissed on the basis of inadequate performance, it is important to document performance appraisal reports, recommendations concerning corrective actions and support provided by the organisation. Sport organisations must be aware of their legal rights and obligations before making important performance management decisions. A limitation of formal performance appraisals is that they tend to overlook important behaviours that contribute informally to an organisation's effectiveness such as citizenship behaviours.

Critical Argument Summary Box

Performance management of volunteers

A case **for** volunteer performance management:

- Volunteers would be provided with clear expectations before accepting a new role.
- Voluntary sport organisations would be better planned and organised.
- Volunteers, particularly those who are new to their role, might feel as though they are being better supported, trained and recognised by their organisation.
- Sport organisations would provide better qualified and trained volunteers to members and therefore a better quality experience for both volunteers and members.
- Volunteers motivated by the opportunity gain work skills would have something to add to their resume.

A case **against** volunteer performance management:
- Volunteer 'work' would become too much like paid work and voluntary sport organisa- tions might become more bureaucratic.
- Potential volunteers might be scared off by high levels of formalisation.
- Volunteers may feel threatened if they know that their performance is being monitored.
- In order to be completed with limited resources, performance management could become a perfunctory process using checklists and providing minimal feedback to volunteers.
- Most voluntary organisations do not have enough volunteers to complete essential tasks and would see performance management as an additional administrative burden.

Concept Check

Performance appraisal

Performance appraisal is a measure of organisational effectiveness. Appraisal of employee performance should be a critical and ongoing HRM activity, as it is through the efforts of individual employees that organisational goals are met.

Rewarding and recognising volunteers and paid staff

Recognising and rewarding individuals for their efforts in contributing to the achievement of organisational goals is as much an issue of motivation and leadership as it is a component of HRM. According to Chelladurai (2006, p. 201) "the purposes of reward systems include attracting and retaining good employees, motivating performance, encouraging skill development, cultivating organisational culture, and reinforcing the organisational structure." There are substantial differences between employed and volunteer staff in the rewards sought, benefits received and the recognition provided by sport organisations. Importantly, rewards may be intrinsic or extrinsic and must be valued in order to motivate individual effort. The rewards and recognition that motivate individual effort vary from one task to another as well as between individuals.

The major element in extrinsic reward systems for paid staff is financial compensation. Other benefits include employer contributions to superannuation, paid leave (recreation, sickness and long service) and salary increases usually linked to performance management. It is not unusual for paid staff to compare their salary and benefits with other employees within the organisation or with people with similar skills, qualifications and workloads in other sport and non-sport organisations. It is important to recognise that staff are also motivated by intrinsic rewards such as responsibility, task significance and variety. Staff who perceive that they are being equitably rewarded are likely to be satisfied and may be more highly motivated to work towards the achievement of organisational goals.

Many reward systems for employees (e.g., pay) are under the control of sport organisations. In contrast to paid staff, volunteers are not paid for what they do within organisational settings to achieve organisational goals. Cuskelly and Harrington (1997) found that social and personal rewards were the most important perceived benefits amongst volunteer sport administrators. Pearce (1993) argued that volunteering is legitimised by emphasising its work facet, but this implies that volunteers receive rewards for their work, in much the same ways as employees receive pay. However, the rewards for volunteering "that seem most important are not under the control of the organisation but derive from the participation itself" (Pearce, 1993, p.181). Volunteering is motivated by enjoyment of the activity, social interaction, and with the satisfaction of contributing to the larger social good. This is not to deny that paid employees also perceive enjoyment and social interaction as important benefits of working for a sport organisation. Reward and recognition systems also have implications for the retention of staff. Expectancy theories, such as the Porter and Lawler (1968) model, suggest that individuals who perceive that the time and effort they put into working for a sport organisation are far greater than the rewards and recognition received are likely to become dissatisfied and may feel less motivated to work and less committed to their organisation.

Retention or replacement

The retention of paid staff and volunteers provides a sense of stability and continuity within sport organisations. The more that staff are retained, the less resources have to be directed towards staff recruitment, selection, orientation and training. However, a certain level of staff turnover is to be expected and is desirable to ensure that sport organisations continue to respond to their members and remain relevant to their external environment. However, high levels of staff turnover combined with shortages in the supply of volunteer labour can significantly disrupt the operations of sport organisations. In extreme cases, high rates of turnover can seriously threaten the continued existence of a sport organisation. A constant challenge in HRM is finding an appropriate balance between the retention and replacement of human resources.

In a study of volunteers, Cuskelly, Taylor, Hoye, and Darcy (2006) found that the average level of annual turnover was 26 per cent and that volunteer retention was perceived significantly more problematic for clubs that reported poor volunteer management practices compared to clubs with relatively good volunteer management practices.

Replacement is a necessary part of HRM to fill vacancies created by the movement of staff from their existing positions due to resignations, retirements, promotions, transfers and terminations. It is important that sport organisations anticipate and plan for voluntary (e.g., resignation or retirement) and involuntary (e.g., secondment, termination) separation that inevitably occurs. When long-serving volunteer board members retire, resign or fail in a bid for re-election, it provides opportunities for organisation renewal and development. The replacement of volunteers and paid staff can bring fresh points of view and a renewed focus on strategic goals to a sport organisation. When staff vacancies occur, the process of HRM can be implemented to ensure an appropriate alignment between a sport organisation's strategic goals and its human resources.

Organisational commitment

The retention of paid staff and volunteers, particularly those who are highly motivated and skilled is of strategic importance to sport organisations. The development of organisational commitment is an important factor in the performance and retention of paid staff and volunteers. Individuals who are more committed tend to perform better on the job and are less likely to be absent and leave their organisation. Organisational commitment is a form of affective attachment to an organisation (Mowday, Porter, & Steers, 1982). It may be experienced at differing levels of intensity and is developed as a result of a wide range of personal and situational factors. Organisational commitment can be a relatively low intensity and calculated relationship (calculative commitment) or a more intense and positive orientation that typically develops within the affective domain (affective commitment). Meyer and Allen (1988, 1991) developed a three-component model of organisational commitment. In their model, *affective* commitment embodies the notion that individuals become committed to an organisation because they *want to*. *Continuance* commitment develops as a result of *having to* be committed due to a lack of alternatives or the sacrifice of a high level of sunk costs if one was to leave an organisation. It incorporates the tenets of calculative commitment and refers to an awareness of the costs associated with leaving an organisation (Meyer & Allen, 1991). The third component of commitment is labelled *normative* commitment and develops as a result of feeling one *ought to* be committed. Normative commitment is based on socialisation, organisational investment and the strength of the reciprocity norm. Fink (1992) discussed the importance of shared accountability, modelling behaviour, empowering others, task interdependence and building group identity in the development of organisational commitment.

The commitment of volunteers may be different to that of paid staff in sport organisations. Volunteers are not remunerated for their 'work' and their commitment tends to be linked to affective rewards; the benefits of being a volunteer are value-based and far less tangible than the benefits of being a paid employee. This is a potential source of conflict in sport organisations that are managed by voluntary boards but utilise employees. Volunteers may question their own level of commitment when someone else is being paid to carry out what they perceive as similar tasks. At the same time, employees may question the commitment of volunteers, who, despite having the best interests of their sport at heart, cannot always be relied upon to follow through on tasks. This management dilemma is compounded by unclear lines of responsibility and authority within sport organisations in which volunteers manage paid staff and, at times, paid staff direct the activities of volunteers. Cuskelly, Boag, and McIntyre (1999) reported that in comparison to volunteers, paid staff reported higher levels of continuance (calculative) commitment. Paid staff seemed to be more acutely aware of the level of sacrifice they would have to make in order to leave their organisation and the lack of availability of alternative organisations for which they could work. They concluded that paid staff seemed to have a greater vested interest in the survival and development of their sport organisations than did volunteers.

Concept Check

Organisational commitment

Organisational commitment is a form of attachment to an organisation which is associated with higher levels of individual performance and lower rates of turnover and absenteeism. HRM policies should aim to enhance the commitment of paid staff and volunteers to their work and to the organisation.

Summary

Human resource management is a management function that is critical to the achievement of strategic goals in sport organisation. Volunteers and paid staff work closely with one another in the management of sport. Volunteers have traditionally been the 'backbone' of sport delivery systems. However, the nexus between volunteers and paid staff has assumed greater importance as the organisation and management of sport moves towards more boardroom and executive office style operations. HRM is a process that involves acquiring, developing and retaining the services of paid staff and volunteers. Differences between paid staff and volunteers in relation to the traditional HRM model were outlined. The importance of the development of organisational commitment was identified as an important factor in the retention of paid and volunteer staff and the achievement of strategic goals.

CASE STUDY: THE RECALCITRANT BOARD MEMBER

Bill Walsh had a long history as a national representative player. He is a highly committed and well qualified coach and has two children who have made national teams in their age groups. Bill has a lot of support amongst the rank-and-file members because of the profile he developed when he was a member of the national team. About two years ago, a casual vacancy occurred on the National Board and Bill was appointed to the fill the unpaid position. Since he has joined the board, Bill has had the worst attendance record of all of the board members. When he has attended meetings, he has rarely followed up on assigned tasks. Outside of board meetings he has frequently been overheard running down board members, the staff of the organisation and at time has been critical of the major sponsors. Both the Executive Director (ED) and the President have had to move into damage control with sponsors after Bill, in his role as a board member, has shared the corporate box with them at national tournaments. As a result of Bill's actions, several of the better performing board members and the ED are threatening to resign. The major sponsors have signalled that they may withdraw early the three-year agreement which expires a little over a year from now. There is no bylaw in the constitution which relates to the performance of board members and there is no precedent within the organisation of terminating the services of an unpaid board member.

Should this situation be handled through a process of performance appraisal? Who will conduct the appraisal? Who will be appraised and what will be appraised? Should the appraisal process be evaluative or developmental? If the decision is made either to ask for Bill's resignation or to fire him, who should do it? How should it be handled? What are the potential problems if the performance appraisal process is poorly handled?

Review questions

- Why should HRM be considered a critical management function in sport organisations?
- Discuss the relative importance of an individual's ability, commitment, effort and organisational support as factors in effectively performing a job as a volunteer or as a paid staff member within a sport organisation.
- Distinguish between a position (job) description and a position (job) specification. Write a brief position description and position specification for the employment of a full-time junior development officer for a provincial-level netball association.

- As the National Development Officer of a medium-sized sport organisation, you have been given the task of human resource manager for the national championships to be staged one year from now. Use the HRM process outlined in this chapter as framework to outline the major tasks and a timeline for how you would go about achieving such a task.
- Should there be different performance management processes for paid and volunteer staff? Why or why not?
- Retention of paid staff and volunteers is an important aspect of human resource management. However, very high and very low levels of turnover can adversely affect the daily operations and strategic direction of a sport organisation. Discuss.

Advancing your understanding

- **Australian Human Resources Institute.** http://www.ahri.com.au/. Manages the Asia Pacific Journal of Human Resources, a peer-reviewed journal that communicates the results of research, theory and examples of practice in the field of human resources in the Asia-Pacific region and published by Sage.
- **Australian Human Resources Management.** http://www.hrmguide.net/australia/. A series of linked websites containing pages of free HR-related articles, features and links.
- **Bruce, P. J. (2007).** *Human resource management casebook.* Australia: Pearson Education. A continuous series of case studies that explore HRM issues for a hypothetical small to medium enterprise.
- **Human Resources Institute New Zealand.** http://www.hrinz.org.nz/. Professional organisation for people who are interested or involved in the management and development of human resources.
- **International Association for Human Resource Information Management (IHRIM).** http://www.ihrim.org/. HR information management, systems issues, trends, and technology.
- **New Zealand Journal of Human Resources Management.** http://www.nzjhrm.org.nz/. A peer-reviewed electronic journal which publishes original material on the development and practice of human resource management in New Zealand and the South Pacific region.

References

Auld, C., & Cuskelly, G. (2000). *Volunteer management: A guide to good practice.* Retrieved from http://www.ausport.gov.au/__data/assets/pdf_file/0005/115556/2._Managing_Volunteers.pdf.

Australian Bureau of Statistics. (2011). Sport and physical recreation, a statistical overview, Australia, 2011 (Cat. No. 4156.0). Canberra: Commonwealth of Australia.

Chelladurai, P. (2006). *Human resource management in sport and recreation* (2nd ed.). Champaign, IL: Human Kinetics.

Cuskelly, G., Boag, A., & McIntyre, N. (1999). Differences in organisational commitment between paid and volunteer administrators in sport. *European Journal of Sport Management, 6,* 39–61.

Cuskelly, G., & Harrington, M. (1997). Volunteers and leisure: Evidence of marginal and career volunteerism in sport. *World Leisure and Recreation Association (WLRA) Journal, 39*(3), 11–18.

Cuskelly, G., Taylor, T., Hoye, R., & Darcy, S. (2006). Volunteers management practices and volunteer retention: A human resource management approach. *Sport Management Review, 9,* 141–163.

Department of Labour. (2010). Employment and Skills Snapshot: Arts and Recreation Services. Retrieved from http://www.dol.govt.nz/services/LMI/tools/skillsinsight/snapshots/arts/arts.pdf

Fink, S. L. (1992). *High commitment workplaces*. New York: Quorum Books.

Kikulis, L. M., Slack, T., & Hinings, B. (1995). Does decision making make a difference? Patterns of change within Canadian National Sporting Organisations. *Journal of Sport Management, 9*, 273–299.

Meyer, J. P., & Allen, N. J. (1988). Links between work experiences and organizational commitment during the first year of employment: A longitudinal analysis. *Journal of Occupational Psychology, 61*(3), 195–209.

Meyer, J. P., & Allen, N. J. (1991). A three component conceptualization of organizational commitment. *Human Resource Management Review, 1*(1),61–89.

Mowday, R. T., Porter, L. W., & Steers, R. M. (1982). *Employee-organization linkages: The psychology of commitment, absenteeism, and turnover*. New York: Academic Press.

Pearce, J. L. (1993). *Volunteers: The organizational behavior of unpaid workers*. London: Routledge.

Pinnington, A., & Lafferty, G. (2003). *Human resource management in Australia*. Victoria, Australia: Oxford University Press.

Porter, L. W., & Lawler III, E. E. (1968). *Managerial attitudes and performance*. Homewood, Ill: Irwin.

Simon, H. A. (1957). *Administrative behavior* (2nd ed.). New York: Free Press.

Sport and Recreation New Zealand. (2000). *Running sport 1: Recruiting and retaining volunteers*. Wellington, NZ: Sport and Recreation New Zealand.

Sport and Recreation New Zealand. (2008). *Sport, recreation and physical activity, participation among New Zealand adults: Volunteers*. Retrieved from http://www.activenzsurvey.org.nz/Results/2007-08-Active-NZ-Survey/National-Report/Volunteers/

Taylor, T., Doherty, A., & McGraw, P. (2008). *Managing people in sport organizations: A human resource perspective*. Oxford: Elsevier.

Chapter 13

Corporate Social Responsibility

Geoff Walters and Richard Tacon

OBJECTIVES

After completing this chapter, you should be able to:

- understand the development of corporate social responsibility (CSR);
- be aware of the strong association between CSR and stakeholder theory;
- discuss the need for sport organisations to manage stakeholder relationships;
- identify different ways that sport organisations can engage and participate with stakeholders.

Key terms

In this chapter, readers will become familiar with the following concepts and terms:
- corporate social responsibility
- corporate citizenship
- stakeholder
- stakeholder identification
- stakeholder management
- stakeholder engagement
- stakeholder participation
- charitable foundation
- profit maximisation
- normative stakeholder theory
- instrumental stakeholder theory

Introduction

Over the last few decades public concern over the role of business in society has grown and is now substantial. Partly as a result of instances of corporate excess and irresponsibility, there is now greater pressure on organisations to be more accountable and to show commitment to society through social and environmental activities. Corporate social responsibility (CSR), broadly referring to the responsibilities that a business has beyond profit maximisation (Carroll, 1979) has become the means through which organisations seek to demonstrate this accountability and commitment to society. Corporate social responsibility is also an important issue within the sport industry as sport organisations have become increasingly influential members of the global community and the concerns of transparency and accountability that are evident within the corporate world now more than ever affect sport (Walker & Kent, 2009).

Despite broad acceptance that CSR relates to the relationship between business and society, key issues remain such as what does it mean to be accountable to society and, critically, who should organisations be accountable to? This latter point is critical for those individuals or organisations that are tasked with implementing CSR. Indeed, it has been argued that there is a need for organisations to identify different stakeholder groups (e.g., Phillips, 2003b; Mitchell, Agle, & Wood, 1997) and, if they are to create long-term competitive advantage and organisational wealth, that they must also manage multiple stakeholder relationships as part of firm strategy (Post, Preston, & Sachs, 2002; Freeman, 2006). This is where stakeholder theory has relevance for organisations and sport organisations alike; it maintains that in addition to shareholders, an organisation should recognise the interests of a wider range of constituents that have a stake in a corporation and a right to inclusion in the governance process, such as customers, employees, suppliers, and those that live in the communities in which organisations operate. It is clear then, that if a key aspect of CSR is engaging with, and having a commitment to multiple stakeholders, then it can be argued that CSR and stakeholder theory are particularly suitable partners.

Concept Check

Corporate social responsibility

Corporate social responsibility (CSR) broadly refers to the responsibilities a business has beyond maximising its profits.

The aim of this chapter is to demonstrate firstly, how stakeholder theorising can illuminate key issues in sport management, and secondly, how CSR has been implemented by sport organisations through stakeholder management strategies. It begins by providing an overview of the development of CSR, how CSR relates to sport, before discussing the strong association between CSR and stakeholder theory. These early sections draw on relevant academic theory. The chapter then focuses on the issue of stakeholder management and how this can be implemented. It is argued that there are three key elements to a stakeholder management strategy. The first is stakeholder identification – sport organisations need to identify which stakeholders are salient. The second and third elements are stakeholder engagement and stakeholder participation (Low & Cowton, 2004) - two techniques available to sport organisations that want to be proactive in the management of stakeholder relationships. This chapter provides an introduction to these three elements by adopting an organisational-level perspective. It will provide examples of how sport organisations identify stakeholders and manage their relationships with different stakeholder groups through both engagement and participation strategies. Certain issues, whilst critical to a broader understanding of organisation-stakeholder relationships, are beyond the scope of this chapter. These include how stakeholders perceive and react to stakeholder management strategies, the complexity of interactions between different stakeholders and whether they feel able to mobilise to increase influence, and the issue of heterogeneity within stakeholder groups.

CASE STUDY: THE AUSTRALIAN FOOTBALL LEAGUE COMMUNITY PROGRAMMES

The Australian Football League (AFL) is the governing body for Australian Rules Football and is also responsible for the organisation of the league competition of the same name – the AFL. Although the main responsibility of the AFL is the organisation of a sports league, the AFL is also involved in running a range of community programmes. The four main programmes clearly demonstrate that the AFL has identified specific stakeholder groups and has developed targeted programmes to address their needs.

- *Multicultural programmes*

The Multicultural Program is a joint initiative between the AFL, AFL Victoria, Victorian Government and the Federal Government through the Department of Immigration and Citizenship. The aim is to work with Multicultural Development Officers, local leagues and clubs to help build strong working relationships with migrant and refugee communities.

- *Disability inclusion*

The AFL is committed to providing equal opportunities for all to participate in Australian rules football and a range of different programmes targeted at disabled communities

- *Indigenous community*

The AFL has a range of programmes focused around issues of health, education, employment and personal development that are targeted at indigenous people.

- *Respect and Responsibility*

The Respect and Responsibility Policy was launched by the AFL in 2005 and is aimed at raising awareness of the issue of violence against women.

Source: http://www.afl.com.au/community%20programs/tabid/17494/default.aspx

Corporate Social Responsibility

CSR is difficult to define. Indeed, even the term itself is not settled and other terms, such as corporate social performance, corporate social responsiveness and corporate citizenship, are often used to describe the same or similar things. CSR has been traced to the Progressive reform movement in the US in the late 1800s and early 1900s, and it has been argued that by the 1920s many business leaders adhered to some conception of responsibility (Windsor, 2001, p. 229). Nevertheless, Bowen (1953) is often attributed with one of the earliest definitions of CSR. His definition saw it as "the obligations of businessmen to pursue those policies, to make those decisions, or to follow those lines of actions which are desirable in terms of the objectives and values of our society" (Bowen, 1953, p. 6). Later in 1979, an influential article defined it as follows: "the social responsibility of business encompasses the economic, legal, ethical and discretionary expectations that society has of organisations at a given point in time" (Carroll, 1979, p. 500). In the 1980s, a range of themes associated with CSR emerged, including stakeholder theory, business ethics theory, corporate citizenship, and cause-related marketing demonstrating that the concept "served as the base-point, building block, or point-of-departure for other related concepts and themes, many of which embraced CSR-thinking and were quite compatible with it" (Carroll, 1999, p. 288).

In the 1990s and 2000s, there were increasing attempts to understand how organisations seek to implement CSR leading to a large body of empirical research. This has led to an emphasis on linking CSR with corporate financial performance and CSR is increasingly seen as a way to add value to the business. This demonstrates a shift from normative justifications for implementing CSR to more instrumental performance-oriented motivations (Lindgreen & Swaen, 2010). However a recent academic analysis suggests that focusing on performance motivations for CSR fails to take into account the full range of effects of business activity. Instead, it proposed that corporate social performance should properly be conceived of as "a set of descriptive categorizations of business activity, focusing on the impacts and outcomes for society, stakeholders and the firm" (Wood, 2010, p. 54). Among those actually working in organisations in different sectors, understandings of, and attitudes towards, CSR are perhaps even more varied. Nevertheless, there appears to be an increasing consensus among academics and business practitioners that CSR relates to an organisation's interaction with a range of stakeholders, such as employees, customers, suppliers, and local communities. Stakeholder management itself is not easily defined, with a series of ongoing debates concerning who an organisation's stakeholders are, how legitimate their various claims are and whether and how organisations ought to respond to them. However, thinking about CSR in relation to organisations and their multiple stakeholders provides a useful framework for assessing organisational performance.

Corporate Social Responsibility and sport

It has been argued that there has been an increase in sport organisations addressing the issue of CSR in recent years (Walters & Tacon, 2010). For example, many individual athletes have set up charitable foundations that provide funding to worthy causes, such as the Lance Armstrong Foundation that funds cancer research (Kott, 2005). CSR activities are also prominent at the level of the professional sports league (see the AFL example above) and the individual team or franchise. Within the UK, there has been a long-standing commitment to CSR with the emergence of the *Football in the Community* schemes in the 1980s and 1990s and the more recent conversion of these schemes to charitable foundations. These foundations deliver social inclusion and educational based initiatives and have demonstrated that football clubs can play a positive role within their communities (Brown, Crabbe, Mellor, Blackshaw, & Stone, 2006). These types of foundation are also extremely prominent across the major leagues in the US. It is also the case that some sports organisations have begun to replicate the trend for CSR reporting. For example, Chelsea Football Club has produced a CSR report separate from the annual accounts.

CSR is also firmly on the agenda of many sport governing bodies. UEFA (Union des Associations Européennes de Football), the governing body for European football, has developed a social responsibility partnership portfolio and is working with a number of charity partners to address specific issues including racism, reconciliation and peace, football for all, violence, health and humanitarian aid. UEFA has also made a commitment to allocate 0.7 per cent of annual revenue to social projects – in line with the commitment made by the developed nations of the world to donate 0.7 per cent of gross national product to development assistance as part of the Millennium Project. There has also been increasing demand for sport events to consider their overall impact and to implement CSR through a variety of initiatives. At both the 2006 Winter Olympics in Turin and the 2006 Super Bowl in Detroit there were a range of CSR initiatives (Babiak & Wolfe, 2006; Cappato & Pennazio, 2006), while FIFA launched *Win in Africa with Africa* in 2006, a CSR initiative aimed at supporting developments within the African continent drawing on the 2010 World Cup in South Africa. There is also a growing need for mega sport events to address environmental concerns.

Despite the growing propensity for sport organisations to address CSR, and in light of the growth in mainstream management literature on CSR over the last 30 years, it is somewhat surprising that academic analysis of the role of sport and social responsibility is a relatively recent trend (e.g., Babiak & Wolfe, 2006; Smith & Westerbeek, 2007; Walters, 2009; Bradish & Cronin, 2009; Godfrey, 2009; Walters & Tacon, 2010). Arguably, this has come about as the role of sport in society has become more prominent and as sport organisations have become increasingly influential members of the global community. The concerns of transparency and accountability evident within the corporate world have transferred to sport. This has led some to suggest that sport organisations cannot ignore CSR and that they have to implement it (Babiak & Wolfe, 2006). Whether or not this is the sole imperative, it is clear that many sport organisations have, over the last few decades, engaged with various CSR imperatives, including philanthropy, community involvement, youth educational activities and youth health initiatives (Babiak & Wolfe, 2009; Walker & Kent, 2009; Walters, 2009).

It has also been argued that sport organisations offer a particularly appropriate context for CSR. Despite the fact that many sports organisations are multi-million pound businesses, they also have a highly significant role that is reflected in the representation of notions of community and tradition. This particular role of sport organisations underpins seven unique characteristics of sport CSR (Smith & Westerbeek, 2007). First, the popularity and global reach of sport can ensure that sport CSR has mass media distribution and communication power. That is, the prominence of sport within the media helps to promote and communicate CSR activities to a wide audience. Second, sport CSR has youth appeal: children are more likely to engage in a CSR programme if it is attached to a sport organisation or a sports personality. Third, sport CSR can be used to deliver positive health impacts through programmes and initiatives designed around physical exercise. Fourth, sport CSR will invariably involve group participation and therefore aid social interaction. This can also lead to a fifth benefit, which is improved cultural understanding and integration. Sixth, particular sport activities may lead to enhanced environmental and sustainability awareness. Finally, participating in sport CSR activities can also provide immediate gratification benefits. It is important to realise that these benefits are by no means automatic. Certainly, there is a need for much greater understanding of the processes through which sport is presumed to lead to various social benefits and much better research evidence. Nevertheless, the seven factors make clear the *potential* for sport organisations to engage effectively in CSR.

Corporate Social Responsibility and stakeholder theory

Stakeholder theory is based on the understanding that a corporation should recognise the interests of a wide range of constituents that have a stake in the organisation, for example customers, employees, suppliers, and communities. Academic literature on stakeholder theory has grown substantially in recent years (Friedman & Miles, 2006), and has built on the seminal work of Freeman (1984, p. 46) who defined a stakeholder as "any group or individual who can affect or is affected by the achievement of the organisations objectives". Moreover, it has also become a key term used in political rhetoric. Despite the ubiquity of the Freeman (1984) definition, it has been criticised for being too broad (Freeman & Phillips, 1996) whilst a number of scholars have attempted to develop a theoretical framework in which to understand stakeholder theory (e.g., Donaldson & Preston, 1995; Phillips, Freeman, & Wicks, 2003).

Given that the central issue within CSR is the nature of the relationship between business and society and how this is defined and acted upon (Blowfield & Murray, 2008, p. 36) many authors have illustrated how stakeholder theory is intimately bound up with CSR (Campbell, 2007; Carroll, 1999; Maignan & Ferrell, 2004). Furthermore, Carroll (1991, p. 43) observed that "there is a natural fit between the idea of corporate social responsibility and an organisation's stakeholders". From an organisational perspective, a stakeholder approach is useful as it "puts 'names and faces' on the societal members or groups who are most urgent to business, and to whom it must be responsive" (Carroll, 1991, p. 43). If it is accepted that CSR broadly refers to the responsibilities that a business has beyond profit maximisation, and this can involve a commitment to multiple stakeholders, then two key issues that organisations face is how to manage multiple stakeholder relationships and balance their interests (Laplume, Sonpar, & Litz, 2008).

Recently, a number of studies have drawn on stakeholder theory as a framework with which to better understand sport, following a call from Friedman, Parent, and Mason (2004). These studies have explored its utility in relation to sport events (Leopkey & Parent, 2009; Parent & Deephouse, 2007), football club governance (Senaux, 2008) and professional road cycling (Morrow & Idle, 2008). Earlier studies focused on stakeholder identification and stakeholder perceptions in intercollegiate athletics (Putler & Wolfe, 1999; Trail & Chelladurai, 2000; Wolfe & Putler, 2002), stakeholder power and legitimacy in Rugby Union (Morgan, 2002) and economic development decision making (Friedman & Mason, 2004). In the academic literature on football (soccer) there has been a discernible interest in stakeholder ideas. Indeed, Morrow (2003, p. 43) suggests that "the stakeholder concept has greater relevance for football clubs than for conventional businesses because of the particular features of certain football club stakeholders" (Morrow, 2003, p. 43). These studies demonstrate that the application of stakeholder theory has relevance for sport organisations. However, from an organisational perspective, the issue of how stakeholder theory maintains both conceptual and empirical relevance is critical. Therefore it can be argued that stakeholder management involves the application of theory within the context of a practical framework that is useful for managers of sport organisations.

Concept Check

Stakeholder theory

Stakeholder theory suggests that a corporation should recognise the interests of a wide range of constituents, beyond shareholders, that have a stake in the organisation.

Stakeholder management

Friedman and Miles (2006) assert that stakeholder management is essentially about managing relationships. There are two fundamental justifications underpinning the need to manage relationships with different stakeholders. Firstly, a normative justification: management should acknowledge diverse stakeholder interests and should attempt to respond to them as a moral requirement for the legitimacy of the management function (Donaldson & Preston, 1995). The main contention of Donaldson and Preston (1995) is that normative stakeholder theory is the moral or philosophical base on which organisations operate and provides the overarching justification for stakeholder theory and is the reason why stakeholder theory should be accepted over alternative conceptions. For example, the seven Clarkson Principles (1995) have been acknowledged as a model of best practice stakeholder management and are essentially normative in the sense that they prescribe what managers should do (Friedman & Miles, 2006).

Secondly, the instrumental perspective: understanding and managing stakeholder relationships and taking the needs of a range of stakeholder organisations into account is critical to firm strategy, long-term competitive advantage and the creation of organisational wealth (Post et al., 2002; Freeman, 2006). The instrumental stakeholder approach clearly believes that there is a connection between the practice of stakeholder management and the achievement of corporate performance goals. As Driver and Thompson (2002, p. 114) argue, a focus on stakeholder interests "brings results in the sense of strengthening the company and economy generally". However, despite contrasting justifications (although not necessarily mutually exclusive) both normative and instrumental stakeholder approaches require the implementation of a stakeholder management strategy that emphasises the importance of developing and maintaining relationships with a network of stakeholder organisations.

Concept Check
Instrumental stakeholder theory
Instrumental stakeholder theory holds that managing stakeholder relationships effectively helps create long-term competitive advantage.

Understanding and managing multiple stakeholder relationships has also been recognised to be at the heart of good governance in sport. However, it has been argued that sport organisations need to work harder to understand the needs of an increasing range of stakeholders (Ferkins, Shilbury, & McDonald, 2005). In the UK, there have been concerns about whether football (soccer) clubs are able to implement stakeholder management strategies. For example, Brown et al. (2006) concede that football clubs have difficulties in engaging with a wide variety of individuals, organisations, and with many different types of community stakeholders. Stakeholder management has been recognised as an issue for sport organisations more generally. In the Governance Guide for NGBs produced by UK Sport, the four principles of good governance implicitly provide guidelines on how to manage stakeholders: accountability of decision makers to stakeholders; participation so that all stakeholders are represented when decisions are taken; responsiveness of the organisation to its stakeholders; and transparency about the information on which decisions have been based, the decisions themselves, and the way those decisions are implemented (UK Sport, 2004, p. 3).

Based on a review of the literature on stakeholder theory, the following three key elements are suggested as a way for a sport organisation to implement a dedicated stakeholder management strategy. The first is stakeholder identification – sport organisations need to identify which stakeholders are salient. Although stakeholder identification does not prescribe how an organisation should manage stakeholder relationships, the identification of the role, objective and nature of the stake of multiple stakeholders is a critical first step for an organisation that intends to implement a stakeholder management model. The second and third elements are stakeholder engagement and stakeholder participation (Low & Cowton, 2004) - two techniques available to sport organisations that want to be proactive in the management of stakeholder relationships.

Stakeholder identification

Argenti (1997) argues that the major problem with stakeholder theory is the lack of clarity over the issue of stakeholder identification. This concern is addressed by several stakeholder scholars (e.g., Phillips, 2003a; 2003b; Mitchell et al., 1997). For example, Phillips (2003a, p. 25) states, "a significant shortcoming in stakeholder thinking is in the discernment of which groups are stakeholders and why – that is, the problem of stakeholder identity". This comprises two fundamental questions: (i) which stakeholders *should* managers pay attention to?; and (ii) which stakeholders do managers *actually* care about? (Laplume et al., 2008). The first, normative, question has resulted in a 'broad vs. narrow' debate in stakeholder theory research (Clarkson, 1995; Phillips, 2003a; Reed, 1999). A broad definition of a stakeholder favours the inclusion of a large number of groups, whereas a narrow definition is limited to those groups who are said to have a morally legitimate claim, appealing to a normative core for stakeholder theory. Phillips (2003a) proposes a middle ground in this debate by focusing on stakeholder legitimacy.

Concept Check
Normative stakeholder theory
Normative stakeholder theory is based on the notion that managers ought to acknowledge stakeholder interests and attempt to respond to them as a moral requirement.

The second, largely empirical, question has been addressed by a number of scholars beginning with Mendelow (1981) who suggested that one way to do this is to rank stakeholders on the level of power they wield and the level of interest they have in organisational governance. According to Mendelow's (1981) framework, stakeholders that have a high level of power and interest in an organisation are deemed to have a significant relationship with the organisation and can be considered key stakeholders. A leading paper by Mitchell et al. (1997) suggested that managers pay attention to stakeholders based on their possession of three key attributes – power, legitimacy and urgency. Power relates to the value of the resources they possess; legitimacy to social acceptability; and urgency to how time-sensitive or critical their claims are. Subsequent research has provided reasonable empirical support for this formulation (Agle, Mitchell, & Sonnenfeld, 1999). However, several other typologies have also been proposed (e.g., Friedman & Miles, 2002; Frooman, 1999; Huang, Ding, & Kao, 2009). Laplume et al. (2008) also advocate research investigating the role of organisational culture in identifying and addressing the saliency of stakeholders (Jones, Felps, & Bigley, 2007).

Whilst Wolfe et al. (2005) argue that within sport it is easy to identify salient stakeholders it could be argued that stakeholder identification is no more straightforward in sport than it is in any other industry and that managers working in sport need to be able to draw on a framework or model in which they can understand which stakeholders are salient. The theoretical framework developed by Mitchell et al. (1997) is one such approach used by Parent and Deephouse (2007) in their case studies of two organising committees at two large sport events. They found that power was the most important element followed by urgency and legitimacy. It has also been shown that identifying stakeholders is an essential role of the board of a sport organisation. This is increasingly recognised and many organisations are producing guidelines to help sports bodies. For example in *Nine Steps to Effective Governance* (SPARC, 2006b), Sport and Recreation New Zealand show how understanding and analysing stakeholder relations is an essential part of the strategic plan.

Concept Check

Stakeholder identification

Stakeholder identification is concerned with which stakeholder group's managers should pay attention to, and which stakeholder group's managers do pay attention to.

Stakeholder identification within National Governing Bodies of sport

In a survey of National Governing Bodies of sport in the UK (Walters et al., 2010) that looked at the levels of power and interest among a range of stakeholders (drawing on the Mendelow (1981) framework), it was found that some stakeholders, such as commercial sponsors, were considered to have comparatively high levels of power, but low levels of interest in an NGB's governance. On the other hand, political actors, such as the Department for Culture, Media and Sport, and sport agencies, such as Sport England and UK Sport, have high levels of interest in corporate governance, but wield comparatively less power. This is reflective of developments in the organisational and policy landscape in which NGBs operate. Houlihan and Green (2009) argue that the Government's modernisation agenda has resulted in the lines of accountability of Sport England and UK Sport being drawn upwards to Government and outwards to commercial sponsors, rather than downwards to key partners, such as national governing bodies. The survey findings suggested that a similar process is evident for national governing bodies with the stakeholders that managers are most concerned about are those that provide key revenue streams such as commercial sponsors and government departments.

Stakeholder engagement

A stakeholder engagement strategy involves an organisation maintaining effective dialogue with stakeholder groups through communication mechanisms, meetings and consultations. However it can be argued that there are different levels of engagement. For example, certain types of engagement can be considered manipulative and misleading and involve one-way dialogue (Friedman & Miles 2006), offering little chance for stakeholders to respond. It has also been argued that an engagement strategy will keep stakeholders at arm's-length from corporate decision-making and as such, they are only able to exert a certain level of influence on an organisation (Low & Cowton, 2004). Despite these concerns, it is still necessary for a sport organisation to implement an engagement strategy.

In the UK one of the key recommendations made by UK Sport in the Modernisation Programme (which aims to promote "greater effectiveness, efficiency and independence" in National Governing Bodies of Sport (UK Sport, 2003, p. 1)) was the need for National Governing Bodies of Sport (NGBs) to communicate effectively with members, participants and wider stakeholder groups (UK Sport, 2003, p. 4). More recent survey research has shown that a high proportion of NGBs are taking definite steps to engage stakeholders actively, for instance by providing information to stakeholders through their website and/or annual report and seeking feedback from stakeholders on particular consultations (Walters et al., 2010). This is evident in the case of New Zealand Football, the governing body for football in New Zealand. Their website provides copies of annual reports and the strategic plan for 2009-2011 demonstrating that part of a stakeholder engagement strategy is to be transparent. The strategic plan also sets out the need to understand the different needs of stakeholder groups, to develop an ongoing stakeholder communication and engagement plan, and to annually survey stakeholders for their feedback on the objectives and goals of New Zealand Football (http://www .nzfootball.co.nz/index.php?id=39).

Such a commitment to stakeholder engagement often requires the creation of a specialist role and it is becoming more common for sport organisations to appoint an individual dedicated to stakeholder engagement. For example, in 2011 the New Zealand Rugby Union advertised for the position of Stakeholder and Community Relations Manager. The overall purpose of the role is to "manage and develop the implementation of stakeholder relations programmes and community relations strategies which enable the NZRU to build and maintain active engagement and positive relationships with a wide range of stakeholders, influencers and communities" (www.nzru.co.nz).

It can also be argued that the management of sport facilities should examine the long-term implications on the stakeholders that have an interest in, or are affected by, the facility, and not just on the operational procedures (Atkin & Brooks, 2003). More recently it has also been argued that there is a need to engage with stakeholders during the development of new sport stadiums (Brown et al., 2006; Walters, 2011). The development of the Emirates Stadium in the UK is a case in point. The stakeholder engagement strategy implemented by Arsenal football club involved resident and supporter consultations, a varied communication strategy, and the Stadium Liaison Committee and Stadium Management Plan. These indicate that the football club sought to manage multiple relationships with different stakeholder communities and maintain regular consultation between the club and community in order to minimise the negative effects of the stadium development. However despite these engagement mechanisms, the majority of stakeholder groups were kept at arms-length from the decision-making processes and therefore had little opportunity to participate in decision-making processes.

Concept Check

Stakeholder engagement

Stakeholder engagement refers to the way in which an organisation maintains an ongoing dialogue with stakeholder groups, for example through meetings and consultations.

Sport and Recreation New Zealand – stakeholder communications

Sport and Recreation New Zealand have produced guidelines for sport organisations on how to develop a strategic plan to communicate with stakeholders. The document *Creating a Stakeholder Communications Plan* (SPARC, 2006a) states that:

"An effective stakeholder communications plan will:
- support your organisation in achieving its stated goals and objectives
- support or improve your operational effectiveness
- support or improve your relationships with those who are important to ensuring your success (often called key stakeholders or your target audience)
- deliver measurable results to your organisation" (p. 3).

The document then goes on to provide an eight-step communications planning framework which is aimed to get sports organisations to think through the various stages required as part of a strategic approach to communications. These eight steps are:

1. Setting communication objectives
2. Setting key messages for your organisation
3. Defining and prioritising key stakeholders (target audiences)
4. Setting additional key messages which are relevant for each stakeholder group and their particular issues/concerns
5. Developing effective communication tactics for each target audience
6. Allocating budget and responsibilities
7. Developing the quarterly communications calendar
8. Assessing results and adapting the plan (SPARC, 2006a, p. 4).

Stakeholder participation

Stakeholder participation moves beyond engagement in that it enables stakeholder groups to have an active involvement in decision-making, often integrating them within the governance or representative structures of an organisation (Low & Cowton, 2004). Such a model is indicative of an inclusive stakeholder approach that emphasises participation and representation as key elements of the management of stakeholder relationships. However stakeholder participation can be problematic in that it can lead to difficulties in deciding which stakeholders deserve representation on a board or committee. Moreover the skills and abilities of the stakeholder representatives on a board may also be a concern leading to internal conflict. This is the case at many sport organisations, where in the face of growing commercial pressures, the abilities of the voluntary board do not match the requirements of the organisation.

Many NGBs within the UK have structures that allow for stakeholder participation. For example it was found that stakeholders have representation on the main board or committee at 67 per cent of NGBs, whilst 66 per cent involve stakeholders on various committees (Walters et al., 2010). In addition, the supporter trust model is a clear example of stakeholder participation in practice. Within the UK and in Europe, there are a large number of supporter trusts at football and at a smaller number of rugby clubs. A supporters' trust is an independent, not-for-profit, democratic co-operatively owned organisation that seeks to influence the governance of a sports organisation through improve supporter representation. Many are able to participate in the governance of a football club through share ownership and by having board representation. In the UK there are 100 trusts that maintain a shareholding at clubs and 45 supporter-directors (Brown, 2008). The most notable successes include the three professional clubs in the Football League that are owned by the supporters trust; Brentford, Exeter City and AFC Wimbledon.

The stakeholder participation model is also prevalent within German football where the ultimate ownership and decision-making power remains under the control of the member association. The German Football Association (Deutsche Fußball-Bund) rules state that the member association retains 50 per cent plus one vote of the incorporated football club, ensuring that the majority ownership of German football clubs cannot be granted to any one individual (Dietl & Franck, 2007). The football club remains under the control of the member association with members (supporters) having the responsibility to elect the chief executive and members of the management board of the football club. However it has led to a limit on foreign investment in German football club which has placed the model under pressure given that there is a belief that foreign investment would make German clubs more competitive in European competition.

Concept Check

Stakeholder participation

Stakeholder participation refers to the way in which stakeholder groups engage actively in decision-making within an organisation, for example through being represented in the governance structures of the organisation.

CASE STUDY: STAKEHOLDER PARTICIPATION IN THE AUSTRALIAN FOOTBALL LEAGUE

In the Australian Football League the majority of the 17 clubs are constituted as membership clubs. Membership has been growing year on year since 2001 and total membership numbers exceeded 600,000 for the first time in 2010 with three clubs having over 50,000 members. Growing membership numbers are important for the AFL clubs and for the league as a whole as it translates into large attendances and revenues and helps to attract corporate sponsorship. Andrew Demetriou, the CEO of the AFL, stated that membership is absolutely fundamental to the AFL: "*membership continues to be the lifeblood of our clubs, and the AFL's single most important indicator of the game's health remains attendances at our matches and the commitment of our supporters to become a member of one of our clubs*" (Walsh, 2010).

Club membership also provides certain voting rights although it is clear that the constitutions vary across the clubs with different policies in relation to member voting rights on issues such as name changes, changes to club colours, relocations, and also in respect to appointing a proportion of board members. Whilst this membership model in the AFL is illustrative of a stakeholder participatory approach, there has been criticism that despite the constitutional rights of members, many AFL clubs do not offer members a real opportunity for genuine participation in the club and that membership is essentially a "glorified stadium entry ticket" (Paterson, 2010, p. 508). Indeed, it has been argued that often members are unaware of their rights and that AFL clubs could do much more.

Summary

As CSR has moved from a position on the periphery of organisational activity to become a central component within mainstream business organisations, it has also been the case that sport organisations have started to address CSR in different ways. This chapter has looked at CSR in sport by drawing on stakeholder theory. With CSR as its core construct, stakeholder theory is highly relevant to the management of sport organisations (Friedman et al., 2004). The chapter has provided an overview of the development of CSR and the theoretical discussions surrounding stakeholder theory, and has sought to identify how stakeholder theorising is a useful tool for sport organisations that are seeking to implement a stakeholder management strategy as part of their commitment to CSR.

This chapter is firmly grounded at the organisational-level. This type of approach suggests that for sport organisations knowledge of the organisation's environment is crucial and through a stakeholder management strategy key issues can be addressed including: who are our stakeholders; how do interests vary within and between stakeholder groups; what is the nature of the relationship between a sport organisation and its stakeholders; what obligations does the organisation owe to its various stakeholders; and how should decision making be oriented to balance the interests of the various stakeholders. In order to effectively address these issues three key elements to stakeholder management have been proposed: stakeholder identification; stakeholder engagement; and stakeholder participation (Low & Cowton, 2004). Whilst stakeholder identification is clearly the first element that sport organisations need to consider as part of a stakeholder management strategy, it is not always as straightforward to distinguish between stakeholder engagement and stakeholder participation. Indeed, they might better be thought of as points on a continuum from low engagement through to active participation. However what is clear is that each sport organisation needs to decide what level of engagement or participation is necessary for each stakeholder group and then manage the relationship accordingly. To conclude, this chapter has shown, first, that stakeholder theorising can illuminate key issues in sport management, and second, how CSR has been implemented by sport organisations through stakeholder management strategies

Review questions

- Why is CSR important for sport organisations?
- Why is it important for sport organisations to identify different stakeholder groups?
- What are the risks of identifying too many different stakeholder groups?
- Should sport organisations seek to apply an engagement strategy or a participation strategy with stakeholders or both?

References

Agle B. R., Mitchell, R. K., & Sonnenfeld, J. A. (1999). Who matters to CEOs? An investigation of stakeholder attributes and salience, corporate performance and CEO values. *Academy of Management Journal*, 42(5), 507–525.

Argenti, J. (1997). Stakeholders: The case against. *Long Range Planning*, 30(3), 442–445.

Atkin, B., & Brooks, A. (2003). *Total facilities management* (2nd ed). London: Blackwell.

Babiak, K., & Wolfe, R. (2006). More than just a game? Corporate social responsibility and Super Bowl XL. *Sport Marketing Quarterly*, 15(4), 214–222.

Babiak, K., & Wolfe, R. (2009). Determinants of corporate social responsibility in professional sport: Internal and external factors. *Journal of Sport Management*, 23, 717–742.

Blowfield, M., & Murray, A. (2008). *Corporate responsibility: A critical introduction.* Oxford: Oxford University Press.

Bowen, H. R. (1953). *Social responsibilities of the businessman.* Boston: Little, Brown.

Bradish, C., & Cronin, J. (2009). Corporate social responsibility in sport. *Journal of Sport Management, 23,* 691–697.

Brown, A. (2008, December). Direct action. *When Saturday Comes, 262.* Retrieved from http://www.wsc.co.uk/content/view/4737/29/

Brown, A., Crabbe, T., Mellor, G., Blackshaw, T., & Stone, C. (2006). *Football and its communities: Final report.* London: The Football Foundation.

Campbell, J. (2007). Why would corporations behave in socially responsible ways? An institutional theory of corporate social responsibility. *Academy of Management Review, 32*(3), 946–967.

Cappato, A., & Pennazio, V. (2006). *Corporate social responsibility in sport: Torino 2006 Olympic Winter Games.* Turin: University of Turin.

Carroll, A. B. (1979). A three-dimensional conceptual model of corporate performance. *Academy of Management Review, 4*(4), 497–505.

Carroll, A. B. (1991).The pyramid of corporate social responsibility: Toward the moral management of organizational stakeholders. *Business Horizons, 34,* 39–48.

Carroll, A. B. (1999). Corporate social responsibility: Evolution of a definitional construct. *Business and Society, 38*(3), 268–295.

Clarkson, M. B. E. (1995). A stakeholder framework of analysing and evaluating corporate social performance. *Academy of Management Review, 20*(1), 92–117.

Dietl, H., & Franck, E. (2007). Governance failure and financial crisis in German football. *Journal of Sports Economics, 8*(6), 662–669.

Donaldson ,T., & Preston, L. E. (1995). The stakeholder theory of the corporation: Concepts, evidence and implications. *Academy of Management Review, 20*(1), 63–91.

Driver, C., & Thompson, G. (2002). Corporate governance and democracy: The stakeholder debate revisited. *Journal of Management and Governance, 6,* 111–130.

Ferkins, L., Shilbury, D., & McDonald, G. (2005). The role of the board in building strategic capability: Towards an integrated model of sport governance research. *Sport Management Review, 8,* 195–225.

Freeman, R. E. (1984). *Strategic management: A stakeholder approach.* Boston: Pitman.

Freeman, R. E. (2006, August). The Wal-Mart effect and business, ethics and society. *Academy of Management Perspectives, 20*(3) 38–40. DOI: 10.5465/AMP.2006.21903479

Freeman, R. E., & Phillips, R. (1996). Efficiency, effectiveness and ethics: A stakeholder view. In N. W. Gasparski, & L. Ryan (Eds.), *Human action in business* (pp. 65–81). New Brunswick: Transaction Publishers.

Friedman, A. L., & Miles, S. V. (2002). Developing stakeholder theory. *Journal of Management Studies, 39*(1), 1–22.

Friedman, A. L., & Miles, S. V. (2006). *Stakeholders: Theory and practice,* Oxford: Oxford University Press.

Friedman, M. T., & Mason, D. S. (2004). A stakeholder approach to understanding economic decision making: Public subsidies for professional sport facilities. *Economic Development Quarterly, 18*(3), 236–254.

Friedman, M. T., Parent, M. M., & Mason, D. S. (2004). Building a framework for issues management in sport through stakeholder theory. *European Sport Management Quarterly, 4*(3), 170–190.

Frooman, J. (1999). Stakeholder influence strategies. *Academy of Management Review, 24*(2), 191–205.

Godfrey, P. (2009). Corporate social responsibility in sport: An overview and key issues. *Journal of Sport Management, 23*(6), 698–716.

Houlihan, B., & Green, M. (2009). Modernization and sport: The reform of Sport England and UK Sport. *Public Administration, 87*(3), 678–698. DOI: 10.1111/j.1467-9299.2008.01733.x

Huang, Y-C., Ding, H-B., & Kao, M-R. (2009). Salient stakeholder voices: Family business and green innovation adoption. *Journal of Management and Organisation, 15*(3), 309–327.

Jones, T. M., Felps, W., & Bigley, G. A. (2007). Ethical theory and stakeholder related decisions: The role of stakeholder culture. *Academy of Management Journal, 32*(1), 137–155.

Kott, A. (2005, January/February). The philanthropic power of sports. *Foundation News and Commentary, 46*(1), 20–25.

Laplume, A. O., Sonpar, K., & Litz, R. A. (2008). Stakeholder theory: Reviewing a theory that moves us. *Journal of Management, 34*(6), 1152–1189.

Leopkey, B., & Parent, M. M. (2009). Risk management issues in large-scale sporting events: A stakeholder perspective. *European Sport Management Quarterly, 9*(2), 187–208.

Lindgreen, A., & Swaen, V. (2010). Corporate Social Responsibility. *International Journal of Management Reviews, 12*(1), 1–7.

Low, C., & Cowton, C. (2004). Beyond stakeholder engagement: The challenges of stakeholder participation in corporate governance. *International Journal of Business Governance and Ethics, 1*(1), 45–55.

Maignan, I., & Ferrell, O. C. (2004). Corporate social responsibility and marketing: An integrative framework. *Journal of the Academy of Marketing Science, 32*(1), 3–19.

Mendelow, A. L. (1981). Environmental scanning: The impact of the stakeholder concept. In *Proceedings of the 2nd International Conference on Information Systems,* (pp. 407–417). Cambridge, MA.

Mitchell, R., Agle, B., & Wood, D. (1997). Toward a theory of stakeholder identification and salience: Defining the principle of who and what really counts. *Academy of Management Review, 22*(4), 853–866.

Morgan, M. (2002). Optimizing the structure of elite competitions in professional sport – lessons from rugby union. *Managing Leisure, 7*(1), 41–60.

Morrow, S. (2003). *The people's game? Football, finance and society.* Basingstoke: Palgrave Macmillan.

Morrow, S., & Idle, C. (2008). Understanding change in professional road cycling. *European Sport Management Quarterly, 8*(4), 315–336.

Parent, M. M., & Deephouse, D. L. (2007). A case study of stakeholder identification and prioritization by managers. *Journal of Business Ethics, 75,* 1–23.

Paterson, J. (2010). AFL club membership: A glorified stadium entry ticket, or a genuine ownership stake in the club? *Company and Securities Law Journal, 28*(8), 507–.

Phillips, R. (2003a). *Stakeholder theory and organisational ethics.* San Francisco, CA: Berret-Koelher.

Phillips, R. (2003b). Stakeholder legitimacy. *Business Ethics Quarterly, 13*(1), 25–41.

Phillips, R., Freeman, R. E., & Wicks, A. (2003). What stakeholder theory is not. *Business Ethics Quarterly, 13*(4), 479–502.

Post, J., Preston, L., & Sachs, S. (2002). Managing the extended enterprise: The new stakeholder view. *California Management Review, 45*(1), 6–28.

Putler, D. S., & Wolfe, R. A. (1999). Perceptions of intercollegiate athletic programmes: Priorities and tradeoffs. *Sociology of Sport Journal, 16,* 301–325.

Reed, D. (1999). Stakeholder management theory: A critical theory perspective. *Business Ethics Quarterly, 9*(3), 453–483.

Senaux, B. (2008). A stakeholder approach to football club governance. *International Journal of Sport Management and Marketing, 4*(1/2), 4–17.

Smith, A., & Westerbeek, H. (2007). Sport as a vehicle for deploying corporate social responsibility. *Journal of Corporate Citizenship, 25,* 43–54.

SPARC. (2006a). *Creating a stakeholder communications plan.* Retrieved from http://www.sparc.co.nz/Documents/Partners/Stakeholder-Comms-Planning.pdf

SPARC. (2006b). *Nine steps to effective governance: Building high performance organisations* (2nd ed.). Retrieved from http://www.sparc.co.nz/Documents/Sector%20Capability/effective_govt_2nd.pdf

Trail, G., & Chelladurai, P. (2000). Perceptions of goals and processes of intercollegiate athletics: A case study. *Journal of Sport Management, 14*(2), 154–178.

UK Sport (2003). *'Investing in change': High level review of the modernisation programme for governing bodies of sport.* London: Deloitte and Touche.

UK Sport (2004). *Good governance: A guide for national governing bodies of sport.* London: Institute of Chartered Secretaries and Administrators.

Walker, M., & Kent, A. (2009). Do fans care? Assessing the influence of corporate social responsibility on consumer attitudes in the sport industry. *Journal of Sport Management, 23,* 743–769.

Walsh, G. (2010, July 16). *Club memberships top 600,000.* Retrieved from http://www.afl.com.au/tabid/208/default.aspx?newsid=98326

Walters, G. (2009). Corporate social responsibility through sport: The community sports trust model as a CSR delivery agency. *Journal of Corporate Citizenship, 35,* 81–94.

Walters, G. (2011). The implementation of a stakeholder management strategy during stadium relocation: A case study of Arsenal football club's move to the Emirates Stadium. *Managing Leisure, 16*(1), 49–64.

Walters, G., & Tacon, R. (2010). Corporate social responsibility in sport: Stakeholder management in the UK football industry. *Journal of Management and Organisation, 16*(4), 566–586.

Windsor, D. (2001). The future of corporate social responsibility. *The International Journal of Organisational Analysis, 9*(3), 225–256.

Wolfe, R. A., & Putler, D. S. (2002). How tight are the ties that bind stakeholder groups? *Organisation Science, 13*(1), 64–80.

Wolfe, R. A., Weick, K. E., Usher, J. M., Terborg, J. R., Poppo, L., Murrell, A. J., … Jourdan, J. S. (2005). Sport and organisational studies: Exploring synergy. *Journal of Management Inquiry, 14*(2), 182–210.

Wood, D. J. (2010). Measuring corporate social performance: A review. *International Journal of Management Reviews, 12*(1), 50–84.

Websites

- The Australian Football League, http://www.afl.com.au
- New Zealand football, http://www.nzfootball.co.nz/index.php?id=39
- Sport and Recreation New Zealand, www.sparc.co.nz

Chapter 14

Sport Sponsorship

Lesley Ferkins, Ron Garland and Trevor Meiklejohn

OBJECTIVES

After completing this chapter, you should be able to:

- describe the nature and role of sponsorship in sport as part of a company's marketing mix;
- be familiar with terminology relating to sport sponsorship and integrated sponsorship marketing;
- understand the key components of the sponsorship management process;
- understand the dual perspectives of sponsor and sponsee in relation to sport sponsorship;
- highlight key influences and measures of sponsorship effectiveness;
- understand the partnership approach to sponsorship and the concept of co-branding;
- discuss elements of ambush marketing.

Key terms

In this chapter, readers will become familiar with the following concepts and terms:
- sponsorship
- sponsorship marketing
- partnership
- sponsor
- sponsorship management
- relationship
- sponsee
- image transfer
- media brand values
- sponsorship property
- networking
- sponsorship rights
- rights holder
- leveraging
- sponsorship contract/agreement
- philanthropy
- competitive advantage

- co-branding
- brand awareness
- sponsorship effectiveness
- ambush marketing
- contra, or in-kind
- cost-benefit analysis

Chapter outline

The aim of this chapter is to introduce readers to the nature of sponsorship in sport along with some of the issues and trends that face sponsors, sport managers, event promoters and the sporting public. The concept of sponsorship is introduced coupled with the role that it plays in sport management. A model for managing sponsorship is presented and the key elements of this sponsorship management model are discussed in detail throughout the chapter. The key elements include; setting sponsorship objectives, corporate evaluation criteria, sponsorship selection, implementation, measuring and evaluation of sponsorship effectiveness. A long-term partnership approach to sponsorship is emphasised in this chapter alongside the concept of co-branding in sponsorship relationships. Ambush marketing is also highlighted with reference to major event sponsorship.

CASE STUDY: HYUNDAI'S SPONSORSHIP OF LONGBOARD SURFING IN NEW ZEALAND

Prepared by Trevor Meiklejohn

Three years ago, after a 19-year break from surfing due to many other priorities such as family, study, career and other sporting pursuits, I was both nervous and excited when I unwrapped a brand new longboard on my 38th birthday. This beautifully hand-crafted, nine-foot longboard, that would have been highly inappropriate for the shortboard surfing teenager that I once was, now seemed the perfect option for this more mature surfer many years later. Accompanying the board was a number of items 'thrown in' by the generous surf shop owner such as a leg rope, wax and, curiously, a 'Hyundai Pro Longboard Tour' DVD. The professionally-produced DVD provides the viewer with a stunning account of the series of longboard surf events held throughout the New Zealand summer in the form of the 'Hyundai Pro Longboard Tour'. Integrated into the DVD is a series of Hyundai television commercials and strong Hyundai branding. The DVD takes the viewer on a New Zealand coastal road trip in a Hyundai SUV to idyllic locations such as Sandy Bay in the far north and Kaikoura in the south where the events are held. Whilst the relaxed and laid-back atmosphere that I once knew in surfing is still evident, each event is highly professional and managed to ensure maximum competitor and spectator satisfaction. The branded control tower, the strategically parked 'Hyundai Pro Longboard Tour' branded vehicles, music, merchandise and uniformed staff indicate a significant shift from the surfing world I once knew. It is clear from the calibre of surfers from all around the world competing in this series, including current and former world champions, that this series is a big deal. One can't help but think that the commercial involvement of Hyundai has played a significant part in this shift. Three years on I am still surfing and have attended a number of 'Hyundai Pro Longboard Tour' events with my family and have also covered many miles searching for that perfect wave. A glance at the sponsorship section of Hyundai's website explaining their sponsorship of surfing, suggests that I may very well fit the target audience of their marketing strategy of which sponsorship plays an important part. Their sponsorship of surfing is explained in the website as follows:

(Continued)

Hyundai have been involved with surfing in New Zealand since 2003 and will continue their support for 2011. Since 2006, the first year of the Hyundai Pro Longboard Tour, Hyundai continue to be large sponsors heavily giving back to the community by providing fantastic prizes, free merchandise and consequently remarkable surfing events to New Zealanders nationwide.

New Zealand's coastline has it all, from perfect beaches, long point breaks and several big wave spots, just to name a few. There is no surprise we now see over 200,000 people taking part in surfing in New Zealand every year. Hyundai have taken the initiative to sponsor such a widely-participated sport and have, for the third year running, held the ever so prestigious Hyundai Pro Longboard Tour within New Zealand.

The recent up-taking of longboarding in New Zealand is due to a combination of many factors, one of which is the Hyundai professional competition circuit. This, in turn, has drawn the original crew as well as the new generation of enthusiasts into the water and back onto the old-school majestic vessel.

The strong sponsorship fit that Hyundai has with surfing in New Zealand is illustrated by the extent to which surfers travel. Sport Research Group in 2006 found that 47% of surfers travel more than 500 kilometres per month in search of waves. In years gone by, the Volkswagen Combi and HQ Holden were iconic surf vehicles. The opportunity exists to fill this space in the future. Hyundai has positioned this sponsorship around their range of SUV (4x4) vehicles in recognition of the fact that the search for quality waves frequently involves long gravel roads, west coast beaches and the odd trip around the rocks.

Hyundai is aiming to build brand preference among surfers and fans of surfing in New Zealand who are in the market for a new vehicle. By sponsoring the Surfing Nationals and the Longboard Tour, Hyundai NZ, 100% owned and operated in New Zealand, hopes to make those people aware of Hyundai's presence and involvement with surfing in New Zealand (Hyundai, 2011).

Introduction

Sponsorship has been around since Roman times when emperors sponsored chariot races. Later, in Europe, the upper classes showed their support for art and culture by giving money to artists and musicians. The inaugural modern Olympic Games, in Athens in 1896, experienced legitimate corporate investment in sport when companies purchased advertising space in the official Olympic Games programme (Sandler & Shani, 1993). Coca-Cola was the first company to purchase official 'sampling rights', at the St Moritz Winter Games in 1928 (Stotlar, 1993) and, in that very same year at the Summer Olympics in Amsterdam, delivered one thousand cases of their product to the U.S. Olympic team, and sold their bottled drink from kiosks located around the Olympic stadium (Coca-Cola, 2011).

In contrast to these early examples, where the investing organisations had commercial motives for their association with sport, sponsorship also has its roots in philanthropy which is characterised by individuals or organisations providing grants and donations of cash or kind to the sport (individual, event or organisation) with little or no return expected by the donor (philanthropist). Whilst philanthropy is still very much part of the environment in which sport operates, sponsorship is now recognised as a strategic business-building tool. This shift in thinking from philanthropy to strategic marketing led to sponsorship investment being used to leverage exposure and profile from all elements of the communications and marketing mix.

The world-wide recession in the mid-1980s, and the more recent global economic crisis, have led to a growing demand for corporate organisations to show a genuine return on investment (ROI) which has, therefore, resulted in a dramatic shift in sponsorship spending and planning. Today, sponsorship is equally as accountable as any other promotional strategy and just as commonly used for building brands. In this current environment there is an increased need for corporates to demonstrate leadership in both commercial performance and social responsibility, both important factors in customer loyalty (Cone, Coughlin, Roper, & Starch, 1994). Competition, mergers, and increased use of technology have businesses struggling to differentiate themselves in today's markets. This, coupled with significant clutter in print, broadcast and internet media, has led to sponsorship being used as a marketing tool to achieve differentiation as well as specific corporate, marketing and business objectives. In addition to the strategic focus now given to sponsorship, there is also a shift from a short-term transactional view of sponsorship, where an organisation provides cash or kind to a property in return for a number of benefits, to a long-term partnership orientation that embraces concepts integral to inter-organisational relationship literature such as co-operation and communication. Consistent with this approach, Farrelly (2010) states that sponsorship provides a collaborative business platform for participating organisations who seek to achieve mutually-beneficial outcomes.

Many recent local and international case studies document the power of well-integrated and leveraged sponsorship properties to build brands and drive tangible business returns. As a component of the marketing mix, the amount spent on sport sponsorship is growing. Factors such as increased restrictions on advertising, higher advertising costs, the consumers' ability to 'zap' or fast-forward through commercials, and increased media coverage of major sponsored events have contributed to this growth (Olson, 2010). Furthermore, the role sport plays in people's lives coupled with sport brands that engage the consumer emotionally, have the potential to 'cut through' the congested promotional landscape. Akaoui (2007) noted the global spend on sponsorship had reached an estimated $US33+ billion of which approximately two-thirds is directed at sporting events, leagues, teams and players (Crompton, 2004; Verity, 2002).

This chapter provides an insight into sponsorship as a bona fide marketing discipline with demonstrated ability to win consumer hearts and minds and gain market share, while, at the same time, delivering positive community benefits. An understanding and appreciation of the role of sport sponsorship in the marketing mix is essential for sport managers as they endeavour to manage their organisations in the modern business environment.

Concept Check

Sponsorship

Sponsorship is generally recognised as the purchase of an exploitable opportunity associated with an activity not normally part of a company's core business that results in tangible benefits for the sponsor as well as benefiting the sponsored party.

Defining sponsorship

Numerous definitions of sponsorship exist in both academic and mainstream sporting literature. In a comprehensive review of sponsorship literature, Walliser (2003) noted that there is some agreement that sponsorship is based on an exchange between sponsor and sponsored, and pursues marketing objectives by exploiting the association between the two. Mullin, Hardy, and Sutton (2007) defined sponsorship as the acquisition of rights in order to affiliate or directly associate with an event or product to derive benefits related to the affiliation. Finally, an earlier and well-used definition comes from Sleight (1989, p. 4) who explained sponsorship as: "A business relationship between a provider of funds, resources or services and an individual, event or organisation which offers in return some rights and association that may be used for commercial advantage".

There are also variations in the literature regarding key terms used to describe the members of a sponsorship relationship; in particular the organisation, event or athlete being sponsored. The sponsoring organisation or the organisation providing cash and/or 'in-kind' goods or services is generally known as the sponsor. The organisation, event or athlete being sponsored has been referred to in sponsorship literature as a sponsee, property, entity or rights holder.

Concept Check
Sponsor and the organisation, event or athlete being sponsored
A sponsor is the purchaser of sponsorship rights. A sponsee, property, entity or rights holder is the recipient of sponsorship from a sponsor.

Role of sport sponsorship

Many reasons have been cited for the role and growth of sport sponsorship. On the one hand, the ever increasing professional sporting environment requires sports to invest heavily in facilities, events, programmes, players and staff, to name a few. Corporate sponsors, as a result of the rights fees they pay for the legal right to use a property's trademarks, logos and intellectual property in promotional activity, are a prime source of revenue for the sport organisation. Long-term sponsor relationships can therefore, provide a steady stream of revenue as well as enhanced exposure for the sport organisation (Dees, Bennett, & Villegas, 2008). On the other hand, sport sponsorship is attractive to corporations because the sport organisations and the events they produce provide highly-involved, passionate and loyal fans enabling the creation of unique and targeted marketing messages. Furthermore, sponsorship can be used to link consumers to the sponsors' brands and influence consumers and business partners to form positive brand images or make purchases from their companies (Farrelly, Quester, & Burton 2006). For international brands such as Gillette, Vodafone and adidas, sport sponsorship is pivotal in their marketing communications campaigns and provide these very different brands with a global brand communication platform (Akaoui, 2007).

A model of sponsorship selection and management

Once a company has made a decision to incorporate sponsorship into its marketing strategy and has specified the outcomes it hopes to achieve, it then usually develops a sponsorship management strategy. Irwin and Asimakopoulos (1992) proposed an excellent six-step approach to sponsorship management. The first step is to conduct a review of the corporate marketing plan, including marketing and communications/corporate objectives and marketing budget locations and, in particular determining the role sponsorship may play in the marketing strategy. The second step sets sponsorship objectives in terms of corporate, product/brand, new business and customer loyalty objectives. The third step establishes evaluation criteria in terms of cost/ROI, match of image, audiences, PR/media, product sales and customer/VIP, for example. The fourth step involves sponsorship selection through proposal screening, proposal grading, selection and allocation of resources. Finalising the sponsorship contract is also essential in this step and will include the length of the sponsorship and the specification of rights provided to the sponsoring organisation. The fifth step involves the implementation or execution of the sponsorship and will include strategies to leverage and maximise the effectiveness of the sponsorship. The sixth and final step evaluates the sponsorship by measuring all activity against objectives. With the role of sport sponsorship discussed above, steps two through six are now detailed with supporting examples.

Understanding why companies sponsor

The second step of the sponsorship management process involves setting sponsorship objectives. Understanding why companies sponsor is an essential element. Based on their review of sponsorship motivations, Chadwick and Thwaites (2004) developed four distinct categories of sponsorship objectives.

- *Marketing communication objectives* – The use of sponsorship as a promotional strategy with a view to increasing sales, raising brand awareness, promoting image transfer and targeting specific markets with tailored messages/offers. Sponsorship, unlike traditional advertising, can engage a consumer by bestowing benefit on an activity that the consumer is already emotionally connected to (Meenaghan, 2001). In simple terms, a consumer's defence mechanisms are low when perceiving sponsorship in comparison to traditional advertising (Mason, 2005). The Rugby World Cup (RWC) held in New Zealand in 2011 provided its leading tier of sponsors, 'World Wide Partners', with many marketing opportunities. Heineken, for example, with its exclusive pourage rights at all RWC events, significantly increased its sales throughout the tournament.
- *Relationship marketing objectives* – The use of sponsorship to build relationships with customers, collaborative partners, key stakeholders and staff. Sponsorship provides a unique environment, in the form of corporate boxes, lounges and marquees, for sponsors to host clients and reward staff outside the normal place of work.
- *Network objectives* – The use of sponsorship to establish relationships with other organisations associated with the property such as other sponsors, the property's customers and the media. Many sport events and sporting organisations have a 'family or network of sponsors' and other important stakeholders which any new sponsor automatically joins, thereby opening doors to many networking opportunities.
- *Resource objectives* – The allocation of key strategic capital and human resources in order to differentiate and create a unique point of difference from competitors in order to achieve a competitive advantage. Timex Watches' long-standing relationship with the iconic endurance event 'Ironman' has seen significant investment and development by Timex in the advanced Ironman watches worn by athletes, as both an essential training tool and a 'badge of honour' for completing the gruelling event. This has enabled Timex to establish and maintain a unique point of difference from its competitors.

Further to the above, Apostolopoulou and Papadimiriou (2004) investigated motivations and objectives for Grand National Sponsors of the 2004 Olympic Games in Athens. In the main, their findings complement the above categories showing that enhancing corporate image, increasing awareness, increasing sales/market share and enhancing employee relations were key motivations for sponsors. They concluded by suggesting that whilst sponsorship motives are varied, a company should not consider a sponsorship unless they have specified the outcomes they hope to achieve from their involvement.

Corporate criteria

The third step of the sponsorship management process above highlights the development of evaluation criteria for sponsorship opportunities. Most sponsors will have a checklist comprised of the following criteria:

- *Is the sport compatible with their company or brand?* For example, the sports that Red Bull is involved with include extreme sports such as cliff diving, big wave surfing and free-style motocross, to name a few, all of which exude the same brand values as Red Bull.
- *Are there any political or commercial risk factors such as boycotts, drug scandals or player misconduct?* For example, continued poor performance or behaviour on or off the field or court, or other controversies surrounding the administration of the sport, are likely to be scooped up by the media. This can negatively affect the sponsor and the integrity and market value of the property. An example of this is the case study by Kahuni, Rowely, and Binsardi (2009) which investigated the 2007 Formula One spying scandal involving the Vodafone McLaren-Mercedes Formula One team.
- *Will there be any conflicts or clash of sponsors in the sport at any level?* Managing conflicts between event sponsors, team sponsors and individual player sponsors, for example, is an ongoing challenge, particularly when sponsors of a property seek to portray a level of association or access benefits they are not entitled to.
- *Is the sport relevant to the company's target audience?* For example, Sanitarium's targeting of the youth market via their sponsorship of the iconic 'Weet-Bix Triathlon.
- *What is the timeframe of the event or sport? Is it a 'one-off' or are there ongoing opportunities?* For example, the four-yearly Rugby World Cup compared to the annual Super Rugby competition.
- *Is the event news-worthy and how often will coverage of the sport reach the audience?* It is reported that 1 billion people, or 15% of the world's population, tuned into the opening ceremony of the 2008 Beijing Olympics.
- *Are there any associated leveraged media opportunities?* For example, Vodafone's sponsorship of the New Zealand Warriors not only provides them with significant live broadcast exposure, but additional media exposure is provided via the Warriors' website, social media and specialised rugby league programmes.
- *Is product sector exclusivity offered?* For example, official sponsors of the 2011 Rugby World Cup, such as Land Rover, had exclusivity in the vehicle market associated with this prestigious tournament.
- *What direct sales opportunities exist?* For example, wine-maker Jacob's Creek, as a major sponsor of the Australian Tennis Open, established the Jacob's Creek Open House – a public wine bar at the event.

- *Is there an existing relationship with the property?* Existing formal and informal relationships are often the foundation upon which more formal relationships are developed (Chadwick & Thwaites, 2004).
- *The importance of geographic proximity.* It is commonly held by sponsors that working with organisations located in the same geographic area is likely to result in more effective sponsorship programmes, as it presents the opportunity to build relationships with key local stakeholders (Chadwick & Thwaites, 2004). The long-standing relationship that the alcohol brand, XXXX, has with Queensland Rugby League that dates back to 1991 is an example of this.

Sponsorship selection and formalising the relationship

The dynamics involved in this fourth important phase of the sponsorship management process are often detailed and time-consuming. While corporate organisations may be scanning the environment for potential properties, sport organisations are often actively soliciting corporate sponsorship in a process that may involve significant research and many meetings, to enable them to understand the marketing objectives of corporates in order to establish a proposal that is able to meet their objectives. The corporate organisation will assess/rank the proposal(s) and, normally, after considerable discussion and negotiation, a contract/agreement is finalised that will specify the rights provided to the sponsor and the corresponding investment required for those rights from them.

Soliciting corporate sponsorship

There is no easy road to securing a corporate sponsor for a property. The organisation doing the seeking usually needs to demonstrate:
- a vision for the sponsor of shared expectation and long-term direction;
- the skill and ability to accomplish the proposition in a professional manner supported by good management;
- the right attitude to tie-in with the sponsor's commercial philosophy;
- the desire and determination to follow through.

At a practical level, sponsorship solicitation calls for a high degree of professionalism, patience and persistence. The sponsorship property and associated benefits must present 'an irresistible marketing opportunity'. Noted prerequisites for success are a thorough understanding of the marketplace and the needs of a potential sponsor, a sound 'marketable property', and a well-prepared proposal containing quantifiable benefits presented with adequate lead-time (Stotlar, 2001).

A sponsorship proposal

As highlighted above, sponsorship proposals are considerably more effective if they tie sponsorship elements specifically to the objectives of the sponsoring organisation. A good proposal may include:
- key details of the opportunity
- an overview of the sponsee's marketing plan and budget
- a list of funders and sponsors confirmed to date
- a comprehensive list of benefits linked to the company and its products

- a timeline and critical path
- credentials of the company and key subcontractors
  To be seriously considered, the sponsorship opportunity usually contains at least six of the following:
- a natural link with the sport or event
- naming rights to an event/sport, or an element the sponsor can 'own'
- sponsorship exclusivity
- opportunities for VIP hospitality or consumer promotion
- it specifically targets one of the sponsor's primary demographics
- promotional media time/space (not just logo exposure)
- creative ideas for utilisation of the sponsorship
- exclusive vending/product rights
- opportunities for retail cross-promotions
- on-site sales

Establishing a close business partnership with a sponsor has been found to be paramount to sponsorship success (Stotlar, 2001). From this perspective, both parties then need to work co-operatively to meet mutually-agreed objectives. From the outset, the sponsee, therefore, needs to exceed their sponsor's expectations; thus, sponsor servicing can be labour-intensive and time-consuming.

Selecting the property

Different sponsorship properties will vary in their ability to achieve a balance of corporate, brand and business development objectives (Mullin et al., 2007). When assessing a sponsorship proposal, potential sponsors will rank the opportunity against all or some of the following categories:
- *Image development:*
  - compatibility with corporate positioning and target audiences
  - industry exclusivity in product/service category
  - emotional appeal to target audiences
  - credible association with company products, staff and clients
  - ability to build leadership and long-term equity in the event
- *Name awareness/brand exposure:*
  - one-off or regular activity
  - sole/exclusive positioning or one of several sponsors
  - ability to 'own' the event or property
  - television and other media exposure (electronic and print)
  - on-site awareness (signage, tickets, print, branded items, logo on player and staff clothing etc.)
- *Property performance/potential/execution/delivery:*
  - track record/potential of property and owners
  - financial soundness/integrity of property
  - experience/expertise of sponsee
  - co-operation of property owners
  - availability of volunteers or external professional managers
  - guaranteed benefits and legal protections
  - guaranteed post-event audit and market research data

- *VIP/customer/staff involvement:*
  - relevance to staff and opportunity for their involvement
  - opportunities for VIP hospitality, including existing and potential customers, trade and key suppliers
  - standard of hospitality/entertainment
  - access to high profile personalities/stars and conditions around this

Sponsorship contract/agreement

A written, binding contract is recognised as a vital building block to a good relationship between sponsor and sponsee, and is essential for the protection of the interests of both. Lack of a contract that clearly sets out the rights and obligations of both parties infinitely increases the chances of misunderstandings and the possibility of the relationship turning sour. A sponsorship contract is a legally-binding document stating the intent of the agreement in plain language, with minimal 'legalese'. The document becomes a working framework for the relationship, respecting the spirit of mutuality and protecting the interests and investments of both parties. A basic contract may include the following details:

- parties to the agreement (sponsor, sponsee, agents or brokers, merchandisers);
- the sponsorship property (organisation, event, team, venue etc.) and any governing bodies and/ or regulations that are to be complied with;
- the term (commencement and duration of sponsorship and option for renewal) and timeframe of the property's activity;
- sponsorship status (e.g., sole, principal naming or title rights, exclusivity);
- granting of rights (use of property logo, trademarks, names and/or intellectual property) with conditions of use and any approval processes required;
- sponsorship benefits (e.g., television, advertising and editorial rights, media monitoring, signage rights, hospitality, merchandise, discounted offers, complimentary access);
- payment schedule (how and when payment is to be made – cash or contra - conditions regarding use of monies);
- termination (breach of contract, remedies and mediation);
- performance (service levels, insurance, indemnities);
- confidentiality (it is usual for both parties to require non-disclosure of the terms and conditions of the agreement).

Owing to the complicated processes involved, legal advice is commonly sought on the preparation of sponsorship contracts, reviewing and negotiating agreements, and especially on complex matters relating to taxation and sponsorship law, which can change frequently.

Concept Check

Contra, or in-kind sponsorship

Contra, or in-kind sponsorship means the supply of a company's products or services in lieu of, or as well as, cash for rights to the sponsorship property.

Sidebar: Auckland Rugby sponsor benefits example

With the above in mind, the Sponsorship Manager for the Auckland Rugby Football Union (ARFU), Emily Travers, provides a summary of the types of rights and benefits received by sponsors of Auckland Rugby. Whilst the level of sponsorship will determine which benefits are received, Travers states that the majority of the forty sponsors of Auckland Rugby receive access to the core benefits but at various levels to reflect their quantum of investment. These benefits may include:

- Subject to the level of sponsorship, status as major sponsor, official sponsor or supplier of the Auckland Team and/or Auckland Rugby Football Union.
- Category exclusivity.
- The non-exclusive right to use the Auckland Rugby logo on promotional material (subject to the approval of the ARFU).
- Signage such as: digital signage, field painting, side-line flags, goal post pads, fixed board signs, changing room/tunnel signage.
- Playing apparel branding – limited branding positions on shorts and jerseys, subject to a maximum square centimetre allowance provided by the governing body (the NZRU).
- Logo placement on ARFU letterhead, posters and promotional advertising.
- Exclusive sponsor hospitality at matches.
- Match tickets.
- Invitations to functions such as the Awards Dinner and special events.
- Creation of and invitations to sponsor functions to provide networking opportunities.
- Access to players and team management (subject to a number of strict terms and conditions in the players' collective with the NZRU).
- Game day recognition including programme advertisements, logo placement, advertising and logo acknowledgement on the big screen, PA system announcements, and "match day sponsor" status.
- Game day fan activation opportunities.
- Recognition and links to the sponsors' websites on the ARFU website and social media pages.
- Access to discounted merchandise and signed memorabilia.
- Access to the ARFU database that includes over 21,000 registered players for promotional activity.
- Rights to club rugby and junior rugby properties.
- Sponsors' trip to one away game with other sponsors of the Auckland Team.
- Reciprocal business.

While the sponsorship contract is vital to ensure accurate fulfilment of a sponsorship, Travers believes there is always scope to develop and foster a partnership beyond the platform of the written agreement. Often, this can be the difference between a good sponsor/rights holder relationship and a great one.

Implementation or execution of the sponsorship

The fifth step of the sponsorship management process involves the implementation or execution of the sponsorship and will include strategies to leverage and maximise the effectiveness of the sponsorship. The process of leveraging is considered vital for organisations to maximise the potential of their sponsorship involvement, and will often involve the allocation of additional funds and resources. Activities such as advertising campaigns to promote the relationship, branding the distribution outlets of the sponsor with the sponsee's logos and imagery are examples of the many leverage options available to a sponsor. Whilst some references in the literature suggest 'dollar for dollar' leveraging support (Meenaghan, 1991), a study of English Professional Football sponsorship by Chadwick and Thwaites (2004) indicated that the benchmark for this spending is 25% of the contract value. This may, however, reflect the very large amounts paid for these properties. In a study that reinforced the importance of leverage activity by a sponsor, Akaoui (2007) found that only those sponsors associated with the Fifa 2006 World Cup that engaged in significant leverage activities during the event were able to establish a dramatic advantage. Those that did not maximize their involvement received little benefit at all.

Concept Check

Leveraging

Leveraging is the process of using the sponsorship property to gain added value, for example, brand exposure via electronic media, publicity and promotions.

Understanding and measuring sponsorship effectiveness

The sixth and final step in the sponsorship management process evaluates sponsorship by measuring all activity against objectives in order to assess effectiveness and to ensure maximum accountability of sponsorship. Meenaghan (1999) suggested that the need for accountability has fed the demand for sponsorship research. Not only can pre- and post-campaign awareness and shifts in consumer perceptions be measured, but, increasingly, revenues from product and/or merchandising directly attributable to brand marketing can be examined against the investment made.

In addition to establishing what is to be measured, the major challenge with sponsorship research is to separate out and measure any change or increase in sales attributable to the sponsorship, as distinct from other elements in the marketing mix. There are endless variations to what can and should be measured relative to the strategic issues and objectives of the sponsorship programme and marketing activity as a whole. For example, it is common for major sponsors of the Olympics and Soccer World Cup to measure any change in consumer perception as a result of their sponsorship of such high-profile activities. A benchmark and tracking programme commonly addresses:

- the correct identification of the sponsor with the event;
- awareness of the product/brand;
- awareness of the sponsorship activity;

- perception of the brand relative to its competitors;
- perception of various attributes associated with the brand.

International research indicates that consumers are likely to be far more receptive to commercial messages accessed through integrated sponsorship campaigns in terms of familiarity, favourability and propensity to purchase (Mullin et al., 2007). Findings from the study by Meenaghan (1999) clearly substantiate the proposition that the ability of sponsorship to generate positive consumer brand attitudes can be powerful and lasting. Dees, Bennett, and Villegas (2008), in their study of College Football sponsorship, reported that individuals who attended games and held positive views towards sponsors were more likely to purchase from those companies, and that the goodwill created as a result of the sponsorship had the most impact on consumers' intentions to support the corporate sponsors via their purchasing behaviours. Furthermore, the sincerity and logical nature of the fit between the sponsoring organisation and the property can also influence the degree of effectiveness of the sponsorship (Olsen, 2010).

> ## Concept Check
>
> ### Brand awareness
>
> Brand awareness is the public profile created by associating a brand or product with a spor event, organisation, team or individual athlete.

Sponsorship cost–benefit analysis

The prior sections indicate that sponsorship has the potential to generate positive benefits for a sponsor. The benefits, however, are usually considered in relation to the investment by the sponsor. Sam, Batty, and Dean (2005) reinforced that sponsorship not only involves the monetary or 'in-kind' investment from a sponsor, but also that considerable time and resource is required/invested in planning, negotiating, managing/leveraging and measuring the effects of sponsorship. Therefore, an understanding of the potential benefits relative to the investment is essential in the sponsorship management process. In the past, measurement of sponsor benefits has been difficult and imprecise, with funds being regarded as 'soft spending' from corporate community or philanthropic budgets. Driven by demand for accountability from management and stakeholders, sponsors now compare their returns against competitive advertising costs and value, with funding allocations coming from the marketing and public relations mix. Sponsors can measure the amount of 'free' publicity they receive and then ascribe a dollar value equivalent to paid advertising exposure (usually adjusted to 25–30 per cent of the full advertising ratecard value). Sponsorship can be measured using three broad methods of evaluation:

- measurement of brand awareness or attitude changes;
- increases in direct sales or market share;
- comparisons between the value of sponsorship-generated media, coverage and brand exposure to the cost of equivalent advertising, space or time.

Such measurements are usually made in light of the cash and/or in-kind investment, leverage costs and other resource commitments in order to determine the true value of the relationship.

Concept Check

Media brand values

Media brand values refer to the dollar value assigned to exposure of branding elements during an event or sponsorship. These values are calculated as a percentage of the television ratecard cost based on the minutes of exposure achieved.

Sponsorship and co-branding – A partnership approach to sponsorship

Urriolagoitia and Planellas (2007) suggested that an increasing number of sponsors and sponsored parties refer to each other as partners. This reflects a move from a short-term 'transactional' view of sponsorship as a marketing communication tactic, to the strategic role of sponsorship in establishing long-term relationships in order to build brands and, inevitably, establish and maintain a competitive advantage. Amis, Slack, and Berrett (1999) found that companies who utilised their sponsorship as a long-term strategic resource were able to develop a distinctive competence and achieve a position of sustainable competitive advantage. This move of sponsorship from a one-off exchange to a long-term relationship creates an opportunity for co-branding (Motion, Leitch, & Brodie, 2003).

Co-branding is defined as "a form of co-operation between two or more brands with significant customer recognition in which all the participant brand names are retained" (Blacket & Boad, 1999, p. 7). The partnership between adidas (major sponsor of the All Blacks) and the New Zealand Rugby Union (NZRU) was examined by Motion et al. (2003) and highlighted the co-branding strategy between these two iconic brands. The relationship, which began in 1999, was essential for both organisations in different ways. For the NZRU it provided significant funds in order to cope with the demands of professional rugby as well as the infrastructure and 'marketing grunt' provided by adidas to take the All Black brand globally. For adidas, the association was vital to gain credibility and market share in the rugby footwear and apparel industry. Co-branding was achieved through joint campaigns emphasising common values of tradition and authenticity to enable adidas to achieve national identity with the All Black brand. Links to former All Black captains and the Haka in commercials, coupled with promotions at events such as 'black out themes', established a new co-branded identity between these two iconic sporting brands.

Concept Check

Co-branding

A type of co-operation between two or more brands where there is significant customer recognition in which the brand names of the participants are retained (Blacket & Boad, 1999).

Ambush marketing

The competitive advantages generated by some companies, that have created a unique marketing proposition as a result of their sponsorship involvement, has seen organisations ambush such companies to either negate such advantages or gain them for themselves. Ambush marketing refers to the unauthorised association by businesses with events, organisations, products, services or athletes through a range of marketing activities (Townley, Harrison, & Couchman, 1998) in order to create the impression they have an official association when, legally, they do not. The term was first coined during the 1984 Los Angeles Olympic Games to describe the marketing activities of non-sponsors such as Kodak, which used a variety of activities to 'ambush' official sponsors Fuji (Sandler & Shani, 1993). McKelvey and Grady (2008) noted that Nikes' ambush of the 1996 Atlanta Olympics is recognised as the 'ambush of all ambushes'. Nike covered the city with billboards, handed out swoosh banners at competitions and erected a massive Nike Centre over-looking the stadium. This activity saved Nike US$50 million in official sponsorship fees and devastated the International Olympic Committee, whilst sending a warning to all other major event managers and rights holders. More specifically, potential ambush activities include sponsorship of the broadcast of the event, purchasing advertising time around the event, thematic advertising and implied allusion, the creation of a counter-attraction, and purchasing advertising space at nearby locations (Crompton, 2004).

To minimise the chance of ambush marketing, event promoters are being asked by sponsors to provide assurances that their investment will be protected vigorously. The demands for 'clean stadia' (i.e., clear of all promotional material other than for the official sponsors), and intense policing of any attempts at ambushing by rival organisations, have been features of more recent major world-wide events. Sponsorship programme protection strategies include: pre-event education and public relations initiatives, on-site policing tactics, contractual language in athlete participation and customer ticket agreements, and the enactment and enforcement of special trademark protection legislation (McKelvey & Grady, 2008). The New Zealand Government passed the Major Events Management Act in 2007 in order to secure the hosting rights for the 2011 RWC, and to both ensure the non-disruptive management of the event and the protection of the official sponsors of the event When events are declared 'major events' legal protections are put in place to prevent unauthorised commercial exploitation at the expense of an event organiser or its official sponsors (Rugby World Cup, 2011).

Concept Check

Ambush marketing

The unauthorised association by businesses with events, organisations, products, services or athletes through a range of marketing activities (Townley et al., 1998).

CASE STUDY: LG ELECTRONICS AND THE NORTHERN MYSTICS ANZ CHAMPIONSHIP NETBALL FRANCHISE

Prepared by Trevor Meiklejohn

A meeting with LG Electronics' Marketing Manager, Kane Silcock, and the Northern Mystics CEO, Mark Cameron, provides a compelling insight into the sponsorship relationship between these two organisations. The reference to a 'partnership agreement' by Kane instead of a sponsorship agreement sets the scene for this mutually-beneficial and enduring relationship that began in 2008. The LG Electronics brand was launched in New Zealand in 2007 and corresponded with a need to increase brand awareness, credibility and market share in a very competitive marketplace. The timing of the introduction of the newly-established Trans-Tasman Netball League 'The ANZ Championship' in 2008 could not have been better, and provided an ideal sponsorship opportunity in the form of the New Zealand franchise with the largest population base, the Northern Mystics. Securing the naming rights for this franchise initially gave the LG brand significant exposure via televised matches, event branding and event leveraging activities, specialist televised netball programmes, community engagement initiatives by the team, plus electronic and print media coverage.

With the awareness of the LG brand enhanced significantly after the first two years of the relationship, the focus of the sponsorship for LG has now moved to product line awareness and education for both electronic retail distributors and the wider public. Leveraging activities, such as LG events for retailers presenting new products like mobile phones, TV, audio, video, kitchen and laundry appliances, IT products and air conditioning in conjunction with high-profile LG Mystics players, have proven very successful. Furthermore, each home game provides the opportunity for LG to demonstrate its products to thousands of passionate and engaged netball fans via its themed interactive display areas at the stadium. Here, LG staff members provide fans with opportunities to trial 3D television sets as well as a myriad of other electronic products that appeal to this target group of potential customers.

The LG brand, as the result of a well-developed marketing strategy of which sponsorship is a core component, has been able to enhance brand awareness, increase product knowledge and gain market share in a relatively short period of time. Co-branding is very evident in this relationship with the two brands becoming synonymous with one another. The recent extension of the sponsorship contract for another three years is testament to the value LG sees in their sponsorship of the Northern Mystics and the long-term view they are taking of the partnership.

Summary

Sponsorship now plays a significant role in the sport marketing landscape. It is a critical resource for sporting organisations in order to survive, grow and prosper in increasingly challenging environments. It has also become a significant element in the marketing strategies of corporate organisations due to its potential to create a unique point of difference in cluttered competitive markets. It creates a platform to target specific markets, enhance brand image and awareness, and increase sales, as well as providing a myriad of relationship and networking opportunities. What is also becoming very clear is that those organisations that take a long-term view of sponsorship, underpinned with a partnership philosophy, are likely to gain greater returns than those who simply view it as a business transaction.

Bottom line – implications for management

- Sporting organisations should seek to understand the marketing objectives of potential sponsors in order to tailor a sponsorship proposal.
- Legal advice should be sought on the preparation of proposals, reviewing and negotiating agreements and especially on complex matters relating to taxation and sponsorship law, which can change frequently.
- A company should not consider a sponsorship unless they have specified the outcomes they hope to achieve from their involvement.
- Brands that engage in significant leverage activities with their sponsored properties are able to gain a greater advantage than those who do not leverage their association.
- Sincerity and the logical nature of the fit between the sponsoring organisation and the property can influence the degree of effectiveness of the sponsorship.
- A long-term partnership view of sponsorship is important for both sponsor and sponsee.

Review questions

- What are the major challenges facing marketers today and why is sport sponsorship a good choice?
- What are some critical success factors to ensure the success of sport sponsorship?
- How do corporates go about selecting a sponsorship?
- What are some factors sport marketers should be aware of when preparing a proposal or making an approach to a potential sponsor?
- How can sponsorship be measured?
- Provide up to five different leverage activities a sponsor may utilise with a sponsored property.

References

Akaoui, J. (2007). Brand experience on the pitch: How the sponsors fared in the World Cup. *Journal of Advertising Research, 47*(2), 147–157.

Amis, J., Slack, T., & Berrett, T. (1999). Sport sponsorship as distinctive competence. *European Journal of Marketing, 33*(3/4), 250–272.

Apostolopoulou, A., & Papadimiriou, D. (2004). "Welcome home": Motivations and objectives of the 2004 Grand National Olympic sponsors. *Sport Marketing Quarterly, 13*, 180–192.

Blacket, T., & Boad, B. (1999). *Co-branding: The science of alliance.* London: Macmillan.

Chadwick, S., & Thwaites, D. (2004). Advances in the management of sport sponsorship: Fact or fiction? Evidence from professional soccer. *Journal of General Management, 30*(1), 39–60.

Coca-Cola (2011). *Coca-Cola and the Olympic Games: Our partnership history.* Retrieved from http://www.thecoca-http://www.thecoca-/colacompany.com/heritage/pdf/Olympics_Partnership.pdf

Cone and Coughlin Communications Inc., Roper & Starch Worldwide Inc. (1994). *The Cone-Roper study: A benchmark survey of consumer awareness and attitudes towards cause-related marketing.* Boston, MA: Cone/Coughlin Communications.

Crompton, J. L. (2004). Conceptualising and alternative operationalizations of the measurement of sponsorship effectiveness in sport. *Leisure Studies, 23*, 267–281.

Dees, W., Bennett, G., & Villegas, J. (2008). Measuring the effectiveness of sponsorship of an elite intercollegiate football program. *Sport Marketing Quarterly, 17*, 79–89.

Farrelly, F. (2010). Not playing the game: Why sport sponsorship relationships break down. *Journal of Sport Management, 24*, 319–337.

Farrelly, F., Quester, P., & Burton, R. (2006). Change in sponsorship value: Competencies and relationships. *Industrial Marketing Management*, 35, 1016–1026.

Hyundai (2011). *Hyundai are a major sponsor of surfing in New Zealand*. Retrieved from http://www.hyundai.co.nz/about-hyundai/sponsorship/hyundai-pro-longboard-tour

Irwin, R. L., & Asimakopoulos, M. (1992). An approach to the evaluation and selection of sport sponsorship proposals. *Sport Marketing Quarterly*, 1(2), 43–51.

Kahuni, A. T., Rowely, J., & Binsardi, A. (2009). Guilty by association: Image 'spill-over' in corporate co-branding. *Corporate Reputation Review*, 12(1), 52–63.

Mason, K. (2005). How corporate sponsorship impacts consumer behaviour. *The Journal of American Academy of Business*, 7(1), 32–35.

McKelvey, S., & Grady, J. (2008). Sponsorship programme protection strategies for special sport events: Are event organizers out-manoeuvring ambush marketers? *Journal of Sport Management*, 22, 550–586.

Meenaghan, T. (1991). The role of sponsorship in the marketing communications mix. *International Journal of Advertising*, 10(1), 35–47.

Meenaghan, T. (1999). Commercial sponsorship: The development of understanding. *International Journal of Sports Marketing & Sponsorship*, 1(1), 19–31.

Meenaghan, T. (2001). Understanding sponsorship effects. *Psychology and Marketing*, 18, 95–122.

Motion, J., Leitch, S., & Brodie, R. J. (2003). Equity in corporate co-branding. The case of adidas and the All Blacks. *European Journal of Marketing*, 37(7/8), 1080–1094.

Mullin, B. J., Hardy, S., & Sutton, W. A. (2007). *Sport marketing* (3rd ed.). Champaign, IL: Human Kinetics.

Olson, E. L. (2010). Does sponsorship work in the same way in different sponsorship contexts? *European Journal of Marketing*, 44(1/2), 180–199.

Rugby World Cup (2011). *Rugby World Cup 2011 in New Zealand: A guide to the Major Events Management Act (2007)*. Retrieved from http://www.rugbyworldcup.com/mm/Document/Tournament/Destination/02/03/72/63/2037263_PDF.pdf

Sam, P., Batty, R., & Dean, R. (2005). A transaction cost approach to sport sponsorship. *Sport Management Review*, 8, 1–17.

Sandler, D. M., & Shani, D. (1993). Sponsorship and the Olympic Games: The consumer perspective. *Sport Marketing Quarterly*, 2(3), 38–43.

Sleight, S. (1989). *Sponsorship: What it is and how to use it*. Sydney: McGraw-Hill.

Stotlar, D. (1993). Sponsorship and the Olympic Winter Games. *Sport Marketing Quarterly*, 2(1), 35–43.

Stotlar, D. (2001). *Developing successful sport sponsorship plans*. Morgantown, WV: Fitness Information Technology.

Townley, S., Harrison, D., & Couchman, N. (1998). The legal and practical prevention of ambush marketing in sports. *Psychology and Marketing*, 15(4), 333–348.

Urriolagoitia, L., & Planellas, M. (2007). Sponsorship as strategic alliances: A life-cycle model approach. *Business Horizons*, 50, 157–166.

Verity, J. (2002). Maximising the potential of sponsorship for global brands. *European Business Journal*, 14(4), 161–173.

Walliser, B. (2003). An international review of sponsorship research: Extension and update. *International Journal of Advertising*, 22, 5–40.

Acknowledgements

This chapter acknowledges and builds on the contribution of Kathy Knott, co-author of the chapter Sport Sponsorship in the first edition of Sport Business Management in New Zealand.

Chapter 15

Sport Development

Nico Schulenkorf and Daryl Adair

OBJECTIVES

After completing this chapter, you should be able to:

- understand the importance of history, tradition, ethics and values for contemporary sport development;
- comprehend the influence of political ideologies on the creation of sport development policies;
- identify core components associated with sport participation and program delivery, together with their potential impacts on society;
- discuss and analyse the opportunities, challenges and limitations in both sport-for-development and Sport for Development and Peace;
- reflect on current issues in sport development, and contemplate areas needing reform.

Key terms

In this chapter, readers will become familiar with the following concepts and terms:
- sport-for-development
- development through sport
- the notion of 'community'
- sport for development and peace (S4DP)

Introduction

Fundamentally, sport development is about providing opportunities for individuals and communities to engage in grassroots physical activities in terms of what can be described as 'the common good'. When appropriately conceived and managed, sport allows participants to optimise their physical fitness levels and has the capacity to provide people of varying ages with valuable social experiences. People who work in sport development, therefore, share a similar goal of motivating individuals to participate in sport for purposes of health promotion and wider social benefit. However, as we will see in this chapter, the purposes, values and desired outcomes of sport development are not static; indeed, the more recent move to sport-for-development indicates a fundamental move away from sport participation as the key objective and towards involvement in sport as a vehicle to achieve desired social outcomes. Indeed, the principal goal of sport-for-development managers today is the deployment of sport and physical activity programs to engage people from varying ethno cultural and socio-economic backgrounds, within which ideals of interpersonal respect, intergroup harmony, and community cohesion are crucial.

This chapter begins with a discussion of how sport became a significant part of community life in Australia and New Zealand, how it was organised, and the policy milieu within which it has operated. It then evaluates contemporary principles and practices underlying sport development today, drawing on international literature and research from within the Australasian context. Importantly, the chapter also provides practical examples of sport-for-development using fieldwork studies from the Oceania region. The chapter is, therefore, divided into four key sections: the origins and evolution of sport development; sport participation and public policies; sport-for-development; and sport for development and peace (S4DP). Finally, conclusions are drawn and recommendations for future research in the area of sport development are provided.

Sport and community development: Origins and evolution

Modern, codified sport is arguably a by-product of reforms that took place in the elite English public schools of the 19th century. The undisciplined, often violent behaviour of schoolboys was at odds with the goal of producing young men who, by virtue of their social position, were set to assume leadership roles in English society. They had status on account of birth and privilege, but too many lacked commitment to study and respect for authority. Sweeping reforms to this elite educational system were introduced during the mid 19th century, part of which involved developing both the mind and the body of pupils, instilling through religion and organised sports an early form of muscular' Christianity (Holt, 1990). Sport, in the reformers' view, was much more than a mere game; it provided important lessons for life, such as striving for victory and accepting defeat – both with good grace. Similarly, sport was thought to build character and provide a productive outlet for young boys to express themselves physically and represent their schools – in the process creating feelings of community among students and promoting a sense of loyalty to the institution (Chandler, 1991). This games ethic' and its associated *esprit de corps* spread around the British Empire during the Victorian era and became a cornerstone for the development of school and community sport in both Australia and New Zealand (Daly, 1982; Mangan, 1986, 1988).

During the 20th century, grassroots sport in Australasia relied on the leadership of schools at the junior level and on suburban or provincial community clubs at the adult level. Cricket and rugby union were of particular interest to schoolmasters who had migrated from England. As team sports they were able to engage a large number of students, while their laws and rules – in which umpires and referees were in full control – provided a sense of discipline and respect for authority that was pedagogically attractive (Crotty, 2000; Ryan, 2011; Stewart, 1992; Vincent, 1998). These early forms of junior sport development, therefore, were about purposeful physical activity in the interests of inculcating moral values. The health dimensions of sport (i.e., appropriate levels of exercise) were a secondary consideration. Community sport for adults centred on the town, suburb or province. They relied overwhelmingly on volunteer administrators, officials and the goodwill of supporters to enable clubs to survive. In rural areas especially, the sport club could be the social hub of a local community (Crawford, 1985b; Indian, 1981). These were male-dominated spaces because, with some exceptions, sport in both Australia and New Zealand was – as in Britain – established by men, for men and in the interests of men (Crawford, 1985a; Phillips, 1996). Community sport development initiatives for women centred on another English import, the game of netball, which was an offshoot of basketball designed specifically for females. There were certainly examples of men and women participating in the same community sport clubs, such as in golf, tennis and rowing, but females almost always played 'second fiddle' to the males, such as in access to facilities, equipment, resources and playing arenas (Adair, 1994; Cashman, 1995; Crawford, 1987).

What, then, were the fundamental claims about sport's value to Australia, New Zealand and nearby Pacific Islands in the 20th century? First, as mentioned, at the school level sport helped to establish a sense of *esprit de corps* among student bodies, while at the community level sport clubs were a focus for the establishment of group identities based on locality. Second, the rise of the amateur ideal in British sport, which was subsequently a cornerstone of the modern Olympic Games, provided an emphasis on 'participation for its own sake', which imbued games with an ethos of selflessness and community spirit (Jobling, 2000; Obel, 2005; Seynard, 2002). This was contrasted with the apparent self-interestedness of sports that involved systematic gaming, wagering or payment of players – the professional mode of sport (Greenwood, 2007). For sports that were part of the Olympic movement in Oceania, the amateur code was followed with evangelical zeal; those who stepped outside of that value system were barred from competing in amateur sports and, therefore, from a range of events at the Olympic and Commonwealth Games (Adair & Vamplew, 1997; Letters & Jobling, 1996; Wilkinson, 1998). However, the boundaries around the amateur ideal began to loosen by the last quarter of the 20th century, leading to a new value system for sport within which community development is no longer inconsistent with commercial sponsorship, business-like operation and remuneration of club representatives (Owen & Weatherston, 2002; Skinner, Stewart, & Edwards, 1999). In part, this has been caused by an increased financial commitment by governments to elite-level sport combined with inadequate levels of public funding for localised sport and associated community development initiatives.

Sport participation and public policies: Contested terrain

For many years, national governments in both Australia and New Zealand had a relatively *laissez faire* view of state involvement in sport. They regarded community sport as a public good, but concluded that its operation and funding were primarily the responsibility of volunteer organisations run by inspired individuals. Sport participation became a more obvious part of public policy in Australia and New Zealand during the 1970s, when national governments introduced ministerial portfolios under the auspices of tourism/recreation and recreation respectively, within which sport was subsume (Lawrence, 2008; Stewart, Nicholson, Smith, & Westerbeek, 2004). In brief, on both sides of the Tasman there was a similar concern about the state of community sport and recreational facilities and levels of mass physical activity and fitness.

In Australia there was also a commitment to nurture performance excellence by improving resources for national representatives, especially those at Olympic and Commonwealth Games. The was mooted in 1973 by the germinal Bloomfield Report, and accelerated thereafter by Australia's 'dismal' showing at the 1976 Montreal Olympics, where the nation failed to win a gold medal. All this provided a catalyst for the establishment, during the 1980s, of the Australian Institute of Sport (AIS) whose principal purpose was to cater to the needs of high performance Olympic athletes. However, this was followed soon after by the inauguration of the Australian Sports Commission (ASC), which had an overarching role of policy and programme initiatives to serve the needs of National Sport Organisations (NSOs) and to oversee the AIS. The ASC also had a remit to encourage sport for all, so when it came to funding priorities the national government's budget allocation to the ASC involved intense debate over the amount that ought to be allocated to sport development priorities versus allocations to elite academies and high performance facilities (Bloomfield, 2003; Ferguson, 2007).

In general terms, national government funding for the AIS and state-based regional academies has remained robust over the past thirty years, support for NSOs has plateaued, but the commitment to mass sport participation has, in relative terms, waned (Green, 2007). This decline has come despite growing evidence of rising sedentary behaviours and obesity levels – particularly among youth (Gill et al., 2009). The Australian government's recent policy response in terms of promoting physical activity for children – the Active After School Communities programme (AASCs) – appears to have had limited impact: instead of *requiring* sport and exercise programs during school hours, funding has been allocated for *voluntary* activities after school (Robotham, 2011). The other weakness of AASCs is the absence of an explicit connection between its programmes and the NSOs and community sport clubs – organisations that might be expected to recruit young people into weekend participation (Australian Independent Sport Panel, 2009).

New Zealand's peak sport agency, the Hillary Commission, was established in the 1980s as a quasi-autonomous, non-government entity with a remit to facilitate the development of sport and physical activity in regions and local communities. By comparison to Australia and its AIS, national pathways to excellence, such as the very modestly funded New Zealand Sports Foundation (NZSF), were poorly established. By the 1990s, the Hillary Commission (HC) programmes were reconfigured to suit a neo-liberal policy paradigm, with the state hoping to devolve responsibility for their operation to entrepreneurial sport and physical activity providers in different regions (Sam & Jackson, 2004). In 2002 a new organisation, Sport and Recreation New Zealand (SPARC), had subsumed both the HC and the NZSF. More centralist than its predecessor, SPARC promised much for sport participation at club and regional levels but, according to Lawrence (2008), has too often struggled to engage with, or meet the needs of, community sport stakeholders. Concurrently, SPARC began to increase its focus on high performance outcomes, with a policy of medal targets at Commonwealth and Olympic Games introduced in an effort to justify government funding of both elite and mass participation sport (Piggin, Jackson, & Lewis, 2009). The assumption in terms of the latter is that medals have a ripple effect in terms of public involvement in sport, a politically convenient claim but none the less a misapprehension that also pervades Australian sport policy discourse (Veal & Frawley, 2009).

In sport development terms, the ASC and SPARC have – perhaps ironically – been more effective beyond 'mainstream' grassroots participation. Both organisations have been at the forefront of programmes intended to improve access to sport and physical activity among groups that, historically, have variously been marginalised or discriminated against. First, there has been a growing awareness of the sport development needs of women, not only in terms of resources to support female participation, but also in respect of women assuming operational and managerial roles within sport (Australian Sports Commission, 2011). A recent policy innovation is for sport organisations to move from separate administrations for men and women to a single umbrella entity. This streamlining is intended to reduce operational expenses and, by combining men and women under a common organisational framework, better support their respective needs. In sports where men and women have similar profiles and resources, such as field hockey, this has worked quite well. But in environments where the power differential is stark, such as in cricket (dominated by men), female influence and the needs of women have received short shrift (Hoye & Stewart, 2002; Stronach & Adair, 2009).

Second, both SPARC and the ASC have introduced programs to better engage with, and provide opportunities for, people with a disability. They have a particular interest in accommodating the needs of elite performers, which is understandable given the performance expectations associated with the Paralympics. However, the participation needs of 'recreational' athletes with a disability remain a challenge, something that is currently undergoing evaluation (Australian Sports Commission, 2010). This area of sport development is particularly weak because there are often limited options for people with disabilities to use public leisure centres or private gyms; staff are generally trained to address the demands of able bodied exercisers and so have little knowledge about how to meet the physical activity needs of people with serious movement constraints (Stumbo, Wang, & Pegg, 2011). A third area in which sport development initiatives have appeared under the banner of the ASC and SPARC is in the area of support for Indigenous athletes, which is evaluated in Chapter 3 of this book.

While the discussion thus far has focused attention on policy interventions at the national level, it needs to be acknowledged that in terms of sport development many of the most innovative and significant programs have been conceived regionally and operate locally. There are now numerous community-based initiatives wherein sport is used as vehicle to engage young people who may be refugees, part of a culturally and linguistically diverse background, or deemed disadvantaged in some way. Programmes such as 'Football United' in New South Wales provide free access to children who wish to play soccer for either fun or competition, but the main focus is developing friendships through intercultural awareness and a sense of belonging in a diverse community (Bunde-Birouste, Bull, & McCarroll, 2010). These programmes have relied on a combination of funding from government agencies under the banner of health of multiculturalism, although there has been some support from businesses interested in fulfilling corporate social responsibility goals. Neither the ASC nor SPARC have contributed significantly to this emerging sport-for-development space; they have mainly been concerned with high performance athletes and the operation of NSOs.

Sport-for-development: Development *through* sport

The recently developed sport-for-development stream focuses on the role that sport can play in contributing to overall community wellbeing. In other words, sport-for-development refers to development achieved *through* sport, where individuals and groups participate to achieve more than just physical outcomes: they also participate with aspirations to realise certain social, cultural, psychological, educational, and economic goals. Despite the different foci of sport-for-development programmes, they all share the common belief that sport projects can and should be designed to positively develop people and communities, and thus to make a welcome difference.

Table 15-1: *Potential benefits of sport-for-development initiatives*	
CATEGORY	POTENTIAL BENEFITS
Social	Community Involvement; Relationship and Friendship Building; Respect and Fair Play; Pride and Spirit; Preventing Crime
Physical	Health and Fitness, incl. Physical Capacity Building; Reduction of Obesity and Chronic Diseases; Reduction of Health Care Costs
Psychological	Mental Health Enhancement; Disaster and Trauma Relief Support; Leadership Skills; Inclusive Social Identity Building; Prestige and Profile
Cultural	Inter-Community Relationships; Peace and Reconciliation; Integration of 'Others' incl. Minority Groups (e.g., Indigenous Peoples, People with Disabilities, Foreigners, Women in Sport etc.); Revitalising of Tradition and Values
Educational	Learning of Values and Life Skills; Improved Academic Achievement; Increased Body-Mind Knowledge; Increased School Attendance
Economic	Destination Promotion; Tourism Enhancement; Urban / Rural Renewal; Jobs and Workplace Skills; Infrastructure Development
Environmental	Showcasing the Environment; Fostering Awareness and Stewardship; Providing a Platform for Social Mobilisation; Building Sustainable Sport Facilities

Central to the success of sport-for-development initiatives is the active involvement of stakeholder communities. In other words, when trying to achieve desired development benefits, community participation provides the key to success in any of the categories listed in Table 15-1 above. Before we can discuss the concept of community participation in more detail, we need to understand how the term 'community' is typically used in this context. Community comes from the Latin *communis*, which translates into something that is deemed common, public, and shared by many or all. A community can thus be described as a specific group or a network of groups organising themselves around specific issues of shared interest and importance (Labonte & Laverack, 2001). Although there is disagreement and contention about the boundaries and forms of communities, the term is generally applied to a set of relationships in which there exist positive bonds of identity and affection between people. Nisbet (1969), for example, describes community as a fusion of feeling, tradition, commitment, membership and psychological strength that leads to shared feelings of togetherness and a sense of commonality and belonging among a group of people. A community may also be seen as a place where group solidarity, participation and coherence can be found (Purdue et al., 2000; Taylor, 2003). In sum, community may be described as a network of social relations marked by mutuality and emotional bonds amongst its members.

That said, 'community' is essentially a subjective individual and collective experience; it is felt and experienced rather than measured and clearly defined (Ife, 1995). Some aspects of an actively engaged community are, however, quite typical, which prompted Shaffer and Anundsen (1993) to develop a five-point definitional framework. They suggest that an inter-reliant community is a dynamic whole that emerges when people in a group do one or more of the following:

Participate in common practices.

Depend upon one another.

Make decisions together.

Identify themselves as part of something larger than the sum of their individual relationships.

Commit themselves for the long term to their own, one another's, and the group's wellbeing.

This five-point definition indicates that the essence of the term 'community' is the idea of having something in common, or being in *Gemeinschaft* [togetherness] with others. It also suggests that in order to develop this, community members need to engage and actively participate *as* a group. Community participation of this type has thus been described as "the creation of opportunities to enable all members of a community and the larger society to actively contribute to and influence the development process and to share equitably in the fruits of development" (Midgley, 1986, p. 24).

Fundamental to the idea of community participation is an emphasis on 'building from below'; in other words, a development initiated within communities. This is the same for projects conducted in highly developed countries such as Australia and New Zealand as it is for developing countries in Pacific Island nations around Oceania. However, what is different in these varying contexts are the local capacities available, and therefore the amount of external support needed to plan, manage, implement, sustain and grow projects. Running a sport-for-development project in Sydney, Australia is dissimilar from managing a sport-for-development project in Port Vila, Vanuatu. In the two scenarios the resources and capacities, the characteristics, knowledge, and skills needed to move to greater levels of community wellbeing are different, as are the program challenges themselves.

CASE STUDY: INCREASING PHYSICAL ACTIVITY IN THE PACIFIC ISLANDS

Many Pacific islanders experience serious health issues, and population non-communicable disease (NCD) risk is among the highest in the world (SEARO, 2008). NCDs include life-threatening diseases such as cardiovascular diseases, diabetes, different types of cancer and depression. It is widely known that a significant proportion of NCD morbidity and premature mortality can be prevented through population-based lifestyle interventions and the control of preventable risk factors (Epping-Jordan, Galea, Tukuitonga, & Beaglehole, 2005; WHO, 2008; WPRO & SPC, 2007). Increasing physical activity (PA) levels and sport participation may well be an effective strategy to reduce NCD risk in the culturally diverse Pacific region (Siefken, MacNiven, Schofield, Bauman, & Waqanivalu, in press).

When trying to increase PA and sport participation levels, women have an important role to play. They often set the role model for the family, they generally determine the family's diet and they have a significant impact on community life, both directly and indirectly through women's associations and church groups. Moreover, health care is considered to be an area of life dominated by women in many low- and middle income countries (Baile, 1989). Thus, it is assumed that focusing PA and health interventions on women is an effective strategy when trying to disseminate the message of healthy lifestyles to the wider community.

Regrettably, it has been found that Pacific women are less likely to be physically active than their male counterparts and as a consequence, they are exposed to higher NCD risk (Ulijaszek, 2001). In order to understand the barriers to sport participation and to reveal the best options to increase women's PA levels in the Pacific islands, the Centre for Physical Activity and Nutrition (CPAN) in Auckland / New Zealand conducted several focus groups with female community members in the region. The researchers believe that to design a locally-relevant health program it requires both technical knowledge from health experts and local knowledge from the community. Focus groups uncovered, for example, that ni-Vanuatu women are more likely to choose walking for leisure time PA over any other sport activity. Furthermore, they favoured a team-approach over individual exercise activities. The local input allowed the researchers to design a novel and culturally relevant team-based walking challenge aimed at increasing the target population's PA behaviour.

(Continued

After the successful program implementation phase, the walking challenge was monitored for three months during which all participants were in direct email contact with the lead researcher who continued to encourage, inform and advise participants on healthy lifestyle behaviour change. For many participants it was the first time they were given the opportunity to engage in a physical activity challenge and many of them took up a regular exercise regimen. Overall, both parties – local women and external researchers – have greatly benefitted from their cooperation during the experience: participants learned how to make healthy choices in their everyday lives and reduce NCD risk factors, whereas the researchers were able to enhance their understanding of the local state of knowledge around physical activities and the cultural particularities regarding programme design and implementation.

For more information visit http://www.thehealthyislander.com

Katja Siefken
Centre for Physical Activity and Nutrition (CPAN)
Auckland University of Technology (AUT), New Zealand

The case study of Vanuatu suggests that if designed in a meaningful and culturally relevant way, community participation can lead to the development of resources and capacities (i.e., community capacity building) with individuals or within specific groups or communities. It also suggests that in a developing world context, disadvantaged communities are often dependent on some form of external support when realising their program implementation efforts. However, the concept of capacity building is not a one-way street, but an approach to development that requires reciprocal engagement and participation. Looking at the case study above, the reciprocal learning experiences of local communities and external aid workers are a great example of this: while the locals received expert advice in regards to planning, implementing, and managing their project, the expatriates learned about the socio-cultural, economic, and political nuances of the environment they were engaged in. Taken together they were able to design a culturally relevant sport-for-development program that addressed the pressing issue of reducing NCD levels by increasing Physical Activity for women in Vanuatu. Overall, it can be said that if the cooperation between locals and external change agents is one of understanding, engagement and respect, then the ability of communities to build their structures, systems, skills and people will be strengthened, so that they are better able to define their program objectives and achieve their targets of conducting, sustaining, growing and leveraging community projects (Schulenkorf, 2010a; Skinner, 1997).

Sport for development and peace: Sport as a vehicle for change

The area in sport-for-development that relies most heavily on the previously discussed concept of community participation is Sport for Development and Peace (S4DP). S4DP is a relatively new stream within the field of international development: it utilises sport as a development tool, though particularly in divided societies and/or seriously disadvantaged communities (Kidd, 2008). Despite the different contexts in which S4DP projects have been implemented in, the concept itself evolved out of the common belief that well-designed, sport-based initiatives incorporating appropriate values from within sport can be powerful, practical, and cost-effective tools to achieve development goals and contribute something towards peace objectives (Coalter, 2010; Schulenkorf, 2010b; Sugden, 2010). The importance of this new field is reflected in the creation of the official United Nations Office on Sport for Development and Peace (UNOSDP) in 2001. With offices in Geneva and New York, the mandate of the UNOSDP is to coordinate the efforts undertaken by the United Nations in promoting sport in a systematic and coherent way as a means to contribute to positive social change. It assists the Special Adviser to the United Nations Secretary-General on Sport for Development and Peace, Willi Lemke, in his worldwide activities as an advocate, facilitator and representative of sports' social purposes (see http://www.un.org/wcm/content/site/sport/).

When discussing the fast growing field of S4DP, it is important to remind ourselves what the word 'peace' actually means. In its most limited meaning, peace equals the absence of war. However, in the case of S4DP the word needs to be given a broader definition and include connotations of personal and community wellbeing as well as the absence of conflict and tension between previously antagonistic groups. While peace is a policy goal that receives almost universal endorsement, it is extremely hard to achieve sustainably, particularly in areas that historically have been suffering from ethnic or cultural hostilities and violent conflicts between opposing groups (Schulenkorf & Edwards, 2010). Examples of this can be found in various parts of the world, such as Northern Ireland, Sri Lanka, Cyprus, South Africa, Yemen, Kenya, Rwanda and Israel and Palestine. Closer to Australia and New Zealand, examples of negative impacts arising from inter-community struggles include the ethnic conflicts in Indonesia, East Timor, Papua New Guinea and Fiji. Also in Australia and New Zealand themselves there have been ongoing debates around reconciliation and social justice between Indigenous and non-Indigenous communities (see chapter 3). There are now several sport-for-development initiatives in this area, such as the Red Dust Role Models program.

CASE STUDY: SUSTAINABLE DEVELOPMENT THROUGH LONG-TERM PARTNERSHIPS
by Alana Thomson, PhD Candidate, UTS.
Red Dust Role Models (RDRM) is a non-profit organisation that delivers sport-for-development programmes in remote Aboriginal and Torres Strait Islander communities. RDRM was founded by its Managing Director, John Van Groningen, and came about in response to concerns for high youth rates of crime, substance abuse and suicide in some remote Indigenous communities. RDRM has established culturally appropriate and locally sanctioned programmes that attempt to communicate to youth the importance of conscious decisions to eat nutritious foods, avoid harmful substances, keep physically active and attend school. Initially, most of the programmes were sport-themed, as sports are popular in the community and therefore effective at capturing attention and engaging the youth. As the programme has grown, it has expanded to include music and the arts, which complement the sport programmes as vehicles for communication.

The RDRM programme has been developed from outside the communities that it operates in. Therefore, partnerships between RDRM and the remote communities are of critical importance to the success of the programme and desired outcomes for locals. RDRM has been a collaborative development between the Programme Director, the organisation's Cultural Advisor Ray Minniecon, its National Board of Directors (which includes several Aboriginal and Torres Strait Islander people), the relevant

(Continued)

government departments for health and education, as well as elders and other representatives from the remote communities.

PURPOSE OF SPORT ROLE MODELS

In terms of the delivery of the RDRM sport programme, the sport role models are utilised as programme leaders while in the community. It is favourable for the sport role models to be well-regarded in their sports as this helps to attract attention among locals. However, it is much more important that the sport role models' attitudes complement the themes of the programme. Therefore, RDRM is mainly interested in recruiting individuals that are genuinely committed to making a difference in the communities, as this is important to the long-term sustainability of the programme. For this reason, many of the sports role models are recruited through personal recommendations within RDRM and will then be familiarised with the programme philosophies and cultural awareness training to enable them work in Aboriginal and Torres Strait Islander communities. This commitment is important to enable the same role models to visit the same localities over time, helping to sustain the long-term profile and authenticity of the RDRM programme, and engage participating communities on a regular basis.

THE IMPORTANCE OF PARTNERSHIPS FOR PROGRAMME SUSTAINABILITY

Partnerships are extremely important across many aspects of the RDRM operations. As outlined above, RDRM works closely with government agencies to ensure that the programme objectives can be met appropriately in target communities. However, in terms of securing funding to enable the ongoing operations of RDRM, partnerships with the for-profit sector are also relied upon. As the Managing Director strongly opposes a "cheque book" mentality of sponsorship, partnerships with the for-profit sector take on distinct characteristics. First, the for-profit sector partners need to demonstrate that they are motivated by social responsibility, rather than commercial interests. There are limited opportunities for marketing or advertising within the remote areas in which the programme conducts tours, so this lack of commercial motivation is a critical factor. Second, the for-profit partners need to commit not only funds, but other organisational capabilities and resources. One example of this is the for-profit partners to commit paid staff to actively support programme tours in the community. This means that a staff member will accompany RDRM into a community and, depending on their skills, may take on a programme leader role, or alternatively take on a programme support role to complete administrative or other tasks that need to be addressed during the tour. Similar to the role models, every staff member is familiarised with the RDRM philosophies and receives cultural awareness training before working in the Indigenous environment.

Third, partnerships with the target communities are pursued with the goal of developing long-term relationships, goals and reciprocal obligations. This is operationalised through a Community Partnerships Proposal (CPP). The CPP outlines the commitments of RDRM, which includes, for example, the commitment of an RDRM tour with role models and other deliverables negotiated with the community. The CPP also outlines the commitments of the community, which includes the assurance that the programme is supported by Aboriginal or Torres Strait Islander elders and other local representatives, the provision of accommodation for RDRM representatives, and a place to carry out the programme and other deliverables depending on each community context. This reciprocal arrangement is important in ensuring that the partnership represents an exchange, rather than a charitable service provided by RDRM. The CPP is seen as contributing towards long-term and sustainable efforts to build both social and health capital within remote communities.

(Continued)

SUMMARY

The social issues facing some remote Aboriginal and Torres Strait Islander communities are profound and extremely sensitive. RDRM has observed that sport, combined with music and the arts, provide a powerful vehicle to communicate important messages to the youth of these communities. However, the effectiveness of the programme is attributable to careful programme design and long-term planning. This has included seeking input from key stakeholders and making important decisions about the types of people and organisations that RDRM enters partnerships with. The establishment and management of partnerships with remote communities is equally important, and RDRM sees the reciprocal arrangements through the CPP as being an effective means by which to manage such a relationship for long-term outcomes.

FURTHER RESOURCES

Red Dust Role Models webpage: www.reddust.org.au

CASE STUDY EXTENSION ACTIVITIES

- From a review of the Red Dust Role Model webpage, identify the major opportunities and constraints of the programme.
- Based on your responses to question 1, make recommendations to ensure future growth and long-term sustainability of the programme.
- Suggest and justify ways to evaluate the RDRM programme in terms of:
    - the delivery of the programme in the communities;
    - the effectiveness of partnerships with for-profit organisations;
    - the effectiveness of partnerships with the target communities.

S4DP utilises and builds on the potential of sport to bring disparate and even separate groups together and contribute to inclusive social change. According to advocates, when people are engaged in appropriately organised sport projects and programmes, they are provided with opportunities to interact in an environment that promotes intergroup trust and the cultivation of respect. Indeed, according to Dyreson (2003), sport is a de facto language that virtually all people in the world can speak and understand, and which – if appropriately structured – has the capacity to positively engage diverse groups. Similarly, Chalip (2006) contends that sport events have the potential to promote dialogue, solidarity, understanding, integration and teamwork, even in conflict ridden contexts where other forms of social and political negotiation have been unsuccessful. For a long time these perspectives were largely anecdotal and, according to critics, therefore idealistic (Coalter, 2010). It was, indeed, hard to find practical evidence of S4DP projects that demonstrated sustainable outcomes in terms of reconciling or re-uniting disparate communities. However, over the past 10 years, as the number of grassroots initiatives has risen, there have also been growing calls for evidence based, independent reporting of the outcomes of S4DP projects, including the need to not only commit to but actually meet key performance indicators. It has become noticeable, therefore, that funding bodies are now expecting improved monitoring of S4DP programs, with project organisers required to demonstrate their operational effectiveness (Lyras & Welty Peachey, in press). A detailed overview of the different sport-for-development projects, their purpose, goals, objectives, and approaches can be found on the web site of the International Platform on Sport and Development (http://www.sportanddev.org) which is orchestrated by the Swiss Academy for Development.

Exercise:

Go to the website of the International Platform on Sport and Development (http://www. sportanddev.org) and identify one of the projects that engage in sport-for-development. What exactly are their goals and objectives, and how are the organisers trying to achieve them? Considering the financial, socio-cultural and geographical context the project is situated in, what could be some of the challenges for locals and international working on combined projects? Provide some suggestions on how the project may be further developed or improved.

Summary

Staged in a socially appropriate and culturally meaningful way, sport participation can contribute to healthy communities both physically and socially. Historically, sport development focused on building character through teamwork, discipline, and loyalty to a school or club. By the late 20th century, sport-for-development initiatives started to provide experiences that went beyond those provided by competitive sport, instead looking at how sport can also play a role in promoting social integration and community cohesion, thereby providing capacity building opportunities for suitably engaged groups and individuals. However, sport-for-development is hardly a panacea for systemic and complex socio-cultural and economic problems in developed societies like Australia and New Zealand, or among developing regions in and around Oceania. Sport-for-development should therefore be looked upon as one of a suite of community-focused initiatives, whether through music, dance, festivals and the arts, all with a goal of intercultural engagement and mutual understanding leading to improved social cohesion.

In the future, sport development and sport-for-development researchers and practitioners could investigate alternative means, ways and patterns in which sport can be delivered. For example, the rise of computer technologies and the rapid increase in social media may warrant the development of new forms of online sport games that combine gaming with physical activity. While the computer industry has started to design products that allow for this connection, research on their effectiveness in developing both socially and physically healthy individuals is yet to emerge. Also, the link between virtual communities and local communities needs to be developed further, and the importance and type of engagement in social relationships on- and offline should be explored. Finally, there is demand for a stronger integration of social, physical, and psychological factors to achieve 'healthy communities' in our diverse society.

Review questions

Historically, what were the main drivers for sport in Australian and New Zealand societies?
What were the fundamental claims about sport's value to Australia, New Zealand and the Pacific Islands in the 20th century?
For what reasons do national governments allocate the majority of public money available in the sports sector to the professional/elite levels? Do you think this approach can be justified?

- What are some of the achievements and remaining challenges for ASC and SPARC in relation to sport development efforts?
- What are the opportunities and challenges of Western 'change agents' working on community development projects in disadvantaged communities?
- Why is it so important that local communities have a say in the development efforts?
- To what degree can Sport for Development and Peace Projects make a difference in conflict settings? What are the opportunities and where are the limits of such intervention programs?
- How do you think Sport for Development and Peace projects can be sustained and leveraged to the wider community?

References

Adair, D. (1994). Rowing and sculling. In W. Vamplew & B. Stoddart (Eds.), *Sport in Australia: A social history* (pp. 172–192). Cambridge: Cambridge University Press.

Adair, D., & Vamplew, W. (1997). *Sport in Australian history*. Melbourne: Oxford University Press.

Australian Independent Sport Panel. (2009). *The future of sport in Australia*. Canberra. Retrieved from http://www.health.gov.au/internet/main/publishing.nsf/Content/1DDA76A44E5F4DD4CA257671000E4C45/$File/Crawford_Report.pdf

Australian Sports Commission. (2010). *Sports CONNECT: Disability Sector Education Resource Project*. Retrieved from http://www.ausport.gov.au/__data/assets/pdf_file/0004/351265/Sports_CONNECT_Education_Report_FINAL.pdf

Australian Sports Commission. (2011). *Government supports women leaders in sport*. Retrieved from http://www.ausport.gov.au/news/releases/story_448309_government_supports_women_leaders_in_sport

Baile, S. (1989). Women and health in developing countries. *OECD Observer, 161*(1), 18–20.

Bloomfield, J. (2003). *Australia's sporting success: The inside story*. Sydney: University of New South Wales Press.

Bunde-Birouste, A., Bull, N., & McCarroll, B. (2010). Moving beyond the "lump-sum": A case study of partnership for positive social change. *Cosmopolitan Civil Societies: An Interdisciplinary Journal, 2*(2), 92–114.

Cashman, R. (1995). *Paradise of sport: The rise of organised sport in Australia*. Melbourne: Oxford University Press.

Chalip, L. (2006). Towards social leverage of sport events. *Journal of Sport and Tourism, 11*(2), 109–127.

Chandler, T. J. L. (1991). Games at Oxbridge and the public schools, 1830–80: The diffusion of an innovation. *International Journal of the History of Sport, 8*(2), 171–204.

Coalter, F. (2010). The politics of sport-for-development: Limited focus programmes and broad gauge problems? *International Review for the Sociology of Sport, 45*(3), 295–314. doi:10.1177/1012690210366791

Crawford, S. A. G. M. (1985a). The game of "glory and hard knocks": A study of the interpenetration of rugby and New Zealand society. *The Journal of Popular Culture, 19*(2), 77–92.

Crawford, S. A. G. M. (1985b). "Muscles and character are there the first object of necessity": An overview of sport and recreation in a colonial setting - Otago province, New Zealand. *International Journal of the History of Sport, 2*(2), 109–126.

Crawford, S. A. G. M. (1987). Pioneering women: Recreational and sporting opportunities in a remote colonial setting. In J. Mangan & R. Park (Eds.), *From "fair sex" to feminism. Sport and the socialization of women in the industrial and post-industrial eras* (pp. 161–181). Oxon: Routledge.

Crotty, M. (2000). Manly and moral: The making of middle class men in the Australian public school. *The International Journal of the History of Sport, 17*(2–3), 10–30.

Daly, J. A. (1982). *Elysian fields: Sport, class and community in colonial South Australia, 1836–1890*. Adelaide: J.A. Daly.

Dyreson, M. (2003). Globalizing the nation-making process: Modern sport in world history. *The International Journal of the History of Sport, 20*(1), 91–106.

Epping-Jordan, J. E., Galea, G., Tukuitonga, C., & Beaglehole, R. (2005). Preventing chronic diseases: Taking stepwise action. *The Lancet, 366*(9497), 1667–1671.

Ferguson, J. A. (2007). *More than sunshine and Vegemite: Success the Australian way*. Broadway, NSW: Halstead Press.

Gill, T. P., Baur, L. A., Bauman, A. E., Steinbeck, K. S., Storlien, L. H., Fiatarone Singh, M. A., ...Caterson I. D. (2009). Childhood obesity in Australia remains a widespread health concern that warrants population-wide prevention Programs. *Medical Journal of Australia, 190*(3), 146–148.

Green, M. (2007). Olympic glory or grassroots development? Sport policy priorities in Australia, Canada and the United Kingdom, 1960–2006. *International Journal of the History of Sport*, 24, 921–953.

Greenwood, B. (2007). 1908: The year rugby league came to New Zealand. *Sport in History*, 27(3), 343–363.

Holt, R. (1990). *Sport and the British: A modern history*. Oxford: Oxford University Press.

Hoye, R. S., & Stewart, B. (2002). Power and organisational change: The case of the Melbourne Women's Hockey Association, 1995–1998. *Sporting Traditions*, 18(2), 47–66.

Ife, J. W. (1995). *Community development: Creating community alternatives - vision, analysis and practice*. Melbourne: Longman Australia.

Indian, M. (1981). Formalisation of urban leisure: Melbourne, 1880–1900. In R. Cashman & M. McKernan (Eds.), *Sport, money, morality and the media* (pp. 272–288). Sydney: NSW University Press.

Jobling, I. (2000). In pursuit of status, respectability and idealism: Pioneers of the Olympic movement in Australasia. *The International Journal of the History of Sport*, 17(2–3), 142–163.

Kidd, B. (2008). A new social movement: Sport for development and peace. *Sport in Society*, 11(4), 370–380.

Labonte, R., & Laverack, G. (2001). Capacity building in health promotion, Part 1: For whom? And for what purpose? *Critical Public Health*, 11(2), 111–127.

Lawrence, H. D. V. (2008). *Government involvement in New Zealand sport – sport policy: A cautionary tale* (MSpLS thesis). Retrieved from The University of Waikato Research Commons. http://researchcommons.waikato.ac.nz/

Letters, M., & Jobling, I. (1996). Forgotten links: Leonard Cuff and the Olympic movement in Australasia, 1894–1905. *Olympika*, 5(1), 91–110.

Lyras, A., & Welty Peachey, J. (in press). Integrating sport-for-development theory and praxis. *Sport Management Review*. doi:10.1016/j.smr.2011.05.006

Mangan, J. (1986). *The games ethic and imperialism: Aspects of the diffusion of an ideal*. Middlesex: Viking Press.

Mangan, J. (1988). *Pleasure, profit, proselytism: British culture and sport at home and abroad 1700–1914*. London: Frank Cass.

Midgley, J. (1986). *Community participation, social development and the state*. New York: Methuen.

Nisbet, R. A. (1969). *The quest for community*. New York: Oxford University Press.

Obel, C. (2005). Amateur rugby's spectator success: Cultivating inter-provincial publics in New Zealand (1902–1995). *Sporting Traditions*, 21(2), 97–118.

Owen, P. D., & Weatherston, C. R. (2002). Professionalization of New Zealand rugby union: Historical background, structural changes and competitive balance. *University of Otago Economics Discussion Papers*, No. 0214, Dec 2002, 1–29.

Phillips, J. (1996). *A man's country? The image of the Pakeha male: A history*. Auckland: Penguin Books.

Piggin, J., Jackson, S. J., & Lewis, M. (2009). Telling the truth in public policy: An analysis of New Zealand sport policy discourse. *Sociology of Sport Journal*, 26(3), 462–482.

Purdue, D., Razzaque, K., Hambleton, R., Stewart, M., Huxham, C., & Vangen, S. (2000). *Community leadership in area regeneration*. Bristol: The Policy Press.

Robotham, J. (2011, January 13). After-school exercise dropping in NSW despite federal push. *Sydney Morning Herald*. Retrieved from http://www.smh.com.au/lifestyle/back-to-school/afterschool-exercise-dropping-in-nsw-despite-federal-push-20110112-19obb.html#ixzz1UQ38MtUP

Ryan, G. (2011). A tale of two dinners: New zealand rugby and the embrace of empire, 1919–32. *International Journal of the History of Sport*, 28(10), 1409–1425.

Sam, M. P., & Jackson, S. J. (2004). Sport policy development in New Zealand. *International Review for the Sociology of Sport*, 39(2), 205–222.

Schulenkorf, N. (2010a). The roles and responsibilities of a change agent in sport event development projects. *Sport Management Review*, 13(2), 118–128. doi:10.1016/j.smr.2009.05.001

Schulenkorf, N. (2010b). Sport events and ethnic reconciliation: Attempting to create social change between Sinhalese, Tamil and Muslim sportspeople in war-torn Sri Lanka. *International Review for the Sociology of Sport*, 45(3), 273–294. doi:10.1177/1012690210366789

Schulenkorf, N., & Edwards, D. (2010). The role of sport events in peace tourism. In O. Moufakkir & I. Kelly (Eds.), *Tourism, Progress and Peace* (pp. 99–117). Oxfordshire, UK: CABI International.

SEARO. (2008). *Health in Asia and the Pacific*. Manila: South East Asian Regional Office of the World Health Organization.

Seynard, J. (2002). From gentleman to the manly: A large step for the amateur. *Sporting Traditions*, 18(2), 1–14.

Shaffer, C., & Anundsen, K. (1993). *Creating community anywhere: Finding support and connection in a fragmented world.* New York: Putnam Pub. Group.

Siefken, K., MacNiven, R., Schofield, G., Bauman, A., & Waqanivalu, T. (in press). A stocktake of physical activity programs in the Pacific Islands. *Health Promotion International.* doi:10.1093/heapro/dar026

Skinner, J. (1997). *Building community strengths: A resource book on capacity building.* London: Community Development Foundation.

Skinner, J., Stewart, B., & Edwards, A. (1999). Amateurism to professionalism: Modelling organisational change in sporting organisations. *Sport Management Review, 2*(2), 173–192.

Stewart, B. (1992). Athleticism revisited: Sport, character building, and Protestant school education in the nineteenth century Melbourne. *Sporting Traditions, 9*(1), 35–50.

Stewart, B., Nicholson, M., Smith, A., & Westerbeek, H. (2004). *Australian sport: Better by design? The evolution of Australian sport policy.* London; New York: Routledge.

Stronach, M., & Adair, D. (2009). 'Brave New World'or 'Sticky Wicket'? Women, management and organizational power in Cricket Australia. *Sport in Society, 12*(7), 910–932.

Stumbo, N. J., Wang, Y., & Pegg, S. (2011). Issues of access: What matters to people with disabilities as they seek leisure experiences. *World Leisure Journal, 53*(2), 91–103.

Sugden, J. (2010). Critical left-realism and sport interventions in divided societies. *International Review for the Sociology of Sport, 45*(3), 258–272. doi:10.1177/1012690210374525

Taylor, M. (2003). *Public policy in the community.* Houndmills, Basingstoke, England: Palgrave Macmillan.

Ulijaszek, S. J. (2001). Socioeconomic status, body size and physical activity of adults on Rarotonga, the Cook Islands. *Annals of Human Biology, 28*(5), 554–563.

Veal, A. J., & Frawley, S. (2009). *'Sport for all' and major sporting events: Trends in sport participation and the Sydney 2000 Olympic Games, the 2003 Rugby World Cup and the Melbourne 2006 Commonwealth Games.* Sydney: UTS, School of Leisure, Sport and Tourism; Australian Centre for Olympic Studies (Working Paper 6). Retrieved from http://www.business.uts.edu.au/lst/downloads/wp6vealfrawley.pdf

Vincent, G. T. (1998). Practical imperialism: The Anglo Welsh rugby tour of New Zealand, 1908. *International Journal of the History of Sport, 15*(1), 123–140.

WHO. (2008). *A framework to monitor and evaluate implementation: Global strategy on diet, physical activity and health.* Geneva, Switzerland: World Health Organization.

Wilkinson, I. R. (1998). School sport and the amateur ideal: The formation of the Schools' Amateur Athletic Association of Victoria. *Sporting Traditions, 15*(1), 51–70.

WPRO, & SPC. (2007). *Prevention and control of noncommunicable diseases: Meeting of Ministers of Health for the Pacific Island Countries (No. 5.2).* Port Vila, Vanuatu: World Health Organization for the Western Pacific Region and Secretariat of the Pacific Community.

Chapter 16

Sport and the Law

Feona Sayles

OBJECTIVES

After completing this chapter, you should be able to:

- identify the main element of a contract;
- explain what is meant by privity of contract and how an exclusion clause operates;
- understand what types of claims may arise from personal injury;
- explain the basic requirements for negligence;
- explain the basic elements of copyright, trademarks and misleading conduct under the *Fair Trading Act 1986 (NZ)* and/or the *Trade Practices Act 1974 (Cth)*.

Key terms

InIn this chapter, readers will become familiar with the following concepts and terms:

- consideration
- capacity
- agreement
- intention to create legal relations
- exclusion clause
- privity
- exclusive contract
- independent contractor
- employee
- negligence
- personal injury
- exemplary damages
- mental injury
- duty of care
- rights of ownership
- original work
- infringing trade mark
- misleading/deceptive conduct

Introduction

There is no such thing as 'sports law'. This may seem like an odd statement with which to begin a chapter on sports law, but it is true. There is no special field of law with rules that are unique to sport. Instead what is commonly known as sports law is the application of law in a variety of areas to the sports situation. These different areas include tort, contract and criminal law as well as rules developed by statutes such as the Fair Trading Act 1986(NZ).

Since almost any area of law may impact on the provision of sport the topic of 'sports law' encompasses a large number of issues. This chapter should therefore not be taken as a complete rendition of sports law; in fact it is only the 'tip of the iceberg'. Issues such as image protection through privacy rights and name suppression are not included. Nor are the problems that can arise through violence in sport. Judicial review and the legal implications of drugs testing are not covered. These areas are important, but it is beyond the scope of this chapter to cover them in sufficient detail.

What is covered in this chapter are some of the fundamental legal issues facing sports providers. Attention is given to contract law as this is the basis of many actions associated with sports law. Problems connected to injuries in sport have also increased in relevance due to recent cases where sports providers have been charged as a result of events going wrong. The final section on intellectual property is included as this is a key area for sports marketing which is in itself a vital aspect of sports management.

CASE STUDY: WHATBALL SPORTS

Andy is the president of ManawatuWhatball Sports who are the 'local branch' for the sport. Whatball itself is a sport that is played nationally and internationally in a number of countries.

The sport is a cross between Netball and Basketball and is played on indoor courts. Although it is essentially a non-contact sport, players occasionally do injure each other. Usually these injuries are a result of the players breaking the rules, but sometimes it is accidental. The game is played at a very fast pace, so players need to be very fit.

Whatball have been approached by the National organisation to host an international competition. Players will be coming from all over the world.

The competition is expected to have international coverage, so there are a number of big companies that are keen to sponsor the event. Whatball has had preliminary meetings with potential sponsor and has now decided that they will have one sponsor (an international shoe company) for the event who will have exclusive rights.

Andy takes it upon himself to negotiate and conclude the contract without first seeing a lawyer. Andy tells his fellow members: "Relax, this is simple."

After the contract is signed with the shoe company Andy is approached by the existing facility sponsors who are excited about the international event and the fact that their logos will be on Television. Andy tells them that the shoe company won't allow it and that Whatball is going to take down the facility sponsors logos during the event. The facility sponsors decide to sue Whatball for breach of contract.

This creates a lot of publicity, some of which reflects badly on the shoe company. One headline screams "Shoe company can't handle rivals". The shoe company contacts Andy and tells him they intend to sue Whatball for a breach of the contract in regard to the exclusive provisions that stated there was to be no conflict with other existing sponsorship contracts. Andy tells them he did not understand what the terms meant. The shoe company asks him "But surely your lawyer would have explained all that to you?" Andy replies, "I didn't think I needed one."

Contract

This is an important area to understand as contracts and the law of contract are relevant to many activities associated with sport management. The first point to note is that while there are some contracts that are required to be in writing (for example contracts that deal with real estate) a contract need not be in writing to be binding. For a binding contract the basic elements required are: agreement, capacity, consideration and an intention to create legal relations.

Capacity means that a party to a contract has the legal ability to agree. The types of people who may not be considered able to agree are people with defective intelligence or minors (people under the age of 8). In New Zealand, the law in relation to contracts with minors is governed by statute – the Minors Contract Act 1969. This act provides that contracts of employment and insurance can be enforced unless inadequate consideration was given by the other party or it would be unconscionable to enforce the contract (s5). Other contracts against minors may be binding if the minor is close to the age of 18 and it would not be unreasonable to hold the minor to the contract (s6). In Australia the situation is not as clear as some States rely on common law rules whilst others have statutes that govern the situation. In States where the common law rules apply this will mean that a contract against a minor can be enforced if it is for necessaries, employment, or education and the contract benefits the minor. If the contract does not fall within one of these categories then it will not be binding – the minor can choose whether they want to keep the contract or not. An example of Australian statute law is the Minors (Property and Contacts) Act 1970 (NSW) which provides that generally contracts with people under the age of 18 are not binding, but there is a presumption that the contract will be binding if the contract is beneficial to the minor (s19).

Consideration means that something of value (either an act or a promise) is exchanged between the parties. Consideration is also sometimes referred to as a burden undertaken for the benefit of another. The promise that is given can be a promise to pay money or to perform a service or to provide a good. You cannot have a contract if only one party is providing consideration nor can you have a contract if there is past consideration. Past consideration exists when a person performs the act or promise before the contract was made.

Intention to create legal relations means that each party intends the contract to be legally enforceable so many 'social or domestic arrangements' are not considered contracts. For example if you were asked to cook dinner for your flatmates and you agree it is unlikely that either you or your flatmates would intend that you would be legally bound and subject to penalties if you failed to cook dinner because you were late home after training.

For there to be agreement there must first be an offer which is then accepted. An offer can be described as a promise to perform a particular obligation without any qualifications to the promise (e.g., I will do this 'only if'...). One note of caution about offers it that once given they cannot be withdrawn if the other party has accepted the offer. This means that in pre-contractual negotiations both parties should be careful to make sure that any 'promises' made are not considered offers. For acceptance of an offer to be effective it must be communicated to the party making the offer and all terms of the offer must have been made clear and known at the time of acceptance. This generally means you cannot 'add' an important condition or term after the contract is concluded.

As well as the above elements to a contract there are some other aspects to contract that should be considered before looking at specific types of contracts. These are:

Privity

This means the contract will only be binding and enforceable between the parties to the contract. T explain, if X makes a contract with Y to do some gardening for Z then Z will not be able to claim agains X if X does not do the gardening. This is because the parties to the contract are X and Y, not Z. Ther some exception to this such as when an agent is involved. An agent is someone who acts on beha of another person called the principal. If the agent makes a contract with another person (the thir party) the contract will be treated as being between the principal and the third party, not betwee the agent and the third party. For someone to be an agent there must be an agency agreement contract between the agent and principal which is subject to the basic elements of contract such capacity (there will be limitations on the contractual capacity of principals or agents who are minor for example).

The implication for sports is that agreements reached by the organisation or the manager of a tea may not be ` on the individual sportspeople unless there is an agreement that the organisation manager can act as agent for the sportsperson. It also means, in the situation of a minor sportsperson any contracts entered into by their parent, organisation or manager will generally not be bindi on that sportsperson. This is because they will either not be a party to the contract or cannot be principal as they lack capacity.

Exclusion clauses

These are clauses designed to limit the liability of one party in the event that something should go wrong. Often these types of clauses are included in contracts when there is a degree of unequal power between the two parties, as a result the courts tend to take the view that the clause will be more harshly construed against the party wishing to rely on it.

Any clause of this nature must be clearly worded so that the meaning of how liability will be removed is not in doubt – particularly if the clause is intended to remove liability for negligence. This means the clause should not be too broad, but can also mean it should not be too specific. An example where an exclusion clause was held not to apply due to the exact wording is *Insight Vacations Pty Ltd v Young* 2011 HCA 16 (11 May 2011) where an exclusion clause that stated no liability 'Where the passenger occupies a motor coach seat' did not apply to a situation where a passenger was injured whilst standing due to a sudden stop by the driver. The Court said the use of the word seat limited the clause to situations where the passengers were actually seated.

There are statutory prohibitions against some types of exclusion clauses, for example a statement saying that in entering a contract person has not relied on the representations of the other party can be taken as an attempt to avoid the Fair Trading Act 1986 (NZ). In this situation the court will look at the overall circumstances of the contract to see if the clause can be relied on.

One type of clause that is becoming more common for sports providers is an attempt to limit liability for harm during an event or in the provision of sports services (for example gyms). While the degree to which a sports provider can be held liable for personal harm will be discussed below, it should be noted here that in New Zealand this type of clause can be considered an attempt to contract out of the Consumer Guarantees Act 1993 (NZ) or s74 Trade Practices Act 1974 (Cth) (AU). Both the CGA and the TPA provide guarantees a minimum standard for services, which if breached can give rise to certain remedies including damages. The rights under the CGA are independent of any contract and cannot be excluded by a clause in the contract. If a sports provider if found to be in breach of the minimum standards of the CGA they will still be liable under this Act despite any exclusion clauses that they will not be liable for harm or damage.

In Australia, the TPA s68 states that a contract cannot exclude liability under s74. However, this restriction on exclusion clauses does not apply if the services relate to "Recreational Services" as defined within s68B. The idea of what type of services will be subject to s68Bhas been discussed in *Kovacevic v Holland Park Holdings Pty Ltd* [2010] QDC 279. In this situation a woman was injured at her gym when she slipped during an exercise class. She fell because the surface of the gym was not suitable for these types of exercise classes. There was an exclusion clause in the membership contract that excluded liability for harm and loss of property. The court first stated that there was a breach of s74as the classes should not have been held on this type of surface. The court then went on to decide if the exclusion clause was void, or if s68B would allow it to operate. The court decided that 'Recreational Services' are ones that relate to sport or other activities where competition is involved or to other physical activities such as mountaineering. They did not consider that the definition of 'Recreational Services' applied to activities where the main aim is to achieve fitness or good health – hence the fitness classes at the gym were not regarded as 'Recreational Services'. Since s68B did apply the exclusion clause was void. The court said that the exclusion clause would also be void on the grounds that it was not limited to 'death or injury' as required by s68B, instead the exclusion clause also related to loss of property. Whether the reasoning as to what is regarded as a 'recreational service' adopted in this case will be taken up in other cases remains to be seen, but even if this was not followed it could still mean that exclusion clauses that do not limit themselves to death or injury may mean that s68B is excluded.

Specific types of contracts

Sponsorship agreements

This type of contract is common amongst sports not matter what level of operation. Some of the considerations that need to be given in executing this type of contract include the expectations and performance ability of both parties in both the long and the short term. These considerations will impact on the clauses that are included as to termination and rights obtained.

In the situation of 'exclusive' sponsorship there needs to be a careful consideration as to whether this is in the best interest of both parties. Also both parties should fully understand the nature of the contract and the limitations it poses to accepting other offers. A lack of understanding was seen in *Magic Merchandise v Lomu* (Baker J, 3/3/1997, HC Auckland CP38/96). The plaintiff claimed to have an exclusive contract with Jonah Lomu to produce a print which depicted the rugby player in various action poses. The print was to be a limited run and each print would be personally autographed by Lomu. A contract was made with Lomu through his agents and also made a contract with the NZRFU (who had to give permission for such an arrangement). The plaintiff then found out that a similar deal had been made for another poster showing Lomu and David Campese which was intended to promote an upcoming match. The plaintiff said the express terms indicating that the contract was exclusive were: it was a limited edition, there were exclusive rights of distribution, and there was a limited period of royalties payable. The Court held that these terms did not expressly confer an exclusive right to use Lomu's image and that the plaintiff would have to rely on whether there were implied terms. The Court allowed the claim to proceed on the basis that implied terms could be shown, but did state that in the opinion of the Court this may be difficult to prove at a full hearing since such terms would probably be implied due to custom and in this case the field of sports marketing was relatively new so may not have gained such customs.

This case highlights a few of the considerations that must be addressed in a sponsorship/marketing contract such as:

- Each party should consider the implications of and the requirements imposed by prior relationships. In Lomu's case permission was needed from the NZRFU.
- Each party should ensure there is full disclosure of existing agreements that may impact on the new contract.
- If a party wants to have exclusive rights they should ensure there are clear express terms as to this in the contract, rather than relying on implied terms.

Difficulties can also occur when a sportsperson is at the beginning stages of their career and enters into an exclusive sponsorship deal as the value offered may not reflect the future value of the athlete once they start to gain prominence through consistent performance. To overcome this the contract can include escalation clauses which mean that the money/benefits obtained increase if the sportsperson is winning or gaining a higher media profile. Another method of gaining future flexibility for the sportsperson is to ensure that any right of renewal will only be granted if it allows for either a re-evaluation of the sportspersons value or for the inclusion of other sponsors.

Service contracts

These contracts may be with the sportsperson (commonly called athletes contracts) or with other individuals associated with the provision of the sport. In both situations the first aspect to consider is whether the subject of the contract will be an employee (a contract of service) or an independent contractor (a contract for service). There are benefits to either type of contract for both the person performing the service and the person engaging the service. The benefits of independent contractor status include maximising earnings and tax advantages while for an employee there are benefits conferred by employment legislation such as the Employment Relations Act 2000 (NZ) and the Holiday Act 2003 (NZ).

In most cases the type of contract will be clear but, as two cases involving player contract show, the exact nature of the relationship may not always be evident. The first case is a New Zealand case *Kirk v ACC* (1993) NZAR 299 where the player had contracts with his soccer club and the NZFA. He went to play soccer in Bangkok and was injured. He tried to claim accident compensation but was refused as he was not an 'earner'. Kirk appealed this decision. The Court held that he was an earner but then considered what type of earner he was – was he an employee or an independent contractor? In both contracts Kirk was required to play and train at certain times. His club contract also included clauses that he had to play to the best of his ability, to keep fit, attend media sessions and have a good standard of appearance. The Court concluded that Kirk was an employee as he had little control over how and when he performed.

In contrast in the case of *Barnard v Australian Soccer Federation* (Federal Court, Queensland, 29/4/1988) a semi-pro player was not considered to be an employee. The dispute had arisen due to the player taking part in both indoor and outdoor competition (which were organised by different associations). The outdoor association had declared that the player could not play for both organisations and that it was a breach of the Trade Practices Act 1974 (TPA) for him to do so. The player and the indoor association claimed that the Act did not apply as the contracts with the two organisations were contracts of employment so were excluded from the definitions within the TPA. The Court decided that the player was not an employee as he did not have to attend training, be fit, or play to the best of his ability – the type of "control" clauses that the Court in *Kirk* decided was decisive of employment. Of interest here is that there were no actual clauses in the contract relating to this. Instead since any clauses of this nature were missing, the Court decided that the omission meant that this type of performance requirement was not a part of the contract. This means that sportspeople should ensure that these clauses are properly included into a contract if the relationship is intended to be one of employment.

Whether the person is an independent contractor or an employee can impact on entitlements such as compensation for injury in Australia (though note that some State legislation often excludes professional sportspeople as workers: For example see s11, Workers' Compensation and Injury Management Act 1981(WA)) and also impact on statutory duties expected from 'employers' as shown in *Department of Labour v Nelson Dive Centre* [2001] DCR 1079, a Health and Safety in

Employment Act 1992 (NZ)case in which an employer was held liable after a failure during a diving instruction course harmed some of the students. In defence of the charges the Dive Centre claimed the dive instructor was not an employee, but a contractor. If correct this would minimise their liability, since a greater duty is owed to other people if the harm occurs through an employee. The court held since Nelson Dive centre had control over the student enrolments and teaching requirements, the diving instructor had a contract of service not for services – the instructor was an employee. Under the HSE if a relationship of employer/employee exists, the employer must:

- protect the employee;
- ensure that they have the correct training and/or supervision;
- ensure that the actions or inactions of an employee do not harm any other person.

In the above case the Dive Centre failed to do this, and so was liable.

While there are a number of issues in relation to employment law that could be discussed it is beyond the scope of this chapter to go through them. Instead this section on contracts will conclude with some important issues in relation to service contracts between sports providers and sports people.

Negligence and personal injury

There are significant differences between Australia and New Zealand in regard to legal liability for personal injury. In New Zealand the application of this area of law has been limited, largely due to the provision of the accident compensation scheme. In Australia there remains the ability to sue for personal injury even where the person is covered for compensation through schemes such as Workcover – but the extent to which sportspeople can sue has be limited in some areas through various legislation that restricts liability for negligence in some situations. This section will first go through the New Zealand situation then explain the limits on negligence in Australia before explaining the tort of negligence itself.

Concept Check

Tort

This is a name given to a group of civil wrongdoings. The law is common law which means it is created by the courts rather than by statute. Some torts include defamation, trespass and negligence.

New Zealand

The accident compensation scheme provides that an injured person cannot sue for damages if the injury is covered by the Injury Prevention, Rehabilitation and Compensation Act 2001(IPRCA), if the injury is not covered by that Act then a common law claim can proceed. In the early 1990s there was some concern that the number of injuries not covered would increase due to a change in wording however the practical effect has been little change to the type of injuries covered. The overall result is that a large number of sports related injuries will be covered and as a result sports providers will no be liable for a claim. Unfortunately while this is the general rule, sports providers cannot completely 'write off' the possibility of a claim for personal injury as there are some exceptions.

Situations where other claims may be possible

Accident not covered

One of the first exceptions is if the injury is not covered by the IPRCA 2001. In order to be covered by the IPRCA 2001 the injured party must be:

- an insured,
- who suffers a personal injury,
- caused by an accident.

Since these elements must act in combination (personal injury caused by an accident) the absence of one or both of the key elements could mean an injured sportsperson is not covered.

The term insured includes earners and non-earners in relation to non-work injuries, so even 'amateur' sportspeople are covered by the IPRCA 2001. A personal injury is a death, a physical injury, or a mental injury which is either caused by physical injuries or by one of the causes listed in s21. It does not include injury from a gradual process, disease or infection, unless it is work related or is caused through: medial misadventure, a physical injury, or treatment to a physical injury. Heart attacks and strokes are also not covered unless work related or due to medical misadventure. An accident is defined as an event or series of events involving an "application of a force or resistance external to the human body" (which is not part of a gradual process) s25 (1)(a).

In some cases the extent of cover will depend on whether the person suffered the harm during the course of employment. This occurred in *Middleton-Echave v ACC*, where an aerobics instructor suffering from a hernia was refused a claim from the corporation. The difficulty in granting compensation was that it was unclear as to whether the hernia was the result of a work related gradual process, or non-work – only work related gradual processes are covered. What is demonstrated from this case is if an amateur sportsperson is suffering injuries associated with exercise or physical activity that are a result of a gradual process the exceptions as to work related injuries will not apply, so they will not be covered under the Act.

Another situation where an injury may not be covered is when the person suffers a non-work related heart attack. For example, aqua aerobic programmes are quite popular – especially for older people who are unable to stand the impact which occurs with land sessions. Unfortunately this age group may be more susceptible to having a heart attack if placed under excessive strain. As the heart attack would not be work related it would not be covered. A pool provider could be liable in this situation if it was shown that the session was more strenuous than recommend for that age/fitness level, or if there are not adequate checks on those people who attend such sessions. A heart attack could also occur when relatively fit sportspeople are subjected to a training programme that goes beyond their capabilities. To avoid this, a trainer or facility provider should make sure that any programme offered is suitable for the age and fitness of the people undertaking it.

Mental injury

There are two ways in which a civil claim for mental injury will be barred, first if it is covered by the Act (as per s21), second if the mental injury arises directly or indirectly from a personal injury that is covered by that Act. The type of mental injury that is covered by the IPRCA scheme is very limited (mostly it will be mental injury in relation to suffering sexual abuse). So the situations where the mental injury to a person can give rise to a civil claim is where no physical injury has occurred or if the physical injury is not covered by the IPRCA (e.g., a stroke in a non-work situation). For example, in *Queenstown Lakes DC v Palmer* [1999] 1 NZLR 549 a man suffered mental injury after witnessing his wife die in a river rafting accident. The court held that he was entitled to lodge a civil claim as it was not based on the physical injury suffered by his wife but on his own mental injury.

In order to be successful in a mental injury civil claim the injured party must show:

- They have a medically identifiable psychiatric illness.
- The injury must have been reasonable foreseeable.
- There must be a sufficiently proximate relationship between the injured person and the defendant. For example, spectators at a sports event would have sufficient proximity to the event organisers.
- There must be sufficient proximity in time and space to the accident or the immediate aftermath. This means that spectators at the scene of the accident would have a claim while people who see it (e.g.) on Television would not.
- The injury must have resulted from a sudden assault on the nervous system. This would mean that stress created over time from a training programme may not be capable of supporting a claim.

Exemplary damages

If the injured person is covered under the Act, a sports provider may still face the prospect of exemplary damages. The purpose of such damages is to punish the defendant for his or her wrongdoing and deter others from acting in a similar way. These damages may not be available if:

- it can be shown that the actions are likely to be the subject of other proceedings, and
- the injured person is *not* covered by the Act (in which case they would still be free to pursue other claims).

If the injured party is covered under the IPRCA, section 319 allows for a claim of exemplary damages, notwithstanding any other proceedings that have or are likely to arise. Damages are usually reserved for conduct which is 'outrageous' and 'grossly negligent and reckless', so sports providers would need to engage in conduct which has a high degree of risk to be liable.

While the actual conduct of the sports provider will be the main consideration, other factors such knowledge of the risk can be important. The knowledge factor has been the subject of recent debate. In the case of *A v Bottrill* [2002] UKPC 44, the Court of Appeal concluded that for a person to be held liable for gross negligence they must have a conscious appreciation of the particular risk not just knowledge of the circumstances. The case then went to the Privy Council on appeal, where it was decided that gross negligence requires only that the defendant knew the circumstances and engaged in a high risk activity there is no need to show that the defendant consciously appreciated the risks involved in their actions. This means the sports provider does not have to actually know that there is a risk: it would be enough that it will be that the conduct is so unreasonable in the circumstances that it created the risk.

A point to note is that the conduct does not have to be that of the actual sports provider - it can be the actions of an employee, in which case liability will be imposed on the employer by way of vicarious liability. So sports providers must take care to ensure that not only do they know of the risks so as to avoid them, but also that their staff know and appreciate the risks.

Concept Check

Vicarious liability

This is where the actions of an employee or agent are treated as being the actions of their employer or principle. The employee or agent must be acting within their actual authority (what they have been told or what has been implied they can do) for the employer or principle to be liable.

Contract

If the injury is a result of a breach of contract the injury party will be barred from suing, but if the contract covered the situation then the injured party could sue. So if a contract had a clause such as 'in the event the sportsperson is injured due to negligence they will have the right to claim damages' the sportsperson will not be barred from suing for damages. It will not be enough that a contractual term which ensures 'safety to the player' has been breached.

Critical Argument Summary Box

Should there be a restriction on Negligence via statutes

For:
- Gives a greater emphasis on people being responsible for their own choices.
- Will eventually lead to increased clarity as to whether liability is present in some circumstances.
- Greater protection for volunteers.

Against:
- Restricting liability can led to unsafe practices.
- Leads to confusion since the restrictions do not apply to all jurisdictions.
- Currently court action may still be needed to find if liability is excluded so still costly.

Australia

In Australia there are various worker compensation schemes and legislation such as Workers' Compensation and Injury Management Act 1981(WA). These schemes provide compensation to workers, but sometimes may exclude professional sportspeople as being classed as workers (though there may be separate schemes for sports injuries).In most States even if a person is eligible for compensation this does not prevent them from being able to take a civil action such the tort of negligence or for a breach of warranty under the Trade Practices Act 1974 (Cth). There may however be some restrictions such as not being able to claim both damages under a civil action and compensation under a statutory scheme (for example the Sporting Injuries Insurance Act 1978 (NSW) s35A prohibits claiming both damages and compensation).

The main limitation that is placed on sportspeople seeking a claim in negligence is due to statutes such as the Civil Liability Act 2002 (NSW) – please note there are differences between each State so this Act is merely an example of how such legislation works. Under the Civil Liability Act 2002 (NSW) a person will not be liable for the tort of negligence when the plaintiff (the person who suffered the harm) was engaged in a dangerous recreational activity and the harm was due to an obvious risk of this activity (s5L). A recreational activity is defined in a similar manner to recreational services under s68B of the Trade Practices Act 1974, so the reasoning in *Kovacevic v Holland Park Holdings Pty Ltd* is followed this would mean activity that has the prime aim of achieving fitness will not fall within the provision. An activity is 'dangerous' when it carries a significant risk of serious harm. One view as to when a risk will be significant is that there is a 'real chance' of it occurring (see *Fallas v Mourlas* [2006] NSWCA 32 at [91]). An obvious risk does not have to have a high probability of occurring and can include risks that are not prominent (s5F). The risk must be obvious to a reasonable person in the position of the plaintiff, so factors such as age may be relevant as to whether the risk was obvious.

The concept of the obvious risk is also relevant to excluding liability for a failure to warn about risks. If the risk is an obvious one there is no duty to warn unless asked, or if there is a legal duty to warn, or if there is the risk of death/injury from professional services (s5H). Section 5G states that a person is presumed to be aware of obvious risks, which has the potential to impact on the defence of *volentinon fit injuria*. This defence requires that the plaintiff was aware of the risks, they understood the risks, and agreed to continue despite the risk involved. The statutory presumption for obvious risks means that a defendant need only focus on whether the person understood risks and voluntarily agreed to take part. A case example that illustrates these concepts is *Woods v Multi Sport Holdings Pty Ltd* (2002) Aust. Tort Reports 81-640 where a person playing indoor cricket suffered an eye injury. The complex had no warning signs about potential risks nor did it provide safety gear. However, the action was not successful as it was felt by the court that the risks involved were so obvious that warnings were not needed.

Liability is also excluded where the harm is the result of an 'inherent risk' – meaning that the risk cannot be avoided even with 'the exercise of reasonable care and skill (5I).

Volunteers will not be liable under a civil claim whilst doing community work in relation to a community organisation (s61). This can provide protection to people such as amateur coaches and referees in relation to claims for negligence just so long as they are acting within the scope of their activities/instructions and are not under the influence of alcohol or drugs.

Other provisions of the Act include the ability to contract out of liability (see the above discussion on exclusion clauses in relation to this concept), limited liability for professionals (s5O), as well as restrictions on the amount that can be claimed (ss12-14) and the situations in which non-economic loss can be claimed (ss16-17).

Negligence

Civil

In most of the situations where a sports provider could face an action for injury, the likely claim would be one of negligence. In pleading this, the injured user would need to show:

* a duty of care was owed, and
* this duty was breached, and
* the breach caused the injuries suffered.

Kelly (1987) states that a duty of care is established when the 'relationship between the parties is such that the defendant should have contemplated that his or her negligent act would lead to the damage suffered'. One case that helps to illustrate whether there is the existence of a duty is *Haylen v NSW Rugby Union Ltd* [2002] NSWSC 114. In this case a young male was injured during a game of rugby. He became a quadriplegic. He did not sue the referee, but he did sue the Rugby Union on the basis that the game itself was dangerous. It was argued that the Union was negligent by "propagating, controlling and organising the game of rugby union and specifically the match in which the Plaintiff was playing when, as the Defendant knew or ought to have known, the rules under which it was played exposed persons playing the said sport to unnecessary risk of injury". The court contemplated the matter and decided that in this case the duty that was being sought was too wide. One of the considerations that a court will have in deciding whether a duty is present is whether the imposition of a duty is desirable. If a duty would create too greater liability than is warranted then the court will say the duty is too wide. As a result the action was not successful.

A breach of a duty is considered to be a departure from the usual standard expected from someone in the position of the defendant. This 'usual standard' means that even if the defendant is inexperienced or lacks the skills needed to obtain the standard, they will be liable just as much as a person with the necessary skills. The reason for this is if a person voluntarily places themselves into a position requiring skills they should take full responsibility for the outcome. The harm that is complained of must be a result of the breach, and not some other action. For a civil action the plaintiff need only show that these requirements happened on the balance of probabilities.

Two case examples where the action was successful include *Smolden v Whitworth*, Times Law Reports, April 1996 in which a 17 year old male who suffered a spinal injury during a game. The boy sued the referee of the game for a negligent application of the rules. It was argued that had the referee been more vigilant is enforcing the rules the injury would not have occurred. The second case is *Albany Golf Club Incorp. v Carey* (1987) Aust. Torts Reports 80-139 where the way in which a golf course had been designed meant certain risks were not obvious. The design was such that there was a line of trees which blocked a practice area. The trees were not very high, but high enough that the practice range could not be seen nor could people on the practice range see beyond the trees. A ball was hit from the practice range and went over the trees hitting a man in the eye. The man sued the golf club and was successful.

In the situation of sport, negligence could arise where spectators at an event are placed in danger. In this situation the event organiser will owe a duty of care to ensure the safety of spectators, and if they put spectators in a place that is unsafe there will be a breach of that duty. The damage that occurs from being put into an unsafe place could include mental injury after just avoiding being harmed.

Criminal

Negligence as a standard for criminal liability is rare as usually criminal law will require intentional or reckless act, there are however some limited exceptions where negligence will suffice for liability. Criminal negligence has similarities with civil negligence in that it must be shown that there is a duty, this duty has been breached and that harm resulted from the breach. In New Zealand the duties where negligence may apply are contained in ss151-153, 155-157 Crimes Act 1961 in Australia these are usually contained within provisions relating to manslaughter (for example s15 Crimes Act (ACT) or s280 Crimes Act (WA)). A major difference between civil negligence and criminal negligence in both Australia and New Zealand is that the breach must be a major departure (rather than just a departure) from the usual standard (see s150A Crime Act 1961(NZ)) so the level of negligence required is *gross* negligence. While civil negligence will make no allowances for inexperience or lack of skills it is possible that gross negligence will take this into consideration. However, it is suggested that if a person undertook a risky task knowing fully that they were not capable of performing it this will not be looked upon favourably.

A New Zealand case example of criminal negligence is *R v Anderson* [2005] 1 NZLR 774. The case involved a bike race that took the cyclists on a steep and winding road. The organiser had given the participants an information sheet that advised them to obey the road rules and to stay left, but had also included information that part of the winding road would be 'closed'. In fact the road was not properly closed; instead it was just a means by which officials could check that people coming through were bone fide participants. A cyclist travelling up the road crossed over the centre line and was killed by an oncoming car. The organiser was charged under s145 Crimes Act 1961 (NZ) (criminal nuisance) on the basis that she did not make it clear that the section of the road where the accident happened would not be closed to other traffic. The charge relied on the legal duty created by s156 Crimes Act 1961 (NZ) (a person in charge of dangerous things).

When the case first went to trial she was found guilty and was fined $10,000. This had been due to the direction from the judge that the knowledge requirement for s145 was that she knew *or* ought to have known if she had thought about it that her omission would cause a risk. On appeal the court decided what had to be shown was that she actually knew the omission could cause harm. Her conviction was quashed. This did not mean she had not breached the duty in s156, and if she had been charged with another offence that did not require the type of 'knowledge' needed for s145 she could have been found guilty – for example it is possible that a manslaughter charge could have been brought.

This case caused concern for a number of sports providers who regularly organise events. The reaction from some has been to attempt to 'contract out' of liability by using exemption clauses in entry documents. This type of clause will not assist the event organiser against criminal charges if it is shown that:

- there was a serious risk present, and
- the organiser knew of the circumstances creating the risk, and
- the organiser neglected to minimise or eliminate the risk, and
- the failure to do this was a major departure from the standard expected.

Sports providers need to make sure events or facilities are safe. They should look at all possible risks and minimise them. If a risk still exists it must be decided whether the risk is too outrageous to take in the circumstances. If it is, then facilities should be closed or events cancelled. To assess the level of care needed in a particular area, sports providers can look at industry standards to give guidance as to what is acceptable.

Intellectual property and sport marketing

This area of law relates to intangible property that has been brought into existence by creative effort. Just like other forms of property it is capable of being owned, so there are certain rights of ownership that are associated with IP and sports marketing. Some of these rights help to protect the owner when the property is 'stolen' or misused by others. The areas associated with IP and sports marketing that this section will look at are: Copyright, Trade Marks and the Fair Trading Act/Trade Practices Act.

Copyright

The Copyright Act 1994 (NZ) and the Copyright Act 1968 (Cth) provides that to qualify for protection it must be shown that there is an 'original work'.

The requirement that a work be 'original' is contained within s14 of the CA 1994(NZ) and s32 CA 1968 (Cth) .What is meant by originality has been further interpreted by the courts in both countries as meaning there must be a degree of skill and work that has been expended by the author, rather than a need for creativity to be a part of the work. In New Zealand and Australia the creation must also be capable of being categorised as one of the following types of 'work': literary, dramatic, musical, or artistic works, photos and engravings, sound recordings, films, broadcasts, and typographical arrangement of published editions. If the creation cannot be categorised within one of these headings it will not be able to gain copyright.

If these requirements are met the author of the copyright work receives rights of ownership that allow the author to show, sell or otherwise use the work as they see fit. The rights of ownership also allow the author to prevent other people from showing, selling or using the work without his/her permission. It should be noted that in some cases the author and the owner may be two different people – for example if a sports club commissioned an artist to design a logo the artist would be the author but the sport club would be the owner.

If copyright material is used without permission then a claim for breach of copyright can be made. If the claim is successful the plaintiff may be able to claim damages or obtain an injunction granted to prevent the defendant from further using the copyright work. To claim that there has been a breach of copyright the owner of the work must show:

a sufficient degree of object similarity, and

a causal connection between the two works.

By showing both of these requirements the owner of the copyright can demonstrate that the infringing copy is derived from the original work. The owner of the copyright need not have to show the whole of the work was copied. It is enough that a substantial part of the original work has been used.

One case where such an action was successful was *Australian Olympic Committee Inc& Sydney Olympics 2000 Bid Ltd v Exerciz Pty Ltd* (unrep) Fed Ct of Australia, NSW No NG784 0f 1993, 9/5/1994. The AOC, who had copyright ownership in the Olympic symbol by way of s5(1) Olympic Insignia Protection Act 1987 (Cth), sought to prevent Exerciz from selling T-Shirts displaying the Olympic logo. The AOC was able to obtain an Anton Pillar Order which allowed them to enter the premises of Exerciz and seize the merchandise.

Trade marks

A trade mark is 'any sign capable of being represented graphically and capable of distinguishing the goods or services of one person from those of another person'. Once they served as an indication of the origin of the product now they are frequently used for marketing purposes, as a form of branding. As with other forms of intellectual property rights a trade mark provides a limited monopoly to the registered holder. This allows the holder to control who can use the mark and to prevent unauthorised users from using the mark as a trade mark (James & Wells (1992) *Guide to the Protection of Innovation & Goodwill* James & Wells: Auckland). Control over the mark is justified on the basis that it protects both the registered holder and the general public from traders trying to capture any goodwill and market power attached to the trade mark. So while the use and protection of the mark is primarily commercial, there is also an element of public protection.

Because the ability to register a trade mark gives the holder legal rights over others there are certain qualifications that must be met before protection is given (refer to the discussion in *Indtex Trading Ltd v Otago Rugby Football Union* (HC, Auckland AP 23-sw01, 10 October 2001, Williams J). A mark must be sufficiently distinctive so at to ensure that the monopoly over the mark does not eliminate all reasonable options open to other traders. For example, if a telephone services company tried to trade mark the word 'telephone' it is unlikely the application would succeed. Another aspect that is considered in registering a mark is the effect that it will have on the public. This is because once a trade mark is registered, it not only allows the holder to prevent others from using the mark it also allows the mark to be shown to the public in an unrestricted way in relation to the class of goods that it is registered for. This means that the mark must not have the ability to confuse the public when placed next to goods of the same class that come from other origins. For example see *Pioneer Hi-Bred Corn Company v Hy-Line Chicks Pty Ltd* [1978] 2 NZLR 50, 56, *Hannaford & Burton v Polaroid Corporation* [1976] 2 NZLR 14, 19, *Levi Strauss & Co v Kimbyr Investments Ltd* [1994] 1 NZLR 332. Once a trade mark has gained registration it may still be removed if a third party applies to have the trade marks revokes due to non-use, offensiveness, genericism or deception/confusion.

The owner of a trade mark gains exclusive rights to use the mark, and so may prevent others from attempting to use that mark or a mark that is very similar in a trade mark sense (which means they are using the mark as a form of identifier) – for example see s89 Trade Marks Act 2002 (NZ). There is some difference as to trade mark protection between Australia and New Zealand. In Australia the right to prevent use only applies if the infringing mark is used in the same category that the original mark i registered in. This results in what is known as trade mark dilution where a famous trade mark that i registered for (e.g.) running shoes could be used by another person for another separate category such as (e.g.) perfume without penalties. This problem has now been overcome in New Zealand by s 89(1 (d) Trade Marks Act 2002 which makes it an infringement to use a famous mark regardless of wha category the famous marks has been registered in.

Trade mark infringement has featured in some sports marketing case such as, *New Zealan Rugby Football Union (Inc) v Saint Publishing Ltd* (HC, Auckland, M 1458/01, 2 October 2001 which involved the publication of a calendar which featured former All Blacks wearing the representative jerseys. The trade mark in question was the insignia on the jerseys. The Cour decided to prevent publication of the calendar because consumers would be confused into thinking that NZRFU had endorsed or was associated with the calendar and the way in which the NZRFU trade mark had been presented was 'use' in a trade mark sense. Another recen successful claim was made by the Otago Rugby Football Union in *Indtex Trading Ltd v Otago Rugb Football Union* (HC, Auckland AP 23-SW01, 10 October 2001) where an application for the trad mark 'Carisbrook Classic Clothing' was rejected due to its similarity with the ORFU trade mark 'Carisbrook Home of Otago Rugby'.

The NZRFU had less success in *New Zealand Rugby Football Union (Inc) v Canterbury International Ltd* (HC, Wellington, CP 167/01, 10 July 2001) the NZRFU was unsuccessful in obtaining an injunction against Canterbury Apparel over use of a silver fern with the words 'The Invincibles' on black rugby style jerseys. The NZRFU had argued that it was a breach of copyright, the Fair Trading Act and that it was trade mark infringement. The Court felt that consumers would not be confused with the product source or be deceived into thinking that NZRFU had endorsed the product. The Court also said that Canterbury had equal rights to use the images of players wearing the jerseys due to the history of its marketing and previous use of such images.

Fair Trading Act 1986 (NZ) / Trade Practices Act 1974(Cth)

Both The Fair Trading Act 1986 (FTA) and the Trade Practices Act 1974 (Cth) have provisions that are designed to protect the *public* from being misled about the activities of traders, though actions are frequently brought by rival traders. This means that the focus is on the conduct of the defendant as to how it impacts on consumers, not other traders.

What is misleading?

The main provision that can be relied on is contained in s 9 FTA 1986 (NZ) and s52 TPA 1974 (Cth) which provides essentially that traders shall not engage in conduct that is misleading. There are some slight differences between the two sections in that the TPA 1974 (Cth) states the entity engaging in the conduct must be a corporation whilst the FTA 1986 (NZ) only requires that it be a 'person in trade'. Also the FTA 1986 (NZ) includes conduct that is *likely* to mislead or deceive.

To show that there is a breach of s9/s52, the key elements are:

- *In trade* – It is possible to be a non-profit organisation but still be classed as being in trade for certain activities. For example a sports club may not be in trade as far as social play is concerned but would be in trade in connection to operating a bar in the clubrooms.
- *Conduct* – This is a broad term which will include omissions and half-truths. So if you 'leave out' important details, you could be liable just as much as if you were making a false claim.
- *Misleading or deceptive* – This will be decided on a case by case basis, with attention being given to the "target audience". If the target audience would gain a wrong idea from the conduct presented then the conduct will be misleading. The target audience is the class of person who would come into contact with the conduct. The target audience is not just the 'reasonable' member of the class. The audience will also include the "very astute and the gullible" (*Taco Company of Australia Pty Ltd v Taco Bell Pty Ltd* (1982) ATPR 40-303), but not the "unusually stupid". If the target audience has special knowledge this can influence as to whether they would be misled. For example, if you are only dealing with elite sportspeople not spectators or beginners you may be able to make some false statements that the elite sportspeople would treat as a 'puff' or a joke. In comparison if your target audience included beginners or spectators they may believe these statements and be misled by them.

Two examples of the two legislations in action are first the *NZ Olympic & Commonwealth Games ssn v Telecom NZ Ltd and Saatchi & Saatchi* (2/5/96, HC Wellington, CP 95/96) where Telecom's use of the Olympic "five ring" logo resulted in a claim under s13(e) (as well as other sections). The action was unsuccessful as it was felt that the average reader would see that it was just a clever marketing technique. The second is *Talmax Pty Ltd v Telstra Corporation Ltd* (1996) ATPR 41-484,in which the defendant had used the image of a well-known swimmer to promote a particular product by way of a photo and comments referring to the swimmer in an article. The action was unsuccessful as it was felt readers who looked at the article in full (rather than just glancing at it) would not be misled into thinking that the swimmer had agreed to use of the image or that the swimmer was endorsing the product.

Major Events Management Act 2007 (NZ)

This legislation was introduced to deal with the problem of ambush marketing and ticket scalping. Ambush marketing is where an organisation will attempt to have a marketing 'free ride' by not paying sponsorship money and instead attaches its own independent marketing to an event. There are two main types of ambush marketing. The first is where the organisation will attempt to associate itself with an event/product. An example of this is the *NZ Olympic & Commonwealth Games Assn v Telecom NZ Ltd and Saatchi & Saatchi* situation where Telecom used its marketing to associate its product with the games. Ambush marketing may also be intrusive. This is where the organisation actually invades the event with its marketing/branding. To protect against these practices, the Major Events Management Act 2007 (MEMA 2007) provides for penalties in situations where an organisation uses 'protected' words and images so as to suggest an association to a major event, and also provides for 'clean zones' where no marketing other than official marketing may occur. There are also penalties for 'pitch invasion' and scalping tickets. To gain any of the protections listed below, the first step that must happen is for the event to be declared a major event by the Governor-General in accordance with s7.

Ambush marketing by association is protected against via s 10 which provides that no person may make a representation that suggests an association between goods/services and a major event. The use of any major event emblems/words will be presumed to be in breach of s10 unless an exception applies. The exceptions include; being given authorisation by the event organiser, use for news reporting/coverage, use for private opinion, and 'honest' business use (s12).

Protection against Ambush marketing by intrusion occurs by way of 'clean zones' which are active during a 'clean period'. The zone will consist of the venue for the major event and the area that is directly proximate to it, (s16(3)). As well as a 'clean zone', the Economic Development Minister may also declare a 'clean transport route' which can be up to 5km from the outer area of 'clean zone' (s16(4)). Both a clean zone and a clean transport route will not include 'excluded land or buildings' (private land and buildings) that are within the areas (s16(5)). No unauthorised person may engage in street selling in a clean zone (s17), no person may advertise (s18) or have advertising that is visible in a clean zone (s19) in a clean zone or advertise in a clean transport route (s20). Exceptions to this prohibition are listed in s22 and include advertising through 'honest business practice', articles of clothing worn by the public (unless there is more than one person with the advertising and wearing the clothing is intended to intrude on the major event) and clothing worn by participants in the major event and volunteers connected to the major event. There is a defence contained in s24, which provides a defence to advertising and media companies who publish an advertisement as part of their normal course of business and have had no idea that such publication would be a breach of s18-20.

Other protections include provisions for Ticket-scalping which is where people buy up tickets to an event and sell them at a very high price once tickets to the event have run out. This practice is prohibited for a major event; since s25 provides that no person may sell or trade tickets for a price higher than the original price. Pitch invasion is also provided for, although it has generally been harmless, it has on occasions resulted on disruptions which could impact on sponsors of the event by creating a negative association. To protect against this, s27 provides that no unauthorised person can go onto or propel and object onto the playing surface of a major event.

Critical Argument Summary Box

Should we have legislation like MEMA

For:
- Greater protection for sponsors.
- Stops 'free loading' via ambush marketing.
- Can protect spectators from unauthorised dealers.
- The legislation provides greater certainty of what is/is not allowed compared to broader areas of law such as the FTA.

Against:
- Not needed as other law is suitable to protect sponsor interests.
- Can punish behaviour that is not overly harmful such as pitch invasion.
- Only applies to certain events so is limited protection.
- Does not prevent other forms of 'free loading' such as price gouging.

Summary

As can be seen by the discussion in this chapter there are many examples of how a sports provider could encounter problems due to underestimating the way in which the law impacts on the performance of their activities. The impact and number of legal issues will increase when the sports provider is in a professional sports environment but this does not mean 'local' sports should ignore potential concerns. A local club could be sued for negligence in much the same way that an organiser of a national event could – and the resulting financial consequences could be more damaging for a local club. So no matter what level of operation, a sports provider should be aware of the legal consequences in performing certain activities.

While it may seem that compliance with the law and the penalties that arise from a failure to comply are sometimes weighted against the provision of some sports activities, law and sport do not need to be 'enemies' of one another. Both have rules and a need to obey the rules so that all participants can benefit through a safe and fair environment. In both situations problems can be overcome by knowing what the rules are.

Knowledge of the 'rules' does not require sports providers to be legal experts. They do not have to know the finer points of how wording within a contract may be interpreted if a dispute arises, nor do they have to know the full process of registering a trade mark. What sports providers do need to know is that these actions can produce certain legal results and should therefore be handled by someone with expertise in law. This does not mean that a sports provider must have lawyer on "speed dial" for each and every activity, but they should have access to legal advice for important actions/events.

The main aim for sports providers is to minimise potential legal problems. This can be achieved if the sports provider is able to identify and understand situations where legal issues may arise and when professional legal advice may be needed.

CASE STUDY: WHATBALL SPORTS

The international Whatball competition has taken place. The competition proved to be very popular with spectators, on the first few nights Andy limited the number of people coming in to watch for safety reasons, but on the final night he decided to let more people come in. "After all", Andy thought, "this will help to make up for the sponsorship money that was lost". The extra people were placed very close to the court. During a very aggressive game some of the players were pushed hard into the extra spectators this caused a minor riot to start as spectators were pushed against another. An elderly woman was amongst these spectators and was so scared by the pushing and crowding that she had a heart attack. Andy, while upset that the woman was harmed comments that 'well mistakes sometimes happen'. Unfortunately for Andy, the elderly woman has a grandson who is a lawyer and is now preparing to sue. If Andy has a better understanding of sport law he may now realise the trouble he is in.

Review questions

- Jill has made a sponsorship contract with Brian a young swimmer aged 171/2 years. The terms of the contract are very generous to Brian and do not require Brian to do anything that could be regarded as exploitive. Would this contract be enforceable?
- What are the elements of a binding contract?
- Marshall's Gym has a membership contract that states it will not be 'liable for any loss/damage to property or harm to any person'. Jackie is injured whilst on the treadmill as the treadmill had not been serviced for a long time and came to an abrupt halt while she was on it. Explain, if Jackie was able to mount a claim based on injury, whether the exclusion clause would prevent liability.
- Sandra is organising a big triathlon. It is the first time she has organised an event like this. She is told by local surf lifesavers that the area of sea marked out for the swimming portion has a dangerous rip. There are no other areas of sea that can be used without altering the entire race. Sandra decided to go ahead with the race as it is. If a race contestant is harmed while swimming could Sandra be held liable?
- Jock has decided to produce jerseys in the same colour and design as the Manawatu Rugby Union design and sell them to tourists coming to Manawatu. Can the MRU stop him from doing this?

Advancing your understanding

Burrows, J. F., Finn, J., Todd, S. M. D. (2002). *Law of contract in New Zealand*. Wellington: LexisNexis Butterworths.

Elliott, C. (2008). Ambush marketing: A wide new sponsorship right. *NZLJ*, 207.

James & Wells (1992). *Guide to the protection of innovation & goodwill*. Auckland: James & Wells.

Sadler, P., & Guthrie, R. (2001). Sports injuries and the right to compensation. *Legal Issues in Business, 3*, 9-14.

Thorpe, Buti, Davies, Fridman, Jonson. (2009). *Sports law*. Victoria, Australia: Oxford University Press.

Todd, S. (Ed). (2001). *The law of torts in New Zealand*. Wellington, New Zealand: Brooker's.

References

Kelly, G. M. (1987). *Sport and the law*. Sydney, NSW: The Law Book Co.

Chapter 17

Sport Event Management: Creating Engaging Experiences

Nico Schulenkorf and Deborah Edwards

OBJECTIVES

After completing this chapter, you should be able to:

- define the term 'sport event experience';
- understand the concepts and theories underpinning the management of sport event experiences for different stakeholders;
- apply management principles and sociological concepts to sport events in an Australian and New Zealand context;
- understand the importance of sport event leverage as a form of maximising positive event experiences and associated benefits;
- identify areas of future research for analysing and designing engaging event experiences.

Introduction

This chapter is concerned with an increasingly popular area of the experience economy, the management of sport events. Sport events represent a temporary drawing together of resources to create a particular experience for participants, spectators and other stakeholders. Depending on the size of the sport event it can take weeks, months, or years of preparation to deliver an experience that is over in a matter of hours or days. Sport event management is fundamentally about creating engaging experiences, and leveraging them to achieve lasting benefits for all those involved. Getting the experience right such that participants, spectators and other stakeholders are satisfied is critically important for the future popularity of any sport event.

This chapter focuses on examining sport event experiences and investigates the meanings attached to them. It combines the areas of event planning, management and design and uses examples from Australia, New Zealand and international contexts to illustrate the significance of sport events in our society. In particular, the chapter presents an overview of how sport activities can be designed to impact positively on people, so that engaging experiences (Pine & Gilmore 2011) can be created. Our starting point is a discussion of the term 'experience'. We then review the literature on sport event experiences, before moving to an analysis of the importance of experiences for different sport event stakeholders. Moreover, we examine the concept of sport event leverage to understand the processes of maximising engaging experiences beyond the sport event. Finally, suggestions for future research in the area of event experiences and sport event leverage are provided.

Defining the sport event experience

Before we discuss sport event experiences in more detail, we need to establish what the term actually means and how it is typically used in the sport event context. In everyday conversation, people may use the term 'experience' as either a verb or a noun. For example:

"We experienced a fantastic atmosphere at the Rugby World Cup." (Verb)
"I have a lot of experience in organising sport events." (Noun)

In both examples, people add a certain meaning to the word 'experience'. Getz (2007) segmented experience into the three dimensions 'conative', 'cognitive' and 'affective'. The 'conative' dimension of experience describes people's actual behaviour, e.g., the experience of running in a marathon. The 'cognitive' dimension refers to awareness, perception, memory, learning, judgement, understanding or making sense of an experience. An example of this is people attending a sport congress and discussing new ideas and research with like-minded others. Finally, the 'affective' dimension includes the feelings, emotions and values attached to a particular experience. Feeling pride and happiness when a favoured team wins a sporting competition falls into this category. These dimensions are not mutually exclusive; in fact, people may be satisfied with their event experience in one dimension, but feel disappointed in another. For instance, it is certainly possible to attend a sport event where you have not learned anything new (cognitive), but the atmosphere and interaction between people was very sociable (affective) resulting in an experience that was, overall, enjoyable.

Whilst an experience lacks tangibility it is not an amorphous construct, it is as real an offering as any service, good, or commodity (Pegg & Patterson, 2010). According to Pine and Gilmore (2011) there are a multiplicity of dimensions to be considered when envisioning engaging experiences such as whether the experience is shared with others, the intensity and duration of the experience, the multisensory nature of the experience (sights, sounds, smells, weather), the level of personal meaningfulness attached to them, prior life experiences and cultural considerations. These dimensions engage individuals on an emotional, physical, intellectual, and or spiritual level in which they are co-creators of their own experience (Pegg & Patterson, 2010; Lusch, Vargo, & Brien, 2007; Pine & Gilmore, 1999, 2011). Fundamentally, experiences are intensely personal and no two people can have the 'same' experience, however they can 'share' similar experiences.

Understanding sport event experiences

The sport event context has two qualities that can facilitate stakeholders' engagement in the co-creation of their experience; a boundary and a theme (Carù & Cova, 2007). The beginning and end nature of sport events acts as a boundary that enables stakeholders to contrast the sport event experience to their daily lives. This boundary also reduces the likelihood of other non-related intrusive elements appearing that can diminish the intensity of the experience (Carù & Cova, 2007). The theme acts as a symbolic packaging of the context (Carù & Cova, 2007), which appeals to the special interests of those involved. The role of sport event management is therefore to create a themed environment from beginning to end which facilitates engaged experiences for all stakeholders involved, including participants, athletes, performers, spectators, volunteers and staff (Berridge, 2007). Importantly, event managers – whether volunteers responsible for a club tournament or professionals working at a major international sport event – require a thorough understanding of their stakeholders and a commitment to providing an engaging sport event. In sport event management, this thorough understanding can be achieved by developing a conceptual and theoretical appreciation of the sport event experience, and by approaching the management of events in a systematic and methodical way.

Building on the work of Klap (2006) we argue there are two broad sets of factors that are required for the creation of engaging events (see Figure 17-1). The first set is the Operational Factors necessary for ensuring that a 'Baseline' or minimum standard is provided. In a sport event context they include factors such as an adequate number of staff, appropriate equipment and facilities, and adequate risk and safety precautions. It is argued that these factors serve to remove dissatisfaction and improve performance, but they cannot be relied upon to generate engaging experiences that are going beyond expectations.

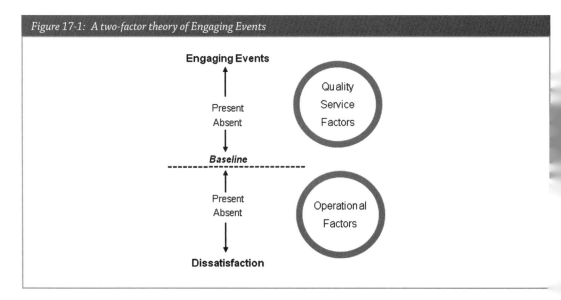

Figure 17-1: A two-factor theory of Engaging Events

The second set of factors is Quality Service Factors. These factors can help lift events above the baseline level to the point where they become engaging. Quality service factors can include organisers enthusiasm, flexibility, and a creative responsiveness to stakeholder needs. In seeking to understand how athletes, performers, spectators, volunteers and staff members experience an event and how they expect an engaging event to be, it is necessary to think beyond the interaction that forms the event 'occasion'. Various authors (Drummond & Anderson, 2004; Lee & Shafer, 2002; Rossman & Elwood Schlatter, 2008) have suggested that the event experience begins well before spectators take their seats or players appear on the field, and also extends beyond the time when the final whistle is blown. Such a holistic view on event experiences should underpin all management activities and we will return to this in the following sections of the chapter.

In analysing event experiences for different stakeholders, Pine and Gilmore (2011) discern two broad dimensions that sit along a continuum; participation (active-passive) and connection (absorption-immersion). When combined these dimensions bring together four realms of experience - entertainment, educational, aesthetic and escapist (Figure 17-2). This model is useful in understanding the creation and meaning of experiences in the sport event context.

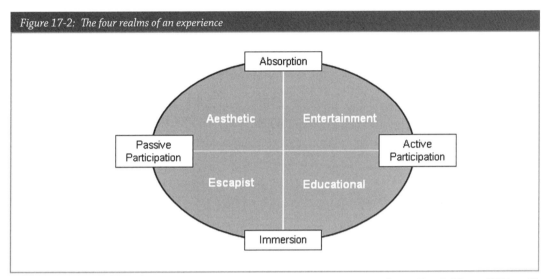

Figure 17-2: The four realms of an experience

Source: Pine & Gilmore (2011, p. 46)

According to Pine and Gilmore (2011) participation can be either active or passive. Active participation would include athletes, performers or judges. Passive participation would include spectators or people who are attending the sport event as observers. However, these spectators also contribute to the atmosphere of the sport event. Connection represents how immersed or absorbed a person is in the sport event. A spectator absorbs the experience of a sport event from a distance whilst athletes are immersed in the activities of the sport event itself as well as the sights, sounds and smells of the spectators around them. The four realms of experience comingle as mutually compatible domains (Pine & Gilmore, 2011). Truly engaging experiences are created when the blurring of different boundaries occurs. Staging engaging experiences therefore requires the incorporation of more than one of the four realms of experience. It begins with embracing an experience-directed mindset, which is not only about the design and production of 'things' but also about the design and orchestration of experiences using these 'things' (Pine & Gilmore, 2011).

Creating engaging experiences

According to Clawson (1963) there is a multi-layered production of 'experience' that consists of five key stages: anticipation; travel to the event; the direct experience; travel from the event; and recollection. Similarly, Drummond and Anderson (2004) divide the event experience into four different stages, namely pre-event; arrival at the venue; engaging in the event; and post-event. Both authors have an extended view of the event experience which provides a framework that can be used for planning and managing various aspects of an event, including the management of stakeholders such as athletes and performers, spectators and fans, sponsors and VIPs, and the media. Furthermore, the extended framework allows for the generation of leverage beyond an event and at times from sources peripheral to the main event. With this holistic view of event management in mind, we now turn to the significant sport event stakeholders and examine how event organisers may satisfy their experience needs. Whilst reading the following discussion, keep in mind the following questions:

- What can be done to enhance the aesthetic value of the sport event? What can make the environment comfortable and inviting? What sense of place can be created to encourage people to stay longer?
- How will the escapist aspect of the sport event draw participants in? How could you encourage stakeholders to be immersed in the event?
- What can the different stakeholders learn from experiencing the event? What activities can help them engage in learning new knowledge and skills?
- What entertainment can the sport event offer to assist stakeholders to enjoy their experience better?

Athletes and performers

In a sports context, athletes and performers are the key to any special event experience. The event is all about them and their contribution, their activity, their show. However, in creating an experience for others, athletes and performers also have their own experiences at events. Typically, this experience begins when athletes and performers first become aware of an event. Depending on the type, size and scale of the occasion, they may have to register, qualify or be invited to participate. Professional athletes are likely to prepare and train long before the first whistle is blown, and they look forward in anticipation to the day when they can perform, compete and show their skills. Importantly, for athletes to experience an engaging event, participation has to be about more than just winning. While in competitive sport the intent of winning may always be present, many people compete for personal reasons such as to gain fitness or a sense of accomplishment, while others engage in events for social or cultural reasons (Filo, Funk, & O'Brien, 2008; Misener & Mason, 2006). They may want to have a good time with their teammates, enjoy each other's company and feel part of a group or sub-culture (Green & Chalip, 1998). Here, sport becomes meaningful because of the sense of community that is created.

For some event performers the competitive element may be completely removed from the sporting agenda. For example, a juggling artist or a dancing group that perform to entertain the crowd are physically engaged at a sporting event, but they often do so without direct competitors or opposing teams. As supporting acts they perform primarily for leisure, social or entertainment reasons. Performing may also provide them with additional self-esteem and a feeling of mastery or professional confidence (Berridge, 2007). Furthermore, performers become part of a larger event community, in which they get to experience and enjoy the main act and additional ancillary activities. For example, artists performing at Opening Ceremonies at Olympic Games become part of the Olympic Movement and get to enjoy the spirit of the Games as 'insiders'.

It is important to remember that athletes are the key to successful sport events, and that their needs and wishes are respected (Drummond & Anderson, 2004). A positive 'can do' relationship need to be established and maintained before, during and after the event. While interaction before and during the event seem to be obvious success-factors, communication in the post-event phase is often neglected. However, in the attempt to sustain relationships and opportunities for future engagements and networking, communication and appraisal after the event is crucial. For example, to recollect positive experiences athletes could be provided with something tangible to take away from the occasion. In addition to potential prize money, trophies, medals and/or awards for winning teams, all individuals could be given certificates for their participation or souvenirs, photos or CDs/DVDs that remind them of their experience. These kinds of memorabilia can reinforce the connection between an athlete and an event, and will help to establish positive and lasting memories.

Spectators and fans

For spectators, the attendance at an event can be motivated by a number of different factors. For instance, parents and grandparents travel to sporting competitions week after week to see their children and grandchildren play. Other families enjoy local events that happen in their states or communities, while the ultra-committed travel around the world to witness special events such as World Championships, Commonwealth Games or Olympic Games. Most spectators agree that it is simply more exciting to be part of a live event in a stadium compared to watching sports at home on TV. Event involvement can be an adventure or a social escape for people; Chen (2006) even suggests that for loyal fans travelling to sport events and experiencing the atmosphere around events can be a described as a 'pilgrimage' of experiences. Again, the sense of community or communitas created at events has a special meaning to people and their respective groups or sub-groups (Chalip, 2006; Green & Chalip, 1998). In fact, it almost seems as if the stadium has become the church of the 21st century – a special and spiritual place for dedicated fans.

Irrespective of the level of dedication and involvement, anyone attending an event is seeking to be entertained through an engaging experience. In other words, entertainment, joy and fun are *generic* experiences that will occur at any type of event irrespective of its purpose (Getz, 2007). In essence, these generic experiences are ambiguous and have nothing to do with the design of a particular event programme, setting or theme. In contrast, *specific* event experiences relate to purposefully planned events that have a particular significance. For example, cultural celebrations are generally about seeking knowledge, learning and understanding, while carnivals are associated with spectacle, revelry and symbolism. Events with a clear purpose, message or theme will leave a more memorable and lasting impression, as they have a special meaning for people.

When planning and designing sport event experiences, organisers need to be aware of these meanings and design the event programme accordingly. In fact, the spectators' experience of any event begins long before the gates open; it begins when they first become aware of the event. Organisers can influence these early stages of the overall experience with a well-designed pre-event build-up, e.g., creative news reports, media advisories and advertising, so that interest is created and people decide to become part of the show (Allen, O'Toole, Harris, & McDonnell, 2011; Drummond & Anderson, 2004; Shukla & Nuntsu, 2005). It may be the creative promotion of a certain sports team, a certain player, a certain tournament or a special event theme that catches their attention. Furthermore, the opportunity for people to seek additional information online through an interactive webpage will help to promote the event, and a hassle-free purchase of online tickets will create a positive impression and expectations in its lead-up. In other words, the website performance as well as online ticketing/ payment options become part of the event experience that will impact on people's opinion regarding the event's organisation and efficiency.

On the day of the event, factors such as public transport options, traffic conditions and parking become part of the audience's experience when travelling to the venue. Upon their arrival at the venue, visual aspects such as decorations or support elements such as information stands, greeting staff and clear signage can make a positive difference. Most important, however, is the direct experience at the event. The event as a service product is the main reason why people attend and it should provide them with a positive and lasting impression. One way of achieving this is through a convincing and stimulating theme that unifies the different areas of an event (Allen et al., 2011; Tassiopoulos, 2005). According to Getz (2007), a convincing theme alters the audience's sense of place, time and reality. This means that the theme should underpin event planning and design; themes should also be made tangible and memorable through 'positive cues' that leave lasting impressions, including factors such as high-quality customer service, creative decorations, extraordinary performances and entertainment, special food and beverages and various other sensory stimulations.

A certain "Wow Factor" may further enhance the audience's experience (Ralston, Ellis, Compton, & Lee, 2007). A Wow Factor is often seen as a guiding principle for event designers who try to impress the audience through 'something well out of the ordinary'. The Wow Factor may be part of the advertising and promotion campaign, or it may come as an element of special surprise to event attendees. While used in different ways, it is always expected to contribute significantly to customer delight, engagement and overall satisfaction. A lot of planning needs to go into the identification of a suitable and the thematically relevant Wow Factor. For a beach theme event, a guest appearance of swimming legend Ian Thorpe or surf champion Kelly Slater is likely to fascinate people. At a 'Rippa Rugby' sport development event in New Zealand, the same can be said for a guest visit of All Black Dan Carter. Alternatively, a wow factor may consist of visual impressions such as special performances of art and spectacle (Getz, 2007; Ralston et al., 2007). Sound or lighting may also contribute to a special atmosphere and style. Light shows or firework displays – if they are well designed and for example supported by special musical elements – may be relevant ideas. Whatever the Wow Factor, it needs to be electrifying!

Finally, because of the high level of affection between sport spectators and their favourite club/ team/sport/event there should always be the opportunity for spectators to purchase memorabilia of their experience. It will help individuals with the recollection of the day and provide an additional hook for emotional engagement. In the end, many sport events are business affairs and organisers can make good money from selling event souvenirs and memorabilia. Targeted post-event promotions and follow-up material received from event organisers may further increase the likelihood of recollection, spending and repeat visitation.

Sponsors, VIPs and the media

Sport events allow sponsors to become involved in several different ways. For example, they can engage as business partners enabling them to provide hospitality to invited guests and special clientele at an event. In other words, sponsors can have their own stands, booths or lounges at events where very important persons (VIPs) are entertained or the public is informed about new products, services or campaigns. Alternatively, sponsors attend an event and become VIPs themselves, being invited by the organisers in return for their (financial) contribution to the occasion. In any case, the primary experience sponsors enjoy at events is around creating business relations or networks with other leaders and potential partners from the sports and business worlds.

Event organisers need to give special attention to their sponsors and other VIPs. Whether they are sport stars, royalty, celebrities, politicians or business leaders, VIPs require special treatment, honour, respect and security. Because of the high demands, entertaining VIPs can be a difficult and delicate process that requires a lot of attention to detail; furthermore, exclusive access to private areas, lounges or VIP boxes is generally expected. In this private environment, VIP treatment includes specific and exclusive hospitality services, exceptional entertainment options, or the provision of high quality technical equipment. While VIPs are generally separated from the ordinary sport spectators, at times organisers can use their attendance to the event's benefit. A public appearance or involvement of VIPs can for example provide sporting events with special flair and importance, e.g., the Queen's visit at Wimbledon Finals or Archbishop Tutu's speech at the opening of the 2010 Football World Cup. In these cases, event organisers have purposely included VIPs as part of their strategy in creating a special experience and increasing the event's profile.

The media is another stakeholder group that can impact significantly on the profile and image of events. The media communicates the success (or otherwise) of events to the wider community and creates a picture of the event experience in people's minds. Clearly, event organisers need to make sure that influential media personnel is very well looked after. If journalists have positive experiences at an event, the likelihood of good publicity increases and the image of the event and its organisers can be positively affected. On the contrary, negative experiences may lead to journalists reporting unenthusiastically about an event which may damage its image or reputation. When part of the media is involved as an official event sponsor, they can expect to have priority access to players, coaches and other VIPs. While an official partnership with a media organisation has the benefit of positive media exposure being everything but guaranteed, the combination of 'official' and 'unofficial' media at one event may potentially cause some conflict over access and priorities. This confirms Nicholson's (2007) view that media management is one of the most important and delicate areas in strategic sport and event management. Accordingly, larger events nowadays employ media managers whose main focus is on entertaining media relations and satisfying demands.

Event staff and volunteers

As discussed, the job of sport event organisers and other staff members is to create a memorable experience for all stakeholders of an event. However, in creating experiences staff also have their own experiences. Ideally, staff members enjoy their involvement in contributing to an event and experience a form of professional accomplishment through their work (Getz, 2007). When looking at creating positive experiences for staff members in more detail, a number of important factors need to be considered. For example, to avoid confusion and complaints organisers need to set the stage by providing clarification of management hierarchies, supervisory roles and reporting responsibilities. Further, a clear understanding of the event as a whole should be instilled in all staff irrespective of their position. Too often frontline staff (such as race marshals or ticketing officers) know little about the overall organisation of an event and so cannot answer questions from the public or respond effectively things go wrong. Here, a staff briefing detailing topics such as the purpose of the event, the overall layout of the venue, and the programme of activities can be a useful supplement to more specific job or task training. Such a briefing is a good way of ensuring staff can exhibit those previously discussed Quality Service Factors (see Figure 17-1) needed to create an engaging event for spectators and fans. For example, confident and satisfied staff members are likely to show more enthusiasm, flexibility and responsiveness to customers, which can impact significantly on visitors' event experience.

Almost all sport events – from community celebrations to Olympic Games – rely on the input and engagement of volunteers. According to Schlenker, Edwards and Wearing (2011) volunteers are the backbone to sport events and their contributions save organisers significant amounts of money. Therefore, providing volunteers with rewarding and engaging experiences in return for their commitment is an important aspect of sport event management. Effective volunteer management requires a detailed understanding of people's motivations and skills. This knowledge can assist sport event organisers to utilise volunteer skills more efficiently, and match individuals with rewarding tasks that create positive volunteer experiences. To further improve efficiency, event organisers are increasingly monitoring volunteers' motivations, previous roles and experiences, skills, interests, availability and training needs through custom-designed volunteer management software packages. These packages not only allow easy storage and retrieval of data but also help generate work schedules and volunteer mail-outs for future events. While software packages may not be needed for smaller one-off community events, they are of invaluable benefit for re-occurring events and large-scale celebrations.

Leveraging sport events for broader long-term benefits

In contrast to regular sport programs, the hosting of sport events in a community is often infrequent and over a limited period of time. Therefore, one of the great challenges for event organisers is to utilise the momentum of sport events to strategically plan for lasting outcomes for the community (Chalip, 2004, 2006; Kellett, Hede, & Chalip, 2008; O'Brien, 2007; O'Brien & Chalip, 2008). This phenomenon is referred to as 'event leverage'. To achieve event leverage, sport event organisers need to move beyond the planning of direct event impacts towards focusing on strategic paths which achieve lasting outcomes for host communities.

Significant opportunities to leverage a sport event exist in economic and social areas. For example in the area of economic leverage, event organisers can employ strategies during the sport event that encourage repeat visitation by event participants and attendees as future tourists to the host region (Chalip & Leyns, 2002; Chalip & McGuirty, 2004; Costa & Chalip, 2005; O'Brien, 2006). Sport events can be used to foster long-term business relationships between the community and sponsors by encouraging future trade, investment and employment. From a social perspective Chalip (2004, 2006) argues that liminality and communitas can be seen as 'raw material' for social leverage, as they result from a sense of celebration and social camaraderie that can exist around events. Liminality is seen to apply to phases of cultural change, in which previous orderings of thought and behaviour are subject to revision and criticism (Turner & Turner, 1978). The key, then, is to leverage liminoid experiences and the sense of togetherness to achieve lasting social benefits for the community beyond events. Sport events in particular provide a promising arena for social leverage because participants and attendees can experience authentic human interactions not bounded by socioeconomic and socio-political position, status, and roles. For example, sport events may be used as a platform to highlight pressing community issues, or to change people's perception regarding certain social problems or values. The staging of the

Homeless World Cup in Melbourne in 2010 is an example of this. Here, organisers aligned the sport event with a particular social issue and they cooperated with the media to showcase and publicise both the challenges and potential of homeless people in the community (see Sherry, 2010).

On the largest scale, sport events such as the Rugby World Cup or the Olympic Games provide significant opportunities for social and cultural leverage. Garcia (2001), for example, examined the potential of the 2000 Olympics to be enhanced by an arts festival. Her study suggests that event augmentations such as cultural festivities do have the potential to extend the appeal and fascination of the focal sport event, as they may expand the social dimensions of the main event and generate multiple socio-cultural narratives and meaningful symbols. However, Garcia found that the actual Sydney Olympics' cultural program was largely unsuccessful in providing this added experience to the community, as there was a lack of strategic integration between the sport and cultural activities; an ambiguous understanding of the roles and function of the cultural program; and an ineffective handling of integrative programming elements. The organisers of the cultural arts festivals were not able to utilise, communicate, and leverage the significant synergies among sport, culture and arts, which means that a great opportunity for additional social experiences was lost.

When attempting to leverage sport events with the intention to reach the wider community, event organisers and communities need to expand their connections with key decision makers to generate additional political, educational, promotional and financial benefits. For example, support from different levels of government may secure political backing, financial contributions and permission for the staging and leveraging of sport events. Similarly, active engagement with local businesses is needed to achieve economic leverage. Event organisers and the host community can, for example, cooperate with local businesses and sponsors to create "an event-related look-and-feel" (Chalip, 2004. p. 230) in the host community. This may be achieved by executing event related products, promotions and theming tactics. For example, during the 2011 Rugby World Cup in New Zealand, the Takapuna community on Auckland's North Shore focused their leverage campaign including event advertising and sponsorship around a "French theme". With the French rugby team training on the North Shore during their World Cup preparations, the Takapuna community 'adopted' the team and decorated their main streets with French flags and colours to show their support. Local businesses bought into the theme and sold French food and different types of fan apparel such as T-shirts, support gear or friendship bands in blue, red and white. However, an opportunity missed was the staging of an ancillary event such as a French food and wine festival, which would have further strengthened the connection between the local community and their adopted team. It would have also allowed for business promotions targeted at Wold Cup visitors and international tourists, who could have been encouraged to spend time and money in the Takapuna community. Overall, the example suggests that long-term strategic planning is required to successfully leverage events for expanded experiences and wider benefits. Event organisers and communities need to work closely together to maximise an event's potential, and to develop direct event impacts into lasting event outcomes.

Future research: Maximising engaging experiences

A number of problems exist in creating and staging experiences. Experiences can become marginally less enjoyable after the first time and even less enjoyable after the second time and so on. This process can lead to what is called the commoditisation of the experience (Pine & Gilmore, 2011). To escape the commoditisation trap research that deepens the understanding of sport event stakeholders can provide insights into ways in which the sport event can be customised to provide entertainment, educational, escapist and aesthetic elements that engage them personally.

Due to the intangible nature of experiences they perish with the performance. Fortunately, however, individuals attach great value to engaging experiences which, can then linger in the memory of the person who was engaged in the sport event. Understanding the relationship individuals have with the sport event and how they co-create their experience is a broadened perspective that spans beyond the immediate sport event. To answer the question of why and how individuals become connected and stay immersed, relevant aspects of the individuals' past and future become key areas of investigation. Research is re-focused from description and explanation of an activity to interpreting and understanding the sport event and its contributors. Such experience-based research will contribute to a multi-relational understanding of stakeholders and can lead to strategies for strengthening the co-creational process before, during and after the sporting event.

Event research has for a long time focused on the examination and assessment of a range of immediate sport event impacts (Anderson & Solberg, 1999; Burnett, 2001; Coalter & Taylor, 2010; Crompton, 2004; Lenskyj, 2002; Richards & Wilson, 2004). However, there is a lack of research that combines and evaluates both the direct impacts and long-term outcomes of the same event. This impact-outcome relationship provides another opportunity for rigorous research and a more holistic evaluation of an event's performance. If sport events are staged to make a significant difference to the host community, post event research is required to assess whether the outcomes and potential legacies have met the goals and objectives of the sport event (Schulenkorf, in press). Finally, the theoretical models of strategic event management and sport event leverage that are emerging (Chalip, 2004; O'Brien & Chalip, 2008) require testing, confirmation and development in order to be used as strategic guidelines for event organisers.

Summary

Staging sport events means providing engaging experiences on a number of dimensions and levels in which stakeholders are co-creators of their experiences. This chapter has shown that event organisers are required to satisfy a variety of stakeholders and provide enjoyable and meaningful experiences for everyone involved in a sport event. Organisers need to create a positive and encouraging environment for performers, stage exciting and memorable events for spectators and fans, and at the same time look after their staff and volunteers as the 'engine' for event management. This chapter first explored the meaning of the term 'experience' and explained its conative, cognitive and affective dimensions. While some event experiences are generic and apply to all events, others are specific to the type of event staged. Depending on the purpose of the occasion, events can for example be designed to celebrate a certain sub-culture or to create a sense of community. Moreover, the chapter highlighted the importance of leveraging sport events by maximising positive impacts to achieve wider benefit for the community. Finally, opportunities for future research and empirical investigations around sport event experiences and leverage were suggested.

People often have the naïve belief that anyone can organise a sport event. As we have seen, this belief does not hold true and instead detailed strategic planning, purposeful design and in-depth research is needed to inform the elements of a quality event experience. Only a solid understanding of different event stakeholders and their varying motivations and experiences will allow organisers to create truly memorable and engaging events.

Review questions

- Discuss the behavioural, emotional and psychological dimensions of 'experience'?
- In what ways can event experiences be truly engaging?
- Identify the operational factors and the service quality factors that would be necessary to stage a local, state and national sporting event.
- Give three examples of a Wow Factor for an end-of-season sport event at your local sports club.
- Using the Rugby World Cup as your example, show how stakeholders may experience the event in different ways, related to the four realms of experience – entertainment, educational, escapist and aesthetic.
- How could event organisers have leveraged Sydney's annual City to Surf event for wider social and economic outcomes?
- In what way could have the Rugby World Cup been leveraged to benefit the city of Christchurch, which was unable to host any Games after the Earthquake disaster in 2010?

References

Allen, J., O'Toole, W., Harris, R., & McDonnell, I. (2011). *Festival and special event management* (5th ed.). Milton, Qld: John Wiley & Sons.

Anderson, J., & Solberg, H. (1999). Leisure events and regional economic impacts. *World Leisure and Recreation, 41*(1), 20–28.

Berridge, G. (2007). *Events design and experience* (1st ed.). Burlington, MA: Butterworth-Heinemann.

Burnett, C. (2001). Social impact assessment and sport development: Social spin-offs of the Australia-South Africa junior sport programme. *International Review for the Sociology of Sport, 36*(1), 41–57.

Carù, A., & Cova, B. (2007). Consumer immersion in an experiential context. In A. Carù & B. Cova (Eds.), *Consuming Experience* (pp. 34–47). London: Routledge.

Chalip, L. (2004). Beyond impact: A general model for host community event leverage. In B. Ritchie & D. Adair (Eds.), *Sport tourism: Interrelationships, impacts and issues* (pp. 226–252). Clevedon: Channel View.

Chalip, L. (2006). Towards social leverage of sport events. *Journal of Sport and Tourism, 11*(2), 109–127.

Chalip, L., & Leyns, A. (2002). Local business leveraging of a sport event: Managing an event for economic benefit. *Journal of Sport Management, 16*(2), 132–158.

Chalip, L., & McGuirty, J. (2004). Bundling sport events with the host destination. *Journal of Sport Tourism, 9*(3), 267–282.

Chen, P.-J. (2006). The attributes, consequences, and values associated with event sport tourists' behavior: A means-end chain approach. *Event Management, 10*(1), 1–22.

Clawson, M. (1963). *Land and water for recreation: Opportunities, problems and policies*. Chicago: Rand McNally.

Coalter, F., & Taylor, J. (2010). *Sport-for-development impact study*. Stirling: Department of Sport Studies, University of Stirling.

Costa, C. A., & Chalip, L. (2005). Adventure sport tourism in rural revitalisation - an ethnographic evaluation. *European Sport Management Quarterly, 5*(3), 257–279.

Crompton, J. L. (2004). Beyond economic impact: An alternative rationale for the public subsidy of major league sports facilities. *Journal of Sport Management, 18*(1), 40–58.

Drummond, S., & Anderson, H. (2004). Service quality and managing your people. In I. Yeoman, M. Robertson, J. Ali-Knight, S. Drummond & U. McMahon-Beattie (Eds.), *Festival and Events Management* (pp. 80–96). Oxford and Burlington: Elsevier ButterworFilo, K., Funk, D., & O'Brien, D. (2008). It's really not about the bike: exploring attraction and attachment to the events of the Lance Armstrong Foundation. *Journal of Sport Management, 22*(5), 501–525.

Garcia, B. (2001). Enhancing sport marketing through cultural and arts programs: Lessons from the Sydney 2000 Olympic Arts Festival. *Sport Management Review, 4*(2), 193–219.

Getz, D. (2007). *Event studies: Theory, research and policy for planned events.* Oxford: Butterworth-Heinemann.

Green, B., & Chalip, L. (1998). Sport tourism as the celebration of subculture. *Annals of Tourism Research, 25*(2), 275–291.

Kellett, P., Hede, A.-M., & Chalip, L. (2008). Social policy for sport events: Leveraging (relationships with) teams from other nations for community benefit. *European Sport Management Quarterly, 8*(2), 101–122.

Klap, A. (2006). Event management. In S. Leberman, C. Collins & L. Trenberth (Eds.), *Sport business management in Aotearoa/New Zealand* (pp. 354–373). South Melbourne, VIC; Thomson Dunmore Press.

Lee, B., & Shafer, C. S. (2002). The dynamic nature of leisure experience: An application of affect control theory. *Journal of Leisure Research, 23*(3), 290–310.

Lenskyj, H. (2002). *The best Olympics ever?: Social impacts of Sydney 2000.* Albany: State University of New York Press.

Lusch, R., Vargo, S., & O'Brien, M. (2007). Competing through service: Insights from service-dominant logic. *Journal of Retailing, 83*(1), 5–18.

Misener, L., & Mason, D. S. (2006). Creating community networks: Can sporting events offer meaningful sources of social capital? *Managing Leisure, 11*(1), 39–56.

Nicholson, M. (2007). *Sport and the media: Managing the nexus.* Oxford: Elsevier.

O'Brien, D. (2006). Event business leveraging: The Sydney 2000 Olympic Games. *Annals of Tourism Research, 33*(1), 240–261.

O'Brien, D. (2007). Points of leverage: Maximising host community benefit from a regional surfing festival. *European Sport Management Quarterly, 7*(2), 141–165.

O'Brien, D., & Chalip, L. (2008). Sport events and strategic leveraging: Pushing towards the triple bottom line. In A. Woodside & D. Martin (Eds.), *Tourism management: Analysis, behaviour and strategy* (pp. 318–338). Wallingford, UK; Cambridge, MA: CABI.

Pegg, S., & Patterson, I. (2010). Rethinking music festivals as a staged event: Gaining insights from understanding visitor motivations and the experiences they seek. *Journal of Convention & Event Tourism, 11*(2), 85–99.

Pine, B. & Gilmore, J. (2011). The experience economy. *Revised edition of: The experience economy: Work is a theatre and every business a stage. (1999).* Boston: Harvard Business School Publishing.

Ralston, L. S., Ellis, G. D., Compton, D. M., & Lee, J. (2007). Staging memorable events and festivals: An integrated model of service and experience factors. *International Journal of Event Management Research, 3*(2), 24–38.

Richards, G., & Wilson, J. (2004). the impact of cultural events on city image: Rotterdam, Cultural Capital of Europe 2001. *Urban Studies, 41*(10), 1931–1951.

Rossman, J. R., & Elwood Schlatter, B. (2008). *Recreation programming: Designing leisure experiences* (4th ed.). Champaign, IL: Sagamore Publishing.

Sherry, E. (2010). (Re)engaging marginalized groups through sport: The Homeless World Cup. *International Review for the Sociology of Sport, 45*(1), 59–71.

Schlenker, K., Edwards, D., & Wearing, S. (2011). Volunteering and events. In S. Page & J. Connell (Eds.), *The Routledge handbook of events* (pp. 316–326) United Kingdom: Taylor & Francis Group.

Schulenkorf, N. (in press). Towards sustainable community development through sport and events: A conceptual framework for sport-for-development projects. *Sport Management Review.* doi: 10.1016/j.smr.2011.06.001

Shukla, N., & Nuntsu, N. (2005). Event marketing. In D. Tassiopolous (Ed.), *Event management: A professional and developmental approach* (2nd ed.). Lansdowne: Juata Academic.

Tassiopoulos, D. (2005). *Event management: A professional and developmental approach* (2nd ed.). Lansdowne: Juata Academic.

Turner, V., & Turner, E. (1978). *Image and pilgrimage in Christian Culture.* New York: Columbia University Press.

Chapter 18

Facility Management

By Robyn Cockburn, Richard Hollier and Lucy Atkinson

OBJECTIVES

After completing this chapter, you should be able to:

- describe the eight-stage process of facility design and development;
- describe facility lifecycle costs;
- describe the features of Environmentally Sustainable Design;
- understand the asset management planning process;
- understand the importance of risk management in the planning process;
- describe the risk management process;
- describe the monitoring process;
- understand the need for performance indicators.

Key terms

In this chapter, readers will become familiar with the following concepts and terms:

asset maintenance
asset management plan
asset register
commissioning
data collection, analysis and processing
design brief
development budget
Environmentally Sustainable Design
facility lifecycle costs
feasibility study
financial viability
health and safety management plan
needs assessment
performance indicators
qualitative indicators
quality management systems
risk analysis

- risk management
- schematic design
- specification documentation
- sustainability
- value management

Introduction

The value of sports facilities in New Zealand alone is estimated at $7 billion in 2009. The annual investment by local government on sports facility development and operation is, on average, $695 million dollars each year (Dalziel, 2011). Analysis of expenditure over the 2003 – 2009 period shows that, on average, the annual spend of local government on sports facilities is $695 million: $530 million on operational expenditure and $165 million on capital expenditure (Dalziel, 2011). There are many other organisations that develop and manage sports facilities so these figures are conservative. Statistics NZ also note that due to varying organisational structures and accounting systems in territorial authorities, the data for some council activities is not available or is estimated. While sports facility management has considerable commonality with generic facility management, there are some unique features that are worthy of focus. The needs of high performance athletes and national competition don't always sit well alongside the needs of everyday recreational users, but there are few facilities in New Zealand and Australia that have the luxury of a targeted sports performance market. Sports facility managers are often required to balance social outcomes with financial performance, and return on investment is a key driver for an increasing number of facility owners – whether these are a club, community trust or territorial local authority. In Australasia, as well as internationally, private companies are being contracted to run sports facilities or components of them. Sports facilities are significant assets that require careful management to ensure efficiencies and long term viability. Identifying risk and managing this through a careful monitoring programme is more likely to result in a good outcome. The content of this chapter is adapted from Cockburn and Atkinson (2004).

Being an effective facility manager requires creative programming, consistent quality, and compliance with legislation and standards. This chapter is intended to provide a better understanding of the plans, decisions and actions taken every day by those working in sports facilities across the country. It is divided into several sections:
- Facility Design and Planning
- Asset Management
- Contract and Lease Management
- Risk Management
- Monitoring and Facility Performance.

Facility design and planning

This section gives an overview of the issues around designing and building new facilities or developing existing assets. It details the key stages, from establishing a project control group, through communi consultation, contracting and project management phases, and finally completion and commissioning (see Table 18-1).

Assessing the needs of a community of users or potential users, and responding to those needs by upgrading a facility or building a new one is a complex and expensive process.

CASE STUDY: SO WHAT'S NEEDED?

A large urban council was experiencing significant demands on its sports fields which were being used in excess of their maximum sustainable capacity. Ground closures occurred regularly, particularly during winter. Council officers worked closely with sporting codes during the planning and research phases, particularly football and rugby union. The research identified a number of factors:

- Increased demand from sports groups due to more people playing sport and population growth.
- High annual rainfall.
- Limited land available for new sports field development.
- Demand from professional sports.
- Increase in training on the fields.

A preliminary assessment showed that installation of a 3G artificial sports field would increase use from 6 hours to 60 hours per week during the winter months. The research carried out was invaluable in providing a better understanding of the sport codes needs and requirements, and what actions were necessary to meet the needs identified, now and in the future. This provided a framework for ongoing planning and policy around the provision of sport and leisure facilities for the Council.

CASE STUDY: WHAT'S THE DEMAND?

A Regional Sports Trust and Council responded to an approach by several indoor sports organisations regarding current facilities. They undertook a preliminary study to assess the need for a multi-sport facility. The objectives of the study were:

- to determine and justify the need for a multi-sport facility or the development of existing facilities in the city (taking into consideration the existing facilities and the needs of the region);
- make recommendations on facility development based on identified current and anticipated future user and community needs; and
- identify potential site(s) for development of facilities.

The report findings were that the current level of facility provision was inhibiting the growth of most indoor sports. Most facilities were inadequate and lacked the ability to provide for their sport at the high performance end. Research into the potential constituency identified several anchor users of a large clear door indoor facility with some sports using separate dedicated indoor activity space.

The effect of a new facility on participation is hard to gauge, but significant unmet demand was identified. A large indoor facility was likely to be attractive for a number of reasons, including the assured access for weekly competition leagues and the ability to involve a large group in the activity at any one time. The primary functions of the new facility would be to provide assured access for weekly competition leagues and provide for projected shortfalls in court numbers and adequate support facilities. The preliminary report recommended that a 6 court facility could fulfil the needs of netball, basketball and volleyball.

Getting the right information

Facility development begins with research around issues such as: who the facility is for; establishing likely use level; management structures and processes, and costs both for design-build and on-going operations.

The process outlined has been divided into eight stages, including several stages where information is reviewed and decisions made.

Table 18-1: The facility planning process		
Establish project team	Set up project control group Develop project plan	
Needs assessment	Overall aims and objectives Review of existing provision Information sources Community consultation Determine needs Develop proposal	Proposal
Decision	Options: Abandon proposal or Upgrade existing facility or Develop new facility	
Feasibility Study	Market analysis Draft management plan Pre design Financial viability Risk assessment	
Decision	Options: Implement or amend Postpone or stage development Abandon proposal	
Design	Management plan Design brief Design team Schematic/concept design Developed and detailed design Contract documentation	Project
Construction	Construction and handover Commissioning period	
Evaluation	Facility operational Project evaluation Post construction analysis	

Source: Based on a diagram from Didcoe & Saxby (2007, p. 2?

Stage 1: Establish the project team

The composition of the project control group (PCG) will be influenced by a number of factors. Consideration needs to be given to representation by stakeholders and funders, facility operators and user groups. A range of skills should also be offered by team members.

The role of the PCG is to direct and monitor the progress of the project, with particular emphasis on programme, quality, cost, and achievement of the approved project plan. They will be supported in this by a professional design team comprising project managers, architects and other design and construction experts.

An early task for this group is the preparation of the project plan which documents the problem statement or value proposition, scope and parameters, objectives, deliverables and key performance indicators, overall timeframes and milestones, and responsibilities. This plan will be updated following completion of the needs assessment and feasibility study to reflect key decisions made.

Stage 2: Needs assessment process

A thorough assessment of needs is fundamental to the success of the entire planning process and of any facility which may ultimately be developed.

On large projects, it is likely that the team leader or chair of the group would seek independent advice on matters relating to accountability, financial management, and health and safety obligations.

As a guide, the feasibility phase of the planning process may cost up to five percent of the total cost of the development, but can determine up to 65 percent of the final cost of the building project, as illustrated in Figure 18-1.

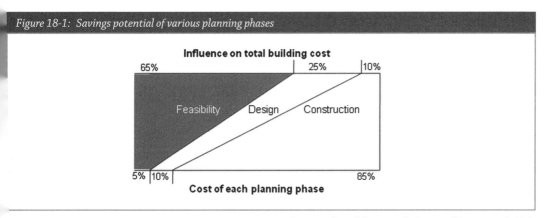

Figure 18-1: *Savings potential of various planning phases*

Source: Adapted from Youth, Sport and Recreation (1991).

Checklist for a needs assessment process

The following checklist outlines the main aspects of a needs assessment process.

Identification of community values and organisation philosophy

Identification and analysis of trends and other social indicators

Review of existing and comparative provision

Evidence of needs clearly established.

Consultation

The community consultation process is core to understanding needs. Quantitative techniques (e.g., surveys, questionnaires) provide an opportunity to identify and quantify need, determine which groups might use a facility, how often, and for what activities. Qualitative consultation techniques (e.g., meetings, focus groups) can provide a more detail understanding on how people might use a facility. A mix of both approaches is useful in a needs assessment to determine what, if anything needs to change and how it needs to change.

If considering an upgrade or change to an existing facility, consultation with current staff is essential to identify issues around current use, gaps in provision and great ideas for improvement.

Stage 3: Decision

The needs assessment process will provide enough information for the project team to decide to proceed – or not to proceed, and will provide direction on the scope and scale of the new facility. Even if it emerges that there is not enough demand for a new facility, information from the assessment can be used to meet other identified recreation programming and resourcing needs and wants.

Concept Check
Research, development and decision-making

The facility design process has many stages alternating between research and development and decision-making.

Stage 4: Feasibility study

A feasibility study will assess the viability of the proposal (in this case, of a new sports facility). It should determine such things as: clear justification for the proposed facility; what features, services and programmes the facility may offer; management structures; location; design and technical aspects; cost-benefit analysis; the social and economic impact the facility is likely to have on the community; and affordability of build and operation. This process is shown in Figure 18-2.

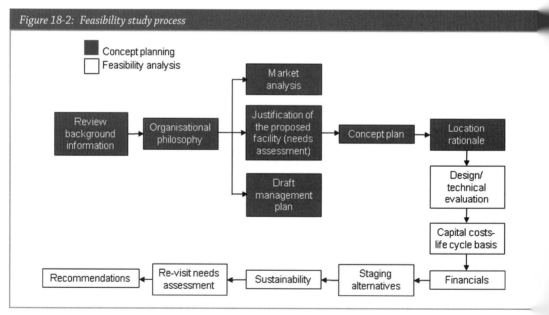

Figure 18-2: Feasibility study process

Source: Didcoe & Saxby (2007, p.

Financial viability

A key component of the feasibility study will be an analysis of the capital costs and sources of capital funding for the project, as well as an analysis of the likely operating expenditure and potential earnings of the facility. Typically the design and construction costs account for only 10% of the overall costs of running a facility over its life, as shown in the figure 18-3.

Figure 18-3: Life cycle costs

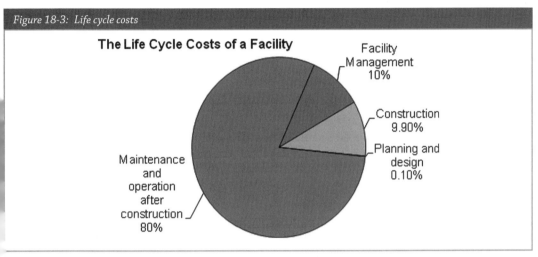

The Life Cycle Costs of a Facility

- Facility Management 10%
- Construction 9.90%
- Planning and design 0.10%
- Maintenance and operation after construction 80%

Source: Adapted from Building Management Authority (1991)

The items highlighted in Table 18-2 should be included as a minimum when assessing financial viability.

Table 18-2: Assessing financial viability

Draft budget checklist (capital costs)

Acquisition of land and site surveys
Administration and legal costs (including consents)
Consultants' fees and planning costs
Site preparation
Access road, parking and support facilities
Construction costs (including provision of infrastructural services, gas, power, water, etc)
Technical systems and utilities
Fixed equipment and furniture (non-fixed items are budgeted separately)
Contingency
Funding sources
The availability of funds throughout the planning, design and construction phases needs to be considered and cash-flow planned accordingly.

(Continued)

Operating expenditure checklist (fixed and variable costs)		Financial projections should be made for a minimum of a three to five-year period, depending on the size of the operation.
		Staff salaries/wages and on-costs
		Administration
		Auditing and insurance
		Depreciation and loan servicing costs
		Advertising and promotion
		Programmes
		Technical systems
		Utilities (usually a high proportion of operating costs)
		Asset management
		Cleaning/maintenance
		Scheduled cyclic building and plant maintenance
		Major building or plant maintenance
		Plant replacement
		Lease or rental costs of equipment
Operating income		Based on usage estimates and anticipated enrolments in programmes. Estimates included in the feasibility study.
		Information from other facilities already operating can give an indication of possible income levels for various programmes or services.
		User fees
		Concessions (locker hire, vending machines)
		Licences (specialist services such as physiotherapy rooms)
Financial forecasts		Statements of (estimated) Income and Expenditure prepared for a pre-determined period. These should be monthly for the first year of operation.
		A sensitivity analysis is a process used to identify financial risks and should also be undertaken at this stage.

Table 18-2: (Continued)

Source: Adapted from Didcoe & Saxby (2007)

There has been a recent trend to taking an overly positive assessment of demand and income when conducting feasibility studies. There is a critical difference between realism and optimism – it's better to be conservative!

Concept Check

Financial viability

Planning, design and construction account for 10% of the costs of the facility over its lifetime

Stage 5: Decision

While it is always a challenge to stop a process part way through, at the conclusion of the feasibility study stage it is crucial that a decision is actively taken on whether or not to proceed. Depending on the financial viability and other mitigating factors, it may be appropriate to amend the proposal, break the project into stages or postpone the development altogether.

Stage 6: Design process

When undertaking the design of a sports facility, the project team needs to develop a design brief, a management plan, and undertake a value management study. Involvement of the facility manager as part of the project team phase has been shown to have a positive impact on design, construction and commissioning.

Example: Design

A senior aquatics facility manager was involved in the development of a new swimming pool. His expertise was invaluable during the design, building and commissioning phases, and resulted in the first pool in New Zealand that opened without any remedial work being carried out to the tiles.

Design brief

The design brief gives the building users the opportunity to influence the design process, and the users' needs should be considered throughout the design process. A good brief will outline the following aspects: administration, including an outline of the process and communication systems; planning; management process; performance expectations; and programme outlines.

Sustainability

Consideration should be given to incorporating requirements for Environmentally Sustainable Design (ESD) in facility design briefs. This will ensure that 'whole of life value for money' principles are considered in the selection and use of materials and that unnecessary energy consumption is avoided. The design team should include appropriate ESD expertise and consider opportunities for a range of sustainable practices including: passive solar design; use of sustainable materials for construction; water reduction and reuse; heat recovery and double glazing. Current Environmentally Sustainable Design is assessed against the following categories: management, indoor environment quality, energy, transport, water, land use and ecology, emissions and innovation.

Example: Sustainability

ESD typically uses green star assessment tools. Green Star assessments are made against criteria set by the Green Building Council of Australia and the New Zealand Green Building Council. However, there are currently no assessment tools specifically for sports facilities so Wellington City Council used these design principles to develop their own assessment tool using the Green star assessment tool illustrated in Figure 18-4.

Recent swimming pool developments have used heat exchangers to convert heat recovered from the air into warm water.

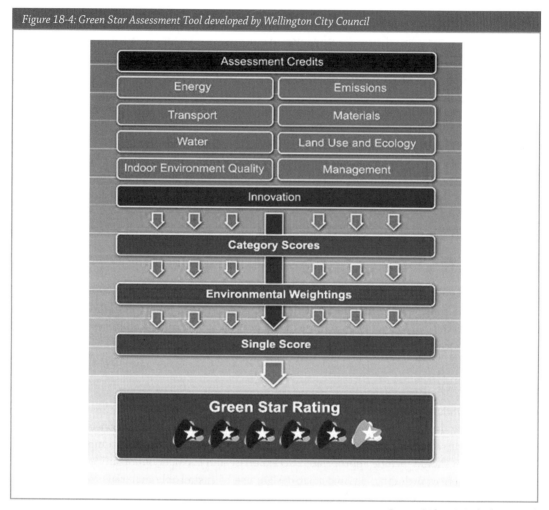

Figure 18-4: Green Star Assessment Tool developed by Wellington City Council

Source: Didcoe & Saxby (2007, p. 7)

Design team procurement

The procurement process follows sign off of the design brief and typically includes development of a Request for Proposal (RFP) document which outlines the scope of work to be undertaken by the design team, the terms and conditions of engagement and the process for engagement (usually utilising a competitive bidding process).

Design team

Consideration is given to the different skill sets required during the design and construction process including project manager, quantity surveyor, planner, architect, engineering (geotechnical, civil, electrical & mechanical, structural, fire and acoustic) and ensures that there is a good alignment and relationship between the client and key members of the professional services team.

The design team has people with a range of expertise and experience in the design of similar facilities; excellent oral/written communication skills; and proven project management experience with complex projects. Moore (1999) concluded that the best design teams were able to balance design leadership with genuine client interest. Standard practice during procurement would be to include reviews of some projects that the design team have undertaken in the past.

Project management plan

A project management plan is prepared to document how the facility will be managed and operated following commissioning. It includes the management structure, staffing requirements, target markets, programmes and services offered, levels of service, use estimates and pricing structure, performance measures. This document, typically prepared by an experienced manager, is utilised to ensure operational requirements are considered during the design process and forms the basis of a facility business plan.

CASE STUDY: WHOLE OF LIFE COST ASSESSMENT

International studies have shown inefficiency between management of the capital cost for a new commercial building and its operational costs (typically 10 times larger than capital cost over 25 years). Normally, the capital cost is heavily managed, while the operational cost is poorly known through design-stage modelling assumptions. Post-occupancy empirical assessments of whole-life cost are rare.

Empirical results suggest aspects directly influenced by the design (such as energy consumption) are only 46% of the total annual cost. The relative annual cost performance of low-impact design, compared with a conventional design on a unit floor area or occupant basis, depends heavily on the proportion of the building utilised for energy intensive activities while location also plays an important role. When considered in terms of whole-life cost, the building performs exceptionally well, with recurrent costs over 100 years calculated as being only four times the capital cost (Mithraratne & Gabe, n.d.).

Schematic or concept design

Schematic or concept design provides a range of designs that meet the brief and which are further refined in collaboration with the project team. At the conclusion of this process, the schematic design report should include: project schedule; cost/estimate analysis; revised budget; and architects, engineers' narratives (mechanical, electrical, plumbing, structural and civil) describing in detail the building systems they are going to use.

Developed and detailed design

The design development step is essentially a refining of the schematic design where the conceptual ideas are refined and further developed to shape the design of the facility. Developed design will enable earlier cost estimates to be refined based on floor areas, use of spaces and selection of materials.

Developed design will generally provide sufficient detail for planning (land use) consenting (known in New Zealand as resource consents) to occur. Once planning consents are obtained the detailed design will be undertaken with drawings detailed enough to enable construction tendering and building consenting.

Value management study

The purpose of a Value Management Study is to bring together the project stakeholders and design team to create a shared understanding of the core values, requirements and key elements of the design brief. In considering the key elements of the design brief, workshop participants are asked to work collaboratively to determine what kinds of spaces are required for each facility/activity; finishing detail, furnishings and equipment; confirm a budget; ensure that core values are appropriately captured and to deliver a 'value for money' solution.

The process is best carried out at the end of developed design, and before detailed design and contract documentation commences. Participants question whether functional requirements, outlined within the Project Plan, have been met by the proposed design, and whether value can be improved by simplifying, combining, relocating or changing anything. Value Management aims to produce results creatively and economically by:

- identifying unnecessary expenditure;
- challenging assumptions;
- generating alternative ideas;
- promoting innovation;
- optimising resources;
- saving time, money and energy;
- simplifying methods and procedures;
- eliminating redundant features;
- updating standards, criteria and objectives;
- improving team performance and other synergies;
- considering whole of life (life cycle) costs.

Contract documentation (or specification documents)

All documents necessary to describe the project to the contractor must be completed during this phase. A review meeting between the architects, engineers and the owner should occur half way through and prior to the final stages of the documentation phase.

Tender bidding and negotiation phase

At this stage an appropriate tender process is decided upon and carried out. Further details are included later in this chapter. Following the tender bidding process, a contractor will be selected by the design team against predetermined criteria. Tenders for public agencies are typically evaluated using a weighted attribute system where the key criteria are identified and each bid ranked. The attributes evaluated usually include: experience/track record; qualifications; methodology; presentation and content; and price.

Concept Check

Good design

Good design is more than drawing. It involves a project team working through a series of discrete stages to clarify values, develop a brief and address sustainability issues.

Stage 7: Construction and handover

All facilities will have technical and commissioning issues, but there are specific issues around aquatic facilities that are potentially problematic. Industry best practice involves consultation with expert aquatic advisors independent of architects throughout the process.

Commissioning

In new and existing facility development projects the contractors, builders and consultants are responsible for ensuring that the facilities, structure, systems and operational components meet the project's specifications and client's operational expectations. This is called the commissioning phase, and should include certifications and tests for:

- Building Code compliance;
- fire systems and evacuation;
- mechanical plant commissioning data, 'as built' drawings, and records;
- electrical systems and load tests;
- client inspections and approvals.

In addition to the 'plant' being tested, the commissioning phase should also involve: handover of as-built drawings and instruction manuals; staff training; and supervised operation of all equipment, preferably in 'real life' situations.

Stage 8: Evaluation

Once the facility is commissioned and operational, it is prudent to track actual performance against the needs identified in Stage 2, and the assumptions identified during the Stage 4 feasibility study. The results of this process can be used to inform future programme and management decisions, and drive additional value from the facility.

Summary

Designing and building new facilities is a complex and expensive process, so money is well spent on the needs assessment and feasibility study stages. The most successful facilities are those which meet the needs and desires of the user groups. Important aspects in facility design are:

- financial information and forward planning – facility operating costs are just as important as the design/building costs
  excellent project management by a skilled and experienced team
  a working relationship that allows plenty of input from potential users (individuals and groups).

Asset management

Introduction

An asset management plan provides a framework to manage a facility or asset in the most efficient way possible. The goal of asset management is to enable the most effective means of delivering the right level of service now and in the future through the creation, acquisition, maintenance, operation, rehabilitation and disposal of assets. In simple terms, an asset management plan is a tool to work out why, when and how much money should be spent on maintenance and improvement work.

Most asset management plans generally identify requirements for maintenance, renewals and improvement work that is needed in the next 10 years, although some organisations require plans that look ahead over the entire life of the asset (20 to 50 years).

CASE STUDY: MANAGING THE ASSETS

Complex facilities like aquatic centres are expensive to build and expensive to run! They have high levels of wear on their fixtures and fittings, plant and equipment, and the only practical way to carry out significant maintenance and upgrades is through scheduled 'shut down' periods. Depending on the age of the pool and the owner's approach to asset management there will be a brief annual closure or a longer closure every two years. During this time plant is replaced and service areas like changing facilities refurbished. The cost of these closures can be up to $1,000,000. A well-developed asset management plan that assesses the life of each asset and the scheduled date for replacement or maintenance enables planning of identified works in a cost effective and efficient way and minimise loss of revenue and risk of plant failure.

The plan in context

Asset Management involves balancing desired levels of service and asset standards against costs and risk. The Asset Management Plan (AMP) outlines how the owners will:

- ensure that assets are managed to deliver the organisation's strategic outcomes;
- ensure that assets provide a specified level of service in the most cost-effective manner;
- provide assurance to stakeholders that the asset is being managed appropriately;
- anticipate, plan and prioritise spending on the asset;
- optimise the life of the asset at the most economic cost over time;
- ensure the smooth operation and continued sustainability of the asset;
- provide a basis for monitoring the performance of the asset;
- identify and minimise environmental risk and liability resulting from the operation of the asset.

Asset Management Plans are a key component of any organisation's planning framework.

Concept Check

Asset management

Asset management plans are a tool for managing maintenance and development of facilities and their equipment and plant.

The asset management process

The key phases of asset management are outlined in Figure 18-5.

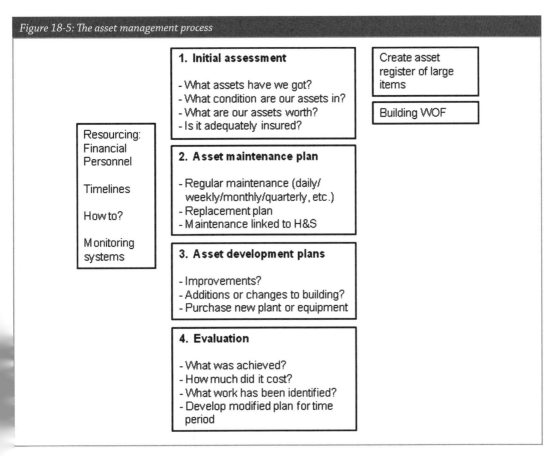

Figure 18-5: The asset management process

Initial assessment

In order to develop asset management plans, an initial assessment has to be undertaken which details all components of the facility. In the case of new facilities, 'as built' drawings or plans of the facility should be available as well as manuals for all technical, plumbing and electrical plant or equipment. Information for existing facilities may require some research; managers should consult with those responsible for the maintenance of plant and equipment, in the absence of 'as built' drawings. Where plans and written specifications are not available, the information is prepared by staff, or in the case of technical plant such as plumbing and electrical, by qualified consultants.

Asset register

Asset registers include all components of the facility, such as, their type, materials, quantity, current condition and estimated current value. Where necessary, consultants may be used to determine the condition and value of technical equipment. The register will also include a number of details about the site, including its legal description, valuation, Certificate of Title, and the year of construction of any buildings. As well as providing necessary information for forward planning and an indication of future capital costs for equipment replacement, information in registers will also be used by the facility's accountant to manage depreciation.

Facility managers may take the opportunity to update insurance policies for the building and plant during the process of developing or updating a register.

Ensuring statutory compliance

The building owner or facility manager is responsible for ensuring that the building meets the requirements of the compliance schedule issued by the relevant local authority when the building was completed. The manager will generally utilise an Independent Qualified Person (IQP) approved by the local authority.

Asset maintenance

Maintenance strategies and objectives need to be developed to guide maintenance planning. The facility manager needs to identify the best blend of planned versus unplanned maintenance in order to minimise risk through breakdown of critical assets (e.g., pool filters, disinfection plant) which can lead to facility closure or unacceptable public health and safety risks.

A planned or pro-active maintenance schedule will identify maintenance regimes for critical or high value assets. Pro-active maintenance is generally more expensive than reactive maintenance because it takes a conservative approach which necessitates maintenance being undertaken well before asset failure or breakdown is likely to occur. It has the advantage of safeguarding against unscheduled facility shutdowns and reduces risk.

A reactive or unplanned maintenance schedule focuses on repair or maintenance when an item fails, (e.g., replace light bulb when it blows). It is generally lower cost as it is not always easy to predict rates of wear and tear and therefore timing of maintenance intervention.

Asset development plan

This part of the plan addresses replacement of assets (e.g., heat pumps), planned additions or improvements to the building, equipment purchases, and other major items of capital expense. In developing the plan, facility managers will consider the needs of future customers, changes in demographics, what competitors are doing, and any other factors which influence demand for the facility.

Design issues that may arise through the monitoring process may also be addressed in this section of the plan, such as, areas that are hard to clean because they are difficult to access.

Evaluation of the Asset Management Plan

An evaluation of the Asset Management Plan is undertaken as part of the annual monitoring and planning process. During this process, the following questions are asked: what did we achieve - an what is still left to achieve; how much did it cost; how accurate are our estimates of wear-and-tear; what adjustments have to be made to the Asset Management Plan for the next period; and, what other things need to happen?

During this part of the process, information obtained from monitoring all aspects of the Asset Management Plan is used to modify and develop the plan for the next identified time period of three to five years.

Monitoring

Written into the plan is usually a requirement for periodic monitoring of the schedule of work. An annual or even six-monthly independent assessment is undertaken to ensure that the Asset Management Plan is being used to maximum advantage.

A careful monitoring process is one way of ensuring that certain procedures occurred, and if they did not occur, or did not go according to plan, to ascertain why. The plan is then modified according to the results gathered in the monitoring process and adapted accordingly. For example, well-maintained plant may last longer than planned for, so the replacement schedule would then be altered.

Managing energy usage

Energy consumption is likely to be one of the biggest on-going expenses for any facility. Managers should be aware of how much energy is consumed, and how efficient the facility is in terms of energy use. They may explore a number of options in terms of energy providers to ensure that they are getting the best value for money for the particular needs of their facility. In addition there are new technologies that allow for load shedding, ground water heat exchange, variable speed drives on pumps, minimising energy use through light sensors or on-demand hot water or maximising use of available natural resources (e.g., light, heat). Consideration of more energy efficient plant should occur as part of the Asset Management Planning process, and new plant retrofitted where appropriate.

Summary

The asset management process has a number of key components – all of which are directed at making good decisions based on sound planning around facility maintenance, development and replacement.

Contract and lease management

It is now common for owners and managers of sports facilities to contract a number of their services out, especially the running of a food outlet or café on the premises. Contracted services may also include cleaning, specific sports programmes, or swim schools.

The principles of negotiation are the same for all contracts, and a process is outlined below under Project Management for Contracts and Leases.

CASE STUDY: THERE'S MONEY IN FOOD...

A community recreation facility opened with a new café. The facility managers decided there was money to be made in food. Their thinking was that a private contractor would stand to take all the profits, which was potential income that the facility needed. Rather than lease the café space to industry specialists, they decided to hire staff and run it themselves.

Well, the scones were hard, the coffee poor, and early patrons lost heart and stopped using the café. The facility started to lose money and they were not benefiting from a fixed price lease for the café space.

After a while, the facility managers saw the error of their ways and tendered for caterers to run the café. It's now a hive of activity and business is sound – for both parties.

Why facility managers contract services

Facility owners or managers may decide to contract out various services or even programmes for a number of reasons. In some local authorities, policy and service delivery is separated as part of a deliberate strategy, and services may be contracted to an internal or external contractor. Cost savings can result when a competitive environment creates improved efficiencies. Lack of skills and experience for some services are better sourced from external providers. Risk to the facility owner is reduced by delivering a service at a known cost. Contracts are let to deliver a service that is not a core part of a facility's business, but is desirable to have (e.g., cafe, equipment repair and maintenance, specialist health services like physiotherapy).

Ethical issues

The letting of contracts in a competitive tendering environment requires skill and ethical behaviour especially where both internal and external tenders are submitted (which sometimes occurs in larger organisations and local authorities). Some of the issues which must be considered are:
* commercial confidentiality;
* process is the same for all participants;
* business performance data for the preceding 3-5 years is provided to all participants;
* existing contracting policies and any variations must be implemented consistently;
* terms and conditions must be fair and equally attractive to all potential tenderers;
* information required should be standard across all contractors to ensure that they are treated fairly during the tender process;
* use of a weighted attributes system that transparently shows the basis for the selection.

Legal and statutory requirements

Many of the legal and statutory requirements of facility owners will also apply to contractors c lessors. Facility managers will seek legal advice when negotiating major contracts for service to ensur that legal and statutory obligations on both sides are spelt out and there is no room for error. This especially important in terms of public liability, facility maintenance responsibilities, food provisio and risk management issues.

Lease and hire agreements

The basic element in this arrangement is that a legally binding lease is prepared between the owner of the facility (the lessor) and the operator of the facility (the lessee).

A lease normally includes a list of the rights and responsibilities of both the lessee and lessor, and penalty clauses for non-compliance with the terms. Once the lease has been signed the terms cannot be changed without the consent of both parties, except where expressly stated in the terms.

The lessor receives a fixed income from the facility or makes a fixed payment, but has no control over its day-to-day management. The lessee has property rights over the facility for a specified time in return for a rent, and may invest funds in a project knowing they have sufficient tenure to generate a suitable return on their investment.

Project management for contracts and leases

Figure 18-6 identifies the key elements of managing contracts and leases.

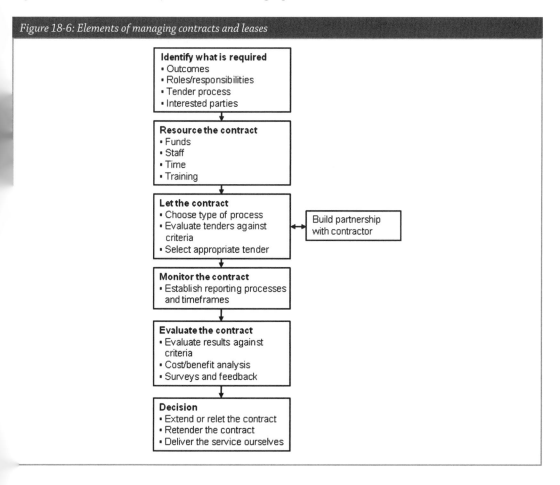

Figure 18-6: Elements of managing contracts and leases

Concept Check

Contracts and leases

Contracts and leases are common. They need to comply with legal and statutory requirements and be negotiated and managed in an ethical manner.

Risk management

Our societies are becoming increasingly litigious and professional sports managers take account of sound
risk management to increase the success of their business and reduce the likelihood of court action.

Good risk management practices are required across all aspects of sport organisations, from
strategic and operational management to planning and delivering events. Whatever the risk, its
management fits well with generic risk management processes (Standards New Zealand, 2010). Figure
18-7 provides an overview of risk management. (The full document from standards New Zealand can
be downloaded from http://www.standards.co.nz for a price).

Figure 18-7: Risk management overview

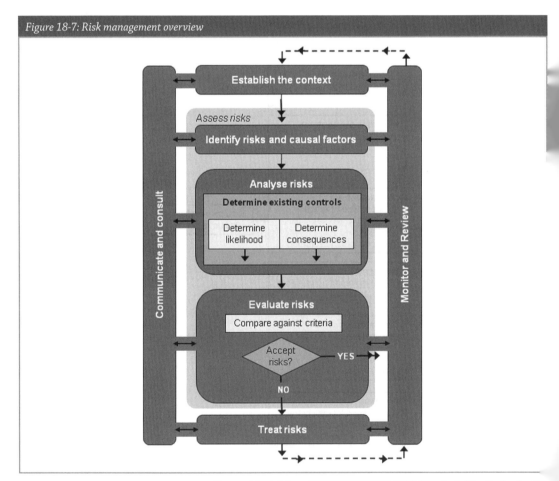

Source: Adapted from AS/NZS ISO 31000:2009 (Standards New Zealand, p.1

CASE STUDY: YOU'RE SWIMMING IN IT!
Microbiological contamination of public swimming pools has been an increasing problem in recent years. Cryptosporidiosis is an infection that causes diarrhoea with stomach cramps and vomiting, it can be severe in people with poor immune systems. The infection comes from faeces of an infected person and enters the body through the mouth to infect other people. Poor personal hygiene and faecal accidents are two ways it can enter the pool environment. When a Cryptosporidium outbreak occurs in the community the impact on pools can be dramatic with loss of income, less confidence by the public in pools and additional costs to manage the decontamination.

The New Zealand Recreation Association and the Water Safety New Zealand combined with public health authorities to develop a protocol for swimming pools that would help minimise the risk and respond effectively if an outbreak occurred. The protocol includes consideration to:
* the role of the Public Health Service in an outbreak;
* the responsibilities of the pool operators and owners;
* public awareness communications including personal hygiene messages;
* identification of 'at risk' groups;
* criteria for closing and re-opening pools if an outbreak occurs;
* treatment procedures for the removal of cryptosporidium;
* cryptosporidium testing procedures including laboratories able to complete tests;
* a faecal accident standard procedure.

Concept Check

Risk management

Risk management is a systematic process of identification, analysis, evaluation and action. It requires people to communicate and monitor.

Who is involved in risk management?

Everyone involved in the facility should in some way be involved in identifying and assessing risks and putting in place plans to manage these in developing a health and safety plan. Risk management requires managers and staff to:
* consider risk management as part of the planning process making sure that specific mention is made in the organisation's vision, strategies, goals, and policy;
* develop overall policies and procedures that identify, assess and mitigate risk;
* develop and put systems in place;
* conduct staff training;
* look at specific interventions to isolate, minimise and eliminate risk;
* always be conscious of potential risk and taking action immediately;
* keep organisation's governing body informed of current and future situations.

Where can risk occur?

Risk is a measure of uncertainty and is inherent in all aspects of managing a facility including:
assets
business

- project
- event
- staff and volunteers
- operations

Evaluating and treating risk

When evaluating risks, facility managers need to make the assessment of likelihood and consequences, and identify the severity of risk and how they will treat it. Typically a Risk Probability Table (Table 18-3) is prepared that identifies the likelihood and frequency of any specific risk occurring. The impact of these are then documented in a Risk Consequences Schedule (Table 18-4). These both contribute to an assessment of criticality.

Concept Check

Risk cost

Risk cost = probability of failure x consequence of failure

Assessment of risk probability and consequences is done against some generally agreed parameters as outlined in Tables 18-3 and 18-4. The rating process assesses the probability of the event occurring using a scale from rare to almost certain.

LEVEL	SCALE	DESCRIPTION	INDICATIVE FREQUENCY
Table 18-3: Risk probability table			
A	Rare	May occur in exceptional circumstances	Once in 100 years
B	Unlikely	Could occur at some time	Once every 30 years
C	Possible	Might occur at some time	Once every 10 years
D	Likely	Will probably occur in most circumstances	Once every 3 years
E	Almost certain	Is excepted to occur in most circumstances	Once a year or more frequently

The next step is to assess consequences of risk, which range from insignificant to catastrophic and include consideration of the following:
- financial impact including direct costs (repair, lost revenue) and indirect costs (legal costs);
- impacts on public health and safety;
- service delivery impact on customers and community;
- environmental and legal compliance;
- environmental damage;
- image, reputation and public support.

The results of this analysis are then mapped on a matrix (Table 18-4) so that the treatment options can be clearly identified. Options include controlling risks cost effectively to reduce probability o consequence, minimising risks through careful monitoring, or insuring against risk, particularl where financial losses are probable.

Table 18-4: Risk consequences schedule					
LIKELIHOOD	CONSEQUENCES				
	1	2	3	4	5
	Negligible	Minor	Moderate	Major	Catastrophic
A. Rare	L	L	L	M	H
B. Unlikely	L	L	M	H	H
C. Possible	L	M	M	H	E
D. Likely	M	M	H	E	E
E. Almost Certain	M	H	H	E	E

The control mechanisms required for each level of risk are as follows:
- Extreme risk requires immediate action.
- High Risk indicates that priority action is required.
- Medium risk requires some planned action.
- Low risk is managed by routine actions.

Implementation

Successful risk management practices depend on a quality management system. Quality management means maintaining an overview of all the processes described below and ensuring a consciousness of risk issues within each process.

Legal and statutory requirements

While the process of risk management is generic, there are some specific areas of risk management that sports managers should consider. Legislative compliance is increasingly complex, with a large number of acts typically impacting on sport management including those outlined below. All legislation is available on-line and searchable by clause at www.legislation.govt.nz or http://www.comlaw.gov.au
- Insurance
- Building design and safety
- Charities and Companies
- Consumer
- Contracts
- Employment
- Health and Safety
- Taxation
- Environment
- Human Rights
- Local Government
- Privacy
- Resource management

Health and safety in employment

Legislation is in place that promotes the health and safety of everyone at work and of other people in or around places of work (in this case, the customers). To achieve this, it requires the employer and the employees to take steps to ensure their own health and safety and that of others.

The Acts require the creation of safe and healthy workplaces and an essential element of the approach is that employees are to be involved in identifying and managing hazards.

The implications of not attending to health and safety

There are always unsafe activities or dangerous areas on premises and potential for these to be hazardous; these must be attended to under the terms of the legislation. The implications for not complying with the law can be significant.

- If one of the duties is breached, the organisation and staff may be prosecuted and fined.
- If any of the other Acts or regulations are breached, a prosecution and fine and/or lawsuits may result.
- If there is negligence, the injured victim may sue for damages.

Employers are bound by the legislation to meet specific requirements. The consequences of not meeting the requirements are that someone may get hurt which could be potentially crippling for the organisation, resulting in personal liability, loss of income, bad publicity, court proceedings, lost jobs, and facility closure. Having a health and safety management plan will minimise the likelihood of any of these outcomes.

Concept Check

Health and safety

Employers are required to take steps to ensure the health and safety of themselves and their employees.

Summary

Risk management is a vital element of good management practice. It is worthwhile investing time and resources to insure the facility against risk through:

- developing organisation-wide risk management policies and procedures;
- training staff and Board members in the appropriate areas of risk management;
- monitoring risk management practice, and improving it where necessary.

Monitoring facility performance

Introduction

Evaluation and monitoring systems need to be built into the planning process. Monitoring focuses on procedures and performance standards that underpin all aspects of the facility and its operation such as, facility design, asset management, contract and lease management, programme design and all other aspects of planning. Types of performance indicators, data collection methods, and how information is used for forward planning, will vary according to what is being measured. The monitoring process is shown in Figure 18-8.

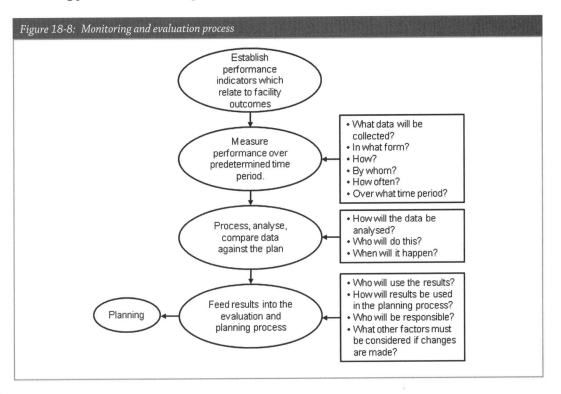

Figure 18-8: Monitoring and evaluation process

CASE STUDY: KEEPING TRACK USING TECHNOLOGY

Software solutions for recreation facilities and services help local government and private organisations automate their operations for maximum efficiency, better customer service and improved accountability to their communities, employees and board or council. More facilities are introducing specific purpose built computer based systems for their facility and revenue management.

Organisations can choose from products that offer automation options for point of sale, facility, league/tournament and membership management, financial administration, club management and the ability for customers to pay on-line. Customer database management enables direct marketing of programmes and can be used effectively for cross selling to specific target markets. For example, those customers enrolled in pre-school learn to swim will likely be interested in other pre-school programmes such as gymnastics, music or drama. Products also offer a choice of deployment, including desktop, hosted and hybrid options. The technology's modular design availability enables organisations to purchase only the solutions they need with the flexibility to add modules seamlessly, as needed.

> CASE STUDY: STAYING TOP OF THE GAME
>
> Award Winning Stadium 2000 has a stadium and range of swimming pools. It monitors its performance using:
> - *financial indicators* (trading surplus, sponsorship and base funding as a percentage of total revenue, percentage subsidy per visit, net cost per resident);
> - *customer satisfaction* (visitor numbers, visits per catchment area, facility use ratio, profile of users);
> - *quality assurance* (Pool Safe, Quality Swim School, staff members of professional associations, staff training and qualifications);
> - *energy* usage and savings;
> - planned and unplanned *repairs and maintenance*.

To develop monitoring systems, identify those things that are 'indicators' of success or failure. Reflect on the business plan and the objectives and key performance indicators developed as part of this process.
- What are the key areas for success?
- What ways can this be tracked?
- What are signs of failure?
- How can these be tracked?
- Where can this information be collected?
- How often does it need collecting, analysing and reporting?
- Who needs to know about variations?
- How will these results be used?

Concept Check

Monitor

Monitor those aspects of the facility that are indicators of success or failure.

Why monitor?

Two of the main reasons for managers to establish good monitoring processes are firstly, that it enables them to compare what is happening with what is desired or what was intended to happen and secondly, that it provides useful information for planning and evaluation processes.

What should be monitored?

The identified 'critical' success areas in each facet of the facility should be monitored. Each facility and its operation will also have some areas of risk (pilferage, equipment damage, slow payers, etc). Careful monitoring of risk will ensure that the costs to the business are minimised. While the steps in the monitoring process will be similar for each facet, the tools used to monitor and the frequency at which data will be collected will vary according to what is being monitored. Staff performance, for example, may be formally monitored twice per year; while critical pool plant may be monitored daily. What is important is that:

- monitoring systems are in place across all aspects of the facility's programmes, services, plant and equipment;
- staff understand the monitoring process and are trained in data collection;
- the information gathered through the process is useful (and is used!).

Establish performance indicators

The use of performance indicators meets both internal (within the organisation) and external (key stakeholders, customers and the general public) expectations of accountability and complies with accepted business practice. Performance indicators benefit a facility in a number of ways, including: early detection of potential problem areas and variations from agreed targets; encouragement of good leadership and motivation via constructive monitoring of staff performance; improved strategic planning; and helping to provide a culture of continuous improvement which benefits both staff performance and customer expectations.

Managers and planners should be very clear about their objectives prior to setting performance indicators; the objectives will dictate what is to be measured, and how it will be measured.

Types of indicators

Indicators used may be one of several types, each of which has specific purposes in terms of the data gathered.

Efficiency indicators: These measure productivity in relation to the output per unit of input and can be particularly useful in making decisions about facility use, for example, the amount of energy (gas/electricity) used to light, heat, cool or ventilate a facility.

Effectiveness indicators: These measure the extent to which the objectives of the service have been met, for example usage per head of population, or numbers of complaints. They can be split into three categories:

- 'pure' effectiveness indicators (number of new people attending)
- excellence indicators (the best service , outstanding cleanliness, unblemished safety record)
- equity indicators (proportions of target groups using the facility).

Qualitative indicators: These measure performance through the customers' eyes, for example, user perceptions of the quality of service or value for money.

Concept Check
Performance

Performance indicators can measure efficiency, effectiveness or quality. Identify what is to be measured, how it is to be analysed and how the results will be used.

Measure performance

Gather data

During this part of the process, managers establish criteria for what is going to be measured, determine the time period over which data is to be measured, establish clear lines of responsibility in terms of the work to be undertaken, and determine appropriate data collection methods. For example, a cleaning checklist is to be completed and any complaints about cleanliness recorded. Alternatively the facility could survey all participants as to how they found out about the facility and its programme.

Analyse and compare data against the plan

Collating and analysing data is a critical part of the process, particularly where it leads into new action plans for the future. An example of this is shown in Table 18-5.

Table 18-5: Plan and outcom			
PLAN INCLUDING OBJECTIVES	PERFORMANCE INDICATORS	RESULTS OF MONITORING	OUTCOME
Encourage more new people to use the facility	25% of all enrolments are first-time users	15% of all found out through the web 10% of new found out through word of mouth 5% new users read local community newspaper article Found out that most were new to the area	Web and word of mouth strongest advertising *Action plan* Build better web profile including links to other newcomers' websites Maximise current users' power: incentive scheme

Use results

Decide beforehand how the results from this process will be used. Information gathered during the monitoring and review process, depending on its level and type, will be used in different ways. For example, financial information is generally reported monthly at management or board level. Information about front-of-house services is part of the facility's ongoing management review process and may be used to make immediate changes such as increased staff training.

If the purpose of the information is established at the beginning, the process of reporting and using that information should flow from that. For example, justification of increased marketing spend can be made based on the impact of user numbers in relation to marketing campaigns.

Summary

Facility managers use a wide range of generic skills – these are covered in other chapters in this text. Key considerations that are unique are facility design and development and the management of significant assets and often technically specialised plant and equipment. Increasingly, components of a facility's services are delivered on contract – the negotiation of compliant and ethical contracts require special focus. Accountability for the performance of a facility to a council or board requires careful monitoring of indicators of success or failure. While the skills are predominantly generic, the balance between return on investment and social outcomes provides for challenges that facility managers relish.

Review questions

- What needs to be considered when undertaking a facility feasibility study?
- What are the stages of a facility development?
- How is the financial viability of a facility development calculated?
- What is the process for establishing an asset management plan?
- What are the principles for negotiating a contract or lease for part of a facility's service?
- What are the key elements of the risk management process and how are these translated in practice?
- How can the effectiveness and efficiency of a sports facility be monitored?

Areas for discussion

- How do political agendas impact on facility management? What are some examples that you are aware of?
- There are some conflicting demands that any sports facility manager needs to balance. Discuss the drive for efficiency and return on investment and how this can be achieved without compromising the social outcomes of the facility. Make reference to a specific facility.
- The process of development and operation of facilities is expensive. Our current concern for environmental sustainability is starting to impact on the design and management. Identify ways facilities can be more environmentally sustainable.
- This chapter has focused extensively on the 'behind the scenes' aspects of facility management, such as, design, asset management, monitoring, and risk management. What do you think the real purpose of managing a facility is? Considering the issues raised in Chapter 15 (Sport Development) and Chapter 17 (Event Management), what is the role of the facility manager? Considerable effort is often focused on raising funds for new facility developments. What facility management issues arise in this situation?

Advancing your understanding

Ammon, R., Southall, R. M., & Blair, D. A. (2004). *Sport facility management: Organizing events and mitigating risks.* Morgantown, WV: Fitness Information Technology.

Chernushenko, D. (2002). *Sustainable sport management: Running an environmentally, socially and economically responsible organization.* Nairobi, Kenya: UNEP.

Locher, E. (1998). Phasing it in: Future facility owners should understand the design and construction process even before they've contacted an architect. *Athletic Business, 22*(8), 38-46.

New Zealand Transport Agency (2009, amended November 2009). *Procurement Manual.* Available from www.nzta.govt.nz/resources/procurement-manual/

Rossman, J. R., & Schlatter, B. (2008). *Recreation programming: Designing leisure experiences.* Champaign, Il: Sagamore Publishing.

SPARC Case studies. Available from www.sparc.org.nz/en-nz/communities-and-clubs/Active-Communities/Sharing-Good-Practice/Graham-Condon-Leisure-Centre---a-partnership-innovation/

References

Building Management Authority, Western Australia. (1991). *How to undertake a feasibility study?* Western Australia: Building Management Authority.

Cockburn, R., & Atkinson, L. (2004). *Recreation facility management manual*. Wellington: New Zealand Recreation Association.

Dalziel, P. (2011). *The economic and social value of sport and recreation to New Zealand. A report produced for Sport and Recreation New Zealand (SPARC)*. AERU Research Unit, Lincoln University, Christchurch.

Didcoe, R., & Saxby, B. (2007). *Feasibility study guide: Sport and recreation facilities*. Western Australia:

Department of Sport and Recreation Western Australia.

Mithraratne, N., & Gabe, J. (n.d.). *Whole-life cost of development decisions: A case study*. Landcare Research Paper: 444.

Moore, D. (1999). *Getting what you need: A practical guide to developing project briefs for new sports facilities*. Wellington, NZ: Hillary Commission.

Standards New Zealand. (2010). *Guidelines for managing risk in sport and recreation organisations: SNZ HB 246:2010*. Wellington, NZ: Standards New Zealand.

Standards New Zealand. (2009). *Risk management: Principles and guidelines: AS/NZS ISO 31000:2009*. Wellington, NZ: Standards New Zealand.

Websites

- Department of Building and Housing, www.dbh.govt.nz
- Australian Sports Facilities, www.ausport.gov.au/information/finding_sport_information/topic/facilities2
- Department of Sport and Recreation, Western Australia, www.dsr.wa.gov.au/facilityresources
- Energy Efficiency and Conservation Authority (NZ), www.eeca.govt.nz
- New Zealand Green Building Council, www.nzgbc.org.nz/main/
- Green Building Council of Australia, www.gbca.org.au
- New Zealand Transport Agency, www.nzta.govt.nz/resources/procurement-manual/
- Panstadia International Quarterly Report, www.panstadia.com
- SPARC – Sport and Recreation Agency, www.sparc.org.nz
- Sport Discus (international sport database), www.sportdiscus.com/
- Sport England Facility Planning, www.sportengland.org/facilities__planning.aspx
- Standards New Zealand, www.standards.co.nz
- The following publications are available to look at, or purchase, from the National Asset Management Steering (NAMS) Group, www.nams.org.nz
    - International Infrastructure Management Manual (Version 4.0, 2011)
    - New Zealand Infrastructure Asset Valuation and Depreciation Guidelines (2006)
    - Developing Levels of Service and Performance Measures Guidelines (2007)
- Optimised Decision-making Guidelines (2004)

Chapter 19

Performance Management in Sport Organisations

Ian O'Boyle

OBJECTIVES

After completing this chapter, you should be able to:

* understand issues facing the modern sport organisation;
* define the various areas of performance in relation to sport management;
* discuss how performance can be measured;
* describe the future for performance management within sport organisations.

Key terms

In this chapter, readers will become familiar with the following concepts and terms:

* performance
* balanced scorecard
* non-profit organisation
* organisation development tool
* measurement
* performance targets
* destination statement

Introduction

Performance management is an initiative that has been implemented within the traditional business environment since the early 1990s. Since then it has evolved to become a fundamental process existing within the sport sector and an integral management system that can aid an organisation in monitoring and assessing its objectives and overall organisational performance. As the modern sport organisation continues to adopt a more professional and 'corporate' approach it is essential that they too implement an effective performance management system within the organisation. The increasing pressure on the modern sport organisation in relation to competitiveness, efficiency and a call for greater transparency further illustrates why a performance management approach is so crucial to these entities. Organisations such as SPARC and Rugby NZ have realised this need and have adopted performance management processes and systems in order to increase and monitor their performance in relation to strategic planning, governance, sports policy and many other areas within these organisations. This chapter analyses key performance areas and challenges facing the modern sport organisation. SPARC is used as a case study throughout the chapter to illustrate how sport organisations are now adopting a performance management approach and the evolution and use of the 'balanced scorecard' as a performance management tool for the modern sport organisation is explained within the chapter.

CASE STUDY: SPORT AND RECREATION NEW ZEALAND (SPARC)

SPARC is the Crown Entity responsible for sport and physical recreation in New Zealand. The organisation was established on 1 January 2003 under the Sport and Recreation New Zealand Act (2002). SPARC provides leadership in research and the development and implementation of policies that recognise the importance of sport and physical recreation to New Zealand. This involves working with other Government agencies to increase participation and strengthen the sport and physical recreation sector, and ensuring these agencies understand the potential that sport and physical recreation offer as a means to achieve their own objectives and outcomes.

SPARC's delivery model is based on partnering with key organisations in the sport and recreation sector (primarily national-level sport and recreation organisations and regional sports trusts) to help achieve desired outcomes.

These partner organisations deliver sport and physical recreation to New Zealanders from the grassroots to the high performance level. SPARC is not primarily a delivery agency, but is responsible for setting direction and providing investment and resources to the sector. SPARC works to:

* *Invest* - target investment to organisations that are the most capable and ready to deliver on desired outcomes.
* *Lead* - provide clear and strong leadership and work in the best interests of the sport and recreation sector through advocacy, policy development and research, and coordination of the sector to be stronger and more effective.
* *Enable* - build the capability of our partners by providing staff, resources, research and examples of good practice across the sector – for example, in coaching, governance and management systems, research and monitoring (SPARC, 2011).

The organisation is a prime example of an entity that has recognised the increased demands that are being replaced on modern sport organisations in relation to competitiveness and a call for greater transparency. In response to this SPARC has formed a leadership team that have a passion and appreciation for sport in New Zealand but also individuals who possess an in-depth corporate knowledge of how to manage such an organisation effectively in the modern environment. This corporate knowledge has led to increased efficiency and positive results in the organisation and in particular within the area of performance management.

SPARC conducts formal performance appraisal processes with individual members of staff every 6 months. Individual's performance within the organisation is based on the expectations of their line manager and the details of their position as outlined within their personal job description. SPARC realises that performance within an organisation begins at an individual level and a formal performance appraisal process ensures individual employee performance can be directly related to the strategic and performance goals of SPARC. Even the CEO of SPARC, Peter Miskimmin, is subject to this formal performance appraisal process. The CEO is responsible to the board and his performance is also analysed every 6 months.

Aside from individual performance evaluation processes, SPARC has also adopted a form of the balanced scorecard in order to assess the performance of the organisation as a whole. The scorecard is essentially based on the on-going strategic plans of SPARC and successes and failures can be seen clearly through the implementation of this performance management tool. A review of the performance within SPARC is conducted on a yearly basis through the use of the balanced scorecard.

The modern sport organisation

The modern sport organisation's administration and daily running requires increasingly specific industrial knowledge. To sustain this development of sport, managers must be equipped with the necessary skills to lead these organisations into the future and a more professional approach must be adopted particularly at executive levels. Managers must familiarise themselves with the various management techniques required to perform well within the modern sporting environment, which often requires adaptation of existing techniques applied in traditional businesses practices.

Sport has evolved to encompass a role in education, healthcare, economic development, the labour market and various social issues. The way in which these organisations are managed, is therefore required to differ from traditional organisational management. The principles, methods and conditions that exist within sport organisations must be analysed before senior management decide on the best style and form of management which suits their organisation. Management must ultimately address two key issues when establishing their future management principles and practices: the nature of the performance that the organisation seeks to achieve; and how this performance is going to be driven.

The modern sport organisation is being confronted with an operating environment that has seen substantial change relating to competitiveness and professionalization. As a result, many organisations have progressed from simply an administrative function to adopting a marketing, on-going strategic and performance approach. Chappelet and Bayle (2005) argue this strategic and performance management style of management is crucial for organisations to define projects, to structure them in a way that will allow them to achieve success, and most importantly to evaluate the project once it is completed in order to draw useful conclusions for the continuation of the project or the establishment of new ones (Chappelet & Bayle, 2005).

It is an obvious fact that sport organisations must clearly define strategic plans and objectives before any performance management system can be put in place. Management itself can be considered as a cyclical process consisting of sub processes that interrelate with each other on a number of different levels (Fischer & Otswald, 2001). In essence, performance management will be impacted directly depending on the strategic direction and objectives operating within a sport organisation.

Strategic and performance management are most commonly applied in the traditional business setting, but can also provide significant benefit to many other institutions such as schools, churches, community meetings, health setting, governmental agencies, political settings and sports organisations (Diaz-Martin, Iglesias, Vázquez, & Ruiz, 2000) as these principles are needed whenever such organisations interact with their environments to produce desired effects.

Sport organisations are predominantly concerned with the effective delivery of their mission. Potentially they may end up earning a profit at year end, but these extra finances must be reinvested within the organisation in order for it to retain its non-profit status. Sport organisations can be compared with traditional business through comparing the members and stakeholders of the organisation to clients and shareholders of a traditional business institution. Sport organisations can take the form of associations, foundations, cooperatives, trusts, societies and even corporations and companies (Kotler & Andreasen, 1991, p. 10).

Concept Check

Transparency

Sport organisations are being required to operate under greater conditions of account-ability, openness and better communication with the general public and various other stakeholders.

Performance within a sport organisation

Measuring the performance of a sport organisation requires a combination of objective and subjective measurements in order to provide a richer and more real vision of the local/regional/national/global performance (Hoye, 2003). The external effects of the sport organisations activities present a major problem relating to performance measurement and as a result it is of utmost importance that an appropriate system of performance measurement is adopted. Within for-profit organisations, the results achieved relating to the amount of finance invested within the entity constitutes the ultimate goal or at least the synthetic measurement of performance and the main objective to be achieved.

Performance measurement within a non-profit organisation such as many involved in the sport industry is often a far more complex issue. Evaluating and controlling the results of a sport organisation is a complex task as these qualitative results are often difficult to express in clear and precise terms Adding to this, sport organisations have various targets and objectives they wish to achieve and within the absence of one dominant goal, it is often difficult to evaluate the performance of a sport organisation based on a synthetic indicator. The notion of efficiency is not always predominant within these organisations and traditional effectiveness is a complex issue with a strong external connation relating to 'societal performance'. The term 'societal performance' can be defined as the social and economic contribution of a sport organisation toward the safe and responsible running of a society In non-profit organisations and in particular sport organisations, disciplinary mechanisms are les present and the survival of the organisation is rarely at stake. As 'societal performance' is often of such a high degree of importance within many sport organisations, the lack of efficiency can often be caused by this factor. As a result of this, the performance of a sport organisation is expected to relate more to effectiveness as opposed to efficiency.

The issue of performance for a sport organisation contains many different layers. Performance fo these organisations can be measured in economic terms, for example the growth of the organisation in financial terms, how profitable the organisation has become; and also in social terms, by evaluating its impact on communities and the environment it serves. It is also clear from literature on this issue that any evaluation of performance relating to a sport organisation requires a multi-criteria approach Sport organisations often combine a mixed and paradoxical approach when it comes to the issue of evaluating performance. Two main issues are most commonly analysed; public service logic, often applied in countries where a ministry of sport exits; and commercial logic (Chappelet & Bayle, 200! Hoye, 2003).

Commercial logic in the context of sports organisations can be defined by several factors. Firstl the increase in the professionalism and intensity of financial issues at stake within elite spor competitions, and this industry in general, could lead to many sport organisations being taken ov by privately run entities that have acknowledged its potential and are seeking to take advantage. Secondly, the way sport is now being consumed is having a major impact on many organisations.

In countries such as New Zealand and Australia where strong sporting infrastructure and culture have been developed, there exists a growing demand for the availability of sporting outlets, various forms of competition within sport, a growth in the number of newly adopted or emerging sports and the appearance of alternative forms of practice that form the basis of a new sporting culture (Ramanantsoa & Thiery-Basle, 1989). A major issue facing the modern sport organisation is adapting and responding to the new and emerging demands relating to sport practice. In New Zealand and Australia, new practices are becoming orientated towards more natural, open terrain and more generally toward open-air, leisure sport such as hiking, climbing, tramping and mountain biking.

State authorities such as SPARC and ASC are now playing a significant role in the way many sport organisations operate within their environment and impact on the decision making process of these organisations. Although they are a major autonomous stakeholder as a result of providing crucial financial resources to these organisations, they also position themselves more and more as a partner and regulator within the sporting environment depending upon various political pressures. Sports organisations are forced to operate in an environment that is constantly becoming more competitive because of pressure brought by the various commercial stakeholders of these entities, such as, event organisers, sport consumers, sport manufacturers and the media. An increasingly heterogeneous and uncertain internal situation is developing within the system of many sport organisations and within the sport movement in general. The non-profit aspect versus the profitability issue of the organisation adds to this complexity facing the modern sport organisation.

The challenge for the modern sport organisation is to establish a system that can meet the varying needs and expectations of their stakeholders, both commercial and public, all the while maintaining adequate service and value to their association. The issue that has faced organisations in recent years has been whether or not they are capable of integrating these centrifugal types of logic while maintaining a certain degree of coherence or culture within their own organisation.

Performance management in sport

Performance management is a relatively new phenomenon within sport organisations but entities such as SPARC and ASC have adopted performance management models similar to The Performance Prism (Neely, 2002), Balanced Scorecard (Kaplan & Norton, 1996) and EFQM model (Wongrassamee, Simmons, & Gardiner, 2003) in order to assist them in achieving their strategic goals and managing their performance effectively. These models have been proven to be successful in the traditional business environment and given that many sport organisations have much in common with the business industry, it is imperative that more sport organisations begin to realize the importance of adopting such initiatives.

Many sport organisations can be described as an organisation, whose main goal is not financial returns, rather the performance of their mission (Chappelet & Bayle, 2005). This is why the issue of performance management is of critical importance for such entities, perhaps even more so than organisations operating within a traditional business environment. Many commentators (Mahony & Howard, 2001; Miller, 1997) on sport suggest that managers involved in this industry are limited by their ability to transfer knowledge of conceptual business practices to the sporting environment. One of the greatest challenges for sport organisations is to ensure that their current and future managers have the necessary skills to lead their organisations in the twenty-first century (Chappelet & Bayle, 2005). Managers within these organisations must familiarise themselves with performance management techniques and adapt them to this unique sector of the management world.

Before any performance management system can be applied within a sport organisation, senior management must fully adopt principles that are based on improving overall organisational performance (Bond, 1999). They must be seen to endorse the new system at all levels within the organisation along with ensuring a consistent relationship with other preexisting initiatives operating within the organisation, such as cross functional integration and focus on the accountability of teams rather than individuals operating within the organisation.

Lyons (2006) claims a sport organisation must focus on its strategies and vision as opposed to the daily internal operations of the organisation. Strategic objectives must be directed by management to ensure that all employees are aware of how their own job description fits in with the strategies and performance goals of the organisation. He goes on to claim that teams themselves are the owners of the performance management system and are accountable for all aspects of that system. Management should allow teams dictate which measures will assist them in the implementation of their roles most effectively. Management must not assume that they are aware what is best for the teams as they will have removed ownership of the system and returned to a command and control style of management, leaving employees powerless (Moffat, 2000).

Concept Check
Non-profit organisation
A non-profit organisation may earn a profit at year end, but in order to retain its non-profit status – this money must be reinvested within the organisation. NPOs do not have shareholders who receive a dividend.

Performance targets

An integral part of the performance management system within both traditional and sporting entities is to set various targets. Performance targeting (Walsh, 2000) has the ability to make positive contributions to any management system. It is important that sport organisations make proper use of performance targets as this technique has a number of limitations and if not implemented properly can have adverse effects on performance. Research has shown that if targeting processes are not carefully designed and implemented, employees can become solely focused on the targets themselves and lose sight of the long term objectives and aims of the organisation (Walsh, 2000; Hood, 2002). This has proven to be one of the major pitfalls when establishing performance targets. In sport organisations and many other public sector entities performance pitfalls can be viewed as of a critical importance due to the special conditions related to responsibility and accountability in the public sector as opposed to the private (Schacter, 2002).

Walsh (2000) argues performance targets are created in order to place attention on particular processes and outcomes relating to a given organisation and also to align the behaviour and actions of individuals to the overall goals and objectives of the organisation, along with the expectations of stakeholders. The case often arises where unintended consequences related to performance target become adverse to the overall performance of the organisation, requiring constant monitoring and review of this process (Van de Walle & Roberts, 2008). The most prominent example of this, as stated above, occurs when individuals become solely focused on targets that are set out for them and lose sight of the overall mission of the sport organisation (Maleyeff, 2003).

Measurement: The Balanced Scorecard

Kaplan and Norton (1992) developed this performance management model that has been used as an effective strategic planning and management tool throughout many organisations and across vast amounts of industries. It has provided senior management with an effective way of monitoring actions and processes undertaken by employees and allowed them to keep record of these actions and consequences in an efficient manner. Although initially only adopted in mostly western countries, it has now spread throughout the global business environment and has been integrated in many non-English speaking nations. Since 2000, use of the Balanced Scorecard and its derivatives such as the Performance Prism (Neely, 2002) and other similar approaches to management, including Results Based Management, have become common in organisations throughout the world. Kurtzman (1997) produced research declaring that almost 70% of companies responding to a questionnaire were measuring performance in a way that was extremely similar to that of the Balanced Scorecard. This method of performance management has been implemented by traditional business and corporations, some government agencies and a hand full of other non-profit organisations. With the increasing parallels between the traditional business and non-profit sport organisation, it is time for this tool to be implemented across the broader spectrum of the sport management sector.

Standardised Balanced Scorecards are relatively easy to implement and can have a positive impact on a sport organisation. However, using one organisation's Balanced Scorecard and attempting to apply it to another organisation can be very difficult and research has suggested that one of the major benefits of the Scorecard lies within the design process itself (Kurtzman, 1997). Problems can arise if the Balanced Scorecard is designed by consultants who may not have had specific knowledge of operations within a sport organisation.

The unique aspect of the Balanced Scorecard which was a new development in the measurement initiatives adopted by for-profit organisations is that it combined financial and non-financial aspects of organisations to give a more detailed view of how the organisation was really performing within its operating environment. In addition, utility and clarity were further enhanced as Kaplan and Norton suggested measures within an organisation should be condensed and grouped together so they could be easily displayed within a four box model (Kaplan & Norton, 1992, 1993). Aside from this new approach to measurement within an organisation, the original definitions of the Balanced Scorecard model were sparse. From its initial inception however, it became clear that selection of measures, both relating to the filtering and clustering process would prove themselves to be the integral activities that management should address in the implementation of this tool. The measures that were to be selected, according to Kaplan and Norton (1992), should be synonymous with issues and initiatives that were relevant within the organisations strategic plans and a simple process of requiring information concerning attitudinal issues would aid in determining which measures should be associated with each perspective (Kaplan & Norton, 1992).

A major issue that became apparent after Kaplan and Norton's initial book, 'The Balanced Scorecard' (Kaplan & Norton, 1996) was that the model did not address the managerial issue of the development of long-term sustainable strategies. Following on from this publication, a second book 'The Strategy Focused Organisation' (Kaplan & Norton, 2000) echoed research previously conducted in this area (Olve & Wetter, 1999) relating to the visual documentation of the links associated with measurement and the development of the 'Strategy Map' (Kaplan & Norton, 2004). This important development within the model inspired a number of very similar variants, improved the model's utility and propelled it into mainstream industries that saw the value in adopting such a performance measurement technique. Modern versions of the Balanced Scorecard can be closely associated with this type of model and the initial samples of the model have become mostly redundant. Modern Balanced Scorecards have also evolved to be more flexible and 'user friendly' and can be applied to almost every type of organisation both in the for-profit and not-for-profit sectors such as many sporting entities.

Kaplan and Norton's (1992) initial design was laid out as a simple 'four box' model that could help organisations ensure they were getting the best results out of all the resources available to them (Kaplan & Norton, 1992). The model suggested that financial measures should not be the only perspective to be analysed. They proposed three other perspectives along with the traditional financial perspective. Learning and Growth; Internal Business Process; and Customer, were also chosen to represent the major stakeholders within an organisation (Mooraj, Oton, & Hostettler, 1999). Research surrounding Balanced Scorecards is vast and some authors have suggested the renaming of these perspectives along with the addition of new perspectives within the model. These arguments have become apparent as a result of recognition that dissimilar but equivalent perspectives would potentially result in a different set of measures. A crucial element of the adoption of this model is that users have confidence that the aspects chosen to be measured are relevant otherwise results can be regarded as insignificant. This has been the predominant factor in 1st generation balanced scorecards becoming redundant as earlier stated (Olve & Wetter, 1999; Kaplan & Norton, 2004; Niven, 2002).

Figure 19-1: 1st generation scorecard

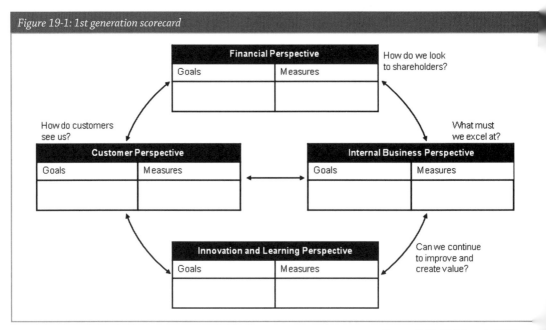

Source: Cobbold & Lawrie (2002, p.

Despite its huge popularity as a concept, literature relating to the design of the 1st generation Balanced Scorecards is sparse. The seldom pieces of literature that do concentrate on the application of the 1st generation Balanced Scorecards (Butler, Letza, & Neale, 1997) and related organisational experiences (Ahn, 2001) generally support the model but also detail the weaknesses in the initial design phase of the approach and suggest improvements that eventually become incorporated in future Balanced Scorecard designs (Epstein & Manzoni, 1997; Eagleson & Waldersee, 2000; Kennerley & Neely, 2000).

Since its initial inception in the early 1990s, many variants and alternatives of the Balanced Scorecard's 'four box' approach have become popular throughout the performance management sector. Many of these variants serve little purpose and have little utility. They are often proposed by those within academia in order to propel other agendas such as green issues (Brignall, 2002) or private consultants who develop similar models in order to increase profits from book sales or conference appearances (Bourne, Franco, & Wilkes, 2003).

Many of these related models are unquestionably similar and research (Cobbold & Lawrie, 2002a) has attempted to establish a pattern in these similarities noting three distinct types of variations. These models can be grouped into 'generations' as part of the evolving process of this performance measurement model (Cobbold & Lawrie, 2002a). The original Kaplan and Norton design along with other models who propose the simplistic 'four box' approach are often classed as the 1st generation Balanced Scorecard. Second Generation Balanced Scorecards saw the emergence of the 'strategy map' which coincided with designs such as the Performance Prism (Neely, 2002) and the Performance Driver model (Olve & Wetter, 1999). More modern designs which incorporate a paragraph relating to the long-term vision of the organisation called 'destination statements' have now become known as 3rd generation Balanced Scorecard models (Cobbold & Lawrie, 2002a).

2nd generation scorecard

One of the major criticisms of the 'first generation' Balanced Scorecards was that it seemed like a solid idea in theory but when put into practice a number of difficulties would arise resulting in many practitioners scrapping the model due to its lack of utility and vagueness. Throughout the 1990s, new design methods began to emerge, some from Kaplan and Norton themselves and others from independent consultants with similar theories and thought processes. These new designs incorporated the 'strategy map' which consisted of a set of objectives strategically placed within the model in order to further assist the organisation in maintaining focus of the organisations long-term visions. Under this new design method, Balanced Scorecards now began to associate strategic aims alongside the pre-existing four perspectives and as a result were able to 'connect the dots' by visual means of the objectives of the organisation and the aspects of the organisation that were to be measured as part of this new initiative.

Kaplan and Norton (1992) argued that for an organisation to be successful financially, they must analyze the ways in which they appear to their shareholders. 2nd generation scorecards did not adopt this synopsis, and instead created a process of associating a limited amount of performance measures to be placed alongside each perspective within the model. Strategic objectives now became a key priority within the model and were used in order to capture the essence of the organisation's strategic operations associated with each performance aspect. The aspects of the organisation that were to be measured were then carefully selected in order to ensure they coincided with these prioritised strategic objectives (Kaplan & Norton, 1993).

Although initially not considered as a major redesign of the pre-existing model, strategic objectives proved to be an integral readjustment to the Balanced Scorecard as these objectives were now directly derived from the organisation's strategic plans. The 'strategy map' element of the revised model comes about as management select the aspects of the organisation they feel are of most importance to measure, then the 'cause-effect' relationship between these aims can be defined through the establishment of links between them. The model can then be derived to measure the strategic performance of an organisation by combing, strategic objectives, the selected measures and the visual assistance of the 'strategy map'. This innovation within the Balanced Scorecard model allows management greater ease of use and provides justification for choosing the selected measures.

These changes in the design and evolution of the Balanced Scorecard were recorded in Kaplan and Norton's (1996) book 'The Strategy Focused Organisation'. They claimed that the balanced Scorecard model had now evolved from a simple performance management tool to a core aspect that should be applied within all organisations (Kaplan & Norton, 1996). Coinciding with their beliefs that the Balanced Scorecard can help an organisation with the implementation of strategic objectives, Kaplan and Norton argued that this model should be at the core of all strategic and performance management activities within an organisation (Kaplan & Norton, 1996).

From 1996 onwards, 2nd generation Balanced Scorecards became popular throughout all sectors and industries and established itself as the leading performance measurement tool an organisation could avail of. A number of criticisms are still apparent with these 2nd generation Balanced Scorecards but they have proved through practical application that they are still more successful when compared with the original Kaplan and Norton models.

3rd generation scorecard

Just before the beginning of the millennium, evolution of the Balanced Scorecard began to occur once again. This resulted in order to address the deficiencies incorporated within the '2nd generation scorecard' designs which failed to acknowledge that opportunities to intervene in the strategic process must be made available in order to anchor objectives in the 'present', real and current management operations. Another major weakness of the '2nd generation designs' is that they ignored the need to 'roll forward' and assess the impact that strategic objectives would have on the organisation.

As a result a further element was added into the mix within the Balanced Scorecard design known as the 'Destination Statement'. This instrument consisted of little more than a brief paragraph of what the 'strategic success' or 'end-date' of the strategic plans would look like. Initial 'destination statements' were constructed with a particular time-line associated with them (e.g., in four years time) detailing which objectives needed to be achieved in this amount of time. Through the application of this new instrument, organizations could now assess how targets were being met on an annual basis and if the strategic vision of the organisation was on its way to being achieved. Management quickly began to understand that if a 'destination statement' was to be incorporated within a Balanced Scorecard model, the selection of strategic objectives and measurement of strategic operations would become an easier exercise for the organisation by allocating targets and measures that could be easily selected to view and track the progress of strategy.

Organisations quickly began to realize that through the implementation of a 'destination statement' senior management and individuals within the workplace were now able to relate their roles directly to the 'destination statement' without constantly making reference to strategic goals that have been set out by the organisation. As a result of this revelation, the design approach of the model was 'reversed' with 'destination statements' attracting the initial attention of the designers as opposed to the final element of the design phase. It was further uncovered through its practical application that establishing a 'destination statement' first, made the selection of strategic objectives and consensus of management and teams within the organisation more efficient.

For a sport organisation to have the ability to make rational decisions relating to its operations and to set targets for strategic objectives, it must develop and be able to articulate exactly what the organisation is aiming to achieve (Senge, 1990; Kotter, 1995). Through the application of a 'destination statement' a sport organisation can detail how exactly it will look within an agreed-upon future time scale (Olve & Wetter, 1999; Shulver, Lawrie, & Andersen, 2000). This instrument often builds upon some existing strategic plans or documents, but it is seldom in practice to find a pre-existing document that can offer the certainty and clarity needed in order to aid a sport organisation in the performance of its strategic objectives.

CASE STUDY: SPARC – ORGANISATIONAL DEVELOPMENT TOOL (ODT)

In keeping with SPARC's refocused emphasis on adopting a performance management approach to their operations, they have developed a tool that assists the organisation in managing their on-going strategic and performance objectives. The organisational development tool has been implemented successfully within SPARC and as a result SPARC has also encouraged many other sporting organisations throughout New Zealand to adopt the ODT.

The ODT is a practical and comprehensive process designed by experts as part of SPARC's focus on developing increasingly successful and sustainable sport and recreation organisations at National, Regional and Club levels.

The ODT supports the development of successful and sustainable sport and recreation organisations by:
- providing a comprehensive 'Warrant of Fitness' to help identify priority areas for improvement;
- establishing a single national standard framework for development and capability work;
- providing a simple way of measuring improvements;
- creating a shared centre of good practice resources.

The ODT offers a comprehensive review of capability and performance that:
- identifies areas of strength and opportunity;
- includes a built-in good practice database;
- provides clear direction for improvement;
- generates quality assessment reports.

One standard approach across all sector organisations provides:
- a network of trained facilitators;
- improved consistency and comparability of results;
- flexibility for wide application with open questions;
- an easy way to monitor and evaluate performance and improvement.

(Continued)

Trained facilitators help organisations work through the tool and produce an assessment report. The tool is supported by a five-step development process as follows:

The tool is offered in three different versions, supporting National Sport Organisations, Regional Sport Organisations and Clubs. All are based on the six-module framework outlined below. This ensures every facet of your organisation is assessed.

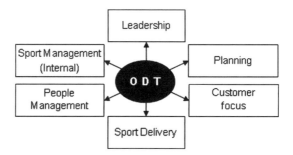

Assessments are led by trained facilitators. A network of facilitators is located within SPARC, Regional Sports Trusts and some National Sport Organisations (SPARC, 2011).

"We found this to be a wonderful tool to assess where we were at and identify areas we needed to address in our planning"– Anne Taylor, Chair, Bowls Waikato.

"The whole process has added significant value to our organisation"– Dave Beeche, CEO, Triathlon NZ.

Concept Check

Destination Statement

A brief statement or paragraph which outlines where it is the organisation sees itself in the coming years. Destination Statements began to be incorporated in 3rd generation balanced scorecards.

Summary

As the modern sport organisation continues to evolve in relation to professionalism, accountability and transparency, it is crucial that the management of these organisations realize the importance of implementing an adequate performance management system throughout the organisation. The gap of knowledge between the traditional business environment and sport organisations appears to slowly be beginning to close, however management within sport organisations must continue to familiarize themselves with best practice of successful systems and business initiatives within the traditional business environment. This knowledge is almost completely transferable to sport organisations and will increase the strategic, performance and overall organizational success of these unique entities.

Looking forward, the Balanced Scorecard is one useful model for performance management in sport organisations, but management within this sector must stay up to date with the inevitably of further evolution of current models. Strategy Maps have been proven to be successful in practical applications and these instruments along with 'destination statements' are evidence of further developments which should be incorporated when utilising a model such as the Balanced Scorecard within sport organisations.

Leading agencies such as SPARC and ASC have begun to use performance management models such as the Balanced Scorecard in order to guide and monitor the performance of their strategies and assist supervisory boards in strategic decision making. It is important that the measurement of data required to satisfy demands of the model can be done efficiently, and annual reports within a sport organisation should begin to focus more on the application and results of the organisation in relation to the effective utility of the performance model being used, such as the Balanced Scorecard. Use of information technology and Balanced Scorecard software are now playing key roles in the operations of wide ranging, successfully performing organisations. It is important sport organisations understand the importance of adopting a performance management culture, and implement suitable models to manage, measure and monitor on-going performance.

Review questions

- What are the major challenges facing the modern sport organisation?
- Sport is entering a new era of greater professionalism and many sporting organisations are adopting a corporate approach. How will this approach prove to be successful for sport organisations in the future?
- Many sport organisations are not concerned with making a profit, rather the effective delivery of their mission. What are some of the key areas of performance within a sport organisation?
- Performance Targets are an integral component of any quality performance management process. How do performance targets help an organisation improve performance? Are there any concerns to be raised relating to performance targets?
- The balanced scorecard has proved to be an effective performance management tool that can positively impact the modern sport organisation. Give a brief description of the evolution of this performance management model.
- In New Zealand, SPARC has shown a good example to other sport organisations through adopting various performance management practices and systems. Describe the Organisational Development Tool (ODT) and its benefits for the organisation which chooses to adopt it.

References

Ahn, H. (2001). Applying the balanced scorecard concept: An experience report. *Long Range Planning, 34*(4), 441–461.

Bond, T. C. (1999). The role of performance measurement in continuous improvement. *International Journal of Operations & Production Management, 19*(12), 1318.

Bourne, M., Franco, M., & Wilkes, J. (2003). Corporate performance management. *Measuring Business Excellence, 7*(3), 15–21.

Brignall, S. (2002). The unbalanced scorecard: A social and environmental critique. In *Proceedings of the 3rd International Conference on Performance Measurement and Management (PMA 2002), Boston, MA, July 2002.*

Butler, A., Letza, S. R., & Neale, B. (1997). Linking the balanced scorecard to strategy. *Long Range Planning, 30*(2), 242–253.

Chappelet, J. –L., & Bayle, E. (2005). *Strategic and performance management of Olympic sport organisations*. Champaign, IL: Human Kinetics.

Cobbold, I., & Lawrie, G. (2002a). *The development of the Balanced Scorecard as a strategic management tool.2GC Conference Paper*. Presented at Performance Measurement Association Conference, Boston, USA, May 2002. Berkshire, UK: 2GC.

Cobbold, I., & Lawrie, G. (2002b). Classification of balanced scorecards based on their effectiveness as strategic control or management control tools. In *PMA 2002 Conference Proceedings*. Performance Management Association.

Diaz-Martin, A., Iglesias, V., Vázquez, R., & Ruiz, A.V. (2000). The use of quality expectations to segment a service market. *Journal of Services Marketing, 14*(2), 132–46.

Eagleson, G. K., & Waldersee, R. (2000). Monitoring the strategically important: Assessing and improving strategic tracking systems. In *Performance Measurement: Past, Present and Future, 2nd International Conference on Performance Measurement, Cambridge, UK.*

Epstein, M. J., & Manzoni, J.-F. (1997). The balanced scorecard and tableau de bord: Translating strategy into action. *Management Accounting (USA), 79*(2), 28–37.

Fischer, G., & Ostwald, J. (2001). Knowledge management: Problems, promises, realities, and challenges. *IEEE Intelligent Systems, 16*(1), 60–72.

Hood, C. (2002). Control, bargains, and cheating: The politics of public-service reform. *Journal of Public Administration Research and Theory, 12*(3), 309–332.

Hoye, R. (2003). The role of the state in sport governance: An analysis of Australian government policy. *Annals of Leisure Research, 6*(3), 209–221.

Kaplan, R. S., & Klein, N. (1995). *Chemical Bank: Implementing the balanced scorecard*. Boston, MA: Harvard Business School Press.

Kaplan, R. S., & Norton, D. P. (1992, Jan/Feb). The balanced scorecard: Measures that drive performance. *Harvard Business Review, 70*(1), 71–79.

Kaplan, R. S., & Norton, D. P. (1993, Sep/Oct). Putting the balanced scorecard to work. *Harvard Business Review, 71*(5), 134–147.

Kaplan, R. S., & Norton, D. P. (1996, Jan/Feb). Using the balanced scorecard as a strategic management system. *Harvard Business Review, 74*(1), 75–85.

Kaplan, R. S., & Norton, D. P. (2004, Feb). Measuring the strategic readiness of intangible assets. *Harvard Business Review, 82*(2): 52–63

Kotler, P., & Andreasen, A. R. (1991). *Strategic marketing for nonprofit organizations* (4th ed.). Englewood Cliffs, NJ: Prentice Hall.

Kotter, J. P. (1995). Leading change: Why transformation efforts fail. *Harvard Business Review On Point* (MarchApril), 1–10.

Kurtzman, J. (1997, February 17). Is your company off course? Now you can find out why. *Fortune,135*(3), 128- 30.

Lyons, P. (2006). Team member involvement in team leader training and performance. *Team Performance Management, 12*(4), 102–14.

Mahony, D., & Howard, D. (2001). Sport business in the next decade: A general overview of expected trends. *Journal of Sport Management, 15*(4), 275–296.

Maleyeff, J. (2003). Benchmarking performance indices: Pitfalls and solutions. *Benchmarking: An International Journal, 10*(1), 9–28.

Miller, L. K. (1997). *Sport business management*. Gaithersburg, MD: Aspen.

Moffat, J. (2000). Representing the command and control process in simulation models of conflict. *Journal of the Operational Research Society, 51*(4), 431–438.

Mooraj, S., Oton, D., & Hostettler, D. (1999). The balanced scorecard: A necessary good or an unnecessary evil? *European Management Journal, 17*(5), 481–91.

Neely, A. (Ed.). (2002). *Business performance measurement: Theory and practice*. Cambridge: Cambridge University Press.

Niven, P. R. (2002). *Balanced scorecard step-by-step: Maximizing performance and maintaining results*. New York: John Wiley & Sons.

Olve, N., & Wetter, M. (1999). *Performance drivers: A practical guide to using the balanced scorecard*. Chichester, UK: John Wiley& Sons.

Ramanantsoa, B., & Thiery-Basle, C. (1989). *Organisations and sport federations, sociology and management*. Paris: PUF.

Schacter, M. (2002). *Not a tool kit. Practitioner's guide to measuring the performance of public programs*. Ottawa, Canada: Institute On Governance.

Senge, P. (1990). *The fifth discipline*. Garden City, NY: Doubleday Currency.

Shulver, M., Lawrie, G., & Andersen, H. (2000). A process for developing strategically relevant measures of intellectual capital. In *Proceedings of the 2nd International Conference on Performance Measurement and Management (PMA 2000), Cambridge, July 2000*.

Sport and Recreation New Zealand. (2011). Retrieved from http://www.sparc.co.nz

Van de Walle, S., & Roberts, A. (2008). Publishing performance information: An illusion of control? In W. Van Dooren & S. Van de Walle (Eds.). *Performance information in the public sector: How it is used* (pp. 211–226). Houndmills: Palgrave.

Walsh, P. (2000). Targets and how to assess performance against them. *Benchmarking: An International Journal, 7*(3), 183–99.

Wongrassamee, S., Simmons, J. E. L., & Gardiner, P. D. (2003). Performance measurement tools: The balanced scorecard and the EFQM excellence model. *Measuring Business Excellence, 7*(1), 14–29.

Chapter 20

Emerging Trends and Developments for Sport Management in the Future

Linda Trenberth, Sarah Leberman and Chris Collins

OBJECTIVES

After completing this chapter, you should be able to:

- describe why the dominant discourse and approach to sport today is a business one;
- compare and contrast developments in sport management in New Zealand and Australia with other sporting nations;
- identify the emerging trends that will have an impact on sport management in the future;
- understand the present and future challenges facing sport managers.

Key terms

In this chapter, readers will become familiar with the following concepts and terms:
- business discourse
- free market
- managerialist critique
- commercialisation
- professionalisation
- high performance sport
- natural justice

Introduction

The aim of this book has been to educate students and practitioners of sport management about business management principles and practices and their application to sport. It is hoped that this attempt has been successful, as an organisation is more likely to achieve its desired results and enhance its prospects for success if it is well managed. Good management may not be the only determinant of success; other factors, such as luck, the weather and politics, for example, can play a part, but management is a major determinant over which there can be some degree of control (Covell, Walker, Sicilano, & Hess, 2003). This, however, must be kept in perspective, as a sports team still has to be good enough to win on the field of play, regardless of how well the organisational details are managed. The bottom-line is that sport managers are responsible for performance both on and off the field

When large sums of money are invested off the field the expectation is that on-field performance will follow. Consider for example, the vast sums of money invested in the 2011 Rugby World Cup in New Zealand. Given that there will be an estimated loss of $39million shared by the Government and the New Zealand Rugby Union, if all tickets are sold, an All Black win will assist in justifying the cost, as many contest the level of expenditure given other pressing issues currently facing the country.

Throughout the book, theory and good practice have been applied to situations that exist in sport. We argue, as do Edwards (1999) and Costa (2005) that sport management practice is likely to be most effective when the sport manager is able to reflect on the theoretical foundations of their experience and, vice versa, that theory will inform their practice. While the management concepts discussed are relevant in many contexts and sport is becoming like any other business, it is accepted throughout the book that sport is unique in ways that sport managers should be cognisant of. However, Costa (2005, p. 132) argues that "we cannot know *a priori* whether there is something unique or distinctive about managing sport. This is itself something we need to determine via research in the field".

It is clear that since the first texts on sport management in New Zealand and Australia came out, there have been dramatic changes in society with profound implications for how sport is managed. The point was made in chapter one that sport will only prosper in so far as its managers can understand and respond to the changes that are shaping the social and economic contexts that it exists within. If a sport business is to be successful, it must address the challenges it faces and implement appropriate strategies in response. But this does not mean that as the commercial value of sporting success for players and all those involved in sport increases, sport managers only understand and apply the dominant bureaucratic, corporate way of managing sport. Slack (1997, p. 89) argued that such a "narrow view limits our ability to understand the complex and paradoxical nature of organisations within the sport industry". Sport leaders and managers must adopt appropriate business ethics alongside the business management approaches to administering sport and be aware that different theoretical positions lead to differing explanations and methods of managing sport that may have very different outcomes. This concluding chapter will look to the future by first reflecting on a dominant discourse and approach to sport today, before comparing the 'state of the play' in New Zealand and Australia with that of other sporting nations. It will then discuss a number of trends that have been identified will influence sport management into the future.

Sport as business discourse

This book concentrates on the business of sport management because it is argued that a dominant discourse of sport these days is a business one (Beech, 2004). However, as we look to the future, it is important to remember the context within which this business orientation has arisen and remind sport managers that they can do more than just support dominant business interests. They should understand and reflect on how sport sociology, ethical frameworks and new metaphors might be considered for understanding and informing decision-making in sport organisations and the social context within which sport exists (Collins, 2007a). The academic home for sport management is itself an issue for debate, as Costa's (2005) research on the status of sport management found. Leading sport management scholars from around the world could not reach consensus on whether sport management should be part of a business degree or sport studies. She also argues that a healthy discipline should consist of multiple discourses, rather than be confined to one.

Concept Check

Discourse

'Discourse' refers to all forms of spoken interaction, formal and informal, and written texts of all kinds. 'Business discourse' means that most of the communication surrounding sport involves language and processes of thinking and reasoning that are centred in the business environment. Sport is talked about in terms of lucrative careers, playing contracts, endorsements and sponsorships. It has been said that the decision-making process in sport should be rooted in solid business principles and practices. But what does this mean? The business discourse of sport needs some analysis.

There are a number of realities that must be taken into account when sport is being managed, and is valuable to remind ourselves that there are a variety of ways of doing and managing sport, depending on the context within which the particular sport organisation is operating – local, regional, national or international (Covell et al., 2003). Management research (Ghoshal, 2005) has also suggested that many of the management theories taught in business schools are in fact destroying good management practices. Ghoshal states (2005, p.76) that "by propagating ideologically inspired amoral theories, business schools have actively freed their students from any sense of moral responsibility". As argued above, it is important that as sport managers the moral or ethical implications of our actions are taken into consideration at each point in time.

In 1994, Trenberth and Collins identified five manifest market conditions driving the institutionalised shift towards formalised training for managers in the sport industry. These included:

* a trend toward increased professionalism in leisure and sport organisations;
* continued development of commercial forms of sport;
* maturation and normalisation of career structures in leisure and sport;
* a mounting awareness of the need for fiscal accountability in the public and non-profit sectors;
* the targeting of management skills by government as a way of enhancing sport systems 'effectiveness'.

Sparks (1995) further identified sustained market growth in some industry sectors, such as adventure tourism and outdoor recreation. Stakeholders such as training authorities and governing bodies responded by taking actions to enhance the performance of their respective organisations (as well as preserve their authority and protect their interests in the service market of leisure and sport by involving more professional managers and creating professional entrance standards for staff Fifteen years later these trends and developments have eventuated and, if anything, the need fo skilled professional sport managers is growing. Rosner and Shropshire (2004, p. 737) go as far as to suggest that "the education of future sports industry leaders must become more business-orientated Those aspiring to be the best sport managers will need the business training of an MBA along with knowledge of the sports industry".

An important condition influencing sport and recreation according to Sparks (1995, p. 96) "has bee: the sustained emphasis by both government and business in recent years on *free-market* solutions t problems of domestic productivity and global position". This process of reorienting national prioritie has brought corporate models of organisation and business norms of productivity into the publi sphere and helped shift interest away from *public administrative* to *corporatist* management strategies and priorities.

Concept Check

Free market

A marketplace that is free of government intervention. Since 1985 it has been the dominant ideology guiding state and federal policies in New Zealand and Australia.

Collins (2007) suggests that the 'managerialist critique' of the welfare state that was undertaken in New Zealand during the late 1980s helped shift the political centre of gravity in the 1990s towards the 'market-oriented ethos' of the New Right. This shift saw a reduction in state expenditure and infrastructure and the privatisation of services as being morally desirable to continued state investment in social welfare. While many state-run social programmes were downsized or eliminated over this period, state funding for sport in particular was preserved on the basis of its perceived market-relevant value in addressing and alleviating social ills and national success which brings international visibility and potential trade opportunities.

Collins (2007, p. 224) argues that a commercial managerialist orientation is now prevails, and that,

> government policy continues to be strongly directed towards corporatist styles of sports management, including strategies to intervene in order to protect 'investment', and achieve high-performance success. Whereas 'facilitation' and 'participation' might have been the buzzwords of the late 1970s and early 1980s, business values such as strategic planning, profitability, key performance indicators, investment, return on investment, intervention and accountability now dominate.

Sport and Recreation New Zealand (SPARC), in particular, talks about 'investing' in sport, rather than merely allocating grants as was the case in the past. Sport organisations are increasingly being called upon to justify requests for funding by demonstrating the return on investment that sport will receive with respect to SPARC's overall goals, especially 'getting New Zealander's more active'. These changes have brought with them a combined emphasis on rationalised measures of sport and leisure industry outputs (value-added, cost–benefit analysis, leisure and sport as a public good) and on sustained industry growth and productivity (measured in both in domestic and globally competitive terms). Government and private-sector initiatives to capitalise on the Beijing 2008 and London 2012 Olympics and build up the New Zealand sport infrastructure are examples of all these changes. Similarly, the Australian government also talks about investment in the development pathway through a strategic whole of sport approach to sports policy (Commonwealth of Australia, 2010)

However, competencies and standardised instruction are not altogether harmonious with either free-market practices or classical liberal notions of education as a process of developing a well informed citizenry (Sparks, 1995). It has to be remembered that these two approaches do not exhaust the possibilities for sport and recreation management education in New Zealand and Australia, as evidenced by the development of specialised programmes in universities around New Zealand and Australia. The role of the state, with its 'managerialist critique' together with the influence during the 1990sof the New Right, has led to a more commercial orientation and policy directed towards commercial styles of sport management (Collins, 2007).

Concept Check

Managerialist critique

The managerialist critique involved a market-orientated ethos and introduced a new semi-autonomous, corporatised approach to sport funding, emphasising business structure, practice and expertise.

The prominent business discourse of sport seems to suggest that there is very little about sport that is intelligible in other than commercial terms. It is interesting to note that in the intense public and political debate surrounding New Zealand's Cricket's (NZC) 2005 Black Cap Tour of Zimbabwe, where significant pressure was applied by Government and public opinion for the NZC to cancel the tour due to human rights abuses, NZC's defence and primary argument for the tour's continuation was based purely on business imperatives and contractual obligations. By contrast the Minister of Foreign Affairs, Phil Goff, expressed concerns about gross human rights in Zimbabwe, and stated that while he understood NZC's position, he noted that it was their financial and business argument against his moral argument (TV One News 6pm, 1 July 2005). Similarly, whilst the Lions Tour to New Zealand was touted primarily as a sporting event, the economic benefits to the country cannot be minimised (see Table 20-1).

Table 20-1: The Lions rugby tour of New Zealand: Facts and figures
• 355,000 people attended matches
• more than 1.1 million TV viewers watched each of the three tests excluding those in pubs and clubs
• 1.26m for 1st test
• 1.20m for 2nd test
• 1.12m for 3rd test (combined TV3 & Sky figures; home viewers)
• 29,000 visitors from Great Britain & Ireland (Source: Department of Labour)
• 84 extra domestic flights scheduled by Air New Zealand
• 1200 passengers accommodated aboard Pacific Sun cruise ship
• 2100 campervans & motorhomes hired during the tour
• 46,000 guest catered for by official corporate hospitality programme Lions Hospitality 2005
• 150,000 fan banners produced for Test matches
• Nine 40-foot containers shipped by DHL from Germany for hospitality purposes
• Estimated direct foreign exchange economic benefit: $120m (Source: Howarth Asia Pacific Ltd)
• Estimated total economic benefit: $250m (Source: Howarth Asia Pacific Ltd)
• www.allblacks.com New Zealand's most popular sport website for June (Source: Nielsen/NetRatings); 5.3 million page impressions; 372,000 unique users; 6500 video downloads per day

Figures for the 2006 Melbourne Commonwealth Games paint a similar picture (see Table 20-2):

Table 20-2: Economic impact of Melbourne Commonwealth Games
• Over 2 million spectators
• Cultural program Festival Melbourne 2006 attracted a further 2 million spectators and 81,000 attended regional festivals in Ballarat, Bendigo, Geelong and Moe
• Estimated total visitor expenditure $247.7 million
• Sponsorship revenue to M2006 from the 2006 games estimated at $95.1 million
• Increase in employment (FTE) 13,584
• Increase in Gross State Product of $.16 million over a 20-year period

Source: KPMG (2006)

Alongside the dominant business discourse and the socially constructed nature of sport, come numerous challenges for those involved in the world of sport (Beech & Chadwick, 2004; Covell et al., 2003; Petroczi, 2009). In recent years there has been a growing concern about issues in sport, such as drug use and drug control, racial vilification, gambling, bribery, violence and injuries, gender discrimination and cheating. While many of the ethical problems associated with sport are access and equity issues that can be linked to entrenched patriarchy and racism in sport and wider society, others stem from what some consider to be the over-commercialisation of sport. As the commercial value of sporting success increases so too are the temptations for players, coaches and promoters to employ dubious means to achieve their goals. A high profile example in 2007 was the BALCO drug scandal in the USA (for more information see http://www.usatoday.com/sports/drugs-in-sports.htm).

MINI-CASE: BALCO DRUG SCANDAL

Victor Conte founded Bay Area Laboratory Co-operative (BALCO) in 1984 to undertake chemical analysis for athletes and sell legal supplements such as ZMA. Three developments in 2003 put the lab at the center of a sprawling drug scandal. First, an anonymous tipster turned over a sample of a substance later identified as a new steroid called THG. Concurrently, a federal investigation of BALCO led to a raid on September 3. Finally, the U.S. Anti-Doping Agency publicly connected the dots, announcing details of its knowledge of THG and saying it had contacted the Justice Department and that its source had identified Conte as the source of the drug. Since then, four men — BALCO founder Victor Conte, BALCO executive James Valente, track coach Remi Korchemny and trainer Greg Anderson — have been indicted, and many athletes in baseball, football and track and field have come under scrutiny, such as, for example, Marion Jones. Because track and field has the most stringent anti-doping rules of those three sports, several athletes have been suspended, and some have been essentially pushed out of the sport. Some athletes have been punished even without a positive drug test, as a result of new guidelines.
Source: http://www.usatoday.com/sports/balco-glance.htm

What is suggested here is that while professionalisation of sport has raised the standards of excellence, and commercialisation has made sport into a viable way of life and a vocation for athletes, coaches, administrators, sport scientists and others, managers must also consider the ethical challenges in sport that are associated with perceiving sport as merely business, and begin to resolve pressing issues. Well directed quality business management practices are required at every level. The future must be planned as far as possible, with the learned experiences of the past guiding the process, while current realities will also direct future hopes. The sport manager of today must be proactive, forward looking and anticipate on-going change. The social context is not static, and never has been. The social world in which sport exists is "continually undergoing all sorts of changes, some of which may be rapid, others slower; some may be ephemeral, others more lasting" (Collins et al., 2007, p. 444). These changes could be, for example, in demographics, in technology or in the economic situation nationally and internationally. Sport leaders need to be innovative in order to deal with, and respond to, change. They also should view sport management holistically as often one issue affects another. For example, a change in customer profile may mean a change in marketing, which may mean a change in specialist staff (Watt, 2003; Chadwick, 2004).

Having reflected briefly on the socially constructed nature of the business of sport and challenges that arise from that, the chapter will now consider international developments and compare New Zealand and Australia with other sporting countries.

International perspectives

While the United Kingdom and the United States of America were previously the home of sport management and, in particular facility management, managers are now turning to the sport models originating in Canada, further developed in Australia and made to fit to scale in New Zealand. As the southern hemisphere consistently outperforms their northern counterparts per head of population, the southern models offer excellent examples of sport management. For example, "Australia with approximately 30percent of the British population has been successful in at least 60 percent of the major Australia-United Kingdom sporting competitions" (Bloomfield, 2003, p. 209).The work of the Australian Sports Commission is a particularly useful example. The core concepts evident in the southern models, demonstrate the significance of key management areas such as planning, organising and leading.

It has been argued that medals are first won in the boardrooms. It is here that clear goals and targets are established for controlling sport development and planning innovative developments Effective planning has led to much success for the southern models. However, the success of Australia at the Sydney Olympics – 4th in the medal tally – is coming at a cost. Many international rivals are interested in finding out how the Australian sport system works, and Britain in particular is attracting and employing Australians to run its various sport organisations, as they can pay higher salaries than are available in Australia. This means many experienced and capable staff are lost from Australia and given the amount of money being invested by the United Kingdom in sport, particularly with the awarding of the 2012 Olympics, other nations need to take heed (Bloomfield, 2003). To some extent this prediction was borne out at the Beijing 2008 Olympics, with Britain coming fourth on the medal table ahead of Germany and Australia (Coakley, Hallinan, Jackson, & Mewett, 2009).

The development of elite sport in countries such as Australia, Canada and the United Kingdom was largely driven by poor performance at major international competitions, primarily the Olympics and Commonwealth Games, and the link to the success or failure at these events has on the nation, in terms of medal tallies, (Green & Houlihan, 2005). The same can be said for New Zealand. The development of the New Zealand Academy of Sport (NZAS) in 2000 was a response to poor performance on the world stage. New Zealand improved its medal haul by four in Beijing compared with Athens, despite the same number of gold and silver medals.

The southern models contain unique policies being developed centrally by both SPARC and the Australian Sports Commission. In New Zealand, these policies are translated into action by the network of regional sport trusts, High Performance Sport New Zealand operations, local authorities and development officers. The Australian Institute of Sport (AIS), state institutes and the Department of Health and Ageing are responsible for sport delivery in Australia (see chapter two). Green and Houlihan (2005) identify four tensions that exist when working in the area of high performance sport. The first is that between elite and club development – the needs of each sector are quite different and need to be catered for within a limited amount of funding set aside for sport by respective governments. Linking with this first tension, are the disparate needs of elite and club athletes in terms of access to resources. The third tension is "between an aspiration towards a professionalized rational-bureaucratic model of management and the voluntaristic and more sectional/political model of decision-making found in many sports" (Green & Houlihan, 2005, p.169). The final tensions, revolves around the increasing pressure to centralise sports, with resistance from the regions.

New Zealand's and Australia's past emphasis on mass participation and training of local volunteers to deliver and administer sport programmes for all ages is already being replicated in Europe. The realisation that the traditional national governing body system does not cater for over 50 per cent of the population has led to this approach where participation is organised through customised sport programmes. In Australia, school sport programmes – for example Sport Search, a sophisticated talent identification programme, career counselling for aspiring athletes and sports participation where children get to experience all the roles from manager, to coach, to referee – shows a well organised sport system. These programmes are now being implemented in Europe. The Scottish Sports Council has, for example, led the way in implementing programmes through an extensive network of over 360 sport development officers. These officers are linked through a structure similar to that operated by the New Zealand Regional Sports Trusts network. *The Sport for All* concept is slowly being replaced by the more focused programmed approach, with a greater emphasis on coordination and delivery by sport professionals instead of volunteers. Despite these examples of general sport participation programmes, Green and Houlihan (2005, p. 189) conclude that "elite sport development and achievement on the one hand and mass participation and club development on the other are deeply incompatible functions within the policy frameworks current in Australia, Canada and the United Kingdom".

The home of excellent coaching has been Europe and in particular Eastern Europe, the Netherlands and Scandinavia. The New Zealand system of coaching education has fallen behind these more rigorous models and that of Australia, unlike their management counterpart. However, the interchange of personnel between the northern and southern hemisphere is leading to the redevelopment of New Zealand programmes. 'Taking Coaching into the Future - The New Zealand Coaching Strategy: for Coaches, by coaches' was released at the end of 2004. Its stated objective is to create a World-class Coaching Environment, which meets the needs of coaches and the athletes they coach. Three objectives underpin this – more time, increased recognition and status, and improved quality for coaches (SPARC, 2004). The strategy was rolled out to regions during 2005 and the impact of the strategy remains to be seen.

It could be argued that sport leadership is being driven by the southern countries through their systematic and innovative approach to sport. The world of rugby provided a classic case in leadership drive and initiative from the southern hemisphere, supported by a professional and well organised approach to managing an explosive change from the amateur world to the new professional game. This caught the traditionalists off guard in the northern hemisphere and the resultant financial and playing disarray of the game in the late 1990s in these countries showed weaknesses in all areas of management – planning, organising, leading and controlling. However, many high-profile New Zealand and Australian players have subsequently been lured away to Europe, offering packages the New Zealand and Australian game cannot match.

The isolation of the southern hemisphere countries has resulted in an eagerness and willingness to travel, frequently and over long distances in pursuit of experience, competition and training, with sports such as cycling establishing a training base in Europe. New ideas are brought home, tried, tested, discarded and refined. There is an alumni of New Zealand and Australian players, coaches and administrators and officials in UK and Irish sport and in other overseas sporting nations such as the Netherlands and Japan. Creating links and networks with New Zealanders and Australians working, playing, coaching and administrating overseas is important for the continued development of sport in this country, though it is important not to lose the talent permanently.

Trends and their implications for sport managers

The differences between the previous amateur world and the 'new world' of professional sport entertainment are stretching the 'old' sport model to breaking point. Traditional sport administrations here and overseas, are often poorly equipped in terms of structure, legislation, knowledge and are often unable to respond quickly enough to the changing world around them. Examples of the 'power and control' struggles that have been occurring between traditional structures and more corporate operations include:

- the ANZ netball competition;
- Indian Premier Cricket League;
- clubs being floated on the stock exchange, such as, UK football clubs;
- revamping rugby league competitions in the UK and Australia;
- SANZAR's professional Super Rugby Union competition;
- proposed Indian Premier hockey league for 2013.

The implications for sport managers of such examples include the need for a stronger understanding of:

- corporate governance;
- financial management;
- corporate social responsibility;
- share and stock market;
- mergers and acquisitions;
- sport law, commercial and international law;
- TV rights and the law;
- technology and its application in sport;
- the intended and unintended consequences of business and policy decisions.

Lessons can also be learned about managing sport from the experience of baseball in the United States (Covell et al., 2003). A Major League Baseball Players' Association strike began in August 1994, with no League Championship Series nor World Series as a result. Baseball eventually went back to play without a contract in May 1995 and a collective bargaining agreement was finally signed in November 1996 after two-and-a-half years. The issue of salary cap and revenue sharing continued with clandestine negotiating. The outcome was that many baseball fans were alienated creating an adverse situation for the viability of the sport in a highly competitive environment. Fans themselves boycotted, and attendances declined dramatically. For many fans the 'ugly' side of the business was exposed, and many saw what they perceived as 'bad' businessmen, greed and less fun. Markle (1997) argues that the customer's emotional bond with baseball was fractured. However, it is worth noting that Covell et al. (2003) indicate that attendance at baseball games major and minor league has increased by over 4 million since 1994. At the time of writing, Italian football looked set for a player strike centred on the introduction of a tax for high income earners (The Globe and Mail, 2011).

The lessons to be learned from this experience for sport managers here and in Europe are that while there is a need to be more professional and businesslike, sport managers need to understand the nature of the business and the disposition of the consumer through demographics, psychographics and socio-economics. The term 'businesslike' should connote intelligence, understanding, emotion and action, not the quick sell, greed and 'flashy business-suit ethics'. Sport managers need to build their business, the product and the *perception* of the product (i.e., goodwill) to be more attractive and appealing. Sport managers must build relationships with sponsors, learn their business needs and become an agency rather than just a salesperson. They should under-promise and over-deliver. What undermines companies usually has less to do with sufficient money, talent, product or information than with a shortage of good judgement and understanding at the top. In terms of business ethics, what has been taken for granted can be no more (Chadwick, 2004; Covell et al., 2003; Watt, 2003).

Drugs and sport

A major trend linked to the growth in financial investment and huge reward for sport performers is the rise in the abuse of performance-enhancing substances with drug controversies continuing to feature in sports news. The abuse has moved from the use of steroids as the mainstay to performance enhancement, to the use of increasingly sophisticated blood-doping techniques using growth hormones that are difficult to detect and the emerging area of genetic enhancement where gene technologies might be used to enhance athletic performance (Cameron & Kerr, 2007). This endemic rise of drug abuse in world sport and advancing technology is leading to new dilemmas for international sport administrators, involving sport ethics and morality, confronting managers with difficult decisions.

The leadership on this major issue has been undertaken by Canada, Australia, New Zealand and the Scandinavian countries, who have all taken a meaningful stance in the 'war' on drugs. The International Olympic Council (IOC) has in the past put up a token of resistance, with few convinced the IOC has the strength of will for a battle against drugs when there is so much financial reward and credibility at stake. Leadership changes at the IOC and in relevant agencies, however, gave cause for hope. Signalling a significant move in the right direction is the World Anti Doping Code, which was introduced prior to the 2004 Athens Olympics by the World Anti Doping Agency (WADA) (www.wada-ama.org). However, sports outside the Olympic movement are still problematic. In particular, professional sports such as the major leagues in the United States of America, which operate under their own anti-doping rules, are often more lenient that WADA.

During 2011, the New Zealand Academy of Sport came under criticism for allowing elite athletes and staff access to its commercial partner Integria Healthcare's supplement programme, which critics argued put athletes at risk of inadvertently taking banned substances. On-going media investigation by the New Zealand Sunday Star Times was critical of the way in which high performance athletes and Academy staff were able to order supplements via the Academy programme, for themselves and partners, and of the conflict of interest that existed for the NZAS with their commercial partner. The criticism eventually led to SPARC undertaking its own investigation with an independent Wellington barrister. At the time of writing, criticism continues via the media, with the Director General of WADA, New Zealander David Howman, reported as being critical at the lack of wisdom and risk the NZAS was exposing itself and athletes to, distancing WADA from any implication of endorsement. Media articles reported that Howman highlighted "the serious legal liabilities that could be faced by our government agencies if they continue to present the controversial programme …as 'safe' from doping risks". (Plumb, 2011). At the time of writing, the matter remains a subject of contested debate, and whatever the validity or otherwise of the criticism, it highlights the complexity of the environment sport managers find themselves operating within, such as, the challenge of holding in balance commercial imperatives, ethical issues and responsibilities toward athletes, sporting bodies, sporting code requirements and legal matters.

Management cannot be divorced from ethics and morality (Ghoshal, 2005) and, where there are no controls, organisations without values and ethics are at risk of being taken over by external forces As Collins et al. (2007, p. 460) note, "the phenomena of sport is not separate from wider society and is in fact frequently a showcase, particularly given the increasing degree of media involvement and the creation of *media sport*". If sport organisations do not adopt responsible positions, external bodies such as the police and governments will force more control on sporting affairs. In 2011, Nick Willis, third over the line, received his silver medal for the1500m from Beijing, after winner Rashid Ramzi tested positive for a banned substance. Issues such as this will test the resolve and abilities of tomorrow's sport leaders.

Sport and the law

This leads to another major issue impacting on world sport, that of the law. Increasingly, sporting organisations' rules and regulations are seen to be arcane and poorly constructed in the face of legal challenges. Participants who have high financial stakes in sport are employing talented lawyers to challenge what might be outdated laws ruled over by poorly equipped administrators. Sport vulnerability to the courts has increasingly resulted in National Sporting Organisations ceding some of their control to the courts. This is leading to a revolution in sport management as world-wide sporting bodies update and rewrite constitutions to bring them in line with civil law. Expensive mistakes by administrators have led to some cases of sport clubs declaring bankruptcy and have led to a whole new approach in decision-making and analysis.

Sport organisations are being increasingly challenged by athletes, coaches and team managers. high profile case in New Zealand related to Olympic team selection practices in 2004 by Yachting New Zealand. Andrew Murdoch and others appealed through the Sports Disputes Tribunal (SDT) the non-selection for the 2004 Athens Olympics. Their appeal was upheld by the (SDT); however, Yachting New Zealand appealed their decision and took the case to the Court of Arbitration for Sport (CAS). CAS found in Yachting New Zealand's favour, supporting the selectors' right to exercise their expert judgement in determining selection for the Olympic Games. A not dissimilar non-selection challenge to the SDT occurred from Ms Hunter-Galvan regarding her non-selection by Athletics New Zealand for the marathon team at the 2008 Beijing Olympics. The Tribunal ruled in favour of the athlete with a decision that the Selectors reconsider Ms Hunter-Galvan's application for nomination, on the basis of their ruling (Sports Tribunal of New Zealand, 2008). This again received considerable media attention with the debate played out in public, and while Ms Hunter-Galvan was eventually included in the Olympic team, her subsequent suspension in 2009 for two years for an anti-doping violation involving the prohibited substance erythropoietin (EPO)(Sports Tribunal of New Zealand, 2009), no doubt undermined any public support she had previously enjoyed.

Challenges from athletes or coaches typically arise around poor process or perceived non-adherence to policy. Sporting dispute tribunals may well rule that while the decision of a particular sporting body was not unreasonable, poor process may have been involved in arriving at the decision, as is demonstrated in the 2011 case boxing coach Mr Jenkins took against Boxing New Zealand. Mr Jenkins challenged Boxing New Zealand's appointment of another coach to the Youth Olympics. The SBT's public statement on the case noted that it

> did not accept that the decisions reached by the BNZ Executive were unreasonable, on the evidence and in law... However, the Tribunal decided Mr Jenkins had been denied natural justice in the way the BNZ Appeals Committee heard his appeal. This included that: Mr Jenkins was not notified when or where the appeal hearing was to be heard; the hearing was heard in private; he was not asked for submissions or supporting evidence; he did not know the matters to be considered; and some factual matters were clarified in the hearing that should have been referred to Mr Jenkins first as he may have had some submissions on them.

> *(Sports Tribunal of New Zealand, 2011)*

Accordingly the SBT ruled that Mr Jenkins had been denied natural justice.

Legal actions have also resulted from player violence on the field of play with convictions of assault arising against individual athletes (Jackson & Mckenzie, 2007; Coakley et al., 2009). Increasing violence towards referees led to a 2010 national campaign in New Zealand to protect, in this case, rugby referees (TVNZ, 2010). Sport has long been thought of as being subject to a different set of rules to those applying in the workplace. However, for some, the sport field *is* the workplace and sport managers need to come to terms with the fact that the rules that are imposed need to reflect the standards that society and the courts expect.

Television, finance, drugs and the law are some of the areas in which there are some obvious trends emerging that will continue to dominate sport management. There are other less dramatic but no less important trends worthy of note for students and practitioners of sport management alike.

Trends and challenges in sport

Sport organisations that have the best chance of growth and survival into the next century are those that take proactive steps to create their own future (Westerbeek & Smith, 2003). Business and sport are coming to grips with changing community lifestyles and expectations, which are reflected in demands for better spectator facilities, as well as more flexibility in scheduling so that fixtures will coincide with the preferred viewing times of the public (Collins et al., 2007). Sport no longer has a captive audience –other choices are on offer – and sport managers will have to do a much better job of understanding changing consumer demands. Sporting organisations need to ask whether they are undertaking the required analysis to understand their customers (Chadwick, 2004). Some of the key issues identified by Chadwick (2004) are highlighted in Table 20-3.

Table 20-3: Trends in sport		
GROUP	DEVELOPMENTS	RELATED EXAMPLE
Sport businesses	• Changing nature of sport product • Globalisation • Commercial development of sport businesses	Flotation of UK soccer clubs on the stock market
Participants	• Image rights • Role of agents & representatives • Litigation	Use of the haka for All Black games and advertising
Resource providers and sport business partners	• Strategic considerations • Cost of securing sports property rights • Exclusivity& control	Merging in 2005 of Harlequin Rugby Union club with Broncos Rugby League club to maximise benefits to both codes both on and off the field
Fans and customers	• Changing social and leisure trends • Service expectations • Market fragmentation	Catering to the aging population in most of the Western world will be an ongoing challenge for sport managers

Source: Adapted from Chadwick (2004, pp. 457-458)

Some of the trends specifically related to the customer base and changing social leisure trends include the following:

- *A decrease in club volunteers:* In an effort to attract support agents, organisations will have to adopt more HRM-type practice as opposed to 'seeing who's around'.
- *A change in working habits:* People want to see services provided around the clock – a trend that will transform both leisure and work patterns. Consumers expect to be able to make their leisure choices at their convenience that fits the demands of family and work lifestyles.
- *Changes in lifestyle:* Different values can be seen to be emerging and people's lifestyle choices are changing. Some of these values include: teamwork; improvement of ability; fair play; concern and respect for others; people connecting people; leadership; community service; love of sport; love of nature; social interaction; egalitarianism; breakdown of class and ethnic barriers; and community development. Sports that fail to reflect these lifestyles and values in their game, risk declining numbers.
- *Pay-for-play:* There is a growing demand for social-level, semi-competitive sports on a pay-for-play basis. Significant growth in these sports (such as touch and indoor netball), support this and reflect consumers' willingness to pay for service.
- *Competing leisure activities:* Clubs are being out-competed by the widespread availability of leisure choices at very competitive prices. The pressures of society generally result in many people having less leisure time and there are more activities demanding the reduced time people have.

- *A shift from teams to individuals:* While the traditional team games remain the great spectator sports, when it comes to participation there has been a dramatic shift in favour of individual activities (e.g., aerobics, gym).
- *Women:* Women have engaged in and defined new forms of activity, characteristically individual ones because their personal time is at a much greater premium than for men.
- *Sport for the ageing:* Historically sport was the preserve of the young, but with the erosion of the traditional pattern, squash clubs, swimming pools, aerobic classes and half-marathons are full of people in their forties and fifties.
- *Watching sport:* While there has been a big increase in participation, there has been an even bigger increase in the number of those watching.
- *Increasing technological innovation:* This not only provides opportunity, but also a variety of threats to many sports. While sporting organisations can leverage off the opportunities this provides, it also provides increased competition for the consumer dollar and time. Computer games, for example, where fans can play 'virtual sports' are becoming increasingly popular, with the possibility of drawing people away from watching the actual game, either live or via television coverage. David Stern, the NBA Commissioner in the United States stated, ". . .my worst fear was . . . that as video games got so graphically close to perfection, and you could create your own players – their hairdos, their shoes – that there might be a battle between seeing games in person or on television and seeing it play out on a video game" (Schiesel, 2005). As a result, sporting organisations in the United States were beginning to look for ways to ensure their own ownership stake in such commercial opportunities. The use of twitter, facebook and blogs are increasingly used by sports organisations to interact with their stakeholders and fans.

All these trends have the potential to drastically reduce the success and viability of sport organisations. They are significant issues that are important for New Zealand's and Australia's future which should be understood and monitored by those in governance and management roles. These factors reinforce the need to have people managing and leading sport who are pro active and innovative, and therefore are able to ride the waves of change that will affect sport in the future.

Into the future

What factors will therefore need to be taken into account by sport managers over the next ten years? Mahony and Howard (2004) commenting on the situation in the United States, suggest that sport managers will need to:

> *Take advantage of new technology.* This not only includes maximising the potential of the internet, but also recognising the impact developments in ticketing and seating, signage and video-based systems will have. As Mahony and Howard (2004) point out many sport organisations are now not only online but developing coherent, long term web strategies. A key technological development of the future will be the convergence of the Internet technology with television. However, improvements in technology can also be counterproductive in that spectators inevitably have more viewing options leading to lower ticket sales and fewer sporting events drawing large audiences. Organisations will need to know who their audiences are and utilise the changing world of technology appropriately when making decisions about investment and usage.

- *Exploit the big events, rivalries and stars.* Australia did this with the Sydney Olympics and 2006 Melbourne Commonwealth Games. New Zealand is doing this with the 2011 Rugby World Cup both on and off the field. Similarly, sporting rivalry between Australia and New Zealand mean that fixtures such as the Bledisloe Cup always attract significant numbers of spectators and sponsors. Australia and New Zealand have begun experimenting with holding their rugby test matches in Hong Kong, to maximise game attendance and media coverage. International sporting stars in the big money sports of rugby, rugby league, golf and sailing, give New Zealand and Australia prominence on the international scene.
- *Improved targeting efforts by small organisations.* Organisations will remain successful as long as they can reach their target market.
- *Tapping new markets.* This will involve both looking of new target groups nationally and seeing the world as a marketplace, rather than limiting the organisation to New Zealand and Australia.
- *Reconnecting with traditional fans/consumers.* Many sport organisations know little about their current fan base. In order to satisfy increasing expectations of service delivery in the competitive sporting market, it is necessary for sport managers to have a very good understanding of who their fans are, what they want and how to attract more. Sport organisations are dealing with 'customers' whose loyalty cannot be taken for granted in a highly competitive world and decisions must be made that are good both for the sport and for the public. However, sport managers must not lose sight of the fact that all decisions relating to the participation and management of sport are underpinned by ethical considerations, and lack of their expression in a changing sporting and external environment causes many problems. The use of twitter, facebook and blogs is providing new opportunities in this area.
- *Financial implications.* In an increasingly tight financial environment the ability to manage the organisations finances to their best effect, will separate the successful organisations from the rest. Creative financing and budget cuts are likely to be part and parcel of this process. Sport organisations will have to decide where their priorities in the long term are, so as to remain financially viable.
- *Synergy.* Strategic alliances in sport are becoming more common. There have been mergers of teams, leagues and clubs, in order to maximize resources and realise their potential. Other mergers that may well become more popular involve sport organisations and the media.

The role of government will also play an important part in the future of sport, particularly the amount of funding provided to sport. Sport organisations in New Zealand and Australia are increasingly being forced to seek funding from sponsorship and pub charities, with government funding being channelled into high performance sport.

Sport managers must be cautious and ensure that they are prepared for change. Sport as a business needs general management/leadership skills, including marketing ability, planning, information and performance management skills. Common problems that exist with planning include: strategic plan not being translated into business; lack of vision, mission statements and goals that do not motivate management plans not produced; lack of staff involvement in strategy formulation processes, leading to lack of ownership and non-implementation; thinking that is too internally focused lacking strategic focus; poor monitoring of plans (bottom-drawer syndrome);rigidity, lack of commonly understood jargon, and failure to specify the specific services/goods provided; and the lack of information based on good market research and environmental analysis on which to plan. Board must clearly define their roles which includes setting the strategic direction, the selection/appraisal/firing of the Executive Director, establishing policy, monitoring and approval of budgets/expenditure.

Individual performance needs to be appraised against plans, competencies and job descriptions, areas need to be identified for training/development, and major accountability mechanisms should be in place. Recruitment should be open and appointments made on technical skills and knowledge of sport. Traditional voting systems can be complicated and sometimes mean that the person most qualified does not get elected. National sport organisations need to focus on the value they add to sport. One area of added value is the potential to assist regional organisations to develop sponsorship, marketing plans, strategic/business plans and management systems.

As highlighted throughout this book, the convergence of sport and business continues to strengthen. There are a range of challenges for sport organisations, participants, resource providers and business partners and for supporters alike. The challenge for the sport manager is to balance the competing challenges and needs of all the relevant stakeholders. Sport businesses are becoming multi-product leisure brands, and broadcasting increasingly has an increasingly dominant role to play in augmenting and promoting the sport product. This adds greatly to the management task for a sport organisation. There is an argument for governments and governing bodies to step in and regulate the commercial development of sport businesses to see that 'fit and proper' persons are running sport (Holtt, Michie, & Oughton, 2003). Participants in sport are increasingly exploiting the commercial value of their images with implications for how they are managed on and off the field and for how they can protect the exploitation of their image rights from organisations to which they are not affiliated, all with implications for sport managers. The issue and value of naming rights at all levels of sport will continue to be a prominent part of the sportscape in years to come. These are only some of the challenges ahead for sport organisations and there will be a variety of ways in which sport organisations deal with them, just as other businesses have to address how social trends, technological developments and globalisation will affect them.

This book has provided a theoretical and applied approach to strengthen the administrative structures of sport. The outcomes of effective management, combined with the thrust of government, business and funding agencies, could help New Zealand and Australia achieve success at major sporting events such as the Olympics, as well as foster participation at the lower levels through the diversity of 'recreational' sport clubs. Sport leaders must acquire and apply managerial skills as tools to enable sport for all to survive and thrive. They must be sensitive to changing trends and be able to make the appropriate moves to benefit their sport and society. The world is increasingly complex and it is clear that to manage sport effectively into the 21st century, sport managers must utilise and manage resources in an efficient way and develop products and services that add value to the customer.

Certainly the indications are that sport and physical activity will continue to be important features of New Zealand and Australian society. Those sport managers who take the trouble to acquire the requisite skills are more likely to add value to their respective organisations, with the benefits flowing on to the participants, supporters, organisers, sponsors, community and nation. Sport has adopted many practices from the business world. Recent research suggests that non-sport organisations can also learn much about organisational success from sports organisations (Wolfe et al., 2005). They argue that sport performance tests the edge, and therefore business may be able to learn from sport. Whether or not this materialises, one thing is for certain the sport industry has exceeded predictions to date and looks set for continued remarkable growth and performance (Mahony & Howard, 2004).

Review questions

- How can sport managers use their skills to be socially responsible as well as to position their organisations to face the increased competition and economic pressures that lie ahead?
- What are some of the major trends emerging in the sport industry and how might they affect the future of sport?
- What are the possible reasons for the declining volunteer input into sport organisations and what possible actions can sport managers take to turn the trend around?
- Why is business often seen as a contaminating influence that erodes the heroic values associated with amateur sporting and local community ideals?
- What, if anything, have other sporting nations learned from New Zealand and Australia about how to manage sport?
- What role should government play in fostering sport at both the recreational and elite level?

References

Beech, J. (2004). Introduction. In J. Beech & S. Chadwick (Eds.), *The business of sport management* (pp. 3–24). Harlow, UK: Prentice Hall.

Beech, J., & Chadwick, S. (2004). *The business of sport management*. Harlow, UK: Prentice Hall.

Bloomfield, J. (2003). *Australia's sporting success: The inside story*. Sydney, NSW: UNSW Press.

Cameron, J., & Kerr, R. (2007). Doping and sport: Dying to win? In C. Collins & S. Jackson (Eds.), *Sport in Aotearoa/New Zealand society* (pp. 402–422). Melbourne: Thomson-Nelson.

Chadwick, S. (2004). The future for sport businesses. In J. Beech & S. Chadwick (Eds.), *The business of sport management* (pp. 452–473). Harlow, UK: Prentice Hall.

Coakley, J. J., Hallinan, C., Jackson, S., & Mewett, P. (2009). *Sports in society: Issues and controversies in Australia and New Zealand*. Sydney: McGraw-Hill.

Collins, C. (2007). Politics, government and sport in Aotearoa/New Zealand. In C. Collins & S. Jackson (Eds.), *Sport in Aotearoa/New Zealand society* (pp. 208–229). Melbourne: Thomson-Nelson.

Collins, C. (2007a). Studying sport in society. In C. Collins & S. Jackson (Eds.), *Sport in Aotearoa/New Zealand society* (pp. 1–22). Melbourne: Thomson-Nelson.

Collins, C., McLeod, T., Thomson, R., & Downey, J. (2007). Challenges ahead: The future and sport in Aotearoa/New Zealand. In C. Collins & S. Jackson (Eds.), *Sport in Aotearoa/New Zealand society* (pp.443–466). Melbourne: Thomson-Nelson.

Commonwealth of Australia. (2010). *Australian sport: The pathway to success*. Canberra, ACT.

Costa, C. A. (2005). The status and future of sport management: A Delphi study. *Journal of Sport Management, 19*, 117–142.

Covell, D., Walker, S., Sicilano, J., & Hess, P. W. (2003). *Managing sports organizations: Responsibility for performance*. Mason, OH: Thomson South-Western.

Edwards, A. (1999). Reflective practice in sport management. *Sport Management Review, 2*, 67–81.

Ghoshal, S. (2005). Bad management theories are destroying good management practices. *Academy of Management Learning & Education, 4*(1), 75–91.

Green, M., & Houlihan, B. (2005). *Elite sports development: Policy, learning and political priorities*. London: Routledge.

Holtt, M., Michie, J., & Oughton, C. (2003). Corporate governance and the football industry. In L. Trenberth (Ed.), *Managing the business of sport* (pp.123–142). Palmerston North, New Zealand: Dunmore Press.

Jackson S., & Mckenzie, A. (2007). Violence and sport in Aotearoa/New Zealand. In C. Collins & S. Jackson (Eds.), *Sport in Aotearoa/New Zealand society* (p422–444). Melbourne: Thomson-Nelson.

KPMG. (2006). *Economic impact study of the Melbourne 2006 Commonwealth Games: Post-event analysis*. Retrieved from: http://www.thebigopportunity. org.uk/uploads/4/0/0/1/4001782/econ_impact_ report_of_melbourne_games.pdf

Mahony, D., & Howard, D. (2004). Sport business in the next decade: A general overview of expected trends. In S. R. Rosner & K. L. Shropshire (Eds.), *The business of sport* (pp. 746–756). Sudbury, MA: Jones and Bartlett Publishers.

Markle, P. (1997). Toronto Blue Jays Baseball Club. Papre presented at the Running Sport Forum for Leaders, 16-17 May pp 1–9, Wellington NZ: Hillary Commission.

Petroczi, A. (2009). The dark side of sport: Challenges for managers in the twenty-first century. *European Sport Management Quarterly, 9*(4), 349–352.

Plumb, S. (2011, September 4). Supplements programme not 'WADA compliant'. *Sunday Star Times*. Retrieved from http://www.stuff.co.nz

Rosner, S. R., & Shropshire, K. L. (2004). *The business of sports*. Sudbury, MA: Jones and Bartlett Publishers.

Schiesel, S. (2005, June 23). Who's got game? Now, it's the fans. Sports teams fret as youths forsake real contests for video version. *International Herald Tribune*, p. 13.

Slack, T. (1997). *Understanding sport organisations: The applications of organisational theory*. Champaign, IL: Human Kinetics.

Sparks, R. (1995). Leisure and sport management in New Zealand: A situation analysis and a proposal. In G. Cushman, C. Simpson, & L. Trenberth (Eds.), *ANZALS Leisure Research Series*, 2, (pp. 94–125). Christchurch, New Zealand: Lincoln University.

Sports Tribunal of New Zealand. (2008). Retrieved 12 September 2011 from http://www.sportstribunal. org.nz/decisions-08/hunter-galvan-decision.pdf

Sports Tribunal of New Zealand. (2009). Retrieved 12 September 2011 from http://www.sportstribunal. org.nz/decisions-09/hunter-galvan-decision09. pdf

Sports Tribunal of New Zealand. (2011). *Media Release: Tribunal finds natural justice not provided to boxing coach in appeal process*. Retrieved September 12, 2011 from http://www.sportstribunal.org.nz/ decisions-11/Jenkins_media_release.pdf

SPARC. (2004). *Taking coaching into the future: The New Zealand coaching strategy – for coaches, by coaches*. Wellington, New Zealand: SPARC.

The Globe and Mail. (2011). Italy set for players' strike after talks fail. Retrieved from www. theglobeandmail.com/sports/soccer/italy-set-for-players-strike-after-talks-fail/article2141713/

Trenberth, L., & Collins, C. (1994). *Sport management in New Zealand: An introduction*. Palmerston North, New Zealand: Dunmore Press.

TVNZ. (2010). Bid to crackdown on abuse of referees. *One News*. Retrieved from http://tvnz. co.nz/national-news/bid-crackdown-abuse-referees-3610792)

Watt, D.C. (2003). *Sports management and administration* (2nd ed.). London: Routledge.

Westerbeek, H., & Smith, A. (2003). Sport Business in the global marketplace. NMew York: Palgrave MacMillan.

Wolfe, R. A., Weick, K. E., Usher, J. M., Terborg, J. R., Poppo, L., Murrell, A. J., Dukerich, J. M., Core, D. C., Dickson, K. E., & Jourdan, J. S. (2005). Sport and organizational studies: Exploring synergy. *Journal of Management Inquiry, 14*(2), 182–210.

Contributor Profiles

Editors

Sarah Leberman is a Professor and the Associate Head of School in the School of Management at Massey University in Palmerston North. She has a PhD in Management and an MA (Applied) in Recreation Administration from Victoria University in Wellington, as well as an MA in Geography from Cambridge University in England. Prior to her academic life she managed the Recreation and Sport Centre at Massey University. In 2008 she gained a Fulbright Senior Scholar Award, which she tenured at the Tucker Centre for Research on Girls and Women in Sport at the University of Minnesota. Her research interests are in the areas of women in sport and leadership, as well as the transfer of learning, and in particular the processes and factors which facilitate this. Sarah is also an Editorial Board member of the Journal of Sport Management. She is actively involved in sport through her role on the New Zealand Olympic Committee Women in Sport Group, and as the manager of the Women's Junior Black Sticks and occasionally also the Women's Black Sticks.

Chris Collins is Chief Executive at the Eastern Institute of Technology, a large public sector tertiary education institution based in Hawke's Bay, New Zealand. He has wide experience in sport, both as a participant, senior level coach, in governance, senior management and as an academic. His undergraduate study was in Physical Education at Otago University, with postgraduate studies completed at Victoria University in Recreation Administration. He spent 17 years employed in the University sector, at Victoria and Massey University, before taking up executive roles in the Institute of Technology sector in 2002. At Massey University he served as the University's Director of Sport and Recreation, responsible for facility development, staffing, facilities and programmes, and for a while also concurrently headed the University's sport management and coaching academic programme, before moving into senior management roles heading student services and as Regional Registrar. Prior to his current Chief Executive role, he was the Dean of the Faculty of Health, Science and Technology, at UCOL Institute of Technology. He has served on the Board of Directors of the New Zealand Academy of Sport – Central, and is a current Board member of the Regional Indoor Sport and Events Centre in Hawke's Bay. He was co-editor of previous texts on sport management in New Zealand, has contributed to numerous other academic publications, and was editor and co-editor of the companion texts 'Sport in New Zealand Society', first published in 2000, with the 2nd edition in 2007.

Linda Trenberth is presently head of the Management Department and Assistant Dean Learning and Teaching at Birkbeck, University of London. Her research interests include workplace bullying and stress, workplace stress and coping, human resource management and performance, and of course sport management. She was an Olympic gymnast and had a significant impact in setting up the very successful sport management programme at Massey University in New Zealand and then at Birkbeck, University of London in the UK. She has published four texts in sport management and has now moved her career in the direction of senior management in Higher Education.

Contributors

Daryl Adair is Associate Professor of Sport Management at University of Technology, Sydney. His research interests include sport and diversity issues, sport and racialisation, and sport engagement by Indigenous Australians. In the past two years he has edited special issues of academic journals around these themes: *Australian Aboriginal Studies* (2009), *Sporting Traditions* (2009), *Sport Management Review* (2010), *International Review for the Sociology of Sport* (2010), *Cosmopolitan Civil Societies* (2010), and *Sport in Society* (2011). His most recent book is the edited volume *Sport, Race and Ethnicity: Narratives of Difference and Diversity*, FIT Publishing (2011).

Lucy Atkinson is a researcher and recreation planner, currently working as a family support worker for CCS Disability Action in Christchurch. Lucy has a Postgraduate Diploma in Disability Studies, specialising in autism (Massey). Her background includes working in local authorities in Wellington and Nelson, physical activity planning and programme development, developing training manuals for the community sector, and developing training for parents of disabled children. Lucy also consults for research and development company Lumin, with recent work including research and programme development for the twelve-court Indoor Community Sports Centre in Wellington. With Robyn Cockburn she developed the *Recreation Facility Management Manual*. Her current areas of interest include community recreation, with a particular emphasis on removing barriers to inclusion. She is also interested in resilience factors in children and families coping after natural disasters.

Chris Auld, Professor and Dean (International) with the Griffith Business School, has published extensively on sport management, especially relating to community sport and sport volunteers. He is a member of the Editorial Advisory Board of the *Annals of Leisure Research*. Chris has undertaken research projects funded by a wide range of government and private sector organisations including: the Australian Research Council, Australian Sports Commission, Hong Kong Sports Development Board, Queensland Academy of Sport, NSW Sport and Recreation, Sport and Recreation Queensland, the Australian Football League, Queensland Department of Communities, and Brisbane City Council. His present research interests include the management of sport volunteers, board performance and governance in third sector organisations, and the impacts of major sport events. In 2010 he was elected as a Senior Fellow and Founding Member of the World Leisure Academy (membership of which is limited to 50 individuals worldwide). Chris was also appointed as one of four members to the Membership Nomination Committee of the Academy.

Patricia (Trish) Bradbury is a Senior Lecturer within the School of Management at Massey University, Albany. She taught in the Sport Management Programme for 18 years and now teaches core management papers. Trish has extensive experience in managing and coaching sport teams and organisations, and has been a director on the Boards of various national and regional sporting bodies. Trish worked with three national sport organisations in Canada prior to taking up residence in New Zealand. Her major research interests concern a variety of aspects of sport management related to events, organisational development, people management, and facilities.

Robyn Cockburn is Director of Lumin Limited, a training and development consultancy offering research, strategy, and development services to the recreation, arts and sports sector. She has a Bachelor of Physical Education (Otago), Master of Arts (Applied) in Recreation Administration (Victoria University of Wellington) and a Postgraduate Certificate in Athlete Career and Education (Victoria University, Melbourne). In addition to experience in recreation facility management Robyn has taught at all levels of tertiary education. Along with Lucy Atkinson, she co-authored the New Zealand Recreation Association's Facility Management Manual. Based on this, she developed and led the Facility Management Development Programme, resulting in people working in facility management receiving a National Diploma in Community Recreation (Facility Management). She is frequently engaged to provide mentoring and coaching for current facility managers. Robyn has been a national board member for a range of different national organisations, including: Physical Education New Zealand, Dance Aotearoa New Zealand, New Zealand Recreation Association and she is currently on the board of the Australia New Zealand Association of Leisure Studies, the first non-academic to hold this position.

Graham Cuskelly, Professor and Dean (Research) in the AASCB (International) accredited Griffith Business School, has a Bachelor of Education (Newcastle), Master of Science (University of North Carolina at Chapel Hill) and PhD from Griffith University. Graham's research interests are predominantly in the organisation and development of community sport, volunteers in sport, and sport governance. He has published his research findings in a number of peer reviewed journals including the *Journal of Sport Management, Sport Management Review, European Sport Management Quarterly, Event Management*, and the *Journal of Sport Behavior*, and he is currently editor of *Sport Management Review*. Graham is a former Editor of *Sport Management Review* and has published two books, *Sport Governance* (Elsevier) with Russell Hoye and *Volunteers in Sport: Theory and Practice* (Routledge) with Russell Hoye and Chris Auld. He has also published research monographs and book chapters on sport organisations and volunteers. As a chief investigator (leader and team member), Graham has been awarded several Australian Research Council Nationally Competitive Research grants and a Canadian Social Sciences and Humanities Research Council grant to study community sport organisations. Graham is currently a member of the board of the Sport Management Association of Australia and New Zealand (SMAANZ) and is a fellow and former national board member of the Australian Council for Health, Physical Education and Recreation (ACHPER).

Deborah Edwards, PhD, is a Senior Research Fellow at the University of Technology, Sydney. Prior to pursuing an academic career in 1987, Deborah worked extensively in the hospitality and hotel sectors in Australia and overseas. Deborah's research has focused on examining the functionality and performance of urban destinations. Deborah has been the principle investigator on a number of significant projects focusing on spatial mapping of tourists in urban destinations, community and event impacts, and destination management. Her work on mapping tourists' spatial movements has been conducted in Sydney, Canberra, Melbourne and London and is the first of its kind in Australia. Deborah has published extensively in the area of events, sustainable tourism and destination management.

Margot Edwards is a Senior Lecturer in the Department of Management at Massey University, Albany. She has an MSc (Hons) in Zoology from the University of Auckland and has completed a PhD examining the impact of gender on the roles and qualities of elite women's hockey coaches. Her research interests include sport and gender, identity, and leadership. Margot has represented Auckland and New Zealand in field hockey and has been active in coaching elite-level youth teams.

Lesley Ferkins is a PhD and Senior Lecturer in sport management at Deakin University, Melbourne. Her area of specialisation is the governance of sport organisations, a primary focus of her teaching and research. Lesley has worked closely with the boards of national and state sport organisations in New Zealand and Australia and has held the position of president of the Sport Management Association of Australia and New Zealand (SMAANZ). Prior to joining Deakin University, Lesley was Postgraduate Head and Senior Lecturer within the School of Sport and Recreation at AUT University in Auckland, New Zealand, and spent nine years at Unitec New Zealand as Programme Director and Senior Lecturer in the School of Sport. Lesley has presented at numerous conferences around the globe and has published in the world's top sport management journals (*Journal of Sport Management* and *Sport Management Review*).

Ron Garland was an Associate Professor of Marketing in the Waikato Management School, University of Waikato, Hamilton, where he taught courses and conducted research in sport marketing as well as consumer behaviour, strategic marketing, services marketing and marketing research. He had published several chapters on marketing issues in sport management texts as well as in *European Sport Management Quarterly* while his mainstream marketing publications appeared in a variety of journals, including *European Journal of Marketing, Marketing Intelligence & Planning*, and *Journal of Financial Services Marketing*. Ron was a former best paper winner in *International Journal of Retail & Distribution Management*.

Chris Gratton is Professor of Sport Economics and Co-Director of the Sport Industry Research Centre (SIRC) at Sheffield Hallam University. He is a specialist in the economic analysis of the sport market. He is co-author (with Peter Taylor) of six books specifically on the sport and leisure industry, and together they have published over 100 articles in academic and professional journals. Their first book, *Sport and Recreation: An Economic Analysis*, was widely regarded as one of the leading texts in the economics of sport. It has been rewritten and published as *The Economics of Sport and Recreation* in August 2000.

Richard Hollier has a background and qualifications in Parks and Recreation Management and Infrastructure Asset Management and was appointed Chairperson of the New Zealand NAMS Group in 2011. He has over 20 years local government management experience in all facets of parks, recreation and community facilities management. Richard was an Associate Director for international consulting practice Maunsell AECOM in Auckland, New Zealand. He had ten years infrastructure asset management experience working on a wide variety of projects in New Zealand, Australia and South Africa including as a contributing author of the International Infrastructure Management Manual, the New Zealand Infrastructure Asset Valuation and Depreciation Guidelines and the Creating Customer Value from Community Assets Manual.

Terry Kilmister has, for the last 25 years, provided corporate governance advice to boards in the public, commercial and not-for-profit sectors in New Zealand, Australia and the USA, and he has worked extensively with sports organisation boards. While living in Australia he formed a close working relationship with the Australian Sports Commission, carrying out many in-depth governance-related assignments on their behalf with many of Australia's premier sports bodies. Terry has also worked with sports organisations in the USA, and in New Zealand with the Hilary Commission and more recently with SPARC. Terry has returned to New Zealand to live and he works on a part-time basis. Together with his partner Graeme Nahkies, Terry is widely published in the field of corporate governance.

Trevor Meiklejohn is a Lecturer at Unitec New Zealand in the Department of Sport. He also manages the relationships that Unitec has with the Blues, Auckland Rugby and the Northern Mystics Netball franchise. Before embarking on an Academic career, Trevor held positions in sport development, marketing, and facility management for regional and national sporting organisations including North Harbour Rugby, the New Zealand Rugby Union and the Millennium Institute of Sport and Health. Trevor's research interests include interorganisational relationships, sponsorship, and brand management. Trevor is a keen surfer, dedicated long distance runner, rugby fan and netball supporter.

Ian O'Boyle has a BSc (University College, Dublin), and an MSc (University of Ulster) and is currently undertaking his PhD, which looks at performance management within sports organisations. In addition to his PhD research, Ian has lectured for various undergraduate courses within the School of Sports Studies at the University of Ulster. He has also taught sport management modules in Stranmillis University College and Northern Regional College in the UK. His passion for sport is fuelled by his own experiences as a Senior Irish International basketball team member and former captain of Junior Irish International teams. Ian's research relates to establishing a connection between traditional business performance management principles and practices and those practiced within sporting entities. He has previously led research analysing the public provision of sports facilities on the island of Ireland and New Zealand, motorsport volunteerism in the UAE, the use of the Balanced Scorecard in non-profit organisations, and performance management in sport organisations.

Farah Rangikoepa Palmer (Ngati Mahuta and Ngati Waiora; Tainui) is a part-time Senior Lecturer in the School of Management, Massey University. She currently lectures on leadership and governance and has research interests in sport sociology, sport management, leadership and governance especially with regards to Māori and women. She is currently a Research Associate of the Māori Business Research Centre (Te Au Rangahau) and the Academy for Māori Research and Scholarship (Te Mata o te Tau) at Massey University. In addition, Dr Palmer writes a weekly sport column for the Otago Daily Times, and mentors professional rugby players in the Manawatu as a Professional Development Manager. Dr Palmer was a member of the New Zealand women's rugby team (Black Ferns) from 1995 to 2006, and captained the team from 1997 to three World Cups (1998, 2002, and 2006). Since retiring she has remained involved in women's rugby as part of the Women's Advisory Committee for the International Rugby Board (IRB), and independent member of the New Zealand Māori Rugby Board and a member of the Māori advisory group to SPARC known as Te Roopu Manaaki. At a community level, she is a member of the Tu Toa Trust (alternative sport/education programme).

and Palmerston North Girls High School Trust (allocating scholarships) and became an Officer of the New Zealand Order of Merit (ONZM) in 2007 for work done in sport and women's rugby. Dr Palmer currently resides in Palmerston North with her partner and son.

Jenny Parry was formerly a Senior Lecturer in the Department of Finance, Banking and Property at Massey University, Palmerston North. For a number of years she was also the Head of Department and Chair of the University's Disciplinary and Scholarship Committees. Jenny taught introductory finance and investment analysis but her research interests were primarily in security design and company financial decision-making. Jenny's PhD research topic was the financing of biotechnology companies. She retired from the University in 2001 to pursue other interests.

Sam Richardson is a Lecturer in the School of Economics and Finance at Massey University, where he teaches first and second year microeconomics. He is a Massey University graduate with Bachelors and Masters degrees in Applied Economics (majoring in Agricultural Economics), and he completed his PhD in Economics in early 2011. His PhD thesis is entitled *Assessing the Economic Justification for Government Involvement in Sports Facilities and Events in New Zealand*, and involved, among other things, estimating the realised economic impacts on New Zealand cities of internationally-oriented sports events and sporting facility construction. Sam is actively researching in the area of the economics of sport, and in particular examining the realised economic impacts of major events and the estimation of benefits of sporting events to attendees.

Feona Sayles is a Lecturer in business law at Massey University, Palmerston North, and has a LLB, LLM and a BBS in sports management. She is also a Barrister and Solicitor of the High Court of New Zealand. Feona's involvement in sports includes providing legal advice to sporting groups, administrative roles, coaching, and playing. She has been a representative player at local, regional and national level.

Nico Schulenkorf, PhD, works as a Lecturer for Sport Management at the University of Technology, Sydney (UTS). His research focuses on the social, cultural and psychological outcomes of sport and event projects, and in particular the role of sport in contributing to social development within and between disadvantaged communities. For several years, Nico has been involved in sport-for-development and health promotion programs in countries such as Sri Lanka, Israel and the Pacific Islands. He has been working with local and international NGOs, Government Agencies, Sport Associations and Ministries in developing capacities to implement, monitor and evaluate development projects. For his long-term contribution to the advancement of social justice on an international level, Nico was awarded the 2008 UTS Vice Chancellor's Human Rights Award.

Richard Tacon is currently undertaking a PhD at Birkbeck, University of London, in which he is examining social capital in voluntary sports clubs. He previously completed an MSc in sport management and the business of football at Birkbeck, prior to which he received a BA Hons in Classics at the University of Cambridge. In 2005, Richard joined the Football Governance Research Centre as a research Officer, where he was involved with the annual State of the Game publications in 2005 and 2006. Richard then became Research and Evidence Officer at the Central Council of Physical Recreation (now the Sport and Recreation Alliance), the umbrella organization for the national governing bodies of sport in the UK, where he worked until 2008. Richard's main research areas are the social impacts of sport, evaluation within sport, and corporate social responsibility in sport.

Sue Walker, PhD, is research manager for SPARC (Sport & Recreation New Zealand) and was the research and information manager for SPARC's predecessor, the Hillary Commission. She also has been the manager of the Health Sponsorship Council's Research and Evaluation Unit, the Department of Internal Affairs' Research and Evaluation Services team, and information manager for the Commerce Commission. Before coming to New Zealand in 1995, Sue worked on an extensive range of projects as a contract researcher in the university, public and private sectors in the UK.

Geoff Walters is a Lecturer in management at Birkbeck, University of London, and a director of the Birkbeck Sport Business Centre. He graduated from Lancaster University Management School and the University of Manchester before completing an Economic and Social Research Council funded PhD at Birkbeck that looked at corporate governance in the football industry and the relevance of stakeholder theory. He has since published numerous articles and book chapters on corporate responsibility in the sport industry and in 2010 was funded by UEFA through the Universities Research Grant Programme to undertake research on CSR in European football.

Index